Microsoft
Word 2010:
Comprehensive

JUDY MARDAR
PC Source

PAMELA R. TOLIVER
Soft-Spec

LABYRINTH
LEARNING™

El Sobrante, CA

Microsoft Word 2010: Comprehensive
by Judy Mardar and Pamela R. Toliver

Copyright © 2011 by Labyrinth Learning

Labyrinth Learning
P.O. Box 20818
El Sobrante, California 24820
800.522.9746
On the web at lablearning.com

President:
Brian Favro

Product Development Manager:
Jason Favro

Managing Editor:
Laura A. Lionello

Production Manager:
Rad Proctor

eLearning Production Manager:
Arl S. Nadel

Editorial/Production Team:
Donna Bacidore, John Barlow,
Scott Benjamin, Belinda Breyer, Alec Fehl,
Sandy Jones, PMG Media

Indexing: Joanne Sprott

Interior Design:
Mark Ong, Side-by-Side Studios

Cover Design:
Words At Work

ITEM: 1-59136-304-7
ISBN-13: 978-1-59136-304-0

Manufactured in the United States of America.

10 9 8 7 6 5 4 3 2

Contents in Brief

Table of Contents

Quick Reference Tables

PAGE SETUP TASKS

SHARING AND SECURITY TASKS

TABLE TASKS

Keyboard Shortcuts

DOCUMENT COMMANDS

New document	`Ctrl`+`N`
Print	`Ctrl`+`P`
Save	`Ctrl`+`S`
Spelling & Grammar check	`F7`
Thesaurus	`Alt`+click desired word

EDITING COMMANDS

Change the font case	`Shift`+`F5`
Copy	`Ctrl`+`C`
Cut	`Ctrl`+`X`
Find	`Ctrl`+`F`
Insert date	`Alt`+`Shift`+`D`
Insert page break	`Ctrl`+`Enter`
Paste	`Ctrl`+`V`
Replace	`Ctrl`+`H`
Show/Hide Ribbon	`Ctrl`+`F1`
Undo	`Ctrl`+`Z`

FORMATTING COMMANDS

Bold	`Ctrl`+`B`
Demote a list one level	`Tab`
Insert a nonbreaking space	`Ctrl`+`Shift`+`Spacebar`
Italic	`Ctrl`+`I`
Promote a list one level	`Shift`+`Tab`
Turn off highlighter	`Esc`
Underline	`Ctrl`+`U`

LINE SPACING COMMANDS

1.5 spacing	`Ctrl`+`1.5`
Double spacing	`Ctrl`+`2`
Single spacing	`Ctrl`+`1`

LONG DOCUMENT COMMANDS

Display the Go To tab	`Ctrl`+`G`
Insert endnote	`Alt`+`Ctrl`+`D`
Insert footnote	`Alt`+`Ctrl`+`F`
Mark Index Entry dialog box	`Alt`+`Shift`+`X`
Update table of contents	`F9`

OTHER COMMANDS

Insert hyperlink	`Ctrl`+`K`
Macros dialog box	`Alt`+`F8`
Move the the next table cell	`Tab`
Move to the previous table cell	`Shift`+`Tab`

Preface

Microsoft® Word 2010: Comprehensive is a complete survey of Microsoft Word, with engaging content that prepares learners to succeed. Our brand new work-readiness skills ensure students have the critical thinking skills necessary to succeed in today's world. The book includes:

- **Introductory Skills** – Introduction to Word, the Help feature, the spelling and grammar checker, AutoCorrect, formatting, editing, tables, and more
- **Intermediate Skills** – Creating newsletters with section breaks, columns, WordArt, clip art, themes, and Building Blocks; creating a policy manual with styles; setting up a mail merge; and creating a promotional brochure with graphic elements
- **Advanced Skills** – Adding tables of contents, indexes, headers and footers, and cross-references; Track Changes; working with SkyDrive; integrating Word with Excel, Power-Point, and the web; and more

Content from this book is also available in two 24+-hr courses and in three 12+-hr courses.

24+ Hour Courses	12+ Hour Courses
Microsoft Word 2010: Introductory Skills	Microsoft Word 2010: Level 1
Microsoft Word 2010: Advanced Skills	Microsoft Word 2010: Level 2
	Microsoft Word 2010: Level 3

For almost two decades, Labyrinth Learning has been publishing easy-to-use textbooks that empower educators to teach complex subjects quickly and effectively, while enabling students to gain confidence, develop practical skills, and compete in a demanding job market. We add comprehensive support materials, assessment and learning management tools, and eLearning components to create true learning solutions for a wide variety of instructor-led, self-paced, and online courses.

Our textbooks follow the *Labyrinth Instruction Design,* our unique and proven approach that makes learning easy and effective for every learner. Our books begin with fundamental concepts and build through a systematic progression of exercises. Quick Reference Tables, precise callouts on screen captures, carefully selected illustrations, and minimal distraction combine to create a learning solution that is highly efficient and effective for both students and instructors.

This course is supported with *comprehensive instructor support* materials that include printable solution guides for side-by-side comparisons, test banks, customizable assessments, customizable PowerPoint presentations, detailed lesson plans, pre-formatted files for integration to leading learning management system, and more. Our unique WebSims allow students to perform realistic exercises for tasks that cannot be performed in the computer lab.

Our *eLab assessment and learning management tool* is available to supplement this course. eLab is an intuitive, affordable, web-based learning system that helps educators spend less time on course management and more time teaching. eLab integrates seamlessly with your Labyrinth textbook.

Visual Conventions

This book uses many visual and typographic cues to guide students through the lessons. This page provides examples and describes the function of each cue.

Type this text	Anything you should type at the keyboard is printed in this typeface.
	Tips, Notes, and Warnings are used throughout the text to draw attention to certain topics.
Command→ Command→ Command, etc.	This convention indicates how to give a command from the Ribbon. The commands are written: Ribbon Tab→Command Group→Command→ Subcommand.
FROM THE KEYBOARD Ctrl+S to save	These margin notes indicate shortcut keys for executing a task described in the text.

Exercise Progression

The exercises in this book build in complexity as students work through a lesson toward mastery of the skills taught.

- **Develop Your Skills** exercises are introduced immediately after concept discussions. They provide detailed, step-by-step tutorials.
- **Reinforce Your Skills** exercises provide additional hands-on practice with moderate assistance.
- **Apply Your Skills** exercises test students' skills by describing the correct results without providing specific instructions on how to achieve them.
- **Critical Thinking and Work-Readiness Skills** exercises are the most challenging. They provide generic instructions, allowing students to use their skills and creativity to achieve the results they envision.

Acknowledgements

We are grateful to the instructors who have used Labyrinth titles and suggested improvements to us over the many years we have been writing and publishing books. This book has benefited greatly from the reviews and suggestions of the following instructors.

Darrell Abbey, *Cascadia Community College*

Joan Adkins, *Nicolet Area Technical College*

Andre Andersen, *Grossmont College*

Tonya Bailey, *Laurel Technical Institute Jim Bandy, Spencerian College*

Margo Bouchard, *University of New Mexico Continuing Education*

Patricia Boyd, *Keefe Technical School*

Sylvia Brown, *Midland College Gene Carbonaro, Long Beach City College*

Earline Cocke, *Northwest Mississippi Community College*

Susan Comtois, *Cambrian College of Applied Arts and Technology Mary Craven, Alabama Southern Community College*

Becky Curtin, *Harper College*

William Eichenlaub, *S.E. Tech, Red Wingm MN*

Janis Engwer, *Lakeland High School and North Idaho College*

Dawn Followell, *Richland Community College*

Debra Hauff, *Merced County Office of Education*

Jennifer Hendry, *Northlands College*

Wayne Henrie, *Ilisagvik College Loretta Jarrell, LTC – Baton Rouge Campus*

Pat Jarvis, *Truckee Meadows Community College*

Laurie Johnson, *Manhattan Area Technical College*

Teresa Jolly, *South Georgia Technical College Gwen Just, Parkland College*

Jodi Kidd, *Ashland County-West Holmes Career Center*

Jeanne Lake, *Marshall Vo-Tech-Saline County Career Center*

Mark Larson, *Wisconsin Learning Center*

Jayne Lowery, *Jackson State Community College*

Tawana Mattox, *Athens Technical College*

Peter Meggison, *Massasoit Community College*

Mitze Mendez, *Seneca*

John Mims, *Central New Mexico Community College Workforce Training Center*

Carmen Morrison, *North Central State College*

Tamara Oakes, *Skagit Valley College, Whidbey Island Campus*

Carrie Pedersen, *Lower Columbia College*

Paul Pendley, *Coastal Bend College*

Joseph Perret, *Pierce College*

Mary Peterhans, *Elgin Community College*

Mary Peterson, *Tennessee Technology Center*

Kari Phillips, *Davis Applied Technology College*

Tonya Pierce, *Ivy Tech Community College-Kokomo*

Kathleen Purcell, *Nova Scotia Community College – IT Campus*

Sharyn Putnik, *Tooele Applied Technology College*

Judy Salerno, *Mohave Community College*

Louis Sanchez, *DeAnza College*

Joann Santillo, *Mahoining County CTC*

Doris Scott, *Traviss Career Center*

Pamela Silvers, *A-B Tech*

Nancy Skinner, *Providence Health & Services*

Lydia Slater, *Rock Valley College*

Amy Smith, *Black Hawk College*

Karen Spray, *Northeast Community College*

Alison Thompson, *Waubonsee Community College*

Julie Tyler, *Great Plains Tech Center*

Cally Youngberg, *Red Wing/Winona State College Southeast Technical*

Sandy Weber, *Gateway Technical College Ericka Wiginton, Southwest Technology Center*

Nick Wright, *Gibbs High School*

Working with Word Basics

LEARNING OBJECTIVES

After studying this lesson, you will be able to:

- Use and customize the Ribbon
- Use the Quick Access toolbar and the Mini toolbar
- Open and close documents
- Navigate in a document
- Use Word Help

In this lesson, you will get an overview of Microsoft Office Word 2010. First you will learn to start Word, and then how to work with the Word interface. You will open and close documents, navigate through a multipage document, and work with Word Help. Finally, you will exit the Word program.

Getting Oriented to Word 2010

My Virtual Campus

Stefanie Bentley has been promoted to marketing assistant at My Virtual Campus, a social networking technology company. My Virtual Campus sells their web application to colleges and universities, allowing students, alumni, faculty, and staff to utilize this social networking website, which is closed to the public and branded for their institution. Her first task is to create a brief summary of what their best-selling website is and how it is used. This effort will provide Stefanie a good opportunity to see just how easy Microsoft Word 2010 is to use when writing her paper, and if she runs into any problems along the way, she will appreciate how much help is at her fingertips.

My Virtual Campus

Our best-selling website, a social networking Intranet established specifically for college communities worldwide, has been gaining popularity at an extraordinary rate.

The website is useful for all types of networking opportunities; for example, social events and career prospects can be publicized, prospective students can check out the campus, professors and students can participate in extended training occasions and collaborate on special projects. It also proves useful when looking for a roommate or offering items for sale. Alumni can post job opportunities for current students and other noteworthy news, and so forth.

In general, here's how it works; you join and create a profile about yourself, choosing how much personal information to enter. Then, you can invite other people to join also. You can chat in real-time with other members, post photos to share, and most importantly, you can control what information others can see about you.

Security is taken very seriously by My Virtual Campus and every step has been taken to ensure your privacy and protect your confidential information.

1.1 Presenting Word 2010

Video Lesson   labyrinthelab.com/videos

Microsoft Office Word 2010 is a dynamic document-authoring program that lets you create and easily modify a variety of documents. Word provides tools to assist you in virtually every aspect of document creation. From desktop publishing to web publishing, Word has the right tool for the job. For these and many other reasons, Word is the most widely used word processing program in homes and businesses.

1.2 Starting Word

The method you use to start Word depends on whether you intend to create a new document or open an existing one. If you intend to create a new document, use one of the following methods to start Word:

- Click the ⊞ button, choose Microsoft Office from the All Programs menu, and then choose Microsoft Word 2010.
- Click the Microsoft Word 2010 🅆 button on the Quick Launch toolbar located at the left edge of the taskbar. (This button may not appear on all computers.)

Use one of the following methods if you intend to open an existing Word document. Once the Word program starts, the desired document will open in a Word window.

- Navigate to the desired document using Windows Explorer or My Computer and double-click the document name.
- Click the ⊞ button and choose Documents. Choose Recently Changed under Favorites, and then double-click the desired document name.

After you start Word, the document window shows. Don't be concerned if your document window looks a little different from this example. The Word screen is customizable.

File tab—This tab leads to file management tasks, including opening, printing, and saving your work. The File tab also leads to Backstage view, which provides information about the document and options to change Word's default settings.

Quick Access toolbar—Frequently used commands appear here, and you can add your own favorites.

Title bar—The name of your document appears here. You see a generic *Documentx* name until you save and name your document.

The Ribbon—This is control central, where you find the tools you need to build, format, and edit your documents.

Insertion point—This is where the action is. When you type, the characters appear at the insertion point.

Zoom control—Dragging the Zoom control or clicking the buttons allows you to zoom in or out on the document.

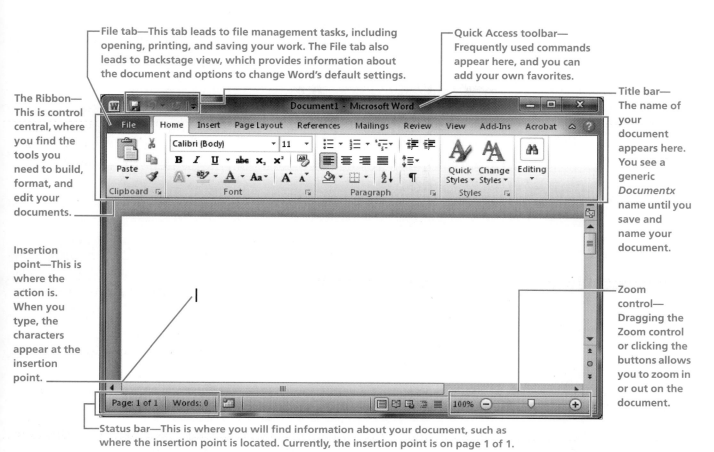

Status bar—This is where you will find information about your document, such as where the insertion point is located. Currently, the insertion point is on page 1 of 1.

TIP

The insertion point is sometimes referred to as the cursor.

Start Word

In this exercise, you will experience starting Word, and you will examine the Word window.

1. If necessary, **start** your computer. The Windows Desktop appears.

2. **Click** the ⊞ button at the left edge of the taskbar, and choose **All Programs**.

3. Choose **Microsoft Office→Microsoft Word 2010** from the menu.

4. Make sure the Word window is **maximized** ▣.

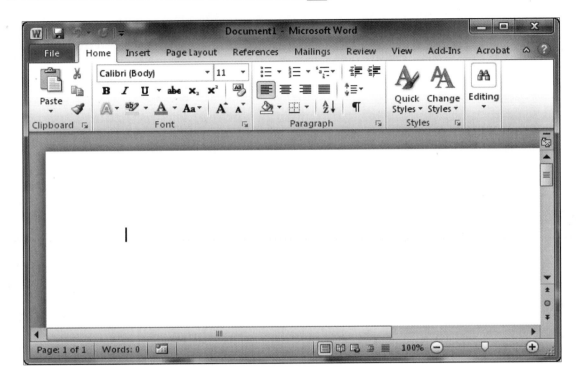

1.3 Opening Documents

Video Lesson labyrinthelab.com/videos

The Open command on the File tab displays the Open dialog box, where you can navigate to a storage location and open previously saved documents. Once a document is open, you can edit or print it.

Opening Older Word Documents

If you open a document created in a previous version of Word, 2007 and earlier, it opens in Compatibility Mode. The term appears in the Title bar, as shown in the illustration. Older Word documents do not understand the new features in Word 2010, so those features are limited or disabled.

When an older document is open, a Convert command is available in Backstage view, which you can use to upgrade the file and make the new features of Word 2010 available.

Storing Your Exercise Files

Throughout this book, you will be referred to files in your "file storage location." You can store your exercise files on various media, such as on a USB flash drive, in the Documents folder, or to a network drive at a school or company. While some figures may display files on a USB flash drive, it is assumed that you will substitute your own location for that shown in the figures. See Storing Your Exercise Files for additional information on alternative storage media. Storing Your Exercise Files is available on the student web page for this book at labpub.com/learn/word10/.

In Windows XP, the folder is called My Documents. In Windows Vista and Windows 7, it is called Documents. Throughout this book we will use the word Documents when referring to this folder.

If you have not yet copied the student exercise files to your local file storage location, follow the instructions in Storing Your Exercise Files, located on the student web page for this book.

Open a Document

In this exercise, you will learn the steps to open an existing document through the Open dialog box.

Before You Begin: Navigate to the student web page for this book at labpub.com/learn/word10 and see the Downloading the Student Exercise Files section of Storing Your Exercise Files for instructions on how to retrieve the student exercise files for this book and to copy them to your file storage location.

1. Follow these steps to open the document:

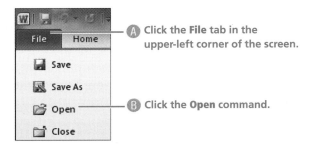

Ⓐ Click the **File** tab in the upper-left corner of the screen.

Ⓑ Click the **Open** command.

NOTE

Later in this lesson, the preceding steps will be written like this: Click the File (or File) tab and choose Open from the menu.

2. When the **Open** dialog box appears, follow these steps to open the My Virtual Campus document:

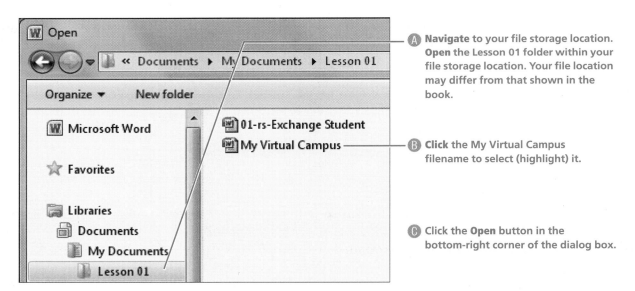

Ⓐ **Navigate** to your file storage location. **Open** the Lesson 01 folder within your file storage location. Your file location may differ from that shown in the book.

Ⓑ **Click** the My Virtual Campus filename to select (highlight) it.

Ⓒ Click the **Open** button in the bottom-right corner of the dialog box.

TIP

You can also double-click on a filename to open it.

3. Make sure the Word window is **maximized** 🔲.

1.4 Working with the Word 2010 Interface

Video Lesson   labyrinthelab.com/videos

The band running across the top of the screen is the Ribbon. This is where you will find the tools for building, formatting, and editing your documents. You can customize the Ribbon by adding new tabs with their own groups and commands.

The Ribbon

The Ribbon consists of three primary areas: tabs, groups, and commands. The tabs include Home, Insert, Page Layout, and so on. A group houses related commands within a tab. Groups on the Home tab, for instance, include Clipboard, Font, Paragraph, Styles, and Editing. An example of a command in the Paragraph group is Increase Indent.

Home tab   Paragraph group   Increase Indent command

Be aware that the arrangement of the buttons on the Ribbon can vary, depending on your screen resolution and how the Word window is sized. Following are two examples of how the Paragraph group might appear on the Ribbon.

Contextual Tabs

Contextual tabs appear in context with the task you are performing. As shown in the following illustration, double-clicking a clip art object in a document activates Picture Tools, with the Format tab in the foreground.

You have to double-click the object the first time to activate the contextual tab; afterward, you only have to click the object once to reactivate it.

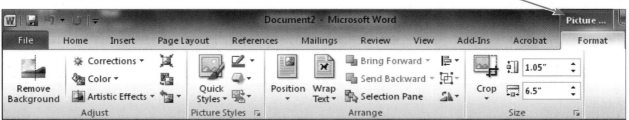

Dialog Box Launcher

Some groups include a dialog box launcher in the bottom-right corner of the group. This means that there are additional commands available for the group. Clicking the launcher opens the dialog box, or it may open a task pane, which, like a dialog box, houses additional commands related to the group.

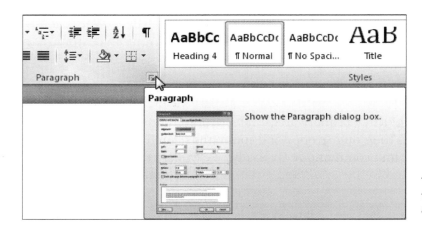

The dialog box launcher displays the dialog box or task pane available for a given command.

Live Preview with Galleries

Live Preview shows what a formatting change looks like without actually applying the format. In the following example, selecting a block of text, and then hovering the mouse pointer over a font in the font gallery, previews how the text will look. Clicking the font name applies the font to the text.

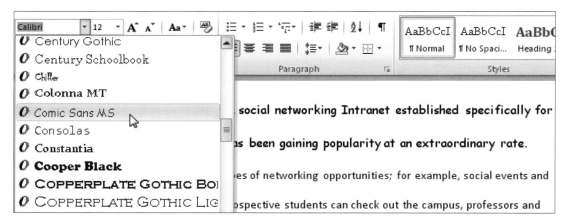

Live Preview of the Comic Sans MS Font

Hide the Ribbon

FROM THE KEYBOARD

Ctrl+F1 to hide/unhide the Ribbon

If you want more room to work, you can temporarily hide the Ribbon by double-clicking the active tab. This collapses the Ribbon, as shown in the following illustration.

Clicking a tab, such as Home, redisplays the full Ribbon temporarily. It collapses again when you click in the document. If you want the Ribbon to remain open, double-click the same tab you used to collapse it, or right-click on the Ribbon and choose Minimize the Ribbon to turn off the feature.

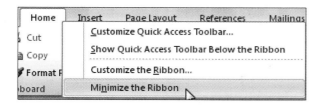

Customize the Ribbon

The Ribbon can now be customized, making it easier for you to have access to the commands that you use frequently all under one tab, if you like. You can add new groups to existing tabs or add new tabs with their own groups and commands. You can always restore the original Ribbon tabs, groups, and commands very easily.

 You cannot add new commands to an existing group on the original Ribbon.

When you choose to add a new tab to the Ribbon, the new tab appears on the right of the active tab; however, you can move it at any time. The new tab includes an empty new group, ready for you to add commands to it. You use the Move Up and Move Down arrows in the Word Options dialog box to reposition existing tabs and groups.

Move Up and
Move Down arrows

DEVELOP YOUR SKILLS 1.4.1
Work with the Ribbon

In this exercise, you will explore the various aspects of the Ribbon, including tabs, contextual tabs, the dialog box launcher, and Live Preview. Finally, you'll hide and unhide the Ribbon, and learn how to customize it.

Display the Insert Tab

1. Click the **Insert** tab on the Ribbon to display the commands available in that category.

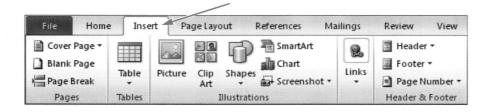

2. Take a moment to investigate some of the other tabs on the Ribbon, and then return to the **Home** tab.

Display Contextual Tabs and Use the Dialog Box Launcher

3. **Double-click** the clip art object at the top of your document to display Picture Tools on the Ribbon.

Selection handles (small circles and squares) surround an object when you click it.

Picture Tools

4. Click anywhere in the **document** to deselect the clip art.

5. Hover the **mouse pointer** over the dialog box launcher in the bottom-right corner of the Font group to display the ToolTip, as shown here.

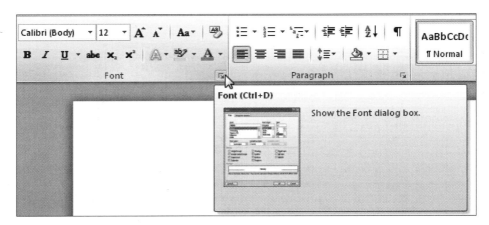

6. Click the **dialog box launcher** to open the Font dialog box.

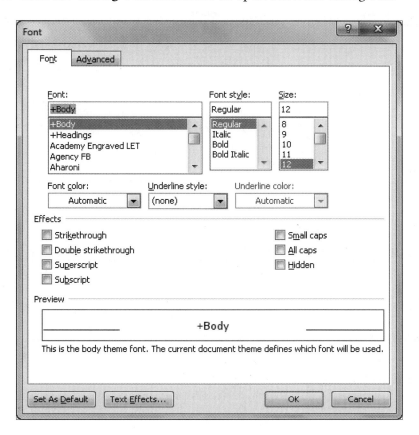

This dialog box provides additional tools for formatting text.

7. Click the **Cancel** button in the bottom-right corner to close the dialog box.

Use Live Preview

8. Position the **mouse pointer** in the white, left margin area of the second paragraph. Then, **double-click** the left mouse button to select (highlight) the entire paragraph, as shown here.
   If you notice a little toolbar fade in, you can ignore it for now. It will fade away on its own.

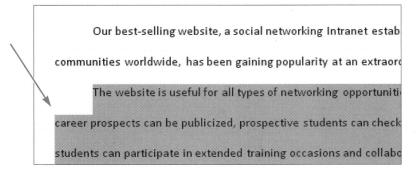

9. Follow these steps to use Live Preview:

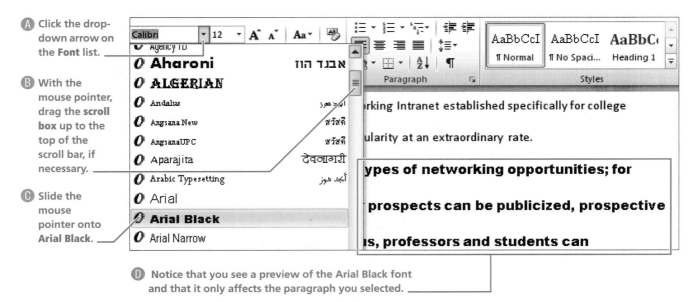

A Click the drop-down arrow on the **Font** list.

B With the mouse pointer, drag the **scroll box** up to the top of the scroll bar, if necessary.

C Slide the mouse pointer onto **Arial Black**.

D Notice that you see a preview of the Arial Black font and that it only affects the paragraph you selected.

10. Take a moment to **preview** a few other fonts.

11. **Click** anywhere in the document to close the font list, and **click** once again to deselect the highlighted text.

Minimize/Restore the Ribbon

12. **Double-click** the Home tab to minimize the Ribbon.

13. **Right-click** a Ribbon tab and choose **Minimize the Ribbon** from the menu to turn off the feature.

Add a New Tab to the Ribbon

14. **Right-click** the Home tab and then choose **Customize the Ribbon**.

15. Follow these steps to add a new tab to the Ribbon:

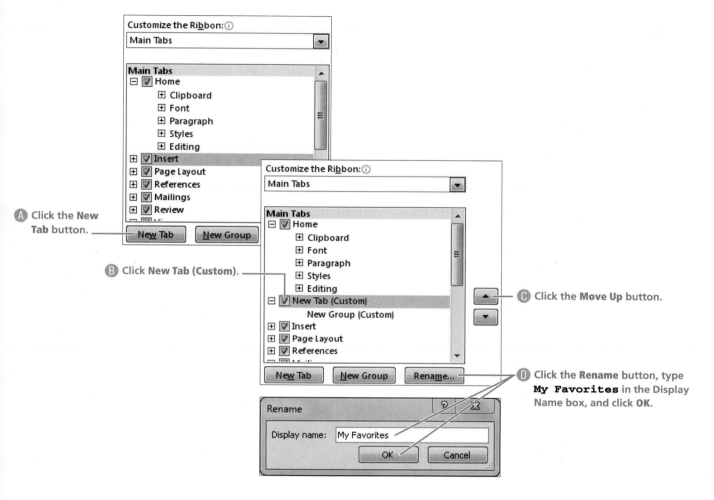

Ⓐ Click the **New Tab** button.

Ⓑ Click **New Tab (Custom)**.

Ⓒ Click the **Move Up** button.

Ⓓ Click the **Rename** button, type **My Favorites** in the Display Name box, and click **OK**.

Notice when you create a new tab, it automatically includes a new group for you to customize with commands.

16. Click **OK** again in the Word Options dialog box, and then click the new **My Favorites** tab. *Notice the new tab is to the left of the Home tab, there are currently no commands on the new tab, and there is a blank New Group awaiting commands to be added to it.*

Add a New Group to the My Favorites Tab

17. Right-click the My Favorites tab and choose **Customize the Ribbon**.

18. Follow these steps to add a new group:

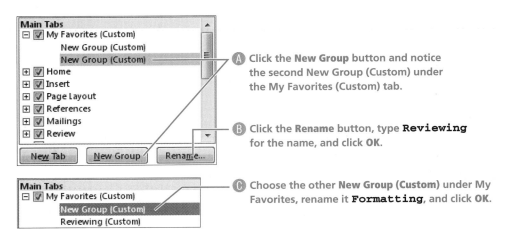

Leave the Word Options box open so you can add commands to your new groups.

Add Commands to Custom Groups

19. If necessary, click the **Formatting (Custom)** group.

20. Follow these steps to add commands to the group:

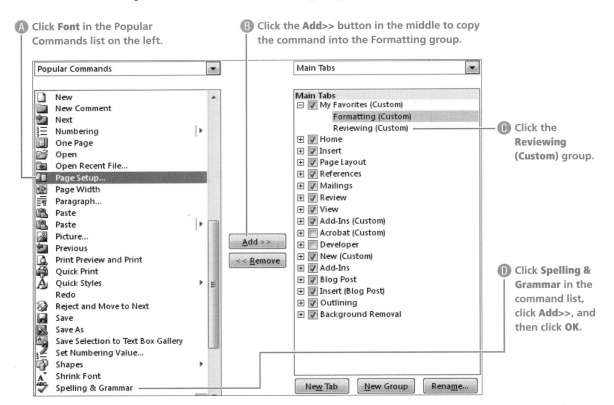

Notice the Ribbon now has a new tab named My Favorites that contains two new groups, Formatting and Reviewing, each containing one command.

21. **Right-click** the Home tab and choose **Customize the Ribbon**.

22. Follow these steps to delete the tab, groups, and commands you made earlier:

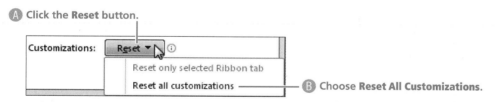

Ⓐ Click the **Reset** button.

Ⓑ Choose **Reset All Customizations**.

23. Click **Yes** in the message box confirming the action, and then click **OK**.

The Quick Access Toolbar

Video Lesson labyrinthelab.com/videos

The Quick Access toolbar in the upper-left corner of the screen contains frequently used commands. It is customizable and operates independently from the Ribbon.

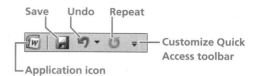

Moving the Quick Access Toolbar

You can place the Quick Access toolbar in one of two positions on the screen. The default position is in the upper-left corner. Clicking the Customize Quick Access toolbar button at the right edge of the toolbar reveals a menu from which you can choose Show Below the Ribbon.

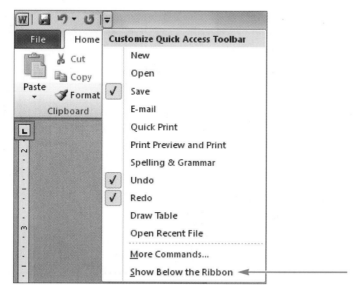

 The Customize Quick Access Toolbar menu conveniently lists a series of frequently used commands that you can add to the toolbar by choosing them from the menu.

Customizing the Quick Access Toolbar

You can add buttons to and remove them from the Quick Access toolbar to suit your needs. You might want to add commands you use regularly so they are always available.

Right-click the Ribbon command you want to add (Center in this example), and choose Add to Quick Access Toolbar from the shortcut menu.

 The terms shortcut, context, pop-up, and drop-down are used interchangeably when referring to a secondary menu that appears.

To remove a button from the Quick Access toolbar, right-click the button and choose Remove from Quick Access Toolbar from the shortcut menu.

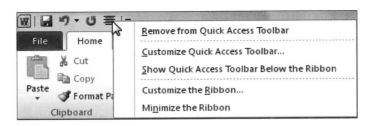

QUICK REFERENCE	WORKING WITH THE QUICK ACCESS TOOLBAR
Task	**Procedure**
Add a button to the toolbar	▪ Right-click the button you want to add. ▪ Choose Add to Quick Access Toolbar from the menu.
Remove a button from the toolbar	▪ Right-click the button you want to remove. ▪ Choose Remove from Quick Access Toolbar from the shortcut menu.
Change the location of the toolbar	▪ Click the Customize Quick Access Toolbar button at the right edge of the toolbar. ▪ Choose Show Below (or Above) the Ribbon.

Work with the Quick Access Toolbar

In this exercise, you will reposition the Quick Access toolbar, and then you will customize it by adding and removing buttons.

Change the Quick Access Toolbar Location

1. Follow these steps to move the Quick Access toolbar below the Ribbon:

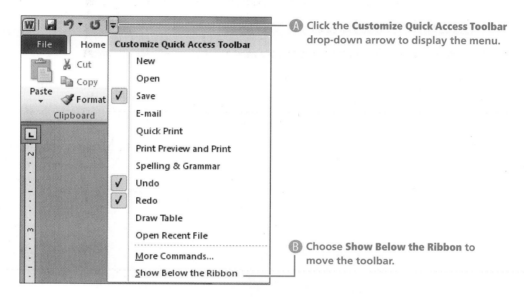

Ⓐ Click the **Customize Quick Access Toolbar** drop-down arrow to display the menu.

Ⓑ Choose **Show Below the Ribbon** to move the toolbar.

The toolbar appears below the Ribbon at the left edge of the window. Now you will return it to its original position.

2. Click the **drop-down arrow** at the right edge of the Quick Access toolbar again, and this time choose **Show Above the Ribbon**.

Add a Button to the Quick Access Toolbar

3. Make sure that the **Home** tab is active, and then follow these steps to add the Bullets button to the toolbar:

Ⓐ **Right-click** the Bullets button in the Paragraph group to display the shortcut menu.

Ⓑ Choose **Add to Quick Access Toolbar.**

The Bullets button now appears on the toolbar.

4. **Right-click** the Bullets ⊞ button on the Quick Access toolbar and choose the **Remove from Quick Access Toolbar** command.

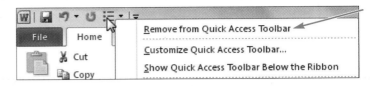

The button disappears from the Quick Access toolbar.

The Mini Toolbar

Video Lesson   labyrinthelab.com/videos

There's another toolbar in Word, and it contains frequently used formatting commands. When you select (highlight) text, the Mini toolbar fades in. After a pause, it fades away. Make it reappear by right-clicking the selected text.

In the following example, clicking the Bold **B** button on the Mini toolbar applies the Bold feature to the selected text.

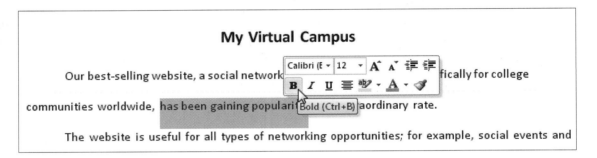

DEVELOP YOUR SKILLS 1.4.3
Use the Mini Toolbar

In this exercise, you will use the Mini toolbar to format text.

1. Follow these steps to italicize a paragraph:

Ⓐ Position the **mouse pointer** in the white margin to the left of the first paragraph and then **double-click** to select (highlight) the paragraph.

Ⓑ When the Mini toolbar fades in, click the **Italic** button.

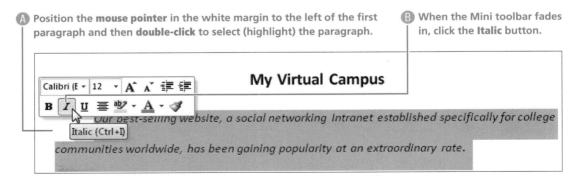

NOTE If this timid little toolbar disappears, right-click the highlighted text and it will reappear.

2. **Click** anywhere in the document to deselect the text and view the formatted paragraph.

3. Select the **first paragraph** again and click the **Italic** button to remove the formatting.

1.5 Navigating in a Word Document

Video Lesson labyrinthelab.com/videos

If you are working in a multipage document, it is helpful to know about various techniques for moving through a document. You can navigate using the scroll bar located at the right side of the screen, or you can use keystrokes.

Navigating with the Scroll Bar

The scroll bar lets you browse through documents; however, it does not move the insertion point. After scrolling, you must click in the document where you want to reposition the insertion point. The following illustration shows the components of the scroll bar.

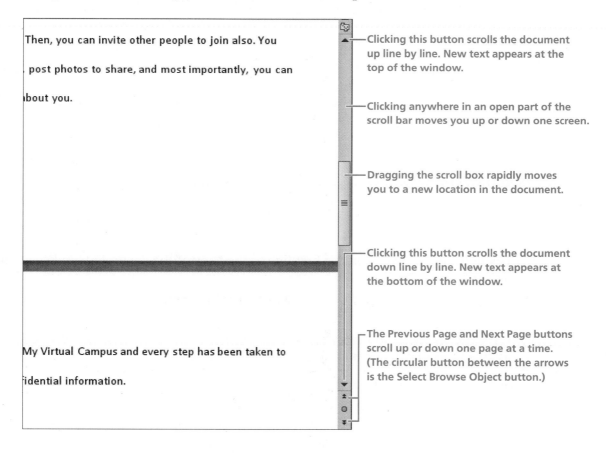

Then, you can invite other people to join also. You post photos to share, and most importantly, you can bout you.

Clicking this button scrolls the document up line by line. New text appears at the top of the window.

Clicking anywhere in an open part of the scroll bar moves you up or down one screen.

Dragging the scroll box rapidly moves you to a new location in the document.

Clicking this button scrolls the document down line by line. New text appears at the bottom of the window.

My Virtual Campus and every step has been taken to idential information.

The Previous Page and Next Page buttons scroll up or down one page at a time. (The circular button between the arrows is the Select Browse Object button.)

Positioning the Insertion Point

When the mouse pointer is in a text area, it resembles an uppercase "I" and it is referred to as an I-beam. The insertion point is positioned at the location where you click the I-beam and it begins flashing. Thus, wherever the insertion point is flashing, that is where the action begins.

DEVELOP YOUR SKILLS 1.5.1

Practice Scrolling and Positioning the Insertion Point

In this exercise, you will use the scroll bar to practice moving through a document, and then you will position the insertion point.

Scroll in the Document

1. Follow these steps to scroll in the document:

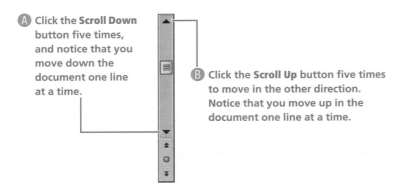

A Click the **Scroll Down** button five times, and notice that you move down the document one line at a time.

B Click the **Scroll Up** button five times to move in the other direction. Notice that you move up in the document one line at a time.

2. Position the **I-beam** Ⅰ mouse pointer in the body of the document.
   Notice that while the mouse pointer looks like an I-beam when it's inside the document, it looks like a white arrow when it is in the document's left margin. The pointer must have the I-beam shape before you can reposition the insertion point.

Position the Insertion Point

3. Click the **I-beam** Ⅰ anywhere in the document to position the blinking insertion point.

4. Move the **mouse pointer** into the left margin area. The white arrow shape is now visible.

5. Position the **I-beam** Ⅰ in the first line of the body of the document, and click the **left** mouse button.
   The insertion point appears just where you clicked. If the background is highlighted, you accidentally selected the text. Deselect by clicking the mouse pointer in the document background.

6. Click the open part of the **scroll bar** below the scroll box to move down one screen, as shown in the illustration to the right.

Use the Scroll Box and the Next Page/Previous Page Buttons

7. Drag the **scroll box** to the bottom of the scroll bar with the mouse pointer.
   Notice that the insertion point is not blinking anywhere on the screen because all you have done is scroll through the document. You have not repositioned the insertion point yet.

8. Click any open part of the **scroll bar** above the scroll box, then click the **I-beam** I at the end of the text to position the insertion point on the last page.

9. Drag the **scroll box** to the top of the scroll bar, and click the **I-beam** I in front of the first word of the first paragraph.

10. Click the **Next Page** ⊻ button to move to the top of page 2.
The insertion point moves with you when you use the Next Page and Previous Page buttons.

11. Click the **Previous Page** ⊼ button to move to the top of page 1.

Navigating with the Keyboard

Video Lesson   labyrinthelab.com/videos

Whether you use the mouse or the keyboard to navigate through a document is a matter of personal preference. Navigating with the keyboard always moves the insertion point, so it will be with you when you arrive at your destination.

The following Quick Reference table provides keystrokes for moving quickly through a document.

QUICK REFERENCE	NAVIGATING WITH THE KEYBOARD		
Press	**To Move**	**Press**	**To Move**
→	One character to the right	Page Down	Down one screen
←	One character to the left	Page Up	Up one screen
Ctrl + →	One word to the right	Ctrl + End	To the end of the document
Ctrl + ←	One word to the left	Ctrl + Home	To the beginning of the document
↓	Down one line	End	To the end of the line
↑	Up one line	Home	To the beginning of the line

DEVELOP YOUR SKILLS 1.5.2
Use the Keyboard to Navigate

In this exercise, you will use the keyboard to practice moving through a document.

Use the Arrow Keys

1. Click the **I-beam** I in the middle of the first line of the first paragraph.

2. Tap the **right arrow** → and **left arrow** ← keys three times to move to the right and left, one character at a time.

3. Tap the **down arrow** ↓ and **up arrow** ↑ keys three times to move down and then up, one row at a time.

Use Additional Keys

4. **Hold down** the Ctrl key and keep it down, then **tap** the Home key to move the insertion point to the beginning of the document. **Release** the Ctrl key.

5. Use the **arrow keys** to position the insertion point in the middle of the first line of the first paragraph.

6. **Hold down** the `Ctrl` key and keep it down, then tap the **left arrow** `←` key three times to move to the left, one word at a time. **Release** the `Ctrl` key.

7. **Hold down** the `Ctrl` key and keep it down, then tap the **right arrow** `→` key three times to move to the right, one word at a time. **Release** the `Ctrl` key.

8. **Tap** the `Home` key to move to the beginning of the line.

9. **Tap** the `End` key to move to the end of the line.

10. Spend a few moments **navigating** with the keyboard. Refer to the preceding Quick Reference table for some additional keystrokes.

11. **Hold down** the `Ctrl` key then **tap** the `End` key to move the insertion point to the end of the document. **Release** the `Ctrl` key.

12. Move the **insertion point** back to the beginning of the document.

1.6 Closing Documents

Video Lesson   labyrinthelab.com/videos

You close a file by clicking the [File] tab and choosing the Close command from the menu. If you haven't saved your document, Word will prompt you to do so.

DEVELOP YOUR SKILLS 1.6.1
Close the Document

In this exercise, you will close a file.

1. **Click** the [File] tab, and then choose **Close** from the menu.

2. If Word asks you if you want to save the changes, click **Don't Save**.

3. If a blank document is open on the screen, use the same technique to **close** it.
   The document window always has this appearance when all documents are closed.

1.7 Starting a New, Blank Document

Video Lesson labyrinthelab.com/videos

You can click the [File] tab, and then choose the New command from the menu to open a new, blank document.

FROM THE KEYBOARD
[Ctrl]+[N] to start a new document

DEVELOP YOUR SKILLS 1.7.1
Start a New Document

In this exercise, you will open a new, blank document. There should not be any documents in the Word window at this time.

1. **Click** the [File] tab, and then choose **New** from the menu.

2. When the New Document dialog box appears, **double-click** the Blank Document icon to display the new document.
   Now you will close the new document and try using the shortcut keystrokes to start another new document.

3. **Click** the [File] tab, and then choose **Close** from the menu.

4. **Hold down** the [Ctrl] key and **tap** the [N] on your keyboard to open a new document.

5. Leave this document **open**.

1.8 Getting Help in Word 2010

Video Lesson labyrinthelab.com/videos

The Microsoft Word Help button appears in the upper-right corner of the Word screen. Clicking the Help button opens the Word Help window where you can browse through a Table of Contents, click links to access a variety of topics, or type a term in the search box and let the system find the answer for you.

Use Word Help

In this exercise you will practice working with several Help techniques.

1. Click the **Help** button in the upper-right corner of the Word window.

2. Follow these steps for an overview of Word Help:

A Some of these toolbar buttons are like ones you may already be familiar with from using a web browser. Click the **mouse pointer** on the top frame of the Word Help window to activate it, and then **hover** the mouse pointer over buttons to see **ToolTips** describing their purpose. The Table of Contents is not visible the first time you use Help; however, you can use the Table of Contents button to display it.

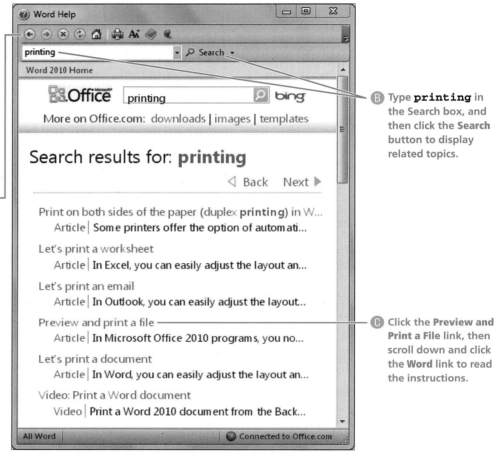

B Type **printing** in the Search box, and then click the **Search** button to display related topics.

C Click the **Preview and Print a File** link, then scroll down and click the **Word** link to read the instructions.

3. Click the **Close** button in the upper-right corner of the Word Help window.

1.9 Exiting from Word

Video Lesson   labyrinthelab.com/videos

Clicking the File tab and then clicking the ⊠ Exit button closes the Word application. It's important to exit Word in an orderly fashion. Turning off your computer before exiting Word could cause you to lose data.

You can also use the Close button in the upper-right corner of the window to close Word.

DEVELOP YOUR SKILLS 1.9.1
Exit from Word

In this exercise, you will exit from Word. Since the blank document on the screen has not been modified, you won't bother saving it.

1. **Click** the File tab.
2. **Click** the ⊠ Exit button at the bottom of the list.
3. When Word prompts you to save changes, click **Don't Save**.
   Word closes and the Windows Desktop appears.

1.10 Concepts Review

Concepts Review   labyrinthelab.com/word10

To check your knowledge of the key concepts introduced in this lesson, complete the Concepts Review quiz by going to the URL listed above. If your classroom is using Labyrinth eLab, you may complete the Concepts Review quiz from within your eLab course.

Reinforce Your Skills

Identify Elements of the Word 2010 Window

In this exercise, you will practice using correct terminology with parts of the Word screen. It's important to use the right terms when talking about the Word application. If, for example, you need to discuss an issue with people in your IT department, they can help you faster if they are clear on what you are talking about.

1. Start **Word 2010**.

2. Using the table to the right of the illustration, write down the correct terms for items **A through E**.

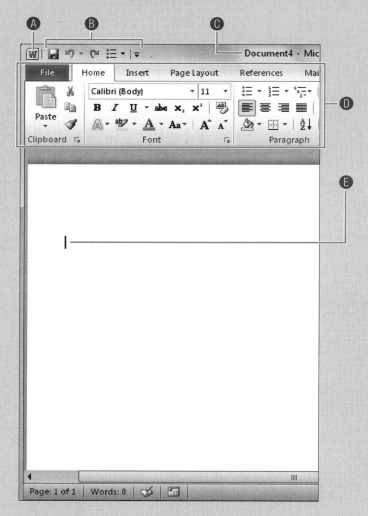

Letter	Term
A	_____
B	_____
C	_____
D	_____
E	_____

Use Word Help

In this exercise, you will work with the Word Help window to find information that can assist you as you work.

1. Click the **Microsoft Word Help**  button in the upper-right corner of the Word window.

Use the Browse Word Help Window

Now you'll review opening a file in another file format. Your links may be in different locations depending on if your computer is online or not.

2. Click the **File Migration** link; then scroll down and click the **Use Word to Open or Save a File in Another File Format** link and read the topic.

3. Scroll up and click the **Word 2010 Home** link at the top of the pane to return to the Browse Word Help pane.

4. Click the **Creating Documents** link in the Word Help window.

5. Click the **Create a Document** link.

6. **Scroll down** to see the major topics that are covered.

Search for Help

7. Follow these steps to locate the Set the Default Font topic:

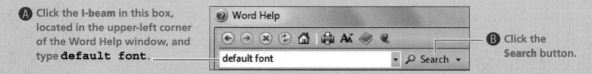

Ⓐ Click the **I-beam** in this box, located in the upper-left corner of the Word Help window, and type **default font**.

Ⓑ Click the **Search** button.

8. Click the **Set the Default Font** link in the Word Help window to view the topic.

9. **Scroll down** and take a moment to read the first few entries.

10. Click the **Close** button in the upper-right corner of the Word Help window.

REINFORCE YOUR SKILLS 1.3
Navigate in a Document

In this exercise, you will use a letter that an exchange student in Paris wrote to his friend. It's a long letter, so it will provide good practice for navigating.

1. **Click** the **File** tab and choose **Open** from the menu.

2. When the Open dialog box appears, if necessary, **navigate** to your file storage location and **open** the Lesson 01 folder.

3. **Double-click** to open the file named rs-Exchange Student.

Navigate with the Scroll Bar

4. Click the **Next Page** ⬇ button at the bottom of the scroll bar to move to the top of page 2.

5. Click the **scroll bar** below the scroll box to move down one screen.

6. Drag the **scroll box** to the top of the scroll bar, and **click** for an insertion point at the beginning of the document.

7. Click the **Scroll Down** ▼ button, and hold the mouse button down to scroll quickly through the document.

8. Click the **Previous Page** ⬆ button enough times to return to the top of the document.

Navigate with the Keyboard

9. Tap the **down arrow** ⬇ key twice to move to the beginning of the first paragraph.

10. **Tap** the End key to move the insertion point to the end of the line.

11. **Tap** the Home key to move to the beginning of the line.

12. **Tap** Ctrl+End to place the insertion point at the end of the document.

13. **Tap** Ctrl+Home to move to the top of the document.

14. If you press and hold the arrow keys, the insertion point moves quickly through the document. **Press and hold** the ⬇ key long enough to move to the beginning of the second paragraph.

15. **Hold down** the Ctrl key and **tap** the → key three times to move to the right, one word at a time.

16. Please leave this document **open** for the next exercise.

Work with the Quick Access Toolbar

In this exercise, you will move the Quick Access toolbar below the Ribbon, and you will customize the toolbar by adding a button to it.

Before You Begin: The rs-Exchange Student document should be open in Word.

1. Follow these steps to move the Quick Access toolbar:

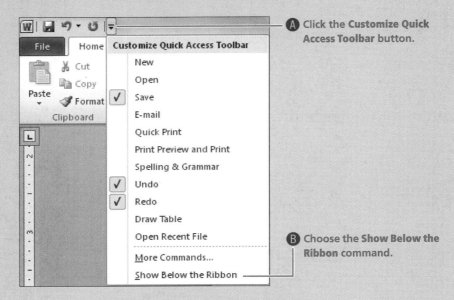

Ⓐ Click the **Customize Quick Access Toolbar** button.

Ⓑ Choose the **Show Below the Ribbon** command.

Now you will return the toolbar to its original position.

2. Click the **drop-down arrow** at the right edge of the toolbar, and choose **Show Above the Ribbon** from the menu.
Next you'll add a button to the Quick Access toolbar.

3. Make sure you're on the **Home** tab. If not, **click** the tab to bring it to the foreground.

4. Follow these steps to add the **Clear Formatting** button to the toolbar:

Ⓐ Right-click the Clear Formatting button in the Font group.

Ⓑ Choose **Add to Quick Access Toolbar** from the menu.

The button now appears on the toolbar.

5. Ask your instructor to inspect your work and initial here to verify the placement of the Clear Formatting button on the toolbar. _____
Next you will remove the button you just added to the toolbar.

6. Place the mouse pointer over the **Clear Formatting** button on the Quick Access toolbar and click the **right** mouse button.

7. Choose **Remove from Quick Access Toolbar** from the menu.

8. Please leave this document **open** for the next exercise.

Apply Your Skills

APPLY YOUR SKILLS 1.1

Use Help to Learn About Print Preview

In this exercise, you will explore Help to learn how to preview a document before printing it.

Before You Begin: The rs-Exchange Student document should be open in Word.

1. Use Help's **Search** feature to locate information about Print Preview.

2. Open the **Print Preview** window by following the instructions in the Help window.

3. Practice using the commands in the **Zoom** group on the Ribbon to view your document in various magnifications.

4. Zoom your document to **250%**, and then ask your instructor to verify the zoom magnification and initial this step. _____

5. **Close** Print Preview, and leave this document **open** for the next exercise.

6. **Close** the Help window.

APPLY YOUR SKILLS 1.2

Ribbon Terminology

In this exercise, you will review terminology relating to the Ribbon. Feel free to refer back in this lesson or to use Word's Help feature to find the correct terms.

1. List the names of the tabs on the Ribbon.

   _____

   _____

   _____

   _____

   _____

   _____

   _____

2. List three commands in the Paragraph group of the Home tab.

   _____

   _____

   _____

3. Define contextual tabs.

   _____

   _____

4. Ask your instructor to verify your answers and initial this exercise. _____

5. Leave the rs-Exchange Student document open for the next exercise.

Customize the Ribbon

In this exercise, you will customize the Ribbon by adding a new tab and group.

1. Add a new **tab** named **Favorites** with a new **group** named **Formatting**.

2. Place the Favorites tab between the **Home** and **Insert** tabs on the Ribbon.

3. Place three **formatting commands** to the new Formatting group.

4. **Restore** all Ribbon defaults by removing any customizations.

5. **Close** the rs-Exchange Student document. If you are prompted to save, do not.

Critical Thinking & Work-Readiness Skills

In the course of working through the following Microsoft Office-based Critical Thinking exercises, you will also be utilizing various work-readiness skills, some of which are listed next to each exercise. Go to labyrinthelab.com/workreadiness to learn more about the work-readiness skills.

1.1 Use Help

Elise Ferrer, one of My Virtual Campus' tech support specialists, has been asked to help with the company's migration from Office 2007 to Office 2010. She decides to provide a "cheat sheet" of online help tutorials to aid the employees using Word. Start Word, create a new, blank document, and use Word's Help feature to locate five basic topics for this purpose. Use a sheet of notebook paper and a pen to record the five links to the online help topics you found.

1.2 Customize the Ribbon

To help the employees in the marketing department work more efficiently, Elise customizes their Ribbons by adding a custom tab. Create a new tab in Word called **Marketing** and position it before the Home tab. Create a group in the custom tab named **Marketing Tasks**. Add five commands to the Marketing Tasks group that you think might be useful for someone working in a marketing department (they will be opening, editing, and formatting documents, in addition to inserting pictures). On a sheet of notebook paper, write down the five commands you selected and explain why you think those particular commands would be helpful for someone in the marketing department. Reset the Ribbon to its default setting when you are finished.

1.3 Customize the Interface

Elise decides to customize the Word interface of her own computer to help her work more efficiently. Practice minimizing and maximizing the Ribbon. Display the Quick Access toolbar both above and below the Ribbon. Add or remove buttons from the Quick Access toolbar. On a sheet of notebook paper, draw a simple sketch of your preferred settings for the Ribbon and Quick Access toolbar. If applicable, exchange papers with a partner and configure your Word interface according to your partner's sketch. Reset the Ribbon and Quick Access toolbar to their default states when you are finished.

Creating and Editing Business Letters

2

In this lesson, you will create business letters while learning proper business document formatting. You will also learn fundamental techniques of entering and editing text, copying and moving text, and saving and printing documents. In addition, you will learn to use Word's AutoCorrect tool to insert frequently used text and control automatic formatting that is applied as you type.

LESSON OUTLINE

LEARNING OBJECTIVES

After studying this lesson, you will be able to:

- Type a professional business letter
- Save a document
- Select and edit text
- Use the AutoCorrect feature
- Set AutoFormat as You Type options
- Copy and move text
- Set Page Layout options
- Preview a document

Student Resources   labyrinthelab.com/word10

Taking Care with Business Letters

Rob Maloney just landed his job as a customer service representative in the Sales Department at My Virtual Campus. He is working for the sales manager, Bruce Carter. A new prospect, Richmond University, has expressed interest in the networking website that My Virtual Campus sells. Mr. Carter has asked Rob to prepare a standard letter for potential new clients, thanking them for their interest and providing information about the website.

Rob starts by referring to his business writing class textbook to ensure that he formats the letter correctly for a good first impression and a professional appearance.

November 24, 2012

Ms. Paige Daniels
Richmond University
15751 Meadow Lane
Chester Allen, VA 23333

Dear Ms. Daniels:

Travis Mayfield referred you to us after he spoke to you about our extraordinary product. I want to take this opportunity to personally thank you for considering My Virtual Campus' social-networking website for your institution. As Travis may have mentioned, we pride ourselves in providing the latest in technology as well as excellent customer service with satisfaction guaranteed.

Enclosed you will find information to review regarding the features of the website. After reading the material, please contact our sales manager, Bruce Carter, at your earliest convenience to discuss your options. Thank you again for considering our amazing website.

Sincerely,

Rob Maloney
Customer Service Representative
Sales Department

rm
Enclosures (2)
cc: Bruce Carter

2.1 Defining Typical Business Letter Styles

Video Lesson labyrinthelab.com/videos

There are several acceptable styles of business letters. The styles discussed in this text include block, modified block standard format, and modified block indented paragraphs. All business letters contain the same or similar elements, but with varied formatting. The following styles are described in this section:

- Block Style
- Modified Block Style—Standard Format
- Modified Block Style—Indented Paragraphs

Block Style

The following illustration outlines the parts of the block style business letter.

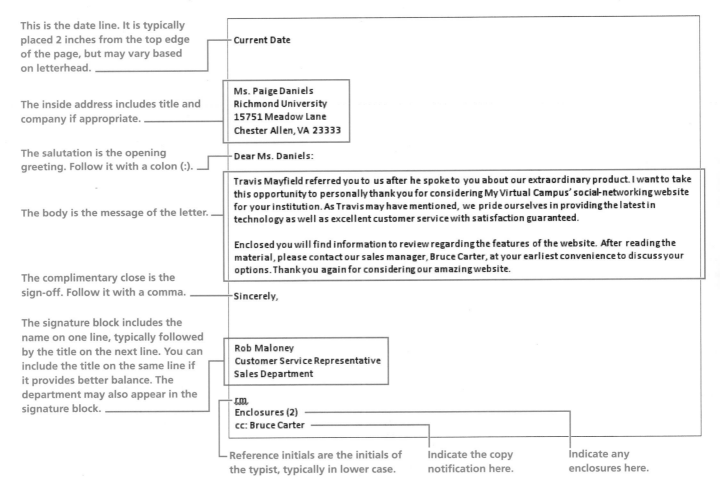

This is the date line. It is typically placed 2 inches from the top edge of the page, but may vary based on letterhead.

Current Date

The inside address includes title and company if appropriate.

Ms. Paige Daniels
Richmond University
15751 Meadow Lane
Chester Allen, VA 23333

The salutation is the opening greeting. Follow it with a colon (:).

Dear Ms. Daniels:

The body is the message of the letter.

Travis Mayfield referred you to us after he spoke to you about our extraordinary product. I want to take this opportunity to personally thank you for considering My Virtual Campus' social-networking website for your institution. As Travis may have mentioned, we pride ourselves in providing the latest in technology as well as excellent customer service with satisfaction guaranteed.

Enclosed you will find information to review regarding the features of the website. After reading the material, please contact our sales manager, Bruce Carter, at your earliest convenience to discuss your options. Thank you again for considering our amazing website.

The complimentary close is the sign-off. Follow it with a comma.

Sincerely,

The signature block includes the name on one line, typically followed by the title on the next line. You can include the title on the same line if it provides better balance. The department may also appear in the signature block.

Rob Maloney
Customer Service Representative
Sales Department

rm
Enclosures (2)
cc: Bruce Carter

Reference initials are the initials of the typist, typically in lower case.

Indicate the copy notification here.

Indicate any enclosures here.

Modified Block Style—Standard Format

The following illustration outlines the differences in the standard modified block style business letter from the block style business letter.

November 24, 2012

The date line, the complimentary close, and the signature block begin at the 3 ½ inch mark on the ruler. All other lines begin at the left margin.

Ms. Paige Daniels
Richmond University
15751 Meadow Lane
Chester Allen, VA 23333

Dear Ms. Daniels:

Travis Mayfield referred you to us after he spoke to you about our extraordinary product. I want to take this opportunity to personally thank you for considering My Virtual Campus' social-networking website for your institution. As Travis may have mentioned, we pride ourselves in providing the latest in technology as well as excellent customer service with satisfaction guaranteed.

Enclosed you will find information to review regarding the features of the website. After reading the material, please contact our sales manager, Bruce Carter, at your earliest convenience to discuss your options. Thank you again for considering our amazing website.

Sincerely,

Rob Maloney
Customer Service Representative
Sales Department

rm
Enclosures (2)
cc: Bruce Carter

Modified Block Style—Indented Paragraphs

The following illustration shows the modified block style business letter with indented paragraphs.

November 24, 2012

Ms. Paige Daniels
Richmond University
15751 Meadow Lane
Chester Allen, VA 23333

Dear Ms. Daniels:

In this format, the first lines of the body paragraphs are indented one-half inch.

    Travis Mayfield referred you to us after he spoke to you about our extraordinary product. I want to take this opportunity to personally thank you for considering My Virtual Campus' social-networking website for your institution. As Travis may have mentioned, we pride ourselves in providing the latest in technology as well as excellent customer service with satisfaction guaranteed.

    Enclosed you will find information to review regarding the features of the website. After reading the material, please contact our sales manager, Bruce Carter, at your earliest convenience to discuss your options. Thank you again for considering our amazing website.

Sincerely,

Rob Maloney
Customer Service Representative
Sales Department

rm
Enclosures (2)
cc: Bruce Carter

2.2 Inserting Text

Video Lesson   labyrinthelab.com/videos

You always insert text into a Word document at the flashing insertion point. Therefore, you must position the insertion point at the desired location before typing.

AutoComplete

Word's AutoComplete feature does some of your typing for you. It recognizes certain words and phrases, such as names of months and names of days, and offers to complete them for you, as shown here.

November (Press ENTER to Insert)
Nove

As you begin typing the month November, AutoComplete offers to finish typing it out.

AutoComplete does not offer to complete the months March through July.

You accept AutoComplete suggestions by tapping Enter. If you choose to ignore the suggestion, just keep typing, and the suggestion will disappear.

Using the Enter Key

You use Enter to begin a new paragraph or to insert blank lines in a document. Word considers anything that ends by tapping Enter to be a paragraph. Thus, short lines such as a date line, an inside address, or even blank lines themselves are considered paragraphs.

Tapping Enter inserts a paragraph ¶ symbol in a document. These symbols are visible when you display formatting marks.

Showing Formatting Marks

The Show/Hide ¶ button in the Paragraph group of the Home tab shows or hides formatting marks. Although they appear on the screen, you will not see them in the printed document. Marks include dots representing spaces between words, paragraph symbols that appear when you tap Enter, and arrows that represent tabs.

Viewing these characters can be important when editing a document. You may need to see the nonprinting characters to determine whether the space between two words was created with the Spacebar or Tab. The following illustrations show the location of the Show/Hide button and the characters that appear when you tap the Spacebar, the Enter key, or the Tab key.

Show/Hide button

These symbols are paragraph marks. They appear whenever you tap Enter.

The dots between words are inserted when you tap the Spacebar.

Tabs are represented by small arrows.

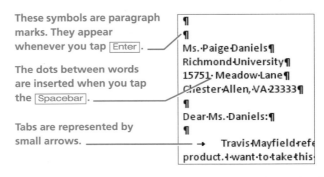

¶
¶
Ms.·Paige·Daniels¶
Richmond·University¶
15751·Meadow·Lane¶
Chester·Allen,·VA·23333¶
¶
Dear·Ms.·Daniels:¶
¶
    →   Travis·Mayfield·refe
product.·I·want·to·take·this

Spacing in Letters

In Word 2007, new default line spacing was introduced. This change adjusted the default line spacing to 1.15 rather than the standard single spacing and added an extra 10 points (a little more than an eighth of an inch) at the end of paragraphs. Therefore, rather that tapping Enter twice at the end of a paragraph, you just tap Enter once, and Word adds the extra spacing.

Apply Traditional Spacing Using the Line Spacing Button

When writing letters, a traditional, more compact look (without the additional spacing) is still considered appropriate. Therefore, when you begin a letter, you may wish to switch to single (1.0) spacing and remove the extra space after paragraphs by choosing the options shown in the following figure.

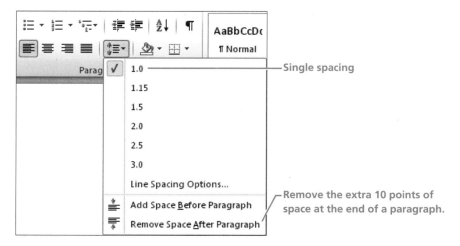

Apply these settings when you wish to type a more compact, traditional letter.

Apply Traditional Spacing Using the No Spacing Style

An alternative to using the Line Spacing button to achieve traditional spacing is to apply the No Spacing style located in the Styles group of the Home tab on the Ribbon, as shown here.

When you begin a new document, click the No Spacing icon on the Ribbon to achieve traditional spacing.

The exercises in this lesson use the Line Spacing button to set traditional spacing; however, feel free to use this alternate method instead if you prefer.

Word Wrap

If you continue typing after the insertion point reaches the end of a line, Word automatically wraps the insertion point to the beginning of the next line. If you let Word Wrap format your paragraph initially, the paragraph will also reformat correctly as you insert or delete text.

Creating an Envelope

Microsoft Word is very smart and versatile when it comes to creating envelopes. For example, when you type a business letter with the recipient's name and address at the top of it, Word recognizes this as the delivery address. Word also gives you two options: print the address directly onto the envelope or insert the envelope at the top of the document in a separate section. The latter option means you can open the letter at any time and the envelope is there, ready for you to print it.

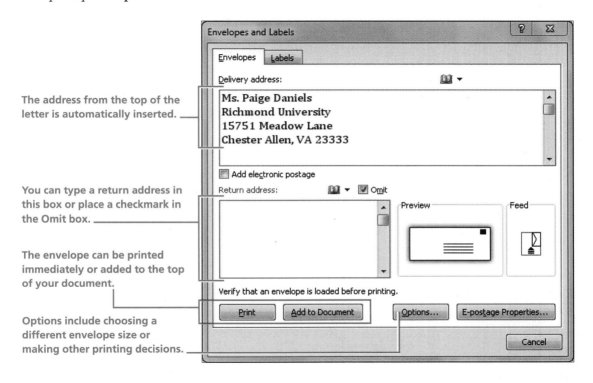

The address from the top of the letter is automatically inserted.

You can type a return address in this box or place a checkmark in the Omit box.

The envelope can be printed immediately or added to the top of your document.

Options include choosing a different envelope size or making other printing decisions.

Return Address

The Envelopes and Labels dialog box allows you to type a return address and keep it as the default. If you don't want the default return address to print on the envelope, you must ensure the Omit checkbox is unchecked in the dialog box.

If a default return address has not been established or the Return Address box is empty, clicking the Omit checkbox is not necessary. By default, the Omit checkbox is already checked.

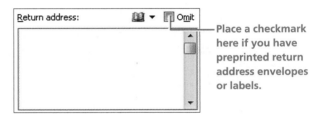

Place a checkmark here if you have preprinted return address envelopes or labels.

When you enter a return address, you will be prompted to save it as the default so you don't have to type it each time you create an envelope.

Type a Letter and an Envelope

In this exercise, you will display formatting marks, adjust spacing, use AutoComplete, work with the Enter key, and let Word Wrap do its job. Finally, you will create an envelope for the letter.

Display Nonprinting Characters and Modify Line Spacing

1. Start **Word**. Make sure the Word window is **maximized** 🔲.

2. Choose **Home→Paragraph→Show/Hide ¶** from the Ribbon, as shown to the right.

   New documents contain a paragraph symbol; you won't see it if you don't turn on the Show/Hide feature. Paragraph symbols carry formatting in them. For a new document, formatting includes default spacing of 1.15 lines and extra space at the end of a paragraph.

   In the next step, you'll select (highlight) the paragraph symbol and reformat it, changing the default line spacing to 1.0 and removing additional space after a paragraph.

3. Position the **I-beam** ⌶ left of the paragraph symbol, **press and hold** the mouse button, **drag** to the right to select (highlight) the paragraph symbol, and then **release** the mouse button.

4. Follow these steps to reformat the paragraph symbol:

   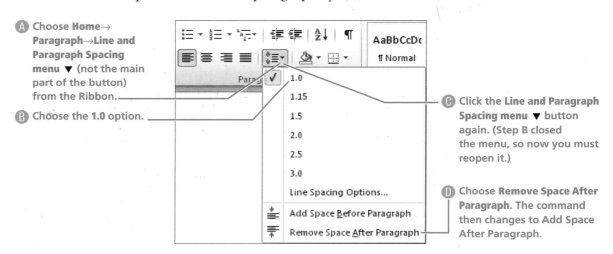

   Ⓐ Choose **Home→Paragraph→Line and Paragraph Spacing menu ▼** (not the main part of the button) from the Ribbon.

   Ⓑ Choose the **1.0** option.

   Ⓒ Click the **Line and Paragraph Spacing menu ▼** button again. (Step B closed the menu, so now you must reopen it.)

   Ⓓ Choose **Remove Space After Paragraph**. The command then changes to Add Space After Paragraph.

Turn On the Ruler and Type the Letter

5. Click the **View Ruler** 🔲 button at the top of the vertical scroll bar to display the ruler.

6. **Tap** Enter five times to place the insertion point 2 inches from the top of the page (at approximately the 1 inch mark on the vertical ruler).

7. Start typing **Nove**, but stop when AutoComplete displays a pop-up tip.
   AutoComplete suggests the word it thinks you are typing and offers to complete it.

8. **Tap** Enter to automatically insert November into the letter.

9. Finish **typing** the date as **November 24, 2012**.

10. Continue **typing** the letter as shown in the following illustration, **tapping** [Enter] wherever you see a paragraph symbol.

If you catch a typo, you can tap the [Backspace] *key enough times to remove the error, and then continue typing.*

```
¶
¶
¶
¶
¶
November·24,·2012¶
¶
¶
¶
Ms.·Paige·Daniels¶
Richmond·University¶
15751··Meadow·Lane¶
Chester·Allen,·VA·23333¶
¶
Dear·Ms.·Daniels:¶
¶
```

11. **Type** the first body paragraph in the following illustration. Let Word Wrap do its thing, and then **tap** [Enter] twice at the end of the paragraph.

```
Travis·Mayfield·referred·you·to·us·after·he·spoke·to·you·yesterday·about·our·extraordinary·product.·I·
want·to·take·this·opportunity·to·thank·you·for·considering·My·Virtual·Campus'·social·networking·
website·for·your·institution.·As·Travis·may·have·mentioned,·we·pride·ourselves·in·providing·the·latest·in·
technology·as·well·as·excellent·customer·service.¶
¶
```

If you see a wavy red line, that is Word's way of telling you that a word *might* be misspelled. If a term is not in Word's dictionary, it is marked as a possible error, even if it is spelled correctly. Wavy green lines indicate possible grammatical errors. Ignore red and green wavy lines for now.

12. Continue **typing** the letter, **tapping** [Enter] where you see a paragraph symbol.

```
I·have·enclosed·information·for·your·review·regarding·the·various·features·of·the·website.·After·reading·
the·material,·please·contact·our·sales·manager,·ASAP,·to·discuss·your·options.·Thank·you·again·for·
considering·our·amazing·website.¶
¶
Yours·truly,¶
¶
¶
¶
Rob·Maloney¶
Customer·Service·Representative¶
Sales·Department¶
```

Create the Envelope

Now you will create an envelope for the letter and add it to the top of the document.

13. **Tap** Ctrl + Home to place the insertion point at the top of the document, then choose **Mailings→Create→Envelopes** from the Ribbon.

14. Follow these steps to add an envelope to the document with no return address:

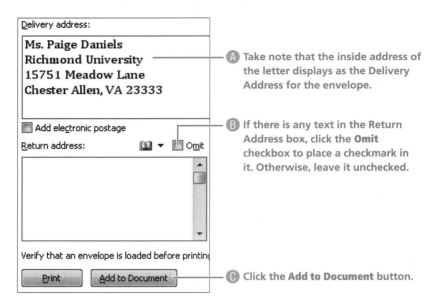

Delivery address:

Ms. Paige Daniels
Richmond University
15751 Meadow Lane
Chester Allen, VA 23333

Ⓐ Take note that the inside address of the letter displays as the Delivery Address for the envelope.

☐ Add electronic postage

Return address: Omit

Ⓑ If there is any text in the Return Address box, click the **Omit** checkbox to place a checkmark in it. Otherwise, leave it unchecked.

Verify that an envelope is loaded before printing

Print   Add to Document

Ⓒ Click the **Add to Document** button.

Notice that the envelope has been added to the top of the document. When you save the document, the envelope is saved with it so you may print it at any time.

15. Click the **Undo** 🔄 button to remove the envelope from the document.

16. Choose **Home→Paragraph→Show/Hide** ¶ to turn off the formatting marks.

Feel free to turn the Show/Hide feature on or off as you see fit throughout this course.

2.3 Saving Your Work

Video Lesson   labyrinthelab.com/videos

It's important to save your documents frequently! Power outages and accidents can result in lost data. Documents are saved to storage locations such as hard drives and USB flash drives.

The Save Command

There are three primary commands used to save Word documents:

- The Save ![save button] button on the Quick Access toolbar
- The File→Save command
- The File→Save As command

FROM THE KEYBOARD
Ctrl+S to save

When you save a document for the first time, the Save As dialog box appears. The following illustration describes significant features of the new Save As dialog box.

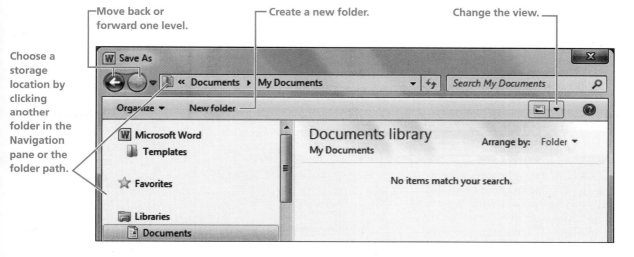

Move back or forward one level.

Create a new folder.

Change the view.

Choose a storage location by clicking another folder in the Navigation pane or the folder path.

Save Compared to Save As

While the Save and Save As commands are quite similar, each has a specific use. If the document was never saved, Word displays the Save As dialog box, where you specify the name and storage location of the document. If the document was previously saved, choosing the Save command again replaces the prior version with the edited one, without displaying the Save As dialog box. You can also use Save As to save a copy of a document, giving it a new filename and/or a new storage location.

Word's DOCX File Format

A file format is a technique for saving computer data. Word 2003 and earlier versions saved documents in the *doc* format. Word 2007 introduced a new file format: *docx*. This is important because users of Word 2003 and prior versions may not be able to read Word files in the *docx* format. However, you can choose to save your document in the older *doc* file format, thus enabling someone with an older version of Word to open the file without installing special software. Also, when you open a document created in Word 2007, the title bar displays

Compatibility Mode next to the actual title. This means certain Word 2010 features not compatible with 2007 are turned off while working in the document.

Word 2003 users can download a compatibility pack from the Microsoft website that allows them to open, edit, save, and create files in the docx file format.

DEVELOP YOUR SKILLS 2.3.1
Save the Letter

In this exercise, you will save the letter you created in the previous exercise.

1. Click the **Save**  button on the Quick Access toolbar.
Word displays the Save As dialog box, since this is the first time you are saving this document. Once the file is named, this button will simply save the current version of the file over the old version.

2. Follow these steps to save the letter:
Keep in mind that your dialog box may contain more files than shown here.

Ⓐ Click in the **Navigation pane**, and open the Lesson 02 folder on your file storage location.

Ⓑ Word always proposes the first line of text as the filename. Type the name **Daniels Letter** and it will replace the proposed name. (If you switched file storage locations, you may need to click in the **File Name** box, **delete** the proposed name with the [Delete] or [Backspace] key, and then **type** the new name.)

Ⓒ Click the **Save** button.

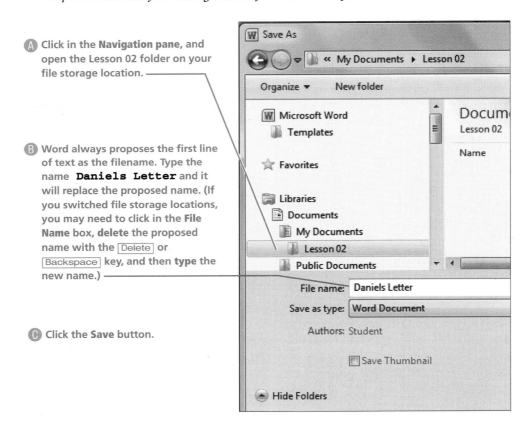

3. Leave the file **open** for the next exercise.

2.4 Selecting Text

Video Lesson   labyrinthelab.com/videos

You must select (highlight) text if you wish to perform some action on it. Suppose you want to delete an entire line. You would select the line first, and then tap ⟨Delete⟩.

Selection Techniques

Word provides many selection techniques; some use the mouse, and some use the keyboard. Use the keyboard techniques if you have difficulty controlling the mouse. Deselect text by clicking in the text area of the document or by tapping an arrow key. The following Quick Reference table illustrates various selection techniques.

QUICK REFERENCE	WORKING WITH SELECTION TECHNIQUES
Item to Be Selected	**Mouse Technique**
One word	Double-click the word.
Continuous block of text	Press and hold the left mouse button while dragging the I-beam over the desired text.
A line	Place the mouse pointer in the margin to the left of the line. Click when the pointer is shaped like an arrow.
A sentence	Hold down ⟨Ctrl⟩ and click the mouse pointer anywhere in the sentence.
One paragraph	Position the mouse pointer in the margin to the left of the paragraph and double-click, or triple-click anywhere in the paragraph.
Multiple paragraphs	Position the mouse pointer in the left margin and drag up or down when the pointer is shaped like an arrow, or drag the I-beam over the desired paragraphs.
Entire document	Triple-click in the left margin, or make sure no text is selected and then press and hold ⟨Ctrl⟩ and click in the left margin.
Nonadjacent areas	Select the first block of text, and then press and hold ⟨Ctrl⟩ while dragging over additional blocks of text.
Item to Be Selected	**Keyboard Technique**
One word	Click at the beginning of the word, and then press and hold ⟨Shift⟩+⟨Ctrl⟩ while tapping ⟨→⟩.
Continuous block of text	Click at the beginning of the text, and then press and hold ⟨Shift⟩ while tapping any arrow key. You can also click at the beginning of the text, press and hold ⟨Shift⟩, and click at the end of the selection.
A line	Press ⟨Shift⟩+⟨End⟩ to select from the insertion point to the end of the line. Press ⟨Shift⟩+⟨Home⟩ to select from the insertion point to the beginning of the line.
Entire document	Press ⟨Ctrl⟩+⟨A⟩ to execute the Select All command, or press ⟨Ctrl⟩ and click in the left margin.

Select Text

In this exercise, you will practice various selection techniques using the letter you just created. Selecting text causes the Mini toolbar to fade in. You can ignore it for now.

Select Using the Left Margin

1. Follow these steps to select text using the left margin:

Ⓐ **Point** outside the margin of the first line of the inside address.

Ⓑ **Click** once to select the entire line.

Ms. Paige Daniels
Richmond University
15751 Meadow Lane
Chester Allen, VA 23333

Ⓒ Make sure the pointer tilts to the **right**, and then **click** once to select this line. (Notice that the previously selected line is no longer selected.)

Dear Ms. Daniels:

Travis Mayfield referred you to us after he spoke to you yesterday about our extraordinary product. I want to take this opportunity to thank you for considering My Virtual Campus' social-networking website for your institution. As Travis may have mentioned, we pride ourselves in providing the latest in technology as well as excellent customer service.

Ⓓ Select this paragraph by **double-clicking** in front of it, using the white selection arrow.

2. Making sure the mouse pointer tilts to the **right** ⬉, **drag** down the left margin. Be sure to **press and hold** the left mouse button as you drag. Then, **click** in the body of the document to deselect the text.

3. Move the **mouse pointer** back to the margin so it is tilting to the **right** ⬉, then **triple-click** anywhere in the left margin.
Word selects the entire document.

4. **Click** once anywhere in the body of the document to deselect it.

Select Words

5. Point on any word with the **I-beam** I, and then **double-click** to select it.

6. **Double-click** a different word, and notice that the previous word is deselected.

Nonadjacent Selections

You can also select multiple locations within a document.

7. **Double-click** to select one word.

8. With one word selected, **press and hold** the ⌨Ctrl key while you **double-click** to select another word, and then **release** the ⌨Ctrl key.
Both selections are active. You can select as many nonadjacent areas of a document as desired using this technique. This can be quite useful when formatting documents.

Drag to Select

9. Follow these steps to drag and select a block of text:

Ⓐ Position the **I-beam** here, just in front of *Travis Mayfield*.... Make sure the I-beam is visible, not the right-tilting arrow.

Ⓑ **Press and hold** down the mouse button, and then **drag to the right** until the phrase *Travis Mayfield referred you to us after he spoke to you* is selected.

Ⓒ **Release** the mouse button; the text remains selected.

I Travis Mayfield referred you to us after he spoke to you yesterday abo
want to take this opportunity to thank you for considering My Virtual (
website for your institution. As Travis may have mentioned, we pride o

2.5 Editing Text

Video Lesson labyrinthelab.com/videos

Word offers many tools for editing documents, allowing you to insert and delete text and undo and redo work.

Inserting and Deleting Text

When you insert text in Word, existing text moves to the right as you type. You must position the insertion point before you begin typing.

Use ⌈Backspace⌉ and ⌈Delete⌉ to remove text. The ⌈Backspace⌉ key deletes *characters* to the left of the insertion point. The ⌈Delete⌉ key removes characters to the *right* of the insertion point. You can also remove an entire block of text by selecting it, and then tapping ⌈Delete⌉ or ⌈Backspace⌉.

Using Undo and Redo

Word's Undo 🔄 button lets you reverse your last editing or formatting change(s). You can reverse simple actions such as accidental text deletions, or you can reverse more complex actions, such as margin changes.

FROM THE KEYBOARD
⌈Ctrl⌉+⌈Z⌉ to undo the last action

The Redo 🔄 button reverses Undo. Use Redo when you undo an action and then change your mind.

The Undo menu ▼ button (see figure at right) displays a list of recent changes. You can undo multiple actions by dragging the mouse pointer over the desired items in the list. However, you must undo changes in the order in which they appear on the list.

Insert and Delete Text and Use Undo and Redo

In this exercise, you will insert and delete text. You will delete characters using both the Backspace *and* Delete *keys, and you will select and delete blocks of text. You will also use the Undo and Redo buttons on the Quick Access toolbar.*

1. In the first line of the first paragraph, **double-click** the word *yesterday,* as shown to the right, and then **tap** Delete to remove the word.

   > spoke to you yesterday about
   > for considering My Virtual Car

2. Click with the **I-beam** (not the right-tilted arrow) at the beginning of the word *thank* in the second line of the first paragraph of the first paragraph, type **personally**, and then **tap** the Spacebar.

3. Position the **insertion point** at the end of the first paragraph between the word *service* and the period at the end of the sentence.

4. **Tap** the Spacebar, and type **with satisfaction guaranteed**.

5. **Drag** to select the first three words of the second paragraph and then type **Enclosed you will find** to replace the selected text.

6. In the same line, position the **insertion point** after the word *your* and **tap** Backspace until the words *for your* are deleted, then type **to**.

7. **Double-click** the word *various* in the same line and **tap** Delete to remove it.

8. In the next line, **double-click** *ASAP,* and type **Bruce Carter, at your earliest convenience,** in its place.

9. Move the **mouse pointer** into the margin to the left of *Yours truly.*
   Remember, the mouse pointer is a white, right-tilted arrow when it's in the left margin.

10. **Click** once to select the line, and then type **Sincerely,** in its place.

Use Undo and Redo

11. You've decided that you prefer *Yours truly,* so click the **Undo** button on the Quick Access toolbar until you return to *Yours truly.*

12. Well, maybe *Sincerely* is better after all. Click the **Redo** button on the Quick Access toolbar until you return to *Sincerely.*

Save Your Changes

13. Click the **Save** button on the Quick Access toolbar to save your changes.

14. Leave the document **open** for the next exercise.

2.6 Working with AutoCorrect

Video Lesson labyrinthelab.com/videos

AutoCorrect is predefined text used for automatically correcting common spelling and capitalization errors. You may have noticed AutoCorrect changing the spelling of certain words while working through the last exercise.

The AutoCorrect feature corrects more than spelling errors. For example, you can set up an AutoCorrect entry to insert the phrase *as soon as possible* whenever you type *asap* and tap the Spacebar or certain other characters such as a Tab, Comma, or Period. AutoCorrect will also capitalize a word it thinks is the beginning of a sentence.

DEVELOP YOUR SKILLS 2.6.1
Use AutoCorrect

In this exercise, you will type some terms that AutoCorrect will fix for you.

1. **Tap** Ctrl + End to move the insertion point to the end of the document.

2. If necessary, **tap** Enter a few times to provide some space to practice.

3. **Type** the word **teh** and **tap** the Tab key.
   AutoCorrect corrects the mistake and capitalizes the word because it thinks it is the first word of a sentence.

4. **Type** the word **adn** and **tap** the Spacebar.

5. Now **select** and Delete the words you were just practicing with.

AutoCorrect Options Smart Tag

Video Lesson labyrinthelab.com/videos

Word uses smart tags, small buttons that pop up automatically, to provide menus of options that are in context with what you are doing at the time. One of those smart tags is the AutoCorrect Options smart tag.

If Word automatically corrects something that you don't want corrected, a smart tag option allows you to undo the change. For example, when Word automatically capitalizes the first C in the cc: line, you can quickly undo the capitalization, as shown here.

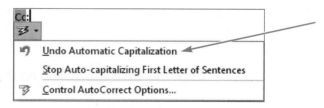

You will see many smart tags as you work. If you do not want to use a smart tag, you can ignore it and it will disappear on its own.

Use the AutoCorrect Smart Tag

In this exercise, you will use the AutoCorrect Options smart tags.

1. Choose **Home→Paragraph→Show/Hide** ¶ to display formatting marks.
   The reference initials should appear on the second blank line following the signature block. Make sure two paragraph symbols appear, as shown here.

   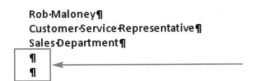

2. If necessary, position the **insertion point** and use Enter to create the blank line(s).

3. Position the **insertion point** next to the second paragraph symbol, and type **rm** as the reference initials, and then **tap** Enter.
   Notice what happened. Autocorrect capitalized the R, and it should not be capitalized.

4. Position the **mouse pointer** over the R, and you should see a small blue rectangle just below the R. Then **drag down** a little, and the AutoCorrect Options screen tip appears.

5. Click the **AutoCorrect Options** smart tag to display the menu shown below. (This is a delicate mouse move, so you may need to try it a couple of times.)

   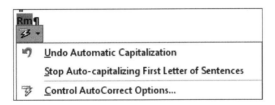

6. Choose **Undo Automatic Capitalization** from the menu.
   Notice that Word marks the initials with a wavy red line, indicating it's a possible spelling error. You can just ignore it.

7. Make sure the **insertion point** is on the blank line below the initials. Then **type** the enclosures notification, **Enclosures (2)**, and **tap** Enter.

8. **Save** 💾 the document and leave it **open** for the next exercise.

Setting AutoCorrect Options

Video Lesson   labyrinthelab.com/videos

To display the AutoCorrect dialog box, choose the File tab to display the Backstage view and then click the Options tab at the bottom of the Navigation pane to open the Word Options window. The AutoCorrect Options button on the Proofing page opens the AutoCorrect dialog box.

Changing AutoCorrect Exceptions

There can be exceptions to the AutoCorrect options you set. For example, when the option Correct Two Initial Capitals is checked and you accidently type the first and second letter in capitals, AutoCorrect automatically corrects it for you. There are three types of exceptions you can set.

- **First Letter**—If you do not type the first letter of a new line as a capital, AutoCorrect fixes it for you automatically. However, you may at times need an exception to this rule. For example, at the bottom of a letter, after you type cc: to indicate a carbon copy, AutoCorrect automatically makes the first letter a capital.

- **Initial Caps**—The opposite of the First Letter option is when you type two capital letters and both should remain capitalized. AutoCorrect automatically corrects the second letter unless you add an exception. For example, when referring to user IDs, you would want the "D" to remain capitalized.

- **Other Corrections**—You can add words here that you do not want AutoCorrect to change, even if they are in the Replace as You Type List at the bottom of the AutoCorrect box. For example, your company may have a unique name or use special terminology.

When you create AutoCorrect entries in Word, the entries are also available for use in Microsoft Excel, PowerPoint, and Access.

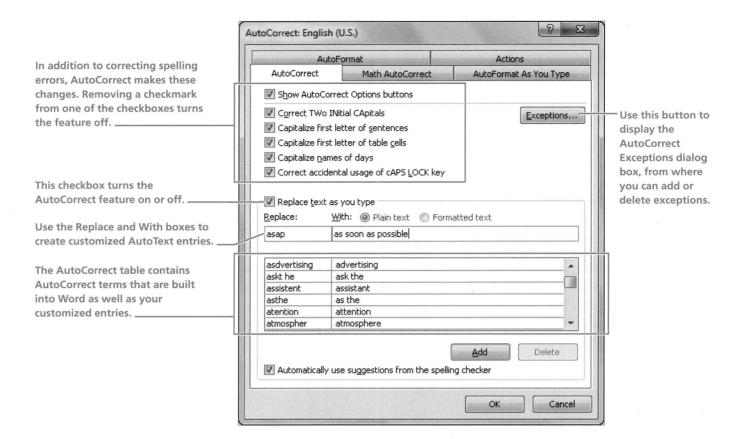

In addition to correcting spelling errors, AutoCorrect makes these changes. Removing a checkmark from one of the checkboxes turns the feature off. ⎯

This checkbox turns the AutoCorrect feature on or off. ⎯

Use the Replace and With boxes to create customized AutoText entries. ⎯

The AutoCorrect table contains AutoCorrect terms that are built into Word as well as your customized entries. ⎯

Use this button to display the AutoCorrect Exceptions dialog box, from where you can add or delete exceptions.

Customizing AutoCorrect

Word's AutoCorrect feature also lets you automatically insert customized text and special characters, and it is useful for replacing abbreviations with full phrases. For example, you could set up AutoCorrect to insert the name of your company whenever you type an abbreviation for it. You can also customize AutoCorrect by deleting entries that are installed with Word; however, please do not delete any in this classroom.

Do not create an AutoCorrect entry with an abbreviation you may want to use on its own; for example, if you used *USA* as an abbreviation for *United States of America,* you could not use *USA* alone because every time you typed it, it would be replaced with *United States of America.*

DEVELOP YOUR SKILLS 2.6.3
Create a Custom AutoCorrect Entry

In this exercise, you will create a custom AutoCorrect entry. It's now time for the copy notification, and you plan to copy Bruce Carter. Since you work for him, you know you'll need to type his name frequently, so it's a perfect candidate for a custom AutoCorrect entry.

1. Click the **File** tab and then click Options at the bottom of the Navigation pane.

2. When the Word Options window opens, follow these steps to display the AutoCorrect dialog box:

Ⓐ Choose **Proofing** from the menu.   Ⓑ Click the **AutoCorrect Options** button.

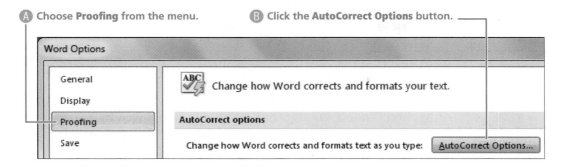

3. When the AutoCorrect dialog box appears, follow these steps to add a custom AutoCorrect entry:

Ⓐ Type **bmc** in the Replace box.

Ⓑ Type **Bruce Carter** in the With box.

Ⓒ Click the Add button.

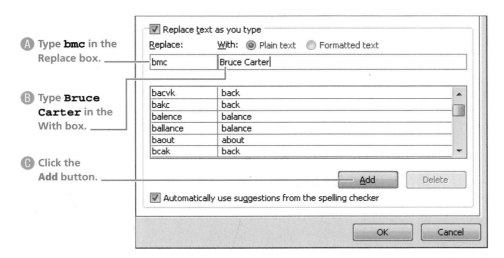

4. Click **OK** twice.

5. Type **cc:** and **tap** the ⎡Spacebar⎤.

6. Use the **AutoCorrect Options** smart tag to undo the automatic capitalization.
   Now you can try out the new AutoCorrect item you added in step 3.

7. Type **bmc** and **tap** ⎡Enter⎤ to automatically type the sales manager's name.

Delete the Custom AutoCorrect Entry

You can easily remove AutoCorrect entries, whether they are new custom entries you added or default entries you did not create originally.

8. Click the **File** tab and then click **Options** at the bottom of the Navigation pane.

9. Choose **Proofing** from the menu, and then click the **AutoCorrect Options** button in the right-hand pane.

10. Type **bmc** in the Replace box, which scrolls the list to Bruce Carter.

11. Click the **Delete** button in the bottom-right corner of the dialog box.

12. Click **OK** twice.

13. **Save** 💾 the letter and leave it **open** for the next exercise.

Setting AutoFormat As You Type Options

Video Lesson   labyrinthelab.com/videos

One of the tabs in the AutoCorrect dialog box is AutoFormat As You Type. You may have noticed certain formatting taking place automatically; this is happening because certain options are already set for you. For example, AutoFormat will replace a typed hyphen (-) with a dash (–), an ordinal (1st) with superscript (1st), or a fraction (1/2) with a fraction character ($\frac{1}{2}$). AutoFormat can also create an automatic bulleted list when you start a line with an asterisk (*), a hyphen (-), or a greater than symbol (>) followed by a space or a tab. Likewise, it creates a numbered list when you start a line with a number followed by a period or a tab.

You can control the formatting that happens automatically as you type by placing or removing checkmarks.

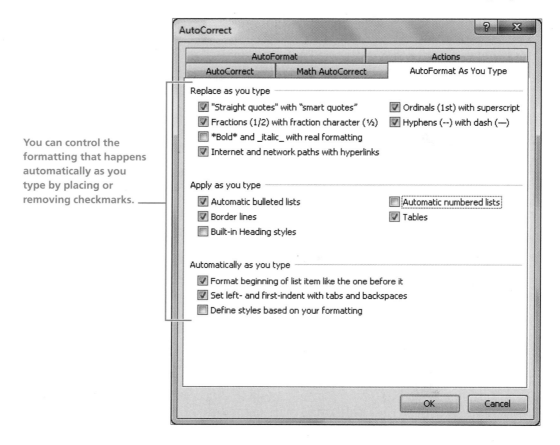

Turn On Automatic Numbering

In this exercise, you will turn on the option that automatically creates a numbered list when you begin a sentence with a number.

1. Click the **File** tab and then click the **Options** tab at the bottom of the Navigation pane.

2. Click **Proofing** on the left and then click the **AutoCorrect Options** button.

3. Follow these steps to turn on automatic numbering:

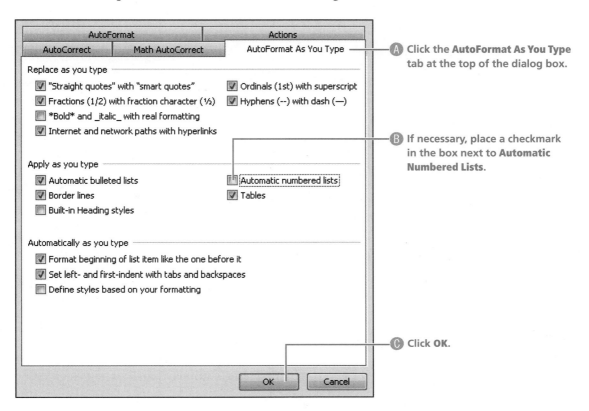

4. Click **OK** again in the Word Options dialog box to close it.

5. Click the **Save** button and leave the document **open** for the next exercise.

2.7 Copying and Moving Text

Video Lesson labyrinthelab.com/videos

FROM THE KEYBOARD

Ctrl+C to copy
Ctrl+X to cut
Ctrl+V to paste

Cut, Copy, and Paste allow you to copy and move text within a document or between documents. The Cut, Copy, and Paste commands are conveniently located on the Ribbon in the Clipboard command group at the left side of the Home tab.

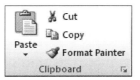

The following table describes these commands.

QUICK REFERENCE	USING CUT, COPY, AND PASTE	
Command	**Description**	**How to Issue the Command**
Cut	The Cut command removes selected text from its original location and places it on the Clipboard.	Click the Cut ✂ button.
Copy	The Copy command places a copy of selected text on the Clipboard, but it also leaves the text in the original location.	Click the Copy 📋 button.
Paste	The Paste command pastes the most recently cut or copied text into the document at the insertion point location.	Click the Paste 📋 button.

Working with the Clipboard

The Clipboard lets you collect multiple items and paste them into another location in the current document or into a different document. It must be visible on the screen to collect the items; otherwise, only one item at a time is saved for pasting. The Clipboard can hold up to 24 items. When the items you cut or copy exceed 24, the Clipboard automatically deletes the oldest item(s).

The dialog box launcher ⬚ that displays the Clipboard task pane is located on the Home tab of the Ribbon.

The following illustration points out the main features of the Clipboard.

In this area, the number of items currently on the Clipboard is displayed.

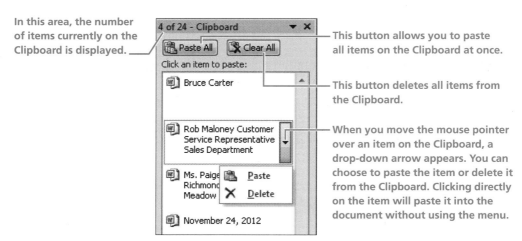

This button allows you to paste all items on the Clipboard at once.

This button deletes all items from the Clipboard.

When you move the mouse pointer over an item on the Clipboard, a drop-down arrow appears. You can choose to paste the item or delete it from the Clipboard. Clicking directly on the item will paste it into the document without using the menu.

Use Cut, Copy, and Paste

In this exercise, you will move and copy information and work with the Clipboard.

1. If necessary, choose **Home→Paragraph→Show/Hide** ¶ from the Ribbon to display the formatting marks.

Copy and Paste Using the Clipboard

2. Choose **Home→Clipboard→dialog box launcher** ⌐ from the Ribbon.

3. Tap ⌐Ctrl⌐+⌐Home⌐, then position the **mouse pointer** in the margin to the left of the date and then **click** to select the line.

4. Choose **Home→Clipboard→Copy** 📋 from the Ribbon.

5. Tap ⌐Ctrl⌐+⌐End⌐ to move the insertion point to the bottom of the document.

6. Follow these steps to paste the date at the bottom of the document:

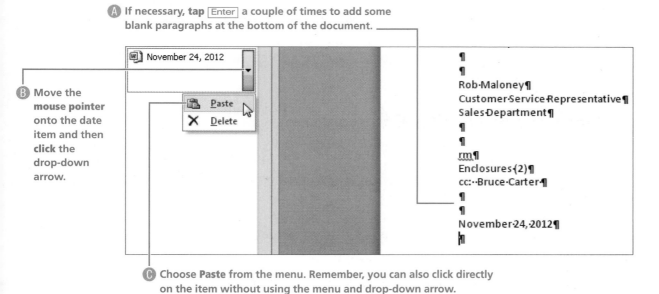

Ⓐ If necessary, tap ⌐Enter⌐ a couple of times to add some blank paragraphs at the bottom of the document.

Ⓑ Move the mouse pointer onto the date item and then **click** the drop-down arrow.

Ⓒ Choose **Paste** from the menu. Remember, you can also click directly on the item without using the menu and drop-down arrow.

Notice the Paste Options smart tag that popped up at the bottom of the pasted text.

7. Click the **smart tag** to view its menu and then click anywhere in the document to close the menu.

8. Tap ⌐Esc⌐ to dismiss the smart tag.

> ⚠️ **TIP** If you don't tap ⌐Esc⌐, the button will disappear on its own.

9. Click **Undo** ↩ to undo the paste.

Move the Inside Address

10. **Scroll up** to the top of the letter, position the **mouse pointer** in the margin to the left of the first line of the inside address, and then **drag** to select all four lines.

11. **Tap** [Ctrl]+[X] to cut the text.
    Notice that using the keyboard shortcut to cut text also puts the item on the Clipboard.

12. **Tap** [Ctrl]+[End] to move the insertion point to the bottom of the document.

13. Click the **inside address** on the Clipboard to paste it at the insertion point.

14. Click **Undo** twice to undo the move and place the address back at the top of the letter.

15. Click the **Close** ☒ button on the Clipboard task pane.

16. Click the **Save** 🖫 button to save the changes.

Editing with Drag and Drop

Video Lesson   labyrinthelab.com/videos

Drag and drop produces the same result as cut, copy, and paste. It is efficient for moving or copying text a short distance within the same page. You select the text you wish to move and then drag it to the desired destination. If you press and hold [Ctrl] while dragging, the text is copied to the destination.

> Drag and drop does not place the selection on the Clipboard.

DEVELOP YOUR SKILLS 2.7.2
Use Drag and Drop

In this exercise, you will use drag and drop to move and copy text.

1. Make sure there are a couple of **blank lines** at the bottom of your document.

2. If necessary, **scroll** so that you can see both the bottom of the document and the *Rob Maloney* line in the signature block.

Drag and Drop Move

3. **Select** the *Rob Maloney* line, and then **release** the mouse button.

4. Place the **mouse pointer** in the highlighted text.
   The pointer now looks like a white arrow.

College Store

Ogden Weber Tech College
200 North Washington Blvd
Ogden, UT 84404
801 627-8353

Store Hours Mon - Thur 7:30 - 7:30
Fri 7:30 - 3:30 Sat & Sun Closed
KEEP YOUR RECEIPT
You Will Need It For Returns

STORE 0001   REG:002   TRAN#:9382
CASHIER:VANESSA J

CROSO

21591363040   N
(1 @ 83.95)   83.95
TOTAL   **83.95**
CASH   **84.00**
CASH CHANGE   0.05-

Thank You For Shopping With Us!
Receipt REQUIRED for All Returns!

www.owatc.edu/bookstore
Like us on Facebook

V202.57   06/12/2014 08:06AM

CUSTOMER COPY

COLLEGE STORE

Ogden Weber Tech College
200 North Washington Blvd
Ogden, UT 84401
80. 727-8353

Store Hours Mon - Thur 7:30 - 7:30
Fri 7:30 - 3:30 Sat & Sun Closed
KEEP YOUR RECEIPT
You Will Need It For Refunds

STORE: 0001   REG 002   TRAN: 9382
CASHIER: VANESSA J.

CROSL

9781783430406
(1) @ 83.95)   83.95
TOTAL   83.95
CASH   84.00
CASH CHANGE   0.05

Thank You For Shopping With Us!
Receipt REQUIRED For All Returns!

www.owatc.edu/bookstore
Like us on Facebook

v202.67   05/12/2014 - 08:06AM

CUSTOMER COPY

5. **Press and hold** the mouse button, and follow these steps to move the text:

A **Drag down** to the bottom of the document, and when you do so, the mouse pointer has a small rectangle at the bottom indicating you are in drag-and-drop mode. ____

B You will also see a dotted insertion point that travels with the mouse pointer. Position it at the **bottom** of the document. ____

¶
Rob·Maloney¶
Customer·Service·Representative¶
Sales·Department¶
¶
¶
rm¶
Enclosures·(2)¶
cc:··Bruce·Carter·¶
¶
¶

C **Release** the mouse button to complete the move.

Now you will undo the move and repeat the process, but this time you'll copy the text.

6. Click the **Undo** 🔙 button to undo the move.

Drag and Drop Copy

7. Make sure the *Rob Maloney* line is still selected.

8. Place the **mouse pointer** inside the selected text, **press and hold** the ⌈Ctrl⌋ key and **drag** the text to the bottom of the document, **release** the mouse button, and then **release** the ⌈Ctrl⌋ key.
   Holding the ⌈Ctrl⌋ key while dragging is what causes the action to be a copy instead of a move. For this reason, you must release the mouse button before the ⌈Ctrl⌋ key; otherwise, the action will become a move.

9. Click **Undo** 🔙 to undo the copy.

10. Leave the document **open** for the next exercise.
    Soon you will learn to switch between documents so you can copy information from one document to another.

2.8 Switching Between Documents

Video Lesson   labyrinthelab.com/videos

There are several techniques for switching between documents. In the next exercise, you will use the taskbar at the bottom of the screen for switching documents. When you have multiple documents open, they will appear as buttons on the taskbar. Clicking a button displays that document in the foreground. In the following illustration, Daniels Letter is the active document. The active document button is lighter than the others.

Viewing Open Documents on the Taskbar

When several documents are open at the same time, they may share one taskbar button. A small image of each open document displays on the screen when you hover the mouse pointer over the taskbar button. You can click the image to display the full document on the screen.

Image of open Word documents

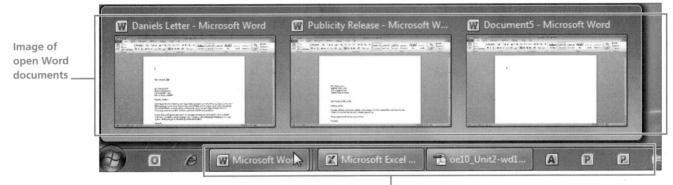

Taskbar buttons for open programs (Notice the Word button has three documents stacked on it.)

Your buttons may be different from the ones shown in the preceding illustration, depending on which program buttons are displayed on your computer's taskbar.

DEVELOP YOUR SKILLS 2.8.1
Switch and Copy Between Documents

In this exercise, you will copy and paste between two documents, using the taskbar buttons to switch between the documents.

1. **Open** the Publicity Release document in the Lesson 02 folder.

2. Follow these steps to switch to the Daniels Letter:

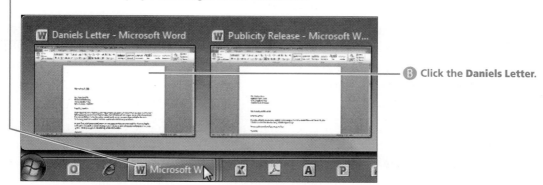

A Hover the **mouse pointer** over the Microsoft Word taskbar button to display small images of the documents.

B Click the **Daniels Letter**.

Copy and Paste the Inside Address

3. **Select** the four lines of the inside address and **tap** Ctrl+C to copy the text.

4. Hover the **mouse pointer** over the Microsoft Word taskbar button again and **click** the image of the Publicity Release document to switch to it.

5. Select the **first three lines**, as shown to the right.

6. **Tap** Ctrl+V to paste the address over the selected text in this document.

Paste the Sales Manager's Name Multiple Times

7. Using the **taskbar**, switch back to the Daniels Letter, and then **select** *Bruce Carter* in the second line of the second paragraph.

8. **Tap** Ctrl+C to copy his name.

9. Using the **taskbar** button, **switch** back to the Publicity Release document.

10. **Select** *SALES MANAGER* in the salutation and then **tap** Ctrl+V to paste *Bruce Carter*. *Notice that the salutation does not look exactly right; it should be a title with a last name. You will fix that in just a moment.*

11. **Select** *SALES MANAGER* in the first paragraph and then **tap** Ctrl+V to paste *Bruce Carter* again.

Once you have copied text, you can paste it multiple times without copying the text again.

12. **Double-click** *Bruce* in the salutation and type **Mr**.

13. **Select** and **copy** *Paige Daniels* at the top of the letter; **paste** it over *YOUR NAME* at the bottom of the document.

Save and Close the Publicity Release Document

14. **Save** 💾 the changes you made in this document and then **close** it.

15. **Save** 💾 the changes to Daniels Letter, but leave it **open** for the next exercise.

2.9 Using Page Layout Options

Video Lesson <u>labyrinthelab.com/videos</u>

The three most commonly used layout options are margins, page orientation, and paper size. All of these are located in the Page Setup group on the Page Layout tab of the Ribbon.

Setting Margins

Margins determine the amount of white space between the text and the edge of the paper. You can set margins for the entire document, a section, or for selected text. The Margins gallery displays preset top, bottom, left, and right margins. The Custom Margins option at the bottom of the gallery opens the Page Setup dialog box.

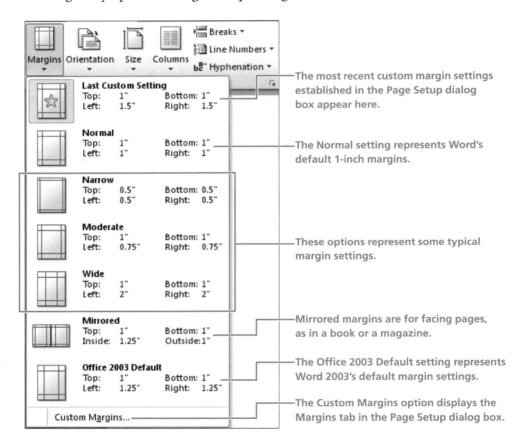

The most recent custom margin settings established in the Page Setup dialog box appear here.

The Normal setting represents Word's default 1-inch margins.

These options represent some typical margin settings.

Mirrored margins are for facing pages, as in a book or a magazine.

The Office 2003 Default setting represents Word 2003's default margin settings.

The Custom Margins option displays the Margins tab in the Page Setup dialog box.

QUICK REFERENCE	SETTING MARGINS
Task	**Procedure**
Change margins from the Margins gallery	■ Choose Page Layout→Page Setup→Margins from the Ribbon. ■ Choose predefined margin settings from the gallery.
Set custom margins	■ Choose Page Layout→Page Setup→Margins from the Ribbon. ■ Choose the Custom Margins command at the bottom of the gallery. ■ Enter settings for top, bottom, left, and right margins.

Set Page Layout Options

In this exercise, you will use the Margins gallery and the Page Setup dialog box to change the document's margins.

1. Choose **Page Layout→Page Setup→Margins** ⊞ from the Ribbon to display Word's Margins gallery.

2. Choose **Narrow** from the gallery and observe the impact on your document.

3. Click the **Margins** ⊞ button again to reopen the gallery and choose **Wide** to see how that affects the document.

4. Open the gallery again; change the margins back to the **Normal** (default) setting.

5. Click the **dialog box launcher** ⊡ at the bottom-right corner of the Page Setup group to open the Page Setup dialog box.
   You can also open the dialog box using the Custom Margins command at the bottom of the Margins gallery.

6. If necessary, click the **Margins** tab at the top of the dialog box.
   Notice the options for changing the top, bottom, left, and right margins.

7. Use the **spinner controls** (up/down arrows) to change the left and right margins to **1.5 inches**.

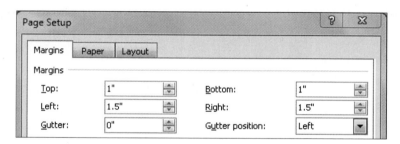

8. Click **OK**; notice the change in your document's margins.

9. Click the **Margins** ⊞ button to display the gallery and choose Normal.

10. **Save** 🖫 the document and leave it **open** for the next exercise.

Setting the Page Orientation

Video Lesson labyrinthelab.com/videos

The page orientation determines how the text is laid out on the paper. The options are vertically (Portrait) or horizontally (Landscape). The default orientation is Portrait. Some common uses for a landscape orientation include brochures, flyers, wide tables, and so forth. The Orientation options are located on the Page Layout tab of the Ribbon.

Setting the Paper Size

Most documents use the standard letter size paper. However, Word supports the use of many other paper sizes, including legal, and also allows you to create custom sizes.

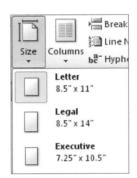

QUICK REFERENCE	SETTING PAGE ORIENTATION AND PAPER SIZE
Task	**Procedure**
Change the page orientation	▪ Choose Page Layout→Page Setup→Orientation from the Ribbon. ▪ Choose the desired page orientation.
Change the paper size	▪ Choose Page Layout→Page Setup→Size from the Ribbon. ▪ Choose the desired size from the menu, or choose the More Paper Sizes command to create a custom paper size.

DEVELOP YOUR SKILLS 2.9.2
Change the Orientation and Paper Size

In this exercise, you will experiment with the page orientation and paper size options.

View Landscape Orientation

1. If necessary, click the **Maximize** 🔲 button.

2. Choose **View→Zoom→One Page** 🔳 from the Ribbon.
   The page is currently in the default orientation of Portrait (vertical). Viewing the entire page allows you to see this clearly.

3. Choose **Page Layout→Page Setup→Orientation** 📄 from the Ribbon.

4. Choose **Landscape** from the menu.
   The page layout changes to horizontal.

5. Click the **Orientation** button again and choose **Portrait** to change the page back to a vertical layout.

View Paper Size Options

6. Choose **Page Layout→Page Setup→Size** from the Ribbon and switch to Legal.
   Notice the paper and envelope sizes available on the menu. The More Paper Sizes command at the bottom of the menu opens the Page Setup dialog box, where you can set a custom paper size if you wish.

7. Choose **Size** again and switch back to **Letter**.

8. Choose **View→Zoom→100%** from the Ribbon to have a larger view of the document.

9. **Save** the document and leave it **open** for the next exercise.

2.10 Working with Combined Print and Print Preview

Video Lesson   labyrinthelab.com/videos

In Word 2010, the Print and Print Preview commands have been combined and are available in Backstage view. The left section is all about the printer and the current page layout options, while the right section is a preview of your document that shows how it will look when printed. You can experiment with different options and see the results immediately.

To display the Print options and Print Preview, choose File→Print.

You can no longer edit while previewing a document.

These options allow you to choose a different printer, view
the printer properties, and set the number of copies to print.

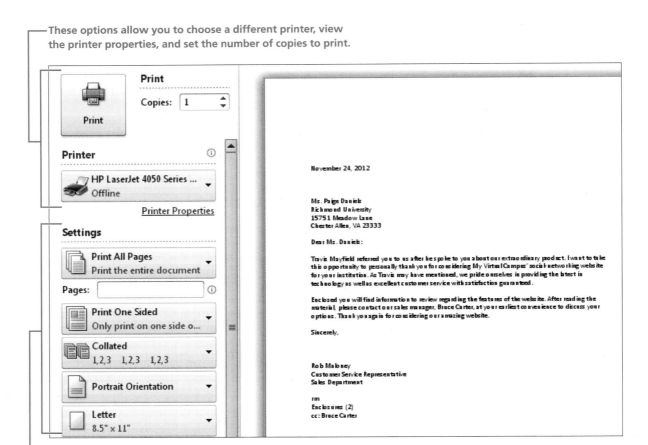

These options allow you to change various page layout options
and see the proposed change on the right in the preview section.

Experiment with Print and Print Preview

In this exercise, you will set printing and page layout options and preview the results.

1. Choose **File→Print**.

Explore Print Options

2. Follow these steps to print multiple copies of the current page:

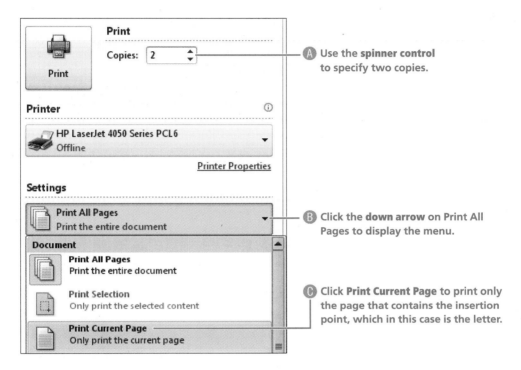

Ⓐ Use the **spinner control** to specify two copies.

Ⓑ Click the **down arrow** on Print All Pages to display the menu.

Ⓒ Click **Print Current Page** to print only the page that contains the insertion point, which in this case is the letter.

Preview Page Setting Changes

3. Follow these steps to preview the document with a different margin setting:

Ⓐ Click the **down arrow** on the Normal Margins setting.

Ⓑ Choose **Office 2003 Default**.

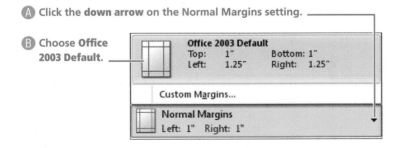

Notice the difference in the margins in the preview.

4. Switch back to the **Normal** margin setting.

5. Change the Orientation to **Landscape** and preview the change in the document.

6. Switch back to the **Portrait** orientation.

7. Click the **File** tab to close Backstage view and return to the document.

8. **Save** 🖫 and **close** the document.

2.11 Concepts Review

Concepts Review	labyrinthelab.com/word10

To check your knowledge of the key concepts introduced in this lesson, complete the Concepts Review quiz by going to the URL listed above. If your classroom is using Labyrinth eLab, you may complete the Concepts Review quiz from within your eLab course.

Reinforce Your Skills

Create a Block-Style Letter

In this exercise, you will practice using traditional spacing for a business letter and letting Word Wrap and AutoComplete take effect. You should control the AutoCorrect feature as needed.

1. If necessary, **tap** Ctrl + N to start a new blank document.

2. Use the **Show/Hide** ¶ button to display formatting marks.

3. Select the **paragraph symbol**, change the line spacing to **1.0**, and then **remove** the space after paragraphs. (You will need to open the menu twice to do this.)

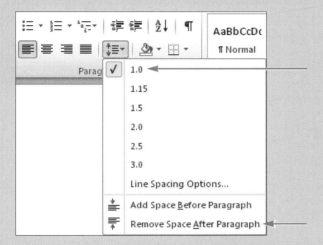

4. **Type** the following letter, **tapping** Enter wherever you see a paragraph symbol. Notice the five paragraph symbols at the top of the document. They position the date at approximately 2 inches from the top of the page.

```
¶
¶
¶
¶
¶
January·11,·2012¶
¶
¶
¶
Ms.·Courtney·Thompson¶
Service·Manager¶
Statesboro·Software·Services¶
810·Ivanhoe·Way¶
Statesboro,·GA·30458¶
¶
Dear·Ms.·Thompson:¶
¶
I·would·like·to·take·this·opportunity·to·thank·you·for·your·excellent·customer·service.·You·were·patient,·
courteous,·and·very·helpful.·The·installation·assistance·you·provided·was·invaluable.¶
¶
I·have·already·put·your·program·to·good·use.·As·you·know,·application·programs·can·boost·personal·
productivity.·Your·program·allows·me·to·manage·my·business·much·more·effectively.·I·am·enclosing·the·
$45·fee·you·requested.·Please·send·me·a·receipt·and·a·catalog.¶
¶
Sincerely,¶
¶
¶
¶
Blake·Evans¶
Administrative·Assistant¶
¶
be¶
Enclosure¶
```

5. Position the **insertion point** just in front of the sentence starting *I am enclosing the $45*, and **tap** Enter twice to create a new paragraph.

6. Position the **insertion point** at the end of the second paragraph, just in front of the paragraph symbol.

7. **Tap** Delete twice to remove the two paragraph symbols separating the new paragraph from the following paragraph.

8. If necessary, **tap** the Spacebar to insert a space between the combined sentences.

9. Position the **insertion point** at the end of the first paragraph before the paragraph mark, and **tap** the Spacebar if there is no space at the end of the sentence.

10. **Type** this sentence: `I also appreciate the overnight delivery.`

11. Add an **envelope**, without a return address, to the top of the letter.

12. **Save** the letter in the Lesson 02 folder, name it `rs-Thompson Letter`, and then **close** it.

Use the Clipboard and Drag and Drop

In this exercise, you will open a document from your file storage location and use the Clipboard to rearrange paragraphs. You will use drag and drop to move blocks of text.

1. **Open** the rs-Professional Contacts document in the Lesson 02 folder.
   Notice that the document contains a list of professional contacts. In the next few steps, you will use the Clipboard to reorganize the contacts by profession: all the attorneys will be grouped together, followed by the designers, and then the bookkeepers.

2. Choose **Home→Clipboard→dialog box launcher** 🔲 from the Ribbon to display the Clipboard.

3. If necessary, click the **Clear All** button to clear the Clipboard.

4. **Select** the first attorney contact, *David Roberts, Attorney,* by clicking in front of the contact in the left margin.
   This will select the entire paragraph, including the paragraph mark.

5. Choose **Home→Clipboard→Cut** ✂ from the Ribbon.
   The item appears on the Clipboard.

6. **Select** the next attorney, *Lisa Wilson,* and **Cut** ✂ it to the Clipboard.

7. **Cut** the remaining attorney contacts to the Clipboard. Use **Undo** ↰ if you make a mistake. However, be careful because even if you use Undo, the item you cut will remain on the Clipboard.

8. Now **Cut** ✂ the designer contacts to the Clipboard.
   The bookkeeper contacts should now be grouped together in the document.

9. Click the **Paste All** button on the Clipboard to paste the attorney and designer contacts.
   Notice that the contacts are pasted in the order they were cut, thus grouping the attorneys together and the designers together.

Create Headings

10. Click to place the **insertion point** in front of the first bookkeeper contact, and **tap** [Enter] twice to create blank lines.

11. Click the **blank line** above the first bookkeeper and type **Bookkeepers**.

12. Use this technique to create headings for attorneys and designers.

Use Drag and Drop

13. Select the *Attorneys* heading, the four attorneys, and the blank line below by **dragging** in the left margin and then **releasing** the mouse button.

14. Position the **mouse pointer** on the selection, and **drag up** until the dotted insertion point is just in front of the Bookkeepers heading.

15. **Release** the mouse button to move the attorneys block above the bookkeepers.

16. Now move the designers above the bookkeepers.

17. **Close** the Clipboard, and then **save** and **close** the file.

Edit a Document

In this exercise, you will edit a document that is marked up for changes.

1. Choose **File→Open**.

2. **Open** the rs-Maine document in the Lesson 02 folder.
   You will edit this document during this exercise. Notice that this document contains formatting that you have not yet learned about. For example, the title is centered and bold, and the paragraphs are formatted with double line spacing. This document is already formatted like this because it is a report.

   - If only one or two characters require deletion, then position the **insertion point** in front of the character(s) and use ⌷Delete⌷ to remove them.
   - If one or more words require deletion, then select the text and use ⌷Delete⌷ to remove the selected text.
   - If a word or phrase needs to be replaced with another word or phrase, then select the desired text and type the replacement text.
   - Use **Undo** ↺ if you make mistakes.

3. When you have finished, **save** the changes and **close** the document.

MAINE – THE PINE TREE STATE

Maine is recognized as one of the most ~~healthy~~ *healthful* states in the nation with temperatures

averaging 70°F and winter temperatures averaging 20°F. It has 3,~~7~~5*00* miles of coastline, is about *summer*

320 miles long and 210 miles wide, with a total area of 33,215 square miles or about as big as all

of the other five New England States combined. It comprises 16 counties with 22 cities, 424

towns, 51 plantations, and 416 unorganized townships. Aroostook county is so large (6,453

square miles) that it covers an area greater than the combined size of Connecticut *and Rhode Island*.

Maine abounds in natural assets—542,629 acres of state and national parks, including the

92-mile Allagash Wilderness Waterway, Acadia National Park (second most visited national

park in the United States), and Baxter State Park (location of Mt. Katahdin and the northern end

of the Appalachian Trail). Maine has one mountain ~~which~~ *that* is approximately one mile high—Mt.

Katahdin (5,268 ft. above sea level) and also claims America's first chartered city: York, 1641.

Maine's blueberry crop is the largest ~~blueberry crop~~ in the nation—98% of the low-bush

blueberries. Potatoes rank third in acreage and third in production nationally. Maine is nationally

famed for its shellfish; over 46 million pounds of ~~shellfish~~ *lobster* were harvested in 1997. The total of *in the United States*

all shellfish and fin fish harvested was approximately 237 million pounds with a total value of

$273 million ~~during the 1997 fishing season.~~ *in 1997*

Apply Your Skills

Create a Modified Block-Style Letter

In this exercise, you will practice the skills needed to create a modified block-style letter. You'll turn on the ruler to ensure the correct spacing for the date, the complimentary close, and the signature block.

1. **Start** a new blank document.
   You will create an AutoCorrect entry for Back Bay Users Group to use in your letter.

2. Click the **File** tab and then click the **Options** button at the bottom of the Navigation pane.

3. In the Options window, choose **Proofing** from the menu on the left.

4. Click the **AutoCorrect Options** button.

5. When the AutoCorrect dialog box appears, type **bbug** in the **Replace** box.

6. Type **Back Bay Users Group** in the **With** box.

7. Click the **Add** button, and then click **OK** twice.

8. If necessary, click the **View Ruler** button at the top of the vertical scroll bar to display the ruler.

9. Create the **modified block-style** business letter shown in the illustration on the next page.

10. Follow these guidelines as you type your letter.
    - Change to **single-spacing** and remove the **after-paragraph spacing**.
    - Space down the proper distance from the top of the page.
    - Use Tab to align the date, closing, and signature block at **3 inches** on the ruler. (You'll need to **tap** Tab six times to indent the lines at 3 inches.)
    - Use correct spacing between paragraphs.
    - Use your **AutoCorrect** shortcut in the first paragraph, rather than typing Back Bay Users Group.

Today's Date

Mrs. Suzanne Lee
8445 South Princeton Street
Chicago, IL 60628

Dear Mrs. Lee:

Thank you for your interest in the Back Bay Users Group. We will be holding an orientation for new members on the first Thursday in April at our headquarters.

Please let us know if you can attend by calling the phone number on this letterhead. Or, if you prefer, you may respond in writing or via email.

Sincerely,

Jack Bell
Membership Chair

XX

11. **Save** 💾 the letter to the Lesson 02 folder on your file storage location as **as-Lee Letter**.

12. **Hide** the ruler using the same button you used to display it.

13. **Delete** the AutoCorrect entry you created in this exercise.

14. **Preview** the letter, then preview how it would look in Landscape orientation with **Narrow** margins.

15. Restore to **Portrait** orientation and **Normal** margins.

16. **Print** the letter if your computer is connected to a printer, and then **save** and **close** the document.

Use the Clipboard and Drag and Drop

In this exercise, you will use the Clipboard and the drag-and-drop technique to rearrange items in a list.

1. **Open** as-Animals in the Lesson 02 folder in your file storage location.

2. Open the **Clipboard**, and use the **Clear All** button, if necessary, to empty it.

3. Use the **Home→Clipboard→Cut** ✂ button to place all the animals on the Clipboard, and then cut all the vegetables to the Clipboard.

4. Position the **insertion point** below the list of minerals, and then use the **Paste All** button to paste the animals and vegetables back in the document.

5. Use the Enter key to put two blank lines between groups and an extra blank line above the minerals, and then **type** an appropriate title at the top of each group.

6. Use **drag and drop** to arrange the groups in this order: Animals, Vegetables, Minerals. Remember, when selecting the text, include the blank line below the group.

7. **Save** 💾 the file and **close** it.

Edit a Document

In this exercise, you will use your editing skills to make specified changes to a letter.

1. **Open** the as-Wilson Letter document in the Lesson 02 folder in your file storage location.

2. **Edit** the document, as shown in the illustration at the end of this exercise.

3. Use Enter to push the entire document down, so that the date is positioned at approximately the **1-inch** mark on the vertical ruler.

4. If necessary, use Tab to move the date, complimentary close, and signature block to the **3-inch** position on the ruler. This will convert the letter from block style to modified block style.

5. When you finish, **save** 💾 the changes, **print** the letter, and **close** the document.

Today's Date

~~Ms. Cynthia Wilson~~ Mr. Roosevelt Jackson
~~118 Upper Terrace~~ 8 Spring street
~~Freehold, NJ 08845~~ Martinville, NJ 08836

Dear ~~Ms. Wilson~~: Mr. Jackson

Thank you for your recent letter concerning back injuries in your office. Yes, injuries are a [back] common problem for office workers today. It was estimated by the U. S. Bureau of Labor Statistics that in one year over ~~490~~,000 employees took time from work due to back injuries. [580]

Encourage your office employees to make certain their work surface is at a ~~suitable~~ height. They should also be encouraged to take frequent breaks from their desks. [comfortable]

Please
~~Feel free to~~ contact my office if you would like more information.

Sincerely,

Elaine Boudreau
Ergonomics Specialist

Critical Thinking & Work-Readiness Skills

In the course of working through the following Microsoft Office-based Critical Thinking exercises, you will also be utilizing various work-readiness skills, some of which are listed next to each exercise. Go to labyrinthelab.com/ workreadiness to learn more about the work-readiness skills.

2.1 Create a Business Letter

WORK-READINESS SKILLS APPLIED

- Writing
- Serving clients/ customers
- Organizing and maintaining information

Stefanie Bentley, the marketing assistant for My Virtual Campus, has received an email from Mary Jones, the student life coordinator from Magnolia College (3000 College Lane, Anywhere, Iowa 22222) asking what's different about the My Virtual Campus service compared to other similar services. Write a response in business letter format stating that My Virtual Campus has the most flexible set of solutions and that you can demonstrate these solutions in an online meeting. Suggest a time and date two weeks from today, and mention that you have enclosed a brochure. Save the letter as **ct-Magnolia** to your Lesson 02 folder. Close the file.

2.2 Use AutoCorrect and AutoFormat

WORK-READINESS SKILLS APPLIED

- Writing
- Serving clients/ customers
- Applying technology to a task

After two weeks with no response from Mary at Magnolia College, Stefanie decides to send a follow-up letter. Create another business letter addressed to Mary (her title and contact details shown above) asking for confirmation that she received your earlier letter and suggesting another time for a meeting. Configure Word's AutoCorrect options to automatically replace **mvc** with *My Virtual Campus* and test it to make sure *mvc* is automatically corrected. Save your document to your Lesson 02 folder as **ct-Follow Up**. Delete the custom AutoCorrect entry so other students can perform this exercise on the same computer later.

2.3 Combine and Switch Between Documents

WORK-READINESS SKILLS APPLIED

- Thinking creatively
- Making decisions
- Organizing and maintaining information

Stefanie decides to blend content from multiple documents so she has a single tool she can use for marketing purposes. Open the files ct-MVC Description Rev 1 and ct-MVC Description Rev 2 from the Lesson 02 folder. Cut, paste, drag and drop, and use any other editing techniques to combine the two descriptions into a single, complete description of My Virtual Campus. You will have to decide which document will contain the updated edits. Save that document to your Lesson 02 folder as **ct-MVC Description Final**.

Creating a Memorandum and a Press Release

In this lesson, you will expand on the basic Word skills you've developed. You will create a memo and a press release and then apply character formatting. You will also get experience with Word's proofing and editing tools, including Spelling & Grammar check. Finally, you will find synonyms in Word's thesaurus and explore other research options.

LESSON OUTLINE

LEARNING OBJECTIVES

After studying this lesson, you will be able to:

- Insert dates and symbols
- Insert and delete page breaks
- Work with proofreading tools
- Use Research options
- Work with formatting features
- Search using the Navigation pane and Find and Replace
- Work with hyperlinks and bookmarks

Preparing a Memorandum

My Virtual Campus continues to grow and is constantly adding the newest advancements in technology. Brett Martin is the public relations representative, and she regularly issues press releases to  members and potential customers, trumpeting forthcoming upgrades. Brett creates a memorandum to which she attaches her latest press release announcing the launch of MyResume, which is being integrated into the website. Memorandums are used for internal communication within a company or organization, whereas business letters are used for external communication. Brett understands the importance of protecting the corporation's proprietary information, so she uses the appropriate trademark designations in her documents.

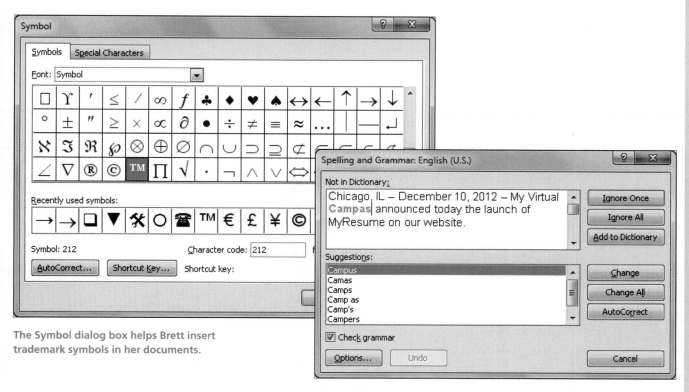

The Symbol dialog box helps Brett insert trademark symbols in her documents.

The Spelling and Grammar tool is a powerful proofreading aid.

3.1 Typing a Memorandum

Video Lesson labyrinthelab.com/videos

There are a variety of acceptable memorandum styles in use today. All memorandum styles contain the same elements but with varied formatting. The style shown in the following figure is a traditional memorandum style with minimal formatting.

The introduction includes headings such as Memo To: and From:. Use a double space between paragraphs, or use the new Microsoft spacing, which automatically adds space after a paragraph. This means you only need to tap Enter once between paragraphs.

The body of the memo comes next.

Extras such as attachment notations go here.

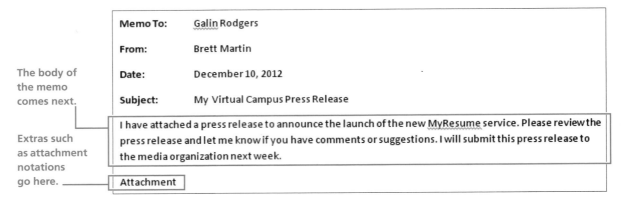

Memo To:	Galin Rodgers
From:	Brett Martin
Date:	December 10, 2012
Subject:	My Virtual Campus Press Release

I have attached a press release to announce the launch of the new MyResume service. Please review the press release and let me know if you have comments or suggestions. I will submit this press release to the media organization next week.

Attachment

Introducing Default Tabs

The Tab key moves the insertion point to the nearest tab stop. In Word, the default tab stops are set every ¹/₂ inch, thus the insertion point moves ¹/₂ inch whenever you tap the Tab key. In this lesson, you will use Word's default tab settings.

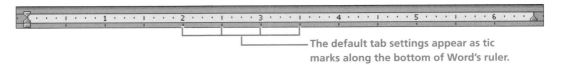

The default tab settings appear as tic marks along the bottom of Word's ruler.

A quick way to turn the ruler on and off is to click the View Ruler button at the top of the scroll bar.

Inserting and Formatting the Date

You use the Insert→Text→Insert Date and Time 🗓 command on the Ribbon to display the Date and Time dialog box. Word lets you insert the current date in a variety of formats. For example, the date could be inserted as 12/10/12, December 10, 2012, or 10 December 2012.

FROM THE KEYBOARD

Alt + Shift + D
to insert a date

The Update Automatically Option

You can insert the date and time as text or as a field. Inserting the date as text has the same effect as typing the date into a document. Fields, however, are updated whenever a document is saved or printed. For example, imagine you create a document on December 10, 2012, and you insert the date as a field. If you open the document the next day, the date will automatically change to December 11, 2012. The date and time are inserted as fields whenever the Update Automatically box is checked, as shown here.

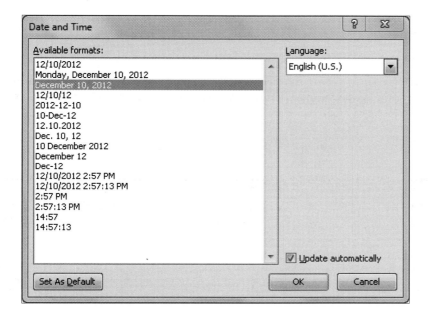

DEVELOP YOUR SKILLS 3.1.1

Set Up a Memo and Insert the Date

In this exercise, you will create a memo and insert the date automatically. You will also try out Word's 1.15 line spacing and the extra space following paragraphs.

Set Up a Memo

1. **Start** a new blank document. Make sure the Word window is **maximized** ▣.

2. If necessary, click the **View Ruler** 🗒 button at the top of the vertical scroll bar to turn on the ruler.

3. **Tap** Enter twice to space down to approximately 2 inches from the top of the page (1-inch mark on the vertical ruler).
   Using Word's default spacing, you don't have to tap Enter as many times as you did in the previous lesson to position the insertion point at 2 inches.

4. Type **Memo To:** and **tap** the Tab key.
   Notice that the insertion point moves to the next $^1/_2$-inch mark on the ruler.

5. If necessary, choose **Home→Paragraph→Show/Hide** ¶ from the Ribbon to display formatting marks.
   Notice the arrow formatting mark that represents the tab.

6. Type **Galin Rodgers** and **tap** Enter once.
   Notice that the word Galin has a red wavy underline, indicating it is not in Word's dictionary.

7. Type **From:** and **tap** Tab twice.
   It is necessary to Tab twice to align the names. The first tab aligns the insertion point at the $^1/_2$-inch mark on the ruler; the second aligns the insertion point at the 1-inch position.

8. Type **Brett Martin** and **tap** Enter once.

9. Type **Date:** and **tap** Tab twice.

Choose a Date Format and Insert the Date

10. Choose **Insert→Text→Insert Date and Time** 📇 from the Ribbon to display the Date and Time dialog box.

11. Follow these steps to insert the date:

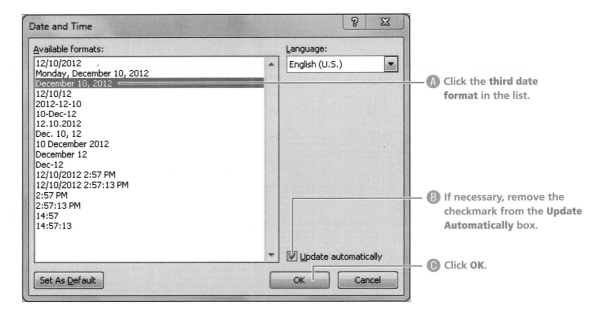

Leaving the Update Automatically box checked instructs Word to insert the date as a field, which means the original date would be lost if you opened and saved the document at a later date. In this instance, you do not want the date to change.

12. Choose **Home→Paragraph→Show/Hide** ¶ to turn off the paragraph marks.

13. Complete the remainder of the memorandum, as shown in the following illustration, using the Tab to align the text in the Subject line. Bear in mind that you only need to **tap** Enter once between paragraphs.

Memo To: Galin Rodgers

From: Brett Martin

Date: December 10, 2012

Subject: My Virtual Campus Press Release

I have attached a press release to announce the launch of the new MyResume service. Please review the press release and let me know if you have comments or suggestions. I will submit this press release to the media organization next week.

Attachment

---

14. Click the **View Ruler** button at the top of the scroll bar to turn off the ruler.

15. Click the **Save** button, and save the document in Lesson 03 folder as **Martin Memo**.

16. Leave the memorandum **open**, as you will modify it throughout this lesson.

Inserting Symbols

Video Lesson   labyrinthelab.com/videos

Word lets you insert a variety of symbols, typographic characters, and international characters not found on the keyboard. You insert symbols via the Symbol dialog box. The following illustration shows how you access the Symbol dialog box. You can also use shortcut key combinations to insert certain symbols; for example, type (c), (r), or (tm) to insert the copyright, registered trademark, or trademark symbols, respectively.

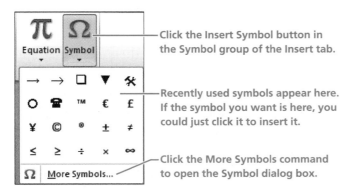

Click the Insert Symbol button in the Symbol group of the Insert tab.

Recently used symbols appear here. If the symbol you want is here, you could just click it to insert it.

Click the More Symbols command to open the Symbol dialog box.

The Special Characters tab displays commonly used special characters, such as the registered trademark (®) symbol and various punctuation symbols.

You can choose from several fonts, each displaying a different set of characters in the dialog box. Some fonts, such as Wingdings, contain interesting and fun symbols.

You can look up or set an AutoCorrect entry (or a keyboard shortcut) that may be used to insert a symbol rather than opening this dialog box.

DEVELOP YOUR SKILLS 3.1.2

Insert Symbols

In this exercise, you will add a trademark symbol and a registered trademark symbol to your document.

1. Position the **insertion point** to the right of *My Virtual Campus* on the *Subject:* line.

2. Click **Insert→Symbols→Insert Symbol** 🔲 from the Ribbon, and choose the **More Symbols** command at the bottom of the menu.

3. When the Symbol dialog box appears, click the **Special Characters** tab.

4. Choose the **registered trademark symbol** (an R inside a circle), and then click the **Insert** button.
   The ® symbol is inserted in the document, and the Symbol dialog box remains open. Word leaves the dialog box open in case you wish to insert additional symbols.

5. Position the **insertion point** to the right of *MyResume* in the main paragraph.
   You may need to drag the dialog box out of the way in order to see the word. To do that, position the mouse pointer on the blue title bar at the top of the dialog box, press and hold the mouse button, drag the dialog box out of the way, and then release the mouse button.

6. Click the **trademark** (™) symbol from Special Characters and then click **Insert**.
   The trademark (™) symbol indicates that a company claims a phrase or icon as its trademark but has not received the federal protection accompanying the registered trademark (®) symbol.

7. Click the **Symbols** tab in the Symbol dialog box, and choose different fonts from the Font list to see other sets of symbols.

8. When you finish experimenting, click the **Close** button to close the dialog box.

9. Click the **Save** 💾 button to save the changes.

3.2 Working with Page Breaks

Video Lesson   labyrinthelab.com/videos

If you are typing text and the insertion point reaches the bottom of a page, Word automatically breaks the page and begins a new page. This is known as an automatic page break. The location of automatic page breaks may change as text is added to or deleted from a document. Automatic page breaks are convenient when working with long documents that have continuously flowing text. For example, imagine you were writing a novel and you decided to insert a new paragraph in the middle of a chapter. With automatic page breaks, you could insert the paragraph and Word would automatically repaginate the entire chapter.

You force a page break by choosing Insert→Pages→Page Break 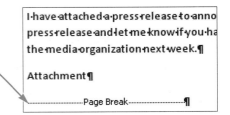 from the Ribbon. A manual page break remains in place unless you remove it. You insert manual page breaks whenever you want to control the starting point of a new page.

FROM THE KEYBOARD
Ctrl+Enter to insert a page break

 If you are working on a first draft or a document you suspect will go through revisions, it is not a good idea to insert manual page breaks because the pages will not repaginate correctly and you may end up with unwanted blank pages.

Removing Manual Page Breaks

In Draft view, a manual page break appears as a horizontal line, including the phrase *Page Break*. You can also see the page break line in Print Layout view if you turn on the Show/Hide feature. You can remove a manual page break by positioning the insertion point on the page break line and tapping Delete, as shown in the illustration to the right.

> I·have·attached·a·press·release·to·anno
> press·release·and·let·me·know·if·you·ha
> the·media·organization·next·week.¶
>
> Attachment¶
>
> ·············Page Break·············¶

Displaying the Word Count

Microsoft Word tracks the number of words, pages, characters, paragraphs, and lines as you type them in a document. The number of words is displayed on the Word Count button on the Status bar; the other counts are available when you double-click the Word Count button.

You may need to count the number of words in a certain paragraph, a certain page, and so forth. To check these statistics, you need to first select the text; you can even select sections of text that are not connected to each other. The word count appears on the Status bar, which shows the number of selected words and the total number of words in the document. For example, a 42-word selection in a document that contains 60 words would display as 42/60.

Page: 1 of 2 | Words: 42/60 —— Word Count button on Status bar

 Select nonadjacent sections by highlighting the first selection, holding down the Ctrl key, and then selecting the additional sections.

Work with Page Breaks

In this exercise, you will practice using manual page breaks. You will insert a page break, thereby creating a new page so you can copy and paste the press release information from another document into your new page.

Insert a Page Break

1. Make sure you are in **Print Layout** view. If you are not sure, click the **View** tab and choose **Print Layout** from the Document Views group at the left edge of the Ribbon. (If the button is highlighted, you are already in Print Layout view.)

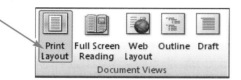

2. **Tap** Ctrl + End to position the insertion point at the bottom of the document and, if necessary, **tap** Enter to generate a blank line below the *Attachment* line.

3. Choose **Insert→Pages→Page Break** from the Ribbon.

4. Select the body paragraph and view the **Word Count** button the Status bar.
   Notice that the numbers 42/60 represent the number of words selected and total number in the document.

5. If necessary, **scroll** to see the bottom portion of page 1 and the top of page 2.

Remove the Page Break

6. **Scroll** up until the *Attachment* line is visible.

7. If necessary, click **Home→Paragraph→Show/Hide** ¶ to display formatting marks and see the page break.

8. **Click** to the left of the page break line, and tap Delete.

9. Try **scrolling** down to the second page and you will see that it is gone.

Reinsert the Page Break

10. Check to see that the **insertion point** is just below the *Attachment* line, and **tap** Ctrl + Enter to reinsert the page break.
    This shortcut keystroke is useful when you use page breaks frequently.

11. Click **Home→Paragraph→Show/Hide** ¶ to hide the formatting marks.
    The insertion point should be positioned at the top of the second page.

12. Click **File→Open** and, if necessary, navigate to your file storage location and **open** Press Release from the Lesson 03 folder.
    Notice that a number of phrases are flagged by the spelling checker (red wavy underlines) and grammar checker (green wavy underlines) in the document. You will take care of those in the next exercise.

13. In the Press Release document, **tap** ⌨Ctrl⌨+⌨A⌨ to select the entire document.

14. **Tap** ⌨Ctrl⌨+⌨C⌨ to copy the document.
    Now you will switch to your memo.

15. On the taskbar, click the **Martin Memo** button to switch back to that document.

16. Make sure your **insertion point** is at the top of page 2.

17. Choose **Home→Clipboard→Paste** 📋 from the Ribbon.
    The press release is pasted on page 2 of your document. Now you will switch back to the press release and close it.

18. Use the **taskbar** button to switch to Press Release.

19. Choose **File→Close** to close the file.
    The Martin Memo should now be in the foreground.

20. **Save** 💾 the file and leave it **open** for the next exercise.

3.3 Working with Proofreading Tools

Video Lesson   labyrinthelab.com/videos

Word's powerful Spelling and Grammar tool helps you avoid embarrassing spelling and grammar errors. Whether you choose to use the default on-the-fly checking, where Word marks possible errors as you type, or you choose to save proofing tasks until you've completed your document content, these tools can help polish your writing. However, these tools are proofreading aids, not the final word. You still need to involve human judgment in a final round of proofing, such as making sure you don't overuse a particular word. The Thesaurus can aid in finding alternate words for you.

- Spelling checker
- Grammar checker
- Research Task Pane

Using the Spelling Checker

Word checks a document for spelling errors by comparing each word to the contents of its built-in dictionary. Word also looks for double words such as *the the,* and a variety of capitalization errors. If you start the spelling checker in the middle of the document, when it reaches the end, a message appears asking if you want to go back and start spell checking from the beginning of the document.

Word can automatically check your spelling as you type. It flags spelling errors by underlining them with wavy red lines. You can correct a flagged error by right-clicking the error and choosing a suggested replacement word or other option from the menu that pops up.

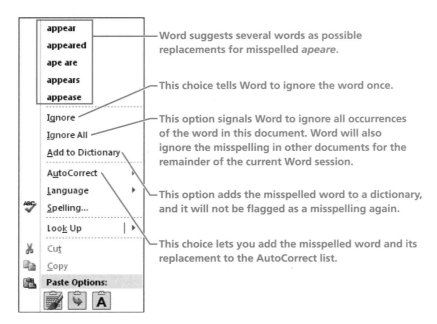

Word suggests several words as possible replacements for misspelled *apeare*.

This choice tells Word to ignore the word once.

This option signals Word to ignore all occurrences of the word in this document. Word will also ignore the misspelling in other documents for the remainder of the current Word session.

This option adds the misspelled word to a dictionary, and it will not be flagged as a misspelling again.

This choice lets you add the misspelled word and its replacement to the AutoCorrect list.

Working with Word's Dictionaries

The main Word dictionary contains thousands of common words; however, it may not include proper names, acronyms, technical terminology, and so forth. When you run the spelling checker and it comes across a word not found in the main dictionary, it marks the word as a possible spelling error. If that word is one that you use often in your writing, you can add it so the spelling checker recognizes it the next time and does not mark it as an error.

Dictionary Options

When the Suggest from Main Dictionary Only checkbox is unchecked, the spelling checker will search for words in the custom dictionaries; however, if that option is checked, it will only search the main dictionary. Adding a word during spell checking adds that word to a custom dictionary. The dictionary options are found on the Proofing page in the Word Options dialog box.

Choose whether Word includes suggestions from custom dictionaries or only the main dictionary.

Access the list of words added to the custom dictionaries.

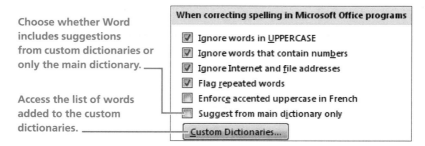

When correcting spelling in Microsoft Office programs

☑ Ignore words in UPPERCASE
☑ Ignore words that contain numbers
☑ Ignore Internet and file addresses
☑ Flag repeated words
☐ Enforce accented uppercase in French
☐ Suggest from main dictionary only
[Custom Dictionaries...]

The options you set for custom dictionaries in Microsoft Word apply to all Office programs.

Remove a Word from a Custom Dictionary

You may add a word to a custom dictionary and then realize it was a mistake. This is not a problem because you can remove it using the Custom Dictionaries dialog box. You simply open the custom dictionary, display the word list, and choose which word to delete.

Choose a word from the list to delete.

Display the list of words currently in the custom dictionary.

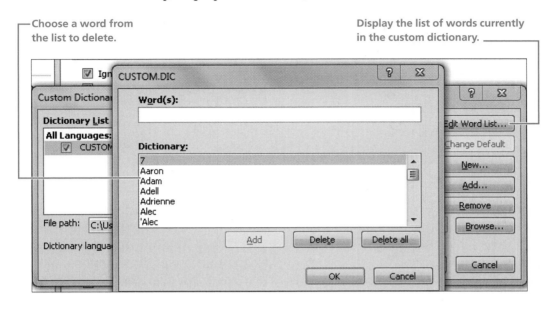

Use Automatic Spelling Checker

In this exercise, you will use the Ignore All option on the spelling checker pop-up menu to remove the red underlines from all occurrences of the words MyResume. You will also delete a repeated word.

Spellcheck Using Ignore All

1. Notice that the word *MyResume* in the first line of page 2 has a wavy red underline. This word appears a number of times in the document.
MyResume *is spelled correctly; it's just that it does not appear in Word's dictionary. As a result, Word flags it as a possible spelling error.*

2. Follow these steps to have the spelling checker ignore all occurrences of *MyResume* and thereby remove the wavy red underline wherever the term appears:

Ⓐ **Right-click** the first occurrence of *MyResume*, and a pop-up menu appears. (The Mini toolbar also shows up, but you can disregard it.)

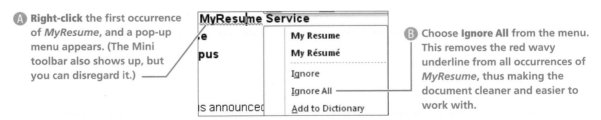

Ⓑ Choose **Ignore All** from the menu. This removes the red wavy underline from all occurrences of *MyResume*, thus making the document cleaner and easier to work with.

Work with Double Word Errors

Word flagged a double word error in the first paragraph of the press release.

3. **Right-click** the word *our* with the wavy red line, and choose the **Delete Repeated Word** command from the menu.

4. **Save** 💾 your file and leave it **open** for the next exercise.

Using the Grammar Checker

Video Lesson   labyrinthelab.com/videos

Word has a sophisticated grammar checker that can help you with your writing skills. Like the spelling checker, the grammar checker can check grammar as you type. The grammar checker flags errors by underlining them with wavy green lines. You can correct a flagged error by right-clicking the error and choosing a replacement phrase or other option from the pop-up menu. Be careful when using the grammar checker. It isn't perfect. There is no substitute for careful proofreading.

Grammar checking is active by default. Grammar checking options are available by clicking the File tab, then clicking the Options tab to display the Word Options window. You can enable or disable the feature by checking or unchecking the boxes shown in the figure to the right.

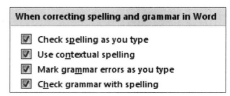

The Spelling and Grammar Dialog Box

FROM THE KEYBOARD

F7 to start the Spelling & Grammar check

Choose Review→Proofing→Spelling and Grammar 📋 from the Ribbon to display the Spelling and Grammar dialog box. You may prefer to focus on your document's content and postpone proofing until you're done. You can use the Spelling and Grammar dialog box for that purpose.

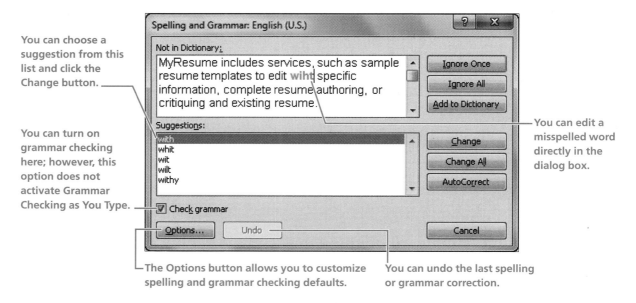

Use the Spelling and Grammar Dialog Box

In this exercise, you will make corrections to the Martin Memo using the Spelling and Grammar dialog box. If you do not see any text underlined in green, the grammar checking options are turned off on your computer. If you see the green grammar check lines in your document, follow the steps to turn the feature on anyway, so you will know where to locate the feature in the future.

1. Click the **File** tab and then click the **Options** tab to display the Word Options window.

2. Choose **Proofing** from the menu on the left.

3. Follow these steps to turn on grammar checking:

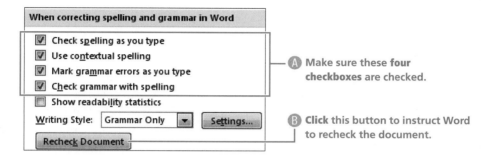

4. When the message box appears, choose **Yes** to dismiss the message, then click **OK** to close the window.
   Since you clicked Recheck Document, notice that MyResume *has wavy red lines again.*

5. Position the **insertion point** at the beginning of the first line on page 2.

6. Choose **Review→Proofing→Spelling and Grammar** ✓ from the Ribbon.
   The Spelling and Grammar dialog box appears, and MyResume *is noted as a possible spelling error.*

7. Click the **Add to Dictionary** button.
   You will delete MyResume *from the Custom Dictionary a little later in this exercise.*

8. The next error is a simple typo; the suggestion with is correct, so click the **Change** button.
   Now Word points out a possible grammatical error.

Use the Grammar Checker

9. Follow these steps to correct the grammatical error:

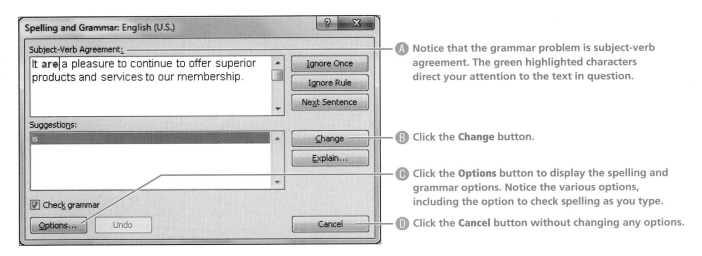

Ⓐ Notice that the grammar problem is subject-verb agreement. The green highlighted characters direct your attention to the text in question.

Ⓑ Click the **Change** button.

Ⓒ Click the **Options** button to display the spelling and grammar options. Notice the various options, including the option to check spelling as you type.

Ⓓ Click the **Cancel** button without changing any options.

10. The next error is a spelling error, and the suggestion *Delivery* is correct, so click the **Change** button.

11. Finish checking the rest of the press release using your own good judgment regarding what changes to make. When *Galin* is flagged, click the **Ignore Once** button.

12. When the message appears indicating that the spelling and grammar check is complete, click **OK**.

Remove a Word from the Custom Dictionary

You will now delete the name MyResume *that you added to the dictionary earlier in this exercise.*

13. Click **File→Options**.

14. Click the **Proofing** tab in the Navigation pane.

15. Follow these steps to display the word list in the Custom Dictionary:

Ⓐ Click the **Custom Dictionaries** button.　　　　Ⓑ Click the **Edit Word List** button.

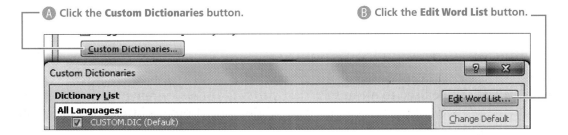

16. Follow these steps to delete *MyResume* from the word list:

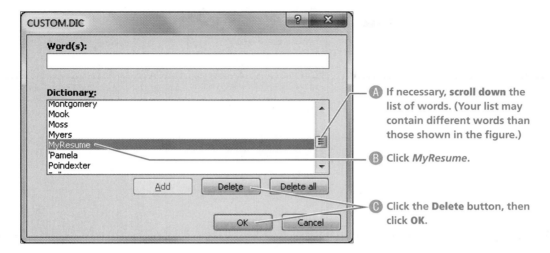

A If necessary, **scroll down** the list of words. (Your list may contain different words than those shown in the figure.)

B Click *MyResume*.

C Click the **Delete** button, then click **OK**.

17. Click **OK** two more times to close the remaining windows.

18. **Save** 💾 the file and leave it **open** for the next exercise.

Using the Thesaurus to Find a Synonym

Video Lesson   labyrinthelab.com/videos

A thesaurus contains words that have the same meaning as another word (synonyms). You can quickly see a list of synonyms for a word by simply right-clicking the word and choosing Synonyms. For a more extensive list with additional options, you can display the Research task pane by choosing Thesaurus from the bottom of the context menu or from the Proofing group on the Review tab of the Ribbon.

FROM THE KEYBOARD
Alt +click the word to look up for Thesaurus

The Thesaurus also contains antonyms, which are words meaning the opposite of other words.

Using the Research Task Pane

The Research task pane goes beyond displaying a list of alternate words. As you know, a word can have different meanings depending upon the context in which it is used. For example, the word *certain* can be used to mean *sure, clear, particular,* or *some.* Using the Thesaurus in the Research task pane, you can look up those additional synonyms by clicking any word displayed in the results list.

In addition to displaying words from the Thesaurus, the Research task pane also provides access to other references, such as a dictionary, business and financial sites, and research sites.

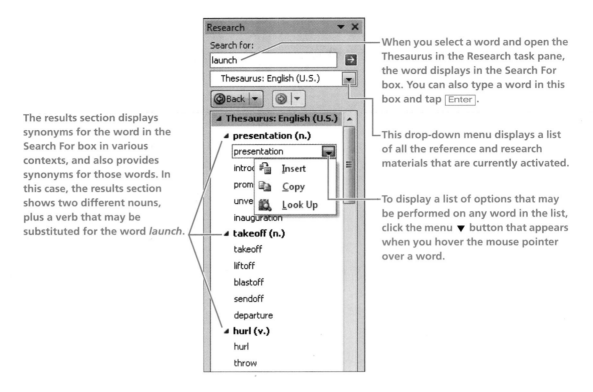

The results section displays synonyms for the word in the Search For box in various contexts, and also provides synonyms for those words. In this case, the results section shows two different nouns, plus a verb that may be substituted for the word *launch*.

When you select a word and open the Thesaurus in the Research task pane, the word displays in the Search For box. You can also type a word in this box and tap Enter.

This drop-down menu displays a list of all the reference and research materials that are currently activated.

To display a list of options that may be performed on any word in the list, click the menu ▼ button that appears when you hover the mouse pointer over a word.

Research Task Pane Options

Word already includes a long list of services in the Research task pane, though you may wish to add your favorites to the list. Certain services in the list are currently activated; however, you can choose which ones to activate and deactivate. When you perform a search, only the services that are currently activated will be researched.

DEVELOP YOUR SKILLS 3.3.3
Use the Thesaurus

In this exercise, you will use the context menu to replace a word with a synonym, and you will experiment with the Thesaurus in the Research task pane. Finally, you will activate and deactivate services in the Research Options.

Choose a Synonym from the Menu

1. **Scroll** to view the press release page.

2. **Right-click** the word *launch* in the first sentence of the *Announcement* paragraph.

3. Follow these steps to replace the word with a synonym:

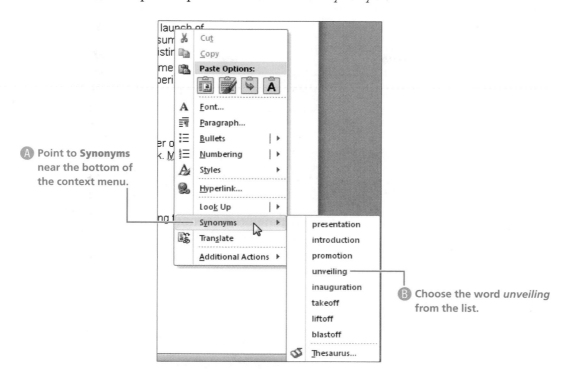

Ⓐ Point to **Synonyms** near the bottom of the context menu.

Ⓑ Choose the word *unveiling* from the list.

Notice that the word launch *in the first paragraph has been changed to* unveiling.

Look Up Synonyms in the Research Task Pane

4. Choose **Review→Proofing→Thesaurus** from the Ribbon.

5. Follow these steps to insert an alternate word for *unveiling*:

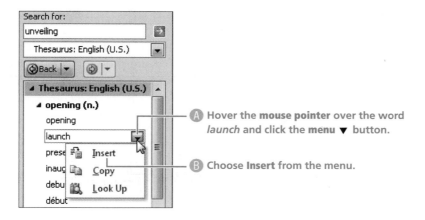

Ⓐ Hover the **mouse pointer** over the word *launch* and click the **menu ▼** button.

Ⓑ Choose **Insert** from the menu.

6. While the Research task pane is still displayed, **click** any word in the results section to view synonyms for that word.

7. Choose **Research Options** from the bottom of the Research task pane.

8. Click the **checkbox** next to Diccionario de la Real Academia Española.

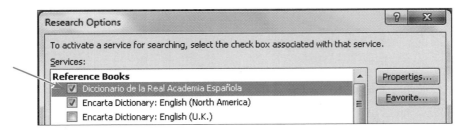

9. Before clicking OK, scroll down through the list to view the available services which may or may not be activated.
   Please do not activate or deactivate services unless are instructed to do so in the classroom.

10. Click the **Thesaurus: English (U.S.) menu ▼** button in the Research task pane to display the list of currently activated services.
    Notice that the list now includes the Spanish dictionary you just activated.

11. Choose **Research Options** again and remove the **checkmark** from the checkbox to deactivate the Diccionario de la Real Academia Española; click **OK**.

12. Click the **Close ☒** button in the upper-right corner of the Research task pane.

3.4 Formatting Text

Video Lesson   labyrinthelab.com/videos

You can format text by changing the font, size, and color, or by applying various enhancements, including bold, italics, and underline. You can change the text formatting before you start typing, or you can select existing text and then make the changes. When you tap Enter, Word continues to use the same formatting until you change it. Two common methods for formatting text include using the Font dialog box or the commands on the Ribbon.

Clearing Text Formatting

TIP

Changes to the font case are not affected by the Clear Formatting command.

Once you have applied formatting, it is very easy to remove. Any selection can be returned to plain text with one click of the Clear Formatting command. You find the Clear Formatting command in the Font group on the Home tab of the Ribbon.

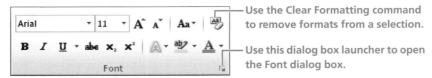

Use the Clear Formatting command to remove formats from a selection.

Use this dialog box launcher to open the Font dialog box.

The following illustration describes the Font dialog box.

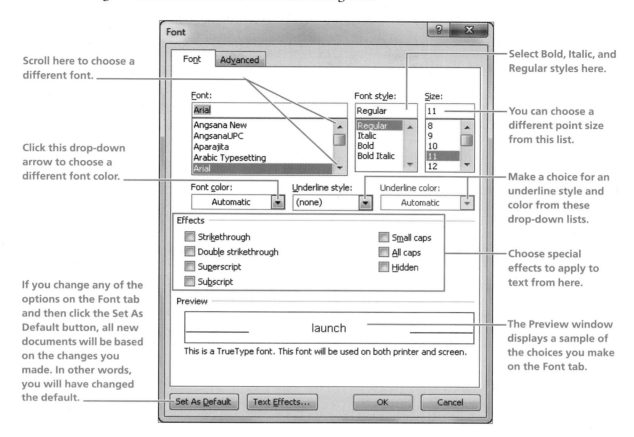

Scroll here to choose a different font.

Click this drop-down arrow to choose a different font color.

If you change any of the options on the Font tab and then click the Set As Default button, all new documents will be based on the changes you made. In other words, you will have changed the default.

Select Bold, Italic, and Regular styles here.

You can choose a different point size from this list.

Make a choice for an underline style and color from these drop-down lists.

Choose special effects to apply to text from here.

The Preview window displays a sample of the choices you make on the Font tab.

3.5 Working with Fonts and Themes

Fonts determine the appearance of the text. There are many fonts installed with Word; some are appropriate for business while others add a more whimsical, personal touch.

A theme is a set of formatting selections including colors, graphic elements, and fonts, all designed to blend well together. The theme-related font choices include one font for body text and one for headings. You will see the actual names of the theme fonts listed in the Font drop-down menu on the Ribbon, but you will see only their generic names, +Body and +Heading, in the Font dialog box. Various themes use different sets of theme fonts.

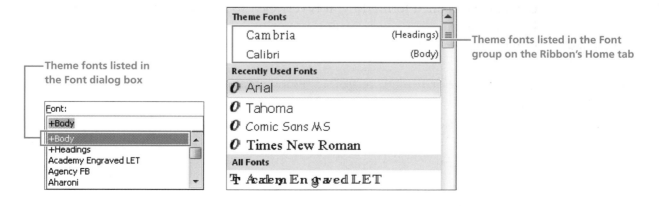

Theme fonts listed in the Font dialog box

Theme fonts listed in the Font group on the Ribbon's Home tab

Changing the Font Case

FROM THE KEYBOARD
[Shift]+[F3] to change font case

Font cases include lowercase, uppercase, sentence case, and capitalize each word. Before beginning to type, if you want the text in uppercase, you can tap the [Caps Lock] key and all text will be capitalized until you tap the key again. Many times though, you may want to change the case after you've already typed the text. In this situation, all you have to do is select the text and apply a different font case. You can change the font case by using the Change Case command in the Font group on the Home tab of the Ribbon or by using [Shift]+[F3] to toggle through the uppercase, lowercase, and capitalize each word commands.

DEVELOP YOUR SKILLS 3.5.1
Format Text

In this exercise, you will use elements from the Font group on the Ribbon, format the text, change the case, and clear formatting.

Format the Press Release Title Lines

1. **Scroll** to the top of the second page.

2. Position the **mouse pointer** in the left margin, and **drag down** to select the first three heading lines.

3. Choose **Home→Font→dialog box launcher** to display the Font dialog box.

4. Follow these steps to change the font and font size:

Ⓐ Scroll down and choose **Arial** from the Font list.

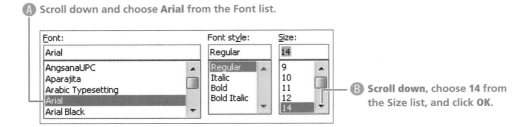

Ⓑ **Scroll down**, choose **14** from the Size list, and click **OK**.

Add Text Enhancements

5. With the three lines still selected, **tap** [Ctrl]+[B] and then **tap** [Ctrl]+[U] to apply bold and underline enhancements to the headings.

6. Click the **Underline** [U] button to remove that enhancement.

7. Follow these steps to apply bold formatting to multiple selections at the same time:

A Position the **mouse pointer** in the margin next to the word *Announcement* and then **click** to select the heading.

B **Hold down** the [Ctrl] key and **click** in the margin next to the other two headings to select them also.

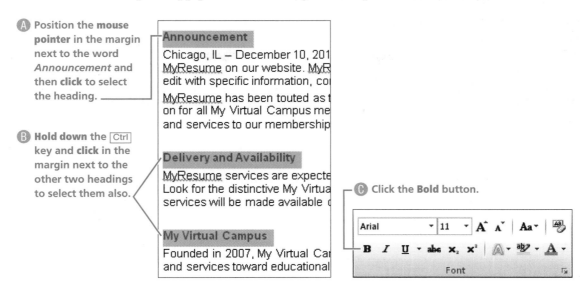

C Click the **Bold** button.

Change the Font Case

8. At the top of the first page, position the **insertion point** at the beginning of the first line, and then **click and drag** over *Memo To*.

9. **Press and hold down** the [Shift] key and **tap** [F3].
   Notice that the text changed to all uppercase with one tap. If you continued holding down the [Shift] key and tapped [F3] again, it would change to all lowercase, followed by Capitalize Each Word with an additional tap.

10. **Double-click** the word *From*, and then choose **Home→Font→Change Case** **Aa** from the Ribbon.

11. Choose **UPPERCASE** from the drop-down menu.

12. Using either method above, change the words *Date* and *Subject* to **uppercase**.
    Don't panic here! The reason that the subject text moved to the next half-inch tab stop is because the word Subject *got bigger when you changed it to uppercase—it's an easy fix.*

13. Position the **insertion point** after the colon following SUBJECT and **tap** [Delete] once to remove the extra tab stop.

Clear Formatting from Selected Text

14. Position the **mouse pointer** in the left margin, and then **triple-click** to select the entire document.

15. Choose **Home→Font→Clear Formatting** from the Ribbon.
    Notice that all formatting is removed from the entire document, including all font changes and text alignments, etc. (This does not include changes to the font case.)

16. Click the **Undo** button to restore all the formatting.

17. **Save** your file and leave it **open** for the next exercise.

The Format Painter

Video Lesson   labyrinthelab.com/videos

The Format Painter 🖌 lets you copy text formats from one location to another. This is convenient if you want the same format(s) applied to text in different locations. The Format Painter copies all text formats, including the font, font size, and color. This saves time and helps create consistent formatting throughout a document. The Format Painter is located in the Clipboard group on the Home tab, and it also appears on the Mini toolbar.

QUICK REFERENCE	COPYING TEXT FORMATS WITH THE FORMAT PAINTER
Task	**Procedure**
Copy text formats with the Format Painter	■ Select the text with the format(s) you wish to copy.
	■ Click the Format Painter once if you want to copy formats to one other location, and double-click if you want to copy to multiple locations.
	■ Select the text at the new location(s) that you want to format. If you double-clicked in the previous step, the Format Painter will remain active, allowing you to select text at multiple locations. You can even scroll through the document to reach the desired location(s).
	■ If you double-clicked, then click the Format Painter button to turn it off.

DEVELOP YOUR SKILLS 3.5.2
Use the Format Painter

In this exercise, you will change the format applied to a heading and use the Format Painter to copy formats from one text block to another.

1. **Scroll** to page 2, if necessary, and **select** the heading *Announcement* just above the first large paragraph of text.

2. When the Mini toolbar appears, follow these steps to apply color to the heading line:

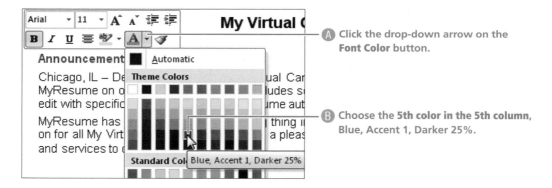

Ⓐ Click the drop-down arrow on the **Font Color** button.

Ⓑ Choose the **5th color in the 5th column**, **Blue, Accent 1, Darker 25%**.

Notice that the color you selected is in the Theme Colors category. These are the theme colors for Word's default *theme.*

3. Keep the text selected and the Mini toolbar active, and follow these steps to apply additional formats to the text:

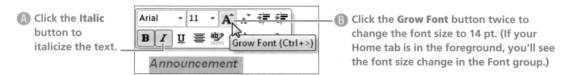

A Click the **Italic** button to italicize the text.

B Click the **Grow Font** button twice to change the font size to 14 pt. (If your Home tab is in the foreground, you'll see the font size change in the Font group.)

Copy Formats to One Location

4. Make sure the heading *Announcement* is selected.

5. Click the **Format Painter** 🖌 button on the Mini toolbar.
   A paintbrush icon is added to the I-beam mouse pointer once it is positioned over the document.

6. Drag the **mouse pointer** across the *Delivery and Availability* heading, and then **release** the mouse button.
   The 14 pt italic blue formats should be copied to the heading. The animated paintbrush icon also vanishes because you clicked the Format Painter button just once in the previous step. If you want to copy formats to multiple locations, you must double-click the Format Painter.

7. Make sure the *Delivery and Availability* heading is still selected.

8. Click the **Format Painter** 🖌 button on the Ribbon and then **select** the last heading, *My Virtual Campus*, to copy the format again.

Copy Formats to More Than One Location

9. **Scroll up** to the top of page 1.

10. **Click** and **drag** over *MEMO TO:* and then click the **Bold** **B** button.
    Be sure to include the colon in the MEMO TO: selection so it is formatted also.

11. Make sure *MEMO TO:* is still selected, and then **double-click** the **Format Painter** 🖌 on the Ribbon.

12. **Drag** over *FROM:* to apply the formatting from *MEMO TO:*.

13. **Drag** over *DATE:* and *SUBJECT:* to format these headings also.

14. Choose **Home→Clipboard→Format Painter** 🖌 to turn it off.

15. **Save** 💾 your file and leave it **open** for the next exercise.

3.6 Working with Find and Replace

Video Lesson   labyrinthelab.com/videos

FROM THE KEYBOARD
Ctrl + F for Find
Ctrl + H for Replace

Word's Find command lets you search a document for a particular word or phrase. You can also search for text formats, page breaks, and a variety of other items. Find is often the quickest way to locate a phrase, format, or item in a document.

The Find and Replace commands appear in the Editing group at the right end of the Home tab.

Searching with the Navigation Pane

The Find command now displays the new Navigation pane on the left side of the screen. You can search for text or other objects in your document, and the items found will conveniently display in the results area, giving you a quick view of everywhere they appear in the document.

Browse Options

By default, the Find command searches for text; however, with a click of the magnifying glass, you can choose to search for other objects, such as graphics, tables, footnotes, and so forth. At the top of the results window are three tabs that allow you to browse the results by the headings, the pages, or the word(s) you typed in the search box.

When you perform a search, the results are displayed in the navigation pane and are also highlighted in the actual document. You can scroll through the document, locating each instance, or simply click any of the results in the navigation pane to jump to that instance in the document.

The magnifying glass displays a menu of search options, including objects such as tables or graphics, which you may search for instead of text.

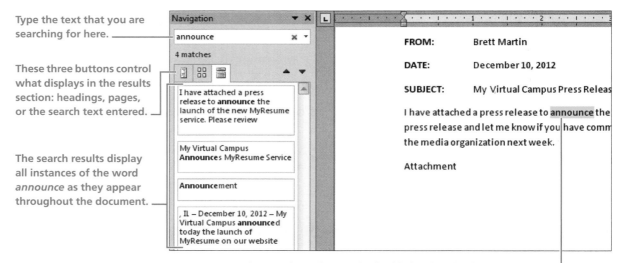

Type the text that you are searching for here.

These three buttons control what displays in the results section: headings, pages, or the search text entered.

The search results display all instances of the word *announce* as they appear throughout the document.

The search results are also highlighted in the document.

Using the Find and Replace Dialog Box

The Replace option in the Editing group on the Home tab displays the Find and Replace dialog box, where you can enter text, an object, or formatting you are searching for and the replacement for the found text, object, or format. You can also use the Go To tab to jump quickly to a specific place such as a page, section, bookmark, and so forth.

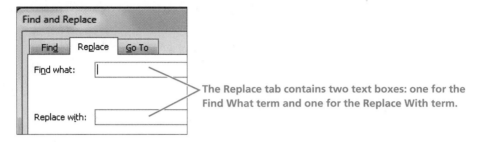

The Replace tab contains two text boxes: one for the Find What term and one for the Replace With term.

If you have already searched for text using the Navigation pane, the text automatically appears in the Find What text box in the Find and Replace dialog box.

Click the Go To button to display a menu of of specific places to jump to.

You type the term you are searching for here.

Click this button if it is labeled More. (The button name toggles between More and Less.) Clicking More displays the bottom half of the dialog box. Clicking Less closes the bottom half.

Notice that the Find and Replace tabs appear within the same dialog box.

Find Next initiates the search.

You can search up or down from the insertion point or through the entire document (All).

The checkboxes let you further qualify your search.

These options allow you to search for formats and other features.

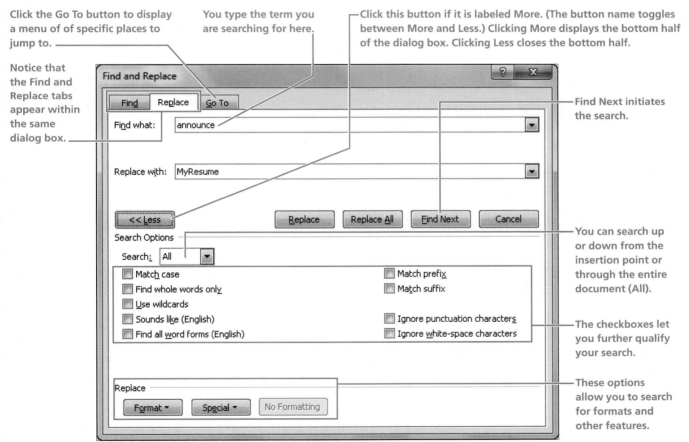

Finding and Replacing Formats

You may want to replace the formats in a document. Perhaps you formatted certain elements with a particular font and now you want to use a different font. Find and Replace finds the formatted elements for you and automatically replaces them.

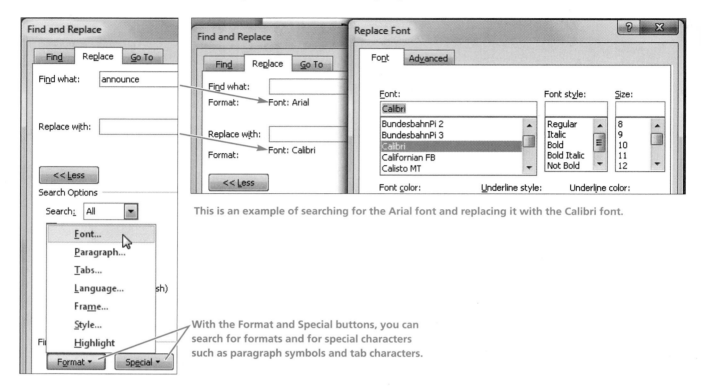

This is an example of searching for the Arial font and replacing it with the Calibri font.

With the Format and Special buttons, you can search for formats and for special characters such as paragraph symbols and tab characters.

DEVELOP YOUR SKILLS 3.6.1
Use Find and Replace

In this exercise, you will search with the Navigation pane, use Find and Replace, and explore some special search options.

Find a Word

1. Position the **insertion point** at the top of page 2, and make sure no text is selected.
2. Choose **Home→Editing→Find** 🔍.

3. Follow these steps to find all occurrences of *website*:

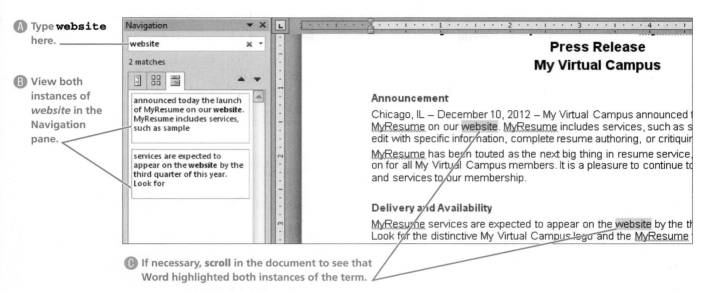

Ⓐ Type **website** here.

Ⓑ View both instances of *website* in the Navigation pane.

Ⓒ If necessary, **scroll** in the document to see that Word highlighted both instances of the term.

4. **Scroll** to the top of the document, and position the **insertion point** anywhere in the first line of the memo.

Find Another Word

5. Click in the **Navigation pane** search box, delete *website*, and type **Announce** (with a capital A) in its place.
   Notice that Word located announce *in the first paragraph of the memo and that* announce *has a lowercase* a, *even though you typed it in uppercase.*

6. Click the second instance in the **Navigation pane** results list and notice that *Announces* is highlighted in the first heading line of the press release.
   Notice that Word found Announce, *even though it is part of* Announces. *By default, the search feature is not case sensitive and doesn't recognize the difference between a whole word and part of a word. You will change this, however, in the next few steps.*

Use the Match Case Option

Now you will use the Find Options and Additional Search Commands menu to display the Find and Replace dialog box, and then use Match Case.

7. Follow these steps to display the Find and Replace dialog box:

Ⓐ Click the **Find Options and Additional Search Commands menu** ▼ button next to the Search Document box and choose **Advanced Find** from the drop-down menu. Notice that the Navigation pane is no longer the active window since you opened the Find and Replace dialog box.

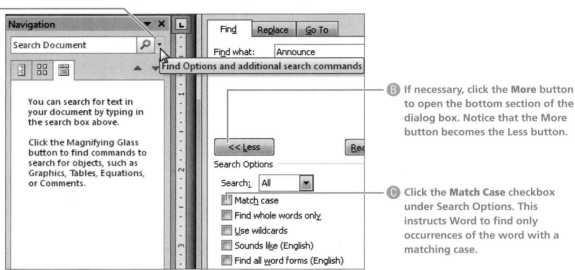

Ⓑ If necessary, click the **More** button to open the bottom section of the dialog box. Notice that the More button becomes the Less button.

Ⓒ Click the **Match Case** checkbox under Search Options. This instructs Word to find only occurrences of the word with a matching case.

8. Click the **Find Next** button, and Word locates the capitalized word *Announcement.*

9. Click **Find Next** again, and Word indicates that the entire document has been searched. *Word skipped over* announced *in lowercase in the next line.*

10. Click **Yes** in the message box.

11. Uncheck the **Match Case** checkbox.

Search for a Whole Word

12. If necessary, **scroll** to the top of the document, and place the **insertion point** anywhere in the first line of the memo.

13. Check the **Find Whole Words Only** checkbox.

14. Click **Find Next** twice, and on the second click Word indicates that the entire document was searched.
    Notice that this time the search did not locate Announces, Announcement, *or* announced.

15. Click **OK** in the message box, and then uncheck the **Find Whole Words Only** checkbox.

16. Delete the word *Announce* in the **Find What** box.

Search for Text Formats

17. Click the **Format** button at the bottom of the dialog box.
    The Format button lets you search for specific fonts, paragraph formats, and other formats.

18. Choose **Font** from the list.

19. Choose **Bold** from the Font Style list, and click **OK**.
    Font: Bold *should appear below the Find What box.*

20. Click the **Find Next** button, and Word selects a word in bold face type.

21. Click the **Less** button to collapse the bottom portion of the dialog box, and then click the **Cancel** button to close the dialog box.

Use Replace

22. Position the **insertion point** at the top of the document, and make sure no text is selected.

23. **Press** Ctrl+H to display the Find and Replace dialog box.
    Notice that the Replace tab is active in the dialog box. The shortcut keystrokes that you use determine which tab displays when the dialog box appears. Make sure the insertion point is in the Find What text box.

24. Click the **More** button to expand the dialog box, and then click the **No Formatting** button at the bottom of the dialog box.
    You need to turn off the Bold formatting option so Find will no longer limit it's results to finding words with Bold formatting.

25. Click the **Less** button to collapse the dialog box.
    The Marketing Department decided to change the name of My Virtual Campus' new feature from MyResume *to* ResumePlus.

26. Type **MyResume** in the Find What box, and then type **ResumePlus** in the Replace With box.

27. Click the **Find Next** button to locate the first occurrence of *MyResume*.

28. Click the **Replace** button to make the replacement.
    Word moves to the next occurrence of MyResume.

Use Replace All

29. Click the **Replace All** button to make all the changes at once.
    The message box informs you that Word made seven replacements.

Use Replace All with caution. You should be confident about the replacements Word will make before you use this feature. Using Replace allows you to monitor each replacement.

30. Click **OK** to dismiss the message, and then **close** the Find and Replace dialog box and observe the *ResumePlus* replacements.

31. **Close** the Navigation pane.

32. **Save** 🖫 the file and leave it **open** for the next exercise.

3.7 Navigating in Documents

Video Lesson   labyrinthelab.com/videos

There are more efficient ways to navigate in a document than always using the arrow keys or the scroll bar. Bookmarks and hyperlinks are especially effective in a long document. You can create and use bookmarks to move to new locations within the same document. You may already be familiar with hyperlinks from using the Internet. (Hyperlinks are those blue, underlined links you use to jump from one place to another). Word gives you the ability to do the same thing. A hyperlink in Word uses bookmarks or heading styles to jump to places that are within the same document.

Setting Up Bookmarks

You can assign a bookmark name to selected text or other objects in a document. Once a bookmark is set up, you can easily navigate to it by choosing the desired bookmark name from the Bookmark dialog box or the Go To tab in the Find and Replace dialog box.

You add new bookmarks to the list by typing a name, with no spaces, in the Bookmark Name text box and clicking the Add button.

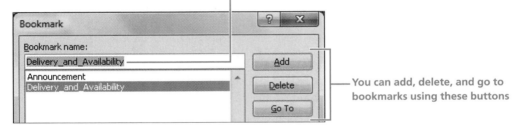

You can add, delete, and go to bookmarks using these buttons

QUICK REFERENCE	USING BOOKMARKS
Task	**Procedure**
Create a bookmark	■ Select the text to use as a bookmark.
	■ Choose Insert→Links→Bookmark from the Ribbon.
	■ Type the bookmark name without spaces.
	■ Click Add.
Jump to a bookmark using the Bookmark dialog box	■ Choose Insert→Links→Bookmark from the Ribbon to open the Bookmark dialog box.
	■ Choose a bookmark name from the list and click the Go To button.
Jump to a bookmark using the Find and Replace dialog box	■ Choose Home→Editing→Find from the Ribbon.
	■ Click the menu ▼ button next to the Search Document box and choose Go To from the list to open the Find and Replace dialog box.
	■ Choose Bookmark from the Go To What box and type or select the Bookmark name, then click the Go To button.

Navigate in Documents

In this exercise, you will create bookmarks and use them to jump to different areas of the document.

Create Bookmarks

1. Before you begin, be sure **page 2** is displayed; then, **select** the word *Delivery* in the second heading.
   Remember, you must first select the text that you want to use as a Bookmark.

2. Choose **Insert→Links→Bookmark** from the Ribbon to display the Bookmark dialog box.

3. Follow these steps to create a Bookmark:

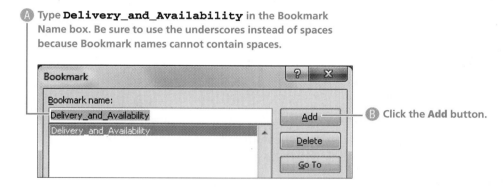

Ⓐ Type **Delivery_and_Availability** in the Bookmark Name box. Be sure to use the underscores instead of spaces because Bookmark names cannot contain spaces.

Ⓑ Click the **Add** button.

4. **Scroll**, if necessary, and **select** the Announcement heading.

5. Choose **Insert→Links→Bookmark** from the Ribbon.

6. Type **Announcement** in the Bookmark Name box, and then click the **Add** button.

Use a Bookmark to Navigate

7. **Press** Ctrl + Home to move the insertion point to the beginning of the document.

8. Choose **Insert→Links→Bookmark** from the Ribbon.

9. Click the Delivery_and_Availability bookmark, and then click the **Go To** button.
   Notice that the Bookmark dialog box remains open just in case you want to jump to somewhere else.

10. Choose the Announcement bookmark and click **Go To**.

11. Click the **Close** ✖ button to close the dialog box.

12. **Press** Ctrl + Home to move the insertion point to the beginning of the document.

Using Hyperlinks

Video Lesson   labyrinthelab.com/videos

A hyperlink is a block of text or a graphic that jumps you to another location when clicked, such as to a Bookmark, to another document, or to a web page. Hyperlinks in Word, just like the hyperlinks in web pages, provide the ability to quickly move to another location within the same document or to another document. To use a hyperlink *within* a document, the location you link to must first be set up as a Bookmark or be formatted in a heading style.

There are four primary types of hyperlinks.

- **Hyperlinks to areas within the current document**—This works much like a Bookmark, jumping the reader to another location in the same document.

- **Hyperlinks to other documents or files**—A hyperlink can open another Word document or even another program, such as Excel or PowerPoint.

- **Hyperlinks to web pages**—You can also create a link in a document to jump to a web page by using a URL address for the hyperlink.

- **Hyperlinks to email addresses**—Certain information may require additional clarification from a specific person; thus, you can create a hyperlink to a specific email address. When the hyperlink is clicked, a new message window opens with the email address already in the To: box.

You can remove a hyperlink if it becomes outdated by using the Hyperlink dialog box or by right-clicking the link to display a context menu.

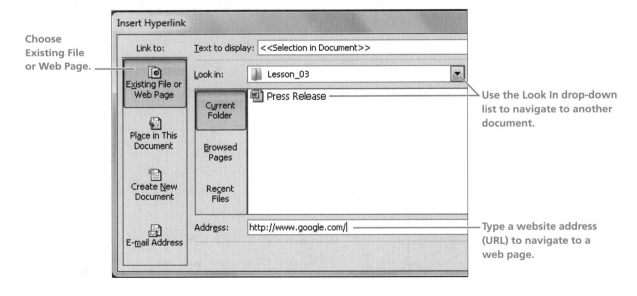

Choose Existing File or Web Page.

Use the Look In drop-down list to navigate to another document.

Type a website address (URL) to navigate to a web page.

DEVELOP YOUR SKILLS 3.7.2

Work with Hyperlinks

In this exercise, you will create a hyperlink and then use it to jump to another document. Then, you will remove a hyperlink.

Create a Hyperlink to Jump to Another Document

1. Select the words *Press Release* in the **Subject** line.

2. Choose **Insert→Links→Hyperlink** 🔵 from the Ribbon.

3. Follow these steps to create a hyperlink to another document:

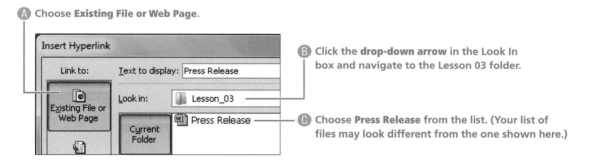

Ⓐ Choose **Existing File or Web Page**.

Ⓑ Click the **drop-down arrow** in the Look In box and navigate to the Lesson 03 folder.

Ⓒ Choose **Press Release** from the list. (Your list of files may look different from the one shown here.)

4. Click **OK** to create the link.
Notice the words Press Release *change to blue, underlined text.*

Use the Hyperlink

5. **Press** and **hold** [Ctrl] and click the **blue** Press Release link.

6. **Close** the Press Release document but leave the Martin Memo **open**.

Remove a Hyperlink Using the Hyperlink Dialog Box

7. **Click** anywhere in the hyperlink.

8. Choose **Insert→Links→Hyperlink**.

9. Click the **Remove Link** button.

10. **Save** and **close** the Martin Memo document.

3.8 Concepts Review

Concepts Review	labyrinthelab.com/word10

To check your knowledge of the key concepts introduced in this lesson, complete the Concepts Review quiz by going to the URL listed above. If your classroom is using Labyrinth eLab, you may complete the Concepts Review quiz from within your eLab course.

Reinforce Your Skills

Practice Formatting

In this exercise, you will practice working with character formats. Use the Font group on the Home Ribbon for steps 3–6 and use the Mini toolbar for steps 7, 8, and 10.

1. **Open** rs-Yard Sale from the Lesson 03 folder.

2. **Tap** Enter a couple times to better align the document on the page.

3. Select the **three heading lines**, and change the font to Arial, bold, and red.

4. **Deselect** the text, and then **select** the first heading line and change it to 18 points.

5. **Select** the second heading line, and make it 14 points.

6. Make the **third heading** line 18 points.

7. Apply **bold** to the date and time in the body.

8. **Select** the body, and change the font to Comic Sans MS or the font of your choice.

9. Place the **insertion point** in front of *Stop* in the body, and **tap** Enter to provide additional space between the heading lines and the body.

10. Change the **heading lines** to a different color of your choice and then change them to uppercase.

11. **Select** the paragraph under the heading lines and note of the number of words in the paragraph versus the entire document.

12. **Save** 💾 the file and **close** it.

Create a Memorandum

In this exercise, you will create a memorandum. You will also apply character formatting.

1. Follow these guidelines to create the memorandum shown at the end of this exercise:
   - **Position** the line *MEMO TO:* approximately 2 inches down from the top of the page.
   - Apply **bold** to the lead words *MEMO TO:*, *FROM:*, *DATE:*, and *SUBJECT:*.
   - Apply **bold** formatting to the time and date in the body paragraph.
   - Type your **initials** at the bottom of the memo.

2. **Save** 💾 the memo in the Lesson 03 folder as **rs-Alexander Memo**, and then **close** it.

MEMO TO:	Trevor Alexander
FROM:	Linda Jackson
DATE:	Today's Date
SUBJECT:	Monthly Sales Meeting

Our monthly sales meeting will be held in the conference room at **10:00 a.m.** on **Thursday, January 24**. Please bring your sales forecast for February and be prepared to discuss any important accounts that you wish to. I will give you a presentation on our new products that are scheduled for release in March. I look forward to seeing you then.

xx

REINFORCE YOUR SKILLS 3.3
Use the Spelling Checker and Find and Replace

In this exercise, you will practice using the Find and Replace feature and then spell check the document.

1. **Open** rs-Birds of Prey from the Lesson 03 folder.

2. **Spell check** the document, making the appropriate changes.

3. Use the **Navigation pane** to highlight all instances of *Birds*.

4. Display the **Find and Replace** dialog box from the Navigation pane.

5. **Replace** all occurrences of *Birds of Prey* with *Bird Watcher*.
   Word automatically italicizes the phrase Bird Watcher *because* Birds of Prey *was italicized.*

6. **Save** 🖫 the document, and then **close** it.

REINFORCE YOUR SKILLS 3.4
Use Hyperlinks and Bookmarks

In this exercise, you will create and use hyperlinks and Bookmarks.

1. **Open** rs-Online Neighborhood Sales Notice from the Lesson 03 folder.

2. Create a **hyperlink** on the word *furniture* in the rs-Online Neighborhood Sales Notice document that will jump to the rs-Furniture document in the Lesson 03 folder.

3. Use the **hyperlink** to open the rs-Furniture document.

4. Create a **bookmark** named **Media_Cabinet** for the piece of furniture on the last page.

5. **Scroll** to locate the dresser and create a bookmark for it.

6. Use the **shortcut keystrokes** to return to the beginning of the document.

7. Use the **Bookmark** dialog box to jump down to view the dresser and then view the media cabinet.

8. **Save** and **close** both the rs-Furniture and the rs-Online Neighborhood Sales Notice documents.

Apply Your Skills

Edit a Business Letter

In this exercise, you will get more practice with Find and Replace and the spelling checker feature. You will also make some formatting changes and practice moving text.

1. **Open** as-Ota Letter from the Lesson 03 folder.
   This letter is set up with traditional letter spacing.

2. **Spell check** the document, making any necessary changes.

3. Use **Find and Replace** to replace all occurrences of *bill* with *account*.

4. Use **Find and Replace** to replace all occurrences of *payment* with *check*.

5. Select the entire document, change the font to **Times New Roman**, and change the font size to **12 points**.

6. Use ⌷Enter⌷ to start the date line at approximately the 2-inch position.

7. Replace *Today's Date* with the current date.

8. Move the **address block** from the bottom of the letter to the space between the last body paragraph and the complimentary close *Sincerely*. If necessary, **insert** or **remove** hard returns until there is a double space between the address block and the last body paragraph and between the address block and the complimentary close *Sincerely*.

9. Insert your typist's **initials** below the signature block.

10. **Save** 💾 the changes, and then **close** the document.

Use the Spelling Checker and Find and Replace

In this exercise, you will practice using the spelling checker and the Find and Replace feature.

1. **Open** as-Collarbone from the Lesson 03 folder.

2. **Spell check** the document. Use your best judgment to determine which replacement words to use for incorrectly spelled words.

3. Use **Find and Replace** to make the following replacements. Write the number of replacements in the third column of the table.

Word	Replace With	Number of Replacements
breaks	fractures	_____
collarbone	clavicle	_____
movement	range-of-motion	_____

4. **Print** the document when you have finished.

5. **Save** 💾 the changes, and then **close** the document.

Format Characters and Insert Special Characters

In this exercise, you will try out various character formats and insert special characters. Then you will insert and delete a page break.

1. **Open** as-Formatting from the Lesson 03 folder.

2. Follow the instructions in the exercise document to format lines and insert special characters.

3. Change the title at the top of the document to **uppercase** and **underline** it.

4. **Save** 💾 the document and **close** it.

Critical Thinking & Work-Readiness Skills

In the course of working through the following Microsoft Office-based Critical Thinking exercises, you will also be utilizing various work-readiness skills, some of which are listed next to each exercise. Go to labyrinthelab.com/workreadiness *to learn more about the work-readiness skills.*

3.1 Use Dates and Symbols

Brett has received positive feedback from early users of MyResume and her press release. She writes a memo to her manager, Rick Smith, reporting some of the feedback. Open ct-Feedback Memo (Lesson 03 folder). Insert a complete and appropriate heading for a memorandum at the top of the document, including To, From, Date, and Subject. Be sure to use the tab stops so the information is nicely formatted and aligned. Add the trademark symbol (™) after *MyResume*. Use Find and Replace to replace all instances of *we have* with **we've**. Save the file to your Lesson 003 folder as **ct-Feedback Final**.

WORK-READINESS SKILLS APPLIED
- Writing
- Serving clients/customers
- Communicating information

3.2 Use Page Breaks and Proofreading Tools

Start with the ct-Feedback Final document you created in the previous exercise and save it to your Lesson 03 folder as **ct-Feedback Points**. Add a final sentence to the first page explaining that specific feedback is on the next page. Insert a page break after the last paragraph and add at least five points of positive feedback from users of MyResume, the online resume builder. Use the spelling and grammar checker throughout the memo, making corrections as necessary. Save your changes.

WORK-READINESS SKILLS APPLIED
- Writing
- Thinking creatively
- Communicating information

3.3 Rewrite and Reformat a Memorandum

Start with the ct-Feedback Points document you created in the previous exercise and save it to your Lesson 03 folder as **ct-Feedback Rewrite**. Use the tools on the Navigation pane to find the first instance of the word *positive* and then replace the word with a synonym you found using the Research task pane. Find and replace the word *potential* with a synonym. Replace at least one other word with a synonym using the Research task pane. Find *MyResume* and turn it into a hyperlink that links to **http://myresume.example.com**. Save your changes.

WORK-READINESS SKILLS APPLIED
- Solving problems
- Selecting technology
- Applying technology to a task

Creating a Simple Report

LEARNING OBJECTIVES

After studying this lesson, you will be able to:

- Create appropriate report formats
- Use paragraph alignment settings
- Use spacing features
- Set custom tab stops
- Format lists
- Apply borders and shading

In this lesson, you will create a simple report. Reports are important documents often used in business and education. You will format your report using various paragraph formatting techniques. Paragraphs are a fundamental part of any Word document. You will learn how to use paragraph alignment techniques, change line spacing, set custom tab stops, and work with Word's indent features. In addition, you will convert text to bulleted and numbered lists and promote and demote the list levels. You will also add interest to the document by applying borders and shading.

Formatting a Research Paper

Kevin Hottel is a business analyst at My Virtual Campus. He has been assigned the task of preparing a report on the importance of computer technology in the 21st

century and how far it has progressed. This report will be a useful tool for management to have as background information. The program manager, John Mathison, asked Kevin to use Word 2010 so he can easily review the report prior to submitting it to his director. After conducting his initial research, Kevin uses paragraph formatting techniques such as borders, bullets, and numbering to prepare an easy-to-read, properly formatted, and professional-looking report.

An Evolution and a Revolution

The Internet is largely responsible for the information explosion we see today. Many people and organizations contributed to its development over many years. The following table shows some high points in the evolution of the Internet.

Year	Event	Responsible Person/Agency
1969	Beginning of the Internet	Advanced Research Projects Agency (ARPANET)
1971	Email invented	ARPANET
1976	Queen Elizabeth sends email	Queen Elizabeth
1990	WWW named	Tim Berners-Lee
1992	"Surfing the Web" coined	Jean Armour Polly
2001	575,000,000 WWW sites	People worldwide

Search Engines

Knowing how to access information on the Internet typically means that you need to be familiar with search engines. Some of the best-known search engines include:

- Google ™
  - Filed for incorporation in September 1998
    This search engine is tops on many people's list.
- Yahoo!®
  - Incorporated in March 1995
    Yahoo! is the oldest directory-type search engine and a favorite of many.
- Ask.com™

Popular Programs

1. Word
   a. A Word-processing program used to create letters, reports, books, memorandums, research papers, and so forth.
2. Excel
3. PowerPoint
4. Access

4.1 Formatting Reports

Video Lesson labyrinthelab.com/videos

There are a variety of acceptable report formats. The following example shows a traditional business report in unbound format. Different report formats can be used for research papers and other types of documents.

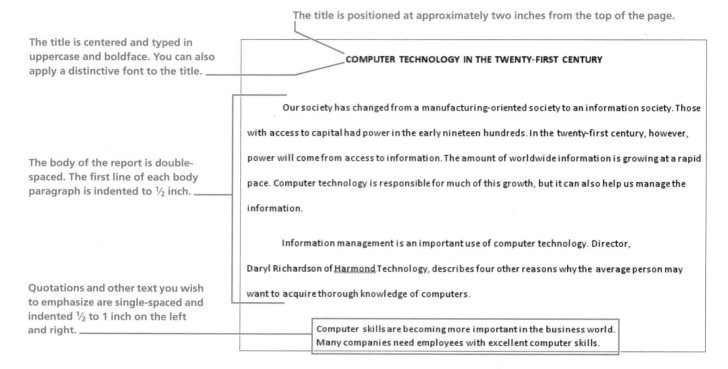

The title is positioned at approximately two inches from the top of the page.

The title is centered and typed in uppercase and boldface. You can also apply a distinctive font to the title.

COMPUTER TECHNOLOGY IN THE TWENTY-FIRST CENTURY

The body of the report is double-spaced. The first line of each body paragraph is indented to ½ inch.

Our society has changed from a manufacturing-oriented society to an information society. Those with access to capital had power in the early nineteen hundreds. In the twenty-first century, however, power will come from access to information. The amount of worldwide information is growing at a rapid pace. Computer technology is responsible for much of this growth, but it can also help us manage the information.

Information management is an important use of computer technology. Director, Daryl Richardson of Harmond Technology, describes four other reasons why the average person may want to acquire thorough knowledge of computers.

Quotations and other text you wish to emphasize are single-spaced and indented ½ to 1 inch on the left and right.

Computer skills are becoming more important in the business world. Many companies need employees with excellent computer skills.

4.2 Using Paragraph Formatting

Paragraph formatting includes paragraph alignment, line spacing, paragraph space settings, and bullets and numbering, to mention a few options.

Selecting paragraphs for formatting purposes is a little different from selecting characters. With character formatting, you select the entire block of text you want to format. In the majority of situations this is necessary. With paragraph formatting, you need only click in the paragraph to *select* it. You can highlight the entire paragraph if you wish, but that is not necessary. On the other hand, if you want to apply formatting to more than one paragraph, you must select at least part of each paragraph.

Paragraph Defined

In Word, a paragraph is created anytime you tap the Enter key. In other words, a paragraph could consist of several lines that end with an Enter or just one line, such as a heading, that ends with an Enter. Tapping Enter to generate a blank line creates a paragraph, even though there is no text in it. What's more, Word stores formats in the paragraph mark.

Paragraph Formatting Compared to Character Formatting

You use character formatting when you wish to format individual words or a selected block of text. Paragraph formatting affects the entire paragraph.

Character formats are available in the Font group of the Home tab on the Ribbon, while paragraph formats appear in the Paragraph group of the Home tab.

Using Paragraph Alignment

Paragraph alignment determines how text aligns between the margins. Left alignment gives the paragraph a straight left margin and a ragged right margin. Center alignment is usually applied to headings. Right alignment generates a straight right and a ragged left margin. Justify provides straight left and right margins. You can use several tools to align paragraphs, including the alignment commands on the Ribbon, the Paragraph dialog box, and the Mini toolbar.

Setting Alignments

The following illustration displays the paragraph alignment commands on the Home tab of the Ribbon. The Center command is also conveniently located on the Mini toolbar.

Align Text Left

Center

Paragraph

Align Text Right

Justify

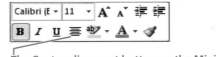

The Center alignment button on the Mini toolbar

Examples

The following illustration shows how the different paragraph alignment settings look in Word.

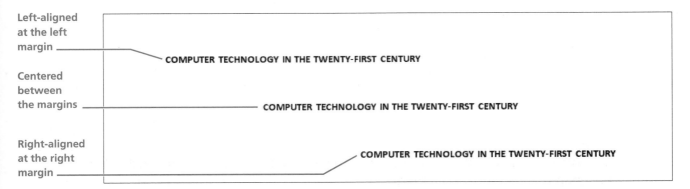

Left-aligned at the left margin

COMPUTER TECHNOLOGY IN THE TWENTY-FIRST CENTURY

Centered between the margins

COMPUTER TECHNOLOGY IN THE TWENTY-FIRST CENTURY

Right-aligned at the right margin

COMPUTER TECHNOLOGY IN THE TWENTY-FIRST CENTURY

Align Text with the Ribbon and Mini Toolbar

In this exercise, you will practice using the alignment buttons in the Paragraph group of the Home tab and the Center button on the Mini toolbar to align your report heading.

1. **Start** a blank document, and make sure the Word window is **maximized** □.

2. If necessary, choose **View→Document Views→Print Layout** 🗐 to switch to Print Layout view.

3. If the ruler does not appear on the screen, click the **View Ruler** 🔳 button at the top of the scroll bar.

4. **Tap** Enter enough times to position the insertion point approximately 2 inches from the top of the page.

Type the Heading

5. Turn on Caps Lock and choose **Home→Font→Bold** **B** from the Ribbon.

6. **Type** the report title, **COMPUTER TECHNOLOGY IN THE TWENTY-FIRST CENTURY.**

7. **Turn off** Bold and Caps Lock, and then **tap** Enter twice.

8. Position the **insertion point** in the report heading.

Align the Heading

9. Choose **Home→Paragraph→Center** ≡ from the Ribbon.

10. Choose **Home→Paragraph→Align Text Right** ≡ from the Ribbon.

11. Choose **Home→Paragraph→Align Text Left** ≣ from the Ribbon.

12. **Right-click** on the heading to display the Mini toolbar.

13. Click the **Center** ≡ button on the toolbar to center the heading.

14. **Save** the file in the Lesson 04 folder as **Computer Report,** leave the file **open,** and continue with the next topic.

Setting Line Spacing

Video Lesson   labyrinthelab.com/videos

FROM THE KEYBOARD
Ctrl+1 for single spacing
Ctrl+5 for 1.5 spacing
Ctrl+2 for double spacing

The Line Spacing ↕≣ button in the Paragraph group of the Home tab lets you set line spacing for one or more paragraphs. Word 2010's default line spacing is 1.15. You apply line spacing by selecting the desired paragraph(s) and then choosing the desired line spacing from the Line Spacing drop-down list, or by using one of the keyboard shortcuts.

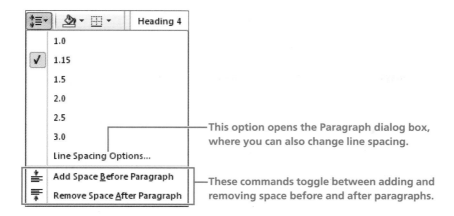

This option opens the Paragraph dialog box, where you can also change line spacing.

These commands toggle between adding and removing space before and after paragraphs.

Inserting a Nonbreaking Space

Most of the time, you take advantage of one of Microsoft Word's oldest and dearest features, Word Wrap, which allows you to keep typing by wrapping the text at the end of each line until you press ⌐Enter⌐ at the end of the paragraph. However, you may want to keep two or more words together on the same line. For example, you should keep a first and last name or a complete date on the same line. For these special cases, you can insert a nonbreaking space to control the word(s) that wrap to the next line. You can use the Symbols group on the Insert tab to insert the special character that creates a nonbreaking space; however, tapping ⌐Ctrl⌐+⌐Shift⌐+⌐Spacebar⌐ is a much quicker method.

Adding Hyphenation

Typically, when you create a document in Word, you let Word Wrap do its thing; that is, it adds all of the text it can on a line until it comes to a word that won't fit. Since that word is too long, it is moved down to the next line. Sometimes this can cause your right margin to become very jagged. To have a more evenly spaced document, you can use the Hyphenation feature found in the Page Setup group on the Page Layout tab of the Ribbon. You have two basic options when activating the Hyphenation menu: automatic or manual hyphenation.

- **Automatic**—The entire document is hyphenated automatically and since you did not enter any manual hyphens, as you edit or revise the document, automatic hyphenation continues as you type.
- **Manual**—You can also set the Hyphenation feature to manual, which goes through the document searching for instances where hyphenation is required. You then get to choose whether or not to hyphenate each word.

DEVELOP YOUR SKILLS 4.2.2
Set Line Spacing

In this exercise, you will begin by changing to double-spacing. Then you will return to single-spacing for several paragraphs in the document.

1. If necessary, choose **Home→Paragraph→Show/Hide** ¶ to display formatting characters.

2. Position the **insertion point** on the second paragraph symbol below the title.

3. Choose **Home→Paragraph→Line and Paragraph Spacing** ⬍☰ from the Ribbon, and click **2.0** for double-spacing.

4. **Tap** the ⎡Tab⎤ key once to create a $^1/_2$-inch indent at the start of the paragraph.

5. Now **type** the following paragraph, but only **tap** ⎡Enter⎤ once after the last line in the paragraph, since double-spacing is in effect.
   The lines will be double-spaced as you type them.

Our society has changed from a manufacturing-oriented society to an information society. Those

with access to capital had power in the early nineteen hundreds. In the twenty-first century, however,

power will come from access to information. The amount of worldwide information is growing at a rapid

pace. **Computer** technology is responsible for much of this growth, but it can also help us manage the

information.

---

6. Make sure you **tap** ⎡Enter⎤ after the last line. **Tap** ⎡Tab⎤ once, and type the following lines.
   Notice that the Word Wrap feature has split the director's first and last name on two lines.

Information management is an important use of computer technology. Director, Daryl

Richardson

---

7. Position the **insertion point** in front of *Richardson* and **tap** ⎡Backspace⎤.
   Notice that now Daryl *and* Richardson *are on the same line but do not have a space separating the first and last name. If you tap the spacebar, it will put* Daryl *back on the previous line.*

Insert a Nonbreaking Space

Now you will insert a special character that will move Daryl *to the next line so his name won't be split on two lines.*

8. Make sure the **flashing insertion point** is between the *l* and the *R* between Daryl's first and last name.

9. **Press** and **hold** ⎡Ctrl⎤+⎡Shift⎤ and **tap** the ⎡Spacebar⎤.
   Notice that the director's complete name is now on the next line with a space separating the first and last name.

10. **Tap** ⎡End⎤, **tap** the ⎡Spacebar⎤, and finish **typing** the rest of the paragraph.
    The completed paragraph should look like the following illustration.

Information management is an important use of computer technology. Director,

Daryl Richardson of Harmond Technology, describes four other reasons why the average person may

want to acquire thorough knowledge of computers.

---

11. **Tap** ⎡Enter⎤ to complete the paragraph, and then change the line spacing to **1.15**.

12. Now **type** the following paragraphs, **tapping** Enter between paragraphs. You don't need to **tap** Enter twice because of the default additional spacing after paragraphs. Do not tab at the beginning of these paragraphs.

Computer skills are becoming more important in the business world. Many companies need employees with excellent computer skills.

Computer skills can often simplify one's personal life. Computers can be used to entertain, to manage finances, and to provide stimulating learning exercises for children.

Using computers can provide a sense of accomplishment. Many people suffer from "computerphobia." Learning to use computers often creates a feeling of connection with the information age.

The Internet and other information resources provide access to a global database of information.

13. **Save** your document, and continue with the next topic.

4.3 Indenting Text

Video Lesson labyrinthelab.com/videos

Indenting offsets text from the margins. You can set indents by using the Paragraph dialog box, dragging the indent markers on the horizontal ruler, or using buttons on the Ribbon.

Adjusting Indents

The Increase Indent and Decrease Indent commands on the Home tab of the Ribbon let you adjust the left indent only. These buttons increase or decrease the left indent to the nearest tab stop. Word's default tab stops are set every half inch, so the left indent changes half an inch each time you click either command.

This paragraph is indented with a first-line indent. It offsets only the first line of a paragraph from the left margin; this produces the same result as tapping the Tab key to start a paragraph.

This paragraph is indented with a left indent, which offsets all lines in a paragraph from the left margin.

Computer skills are becoming more important in the business world. Many companies need employees with excellent computer skills.

Computer skills can often simplify one's personal life. Computers can be used to entertain, to manage finances, and to provide stimulating learning exercises for children.

Using computers can provide a sense of accomplishment. Many people suffer from "computerphobia." Learning to use computers often creates a feeling of connection with the information age.

The Internet and other information resources provide access to a global database of information.

This is a hanging indent, which leaves the first line of the paragraph at the left margin but indents all other lines.

This paragraph is indented from both the left and right margins. A right indent offsets all lines from the right margin. This is most often used to offset a special notation or quote in the middle of the page and is usually accompanied by a left indent.

Experiment with Left Indents

In this exercise, you will use the Increase Indent and Decrease Indent buttons to indent the last four paragraphs.

Indent One Paragraph

1. **Click** in one of the four paragraphs you just typed.

2. Choose **Home→Paragraph→Increase Indent** from the Ribbon.
   The paragraph should be indented $^1/_2$ inch on the left.

3. Choose **Home→Paragraph→Decrease Indent** from the Ribbon to remove the indent.

Indent Several Paragraphs

4. Position the **mouse pointer** in the left margin next to the first paragraph beginning with *Computer skills*, then **drag down** to select it and the next paragraph.

5. Choose **Home→Paragraph→Increase Indent** twice to create a 1-inch left indent on each of the selected paragraphs.
   Notice that the indent markers on the ruler change position when you use the Increase Indent button. You will learn more about that in the next topic.

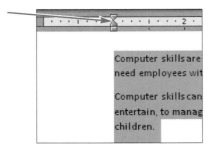

6. Now click **Decrease Indent** twice to remove the indents.
   Again, notice the indent markers on the ruler.

7. **Save** the file. You will continue to work with indents in the next exercise.

Setting Custom Indents on the Ruler

Video Lesson   labyrinthelab.com/videos

You can set indents by dragging the indent markers on the horizontal ruler. The following illustration shows the ruler and the indent markers.

Indent Markers

The indent markers at the left edge of the ruler are made up of two pieces: a top piece and a bottom piece (see the following illustration). You can drag these two pieces independently of each other. The top piece controls the first line of the paragraph when you drag it to the left or right. The bottom piece is a little trickier. It is made up of two sections, but the sections do not come apart. The bottom piece functions differently, depending on whether you place the tip of the mouse in the triangle or the rectangle. Dragging the bottom triangle affects the *rest* of the paragraph (everything but the first line). Dragging the rectangle affects *both triangles*, positioning the first line and all subsequent lines of the paragraph simultaneously.

You use the indent marker at the right end of the ruler 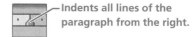 to indent the paragraph from the right.

Indents the first line of a paragraph.
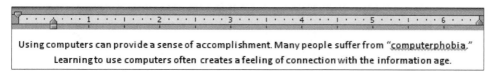
Dragging the top triangle to the right makes a hanging indent (see note below).
Indents all lines of a paragraph from the left.
Indents all lines of the paragraph from the right.

NOTE

Hanging indents are not often used, so many people are not familiar with the term. The following illustration shows an example of a hanging indent, where the first line is *outdented* and the remaining lines of the paragraph are *indented*.

Using computers can provide a sense of accomplishment. Many people suffer from "computerphobia." Learning to use computers often creates a feeling of connection with the information age.

DEVELOP YOUR SKILLS 4.3.2
Use the Indent Marker to Indent Paragraphs

In this exercise, you will practice using the indent markers on the horizontal ruler.

Set Left and Right Indents

1. **Select** all four paragraphs at the bottom of the document.

2. Follow these steps to adjust the left and right indents:

Ⓐ Position the **mouse pointer** on the Left Indent marker (the bottom rectangle).

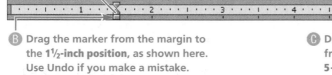

Ⓑ Drag the marker from the margin to the 1½-inch position, as shown here. Use Undo if you make a mistake.

Ⓒ Drag the Right Indent marker from the right margin to the 5-inch position.

Experiment with the Indent Markers

In this section of the exercise, you will focus on the first single-spaced, indented paragraph and experiment further with the indent markers.

3. Make sure all four paragraphs are still **selected**.

4. Position the **mouse pointer** on the First Line Indent marker (the top triangle), and **drag** it to the right to the 2-inch mark on the ruler.
   This indents the first line of each paragraph. Remember, the top and bottom pieces can move independently of each other.

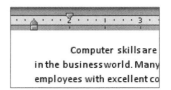

Computer skills are in the business world. Many employees with excellent co

5. Position the **mouse pointer** on the Left Indent marker (rectangle), and **drag** it to the right to the 2-inch mark on the ruler.

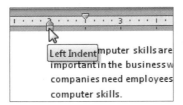

This causes the top and bottom pieces to move simultaneously. Whether they are lined up on top of each other or not, the top and bottom indent markers move simultaneously when you drag the rectangle.

6. Place the **mouse pointer** on the top triangle, and **drag** it left to the 2-inch mark. *The two pieces should be on top of each other.*

7. Feel free to experiment with the indent markers.

8. When you finish, place both pieces of the left markers at the **1-inch** position and the Right Indent marker at **5½ inches**, as shown in the following illustration.

9. **Save** the file, and leave it **open** for the next exercise.

4.4 Using Custom Tab Stops

Video Lesson   labyrinthelab.com/videos

Default tab stops are set every ½ inch, so the insertion point moves ½ inch whenever you tap the [Tab] key. You can change the tab stops if you want the insertion point to move a smaller or larger distance when you tap [Tab] or when you want to use a special tab, such as a center tab or a right-align tab. Custom tab stops are also useful for creating leader lines. For example, the dots you see in a table of contents leading to the page numbers are an example of leader lines on a right-aligned tab.

Never use the spacebar to line up columns of text. Even if it looks right on the screen, it will not print correctly.

Setting Custom Tab Stops with the Ruler

Word provides four types of custom tab stops: left, right, center, and decimal. You can set all four types using the horizontal ruler. You set tabs by choosing the desired tab type from the Tabs box at the left end of the ruler. Then you click at the desired location on the ruler to set the tab. The tab is set for the selected paragraph and for each line thereafter as long as you keep tapping the [Enter] key. You can move a custom tab stop by dragging it to a different location on the ruler.

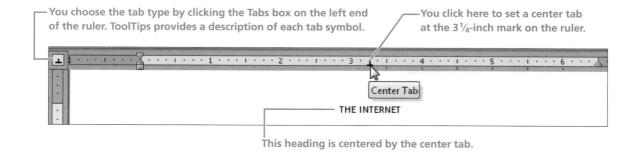

You choose the tab type by clicking the Tabs box on the left end of the ruler. ToolTips provides a description of each tab symbol.

You click here to set a center tab at the 3¼-inch mark on the ruler.

Center Tab

THE INTERNET

This heading is centered by the center tab.

Set Tabs Using the Ruler

In this exercise, you will use custom tabs to set up text in a columnar format.

1. Move the **insertion point** to the bottom of the page and, if necessary, **tap** [Enter] to generate a blank line at the bottom of the document.

2. **Tap** [Ctrl]+[Enter] to insert a page break.

3. Set the left and right indent markers at the **margins**, as shown here.

4. Choose **Home→Paragraph→Show/Hide ¶** from the Ribbon to turn on formatting marks.

5. Select the paragraph symbol at the top of **page 2**.
   Remember, paragraph symbols carry formatting, so you must select the symbol to format it.

6. Choose **Home→Paragraph→Line and Paragraph Spacing** 📑 from the Ribbon, and choose **Remove Space After Paragraph** from the menu.

7. Choose **Home→Paragraph→Show/Hide ¶** from the Ribbon to turn off formatting marks.

Set Custom Tabs

You will set a center tab for the heading on page 2. Although you may be more likely to use the Center align button for this purpose, this will be good practice in setting tabs.

8. Follow these steps to set and use a center tab:

Ⓐ **Click** this box until the Center Tab symbol appears, as shown here. Hover the **mouse pointer** over the tab symbol to display a ToolTip to verify that you selected the Center Tab.

Ⓑ **Click** just under the 3¼-inch mark on the ruler to set a center tab; 3¼ inches is the center of the line.

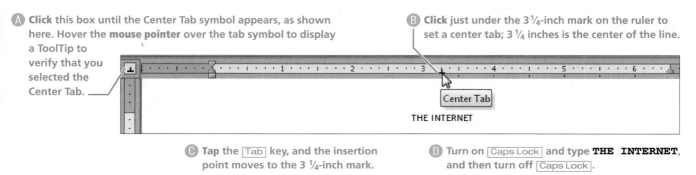

Center Tab

THE INTERNET

Ⓒ **Tap** the [Tab] key, and the insertion point moves to the 3¼-inch mark.

Ⓓ Turn on [Caps Lock] and type **THE INTERNET**, and then turn off [Caps Lock].

9. **Tap** [Enter] twice.

   Notice that the center tab is still in effect. Custom tab stops are paragraph formats, so they are carried to new paragraphs when you tap [Enter]. (Remember, Word stores formatting in paragraph marks.) Keep in mind that you could leave the custom tab stops in the new paragraph, even though you will not use them. However, you will remove them to keep your document from becoming cluttered.

10. **Save** your file, and leave it **open** for the next exercise.

Working with the Tabs Dialog Box

Video Lesson   labyrinthelab.com/videos

You can also set custom tab stops in the Tabs dialog box. You access the dialog box by clicking the dialog box launcher in the Paragraph group of the Home tab and then clicking the Tabs button. In the dialog box, you can specify precise positions for custom tabs, clear custom tab stops, and set leader tabs.

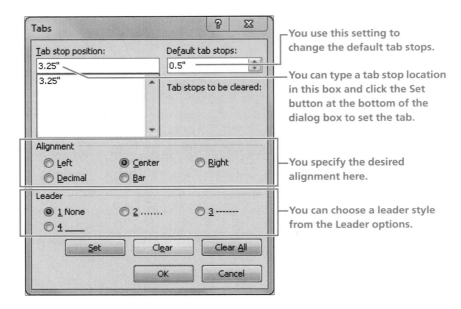

DEVELOP YOUR SKILLS 4.4.2
Use the Tabs Dialog Box

In this exercise, you will use the Tabs dialog box to clear tabs and to set custom tabs.

Clear Tab Stops

1. Make sure the **insertion point** is in the second line below the heading line.

2. Click the **dialog box launcher** 🔲 in the bottom-right corner of the Paragraph group on the Home tab.

3. Follow these steps to clear the custom tab stop:

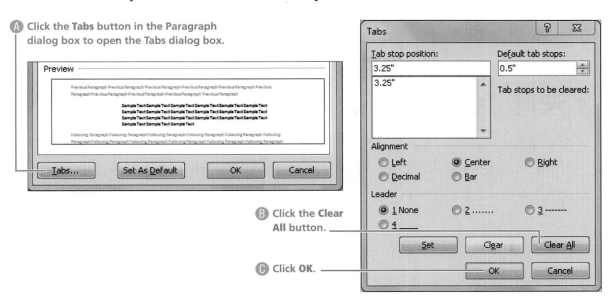

Ⓐ Click the **Tabs** button in the Paragraph dialog box to open the Tabs dialog box.

Ⓑ Click the **Clear All** button.

Ⓒ Click **OK**.

Next, you will type a heading and introductory paragraph for your tabular table.

4. Type **An Evolution and a Revolution**, and then **tap** Enter.

5. **Type** the following paragraph:

> The Internet is largely responsible for the information explosion we see today. Many people and organizations contributed to its development over many years. The following table shows some high points in the evolution of the Internet.

Now you will set the tabs for a to display text in columns.

Set Custom Tabs with the Dialog Box

6. **Tap** Enter twice, and then click the **dialog box launcher** ⬚ in the Paragraph group on the Home tab.

7. Click the **Tabs** button in the bottom-left corner to display the Tabs dialog box.

8. Follow these steps to set three left tabs:

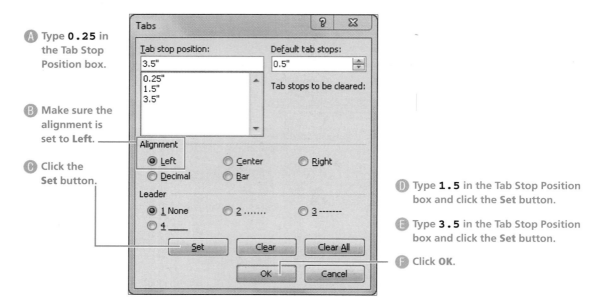

Ⓐ Type **0.25** in the Tab Stop Position box.

Ⓑ Make sure the alignment is set to **Left**.

Ⓒ Click the **Set** button.

Ⓓ Type **1.5** in the Tab Stop Position box and click the **Set** button.

Ⓔ Type **3.5** in the Tab Stop Position box and click the **Set** button.

Ⓕ Click **OK**.

Notice the tab symbols on the ruler. Now you will type the table column headings.

9. **Tap** the ⟨Tab⟩ key and type **Year**.

10. **Tap** ⟨Tab⟩ and type **Event**.

11. **Tap** ⟨Tab⟩ and type **Responsible Person/Agency**, and then **tap** ⟨Enter⟩.
    Notice that the insertion point moves to the left margin of the next line. Even though the tab stops are carried to the new paragraph, you must tap ⟨Tab⟩ to actually use the tab stop.

12. **Tap** ⟨Tab⟩ to align the insertion point below *Year*.

13. Continue **typing** and **tabbing** to create the text as shown in the following illustration. Remember to **tap** ⟨Tab⟩ at the beginning of each line.

Year	Event	Responsible Person/Agency
1969	Beginning of the Internet	Advanced Research Projects Agency (ARPANET)
1971	Email invented	ARPANET
1976	Queen Elizabeth sends email	Queen Elizabeth
1990	WWW named	Tim Berners-Lee
1992	"Surfing the Web" coined	Jean Armour Polly
2001	575,000,000 WWW sites	People worldwide

14. When you finish, apply **Bold** **B** to the column headings.

15. **Save** your file, but leave it **open** for the next exercise.

Modifying Tab Stops with the Ruler

Video Lesson   labyrinthelab.com/videos

To adjust a tab setting on the ruler, you select the lines containing the tab stops you want to change, and then simply drag the tab symbol to the new location. To delete a tab stop, you just drag the tab symbol off the ruler.

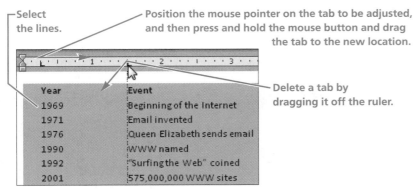

Select the lines.

Position the mouse pointer on the tab to be adjusted, and then press and hold the mouse button and drag the tab to the new location.

Delete a tab by dragging it off the ruler.

If you accidently drag a tab stop off the ruler while trying to move it, just click Undo.

DEVELOP YOUR SKILLS 4.4.3
Modify and Delete Tab Stops from the Ruler

In this exercise, you will use the ruler to modify the tab stop for the second column. Then you will delete tab stops.

Reposition a Tab Stop

1. Position the **mouse pointer** in the margin next to the column heading line, then **drag down** to select all the lines through the 2001 line.
   Be careful to only select the lines containing the tab stops you want to change. Do not select any blank lines above or below the selection. Now you are ready to adjust the tab position.

2. Position the **mouse pointer** on the tab stop at the 1½-inch position, **press** and **hold** the mouse button, and **drag** to the left to the 1¼-inch position, and then **release** the mouse button. (Use Undo if you make a mistake.)

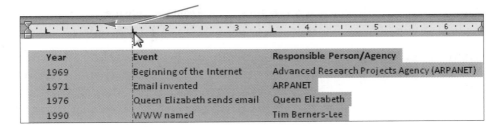

   The entire column moves to the left.

3. Position the **insertion point** at the end of the last line, and **tap** Enter twice.

4. Make sure your **insertion point** is on the second blank line.

5. Position the **mouse pointer** over the tab symbol at the $1/4$-inch position, and then **press** and **hold** the mouse button and drag straight down into the document.

6. **Release** the mouse button, and the tab is no longer on the ruler.

7. **Repeat** that process to remove the remaining tabs at $1\frac{1}{4}$ inches and $3\frac{1}{2}$ inches.

8. **Save** the file but leave it **open**, as you will use it in the next exercise.

4.5 Using Bulleted and Numbered Lists

Video Lesson   labyrinthelab.com/videos

Using bulleted or numbered lists is an effective way to make items of interest stand out in a document. You can turn them on before you begin typing, or apply the desired command after you type the list. For example, rather than listing items in a paragraph separated by commas, entering them as a bulleted or numbered list makes them much simpler to read. Numbered lists are automatically renumbered if you insert or delete an item. A good example of when to use a numbered list is when the sequence is important, as in a series of steps. The items in a bulleted list have no sequence.

Converting Text to Lists

You can type all of your text first in regular paragraph format and then add bullets or numbers later simply by selecting the text and clicking the desired command. Remember, text is considered a paragraph each time you press the [Enter] key; thus, when you type a list of names, for instance, each line is considered a paragraph. When you create a bulleted or numbered list, Word applies a hanging indent, where the line with the bullet or number remains at the left and the text is indented under the first line of text.

This is a hanging indent, which leaves the first line with the bullet at the left margin (in this case) but indents all other lines. ———

- Computer skills are becoming more important in the business world. Many companies need employees with excellent computer skills.
- Computer skills can often simplify one's personal life.
- Computers can be used to entertain, to manage finances, and to provide stimulating learning exercises for children.

In the preceding figure, notice that the remaining lines in the first bulleted paragraph are aligned under the word *Computer* rather than being aligned back out to the left, under the bullet. Note that all bulleted lines do not have to start at the margin; they can be indented to the right. However, a hanging indent is still created for the subsequent lines.

Promoting and Demoting List Items

Demoting a list item increases the indent level by shifting text to the right. Similarly, promoting decreases the indent level and moves the text (with its bullet or number) back to the left. When you demote items in a numbered list, it creates an outline effect, indicating the level of importance of the items in the list. In addition to using the indent buttons on the Ribbon, you can use the ⌐Tab⌐ key to demote an item and ⌐Shift⌐+⌐Tab⌐ to promote a list item. When you tap ⌐Enter⌐, Word maintains the same list level as the previous paragraph.

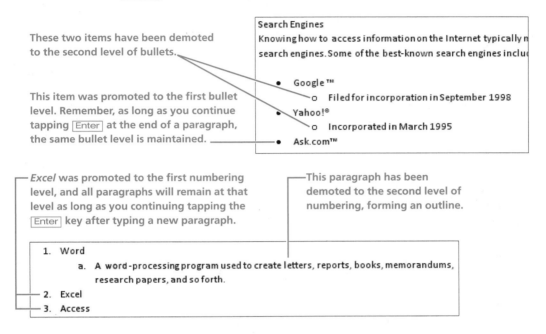

These two items have been demoted to the second level of bullets.

This item was promoted to the first bullet level. Remember, as long as you continue tapping ⌐Enter⌐ at the end of a paragraph, the same bullet level is maintained.

Excel was promoted to the first numbering level, and all paragraphs will remain at that level as long as you continuing tapping the ⌐Enter⌐ key after typing a new paragraph.

This paragraph has been demoted to the second level of numbering, forming an outline.

Turning Off Bullets and Numbering

When you are finished with the list, you should tap ⌐Enter⌐ to position the insertion point on the next line. You then turn off the bullets or numbering command using the buttons on the Ribbon or by simply tapping ⌐Enter⌐ once more.

QUICK REFERENCE	WORKING WITH LISTS
Task	**Procedure**
Convert text to a bulleted or numbered list	■ Select the text to be formatted as a list. ■ Choose Home→Paragraph→Bullets ▤. *or* ■ Choose Home→Paragraph→Numbering ▤.

Task	Procedure
Turn off bullets and numbering	■ Tap [Enter] at the end of the last list item. ■ Choose the Bullets [icon] or Numbering [icon] button. *or* ■ Tap [Enter] one more time.
Demote items in a list	■ Select the items to demote one level to the right. ■ Choose Home→Paragraph→Increase Indent [icon]. *or* ■ Tap the [Tab] key.
Promote items in a list	■ Select the items to promote one level to the left. ■ Choose Home→Paragraph→Decrease Indent [icon]. *or* ■ Hold down [Shift] and tap [Tab].

DEVELOP YOUR SKILLS 4.5.1

Work with Bullets and Numbering

In this exercise, you will convert a list to bullets, promote and demote levels, and create a numbered list.

Create a Bulleted List

1. Make sure the **insertion point** is two lines below the tabbed text table. Then **type** the following heading and introductory paragraph:

> Search Engines
> Knowing how to access information on the Internet typically means that you need to be familiar with search engines. Some of the best-known search engines include:

2. **Tap** [Enter] twice at the end of the paragraph.

3. Type **Google(tm)** as the first search engine and then **tap** [Enter] to position the insertion point on the next line.
   Notice that after you type the (tm), *Word automatically replaces it with the* ™ *symbol.*

4. Finish typing the list as shown, **tapping** [Enter] after each item.

> Google ™
> Filed for incorporation in September 1998
> Yahoo!®
> Incorporated in March 1995

Convert Text to a Bulleted List

5. Position the **mouse pointer** in the margin area to the left of the *Google*™ line and **drag down** to select all four lines in the list.

6. Choose **Home→Paragraph→Bullets** ☷ from the Ribbon.
   Notice all four lines have bullets and are on the same level; you will fix that in just a minute by demoting certain lines.

Demote a List Item

7. **Select** the second bulleted line, *Filed for incorporation in September 1998.*

8. **Tap** `Tab` to demote the line one level under the Google™ heading.

9. **Select** the last line and then click the **Increase Indent button** ☷ on the Ribbon.

10. Position the **insertion point** at the end of the last line and **tap** `Enter`.
    Notice that the new line is still at the indented level. In this case, it needs to be promoted one level so you can type a new search engine.

Promote a List Item

11. **Hold down** `Shift` and then **tap** `Tab` to promote the new line.
    The new line moves one level to the left so it matches the other search engines.

12. Type **Ask.com(tm)** and **tap** `Enter`.

13. **Tap** `Enter` three times to turn off the bullets and leave an extra blank line after the list.

Create a Numbered List

14. Type **Popular Programs** and **tap** `Enter`.

15. Choose **Home→Paragraph→Numbering** ☷ from the Ribbon.

16. **Type** the list, demoting and promoting as shown, and then **tap** `Enter` twice after the final list entry.

```
1.  Word
      a.  A word-processing program used to create letters, reports, books, memorandums,
          research papers, and so forth.
2.  Excel
3.  Access
```

17. Position the **insertion point** after *Excel* and **tap** `Enter`.
    Notice that there is now a new line three and Access *became line four.*

18. Type **PowerPoint** as the new line three.

19. **Save** the document and leave it **open** for the next exercise.

Using the Bullets and Numbering Libraries

Video Lesson   labyrinthelab.com/videos

The menu buttons ⬝ on the Bullets and Numbering buttons provide access to bullets and numbering libraries, where you can choose a style for your bulleted or numbered list or define new formats.

The bullets and numbering libraries shown in the following illustrations display the available built-in styles.

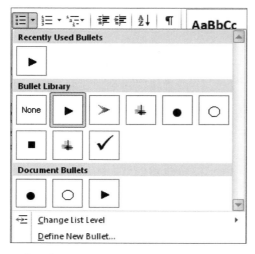

Bullet Library

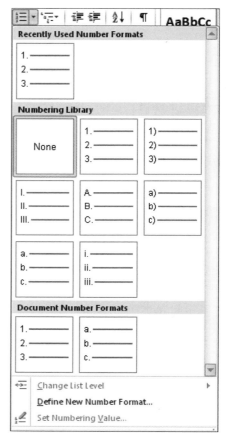

Numbering Library

Change the Bullet Style

In this exercise, you will choose a different bullet style from the bullets gallery.

1. Select the **first bulleted line**.

2. While **holding down** the ⌈Ctrl⌉ key, **select** the *Yahoo!* and *Ask.com* lines, as shown here.

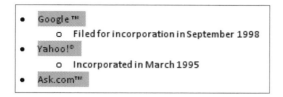

3. Click the drop-down arrow on the **Bullets** ▤ ▾ button and choose the circle bullet. *The position of the circle bullet in the library may vary.*

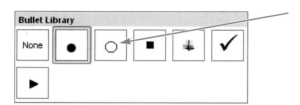

4. **Save** your file, and leave it **open** for the next exercise.

Customizing Bullet and Number Styles

Video Lesson labyrinthelab.com/videos

Bullet styles can be customized by defining a symbol, picture, font, or alignment. You can also customize the number style, font, and alignment. You can define a new bullet or number format by clicking the drop-down arrow on the Bullets or Numbering button and choosing Define New Bullet or Define New Number Format from the list.

You can choose from a variety of symbols, pictures, and fonts.

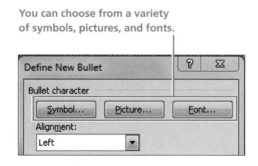

You can select a number style from this list.

You can choose from a variety of fonts to customize your numbering style.

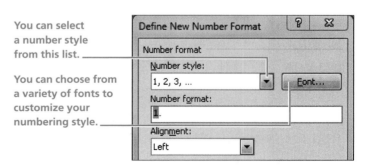

Restart or Continue Numbering

Many documents have more than one numbered list. Sometimes you may want the numbering to continue sequentially from one list to the next. For example, if one list ends with the number 4 you may want the next list to begin with the number 5. If you type a paragraph after the first list, when you begin the next list in your document, Word assumes you want to restart numbering at 1. If you want to continue numbering from the previous list, Word provides an AutoCorrect smart tag when you start additional numbered lists in a document. You can click the AutoCorrect Options smart tag and choose Continue Numbering.

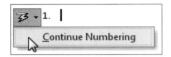

Experiment with Custom Bullets

In this exercise, you will work with the Define New Bullet dialog box.

1. **Click** anywhere in one of the three bulleted search engine lines.

2. Choose **Home→Paragraph→ Bullets** menu ▼ to display the Bullets library, and then choose **Define New Bullet** from the bottom of the menu.

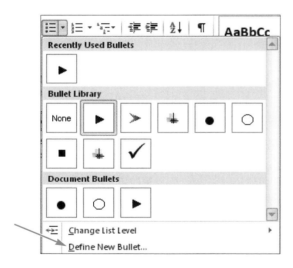

3. Follow these steps to define a picture as a new bullet:

Ⓐ Click the **Picture** button to display the Picture Bullet dialog box.

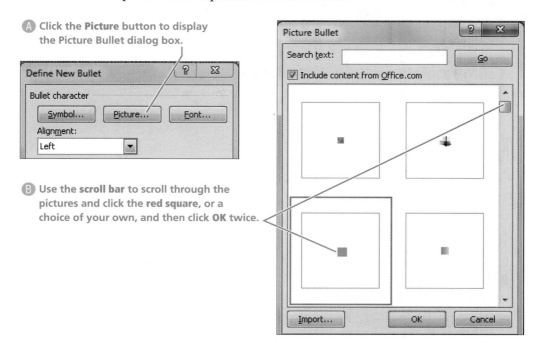

Ⓑ Use the **scroll bar** to scroll through the pictures and click the **red square**, or a choice of your own, and then click **OK** twice.

Notice that all the Level 1 bullets have changed to the new custom bullet.

4. Choose **Home→Paragraph→Bullets** menu ▼ to display the Bullet Library.

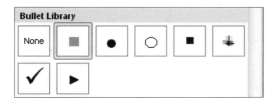

Notice that the new custom bullet now appears in the library, although its location and the number of bullets in the library on your screen may differ from the preceding illustration.

5. Click anywhere in the document to **close** the library.

If you wish to remove a bullet from the library, right-click it and choose Remove from the context menu.

6. Click the *Google* line and then click the **Bullets** menu button one more time and choose the original black bullet.

7. **Save** the document and leave it **open** for the next exercise.

4.6 Setting Line Breaks

Video Lesson   labyrinthelab.com/videos

When working with bullets and numbering, tapping Enter generates a new bullet or number. What if you want to type something relative to a bulleted or numbered item on the next line(s) without generating a new bullet or number? A manual *line break* starts a new line (without inserting a paragraph mark) and continues the text on the new line. The new line is part of the same paragraph as the preceding line. Line breaks are inserted with the Shift + Enter keystroke combination.

•→ Google.™¶ ——— Tapping Enter generates a paragraph symbol and a new bullet.
•→ ¶
•→ Yahoo!®↵ ——— Tapping Shift + Enter displays an arrow symbol and moves
    ¶ the insertion point to the next line without creating a bullet.

DEVELOP YOUR SKILLS 4.6.1
Insert Line Breaks in a List

In this exercise, you will use line breaks to add descriptive information about the items in the search engine list.

1. Place the **insertion point** after *1998* in your bulleted list.

2. **Tap** Shift + Enter to generate a line break rather than a paragraph break.

3. If necessary, click the **Show/Hide ¶** button to see the line break, which appears as a small arrow at the end of the line. Then click **Show/Hide** again to turn off formatting marks.

4. **Type** the following: **This search engine is tops on many people's list.**
   If you were to tap Enter at this point, Word would generate a new bullet because you started a new paragraph.

5. **Click** at the end of *1995* in the line under *Yahoo!* and **tap** Shift + Enter to generate a line break.

6. **Type** the following: **Yahoo! is the oldest directory-type search engine and a favorite of many.**

7. **Save** your file and leave it **open**, as you will use it in the next exercise.

Using the Paragraph Space Settings

Video Lesson   labyrinthelab.com/videos

The following illustration of the Paragraph group on the Page Layout tab shows the default 10-point after-paragraph spacing. You can use the spinner controls on the Before and After Spacing buttons to adjust the amount of space. You can also use the spacing controls in the Paragraph dialog box in the same way.

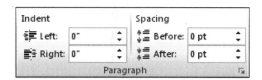

Paragraph spacing controls on the Ribbon in the Paragraph group on the Page Layout tab.

Paragraph spacing controls in the Paragraph dialog box.

Paragraph Spacing Defined

A point (pt) is just 1/72nd of an inch. This fine unit of measure, common in printing, facilitates great precision. Word uses points for type size and other settings, such as paragraph spacing.

72 points = 1 inch   36 points = $^1/_2$ inch   24 points = $^1/_3$ inch

DEVELOP YOUR SKILLS 4.6.2

Set Paragraph Spacing

In this exercise, you will add 4 points of paragraph spacing between the headings and the introductory paragraphs on page 2.

1. **Select** the heading *An Evolution and a Revolution* near the top of page 2.

2. Click the **Page Layout** tab to display its Paragraph group.

3. In the Spacing area, click in the **After** box and type **4**, and then **tap** Enter.
   Notice the additional space following the heading.

The spinner controls in the Spacing area use 6 point increments for spacing. If you wish to use a different measurement, you must enter it manually.

4. **Select** the *Search Engines* heading, and then type **4** in the After box and **tap** Enter.

5. Use the same technique to add **4 points** of extra space after the heading *Popular Programs*. *You could have used the Format Painter to copy the formatting from the first heading, but this was a good opportunity to practice with the spacing controls.*

6. **Save** the file, and leave it **open** for the next exercise.

4.7 Using Borders and Shading

Video Lesson   labyrinthelab.com/videos

You can apply borders and shading to selected text, paragraphs, and objects, such as tables or drawing shapes. Page borders are also available to outline an entire page. In this lesson, you will concentrate on applying borders to paragraphs. Paragraph borders are the lines applied to the top, bottom, left, and right edges of a selected paragraph, and they extend from the left to right margin. Thus, if you only want a border surrounding a specific amount of text, you must select only that text and be careful not to select the paragraph mark. You can choose the style, color, and thickness of borders, and you can also select various shading patterns and colors.

The Borders Button

Clicking the Borders [icon] menu ▼ button in the Paragraph group of the Home tab on the Ribbon displays a menu of border options. The Borders and Shading command at the bottom of the menu opens the Borders and Shading dialog box.

The borders button has a memory. It displays the last choice you made from the menu on the button face. That way you can apply the same type of border several times in a row without opening the menu. The button name changes accordingly.

Example

The border button that appears when you first start Word is named Bottom Border; it looks like this: [icon]

If you apply an outside border, as an example, the button is named Outside Border; it looks like this: [icon]

The Shading Button

The [Shading ▼] button located in the Paragraph group of the Home tab provides a quick way to apply shading. Shading is the background color of the selected area. For example, if you select text, it is the background color behind the text. However, if you apply a paragraph border, it is the background color inside the border that extends from margin to margin.

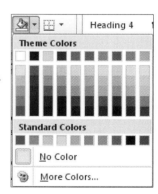

The Borders and Shading Dialog Box

Video Lesson   labyrinthelab.com/videos

Choose Borders and Shading from the Borders [icon] menu ▼ on the Ribbon to display the dialog box. The following illustrations show the features available in the Borders tab and the Shading tab of the dialog box.

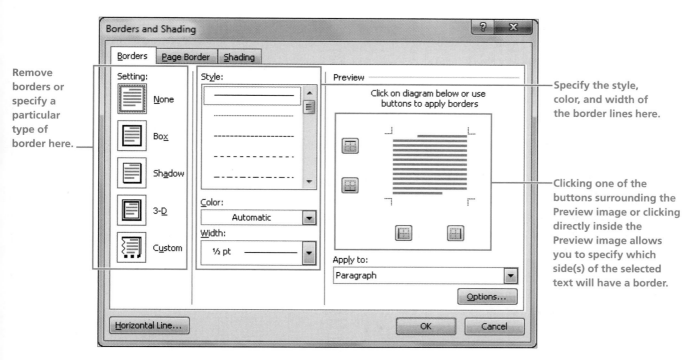

Remove borders or specify a particular type of border here.

Specify the style, color, and width of the border lines here.

Clicking one of the buttons surrounding the Preview image or clicking directly inside the Preview image allows you to specify which side(s) of the selected text will have a border.

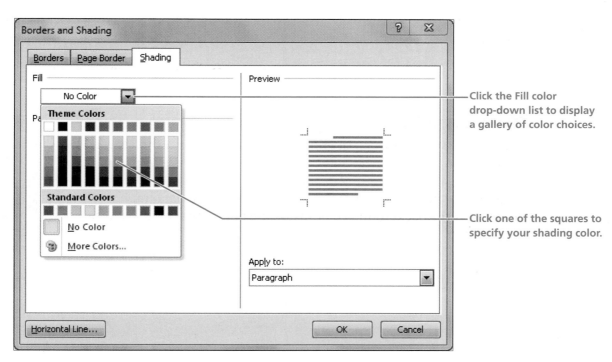

Click the Fill color drop-down list to display a gallery of color choices.

Click one of the squares to specify your shading color.

Apply a Border and Shading to Headings

In this exercise, you will apply borders and shading to the paragraph headings on page 2, using the Borders and Shading dialog box.

1. **Click** anywhere in the line *An Evolution and a Revolution*.

2. Choose **Home→Paragraph→Borders** ▦ ▾ menu ▾ from the Ribbon, and then choose the **Borders and Shading** command at the bottom of the gallery to display the dialog box.

3. Make sure the **Borders** tab at the top of the dialog box is in the foreground.

4. Follow these steps to apply a border to the first heading:

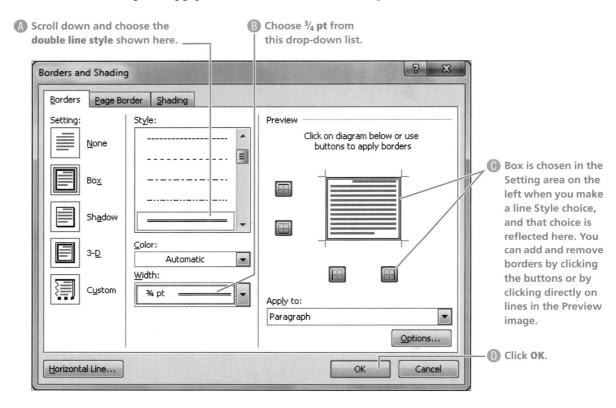

Ⓐ Scroll down and choose the **double line style** shown here.

Ⓑ Choose ¾ pt from this drop-down list.

Ⓒ Box is chosen in the Setting area on the left when you make a line Style choice, and that choice is reflected here. You can add and remove borders by clicking the buttons or by clicking directly on lines in the Preview image.

Ⓓ Click **OK**.

Notice that the border extends between the margins. Paragraph borders fill the space between the margins, unless the paragraph(s) are indented.

5. Choose **Home→Paragraph→Borders** ▦ ▾ menu ▾ from the Ribbon; choose the **Borders and Shading** command at the bottom of the gallery.

6. Click the **Shading** tab, and then click the **Fill** color drop-down list.

7. Choose **Tan, Background 2, Darker 10%** from the list, as shown in the following illustration, and then click **OK**.

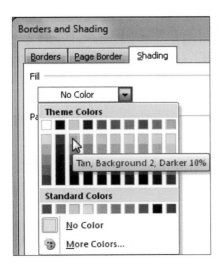

Use the Format Painter to Copy the Heading Formats

8. Make sure your **insertion point** is still in the heading *An Evolution and a Revolution.*

9. Double-click the **Format Painter** . Remember, double-clicking keeps the Format Painter turned on.

10. **Select** the *Search Engines* heading, and then **select** the *Popular Programs* heading to format the headings.

11. Click **Format Painter** again to turn it off.

12. **Save** the file, and leave it **open** for the next exercise.

4.8 Inserting Page Numbers

Video Lesson   labyrinthelab.com/videos

You can insert page numbers at various positions on a page. Page numbers are inserted at the top or the bottom of the page and may be aligned at the left margin, centered, or right-aligned.

A page numbering gallery offers a variety of page numbering designs. Choose Insert→Header & Footer→Page Number from the Ribbon to display a menu of positions for your page numbers. Choose a position, and then click the desired style to insert page numbers in your document.

Insert Page Numbers

In this exercise, you will insert page numbers in your report.

1. Choose **Insert→Header & Footer→Page Number** 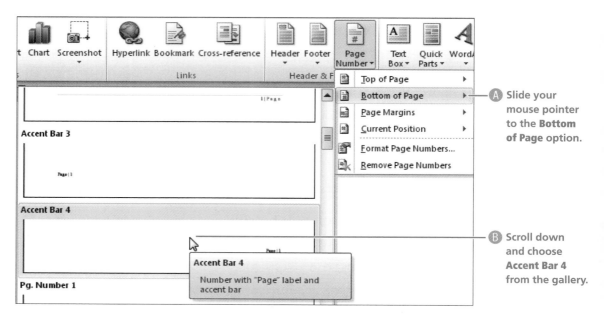 from the Ribbon.

2. Follow these steps to insert page numbering:

A — Slide your mouse pointer to the **Bottom of Page** option.

B — Scroll down and choose **Accent Bar 4** from the gallery.

3. **Double-click** the body of the document to close the footer area.

4. **Scroll** through the document and **observe** the page numbering.
   The numbering appears grayed out, but it will print like normal text.

5. **Save** your report and **close** it.

4.9 Concepts Review

Concepts Review   labyrinthelab.com/word10

To check your knowledge of the key concepts introduced in this lesson, complete the Concepts Review quiz by going to the URL listed above. If your classroom is using Labyrinth eLab, you may complete the Concepts Review quiz from within your eLab course.

Reinforce Your Skills

Create a Policies and Procedures Document

In this exercise, you will use multiple lists to create a policies and procedures page. You will also use Word's demote, promote, and indent commands to organize the lists.

Add Numbering

1. **Open** the rs-Outdoor Adventures file from the Lesson 04 folder.

2. **Select** the three lines of text under the *Medical* heading.

3. Choose **Home→Paragraph→Numbering** [icon] from the Ribbon to convert the text to a numbered list.

4. Convert the lines of text under the *Refunds* and *Cancellations* headings to a **numbered list**.

Add Bullets

5. **Select** the first heading, **hold down** the [Ctrl] key, and **select** the remaining two headings.

6. Choose **Home→Paragraph→Bullets** [icon] from the Ribbon.

7. **Tap** [Enter] after the *Inclement weather conditions* line, then **tap** [Tab].

8. Type **Over 100 degrees** and **tap** [Enter].

9. Type **Below 60 degrees**, **tap** [Enter], and **tap** [Shift]+[Tab].

10. Finish **typing** the document as shown at the end of the exercise on the following page.

Define a Custom Bullet

11. **Select** the three bulleted headings.

12. Choose **Home→Paragraph→Bullets** [icon] menu ▼ from the Ribbon.

13. Open the **Define New Bullet** dialog box and choose a new picture of your choice for the selected bullets.

Work with Indents

14. **Select** the numbered lists below each heading.

15. Chose **Home→Paragraph→Increase Indent** ⊞ once to line up the numbered lists under their heading.

16. **Select** the body of the document, excluding the title and subtitle.

17. Chose **Home→Paragraph→Increase Indent** ⊞ to reposition the body, as shown below.

18. **Save** the file and then **close** it.

OUTDOOR ADVENTURES

Policies and Procedures

■ Medical

    1. All guests must have medical insurance
    2. All guests must sign an injury waiver
    3. All guests agree to pay out-of-pocket medical expenses

■ Refunds

    1. A full refund will be given for cancellations with 60-day notice
    2. A 50% refund will be given for cancellations with 30-day notice
    3. No refund for cancellations with less than 30-day notice

■ Cancellations

    1. Inclement weather conditions
        a. Over 100 degrees
        b. Below 60 degrees
    2. Poor water flow
        a. Water level drops to 20 feet
    3. Insufficient number of guests
        a. Ten-guest minimum

REINFORCE YOUR SKILLS 4.2

Create a Tabular Phone List

In this exercise, you will use tabs, paragraph alignment, and line breaks to create the phone list shown at the end of this exercise.

1. **Press** Ctrl + N to open a blank document.

2. If necessary, display the **ruler** at the top of the screen.

3. Because you know this list will be rather short, **tap** Enter four times to position the insertion point approximately $2\,^1/_2$ inches from the top of the page.

4. Type **My Virtual Campus.**

5. **Tap** Enter twice.

6. Make sure the **left tab** symbol displays here. If not, **click** the box until it appears.

7. Use the **Ruler** to set a left tab at ¹/₂ inch.

8. Now change the tab type to a **right-align tab**; click the **box** until the symbol shown here appears.

9. Set a **right-align** tab at the **6-inch** mark on the ruler.

Add a Leader to a Tab

10. Click the **dialog box launcher** 🔲 in the bottom-right corner of the Paragraph group on the Home tab.

11. When the Paragraph dialog box appears, click the **Tabs** button in the bottom-left corner.

12. Follow these steps to set a tab leader line:

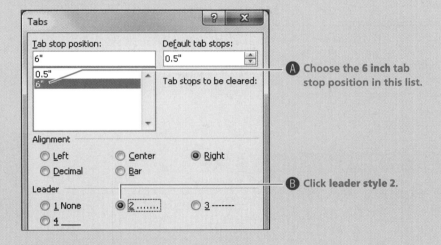

13. Click **OK**.

14. **Tap** the Tab key, and type **Advertising Department**.

15. **Tap** Tab to position the insertion point at the right-align tab, type **312–555–1234**, and then **tap** Enter.

16. Following the illustration at the end of the exercise, continue **typing** the list to the end of the *Accounting* line. Remember to **tap** Tab at the beginning of each new line.

17. Notice the line break symbol at the end of the Accounting line.

18. Insert a line break by **tapping** Shift + Enter.

19. Type **Billing** on the next line.

Because Word does not consider a line break to be a paragraph, it does not take on the additional after-paragraph spacing that Word 2010 adds by default.

20. Tap Enter, and then **tap** Tab and type the last line of the list.

21. **Select** and **center** the title and change the font size to **18 points**.

22. **Save** the document in the Lesson 04 folder as **rs-Phone Directory**, and then **close** it.

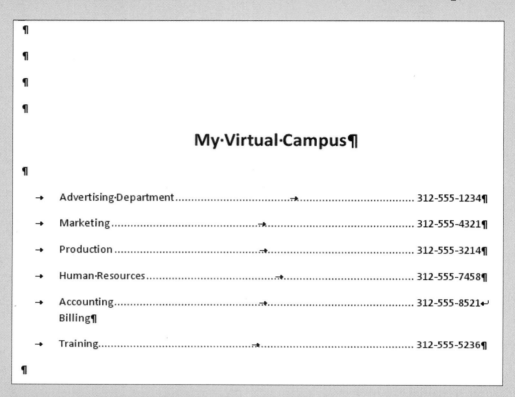

Create a Report with Indents and Bullets

In this exercise, you will open a document from your exercise files. You will format the document until it matches the document on the following page.

1. **Open** rs-Electric Cars from the Lesson 04 folder.

2. Look at the document at the end of this exercise on the following page, and notice the title shown at the top of the document. Insert the **title** at the top margin (1 inch from the top of the page).

3. **Tap** Enter twice after the title.

4. **Format** the title with a 14-point bold font, and center-align the title.

5. Select the first **three body paragraphs**, and apply **double-spacing** to them. Turning on the Show/Hide feature will help you distinguish among the first three paragraphs.

6. Adjust the **first line indent** of the first three body paragraphs to $1/2$ inch.

7. Position the **insertion point** at the end of the first line and **remove the space** after the word *United*.

8. Insert a **nonbreaking space** between the words *United* and *States*.

9. **Select** the next six paragraphs, starting with *Affordability*.

10. Apply the **bullet style** shown to the six paragraphs.

11. Use Tab to demote the bulleted paragraphs below each heading.

12. **Indent** the last paragraph 1 inch on both the left and right, as shown.
    Your completed document should match the example at the end of this exercise.

13. **Save** the changes to the document, and **close** it.

ELECTRIC CARS

Many people are not aware that electric cars have been used almost ninety years in the United States. In fact, before the introduction of the gasoline automobile, approximately 50,000 electric cars soared down American streets. Presently, electric cars are gaining attention as an effective means of improving our air quality, reducing pollution, and reducing the need to import oil into the United States.

Often referred to as "zero-emission vehicles," electric cars have the distinct advantage of releasing little or no pollution, thereby reducing the amount of carbon monoxide in our air. Electric cars are also quieter than gasoline-fueled cars, and the batteries that power these cars have the potential to be recharged through renewable sources such as wind and solar power.

Steven Lough of Eco-Motion Electric Cars in Seattle, WA, highlights a few of the many benefits of electric cars. A summary of his points follows:

- Affordability
  - Electric cars are affordable.
- Efficiency
  - Electric cars are three times more efficient per dollar than gasoline-fueled cars. They improve air quality, limit pollution, and lessen U.S. dependence on imported oil.
- Batteries
  - Electric cars will improve over time. Already new batteries—including metal-nickel-hydride batteries and lithium batteries—are being researched. In the coming years these batteries will be available, doubling and tripling the per charge rate of these automobiles.

Lough adds a powerful statement, saying that:

> There are alternatives [to gasoline automobiles and the pollution and expense associated with them]...There are carpooling, public transportation, bicycles, telecommunications, and yes, electric cars.

Apply Your Skills

Use Borders, Shading, and Lists in a Flyer

In this exercise, you will create a flyer that Lakeville Community Hospital will distribute through their Health Education Department. You will add borders and shading to headings, use paragraph alignment, and create bulleted lists. When you complete the exercise, your document should look like the figure at the end of this exercise.

1. **Open** the file as-Osteoporosis from the Lesson 04 folder.

2. **Select** the title and subtitle, and **format** them with bold, center alignment, and 16-point font.

3. **Format** the next line, *What is Osteoporosis?*, with bold and 12-point font.

4. **Indent** the next paragraph 1 inch from both the left and the right margins.

Add a Border

5. Select the next line, and click the drop-down arrow on the **Borders** command in the Paragraph group of the Home tab to apply an **Outside Border**. Word will apply the border line style that was last used during the current Word session.
   Remember that the appearance of the Borders button reflects the last choice made from the menu during the current Word session.

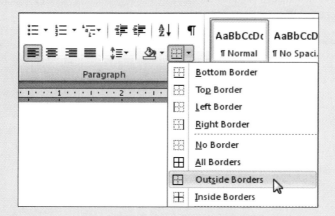

Add Shading

Make sure the line is still selected.

6. Click the drop-down arrow on the **Shading** 🖌 command next to the Borders command.

7. Choose the **shading** you prefer from the gallery.

8. Choose **Home→Clipboard→Format Painter** 🖌 to copy the formatting to the heading *What Can You Do to Help Prevent Falls?*

Add Bullets to Lists

9. **Select** *Get enough calcium* through *Know whether you are at risk*.

10. Apply **bullets** to the list.

11. Apply **bullets** to the seven lines at the end of the document.

12. **Select** both bulleted lists and apply a **different bullet style** of your choice.

13. **Save** the file and **close** it.

Lakeville Community Hospital
Partners in Prevention

What is Osteoporosis?

Osteoporosis is a disorder that causes your bones to become increasingly porous, brittle, and subject to fracture. Women are four times more likely to suffer from osteoporosis than men. However, there are steps you can take to reduce the risk of bone loss and fracture.

WHAT CAN YOU DO TO PREVENT OSTEOPOROSIS?

- Get enough calcium
- Take vitamin D
- Make activity and exercise part of each day
- Stop smoking
- Cut down on caffeine, salt, and alcohol intake
- Know whether you are at risk

WHAT CAN YOU DO TO HELP PREVENT FALLS?

- Have your vision checked
- Stay active to help maintain balance, strength, and coordination
- Wear low-heeled shoes with non-slip soles
- Tie your shoe laces
- Replace slippers that are stretched out of shape and are too loose
- Eliminate all tripping hazards in your home
- Install grab bars and handrails

Use Line Spacing, Numbering, and Indenting

In this exercise, you will format a document with variable line spacing, a numbered list, and indents.

1. **Open** the as-Success document from the Lesson 04 folder.

2. Follow these guidelines to format the document as shown at the end of this exercise:

   - Run the **spelling checker**, making changes as necessary.
   - **Tap** Enter enough times to place the insertion point at approximately the 1-inch mark in the vertical ruler.
   - Change the **title** to uppercase, bold, with a 16-point font.
   - Center the **title**; tap Enter twice after the title.
   - Use **single-spacing** and **double-spacing** as necessary to format the document as shown.
   - Set the **First Line** indent of the two body paragraphs to $1/2$ inch, as shown.
   - Replace the **space** after the name *Ralph* with a nonbreaking space.
   - Adjust the **indents** of the numbered paragraphs and the quotation, as shown.

3. **Save** the document and then **close** it.

SUCCESS

The quest for success is a driving force in the lives of many Americans. This force drives the business world and often results in huge personal fortunes. However, success can come in many forms, some of which are listed below.

   1. Many people in America view success monetarily.

   2. Our society also views public figures such as movie stars, athletes, and other celebrities as being successful.

   3. Educational achievement, such as earning an advanced degree, is often perceived as successful.

It is easy to see that success means many things to many people. The well-known poet, Ralph Waldo Emerson, provides this elegant definition of success:

> To laugh often and much; to win the respect of intelligent people and the affection of children; to earn the appreciation of honest critics and endure the betrayal of false friends; to appreciate beauty; to find the best in others; to leave the world a bit better, whether by a healthy child, a garden patch, or a redeemed social condition; to know even one life has breathed easier because you have lived. This is to have succeeded.

Critical Thinking & Work-Readiness Skills

In the course of working through the following Microsoft Office-based Critical Thinking exercises, you will also be utilizing various work-readiness skills, some of which are listed next to each exercise. Go to labyrinthelab.com/ workreadiness to learn more about the work-readiness skills.

4.1 Format a Report

Brett is creating a short report on the benefits of new wireless technology—and how it will affect My Virtual Campus users. Open ct-Wireless (Lesson 04 folder) and save a copy of it as **ct-Wireless Report**. Add a centered heading with the text **The New Wireless**. Set the line spacing of all paragraphs to 1.5. Experiment with different paragraph alignments and choose the alignment you feel is the most appropriate. Save your changes. If working in a group, discuss why you believe your choice of alignment is the best choice. If working alone, type your answer in a Word document named **ct-Questions** saved to your Lesson 04 folder.

WORK-READINESS SKILLS APPLIED
- Thinking creatively
- Writing
- Serving clients/ customers

4.2 Add Custom Bullets and Shading

Brett wants to add some custom bullets and shading to the report to make it more readable and interesting to others. Start with the ct-Wireless Report you created in the previous exercise and save a copy of it to your Lesson 04 folder as **ct-Wireless Tabs**. Add a bulleted list at the bottom with at least three benefits of the new wireless technology (be creative with these) and change the default bullet to a checkmark. Add a border and background shading to the heading. Save your changes.

WORK-READINESS SKILLS APPLIED
- Writing
- Thinking creatively
- Serving clients/ customers

4.3 Finalize Report Formatting

Brett is ready to put the finishing touches on the report before distributing it. Start with the ct-Wireless Tabs you created in the previous exercise and save a copy of it to your Lesson 04 folder as **ct-Wireless Final**. Experiment with various paragraph/heading alignments and line spacing. Change the bullets to something other than checkmarks and change the left indent of the bulleted items. Feel free to change the font style and size, too! Use these options to format the report so it is easy to read and maintains a professional feel, yet looks distinctly different from the original ct-Wireless Tabs version. Save your changes.

WORK-READINESS SKILLS APPLIED
- Thinking creatively
- Making decisions
- Selecting technology

Working with Tables and Forms

LESSON OUTLINE

LEARNING OBJECTIVES

After studying this lesson, you will be able to:

- Insert a table in a document
- Modify, sort, and format tables
- Perform calculations in tables
- Apply built-in table styles
- Create, modify, and use forms
- Set editing restrictions in forms

A table is one of Word's most useful tools for organizing and formatting text and numbers. Tables are flexible and easy to use. Word provides a variety of features that let you set up, modify, and format tables. In this lesson, you will merge and split table cells, sort rows, quickly apply table styles, and perform calculations within tables. You will also create a form by inserting form fields and learn how to protect the form so only the user can enter data.

Student Resources   labyrinthelab.com/word10

Creating Student Tables and a Form

Bethanie Harmon is an administrative assistant for the Product Development Team at My Virtual Campus. The team is always looking for new ideas to enhance the websites. Bethanie has a few ideas of her own that may be useful for students: a survey to help them determine how much money they might need for personal expenses, a list of expenses with totals, and a simple layout for viewing their class schedules. She decides to create tables and a form to present her ideas at the next product development meeting.

Although it has been awhile since Bethanie has created a table, she is up to the task. She knows Word has powerful table and form tools, and she knows it won't take long to brush up her skills and get the tables and the form created.

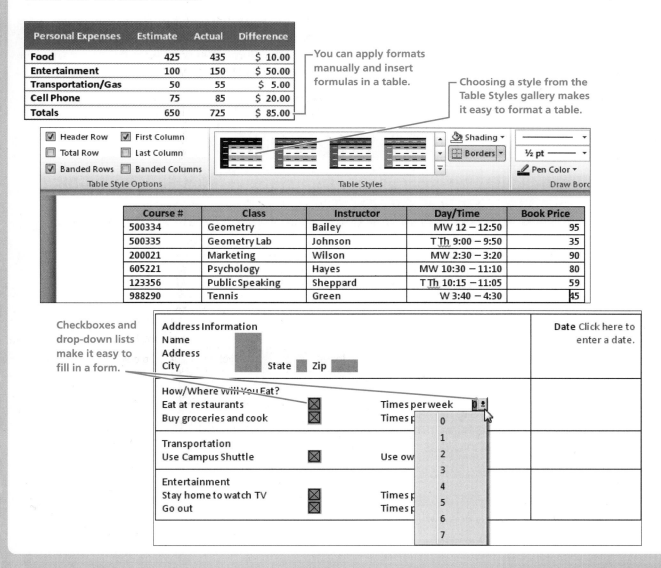

Personal Expenses	Estimate	Actual	Difference
Food	425	435	$ 10.00
Entertainment	100	150	$ 50.00
Transportation/Gas	50	55	$ 5.00
Cell Phone	75	85	$ 20.00
Totals	650	725	$ 85.00

You can apply formats manually and insert formulas in a table.

Choosing a style from the Table Styles gallery makes it easy to format a table.

☑ Header Row ☑ First Column
☐ Total Row ☐ Last Column
☑ Banded Rows ☐ Banded Columns

Table Style Options   Table Styles   Draw Bord

Shading ▾   Borders ▾   ½ pt ──── ▾   Pen Color ▾

Course #	Class	Instructor	Day/Time	Book Price
500334	Geometry	Bailey	MW 12 − 12:50	95
500335	Geometry Lab	Johnson	T Th 9:00 − 9:50	35
200021	Marketing	Wilson	MW 2:30 − 3:20	90
605221	Psychology	Hayes	MW 10:30 − 11:10	80
123356	Public Speaking	Sheppard	T Th 10:15 − 11:05	59
988290	Tennis	Green	W 3:40 − 4:30	45

Checkboxes and drop-down lists make it easy to fill in a form.

Address Information
Name
Address
City   State   Zip

Date Click here to enter a date.

How/Where will You Eat?
Eat at restaurants ☒   Times per week 0 ±
Buy groceries and cook ☒   Times p   0
                                    1
Transportation   2
Use Campus Shuttle ☒   Use ow   3
                                    4
Entertainment   5
Stay home to watch TV ☒   Times p 6
Go out ☒   Times p 7

5.1 Introducing Tables

Video Lesson   labyrinthelab.com/videos

Tables are a convenient way to lay out data in a columnar format without relying on tab stops, which can sometimes cause a little frustration. You can perform simple calculations in a Word table, although you cannot include the complex calculations that you can perform in Excel. In addition to using a table for a simple columnar layout with calculations, tables may be used to create a resumé or a company letterhead with a logo, or to present information in a format similar to the Quick Reference tables found in this book.

Viewing Gridlines

Certain tables, such as resumes, are most appropriate without applying borders around the cells. However, when creating the tables, it may be easier to maneuver around if there are lines. This is where gridlines come into play. Gridlines appear on the screen as blue dotted lines around each cell in the table, but they do not print. You view table gridlines using the View Gridlines command in the Table group on the Layout tab under Table Tools.

If borders have been applied to a table, the gridlines will not be visible; thus, you must remove all borders first to have the gridlines displayed.

Navigating in a Table

FROM THE KEYBOARD
Tab to move to the next cell
Shift+Tab to move to the previous cell

Tables are made up of cells (rectangles) displayed in a grid with horizontal rows and vertical columns. You can select one or more cells, rows, or columns and then insert, edit, or format them just like you do other text in a document. Tapping Tab when the insertion point is in the last cell of a table automatically adds a new row to the bottom.

DEVELOP YOUR SKILLS 5.1.1
Navigate and Enter Data

In this exercise, you will practice navigating in a table and enter data in it.

Navigate in a Table

1. **Open** the Student Tables document in the Lesson 05 folder.
2. Click in the first cell of the **Expense** table to position the insertion point.
3. **Tap** Tab two times to move to the end of the first row.
4. **Tap** Tab again to move to the beginning of the second row.
5. **Tap** Shift+Tab twice to move backwards, one cell at a time.
6. Position the **insertion point** in the last cell in the last row and **tap** Tab.
   A new row is added to the end of the table.
7. Click **Undo** ↶ to remove the new row.

Enter Data

8. Position the **insertion point** in the first cell and then **type** the information shown in the following table. Remember to use Tab to move forward from cell to cell.

Personal Expenses	Estimate	Actual
Food	425	435
Entertainment	100	150
Transportation/Gas	50	55
Cell Phone	75	85

9. **Save** the file and leave it **open** for the next exercise.

5.2 Inserting Tables

Video Lesson labyrinthelab.com/videos

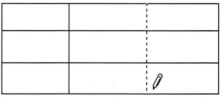

You can insert a table using the Table 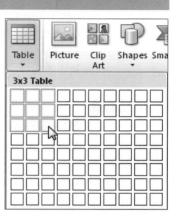 button on the Insert tab of the Ribbon. The Table button displays a grid that lets you specify the number of columns and rows for your table by dragging over the cells in the grid. The new table is inserted in the document wherever the insertion point is located.

You can also insert a table using the Insert Table dialog box found on the Tables menu in the Insert group of the Ribbon. You choose various options in the dialog box for the table. Also on the Tables drop-down list is a Quick Table menu from which you can choose predesigned tables such as calendars.

Drawing a Table

When you draw a table, you start by choosing the Draw Table command from the Insert Table menu on the Insert tab of the Ribbon. The mouse pointer changes to a pen shape so you can begin drawing the table. First, you draw a simple rectangle. Once you have the overall size of the table, you click and drag inside the rectangle to draw the lines for the rows and columns.

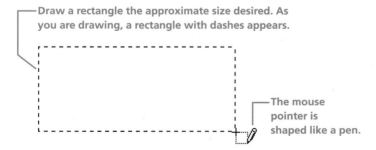

Draw a rectangle the approximate size desired. As you are drawing, a rectangle with dashes appears.

The mouse pointer is shaped like a pen.

Using the same drag method with the pen shape, you draw the row and column lines at the desired locations.

TIP Although you can choose the number of rows for the table before you enter the data, it is not absolutely necessary to do so, since tapping the Tab key in the last cell will add a new row to the table.

Task	Procedure
Insert a table	■ Choose Insert→Tables→Table ⊞ from the Ribbon.
	■ Drag in the grid to select the desired number of columns and rows.
Insert a table using the Insert Table dialog box	■ Choose Insert→Tables→Insert Table from the Ribbon.
	■ Set the number of rows and number of columns.
	■ Click OK.
Insert a quick table	■ Choose Insert→Tables→Insert Table from the Ribbon.
	■ Choose the desired quick table.
Draw a table	■ Choose Insert→Tables→Draw Table from the Ribbon.
	■ Click and drag to draw a rectangle for the table.
	■ Drag to draw the row and column lines inside the rectangle.

DEVELOP YOUR SKILLS 5.2.1

Insert a Table

In this exercise, you will create a table with three columns and three rows. You will also add additional rows to the table.

1. Position the **insertion point** at the end of the *Schedule Planning* heading on page 3 and **tap** [Enter].

2. Choose **Insert→Tables→Table** ⊞ from the Ribbon.

3. Follow these steps to create a three-column, three-row table:

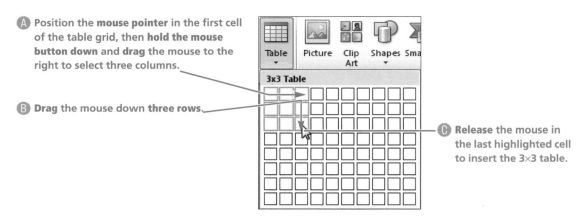

Ⓐ Position the **mouse pointer** in the first cell of the table grid, then **hold the mouse button down** and **drag** the mouse to the right to select three columns.

Ⓑ **Drag** the mouse down **three rows**.

Ⓒ **Release** the mouse in the last highlighted cell to insert the 3×3 table.

4. Position the **insertion point** in the first cell of the table.

5. **Enter** the information shown in the following table using ⌈Tab⌉ to move to the next cell and to add new rows as required.

Course	Days	Units
Math	MWF	3
Science	MWF	3
International Tourism	TTH	2
Biology	TH	3
Biology Lab	W	1

Remember, when you tap ⌈Tab⌉ in the last cell of a table, Word automatically adds an additional row to the table.

Copy the Heading Format

6. **Scroll** up to page 1 to **select** *Expense Table* and choose **Home→Clipboard→Format Painter** to activate the tool and copy the selected formatting.

7. **Select** *Schedule Planning* to apply the copied formatting to the heading.

8. **Save** the file and leave it **open** for the next exercise.

5.3 Using Table Tools

Video Lesson   labyrinthelab.com/videos

Table Tools consist of tabs on the Ribbon that are *contextual*, meaning they appear in context with the task you are performing. They are comprised of the Design tab and the Layout tab. In order to display the tabs, the insertion point must be inside a table.

Exploring the Layout and Design Tabs

The contextual Layout tab under Table Tools contains command groups associated with the layout (structure) as opposed to the design (attractiveness) of a table. For example, layout options include the following: changing the alignment, inserting and deleting columns or rows, inserting formulas, converting text to tables, and sorting table contents. The Design tab under Table Tools offers commands that include table styles, shading and borders, and other style options.

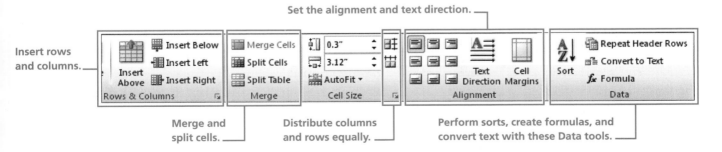

5.4 Converting Tables

Table conversions include converting text to a table or an existing table to regular text. Tabs and spaces are commonly used as separators, such as a tab or a space, between words. One advantage to converting text to a table is the formatting options. For example, in a table, you can add borders around each cell; you cannot do that with text typed in a columnar layout using the Tab key.

Converting Text to a Table

The Convert Text to Table command is found in the Tables group on the Insert tab of the Ribbon; if no text is selected, the command will not be active. One of the most common types of text-to-table conversions uses typed text that is currently laid out in a columnar fashion separated with tabs. When you convert, you are telling Word to replace each tab with a new table column.

There must only be one tab character between each column for the conversion to work properly; thus, turn on the Show/Hide formatting marks prior to converting and remove any extra tabs.

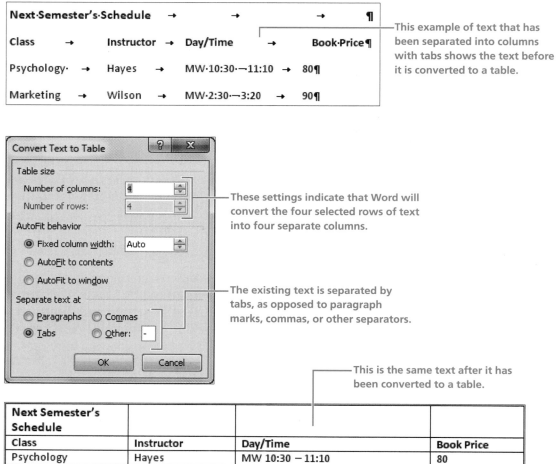

This example of text that has been separated into columns with tabs shows the text before it is converted to a table.

These settings indicate that Word will convert the four selected rows of text into four separate columns.

The existing text is separated by tabs, as opposed to paragraph marks, commas, or other separators.

This is the same text after it has been converted to a table.

Next Semester's Schedule			
Class	Instructor	Day/Time	Book Price
Psychology	Hayes	MW 10:30 — 11:10	80
Marketing	Wilson	MW 2:30 — 3:20	90

Converting a Table to Text

Just like converting text to a table, you can have Word convert an existing table to regular text. You can specify whether the text should be separated by a space or a tab. The Convert to Text command is on the Layout tab under Table Tools on the Ribbon and is only visible when the insertion point is inside a table.

 The insertion point must be in the table; however, you do not have to select anything in the table in order to convert it to regular text.

The default for separation is Tabs; however, you can choose other separators here. ⟶

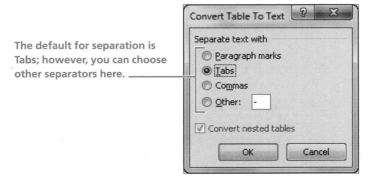

QUICK REFERENCE	CONVERTING TEXT TO TABLES AND TABLES TO TEXT
Task	**Procedure**
Convert text to a table	▪ Turn on paragraph formatting marks, if necessary.
	▪ Ensure there is only one tab separating the columns in all rows.
	▪ Select all lines to be converted.
	▪ Choose Insert→Tables→Table→Convert Text to Table.
	▪ Choose the desired text separator and the number of columns.
	▪ Click OK.
Convert a table to text	▪ Click in any cell of a table.
	▪ Choose Table Tools→Layout→Data→Convert to Text.
	▪ Choose the desired text separator.
	▪ Click OK.

DEVELOP YOUR SKILLS 5.4.1
Convert Text to a Table

In this exercise, you will convert text that is currently in a columnar format, separated by tabs, into a table. For extra practice, you will also convert the table back to regular text.

Convert Text to a Table

1. **Scroll** to the top of page 2 in the document.

2. Choose **Home→Paragraph→Show/Hide ¶** from the Ribbon.
   You may leave the formatting marks displayed for the entire lesson, or you may turn them off at any time.

3. Position the **mouse pointer** in the left margin next to the *Next Semester's Schedule* heading and then **drag down** to select the lines through *Tennis*.

4. Choose **Insert→Tables→Table→Convert Text to Table** to open the Convert Text to Table dialog box.

5. Follow these steps to create a table from the selected text:

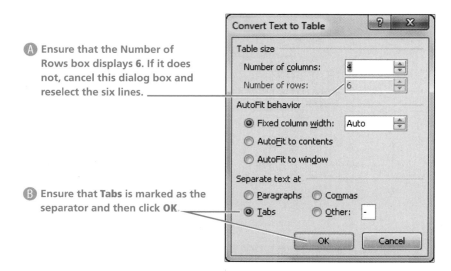

Ⓐ Ensure that the Number of Rows box displays **6**. If it does not, cancel this dialog box and reselect the six lines.

Ⓑ Ensure that **Tabs** is marked as the separator and then click **OK**.

Notice that the text is now in a table with four equal-width columns. Don't worry about the Next Semester's Schedule *heading being in just one cell. You will fix this problem a little later.*

Convert a Table to Text

6. **Click** in any cell in the table.

7. Choose **Table Tools→Layout→Data→Convert to Text**.

8. Verify that **Tabs** is chosen and then click **OK**.
   The table is converted back to regular text separated by tabs.

9. Click **Undo** 🔄 to return the text to the table format.

5.5 Selecting Data in a Table

Video Lesson   labyrinthelab.com/videos

The shape of the mouse pointer changes depending upon whether you are selecting a cell, row, column, the entire table, or certain text within a cell. Each cell contains its own small left margin area. You use the cell's margin to select one or more cells in a row rather than the entire row; the same is true for selecting cells in a column. The following figures illustrate the various pointer shapes that appear when you select different parts of a table.

Point in the margin area of a cell until the mouse pointer changes to a right-tilting, black arrow and then click to select one cell or drag to select multiple cells.

Position the mouse pointer at the top of a column, outside the table, until it becomes a down-pointing, black arrow and then click to select one column or drag to select multiple columns.

Position the mouse pointer just outside the table in the left margin until it becomes a right-tilting, white arrow and then click to select one row or drag to select multiple rows.

Click the square move handle in the upper-left corner of the table to select the entire table. The mouse pointer must be in the table for the handle to appear.

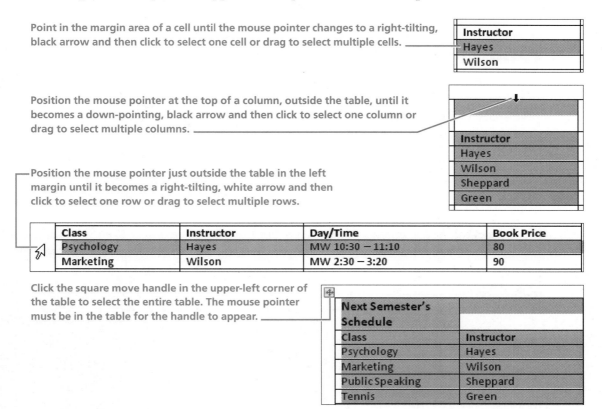

The column widths appear different from what you see on your screen. This is because they have been resized. You will resize your columns a little later in this lesson.

5.6 Aligning Data in a Table

Data can be aligned horizontally or vertically within cells. You can also change the direction of the text within the cells. These commands are found in the Alignment group on the Layout tab when the insertion point is positioned inside a table.

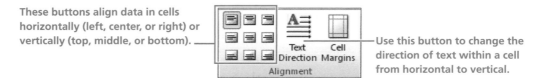

These buttons align data in cells horizontally (left, center, or right) or vertically (top, middle, or bottom).

Use this button to change the direction of text within a cell from horizontal to vertical.

Changing the Text Direction

The default text direction is horizontal. In some instances, you may want the column headings to be vertical with the text facing to the left or to the right. Switching the text to vertical can save space if the table has many columns. The cell height increases automatically to accommodate the change. The same alignment options are available whether the text is vertical or horizontal.

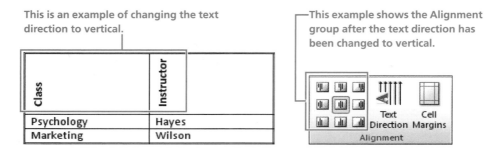

This is an example of changing the text direction to vertical.

This example shows the Alignment group after the text direction has been changed to vertical.

DEVELOP YOUR SKILLS 5.6.1
Select and Align Table Data

In this exercise, you will center-align column headings, right-align the Day/Time and Book Price data, and change the text direction.

1. Follow these steps to select and center the heading's row:

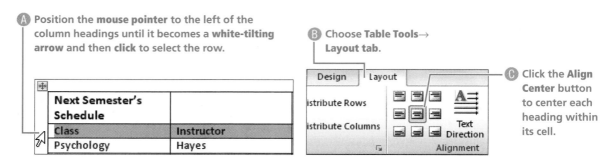

Ⓐ Position the **mouse pointer** to the left of the column headings until it becomes a **white-tilting arrow** and then **click** to select the row.

Ⓑ Choose **Table Tools→ Layout tab.**

Ⓒ Click the **Align Center** button to center each heading within its cell.

2. Follow these steps to select the *Day/Time* and *Book Price* data cells:

Ⓐ Position the **mouse pointer** in the left margin area of the first data cell in the *Day/Time* column.

Ⓑ **Press and hold** the mouse button down, **drag diagonally** to the last *Book Price* number, and then **release** the mouse button.

Day/Time	Book Price
MW 10:30 −11:10	80
MW 2:30 − 3:20	90
T Th 10:15 −11:05	35
W 3:40 − 4:30	45

3. Choose **Layout→Alignment→Align Center Right** ▤ from the Ribbon.
   Notice how the data is now lined up evenly on the right side of each cell.

4. **Scroll** up to view the Expense Table and then **select** all the number cells in the Estimate and Actual columns.

5. Choose **Layout→Alignment→Align Center Right** ▤ from the Ribbon.

Change the Text Direction

6. **Select** the column heading row.

7. Choose **Layout→Alignment→Text Direction** ▤ twice to change the direction to vertical, with the text facing to the right.
   Notice how the row increases in height automatically to accommodate the vertical text.

8. Click **Undo** ↺ twice to change back to the horizontal alignment.
   The row height is also reversed back to the normal text height.

9. **Save** ▤ the file and leave it **open** for the next exercise.

5.7 Merging and Splitting Cells

Video Lesson labyrinthelab.com/videos

The Merge Cells ▦ button in the Layout→Merge group on the Ribbon lets you merge any rectangular block of table cells. Merged cells behave as one large cell. This option is often used to center a heading across the top of a table. You merge cells by selecting the desired cells and then clicking the Merge Cells button.

The Split Cells ▦ button in the Layout→Merge group on the Ribbon lets you split one cell into multiple cells. You can split a merged cell or a cell that has never been merged. A dialog box appears when you click the Split Cells button, which lets you specify the number of columns and rows to create from the split cell.

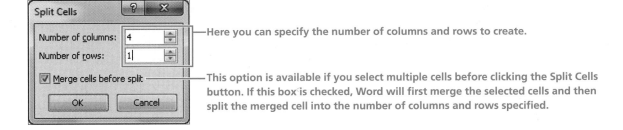

Here you can specify the number of columns and rows to create.

This option is available if you select multiple cells before clicking the Split Cells button. If this box is checked, Word will first merge the selected cells and then split the merged cell into the number of columns and rows specified.

Task	Procedure
Merge cells	■ Select the cells you want to merge. ■ Choose Layout→Merge→Merge Cells ▦ from the Ribbon.
Split cells	■ Select the cell you want to split. ■ Choose Layout→Merge→Split Cells ▦ from the Ribbon. ■ Choose the number of rows or columns to split the cell into. ■ Click OK.

DEVELOP YOUR SKILLS 5.7.1
Merge and Split Cells in a Table

In this exercise, you will merge the cells in the first row to create one cell, where you will center the title across the width of the table. Finally, you will convert the title to regular text.

1. Scroll to **page 2**.

2. Follow these steps to merge the first row of the Next Semester's Schedule tab into one cell and center the title:

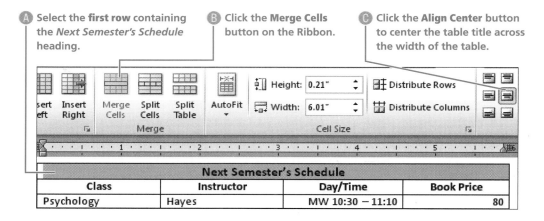

Ⓐ Select the **first row** containing the *Next Semester's Schedule* heading.

Ⓑ Click the **Merge Cells** button on the Ribbon.

Ⓒ Click the **Align Center** button to center the table title across the width of the table.

Next Semester's Schedule			
Class	**Instructor**	**Day/Time**	**Book Price**
Psychology	Hayes	MW 10:30 − 11:10	80

3. With the first row still selected, choose **Layout→Data→Convert to Text**.

4. Verify that *Paragraph marks* is chosen and then click **OK**.
   The title is now regular text and is no longer part of the table.

5. **Save** 💾 the file, and leave it **open** for the next exercise.

5.8 Adding Borders and Shading to a Table

Video Lesson   labyrinthelab.com/videos

You can apply borders and shading to a table through the Borders and Shading dialog box. Alternatively, you can use the Shading and Borders drop-down lists in the Table Styles group on the Design tab. These buttons are interesting to work with because they have a memory. They remember the last option you chose from their menus during the current Word session, and they reflect that option on the button face. This allows you to apply the same formatting multiple times, just by clicking the button face repeatedly rather than opening the menu each time.

DEVELOP YOUR SKILLS 5.8.1
Work with Borders and Shading

In this exercise, you will remove all borders from your table, and then you will reapply the borders. Finally, you will add shading to your heading row.

1. Click the **move handle** in the upper-left corner of the table to select the entire table. Remember, the mouse pointer must be in the table for the move handle to appear.

Class	Instructor	Day/Time	Book Price
Psychology	Hayes	MW 10:30 − 11:10	80
Marketing	Wilson	MW 2:30 − 3:20	90
Public Speaking	Sheppard	T Th 10:15 − 11:05	35
Tennis	Green	W 3:40 − 4:30	45

2. Choose **Design→Table Styles→ Borders ▾** menu ▾ from the Ribbon.

3. Choose **No Border** from the drop-down menu.
   This removes borders from the table. Notice that the button face reflects the No Border icon. Now you'll reapply borders to the table.

4. Make sure the table is still selected, and then click the **Borders menu ▾** again, and then choose **All Borders** from the menu.

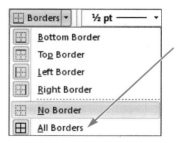

Format the Heading Rows

5. Select the **first row** of the table.

6. Choose **Design→Table Styles→** 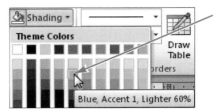 **menu ▼** from the Ribbon.

7. Choose the shading color in the **fifth column, third row**, Blue, Accent 1, Lighter 60%, as shown at right.

8. **Save** 🖫 your document, and leave it **open** for the next topic.

5.9 Sorting Data in a Table

Video Lesson labyrinthelab.com/videos

The Sort 🔡 button in the Data group on the Layout tab opens the Sort dialog box, which provides options to sort one or more columns in ascending or descending order and choose whether the first row of the table contains column headings. You can choose to sort a table by up to three levels. For example, say you have a table containing column headings for city, state, and zip. You can have Word sort the table first by state, then by city within state, then by zip code within city, for a three-level sort.

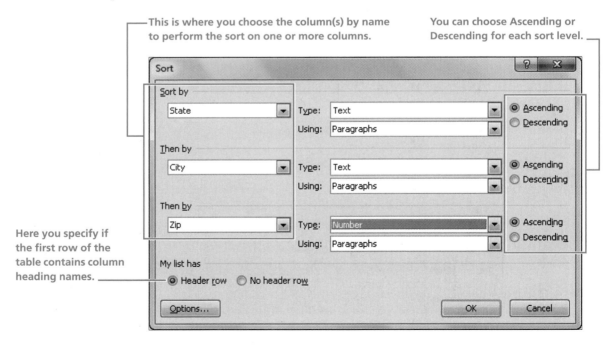

If the first row contains column headings and you do not specify that the table has a *Header row*, then *Column A, Column B,* and *Column C* will display in the Sort By boxes. When you perform the sort, the actual heading names will be sorted along with the data.

Task	Procedure
Sort a table	■ Click in the table. ■ Choose Layout→Data→Sort ⬚ from the Ribbon. ■ Under My List Has, choose Header Row or No Header Row. ■ Under Sort By, select the column or field you want to sort by. ■ For a two-level sort, under the first Then By, choose the column or field you want to sort by. ■ For a three-level sort, under the second Then By, choose the column or field you want to sort by. ■ Choose the Type of information being sorted. ■ Choose Ascending or Descending for each sort level. ■ Click OK.

DEVELOP YOUR SKILLS 5.9.1
Sort Table Rows

In this exercise, you will practice sorting the Next Semester's Schedule table.

1. Position the **insertion point** in any cell in the Next Semester's Schedule table.

2. Choose **Layout→Data→Sort** ⬚ from the Ribbon.
   Word displays the Sort dialog box.

3. Follow these steps to sort the table:

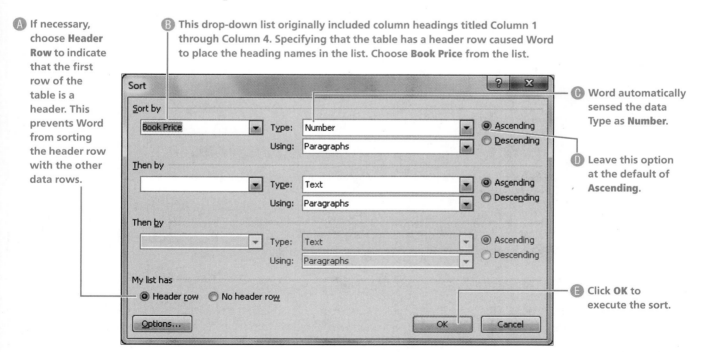

A If necessary, choose **Header Row** to indicate that the first row of the table is a header. This prevents Word from sorting the header row with the other data rows.

B This drop-down list originally included column headings titled Column 1 through Column 4. Specifying that the table has a header row caused Word to place the heading names in the list. Choose **Book Price** from the list.

C Word automatically sensed the data Type as **Number**.

D Leave this option at the default of **Ascending**.

E Click **OK** to execute the sort.

Notice that Word sorts the table rows based on the Book Price column and that now the entire table is selected.

4. Choose **Layout→Data→Sort** 🔼 from the Ribbon again.

5. When the Sort dialog box appears, once again make sure **Header Row** is chosen in the bottom-left corner of the dialog box.

6. Choose **Class** from the Sort By list in the upper-left corner of the dialog box, and keep the **Ascending** option as it is.

7. Click **OK** to sort the table.
   Your table is now sorted in ascending order by Class.

8. **Save** 💾 the document, and leave it **open** for the next exercise.

5.10 Inserting Rows and Columns

Video Lesson labyrinthelab.com/videos

You can insert columns to the left or right of existing columns and insert rows above or below existing rows. If you wish to insert multiple columns or rows, you must first select the same number of existing columns or rows you wish to insert. For example, to insert two new rows, you must select two existing rows. You can use the buttons on the Ribbon in the Rows & Columns group on the Layout tab to insert columns and rows, or you can use the drop-down menu that appears when you right-click a selected column or row.

Moving Rows and Columns

You can move a row or column by using the Cut and Paste commands or by using the mouse to drag and drop. When you select the entire row or column and move it to another location, Word automatically makes room for the selection by moving the other rows down or the other columns to the right. However, if you only select the individual cells within a row or column, when you paste, Word replaces any existing information in the cells. You can prevent data loss by inserting a blank row or column prior to moving.

QUICK REFERENCE	WORKING WITH COLUMNS AND ROWS
Task	**Procedure**
Insert rows	■ Click in the desired row or select the same number of rows that you wish to insert. ■ Choose Layout→Rows & Columns. ■ Choose either Insert Above or Insert Below.
Insert columns	■ Click in the desired column or select the same number of columns that you wish to insert. ■ Choose Layout→Rows & Columns. ■ Choose either Insert Left or Insert Right.

Task	Procedure
Delete rows or columns	▪ Select the desired rows or columns. ▪ Choose Layout→Rows & Columns→Delete. ▪ From the Delete drop-down menu, choose Delete Cells, Delete Columns, Delete Rows, or Delete Table.
Move a row or column using Cut and Paste	▪ Select the entire row(s) or column(s) as desired. ▪ Choose Home→Clipboard→Cut. *or* ▪ Tap Ctrl+x. ▪ Select the row to paste the data above. *or* ▪ Select the column to paste the data to left of. ▪ Choose Home→Clipboard→Paste.
Move a row or column using drag and drop	▪ Select the entire row(s) or column(s) as desired. ▪ Point the mouse in the first cell and drag to the first cell in the desired row or column (you will see a dotted insertion point that travels with the mouse pointer). ▪ Release the mouse button when the dotted insertion point is at the beginning of the first cell in the desired row or column.

DEVELOP YOUR SKILLS 5.10.1

Insert Rows and a Column

In this exercise, you will practice inserting multiple rows and a new column in the table.

Insert Rows

1. Position the **mouse pointer** to the left of the **Marketing** row until it becomes the white-tilting arrow.

2. **Click** and then **drag down** to select the Marketing and Psychology rows.

3. Choose **Layout→Rows & Columns→Insert Above** 🔲 to insert two new rows above the Marketing row.

4. Add the following data to the new blank rows:

Geometry	Bailey	MW 12 – 12:50	95
Geometry Lab	Johnson	T Th 9:00 – 9:50	35

Insert a Column

5. **Click** in any cell in the first column.

6. Choose **Layout→Rows & Columns→Insert Left** 🔲 from the Ribbon.
   A new, blank column is inserted at the beginning of the table. Don't worry about the column spacing; you will fix it later.

7. Type **Course #** as the new column heading.

8. **Enter** the following data in the blank column:

Course #
500334
500335
200021
605221
123356
988290

9. **Scroll back up** to the Expense Table on page 1 and then position the **insertion point** in the *Actual* column.

10. Choose **Layout→Rows & Columns→Insert Right** from the Ribbon.

11. Type **Difference** as the new column heading.

12. **Save** the file, and leave it **open** for the next topic.

5.11 Performing Calculations in Tables

Video Lesson labyrinthelab.com/videos

The Formula dialog box is displayed by choosing Layout→Data→Formula fx from the Ribbon. When the dialog box opens, the Formula box displays the Sum function. The Sum function recognizes whether there are figures entered in the cells above or to the left of the formula cell and indicates that in the formula automatically. However, sometimes you may need a formula for something other than adding. In that case, you must use cell addresses in the formula. Although the columns and rows are not lettered or numbered as they are in Excel, you must use *cell addresses* for certain calculations in a table. The first cell in a table is considered to be cell A1 (first column, first row). Word's formulas are not nearly as sophisticated as Excel's; however, they are adequate for simple calculations.

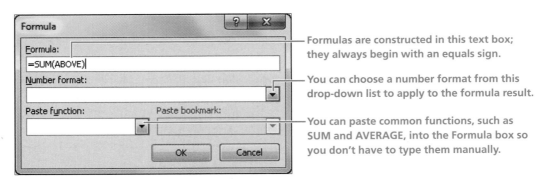

Formulas are constructed in this text box; they always begin with an equals sign.

You can choose a number format from this drop-down list to apply to the formula result.

You can paste common functions, such as SUM and AVERAGE, into the Formula box so you don't have to type them manually.

Constructing Formulas

You construct formulas by typing directly into the Formula dialog box. In Word, formulas can contain a combination of the following elements:

- **Arithmetic operators**—The most common arithmetic operators are + (addition), – (subtraction), / (division), and * (multiplication). For more complex formulas, use Microsoft Excel, then copy and paste the Excel table into the Word document.

- **Cell addresses**—In Word tables, the columns are labeled A, B, C, etc., and the rows are numbered 1, 2, 3, etc. Each cell has an address formed by the column letter and row number. For example, cell A1 refers to the cell in column A and row 1. You can use cell references in formulas. For example, the formula =D2–C2 subtracts the number in cell C2 from the number in cell D2. It is not necessary to type the column letter in uppercase when creating the formula.

- **Functions**—Functions are predefined formulas that perform calculations on cells. The most common functions are SUM, AVERAGE, MIN, and MAX.

  A function is followed by a set of parentheses in which you enter arguments. Arguments include numbers, cell addresses, a range of cells, or direction references (see next bullet). A range of cells is separated by a colon. For example, to include cells C2, C3, and C4 only in a formula, you would type C2:C4.

- **Direction references**—In Word, functions can use direction references to indicate cell ranges. The direction references are ABOVE, BELOW, LEFT, and RIGHT. As an example, the formula =SUM(ABOVE) would sum all numbers above the cell containing the formula.

Word formulas do not recalculate automatically if you change a number in a cell; thus, you must re-create the formula to display the new total.

QUICK REFERENCE	CONSTRUCTING FORMULAS
Task	**Procedure**
Create a formula	▪ Choose Layout→Data→Formula $f\!x$ from the Ribbon. ▪ Delete the formula in the formula box. ▪ Type an equals (=) sign. ▪ Construct the formula using cell addresses. ▪ Use the appropriate operator: + (add), – (subtract), * (multiply), / (divide).
Calculate with a function	▪ Choose Layout→Data→Formula $f\!x$ from the Ribbon. ▪ Delete the formula in the formula box. ▪ Type an equals (=) sign. ▪ Choose a function from the Paste Function list. ▪ Enter the arguments within the parentheses.

Construct Formulas

In this exercise, you will use formulas to calculate the difference for each expense item and then calculate the totals for the Estimate, Actual, and Difference columns.

1. Click in the **Difference** column of the Expense table for the Food row.
   This cell is named D2 because it is the fourth column (D) in the second row (2).

2. Choose **Layout→Data→Formula** fx from the Ribbon.

Create a Formula to Subtract the Estimate from the Actual Expense

3. Follow these steps to create a formula to subtract the Estimate from the Actual expense:

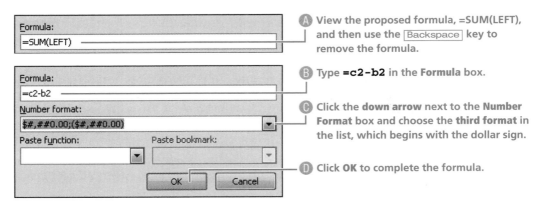

Ⓐ View the proposed formula, =SUM(LEFT), and then use the Backspace key to remove the formula.

Ⓑ Type **=c2-b2** in the **Formula** box.

Ⓒ Click the **down arrow** next to the **Number Format** box and choose the **third format** in the list, which begins with the dollar sign.

Ⓓ Click **OK** to complete the formula.

This formula subtracts the estimated food expense (column b, row 2) from the actual food expense (column c, row 2). Notice that the result, $10.00, displays with a dollar sign and two decimal places.

If you wish to display the dollar format without the two decimal places, you must delete them manually from each cell.

4. **Click** in the cell beneath the one with the formula.

5. Choose **Layout→Data→Formula** fx from the Ribbon.

6. **Remove** the proposed formula and type **=c3-b3**.

7. Click the **Number Format** drop-down menu ▾ button, choose the format with the **dollar sign**, and click **OK**.

8. **Enter** formulas in the remaining rows in the Difference column.

Create a Formula to Total the Columns

9. Position the **insertion point** in the last cell of the table and **tap** Tab to create a new blank row.

10. Type **Totals** in the first cell of the new blank row, and then **tap** Tab to move to the next cell in the Totals row.

11. Choose **Layout→Data→Formula** fx from the Ribbon.
    Word assumes you want to add the numbers above the formula cell.

12. Click **OK**.

   The result should be 650. Notice that the total does not have the dollar sign or decimals since you did not specify any special formatting.

13. Use the default formula again to calculate the total for *Actual* column with no formatting.

14. Calculate the **total** for the Difference column and add the currency formatting.

15. **Save** 💾 the file, and leave it **open** for the next exercise.

5.12 Sizing Rows and Columns

Video Lesson   labyrinthelab.com/videos

You can easily resize columns and rows in a table. Word 2010 offers a variety of techniques for this.

Dragging to Adjust Row Heights and Column Widths

The adjust ↔ pointer appears whenever you position the mouse pointer on a row or column gridline. You can adjust the column width and row height by dragging the gridline. When you drag a column gridline, the width of the column to the left of the gridline adjusts. When you drag a row gridline, the height of the row above the gridline adjusts. If you adjust the left gridline of the first column, all other columns automatically adjust to accommodate the new width of the first column.

You can adjust the width of the first column by dragging this gridline.

Personal Expenses	Estimate	Actual
Food	425	435
Entertainment	100	150
Transportation/Gas	50	55
Cell Phone	75	85

You can also adjust column width and row height by dragging column and row markers on the ruler.

Double-clicking the border between two columns adjusts the column to the left to *best fit*, meaning the column will be as wide as it needs to be, based on the width of its contents. You can select several columns and double-click to best fit the selected columns all at once.

Distributing Rows and Columns

The Distribute Rows ⊞ and Distribute Columns ⊞ buttons in the Cell Size group of the Layout tab let you equally allocate the space in a table among the rows and columns. For example, if a table is six inches wide and has three columns, the Distribute Columns command will adjust the width of each column to two inches.

Adjust Column Widths

Drag to Adjust Column Width

1. Follow these steps to change the width of the first column:

Ⓐ Position the **mouse pointer** on the border between the first two columns. The mouse pointer changes to the adjust pointer (a double-headed black arrow).

Ⓑ **Drag to the right** about a half inch, and then **release** the mouse button to change the column width.

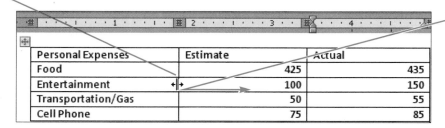

Notice that the second column is much narrower than the last two columns. You will remedy that right now.

Evenly Distribute Columns and Rows

2. Follow these steps to distribute the last three columns evenly:

Ⓐ Position the **mouse pointer** at the top of the Estimate column until it becomes a **black down arrow**.

Ⓑ **Drag to the right** to select all three columns.

Estimate	Actual	Difference
425	435	$ 10.00
100	150	$ 50.00
50	55	$ 5.00
75	85	$ 20.00
650	725	$ 85.00

3. Choose **Layout→Cell Size→Distribute Columns** ⊞ from the Ribbon to make the selected columns the same size.

4. **Scroll** to the Next Semester's Schedule table on **page 2**.

5. **Select** the entire table and distribute the columns evenly.

6. **Scroll up** again to the Expense table.

7. Follow these steps to adjust all columns in the Expense table to their best fit:

Ⓐ Click the **square move handle** to select the entire table.

Personal Expenses	Estimate	Actual	Difference
Food	425	435	$ 10.00
Entertainment	100	150	$ 50.00
Transportation/Gas	50	55	$ 5.00
Cell Phone	75	85	$ 20.00
Totals	650	725	$ 85.00

Ⓑ Position the **mouse pointer** on one of the column gridlines until it becomes the adjust pointer and then **double-click**.

All columns are now as wide as they need to be, based on the width of their contents.

8. **Save** 🖫 the file, and leave it **open** for the next exercise.

5.13 Using Table Styles to Format a Table

Video Lesson   labyrinthelab.com/videos

The Table Styles group located on the Design tab lets you choose from a variety of predefined table formats. These formats automatically apply borders, shading, font colors, font sizes, and other formats to tables. You may be pleasantly surprised to see the professional-looking formatting that results when you apply Table Styles.

After you apply a Table Style, you can continue to customize the formatting of the table if you wish, adding additional borders, for example.

Checking or unchecking these options determines if special formatting will be applied to specific areas of a table, such as the header row or the total row.

☑ Header Row   ☑ First Column
☐ Total Row   ☐ Last Column
☑ Banded Rows ☐ Banded Columns
Table Style Options

Table Styles

🖎 Shad
▦ Bord

Light Shading - Accent 1

These arrows allow you to scroll through the list of available styles.

The More button lets you see a larger gallery of the available styles all at once.

When you position the mouse pointer over a style sample, Live Preview allows you to quickly preview a variety of styles without actually applying one.

Personal Expenses	Estimate	Actual	Difference
Food	425	435	$ 10.00
Entertainment	100	150	$ 50.00
Transportation/Gas	50	55	$ 5.00
Cell Phone	75	85	$ 20.00
Totals	650	725	$ 85.00

Apply Table Styles

In this exercise, you will add polish to your table by applying one of Word's built-in table styles.

1. Make sure the **insertion point** is in the **Expense** table.

2. Choose **Design→Table Styles** from the Ribbon.

Observe the Table Style Gallery

3. Position the **mouse pointer** in the Table Styles gallery, and move from one style to another. Notice that Live Preview displays how the style would look if applied to your table.

4. Use the **middle scroll arrow**, as shown at right, to scroll down and view other built-in table styles.

5. Again, use **Live Preview** to examine additional styles.

6. Click the **More** ⊡ button to display a larger sampling of styles, and then scroll through the gallery.

7. **Click** outside the table to close the gallery, and then **click** the table again.

8. Use the **scroll buttons** to scroll to the second row of table styles.

Apply a Table Style

9. If necessary, place a checkmark in the **Header Row** and **First Column** checkboxes in the Table Style Options group, as shown at right, to apply special formatting to those areas of your table. **Check** or **uncheck** the remaining boxes, as shown in the illustration.

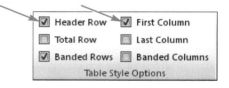

10. Choose the **Light List – Accent 1** style to apply that style to your table.

The location may vary based on your screen size and resolution. You can use ToolTips to locate the style, or feel free to choose another style.

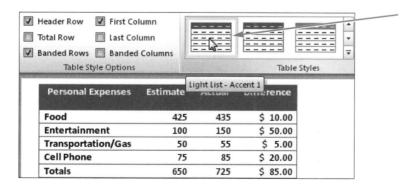

Notice the special formatting on the header row, and notice that bold was applied to the first column. That's the result of options you chose in the Table Style Options group.

Use the Move Handle to Reposition the Table

You used the move handle ⊞ earlier in this lesson to select an entire table. Now you will use it to move your table back to the center of the page.

11. Position the **mouse pointer** over the move handle, and the pointer changes to a four-headed black arrow.

12. **Press** and **hold** the mouse button, **drag** the table to the horizontal center of the page, and then **release** the mouse button.

Adjust Row Height

You've experienced dragging the border of a column to change its width. Now you'll use a similar technique to change row height.

13. Follow these steps to change the height of the first row:

Ⓐ Position the mouse pointer on the row border below the first row.

Personal Expenses	Estimate	Actual	Difference
Food		425	435	$ 10.00
Entertainment		100	150	$ 50.00

Ⓑ When the mouse pointer changes to a **double-headed black arrow,** press the mouse button and drag down, until the row is approximately a quarter to a half inch tall, and then release the mouse button.

14. **Select** the first row with the headings.

15. Choose **Layout→Alignment→Align Center**.
    Notice that the text is centered in the middle of the row and the center of each cell.

16. **Save** 💾 the document, and **close** it.

5.14 Working with Forms

Video Lesson   labyrinthelab.com/videos

Many organizations use forms to collect data. Forms contain both fields, where users enter information, and objects such as checkboxes and drop-down lists to assist users with data entry. With Word, you can easily set up forms, based on tables, to meet the needs of your organization and distribute them in any of the following formats:

■ **Printed**—Printed forms are printed and filled out on paper.

■ **Electronic**—Electronic forms are distributed to Word users and filled out in Word. They are often available via a network or sent in an email.

■ **Internet-Based**—Internet-based forms are posted to a website and filled out using a web browser. The data is stored in an electronic database. Word lets you set up forms and save them as web pages.

Address Information Name Address City ▮ State ▮ Zip ▮		Date Click here to enter a date.
How/Where Will You Eat? Eat at restaurants ☒ Times per week ▮⬍ Buy groceries and cook ☒ Times ▮	0 1 2	
Transportation Use Campus Shuttle ☒ Use ow	3 4	
Entertainment Stay home to watch TV ☒ Times ▮ Go out ☒ Times ▮	5 6 7	

Setting Up Forms

You can set up forms using the same tools and techniques used to set up any other type of document. However, certain Word features are particularly useful with forms. For example, tables are frequently used to set up forms because they allow you to lay out forms with an orderly structure. Creating a form in a table is much easier to work with than using tabs. Word also provides tools in the Controls group on the Developer tab of the Ribbon that can be used to design forms.

DEVELOP YOUR SKILLS 5.14.1
Set Up the Form

In this exercise, you will add a table and custom tab stops to align objects in the form.

1. **Open** the Student Survey document from the Lesson 5 folder.
2. **Select** the title *Georgia South College*.
3. Using the Mini toolbar, change the font size to **16 points**.
4. **Select** *Students Helping Students Response Form*.
5. Choose the **Home→Font→Font Size** 11 ▾ **menu** ▾ button from the Ribbon and choose **14 points** from the menu.
6. Turn on **Bold** **B** and **Italics** *I*.
7. Position the **insertion point** on the line under the subtitle.

Insert a Table
You will use this table as the basis for the form.

8. Choose **Insert→Tables→Table** ▦ from the Ribbon and select **two columns** and **two rows**.
   You will insert additional rows as needed for the form by using the [Tab] *key at the end of each row.*
9. Select the entire table and choose **Table Tools→Layout→Alignment→Cell Margins** and change the Top and Bottom to **.08"**.

10. Position the **mouse pointer** on the line between the two columns and drag it to the **right** to the 5-inch mark on the ruler.
This creates a wide first column.

11. If necessary, click the **Show/Hide** ¶ button to turn on the formatting marks.
Seeing the formatting marks makes it easier for you to see exactly what you are doing in the form.

12. Follow these steps to begin adding text to the form.

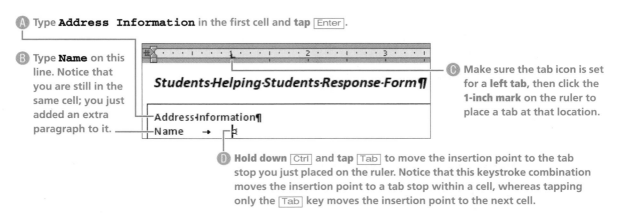

Ⓐ Type **Address Information** in the first cell and **tap** Enter.

Ⓑ Type **Name** on this line. Notice that you are still in the same cell; you just added an extra paragraph to it.

Ⓒ Make sure the tab icon is set for a **left tab**, then click the **1-inch mark** on the ruler to place a tab at that location.

Ⓓ **Hold down** Ctrl and **tap** Tab to move the insertion point to the tab stop you just placed on the ruler. Notice that this keystroke combination moves the insertion point to a tab stop within a cell, whereas tapping only the Tab key moves the insertion point to the next cell.

13. **Save** 💾 the document and leave it **open** to continue with the next topic.

Understanding Form Fields

Video Lesson   labyrinthelab.com/videos

Fields in a form are made up of controls. There are three types of controls you can use in a form: content controls, legacy forms, and ActiveX controls. The type of document you are creating and who will be using it determine which control set to use in the form. See the following table for descriptions of each type of control.

FORM CONTROLS	
Type	**Description**
Content Controls	These controls were introduced in Word 2007. The group contains additional controls that did not exist in the legacy tools. However, these do not work with Word 2003 and older versions of the application. They also have limitations on data restriction properties. For example, you can insert a Plain Text Content Control but there is not an option to limit the maximum length for the entry.
Legacy Forms	This older set of form fields is still available. This set does not include the newer controls, such as the Date Picker and Picture controls, but these fields can be used in any Word version and allow data restrictions to be set.
ActiveX Controls	This set of controls is reserved for documents that will be used in a web page.

Using the Form

After you create the form, you should protect it to prevent anyone from making changes to it. You do this by setting a protection that only allows the users to fill in the form. When a protected form is opened, the first form field is highlighted, ready to receive data. Then, you use ⌈Tab⌉ and ⌈Shift⌉+⌈Tab⌉ to move to the next or previous field. In this lesson, you will use a combination of content controls and legacy forms form fields for practice.

When you mix control types in a form, you lose some functionality. For example, you have to click in the field, rather than use the ⌈Tab⌉ key, when moving from a content control to a legacy form field.

The Developer Tab

All three types of controls are found in the Controls group on the Developer tab of the Ribbon. The Developer tab does not appear on the Ribbon by default. You must activate it by placing a checkmark next to *Developer* in the Word Options dialog box. You can open the Word Options dialog box using the File tab or by right-clicking any tab or command on the Ribbon and choosing Customize the Ribbon. Once you turn it on, the Developer tab remains visible unless you uncheck the option or reinstall Microsoft Office.

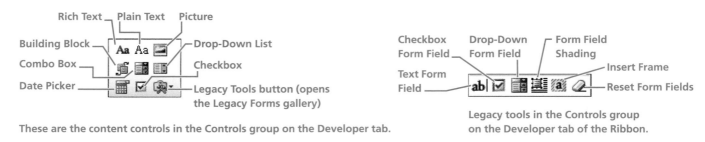

These are the content controls in the Controls group on the Developer tab.

Legacy tools in the Controls group on the Developer tab of the Ribbon.

QUICK REFERENCE	INSERTING FORM FIELDS
Task	**Procedure**
Insert a content control in a form	■ Choose Developer→Controls. ■ Choose the desired content control to insert.
Insert a form field from the Legacy Tools	■ Choose Developer→Controls→Legacy Tools. ■ Click the desired form field to insert it in a document.

Insert Form Fields

In this exercise, you will display the Developer tab on the Ribbon. You will then use a combination of content control and legacy forms controls to insert text fields, checkboxes, and drop-down form fields in your document.

Display the Developer Tab

1. **Right-click** the Home tab and choose **Customize the Ribbon**.

2. Place a checkmark in the **Developer** checkbox, as shown here.

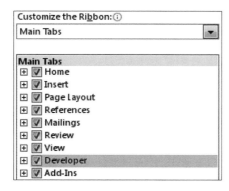

3. Click **OK** to display the Developer tab on the Ribbon.

4. If necessary, click the **Show/Hide** ¶ button to turn on the formatting marks.

Insert a Legacy Forms Text Form Field

5. Position the **insertion point** at the 1-inch tab stop in the first cell of the second row.

6. Choose **Developer→Controls→Legacy Tools→Text Form Field** ab from the Ribbon.
   If formatting marks and shading are turned on, the Legacy Text Form Field control will display little circles in a shaded cell, indicating that it is a form field.

7. If a shaded box is not visible, follow these steps; otherwise, go to the next step.
   - Choose **Developer→Controls→Legacy Tools** from the Ribbon.
   - Click the **Form Field Shading** button to display the shaded field.

   You won't actually enter data in the fields until the form is complete and has been protected. When you eventually enter data, the length of the text field increases to accommodate the text you type, unless you restrict the field length with property settings.

Insert Additional Text Form Fields

8. If necessary, click to the right of the field, **tap** Enter, and type **Address**.
   Notice that a custom tab stop is set at the 1" position on the ruler. Custom tab stops are paragraph formats, so they are carried to new paragraphs when you tap Enter.

9. **Press** Ctrl+Tab, and choose **Developer→Controls→Legacy Tools** from the Ribbon.

10. Click the **Text Form Field** abl button to insert another text field, and then **tap** Enter.

11. Follow these steps to insert the text fields for City, State, and Zip:

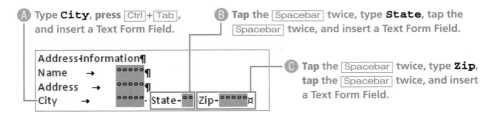

A Type **City**, press Ctrl+Tab, and insert a Text Form Field.

B Tap the Spacebar twice, type **State**, tap the Spacebar twice, and insert a Text Form Field.

Address·Information¶
Name → °°°°°¶
Address → °°°°°¶
City → °°°°°. State-°° Zip-°°°°°¤

C Tap the Spacebar twice, type **Zip**, tap the Spacebar twice, and insert a Text Form Field.

Insert a Text Form Field for the Date

12. **Tap** the Tab key to move the insertion point to the next table cell on the right.

13. Choose **Home→Paragraph→Align Text Right** ▤ from the Ribbon to position the insertion point at the right side of the cell.

14. Type **Date** and **tap** the Spacebar twice.

15. Choose **Developer→Controls→Date Picker Content Control** ▦ from the Ribbon.

16. Follow these steps to insert the current date into the form:

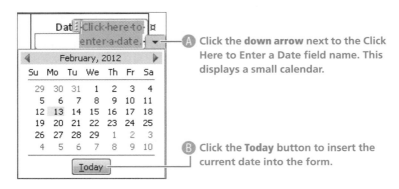

A Click the **down arrow** next to the Click Here to Enter a Date field name. This displays a small calendar.

B Click the **Today** button to insert the current date into the form.

17. **Save** 🖫 the file, and leave it **open** for the next exercise.

Using the Checkbox and Drop-Down List Fields

Video Lesson labyrinthelab.com/videos

In addition to a Text Form Field, Word provides a Checkbox Form Field and a Drop-Down List Form Field. These fields make it easy for users to respond to survey questions and simplify data analysis for the form's creator. Drop-down fields, for example, allow you to enter specific choices to be displayed in a list, while checkboxes restrict answers to a yes/no type of response. You can choose the default entries for each field you place on a form.

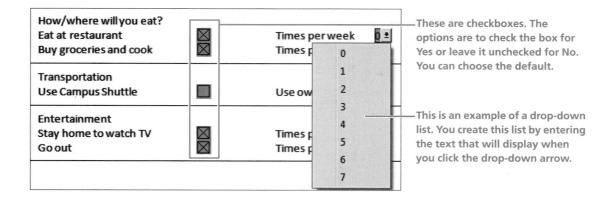

These are checkboxes. The options are to check the box for Yes or leave it unchecked for No. You can choose the default.

This is an example of a drop-down list. You create this list by entering the text that will display when you click the drop-down arrow.

Add Checkboxes and Drop-Down Lists to the Form

In this exercise, you will continue adding form fields to the document, including checkboxes and drop-down lists.

1. Position the **insertion point** in the first cell of the second row.

2. **Drag** the 1-inch tab stop off the ruler.

3. Place **left tab stops** at the 2-inch, 3-inch and 4.25-inch positions on the ruler.

4. Type **How/Where Will You Eat?**, tap Enter, and type **Eat at restaurants**.

5. Follow these steps to insert information in row 2:

Ⓐ Remember to use Ctrl + Tab between the labels and the form fields.

Ⓑ Place Check Box Form Fields here. Be sure to use the checkbox form field in Legacy Tools.

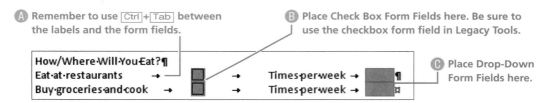

Ⓒ Place Drop-Down Form Fields here.

At this point, nothing happens to these form fields if you click them. They do not become active until you restrict and protect the document as a form, which you will do a little later in this lesson.

6. **Tap** Tab twice to move the insertion point to the first cell in the third row.
   Notice the new row maintains the same custom tab stops you placed in the previous row.

7. Use these guidelines to insert labels and checkboxes in the last two rows of the form, as shown in the illustration:

- **Type** the text and insert checkboxes as shown.
- Insert **Legacy Forms** drop-down form fields for the *Times Per Week* data.
- Use Ctrl + Tab between labels and form fields.
- **Tap** Tab to move between cells.

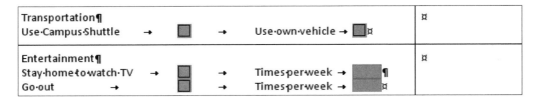

8. **Save** the changes and leave the form **open** for the next exercise.

Applying Field Properties

Video Lesson   labyrinthelab.com/videos

Each field type has various properties associated with it. For example, you can restrict the type and set the maximum length for data entered in text fields. You can also limit users to entering only dates in a field specified as a Date type, and you can have Word automatically format it to a particular date format. Although you cannot prevent all errors during data entry, property restrictions help in that effort.

Modifying Text in a Content Control

The default text is displayed in a content control; for example, the following illustration shows the default text, *Click here to enter text*. This text is replaced when the user selects it and types data in the form. To modify the default text that displays in a content control, you must be in Design Mode. Once in Design Mode, you drag over the text and type the replacement.

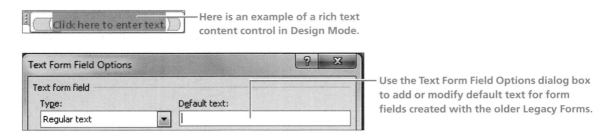

Here is an example of a rich text content control in Design Mode.

Use the Text Form Field Options dialog box to add or modify default text for form fields created with the older Legacy Forms.

To display and edit text in a legacy control, you must open the Text Form Field Options dialog box and enter or modify the text in the Default Text box. The user must select the default text before entering the actual data in the form.

DEVELOP YOUR SKILLS 5.14.4
Set Field Properties

In this exercise, you will set field properties for the various field types.

1. Follow these steps to add default instructional text to the Name field:

Ⓐ **Double-click** the Name field to open the Text Form Field Options dialog box.

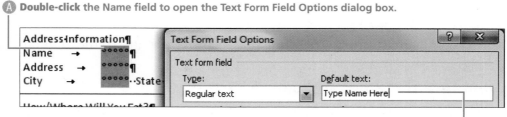

Ⓑ Make sure the insertion point is in the Default Text box and type **Type Name Here**.

2. Click **OK** to accept the default text and close the dialog box.

3. Click the **Date** field at the top of the right column.

4. Choose **Developer→Controls→Properties** from the Ribbon.

5. Choose the **d-mmm-yy** format from the Display the Date Like This list, as shown here.

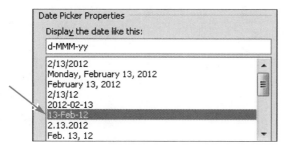

After you specify the date format, when you type a date in the field, Word will apply this specific format.

6. Click **OK** to complete the property settings, then click **Undo** 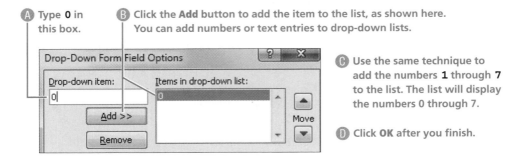 to return to the default format.

7. **Double-click** the State field, set Maximum Length to **2**, choose Uppercase from the Text Format list, and click **OK**.
This forces users to enter the state abbreviations.

8. **Double-click** the Zip field, set the Maximum Length to **10**, and click **OK**.

Set Drop-Down List Properties

9. **Double-click** the *Times per week* field for the *Eat at restaurants* line.

10. Follow these steps to specify the list items:

Ⓐ Type **0** in this box.

Ⓑ Click the **Add** button to add the item to the list, as shown here. You can add numbers or text entries to drop-down lists.

Ⓒ Use the same technique to add the numbers **1** through **7** to the list. The list will display the numbers 0 through 7.

Ⓓ Click **OK** after you finish.

11. **Double-click** the field next to *Times per week* on the *Buy groceries and cook* line.

12. Using the same technique as **step 10**, specify 0 through 7 in the drop-down list for the other *Times per week* fields.

Complete the Form Design

13. **Select** the table, and choose **Home→Paragraph→Borders** menu ▾ from the Ribbon and choose **Inside Borders**.

14. If necessary, click the **Show/Hide** ¶ button to turn off the formatting marks.

15. If necessary, choose **Developer→Controls→Legacy Tools→Form Field Shading** to turn off field shading.

16. **Save** the changes, and continue with the next topic.

Protecting Forms

Video Lesson   labyrinthelab.com/videos

The Restrict Editing feature can prevent users from making changes other than in the form fields. Protecting forms also triggers the form fields to behave like form fields. For example, tapping the Tab key will move the insertion point to the next form field, and clicking a checkbox will insert or remove an X. You unprotect a form when designing or modifying it, and you protect it when you are ready to use it.

Task	Procedure
Protect a form	■ Choose Developer→Protect→Restrict Editing from the Ribbon.
	■ In the Restrict Formatting and Editing task pane, check the Allow Only This Type of Editing in the Document checkbox.
	■ Choose Filling in Forms from the drop-down list.
	■ Click the Yes, Start Enforcing Protection button.
	■ Add and confirm a password, and click OK to use password protection. Otherwise, leave the password fields blank, and click OK to dismiss the dialog box.
Stop protection	■ Click the Stop Protection button in the Restrict Formatting and Editing task pane.
	■ Enter a password if prompted to do so, and then click OK.

Distributing and Using Forms

You can simply print and distribute paper forms to users. Electronic forms should be protected, and they are typically distributed via email. Users can fill out an electronic form online and return the completed form to the person responsible for collecting the data.

Protect and Use the Form

In this exercise, you will protect the form and then enter data in the special form fields you inserted in the document.

Protect and Save the Form

1. Choose **Developer→Protect→Restrict Editing** 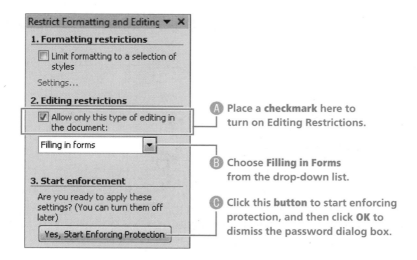 from the Ribbon.
   The Restrict Formatting and Editing task pane opens.

2. Follow these steps to protect the form:

Ⓐ Place a **checkmark** here to turn on Editing Restrictions.

Ⓑ Choose **Filling in Forms** from the drop-down list.

Ⓒ Click this **button** to start enforcing protection, and then click **OK** to dismiss the password dialog box.

3. **Tap** the ⎡Tab⎤ key three times to move the insertion point from one field to another.

4. **Tap** ⎡Shift⎤+⎡Tab⎤ to move backwards through the fields to the Name field.

Fill Out the Form

5. Type **Eugene Washington**, and then **tap** the [Tab] key.

6. Type **5250 Ramiro Avenue**, and **tap** the [Tab] key.

7. Type **Richmond,** and **tap** the [Tab] key.

8. Try entering **California** in the State field, **tap** [Tab], and notice that Word restricts the number of characters to two and automatically changed them to uppercase letters.
   This is because you set the maximum field length property of this field to 2 and the text format property to Uppercase.

9. Type **94803** in the Zip field.

10. **Tap** [Tab], click the drop-down arrow in the **Date Picker**, and click the **Today** button in the small calendar.

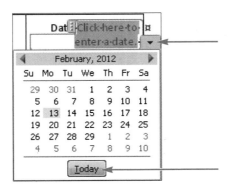

11. Follow these steps to complete the next row:

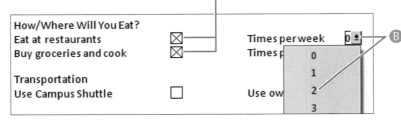

A **Click** the *Eat at restaurants* and *Buy groceries and cook* checkboxes to place Xs in them.

B **Click** the first *Times per week* drop-down field and choose **2** from the list; then repeat for the second *Times per week* in this row and choose **5**.

12. Finish filling in the form as shown in the illustration.

Transportation			
Use Campus Shuttle	☐	Use own vehicle	☒
Entertainment			
Stay home to watch TV	☒	Times per week	5
Go out	☒	Times per week	2

13. **Save** 🖫 the changes, **close** the document, and then **close** the Restrict Formatting and Editing task pane.

14. Reopen the document and then try **clicking** on the title at the top of the form or on any of the text headings.
    Word does not respond. When a form is protected, you can only position the insertion point in fields. Also, notice that the text form field next to Name *is now highlighted and ready for text to be entered because it is the first form field to fill in.*

5.15 Concepts Review

Concepts Review	labyrinthelab.com/word10

To check your knowledge of the key concepts introduced in this lesson, complete the Concepts Review quiz by going to the URL listed above. If your classroom is using Labyrinth eLab, you may complete the Concepts Review quiz from within your eLab course.

Reinforce Your Skills

Convert Text, Format, and Sort a Table

In this exercise, you will convert text to a table, apply a table style, and merge cells. Finally, you will perform a multilevel sort, sorting by Last Name, then State.

1. **Open** the rs-Contractors document from the Lesson 05 folder.

2. Beginning with the title, *Independent Contractors for Fast Track*, **select** all of the lines through Steven Johns.

3. Convert the selected lines of text to a **table**, separating text at tabs.
   (Hint: Use Insert→Tables→Table from the Ribbon.)

Apply a Table Style and Merge Cells

4. Use the **scroll down** button in the Table Styles group to scroll down to the fourth row and apply the **Medium Shading 1 - Accent 4** style. The location may vary. If necessary, use ToolTips to locate the style or choose a different style of your choice.

5. Uncheck the **First Column** checkbox in the Table Style Options group on the Layout tab.

6. Use the **Layout→Merge** group to merge the title row, *Independent Contractors for Fast Track*, into one large cell.

7. **Center** the title in the first row.

Sort Rows

8. **Select** the table rows beginning with the column heading. (Do not select the first row containing the table title.)

9. Choose **Layout→Data→Sort** from the Ribbon.

10. Specify that the selection contains a **Header Row**.

11. Choose **Last Name** and then **State** for the sort keys, leaving both set on **Ascending**.

12. Click **OK** and examine the results to verify that the table sorted as you specified in step 11.

13. **Save** the document and then **close** it.

Independent Contractors for Fast Track					
First Name	Last Name	Rate	Availability	Phone	State
Teresa	Beach	$40/hour	Immediate	213-235-9988	CA
Janet	Bester	$30/hour	April 21	804-450-9090	VA
Julie	Carroll	$35/hour	April 15	510-236-0090	CA
Steven	Johns	$55/hour	Immediate	510-234-8980	CA
Pat	Thomas	$40/hour	May 1	954-223-4565	FL

Format a Table and Use Calculations

In this exercise, you will format the table at the end of the exercise. You will decrease the width of the first three columns and increase the width of the last column. You will also create formulas in a total row.

1. **Open** the rs-Auto Parts document from the Lesson 05 folder.

Format the Table

2. **Select** the first row, and use the **Mini toolbar** to apply bold and center alignment formatting.

3. Select the **second column** by clicking just above the top border of the column when the mouse pointer is a down-pointing black arrow.

4. Use the **Mini toolbar** to center the data in the column.

5. Select the **number cells** in the third column.

6. Choose **Layout→Alignment→Align Top Right** ⊟ from the Ribbon

7. Select the **first three columns**.

8. **Double-click** the border between two of the selected columns to best fit the contents within the columns.

9. Position the **mouse pointer** on the right border of the table. When the mouse pointer changes to a double-headed black arrow, **drag to the right** until the right edge of the table is at the **5 ½-inch mark** on the ruler.

Use Formulas in the Table

10. Add a **new row** to the bottom of the table and type **Total** in the first cell.

11. Use ⎡Tab⎤ to move to the next cell in the last row.

12. Choose **Layout→Data→Formula** *ƒx* from the Ribbon.
    The formula in the Formula dialog box automatically defaults to the Function SUM(ABOVE).

13. Leave the formula as is, and click **OK** to insert the formula in the cell.

14. Use ⎡Tab⎤ to move to the next cell, and click the **Formula** *ƒx* button again.

15. Leave the formula at **SUM(ABOVE)**, and choose the third **number format** from the drop-down list.

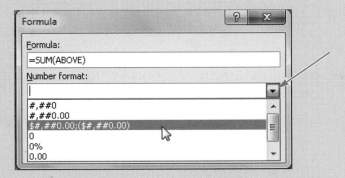

16. Click **OK** to insert the formula.

17. **Double-click** the column border on the right side of the **Cost** column to widen it.

Apply a Table Style

18. Make sure the **insertion point** is in the table.

19. Choose **Design→Table Styles** from the Ribbon.

20. Apply the **third style** in the first row of the gallery—Light Shading, Accent 1—or choose a different table style.

21. In the Table Style Options group on the Design tab, if necessary, check **Header Row, First Column**, and **Banded Rows**. Remove any other checkmarks.

22. **Save** and **close** the file.

Item	Quantity	Cost	Description
Oil Pump	20	$78.20	Lubricates the engine by pumping motor oil.
Oil Filter	20	4.95	Cleans the oil as it circulates through the engine.
Battery	10	45.00	Provides electric current to start the engine.
Starter	10	150.00	Receives energy from the battery, and turns the crankshaft to start the engine.
Muffler	30	79.00	Muffles the sound produced by the engine.
Radiator	5	230.00	Holds and cools the antifreeze.
Total	95	$ 587.15	

REINFORCE YOUR SKILLS 5.3
Insert Fields in a Form

In this exercise, you will create an electronic discount voucher form that fits on a postcard. This provides for an easy mailing campaign.

Set Up the Margins and Paper Size

1. Start a **new** document.

2. Choose **Page Layout→Page Setup→Orientation** from the Ribbon, and then choose **Landscape** from the menu.

3. Choose **Page Layout→Page Setup→Margins** from the Ribbon, and then choose **Narrow** from the gallery to apply 0.5 margins.

4. Choose **Page Layout→Page Setup→Size** from the Ribbon, and choose **More Paper Sizes** at the bottom of the gallery.

5. In the Paper tab, set the page width to **5"** and the height to **3"**, and then click **OK** to close the dialog box.

6. Choose **Home→Paragraph→Line and Paragraph Spacing** from the Ribbon, set the line spacing to **1.0**, and remove the after-paragraph spacing.

7. Type **TrainRight Discount Voucher** and **tap** Enter .

Add a Table

8. Choose **Insert→Tables→Table** ⊞ from the Ribbon, and insert a **two-column, two-row** table.

9. **Click** below the table, and type **Return card by August 15 to receive discount credit!**

10. Choose **Home→Paragraph→Center** ≣ from the Ribbon to center the line below the table.

11. Select the **title** on the first line, format the text as **Calibri 12 pt bold**, and apply the text **color** of your choice.

12. Choose **Home→Paragraph→Center** ≣ from the Ribbon to center the heading.

Insert Text and Fields

13. Select the table, and choose **Home→Paragraph** from the Ribbon.

14. Click the **dialog box launcher** in the bottom-right corner of the Paragraph group.
    The Paragraph dialog box appears.

15. In the **Spacing** portion of the Indents and Spacing tab, replace the 0 with a **3** in the Before spacing box, and click **OK**.
    This will create a little extra space between paragraphs as you enter text and fields in the table.

16. Select the **entire table**, if necessary, and set the font size to **9 pt**.

17. Set a left tab stop at the ¼ **mark** on the ruler in the first cell.

18. **Type** text and insert **legacy form fields** in the table cells, as shown in the following illustration. The fields in the first table cell are checkbox fields. Use ⌈Ctrl⌉+⌈Tab⌉ after each checkbox and then type the entry. The Credit Card Type field is a drop-down list field. All fields in the right column of the table are text fields. Use two spaces between labels and form fields except for the checkboxes.

19. **Save** 🖫 the file as **rs-Voucher** in the Lesson 05 folder, and leave it **open** for the next exercise.
    The form looks ready for use, but it won't be until you protect it in the next exercise.

Set Properties for Form Fields

In this exercise, you will set the field properties for the form fields you inserted in the previous exercise. You will also format the table and protect the form.

Before you begin: Be sure to complete Reinforce Your Skills 5.3. The rs-Voucher document should be open.

Set Field Properties

1. **Double-click** the Credit Card Type field.
   The Drop-Down Form Options dialog box opens.

2. Add the following items to create the drop-down list and then click **OK**: `Visa`, `Mastercard`, `Discover`, and `American Express`.

3. **Double-click** the State field, set the maximum length to **2**, and set the text format to **Uppercase**.

4. Set the maximum length of the **Zip** field to **10**.

Format the Table

5. Reduce the width of the first column by approximately $1/2$ **inch** by dragging the border between the two columns.

6. Select the entire table, and **remove all borders**.

Protect and Save the Form

7. Choose **Developer→Protect→Restrict Editing** ![icon] from the Ribbon.

8. Follow these steps to protect the form:

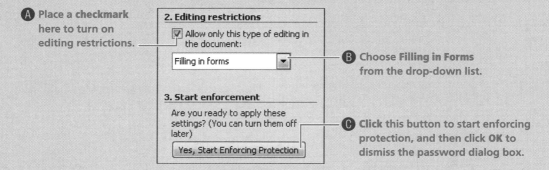

A Place a checkmark here to turn on editing restrictions.

2. Editing restrictions
☑ Allow only this type of editing in the document:
| Filling in forms ▼ |

B Choose **Filling in Forms** from the drop-down list.

3. Start enforcement
Are you ready to apply these settings? (You can turn them off later)
| Yes, Start Enforcing Protection |

C Click this button to start enforcing protection, and then click **OK** to dismiss the password dialog box.

Use the Form

Now that you've protected it, the form is ready for use.

9. Complete the form, as shown in the following illustration.

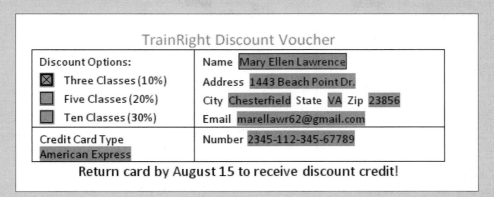

10. Click the **File** tab and choose **Save As**, save the file as **rs-Final Voucher** in your Lesson 05 folder, and then **close** it.

Apply Your Skills

Create a Table with No Borders and Align Data

In this exercise, you will convert text to a table and format it to resemble the table at the end of the exercise.

1. **Open** the as-Word Versions document from the Lesson 05 folder.

2. Use these guidelines to create the following table:
   - **Convert** the text to a table separated by tabs.
   - **Remove all borders** from the table, then **center-align** all of the entries.
   - Apply a **table style** of your choice.
   - **Bold** the first row and apply a **shading** color of your choice.
   - If necessary, use the move handle to **center** the table horizontally on the page.

Company	Word Version	Contact
BPI	Word 2007	David Katz
Exxon	Word 2003	Maria Velasquez
City of Oakland	Word 2003	Michael Gunn
Centron	Word 2007	Ralph Watson
Constructo	Word 2002	Ben Johnson

3. **Save** and **close** the file.

Create Formulas and Format a Table

In this exercise, you will format a table, align data, merge cells, and enter a formula.

1. Follow these guidelines to format the table shown at the end of this exercise.
   - **Open** the as-Order Tracking document from the Lesson 05 folder.
   - Adjust all columns to their **best fit**.
   - **Merge** the cells in the first row.
   - Type **Total Orders** in the first cell of the last row, and place a **formula** in the last cell of the last row to **total** the numbers in the last column.
   - **Align** the data as shown in the example.
   - **Center-align** the table on the page using the **move handle**.

Order Tracking Sheet				
Customer ID	Order Status	Item #	In Stock?	Order Total
233	I	S230	Y	$23.45
234	S	A321	Y	$45.87
341	S	A423	Y	$100.91
567	I	S345	N	$43.23
879	H	D567	N	$78.92
Total Orders				$ 292.38

2. **Save** and **close** the file.

Create an Electronic Form

In this exercise, you will create an electronic form that includes text fields, checkboxes, and drop-down lists.

1. If necessary, start a **new** document.

2. Set the page orientation to **Landscape**, the paper width to **7 inches**, the paper height to **5 inches**, and all four margins to **0.75 inch**.

3. Insert a table with **two columns** and **eight rows**.

4. Set the top and bottom cell margins to **0.05"**.

5. Use these guidelines to set up the form shown at the end of this exercise:

   - Set **tabs** at suitable locations for the social security number, driver's license number, and the three investment objectives.

   - Enter the items in the **table rows** as shown, using appropriate spacing between labels and fields.

   - Insert **legacy form fields** as shown. The Investment Experience and Risk Tolerance fields should use drop-down lists. Use the list entries **Little**, **Moderate**, and **Extensive** for the Investment Experience list. Use the list entries **Conservative**, **Moderate**, and **Aggressive** for the Risk Tolerance list. Use the Date Picker content control for the Date field. All other fields are either text fields or checkbox fields.

   - Set the maximum field length of the State field to **2** (formatted as Uppercase), the Zip field to **10**, the Social Security Number field to **11**, and the Driver's License Number field to **8**.

   - Format the Annual Income and Net Worth fields with a **Number** type and a **Currency** number format.

   - Choose **Design→Table Styles** from the Ribbon; apply the **table style** of your choice from the Table Styles gallery.

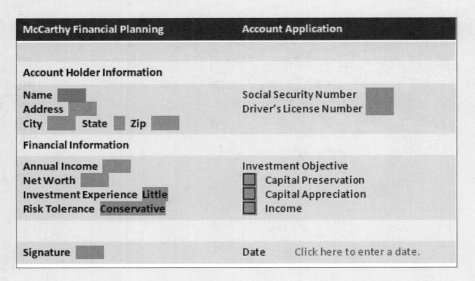

6. **Protect** the form without using a password.

7. **Save** the form as **as-McCarthy** in the Lesson 05 folder.

Critical Thinking & Work-Readiness Skills

In the course of working through the following Microsoft Office-based Critical Thinking exercises, you will also be utilizing various work-readiness skills, some of which are listed next to each exercise. Go to labyrinthelab.com/ workreadiness *to learn more about the work-readiness skills.*

5.1 Create a Product Comparison Matrix

WORK-READINESS SKILLS APPLIED

- Serving clients/ customers
- Solving problems
- Thinking creatively

Bethanie has been asked to create a product comparison matrix highlighting the differences between My Virtual Campus and their leading competitor, University LAN (U-LAN). Open a new document. Start with a 3×3 table (add rows as needed). Type **My Virtual Campus** and **U-LAN** as the headings for each of the last two columns. Create a list of features (make them up) down the first column and indicate with a **yes** or **no** if My Virtual Campus or U-LAN includes that feature. For example, you may indicate that My Virtual Campus supports video chat while U-LAN does not. Format the table as you see fit to make it attractive yet easy to read. Save the file to your Lesson 05 folder as **ct-Product Matrix**.

5.2 Create a Form

WORK-READINESS SKILLS APPLIED

- Serving clients/ customers
- Thinking creatively
- Participating as a member of a team

Bethanie has been asked to create a customer survey form. If applicable, work with a partner to brainstorm a list of questions to ask, such as name, email address, college, date, favorite My Virtual Campus feature, etc. Create a table to help lay out your questions and then create the form fields that will allow users to easily answer the questions. At a minimum, use plain text, a drop-down list, the date picker, and checkbox controls. Use other controls as necessary. Format the table and form so it is easy to use. Save the file to your Lesson 05 folder as **ct-Survey Form**.

5.3 Modify a Form

WORK-READINESS SKILLS APPLIED

- Participating as a member of a team
- Thinking creatively
- Exercising leadership

Start with the ct-Survey Form you created in the previous exercise. Insert a new top row, merge the cells, and type a title for the form. Save the form to your Lesson 05 folder with the new name **ct-Form Final**. Exchange forms with a partner and test each others' forms. Offer constructive suggestions for improvement. Based on your partner's feedback, modify your form. Rearrange the form fields, change the formatting, add or remove a question, etc. Save your changes.

Creating a Newsletter

LEARNING OBJECTIVES

After studying this lesson, you will be able to:

- Insert section breaks in documents
- Use WordArt and clip art
- Create and manipulate newsletter-style columns
- Use building blocks
- Apply themes
- Insert pictures from files
- Edit pictures

In this lesson, you will use Word's Columns feature to create a newsletter. WordArt and clip art will add eye-appeal to the newsletter. You will also have an opportunity to work with Word's Building Blocks and Themes, which make creating professional-looking documents fast and easy. You will also work with basic picture-editing tools to add special touches to your graphics.

Creating a Client Newsletter

Welcome to Green Clean, a janitorial product supplier and cleaning service contractor to small businesses, shopping plazas, and office buildings. Green Clean uses environmentally friendly cleaning products and incorporates sustainability practices wherever possible, including efficient energy and water use, recycling and waste reduction, and reduced petroleum use in vehicles. In addition to providing green cleaning services, the company also sells its eco-friendly product directly to customers.

Jenna Mann is an administrative assistant for the Green Clean company. It is nearing the beginning of a new quarter, and Jenna is setting up the quarterly newsletter that will go to clients to keep them up to date on the happenings at Green Clean. Jenna will add pizzazz to the two-column newsletter by inserting WordArt and clip art images and using the Themes gallery to add color and other visual interest.

These are examples of WordArt and clip art.

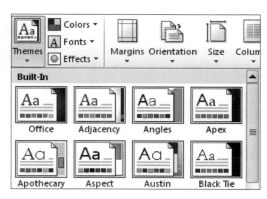

The Word Themes gallery provides a quick way to change a color scheme.

6.1 Working with Section Breaks

Video Lesson   labyrinthelab.com/videos

In Word, whenever you make a page-formatting change that doesn't apply to the whole document, you need one or more section breaks to define the portion of the document affected by the change. Changing margins is an example. If you have 1-inch margins in your document and you want a portion of the document to have 1.5-inch margins, you need one or more section breaks to separate that portion of the document. Otherwise, when you change the margins, they change for the entire document.

Inserting Section Breaks

You use Page Layout→Page Setup→Breaks ▤ to insert section breaks. There are four types of section breaks.

QUICK REFERENCE	WORKING WITH SECTION BREAKS
Type of Section Break	**Purpose**
Next Page	Inserts a section break and starts the new section on the next page
Continuous	Inserts a section break and starts the new section on the same page
Odd Page	Inserts a section break and starts the new section on the next odd numbered page; Word may feed a blank page to force the odd page section break
Even Page	Inserts a section break and starts the new section on the next even numbered page; Word may feed a blank page to force the even page section break

The example in this lesson is a columnar newsletter. The titles at the top of the document will be typed between the margins, which Word considers as just one column. Then the actual newsletter will be in two columns. This results in two separate sections. You display section numbers on the status bar by choosing Section from the pop-up menu when you right-click on the status bar.

The illustration on the next page shows the use of continuous section breaks that are sectioning off the two-column portion of a document.

Deleting Section Breaks

When you have the formatting marks turned on, a break is easily identified. Deleting a section break is as simple as clicking on it and tapping the [Delete] key. When you delete a section break, the section above the break takes on the same formatting as the section below the break.

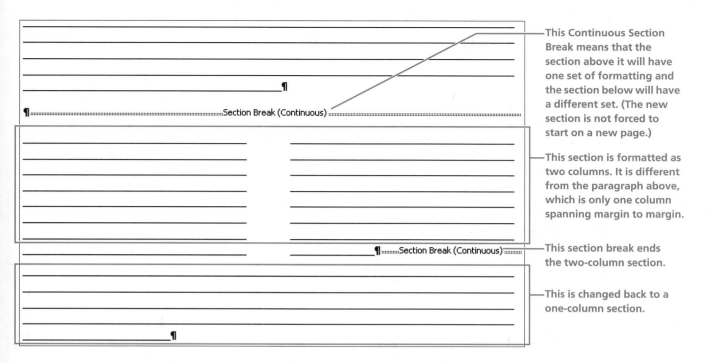

This Continuous Section Break means that the section above it will have one set of formatting and the section below will have a different set. (The new section is not forced to start on a new page.)

This section is formatted as two columns. It is different from the paragraph above, which is only one column spanning margin to margin.

This section break ends the two-column section.

This is changed back to a one-column section.

Insert a Section Break

In this exercise, you will begin developing a newsletter by inserting three title lines and a section break.

1. If necessary, start a **new** blank document, and then make sure the Word window is **maximized**.

2. If necessary, choose **Home→Paragraph→Show/Hide** ¶ from the Ribbon to display formatting marks.
   You need to display formatting marks in order to see a section break.

3. Type **Quarterly Newsletter** and **tap** [Enter].

4. **Type** the following heading lines:

5. **Tap** [Enter] three times, then **right-click** the status bar and choose **Section** from the pop-up menu to display the section numbers on the status bar.

Insert a Continuous Section Break

6. Choose **Page Layout→Page Setup→Breaks** 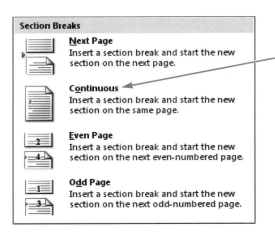 from the Ribbon, and then choose **Continuous** from the menu.

Now you can use different page formatting above and below the break.

Delete a Section Break

7. Position the **insertion point** on the Section Break and **tap** Delete.

8. Click **Undo** from the Quick Access toolbar to place the Section Break back into the document.

9. **Save** the file as **Green Clean Newsletter** in the Lesson 06 folder, and leave it **open** for the next exercise.

6.2 Using WordArt

Video Lesson   labyrinthelab.com/videos

Word provides a great tool, called WordArt, for creating smart-looking text objects. You can use the built-in designs as they are, or you can customize them.

Inserting WordArt

The Insert→Text→WordArt command reveals the WordArt gallery. Once you choose a style from the gallery, you can format and resize it. The following illustration displays the WordArt gallery.

Wrapping Text Around Objects

You edit and format WordArt objects using the WordArt Tools located on the Format contextual tab. Included in the formatting options is Text Wrapping, which controls the relationship of the text surrounding an object, such as a

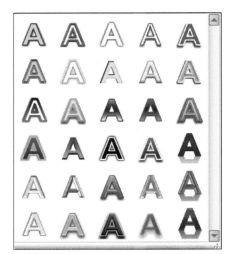

The WordArt gallery contains numerous styles with various preset colors.

WordArt object. Among the wrapping options are having the object move along with the text around it, using the In Line with Text option, or having the text stay in place by selecting the In Front of Text option, where you drag the object anywhere on the page.

The terms *object* and *image* are both used when referring to graphical elements such as WordArt, clip art, and pictures.

Notice the Drawing Tools→Format contextual tab that appears when a WordArt object is selected. It contains a wide variety of tools you can use to format a WordArt object.

The WordArt object has a series of circles and squares (selection handles) surrounding it that indicates the object is selected for your next command. The handles are used to resize the object.

A WordArt object must be selected to make the Format contextual tab visible.

Sizing WordArt

The small circles that surround an object when it's selected (selection handles) are also known as sizing handles. There is also a rotating handle. It is the small green circle at the top of the object. You can drag the rotate handle left or right to rotate the object.

You will also notice this rotating handle on other objects that you insert, such as clip art and shapes.

When you position the mouse pointer on a sizing handle, the pointer changes to a double-headed white arrow, which you can drag to increase or decrease the size of the object. Sizing from a corner handle changes the length and width relative to their original proportions.

The mouse pointer as it appears on a WordArt sizing handle

Insert and Edit a WordArt Object

In this exercise, you will use the newsletter title as the WordArt object. You will then wrap text around the WordArt object, change the background color, and add a text effect.

1. Select *Quarterly Newsletter* in the first line of the document, but do **not** select the paragraph mark at the end of the line.

2. Choose **Insert→Text→WordArt** 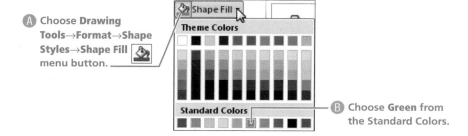 from the Ribbon, and then choose **Fill - Olive Green, Accent 3, Powder Bevel**.

   Notice the text is wrapped around the object. In this case, you do not want the text wrapped around; you want it on its own line. You will fix this problem next.

3. Make sure the object is still selected.

4. Choose **Drawing Tools→Format→Arrange→Wrap Text** from the Ribbon.

5. Choose **In Line with Text** from the drop-down list.

Format the WordArt Object

First, you will change the WordArt fill color.

6. If necessary, select the **WordArt** object.

7. Follow these steps to change the WordArt object background color:

A Choose **Drawing Tools→Format→Shape Styles→Shape Fill** menu button.

B Choose **Green** from the Standard Colors.

8. Choose **Format→WordArt Styles→** $\boxed{\underline{A}\ \text{Text Fill}\ \blacktriangledown}$ menu from the Ribbon.

9. Choose **White, Background 1** from the Theme Colors group.

   Now you will add a text effect to the WordArt.

10. Choose **Format→WordArt Styles→Text Effects** 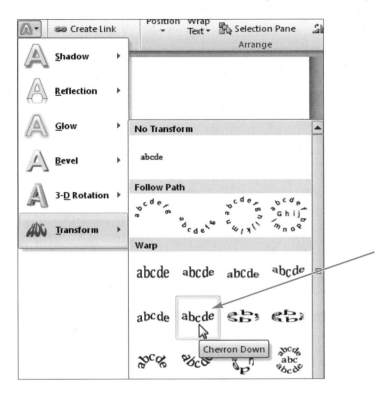 from the Ribbon, and then choose the **second effect** in the **second row** (Chevron Down) of the Transform group.

Format the Headings

Finally, you will center the headings and format the Green Clean heading.

11. Position the **insertion point** in the left margin area next to the WordArt object, then **click and drag down** to select it plus the other two headings.

12. Choose **Home→Paragraph→Center** from the Ribbon.

13. Format *Green Clean* with the **Cambria, Bold, 18 pt** font.

14. Compare your document headings with the illustration at the end of the exercise.

15. **Save** your document and leave it **open** for the next exercise.

6.3 Using Clip Art

Video Lesson labyrinthelab.com/videos

Word 2010 includes a clip art collection installed on your hard drive. Even more clip art items are available online. Once you insert an image, you can change its size, degree of rotation, or location on the page.

Finding Clip Art

You insert clip art by choosing Insert→Illustrations→Clip Art from the Ribbon. When you do so, Word displays the Clip Art task pane, where you can search for images by entering keywords. When you search for a keyword, the task pane displays thumbnails of all images located by your search. You can expand the search to include images on Office.com.

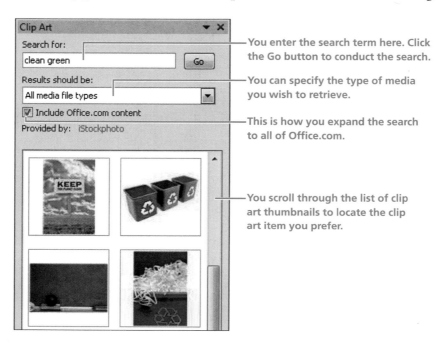

You enter the search term here. Click the Go button to conduct the search.

You can specify the type of media you wish to retrieve.

This is how you expand the search to all of Office.com.

You scroll through the list of clip art thumbnails to locate the clip art item you prefer.

Media Types

There are four media types to choose from:

- Illustrations—images drawn by graphic artists
- Photographs—photographic images
- Videos—simple animated pictures or brief video clips
- Audio—sound effects, such as the noise made by a car horn

Organizing Clip Art

The Clip Organizer is a special place to save your favorite images. It is found in the Microsoft Office Tools folder in Microsoft Office on the Start menu. You can copy and then paste the images directly into the Favorites collection in the Clip Organizer or use the File command in the Clip Organizer to pick and choose images you have saved on your computer. You can also create your own collection in the organizer to keep yourself more organized as you save more and more images.

QUICK REFERENCE	USING THE CLIP ORGANIZER
Task	**Procedure**
Open the Clip Organizer	■ Click the Start button. ■ Choose All Programs→Microsoft Office→Microsoft Office 2010 Tools from the menu. ■ Choose Microsoft Clip Organizer.
Copy a file into the Clip Organizer	■ Open the Clip Organizer. ■ Select the image in the document you will to place in the organizer. ■ Tap Ctrl+C. ■ Switch to the open Clip Organizer window. ■ Click the desired collection where to save the image. ■ Click Edit→Paste from the menu.
Add an image from within the Clip Organizer	■ Open the Clip Organizer. ■ Click on the collection (folder) in the left pane where you want to store the image. ■ Click File→Add Clips to Organizer from the menu. ■ Choose One of My Own. ■ Navigate to the file storage location. ■ Click the desired image to add to the organizer. ■ Click the Add button.

Sizing and Rotating Clip Art

Like WordArt, clip art has the sizing handles to rotate objects. As in WordArt, if you place the mouse pointer on a sizing handle, it changes to a double-headed white arrow, which you can drag to resize the object. You also can use the green circle rotate handle at the top of the selected image to rotate it.

The mouse pointer as it appears on a clip art sizing handle

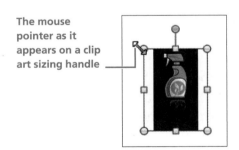

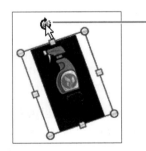

The mouse pointer as it appears on the clip art rotate handle

Moving Clip Art

When you insert clip art, it is positioned in line with text. This means you can use the left, right, or center alignment buttons in the Paragraph group on the Home tab of the Ribbon to reposition the image. However, if you want full control to move the clip art freely, you must change the layout mode to in front of text, found on the Wrap Text drop-down menu in the Arrange group on the Ribbon. To

Four-headed arrow pointer shape to move a clip art or other object

move the object by dragging, you point to the object until the mouse pointer becomes the four-headed arrow, and then drag it to a new location.

WORKING WITH CLIP ART

Task	Procedure
Insert clip art	Choose Insert→Illustrations→Clip Art 🔲 from the Ribbon.
Size clip art	With the object selected, place the mouse pointer on a sizing handle. When the pointer changes to a double-headed arrow, drag to resize the object.
Rotate clip art	With the object selected, place the mouse pointer on the green rotate handle. When the pointer changes to a circular arrow, drag right or left to rotate the object.

DEVELOP YOUR SKILLS 6.3.1
Insert and Resize Clip Art

In this exercise, you will search for a piece of clip art online and place it in your document. You will then resize the clip art image by using the Layout dialog box and by dragging a sizing handle. Finally, you will practice moving an object.

1. Click the **insertion point** next to the paragraph symbol below the Current Quarter heading.
   This is where you'll place your clip art image.

2. Choose **Insert→Illustrations→Clip Art** 🔲 from the Ribbon to display the Clip Art task pane.

3. Follow these steps to search for a piece of Clip Art:

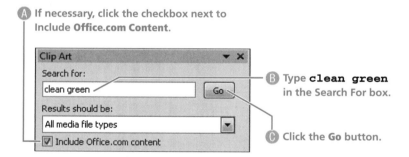

Ⓐ If necessary, click the checkbox next to Include **Office.com Content**.

Ⓑ Type **clean green** in the Search For box.

Ⓒ Click the **Go** button.

4. When the list of search results appears, **scroll** to locate the following clip art image. If this particular image is not available, choose a different image, preferably one that's appropriate for a newsletter from a "green" company.

5. Click directly on the **thumbnail image** to insert it in the document.
   The image could be very large or very small when you first insert it. This is due to how the original artwork was created. Most of the time, you will need to resize a clip art image once you have inserted it, just as you do here. You will resize it in the next section of this exercise.

6. Click the **Close** ✖ button in the upper-right corner of the Clip Art task pane.

7. If necessary, click the **View Ruler** 🗔 button at the top of the vertical scroll bar to turn on the ruler.

Use the Layout Dialog Box to Resize an Image

8. Be sure the **image** is selected.

9. Choose **Picture Tools→Format→Size→dialog box launcher** 🔲 to open the Layout dialog box.

10. Follow these steps to resize the clip art image:

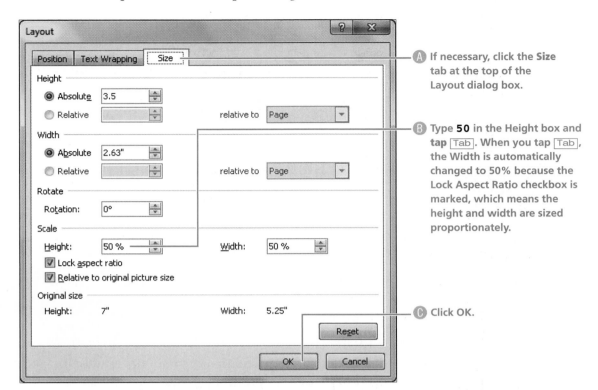

(A) If necessary, click the **Size** tab at the top of the Layout dialog box.

(B) Type **50** in the Height box and tap Tab. When you tap Tab, the Width is automatically changed to 50% because the Lock Aspect Ratio checkbox is marked, which means the height and width are sized proportionately.

(C) Click OK.

You can also use the spinner controls to change the height, which in turn automatically changes the width.

Resize an Image with a Sizing Handle

11. Follow these steps to resize the image to about 1 inch wide:

(A) Position the **mouse pointer** on the sizing handle in the **upper-left corner** of the image. The pointer changes to a double-headed white arrow. (Note: Your double-headed arrow may appear black instead of white.)

(B) **Press and hold the mouse button down,** and **drag diagonally** toward the center of the image. You will see a shadow of the image as you drag it to its new size.

(C) You can judge the size by watching the ruler at the top of the window; when the image is just about **1 inch wide,** release the mouse button.

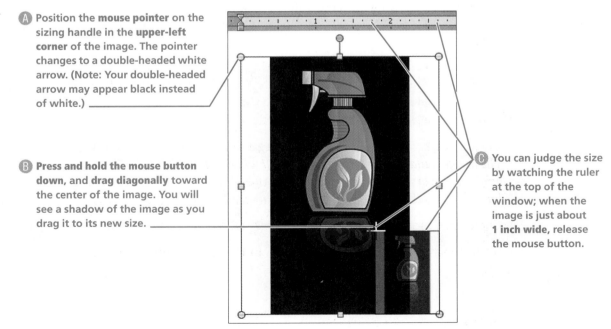

When you resize using a corner sizing handle, the image retains its width-to-height ratio.

Move the Clip Art Image

12. Choose **Format→Arrange→Wrap Text** ![wrap text icon] from the Ribbon.

13. Choose **In Front of Text** from the drop-down menu.

14. **Drag** the image to the center, and then **release** the mouse button.

15. **Undo** ![undo icon] twice to move the image back to the left margin and change the text wrapping to In Line with Text.

16. Choose **Home→Paragraph→Center** ![center icon] to center the image on the page.

 If you used a clip art image other than the one shown above, size it so it's about two inches tall.

17. **Save** ![save icon] the file, and leave it **open** for the next exercise.

6.4 Working with Picture Styles

Video Lesson   labyrinthelab.com/videos

Using the Picture Styles is a quick way to enhance your images by adding borders, shadows, and directionality. There are many options from which to choose using the Picture Style gallery on the Format tab of the Picture Tools on the Ribbon. Picture Styles also include options to change border color, add special effects, and change the layout of an image. The Format tab is activated when a picture is selected.

Applying a Style

You can scroll through the selections in the gallery in the Picture Styles group, or click the More button to see the complete gallery. When you hover the mouse pointer over a style in the gallery, the image previews the new style; if you like it, simply click to apply the new Picture Style to the image.

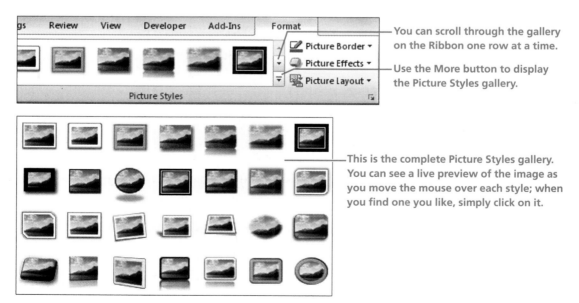

You can scroll through the gallery on the Ribbon one row at a time.

Use the More button to display the Picture Styles gallery.

This is the complete Picture Styles gallery. You can see a live preview of the image as you move the mouse over each style; when you find one you like, simply click on it.

Changing the Border Color on a Picture

The Picture Border colors are displayed by choosing Format→Picture Styles→Picture Border from the Ribbon. The Picture Tools tab is activated when an image is selected. You can choose a color from the Theme Colors group, which provides many shades of related colors, or from the Standard Colors group.

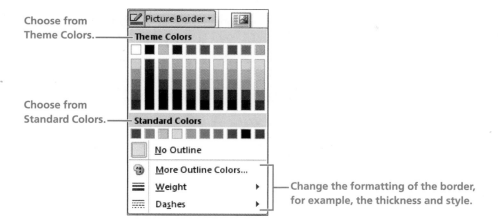

Choose from Theme Colors.

Choose from Standard Colors.

Change the formatting of the border, for example, the thickness and style.

Setting a Transparent Color

Pictures are made up of tiny pixels of many different colors. That is what causes shade variation in the graphic. When you click on a color in the object to make it transparent, all pixels of that same color are also made transparent. The mouse shape changes to a pen when you choose Set Transparent Color from the Colors drop-down menu in the Adjust group on the Ribbon.

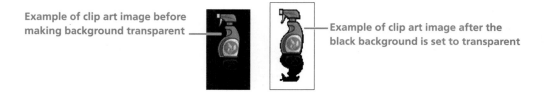

Example of clip art image before making background transparent

Example of clip art image after the black background is set to transparent

Applying an Artistic Effect

You can take your picture styling to the next level using special artistic effects. When an image is selected, a gallery of available artistic effects is found in the Adjust group on the Format tab under Picture Tools on the Ribbon. Some of the artistic effects include a pencil sketch, line drawing, a texturizer, and so forth.

QUICK REFERENCE	WORKING WITH PICTURE STYLES
Task	**Procedure**
Apply a style to clip art	▪ Select the object, and then choose Format→Picture Styles from the Ribbon. ▪ Click the desired style to apply it to the clip art.

Task	Procedure
Change the border color on a picture	■ Select the object, and then choose Format→Picture Styles→Picture Border from the Ribbon. ■ Click the desired Theme or Standard color to apply it to the picture.
Set a transparent color	■ Select the object, choose Format→Adjust→Color from the Ribbon, and then choose Set Transparent Color from the drop-down menu. ■ Click on the color on the image to make it transparent.
Apply an artistic effect	■ Select the object and choose Format→Adjust→Artistic Effects. ■ Choose the desired effect from the gallery.

DEVELOP YOUR SKILLS 6.4.1
Format Pictures with Style

In this exercise, you will remove the black background from the image, add an oval frame around the clip art, and change the frame color to blue.

Set a Transparent Color

1. If necessary, select the **clip art image**.

2. Choose **Format→Adjust→Color** from the Ribbon.

3. Choose **Set Transparent Color** from the drop-down menu.
   Notice when you move the mouse pointer onto the document, it appears as a pen.

4. Click in the **black area** on the clip art image.
   The background around the image should now be white, and all you see is a green bottle and its shadow.

Add an Oval Frame Picture Style

5. If necessary, select the **clip art object**.

6. Follow these steps to apply a new style to the image:

Ⓐ Choose **Picture Tools→Format→Picture Styles** and then **scroll down** to the second row.

Ⓑ Click the **Beveled Oval, Black Picture Style** from the gallery.

Format the Border Color and Weight

7. Be sure the **object** is still selected.

8. Choose **Format→Picture Styles→Picture Border** from the Ribbon.

9. Follow these steps to change the border to a wide blue one:

Ⓐ Select the **Blue** color from the Standard Colors gallery.

Ⓑ Display the **Picture Border** drop-down menu again and choose **Weight** from the list to display the weight options.

Ⓒ Choose the **3 pt** thickness to apply to the **oval border**.

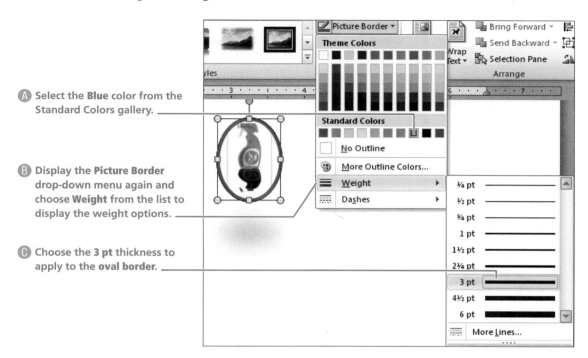

10. **Save** 🖫 the file; leave it **open** for the next exercise.

6.5 Performing Basic Picture Editing

Video Lesson labyrinthelab.com/videos

You can perform basic picture editing tasks with Word. For example, you can crop out parts of a picture. You can also rotate the image, adjust its brightness and contrast, and change its size without using a specialized image-editing program, such as Adobe Photoshop. If you aren't satisfied with the altered image, you can always reset the picture to its original form. If you want to perform more extensive editing to the image, you will need to use a special graphics program designed for that purpose, and then insert the finished image into Word.

Inserting a Picture from a File

In addition to being able to access photographs via the Clip Art task pane, you can also insert pictures directly from files. For example, you can insert a picture taken with a digital camera and stored on your computer or a graphic element copied from another source and saved on your computer.

Inserting a Screenshot

A screenshot is a picture of a complete or a portion of a screen. It can be a picture of the Windows Desktop, another Word file, or any other program window. For a shot of only a portion of the screen, you use Screen Clipping from the drop-down menu of the Screenshot command in the Illustrations group of the Insert tab. For a shot of a whole screen, you use the Screenshot command in the Illustrations group.

Insert a Picture from a File

In this exercise, you will insert a picture and display the Picture Tools Format tab.

1. If necessary, select the **clip art object** you placed in the document and **tap** ⬚Delete.

2. Choose **Insert→Illustrations→Picture** 🖼 from the Ribbon.

3. Navigate to the Lesson 06 folder, and **double-click** the GreenClean picture file to insert it.

4. Take a moment to practice with the picture's sizing handles and Rotate handle. After practicing, **rotate** and **resize** the image to its approximate original size and position. *Notice that when the picture is selected (handles visible), the contextual Format tab appears on the Ribbon. If you click away from the image, the contextual tab disappears.*

5. Click in the **document** to hide the contextual Format tab.

6. **Double-click** the image to display the Format tab in the foreground.

7. Leave the file **open** for the next topic.

Adjusting Brightness and Contrast

Video Lesson labyrinthelab.com/videos

The brightness and contrast settings adjust how the picture appears on the screen and in print. You can use just one of these controls or both simultaneously. The Brightness and Contrast gallery is found on the Corrections drop-down menu in the Adjust group on the Ribbon. For more customized control, you can right-click the image and choose Format Picture to open the Format Picture dialog box.

- **Brightness**—This setting controls how bright each element in the picture looks. Turning up the brightness makes each element appear closer to white. Turning down the brightness makes each element appear closer to black.

- **Contrast**—This setting controls the difference between the darkest and lightest elements of the picture. A high-contrast image has elements that appear very white and very dark. A low-contrast image has elements that appear to have similar shades.

The original image

The same image with a -20% brightness and normal contrast setting

Cropping Pictures

Cropping allows you to hide parts of a picture. Choosing the Crop tool from Picture Tools→Format→Size places crop handles around the object. You drag a handle to hide the unwanted portion of the picture. You can also uncrop a picture, if necessary. As you are cropping a picture, the part you drag over to crop out appears in a gray shadow until you click in the document; then the picture appears with only the part that you did not crop.

Cropping a picture in Word does not affect the original picture in any way. The area hidden by cropping is not deleted.

The image, displaying crop handles before cropping

The image after cropping with Crop handles visible

QUICK REFERENCE	WORKING WITH BASIC PICTURE EDITING TASKS
Task	**Procedure**
Insert a picture from a file	▪ Position the insertion point where you want the picture to appear. ▪ Choose Insert→Illustrations→Picture from the Ribbon. ▪ Navigate to the desired picture, select it, and click the Insert button.
Insert a screenshot of a whole window	▪ Have the program window you wish to capture open. ▪ Choose Insert→Illustrations→Screenshot. ▪ Choose the window to capture from the Available Windows menu.
Insert a partial screenshot of a window	▪ Have the program window you wish to capture open. ▪ Choose Insert→Illustrations→Screenshot menu button. ▪ Choose Screen Clipping from the drop-down menu. ▪ Choose the window to capture from the Available Windows menu. ▪ Use the mouse to draw a rectangle around the portion of the window you wish to capture.

Task	Procedure
Adjust brightness and contrast	■ Select the picture to be adjusted. ■ If necessary, click the contextual Format tab to bring it to the foreground. ■ Click Corrections in the Adjust group, and then choose the desired effect from the gallery.
Crop or uncrop a picture	■ Select the picture to be cropped. ■ If necessary, click the contextual Format tab to bring it to the foreground. ■ Click the Crop [icon] button in the Size group of the Format tab. ■ Place the mouse pointer on a handle on the picture, and drag to crop (or uncrop) the picture.
Undo picture adjustments	■ Select the picture that was modified. ■ If necessary, click the contextual Format tab to bring it to the foreground. ■ Click the Reset Picture [icon] button in the Adjust group.

Compressing a Picture

Pictures and other graphics are usually very large, which increases the overall size of your Word document. Options for reducing the size of your document include compressing the selected image or all images in the document. Once images are compressed, it frees up room on your hard drive, or speeds up the download process on a web page. You can also choose whether to delete the portions of graphics that were cropped, which in turn frees up more space.

File Types to Compress

There are only certain types of graphics that can be compressed. Photographs and other high-resolution images are good examples of files that can be optimized, meaning the file size is reduced; they include .jpg, .tif, .bmp, and .png, to name a few. Others, such as drawing types with extensions such as .wmf, .emf, and eps, cannot be compressed.

You can use a graphics-editing program, such as Adobe Photoshop, to resize drawing images, and then use the Insert→Picture command to bring them into your Word document already optimized.

Task	Procedure
Compress a picture	■ Double-click the picture to display the Format tab on the Ribbon. ■ Choose Format→Adjust→Compress Pictures to open the Compress Pictures dialog box. ■ Choose the desired compression options in the dialog box and click OK.

Edit a Picture

In this exercise, you will practice adjusting the brightness and contrast of a picture, and experiment with cropping and uncropping it.

1. Make sure the GreenClean picture is selected (handles are visible), and the contextual Format tab is in the foreground.

Preview Brightness Settings

2. Follow these steps to practice brightness adjustments:

Ⓐ Choose **Picture Tools→ Format→Adjust→Corrections button** to display the menu of options.

Ⓑ Hover the **mouse pointer** over the various settings, and Live Preview displays the brightness and contrast effects. Then **click** in the document to close the menu without making a change.

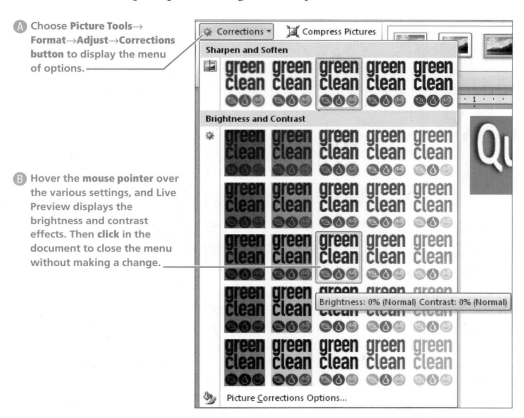

Crop the Image

3. Choose **Format→Size→Crop** from the Ribbon.

4. Follow these steps to crop the words *green clean* off the top of the image:

Ⓐ Notice the **cropping handles** that surround the image.

Ⓑ Move the **mouse pointer** to a corner handle, and notice that the pointer changes to a right angle.

Ⓒ Move the **mouse pointer** to the top-center cropping handle, and the pointer changes to a small upside-down T. **Click and drag down** until the words *green clean* are grayed out. Release the mouse button and click somewhere outside the picture.

Uncrop the Image

When you crop an image in Word, the original is untouched. This makes it easy to uncrop the image later.

5. Select the **image** and choose **Picture Tools→Format→Size→Crop**, then **drag** the top-center handle again and **drag** it up to uncrop the image.

6. Click **Undo** ↰ to crop the words out of the picture, and then click in the **document**. *Remember that cropped-out words are still part of the picture and, therefore, make the overall size of the file larger.*

Compress the Picture

Now you will delete the cropped-out portion of the picture to reduce the file size.

7. **Double-click** on the company logo to select it and display the **Picture Tools→Format** tab.

8. Choose **Format→Adjust→Compress Pictures** from the Ribbon.

9. Ensure there are **checkmarks** in the Apply Only to This Picture and Delete Cropped Areas of Pictures checkboxes; click **OK**.

10. **Save** 💾 the document and leave it **open** for the next exercise.

6.6 Working with Newsletter-Style Columns

Video Lesson   labyrinthelab.com/videos

You can use newsletter-style columns to arrange text in multiple columns. In a newsletter layout, text flows down one column and wraps to the top of the next column. Word automatically reformats column layout as you add or delete text.

Setting Up Columns

You choose Page Layout→Page Setup→Columns ▦ to quickly specify the number or layout of your columns. When you specify the number of columns for the selected text, all columns are of equal width.

Customizing Column Widths

You can choose the More Columns command from the Columns menu to display the Columns dialog box, where you can set up more sophisticated column layouts. For example, you can insert a line between columns and customize the width of each column.

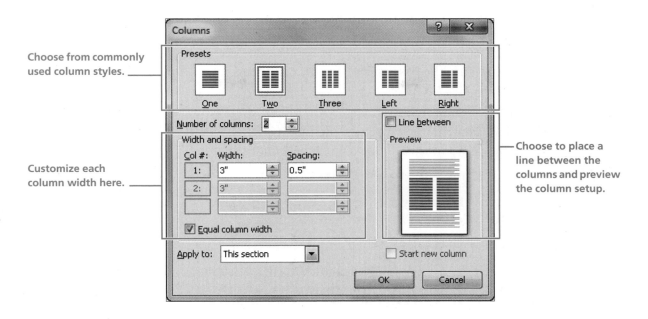

Choose from commonly used column styles.

Customize each column width here.

Choose to place a line between the columns and preview the column setup.

The appearance of the Columns button may vary based on your screen resolution.

DEVELOP YOUR SKILLS 6.6.1
Set Up Columns

In this exercise, you will open a document containing the content for your newsletter and copy it into the current document. Then you will format section two of your document with two columns, and finally you will insert a line between the columns.

1. **Open** the Newsletter Text file from the Lesson 06 folder.

2. **Tap** ⎡Ctrl⎤+⎡A⎤ to select the entire document.

3. **Press** ⎡Ctrl⎤+⎡C⎤ to copy the text of the document.

4. Switch back to the Green Clean Newsletter using the button on the **taskbar**.

5. Position the **insertion point** next to the paragraph mark under the section break.

6. **Tap** $\boxed{\text{Ctrl}}$ + $\boxed{\text{V}}$ to paste the newsletter text into your document.

7. Make sure the **insertion point** is in the second section of the document.

8. Choose **Page Layout→Page Setup→Columns** 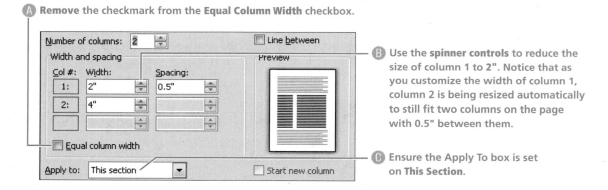 from the Ribbon, and then choose **Two** from the menu.
    The text of the newsletter is now arranged in two columns.

Add a Line Between Columns

9. Choose **Page Layout→Page Setup→Columns** from the Ribbon, and then choose **More Columns** from the menu to display the Columns dialog box.

10. Place a checkmark in the **Line Between** checkbox.

11. Click **OK** to insert the line and then click **Undo** to remove the line.

Customize Column Widths

12. Choose **Page Layout→Page Setup→Columns** from the Ribbon, and then choose **More Columns** from the menu to display the Columns dialog box.

13. Follow these steps to customize the column widths:

Ⓐ **Remove** the checkmark from the **Equal Column Width** checkbox.

Ⓑ Use the **spinner controls** to reduce the size of column 1 to 2". Notice that as you customize the width of column 1, column 2 is being resized automatically to still fit two columns on the page with 0.5" between them.

Ⓒ Ensure the Apply To box is set on **This Section**.

14. Click **OK**.
    The columns don't really look good this way, and while you could Undo 🔁 *at this point, if you changed your mind at a later time, there is still a very quick way to return the columns back to equal size.*

15. Choose **Page Layout→Page Setup→Columns** from the Ribbon, and then choose **More Columns** from the menu to display the Columns dialog box.

16. Click the checkbox next to **Equal Column Width**, and then click **OK**.

17. Scroll through the document to see how it looks.
    It looks like it would be a good idea to balance the columns on the second page. You will do that in the next topic.

18. **Close** the Newsletter Text file without saving, then **save** the Green Clean Newsletter file and leave it **open** for the next topic.

Working with Column Breaks

Video Lesson   labyrinthelab.com/videos

You can manually force a column to end by inserting a column break, thus moving text at the break point to the top of the next column. This technique is often used to place headings at the top of columns and to balance columns on the last page of a multicolumn document.

You insert column breaks by choosing Page Layout→Page Setup→Breaks ▤ from the Ribbon, and then choosing Column from the menu.

Column Breaks Compared to Section Breaks

You may recall that a section break designates the place in a document where some type of new page formatting begins. A column break gives you the ability to control the length of columns *within* a multicolumn section in a document.

QUICK REFERENCE	INSERTING COLUMN BREAKS
Task	**Procedure**
Insert a column break	■ Choose Page Layout→Page Setup→Breaks ▤ from the Ribbon. ■ Choose Column from the menu.

DEVELOP YOUR SKILLS 6.6.2
Insert and Remove a Column Break

In this exercise, you will balance your newsletter by inserting a manual column break.

1. Scroll to the bottom of **page 1**, and notice that the heading for the next paragraph is at the bottom of column 1.

2. Position the **insertion point** just in front of the *Wanting to Go Green, But Don't Know Where to Start?* heading.

3. Choose **Page Layout→Page Setup→Breaks** from the Ribbon, and then choose **Column** from the menu.
   This moves the Wanting to Go Green, But Don't Know Where to Start? *heading to the top of the next column.*

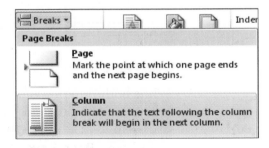

4. If necessary, choose **Home→Paragraph→Show/Hide** from the Ribbon to display the column break.

patronage·over·the·past·fifteen·years·and·look·
forward·to·servicing·you·for·many·years·to·
come.¶
·······························Column Break·······························

Delete the Column Break

5. Position the **insertion point** at the left end of the column break.

6. **Tap** ⎡Delete⎤ to remove the break.

7. Click **Undo** 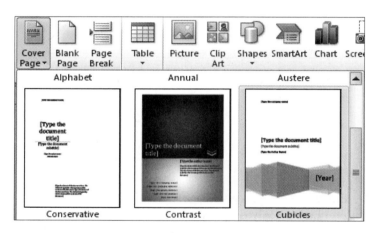 to reinstate the column break.

8. **Save** 🖫 your newsletter, and leave it **open** for the next topic.

6.7 Using Building Blocks

Video Lesson   labyrinthelab.com/videos

The Building Blocks feature allows you to insert pre-designed content into your documents, including cover pages, headers and footers, watermarks, equations, and blocks of text. You can choose from the many built-in Building Blocks, or you can transform your own frequently used content into custom Building Blocks. Building Blocks appear in various galleries throughout the Ribbon, such as cover pages and page numbers. You can modify existing Building Blocks, delete custom Building Blocks, and sort the list in various ways.

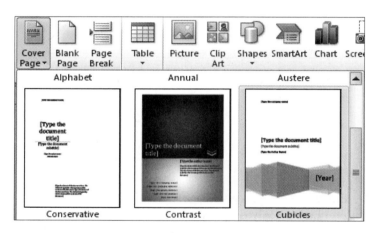

These predesigned cover pages in the Cover Page gallery are examples of Building Blocks.

Using Building Blocks Versus AutoCorrect

While both Building Blocks and AutoCorrect provide easy ways to insert often-used or large amounts of text or objects, the main difference between them is most noticeable in how you use them to insert something into a document. When you type an AutoCorrect name and tap ⎡Enter⎤, ⎡Tab⎤, or ⎡Spacebar⎤, or type a period or comma, the entry is automatically inserted into the document. However, typing a Building Block name requires you to perform another command to insert an entry. The following Quick Reference table explains the procedure for using either fabulous feature. Typically, though not always, Building Blocks are much larger entries, sometimes even a complete "boilerplate" document.

Task	Procedure
Insert an AutoCorrect entry	■ Type the AutoCorrect entry name. ■ Tap `Spacebar`, `Enter`, or `Tab`, or type a period or a comma.
Insert a Building Block	■ Type the Building Block name. ■ Tap the `F3` key. *or* ■ Choose Insert→Text→Quick Parts ▤ from the Ribbon, and then choose the entry from the list.
Insert a text box, header, footer, equation, or watermark Building Block using the Building Blocks Organizer	■ Choose Insert→Text→Quick Parts ▤ from the Ribbon, and then choose Building Blocks Organizer from the menu, select the name in the list, and click Insert.
Insert a cover page Building Block	■ Choose Insert→Pages→Cover Page ▤ from the Ribbon. ■ Choose the desired cover page from the gallery.

Use a Built-In Building Block

In this exercise, you will add a cover page Building Block to your newsletter.

1. Choose **Insert→Pages→Cover Page** ▤ from the Ribbon.

2. When the cover page gallery appears, scroll down and choose the **Cubicles** cover page style shown here.

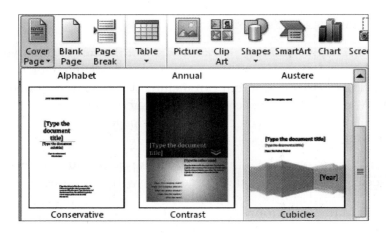

A cover page is attached to the beginning of the document.

Next you will type a title and subtitle, add a company logo for your cover page, and delete any unwanted objects from the cover page.

3. If necessary, click the **document title object**, as shown in the following illustration, and then type **Green Clean**.

4. Click the **document subtitle object** just below the title, and type **Environmentally Friendly Products and Practices**.

Delete Unwanted Objects

Now you will delete objects that you won't use on your cover page. There is an Author object just below the Subtitle object.

5. Click the object just **below** the subtitle object and you will see a tab labeled Author.

6. Click directly on the **Author** tab to select the object, as shown at right.

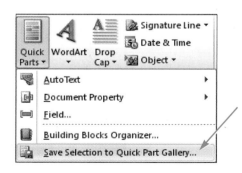

7. **Tap** the Delete key.

8. Choose **Home→Paragraph→Show/Hide** ¶ to turn off the formatting marks.

9. Use the same technique to delete the **Company** object in the upper-left corner of the page and the **Year** object in the bottom-right corner of the page.

10. **Save** 💾 the file, and leave it **open** for the next topic.

Creating Custom Building Blocks

Video Lesson   labyrinthelab.com/videos

You can create your own custom Building Blocks. You select the content that you want to convert to a Building Block, and then you choose the Save Selection to Quick Part Gallery command on the Quick Parts menu. Content can include a wide variety of items such as text, a clip art image, or a WordArt object. You can also assign a custom Building Block to another gallery on the Ribbon. For example, if you created a cover page specific to your company, it would make sense to assign it to the Cover Page gallery.

Inserting a Building Block from the Quick Parts Gallery

The Quick Parts gallery in the Text group on the Insert tab of the Ribbon provides a convenient location for your custom Building Blocks. Inserting an item you saved in the Quick Parts gallery is as simple as clicking on it in the gallery.

Modifying a Custom Building Block

There are two different types of modifications to Building Blocks: changing the properties or modifying the actual content and formatting. If you want to change the name, gallery, where to save it, and so forth, you do so in the Modify Building Block dialog box. However, if you want to modify the actual content, you make the desired changes, select the content, and save the selection with the same name. You will be asked if you want to redefine the existing entry.

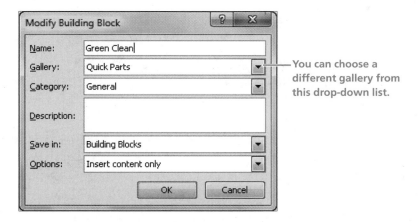

You can choose a different gallery from this drop-down list.

DEVELOP YOUR SKILLS 6.7.2

Create a Custom Building Block

In this exercise, you will type the contact information for the Green Clean company. You will then select it and save it to the Quick Parts gallery.

1. If necessary, choose **Home→Paragraph→Show/Hide** ¶ to turn on the formatting marks, and then **tap** Ctrl + End to place the insertion point at the end of the document.

2. Select the **first paragraph symbol** below the *Management Team and Strategy* paragraph. (If necessary, tap Enter to generate a paragraph symbol.)

3. Choose **Home→Paragraph→Line Spacing** from the Ribbon, and then choose **1.0** spacing.
   The menu closes.

4. Open the menu again, and choose **Remove Space After Paragraph**.

5. Choose **Home→Paragraph→Show/Hide** ¶ from the Ribbon to turn off formatting marks.

6. **Type** the following information:

   Green Clean
   719 Coronado Drive
   San Diego, CA 92102

7. Select the **three lines** that you just typed.

8. Choose **Insert→Text→Quick Parts** 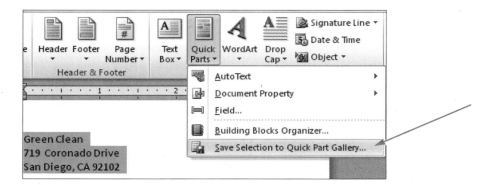 from the Ribbon, and then choose **Save Selection to Quick Part Gallery**, as shown here.

9. When the Create New Building Block dialog box appears, click **OK** to save the address information.

Insert the Custom Building Block

Now you will delete the address from the newsletter so you can test your new Building Block.

10. Make sure the address is still selected, and then **tap** Delete to remove it.

11. Choose **Insert→Text→Quick Parts**  from the Ribbon, and then click your new **Building Block** at the top of the menu to insert it in the document.

Modify Building Block Properties

12. Choose **Insert→Text→Quick Parts** from the Ribbon.

13. **Right-click** the Green Clean Building Block at the top of the list, and choose **Edit Properties** in the menu to open the Modify Building Block dialog box.

14. Follow these steps to change the name of the Building Block:

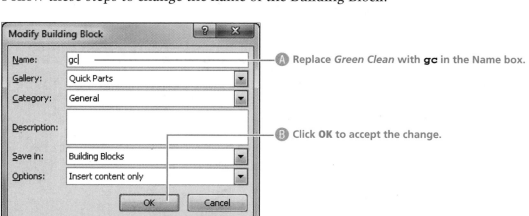

15. Click **Yes** in the message box asking if you want to redefine the entry.

16. Position the **insertion point** at the end of the street address, **tap** the ⌑Spacebar⌑, and type **Suite 200**.

17. **Double-click** on the zip code in the address in the document at the bottom of the page and type **92108**.

18. Select the **three-line** name and address.

19. Choose **Insert→Text→Quick Parts** 🗐 from the Ribbon, and then choose **Save Selection to Quick Parts Gallery**.

20. Type **gc** for the Building Block name and click **OK**.

21. Click **Yes** in the message box to redefine the entry.

22. If necessary, select the **three-line** name and address at the bottom of the column and **tap** ⌑Delete⌑.

23. **Save** 💾 your newsletter, and leave it **open** for the next exercise.

Sorting the Building Blocks List

Video Lesson   labyrinthelab.com/videos

When you open the Building Blocks Organizer, you can sort the list using any of the column headings. Click a heading to sort in Ascending order.

Deleting a Custom Building Block

You delete a Building Block through the Building Blocks Organizer. You can also insert a Building Block from within the Organizer and edit building block properties.

You can click any of the column headings to sort the list.

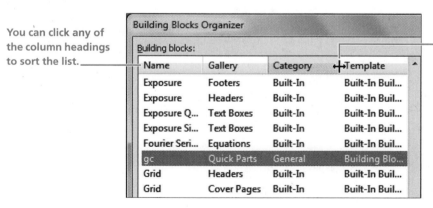

To modify a column width, place the mouse pointer on the border between two columns; the mouse pointer changes to a double-headed arrow. You can then press and hold the mouse button and drag to the left or right to narrow or widen the column.

Task	Procedure
Create a custom Building Block	■ Select the content you want to convert to a Building Block. ■ Choose Insert→Text→Quick Parts ▦ from the Ribbon. ■ Choose Save Selection to Quick Part Gallery from the menu. ■ Make any desired changes in the Create New Building Block dialog box.
Delete a custom Building Block	■ Open the gallery containing the Building Block to be deleted. ■ Right-click the custom Building Block. ■ Choose Organize and Delete from the pop-up menu. *The custom Building Block is highlighted in the Building Block Organizer.* ■ Click Delete.
Sort the Building Block List	■ Choose Insert→Text→Quick Parts ▦ from the Ribbon. ■ Choose Building Blocks Organizer from the menu. ■ Click any of the column headers to sort in Ascending order; click a second time to sort in Descending order.

DEVELOP YOUR SKILLS 6.7.3
Delete a Custom Building Block

In this exercise, you will practice sorting the Building Blocks list and then delete the Building Block you created in the preceding exercise.

1. Choose **Insert→Text→Quick Parts** ▦ from the Ribbon.

2. Follow these steps to begin the deletion:

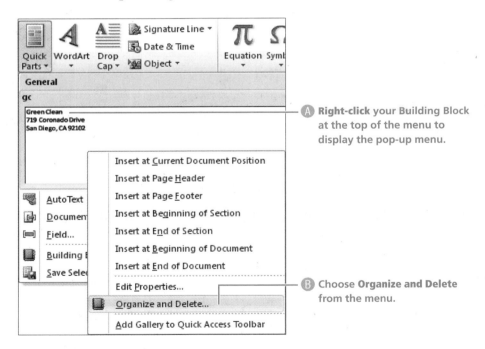

Ⓐ **Right-click** your Building Block at the top of the menu to display the pop-up menu.

Ⓑ Choose **Organize and Delete** from the menu.

The Building Blocks Organizer appears with the Green Clean Building Block highlighted in the list.

3. Click the **column headers** for each column, ending with Name column.

4. Scroll, if necessary, to locate and select the **gc** Building Block.

5. Click the **Delete** button at the bottom of the dialog box to delete the item.

6. When the message box appears verifying that you want to delete the Building Block, click **Yes**.

7. Click the **Close** button in the bottom-right corner of the dialog box.

8. **Save** 🖫 your newsletter, and leave it **open** for the next exercise.

Working with Preformatted Text Boxes

Video Lesson   labyrinthelab.com/videos

A preformatted text box is a box that you can type text in. However, the big difference is that it is already preformatted for you. Perhaps you have seen a quote in a magazine set in the middle of a page or some extra information the author wants to stand out from the rest of the article. These are referred to as pull quotes and sidebars. When you insert a preformatted text box, it has a designated place on the page and will be inserted on the page where the insertion point is located, if there is room; otherwise, it will be placed on a new page. You may move and resize the text box once it is inserted. When you type in it, the text will be wrapped automatically. The preformatted text boxes are found in the Building Blocks Organizer.

QUICK REFERENCE	INSERTING A PREFORMATTED TEXT BOX
Task	**Procedure**
Insert a preformatted text box	■ Choose Insert→Text→Quick Parts 📄 from the Ribbon.
	■ Choose Building Blocks Organizer from the menu.
	■ Select the desired text box, and then click Insert.
	■ Move or resize the text box as desired after it is inserted in the document.
	■ Type the desired text in the box.

DEVELOP YOUR SKILLS 6.7.4
Insert a Preformatted Text Box

In this exercise, you will insert a pull quote preformatted text box. You will then resize and move it, and finally type a testimonial from a customer in it.

1. **Tap** Ctrl + End to ensure the insertion point is at the bottom of the document.

2. Choose **Insert→Text→Quick Parts** 📄 from the Ribbon.

3. Choose **Building Blocks Organizer** from the menu.

4. Follow these steps to insert the Mod Quote text box:

Ⓐ Click the **Name** column heading to sort the Building Blocks list in ascending order.

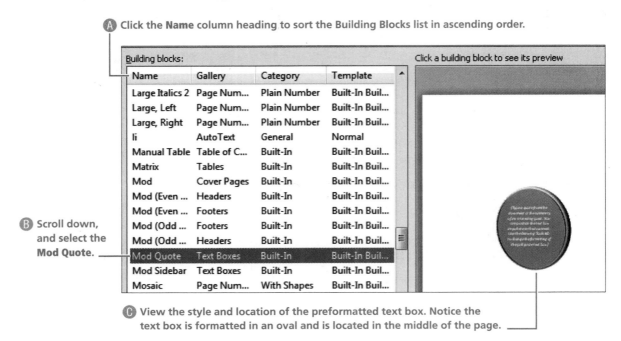

Ⓑ Scroll down, and select the **Mod Quote**.

Ⓒ View the style and location of the preformatted text box. Notice the text box is formatted in an oval and is located in the middle of the page.

5. Click the **Insert** button.
   Don't worry about where the pull quote text box is located for the moment. You will enter text in the box, and then resize and move it to a better location.

6. Begin **typing** (you do not have to click it first) the following in the text box:

   `We appreciate all you do for us AND for our environment!`
   `Thank you for such excellent customer service.` `Enter`

   `Daniels & Daniels, Inc.`

Format the Text in the Text Box

7. Select the text in the **pull quote**.

8. Using the Mini toolbar, change the Font Size to **10**.
   Because it is smaller now, pull quote will fit on the previous page in the middle, where it was preformatted to go.

Resize the Text Box

9. Follow these steps to reduce the size of the text box:

Ⓐ Position the **mouse pointer** on the **left-corner** sizing handle.

Ⓑ **Drag down** toward the center of the object until the shadow of the circle is about 2½ **inches** on the ruler.

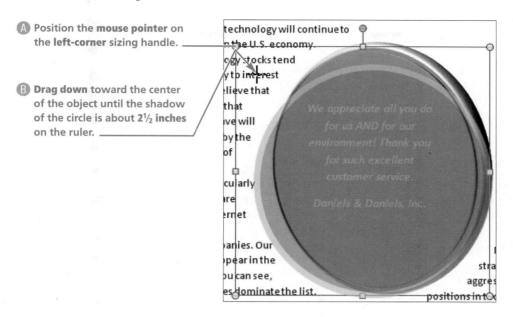

Move the Text Box to a Different Location

Next, you will move the text box to a more appropriate location for this document. Also, don't be surprised if you need to tweak the size slightly; it's a little difficult to judge the size when you cannot see the text while you are resizing the object.

10. If necessary, **scroll up** to see that the preformatted text box has automatically moved up to the middle of the third page.

   The object moved here because it was preformatted to be located in the middle of the page. You will move it now to the empty space at the bottom of the right-side column on page 3.

11. Select the **text box**.

12. Position the **mouse pointer** on the edge of the text box so it becomes the four-headed arrow.

13. Drag the **text box** down to the bottom of the column as shown in the illustration, and then release the mouse button.

14. If necessary, **resize** the text box to display all the text inside it.

15. **Save** 💾 the document and leave it **open** for the next topic.

6.8 Applying Themes

Video Lesson   labyrinthelab.com/videos

Word has a great feature that can instantly add color and visual variety to your documents. A *Theme* is a combination of colors, fonts, and graphic elements that you can apply to any document. You apply Themes from the Themes Gallery in the Themes group of the Page Layout tab. When you hover the mouse pointer over a Theme in the gallery, Live Preview displays the effect of the Theme before you apply it.

Customizing a Theme

You can customize any Theme to match your creative side. You can change the colors in a Theme, choose new fonts, and even add Theme effects such as line thickness, fill color, and so forth.

Changing Theme Colors

Built-in color schemes in a Theme have been coordinated to work together. You can modify the colors using Theme Colors in the Themes group on the Page Layout tab of the Ribbon. When you change a Theme color, it does not change the built-in Theme; it only modifies the colors in your current document. The colors not only affect the font color, but colors in tables, drawing shapes, and charts are all part of the schemes as well.

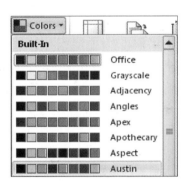

Each one of these sets is a complete color scheme affecting text and fill colors in your document.

Changing Theme Fonts

Themes are created using a set of coordinated fonts. A Theme font set includes either a specific font type in two different sizes for the heading and body text or two different fonts that blend nicely. The Theme Fonts gallery is found in the Themes group on the Page Layout tab of the Ribbon.

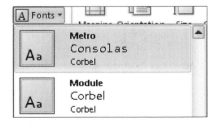

Font sets may include the same font of different sizes or two different fonts.

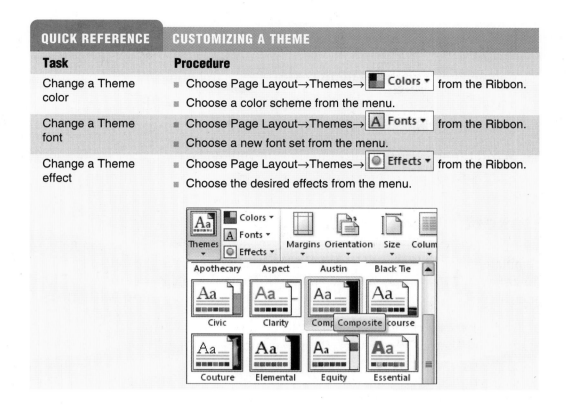

QUICK REFERENCE	CUSTOMIZING A THEME
Task	**Procedure**
Change a Theme color	■ Choose Page Layout→Themes→ Colors ▼ from the Ribbon. ■ Choose a color scheme from the menu.
Change a Theme font	■ Choose Page Layout→Themes→ A Fonts ▼ from the Ribbon. ■ Choose a new font set from the menu.
Change a Theme effect	■ Choose Page Layout→Themes→ Effects ▼ from the Ribbon. ■ Choose the desired effects from the menu.

DEVELOP YOUR SKILLS 6.8.1

Apply a Theme to Your Newsletter

In this exercise, you will use Live Preview to examine a variety of Themes, and then you will apply a Theme to your newsletter.

1. **Scroll up** to the cover page and make sure the titles are visible on the screen.
   The effect of Themes will be particularly easy to see on this page.

2. Choose **Page Layout→Themes→Themes** [Aa] from the Ribbon to display the Themes gallery.

3. Hover the **mouse pointer** over several different Themes and observe the changes in your document.

4. Click the **Composite Theme** (the third one in the third row) to apply it to the document.

5. **Scroll** through your document to see the impact of the new Theme.

Change the Theme Colors

6. Scroll to the **last page** to view the color change in the chart and table.

7. Choose **Page Layout→Themes→** Colors ▼ from the Ribbon.

8. Move the **mouse pointer** around several of the color schemes to view the Live Preview in your document.

9. Choose **Civic** from the menu.

Change the Fonts in a Theme

10. Scroll to the **first page** to view the font changes in the title and subtitle.

11. Choose **Page Layout→Themes→** A Fonts ▾ from the Ribbon.

12. **Scroll** through the list of font sets to view the Live Preview.

13. Choose the **Metro** font set for your document.

14. **Scroll** through the document to view the font and color changes in the document.

15. **Save** 🖫 the file, and leave it **open** for the next topic.

Resetting a Theme

You can always return to the original look of your document by choosing Reset to Theme from Template from the bottom of the Themes menu, as shown in the following illustration. On the other hand, if you simply want to apply a different Theme, it isn't necessary to reset it first. You can just apply one Theme after another, thus overriding the previous Theme.

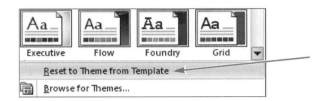

DEVELOP YOUR SKILLS 6.8.2
Reset the Theme

In this exercise, you will reset the document back to its original look.

1. Choose **Page Layout→Themes→Themes** 🖺 from the Ribbon to display the menu.

2. Choose **Reset to Theme from Template** at the bottom of the menu.

3. **Scroll** through the document and observe the original colors and fonts.

Inserting Drop Caps

Video Lesson labyrinthelab.com/videos

A Drop Cap command creates a large first letter of a paragraph. You have the option of leaving it in the paragraph itself with the text wrapped around it, or placing the large letter out in the margin next to the paragraph. Other options include changing the font for the drop cap, modifying the number of lines to drop, and setting the distance from the other text. You must be careful to select only the first letter of a word before applying a drop cap to it. If you select the entire word, the Drop Cap command will make the entire word very large.

This is an example of a drop cap within the paragraph with the rest of the text wrapped around it.

We have exciting news to share! After experiencing much success in the Richmond Metropolitan area, Green Clean has decided to expand into the Charlottesville area. The expansion will include new office space, ergonomically correct, of course, and a brand new retail facility to house all our earth-friendly products. We hope to be up and running in Charlottesville by mid-year. Naturally, we will continue our excellent customer service here in the Richmond market without any interruption in service.

This is an example of a drop cap set out in the margin. Notice that the text does not wrap around the drop cap.

We have exciting news to share! After experiencing much success in the Richmond Metropolitan area, Green Clean has decided to expand into the Charlottesville area. The expansion will include new office space, ergonomically correct, of course, and a brand new retail facility to house all our earth-friendly products. We hope to be up and running in Charlottesville by mid-year. Naturally, we will continue our excellent customer service here in the Richmond market without any interruption in service.

DEVELOP YOUR SKILLS 6.8.3
Insert a Drop Cap

In this exercise, you will insert drop caps in the newsletter

1. Scroll to **page 2** and select the *W* in the word *What's* in the first column on the left.

2. Choose **Insert→Text** from the Ribbon.

3. Follow these steps to apply the Drop Cap feature:

Ⓐ Click the **Drop Cap** button in the Text group on the Ribbon.

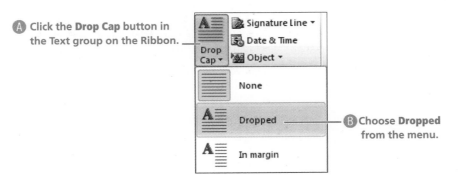

Ⓑ Choose **Dropped** from the menu.

4. **Save** 💾 the file, and leave it **open**.

6.9 Working with Views

Video Lesson labyrinthelab.com/videos

Word lets you view your document in several ways. Each view is optimized for specific types of work, thus allowing you to work efficiently. The views change the way documents appear on the screen but have no impact on the appearance of printed documents. You can choose the desired view from the View tab on the Ribbon or from the View buttons at the right end of the status bar at the bottom of the Word window.

Document views that appear on the View tab of the Ribbon

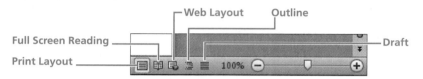

View buttons that appear at the bottom-right side of the Word window

DOCUMENT VIEWS	
View	**Description**
Print Layout	This is the default view in Word 2010. In this view, documents look very similar to the way they will look when printed. It is the most versatile view, allowing you to see such things as graphics, headers and footers, and multicolumn layout. You will probably use this view most of the time.
Full Screen Reading	Full Screen Reading makes it easy to read documents on the screen. It removes elements such as the Ribbon and the status bar in order to display more of your document. This view contains the View Options button, which offers varying display options within the window.
Web Layout	Web Layout displays your document as it would look as a web page. Text, graphics, and background patterns are visible. The document appears on one long page without page breaks.
Outline	Outline view is useful for organizing long documents.
Draft	This view simplifies page layout by eliminating elements such as headers and footers, graphic elements, and the display of multiple columns. This view can be useful when you want to focus on content and ignore surrounding elements.

Change the View

In this exercise, you will try out various views available in Word. You may wish to refer to the view descriptions in the previous table as you look at the view.

1. Locate the buttons 📄📖📑📑📑 at the right end of the **status bar** at the bottom of the window.
   The first button is the Print Layout button, which is the current view.

2. Click the second button, **Full Screen Reading** 📖, and your newsletter will look quite different.
   The column layout may not display accurately in this view. If not, you'll see how to change that in the next steps.

3. Click the **View Options** 📇 button in the upper-right corner of the screen.

4. Choose **Show Printed Page** from the menu if the feature is not turned on. (The icon will have a yellow highlight if it's turned on.)

5. Click the **Next Page** ▶ button at the top-middle section of the screen.
   Now your columns are visible.

6. Click the **View Options** 📇 button again, and click **Show Printed Page** again to turn off the view.

7. Click the **Close** ✖ button in the upper-right corner of the screen to return to Print Layout view.

8. Click the **View** tab and notice the corresponding views in the Document Views group.

9. Click **Full Screen Reading** 📖 in the Document Views group.

10. Click the **Close** ✖ button in the upper-right corner of the window to return to Word's default view.

Using Zoom Controls

Video Lesson   labyrinthelab.com/videos

The Zoom commands in the Zoom group of the View tab provide the ability to change the magnification of your document and control the number of pages that you can display at one time on the screen.

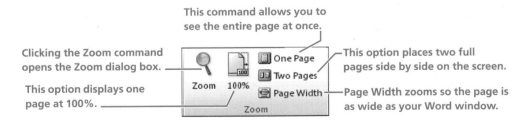

This command allows you to see the entire page at once.

Clicking the Zoom command opens the Zoom dialog box.

This option displays one page at 100%.

This option places two full pages side by side on the screen.

Page Width zooms so the page is as wide as your Word window.

In the Zoom dialog box, you can choose from preset degrees of magnification or specify your own. You can also control the number of pages to display at one time.

You click one of these option buttons to choose a preset degree of magnification.

You can use the spinner controls in the Percent box to choose a customized percent of magnification.

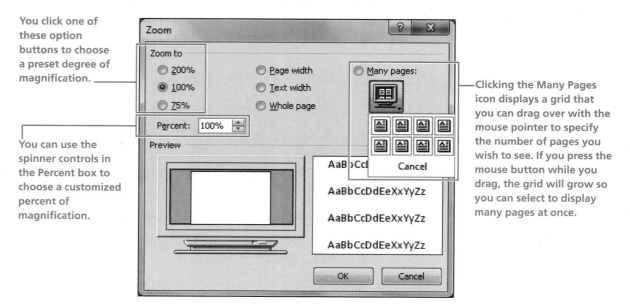

Clicking the Many Pages icon displays a grid that you can drag over with the mouse pointer to specify the number of pages you wish to see. If you press the mouse button while you drag, the grid will grow so you can select to display many pages at once.

The Zoom bar in the bottom-right corner of the Word window provides a quick way to change your document's magnification.

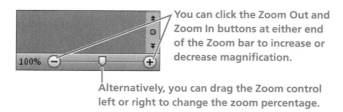

You can click the Zoom Out and Zoom In buttons at either end of the Zoom bar to increase or decrease magnification.

Alternatively, you can drag the Zoom control left or right to change the zoom percentage.

QUICK REFERENCE	SETTING DOCUMENT VIEWS
Task	**Procedure**
Change the document view	■ Use the View buttons on the right side of the status bar. *or* ■ Choose View→Document Views from the Ribbon, and click the desired view in the group.
Zoom the view	■ Use the Zoom bar on the right side of the status bar to change magnification. *or* ■ Choose View→Zoom from the Ribbon, and click the desired option from the group.

Use the Zoom Controls

In this exercise, you will use your newsletter to practice with the Zoom controls.

1. Position the **insertion point** at the top of the page following the cover page.

2. Choose **View→Zoom→Zoom** 🔍 from the Ribbon.

3. Follow these steps to display all three pages of the newsletter at once:

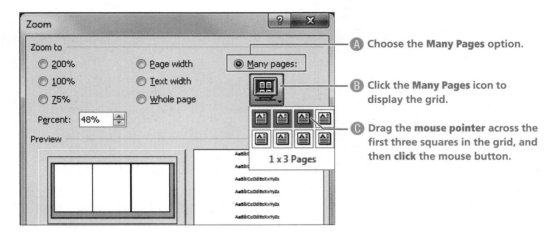

A Choose the **Many Pages** option.

B Click the **Many Pages** icon to display the grid.

C Drag the **mouse pointer** across the first three squares in the grid, and then **click** the mouse button.

4. Click **OK** to view the three pages.

5. Take a moment to test the other options in the Zoom group on the Ribbon, and then choose the **One Page** button.
   Next you'll test the zoom bar in the bottom-right corner of the Word window.

6. Follow these steps to change magnification via the zoom bar:

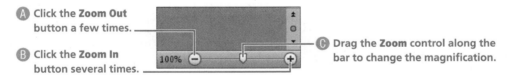

A Click the **Zoom Out** button a few times.

B Click the **Zoom In** button several times.

C Drag the **Zoom** control along the bar to change the magnification.

7. Return the magnification to **100%** using the controls on the Zoom bar.

8. **Save** 💾 your file, and **close** it.

6.10 Concepts Review

Concepts Review	labyrinthelab.com/word10

To check your knowledge of the key concepts introduced in this lesson, complete the Concepts Review quiz by going to the URL listed above. If your classroom is using Labyrinth eLab, you may complete the Concepts Review quiz from within your eLab course.

Reinforce Your Skills

Produce a Winter Holiday Newsletter

In this exercise, you will create a newsletter with a WordArt heading, a section break, and a two-column layout. Then you will add a cover page and modify the Theme.

1. Start a **new** blank document.

2. If necessary, click the **Show/Hide ¶** button to display formatting characters.

Insert WordArt

3. Choose **Insert→Text→WordArt** [A] from the Ribbon and choose the option in the **first column** in the **first row** (Fill - Tan, Text 2, Outline - Background 2).

4. Choose **Format→WordArt Styles→Text Effects** from the Ribbon.

5. Choose **Transform** from the menu, and then select **Warp→Chevron Up** from the gallery.

6. Select the **text** in the WordArt object, type **The Hope Report**, and click **outside** the object to view the new effect.

7. Select the **WordArt object**, and then choose **Format→Shape Styles→Shape Fill** [icon] **menu ▾** from the Ribbon.

8. Click a color of your choice to change the WordArt color.

Insert a Continuous Section Break

9. **Double-click** in the document right under the WordArt object and **tap** [Enter].

10. Choose **Page Layout→Page Setup→Breaks** [icon] from the Ribbon.

11. Choose **Continuous** from the menu.

12. Select the **WordArt object**, and drag it over to the center of the page and down just a little from the top of the page.

Insert the Newsletter Text

13. Position the **insertion point** next to the paragraph symbol below the section break.

14. **Open** the rs-New Year document from your Lesson 06 folder.

15. Use [Ctrl]+[A] and then [Ctrl]+[C] to select and copy the entire document.

16. Switch back to your new document using the button on the **taskbar**.

17. Use [Ctrl]+[V] to paste the text.

18. Make sure the **insertion point** is in the second section of the document.

19. Choose **Page Layout→Page Setup→Columns** [icon] from the Ribbon.

20. Choose **Two** from the menu.

Insert a Cover Page

21. Choose **Insert→Pages→Cover Page** 📄 from the Ribbon.

22. **Scroll down** and click the **Mod** design to add a cover page to your newsletter.

23. **Scroll up** and click the **Title** object, then type **The Hope Report** in the Title box of the cover page.

24. Hover the **mouse pointer** over the line below the title, which reads *Type the Document Subtitle.*

25. Click the **object**, and then type **December 2012**.

Delete Unnecessary Objects

26. **Click** the object beginning with the text *Type the abstract….*

27. Click directly on the tab labeled **Abstract** to select the entire object, and then **tap** the ⌨Delete key.

28. Use the same technique to delete the next two objects, the **Author** and **Date** objects.

Apply a New Theme

29. Choose **Page Layout→Themes→Themes** 🅰 from the Ribbon.

30. Click the **Verve** theme in the gallery to apply it to your newsletter.
Notice the color and font changes that are applied to the newsletter.

Insert a Column Break

31. Position the **insertion point** to the left of the heading *What a Magic Show!*

32. Choose **Page Layout→Page Setup→Breaks** 📄 from the Ribbon.

33. Choose **Column** from the menu to move the heading and its entire paragraph to the top of the second column.

Insert Drop Caps

34. Select the *T* in the word *This* in the first paragraph.

35. Choose **Insert→Text→Drop Cap** from the Ribbon.

36. Choose **Dropped** from the menu.

37. Using the same technique, insert a **dropped cap** for the *O* in the word *Our* in the first paragraph of the second column.

38. **Close** the rs-New Year document without saving any changes.

39. **Save** 💾 the document as **rs-Hope Report**, and then **close** it.

Create a Real Estate Newsletter

In this exercise, you will convert a document to a newsletter format and insert a section break and clip art.

1. **Open** rs-RE News from your Lesson 06 folder.

2. If necessary, click the **Show/Hide ¶** button to display formatting characters.

3. Position the **insertion point** to the left of the heading *How the Market Looks*.

4. Insert a **continuous** section break.

5. Select the **first heading line** at the top of the document, and format it with Cambria (Headings) bold 20 pt.

6. Format the **second line** with Cambria (Headings) italic 14 pt.

7. **Center** both heading lines.

Use and Format a Column Layout

8. Click the **insertion point** in the second section of the document, and apply a **two-column layout** to the text.

9. Format the four headings in the second section with **bold 12 pt**.

10. Position the **insertion point** to the left of the heading *Increase the Value of Your Home* in the first column.

11. Insert a **column** break to place the heading and its entire paragraph in column 2.

Insert and Format a Picture

12. Make sure the **insertion point** is at the top of the second column, and **tap** [Enter] to create a blank line.

13. Place the **insertion point** on the blank line, and then insert a **clip art picture** of a house.

14. **Close ✕** the Clip Art task pane.

15. **Size** the clip art appropriately for the page.

16. Make sure the **image** is selected.

17. Choose **Format→Size→Crop** from the Ribbon.

18. **Crop** the picture from both sides to remove any extra background area without removing the actual house.

19. Choose **Format→Picture Styles** from the Ribbon.

20. Choose a **Picture Style** from the gallery.

21. Choose **Format→Picture Styles→Picture Border** from the Ribbon.

22. Choose a **border color** from the gallery.

23. Turn **off** the formatting marks.

24. **Save** your file in your Lesson 06 folder, and **close** it.

Edit a Picture

In this exercise, you will open a flier and add a picture to it and make editing changes to the picture.

1. **Open** rs-Bandelier from the Lesson 06 folder.

2. **Tap** `Ctrl` + `End` to position the insertion point at the end of the document.

3. Choose **Insert→Illustrations→Picture** from the Ribbon.

4. **Insert** the rs-Bandelier Long House picture in your document. It's located in the Lesson 06 folder.

Change the Brightness and Contrast

5. Make sure the **picture** is selected.

6. Choose **Format→Adjust→Corrections** from the Ribbon.

7. Choose **Picture Correction Options** from the menu.

8. Use the spinner arrow next to **Brightness** to adjust to +40%.

9. Use the spinner arrow next to **Contrast** to adjust it to –40%; click the **Close** button.

10. Choose **Format→Adjust→Reset Picture** from the Ribbon to set the picture at its original brightness and contrast.

Crop the Picture

11. Choose **Format→Size→Crop** from the Ribbon.
    Notice the cropping handles (thick black lines) surrounding the picture.

12. Place the opening of the **Crop** tool over the top-center handle, and then **drag** to crop the top half of the photo so only a portion of the blue sky is visible in the upper-right corner.

13. Using the **top-right handle** on the photo, **drag** to the left so only the left side of the photo is visible.
    You can uncrop portions of a cropped picture at any time.

14. Use the **Crop** tool to uncrop the picture back to its original proportions.

15. Choose **Format→Size→Crop** to put away the Crop tool.

Rotate the Photo

16. Make sure the **picture** is still selected, and then use the green **Rotate** handle at the top of the image to rotate the picture **90°** to the right.

17. Click the **Undo** button to return it to its original position.

Use Picture Styles

18. With the **picture** selected, choose **Format→Picture Styles** from the Ribbon.

19. Click the **More** ☐ button on the Picture Styles gallery to display the entire gallery.

20. Choose the **sixth style** in the last row, Metal Rounded Rectangle. The actual location may vary in your gallery.

21. Make sure the **picture** is still selected.

22. Choose **Home→Paragraph→Center** ☰ from the Ribbon.

23. **Resize** the picture to your satisfaction.

24. **Save** 🖫 the file, and **close** it.

Apply Your Skills

Format a Two-Column Newsletter

In this exercise, you will open a document and convert the first heading line to WordArt. Then you will lay out the document in two columns, format the WordArt, and apply a Theme.

1. **Open** as-Conservation from your Lesson 06 folder.

2. If necessary, choose **Home→Paragraph→Show/Hide** ¶ from the Ribbon to display formatting marks.

3. Follow these guidelines to create your newsletter:

   ■ Convert the **first heading line** to WordArt style Fill - Blue, Accent 1, Metal Bevel, Reflection (fifth column, sixth row).

   ■ **Recolor** the WordArt object with the Shape Fill color of your choice.

   ■ Format the **next two heading lines** with center alignment, Cambria font, bold 12pt.

   ■ Insert a **continuous** section break to the left of the first heading in the body of the newsletter.

   ■ Set up a **two-column** layout in the second section.

   ■ Insert a **column** break to the left of the paragraph beginning *If your home is in....*

   ■ Apply the **Solstice Theme** to your newsletter.

   ■ Insert a **clip art image** of a frog, or another wetland creature of your choice, on the second blank line below the third heading line. Size the image appropriately for the page. Center the image, and rotate it to your satisfaction.

   ■ Insert **dropped caps** to the first letter of the three paragraph headings.

   Hint: You may need to resize the frog image again to make the columns break appropriately.

   ■ Turn **off** the formatting marks.

   ■ **Save** 🖫 the file, and then **close** it.

Create Custom Building Blocks

In this exercise, you will create custom Building Blocks out of text, a clip art image, and a WordArt object.

1. **Open** as-Quick Parts from your Lesson 06 folder.

2. **Save** each of the items in the document (text, clip art, and WordArt) as three separate **Building Blocks**.

3. Leave the **inside address** Building Block name as Bailey, Stevens.

4. Name the **clip art** Building Block **Building Clip**.

5. Name the **WordArt** Building Block **Bailey WordArt**.

6. Start a **new** blank document, where you will create a letterhead for the firm Bailey, Stevens, and Sheppard.

7. **Insert** your Building Blocks into the document in this order: Bailey WordArt, Building Clip, Bailey, Stevens. Place each Building Block on a separate line, and add space between Building Blocks as you deem appropriate.

8. **Size** the clip art as you wish and center align the items.

9. When you complete the letterhead, **delete** your custom Building Blocks from the Quick Parts menu.

10. **Save** your new document as **as-Bailey Letterhead** in your Lesson 06 folder, and then **close** it.

Critical Thinking & Work-Readiness Skills

In the course of working through the following Microsoft Office-based Critical Thinking exercises, you will also be utilizing various work-readiness skills, some of which are listed next to each exercise. Go to labyrinthelab.com/workreadiness to learn more about the work-readiness skills.

6.1 Design a Newsletter

Jenna is tasked with designing and publishing a newsletter to keep everyone informed of important or motivational, fun developments regarding Green Clean. While the newsletter will often be viewed online, there will also be a printed edition available in break rooms and sent to important customers and prospects. Design a one-page newsletter with three columns, inserting column breaks as necessary. Include at least four newsletter items, such as President's Corner, Welcome New Customers, Customer Feedback, Birthday List, Department News, or your own creative ideas. Use at least one piece of decorative WordArt and at least two pieces of clip art. Wrap text around each. Be creative with the text or use placeholder "dummy" text. Save the file as **ct-Newsletter Design** to your Lesson 06 folder.

WORK-READINESS SKILLS APPLIED

- Serving clients/customers
- Seeing things in the mind's eye
- Thinking creatively

6.2 Improve Your Newsletter

Jenna wants to spice up her newsletter a little before distributing it. If necessary, open the ct-Newsletter Design file you created in the previous exercise. Have a partner look at your newsletter and offer comments and suggestions for improvement, such as adjusting column widths, fonts, and colors. Make changes based on your partner's feedback. Add a preformatted text box to identify the month or issue number of the newsletter and save it as a Building Block you can use for future newsletters. Save your file as **ct-Newsletter Design2** in your Lesson 06 folder.

WORK-READINESS SKILLS APPLIED

- Taking responsibility
- Thinking creatively
- Participating as a member of a team

6.3 Use Themes, Drop Caps, and More in Your Newsletter

Open the ct-Newsletter Design2 file, if necessary, and save a copy of it to your Lesson 06 folder with the new name **ct-Newsletter Design Final**. Experiment with applying themes, including customized themes. Insert dropped caps at the beginning of each paragraph and see how you like it. Use zoom controls to help you get the look just right. Save your changes. How do these finishing touches help you convey the positive message the newsletter is supposed to convey? If working in a group, discuss this question. If working alone, type your answer in a Word document named **ct-Questions** saved to your Lesson 06 folder.

WORK-READINESS SKILLS APPLIED

- Thinking creatively
- Making decisions
- Serving clients/customers

Creating a Manual and Using Mail Merge

LEARNING OBJECTIVES

After studying this lesson, you will be able to:

- Format documents with styles
- Create custom styles
- Modify styles
- Control document margins
- Use helpful techniques for navigating and viewing documents
- Set up a Mail Merge document and labels

Word provides a variety of tools that are particularly suited to working with multipage documents. Styles offer a powerful means of ensuring formatting consistency throughout large documents. Special navigation features make it easy to move around long documents, and the Split and Arrange All views make it easy to work with long documents and multiple documents. In this lesson, you will work with these tools as you create an employee policy manual. You will also use Mail Merge to create a form letter to send to employees and set up mailing labels for envelopes.

Formatting and Distributing a Policy Manual

Jenna Mann is the administrative assistant for Green Clean, a successful, environmentally conscience janitorial service company. She has been tasked with the job of producing an employee policy manual to distribute to all Green Clean employees. Jenna's Microsoft Office expertise lets her take advantage of the variety of tools Word offers. She uses Word's built-in styles to format the manual's headings, thus ensuring consistent formatting throughout the document. If she decides to modify a style, Word automatically updates all text associated with that style. When she's finished with the policy manual, Jenna will use Mail Merge to insert the employee's name into a form letter and create mailing labels. Mail Merge will save Jenna many hours that she would have otherwise spent addressing each letter individually.

Purpose of This Manual

The purpose of this manual is to inform you about Green Clean's business practices, employment policies, and benefits provided to you as a valued Green Clean employee. No employee manual can answer every question, so you should feel free to ask questions of your supervisor. Also, feel free to contact the Human Resources department if you have any questions or concerns. It is our desire to keep an open line of communication between you and the company.

Notice

Green Clean reserves the right to modify, amend, and update the policies outlined in this manual at any time. No oral or written statement by a supervisor, manager, or department head may be interpreted as a change in policy, nor will it constitute an agreement with an employee. This manual represents the sole agreement with respect to benefits between the employee and Green Clean. If this manual is updated, you will be given replacement pages for those that have become outdated. A copy will also be placed on our intranet site.

Your Green Clean Benefits

You may not have thought about it, but the value of your benefits amounts to a considerable sum each year in addition to the salary you earn. These are just some of the benefits Green Clean provides to eligible employees each year:

- Credit union membership
- Dental insurance
- Disability leave of absence
- Education assistance
- Employee assistance program
- Group-term life insurance
- Health insurance
- Paid holidays
- Paid vacations

Word 2010's Quick Styles gallery makes it easy to apply professional formatting to a document in mere seconds.

7.1 Formatting Text with Styles

Video Lesson   labyrinthelab.com/videos

A *style* is one of the most powerful formatting tools in Word. A style is a group of formats identified by a unique style name, such as Heading 1. It enables you to rapidly apply multiple formats to a block of text. Styles not only create consistent formatting throughout a document, they allow you to make global formatting changes by modifying the style definition. When you modify a style, the changes are applied to all text formatted with that style.

Remember, anything that ends with a paragraph symbol is considered a paragraph. A heading line is considered a paragraph because it ends with a paragraph symbol.

Types of Styles

Word supports several kinds of styles, as discussed below.

- **Character styles**—Character styles are applied to the word the insertion point is in or to a selected group of words. Character styles can only contain character formats, not paragraph formats. You can apply character styles to text *within* a paragraph that is formatted with a paragraph style. The character style overrides the formats applied by the paragraph style.

- **Paragraph styles**—Paragraph styles are applied to all text in selected paragraphs or to the paragraph containing the insertion point. You can use any character or paragraph formats in a paragraph style. For example, you may want to format a heading with a large, bold font (character formatting) and apply paragraph spacing before and after the heading (paragraph formatting).

When you create a new style, whether it's a character or a paragraph style, you use the Create New Style from Formatting dialog box. A character style is being created in the following illustration.

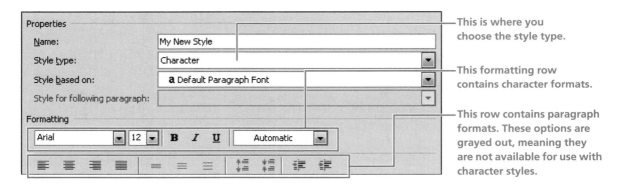

This is where you choose the style type.

This formatting row contains character formats.

This row contains paragraph formats. These options are grayed out, meaning they are not available for use with character styles.

- **Linked styles**—Linked styles (paragraph and character) can behave as either character or paragraph styles. If you simply position the insertion point in a paragraph and apply a linked style, it formats the entire paragraph. If you select a word or several words first, and then apply the style, it applies only to the selected words.

- **List styles**—This feature makes it easy to convert text to a list and to ensure consistency among multiple lists in a document.

- **Table styles**—Table styles can provide consistent formats for multiple tables within a document.

The Normal Style

You are always working within a style in Word. The default style for Word is the *Normal* style. It contains the default formatting that you are familiar with, such as the default Calibri font, the 1.15 line spacing, and so forth.

Quick Styles

Word's Quick Styles gallery contains a group of styles designed to complement each other, and they are based on the current document theme. The gallery contains styles for headings, titles, lists, and special character formatting. Live Preview makes it easy to test a variety of styles in your document before you actually apply the style. The Quick Styles gallery is in the Styles group on the Home tab. When you use a style from the gallery, it then becomes visible in the gallery on the Ribbon without scrolling or opening the gallery. This makes it convenient should you wish to apply the same style several times in a row.

The Quick Styles gallery.

Use these buttons to scroll up and down in the gallery.

The More button displays the entire gallery at once.

The Quick Styles gallery does not contain all of Word's built-in styles. There are many more styles available, as you will see later in this lesson.

DEVELOP YOUR SKILLS 7.1.1
Preview Quick Styles

In this exercise, you will open a document that contains the content for Green Clean's employee policy manual. Then you will use Live Preview and Quick Styles to decide on the styles you wish to use to give the manual a professional, polished look.

1. Start **Word**, and make sure the Word window is **maximized** ⬚.

2. **Open** the Employee Policy Manual document from your Lesson 07 folder.
   This document uses Word's default formatting, with the exception of headings, which are bolded to make them easy to locate.

3. Position the **insertion point** in the first line of the document.

4. Follow these steps to examine the Quick Styles gallery in the **Home→Styles** group on the Ribbon:

Ⓐ **Scroll down** row-by-row through the gallery. (This is tedious, and makes it difficult to get an idea of all the styles available.)

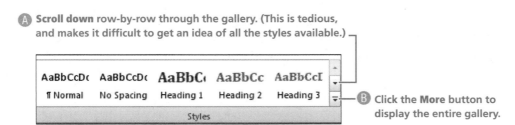

Ⓑ Click the **More** button to display the entire gallery.

5. Hover the **mouse pointer** over the Heading 1, Heading 2, and Title styles to see the Live Preview effect.
One of these styles would be appropriate for the first main heading in the document.

6. Hover the **mouse pointer** over some of the other styles.
You can tell which styles are strictly character (versus paragraph) styles. During Live Preview, they only affect the word where the insertion point is located. With character styles, if you intend to format more than one word, you must select the words prior to applying the style.

Apply the Title Style

7. Click the **Title** style to apply it to the heading.

8. Position the **insertion point** in the next heading line, *You're Part of Our Team*.

Apply Heading 1 and Heading 2 Styles

9. Follow these steps to apply a Heading 1 style to the selected heading:

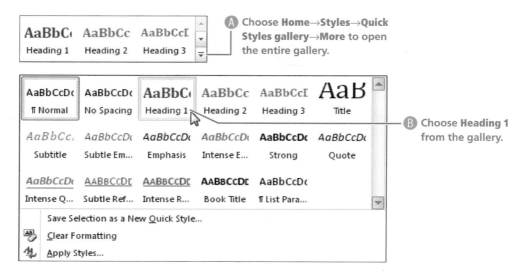

10. Apply **Heading 1** to the other bolded headings on page 1.

11. **Scroll** to the top of the second page, place the **insertion point** in the first heading, and apply the **Heading 1 style**.

12. Position the **insertion point** in the next heading line *Notice*, and apply the **Heading 2** style from the gallery.

13. Apply **Heading 1** to the next heading, *Your Green Clean Benefits*.

Convert Text to a List Style

14. On the **second page**, select the benefits from *Credit union membership* through *Paid vacations*.

15. Open the gallery, and choose the **List Paragraph** style—the last one in the gallery.
Notice that the List Paragraph style is now visible in the gallery on the Ribbon without scrolling or opening the gallery.

16. For each of the next three pages, apply the **Heading 1** style to the first heading on the page and the **Heading 2** style to the remaining headings on the page.

17. **Save** the file and leave it **open**; you will use it throughout the rest of the lesson.

Viewing All Styles

Video Lesson   labyrinthelab.com/videos

Clicking the dialog box launcher ⬜ in the bottom-right corner of the Styles group displays the Styles task pane. It lists all the styles present in the current Quick Styles gallery.

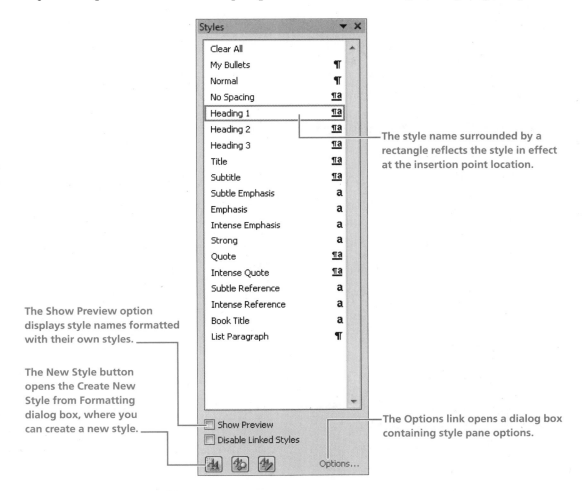

The style name surrounded by a rectangle reflects the style in effect at the insertion point location.

The Show Preview option displays style names formatted with their own styles.

The New Style button opens the Create New Style from Formatting dialog box, where you can create a new style.

The Options link opens a dialog box containing style pane options.

Reveal Style Formatting

To see all of the formats involved in a style, hover the mouse pointer over the style name in the Styles pane, and a pop-up menu appears, describing the font and paragraph formatting contained in the style.

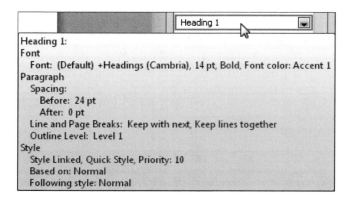

Changing the Quick Style Set

Word comes with a variety of Quick Style sets that you can display in the Quick Styles gallery. This enhances the array of styles available directly from the Ribbon. All of the styles in a set are coordinated to work together. Selecting a new style set affects only the current document you are viewing. If you switch to a different open document, the style set chosen for that document will display.

When you click the Change Styles ![AA] button in the Styles group, Word displays a menu from which you can choose the Style Set command to display a submenu of Word's built-in sets.

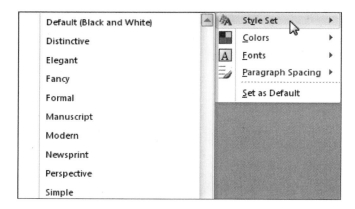

Change the Style Set

In this exercise, you will explore Word's style sets and apply a new style set.

1. **Scroll** to the top of the document.
2. Choose **Home→Styles→Change Styles** ![AA] from the Ribbon.

3. Follow these steps to choose a new style set:

Ⓐ Click **Style Set** from the menu to display the style sets.

Ⓑ View the **Live Preview** of various style sets, and then click **Formal** to apply that style to the document.

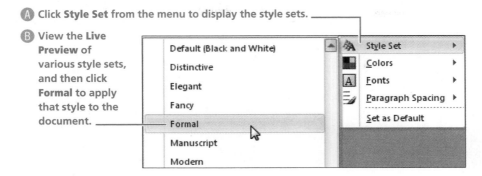

4. **Scroll** through the document to see the impact of the new style.

5. Open the **Quick Styles** gallery to see the formatting of the other styles in the **Formal** set.

6. **Click** in the document to close the gallery.

Apply the Word 2010 Style Set

7. Choose **Home→Styles→Change Styles** ⃟ from the Ribbon.

8. Choose **Style Set** from the menu, and then choose **Word 2010** from the submenu to return to the original look.

Creating a New Custom Style

Video Lesson   labyrinthelab.com/videos

Thus far, you have applied built-in styles. However, there may be situations where the built-in styles do not meet your needs. For example, you may have corporate formatting standards set for different types of documents. You can create custom styles to meet those standards.

There are two approaches you can take to create custom styles. The method you choose is a matter of personal preference; both are equally effective.

- **Define a style by definition**—When creating a custom style in the Create New Style from Formatting dialog box, one option is to open the dialog box and choose all formats from within the dialog box.

- **Define a style by example**—The other option is to format a block of text with the formats you wish to include in your style. Then select the text, and when you open the dialog box, you will see that Word copies the formats from the selected text into the dialog box. At this point, you can make additional formatting selections if you wish.

Making Detailed Style Settings

Clicking the New Style ⃟ button at the bottom of the Styles task pane displays the Create New Style from Formatting dialog box. You can use this dialog box to set all of the formatting for a new style, or use it to tweak the formatting of a style you are creating from selected text. For example, after setting all the formatting to create a style by example, you may want to open this dialog box to choose the style for the following paragraph.

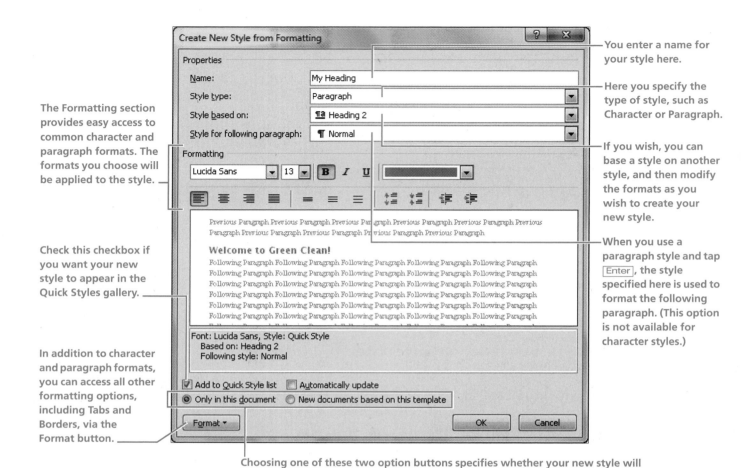

The Formatting section provides easy access to common character and paragraph formats. The formats you choose will be applied to the style.

You enter a name for your style here.

Here you specify the type of style, such as Character or Paragraph.

If you wish, you can base a style on another style, and then modify the formats as you wish to create your new style.

When you use a paragraph style and tap Enter, the style specified here is used to format the following paragraph. (This option is not available for character styles.)

Check this checkbox if you want your new style to appear in the Quick Styles gallery.

In addition to character and paragraph formats, you can access all other formatting options, including Tabs and Borders, via the Format button.

Choosing one of these two option buttons specifies whether your new style will be available in this document only or in all documents based on the current template. In our example, that is the default Normal template. This means your new style would be available in all new documents based on the Normal style.

Create a New Style

In this exercise, you will create a new character style and apply the style to selected blocks of text.

Create a Custom Style

1. On the **first page**, locate the heading *Green Clean Is Committed to Two Goals*.

2. In the first paragraph below the heading, **select** the words *best quality, eco-friendly products and services*.

3. Using the Mini toolbar, apply **Bold** **B** and **Underline** **U** to the selected text.

4. If necessary, choose **Home→Styles→dialog box launcher** in the bottom-right corner of the Styles group on the Home tab to display the Styles task pane.

5. Click the **New Style** button, the far left button at the bottom of the Styles task pane, to display the **Create New Style from Formatting** dialog box.

6. Follow these steps to complete the new style by definition:

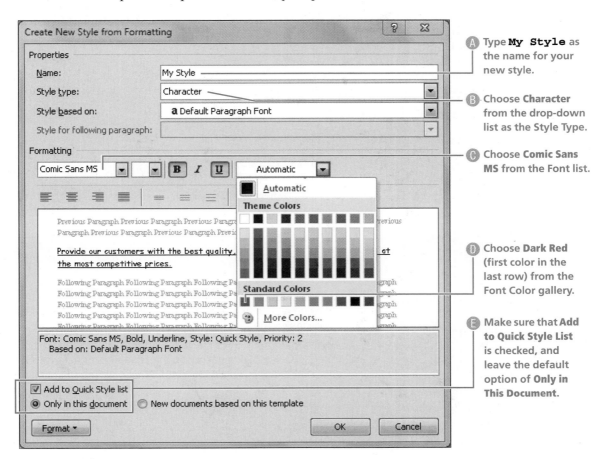

A. Type **My Style** as the name for your new style.

B. Choose **Character** from the drop-down list as the Style Type.

C. Choose **Comic Sans MS** from the Font list.

D. Choose **Dark Red** (first color in the last row) from the Font Color gallery.

E. Make sure that **Add to Quick Style List** is checked, and leave the default option of **Only in This Document**.

7. Click **OK** to finish creating the style and to apply it to the selected text.

Apply Your New Style

8. **Select** the words *above average compensation* in the next paragraph.

9. In the Quick Styles gallery, click your new **My Style** to apply it to the selected text.

10. **Click** anywhere in the document to deselect the text.

11. **Save** 🖫 your file, and continue with the next topic.

Modifying, Removing, and Deleting Styles

Video Lesson   labyrinthelab.com/videos

You can modify built-in styles as well as styles that you create. The ability to modify styles is one of the great powers of Word. Imagine, for example, that you used a heading style that contained a font change, point size change, font color change, bold, and italic, and you applied that style to twenty headings in a long document. Later you decide that you don't like the italic formatting. Rather than going to all twenty headings and removing italics, just modify the style, and all text with that style applied will update immediately.

You can remove a style from the Quick Styles gallery without removing it from the Styles task pane. You can leave it in the task pane for future use, or if you prefer you can delete it from the task pane. Take a moment to examine several of the commands in a style's menu in the Styles task pane.

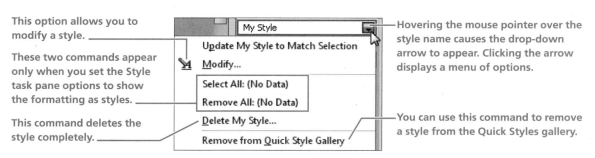

This option allows you to modify a style.

These two commands appear only when you set the Style task pane options to show the formatting as styles.

This command deletes the style completely.

Hovering the mouse pointer over the style name causes the drop-down arrow to appear. Clicking the arrow displays a menu of options.

You can use this command to remove a style from the Quick Styles gallery.

QUICK REFERENCE	USING WORD STYLES
Task	**Procedure**
Apply a style	■ Apply a character style by selecting the words to be formatted and then choosing a style from the Quick Styles gallery on the Home tab or from the Styles task pane.
	■ Apply a paragraph style by clicking in the paragraph and then choosing a style from the Quick Styles gallery on the Home tab or from the Styles task pane. If you want to apply a style to more than one paragraph at a time, you must select the paragraphs.
Create a new style by definition	■ Click the New Style button at the bottom of the Styles task pane to open the Create New Style from Formatting dialog box.
	■ Choose all desired formats from within the dialog box.
Create a new style by example	■ Format a block of text with the desired formats.
	■ Click the New Style button at the bottom of the Styles task pane to open the Create New Style from Formatting dialog box. Word copies the formats from the block of formatted text.
	■ You can make additional format changes within the dialog box if you wish.
Modify a style	■ In the Styles task pane, hover the mouse pointer over the style to be modified.
	■ When the drop-down arrow appears, click it to display the menu.
	■ Choose Modify from the menu to display the Modify Style dialog box.
Add a style to the Quick Styles gallery	■ In the Styles task pane, hover the mouse pointer over the style to be added.
	■ When the drop-down arrow appears, click it to display the menu.
	■ Choose Add to Quick Style Gallery from the menu.
Remove a style from the Quick Styles gallery	■ In the Styles task pane, hover the mouse pointer over the style to be removed.
	■ When the drop-down arrow appears, click it to display the menu.
	■ Choose Remove from Quick Style Gallery from the menu.
Delete a custom style	■ In the Styles task pane, hover the mouse pointer over the style to be deleted.
	■ When the drop-down arrow appears, click it to display the menu.
	■ Choose Delete [style name] from the menu.

Modify and Remove a Quick Styles

In this exercise, you will modify a style to see how it impacts all text formatted with that style. Then you will remove the style from the Quick Styles gallery. The Styles task pane should still be open.

1. Hover the **mouse pointer** over My Style in the Styles task pane to display the drop-down arrow.

2. **Click** the arrow to display the menu.

3. Choose the **Modify** command from the menu to open the Modify Style dialog box.
   This dialog box contains the same elements as the Create New Style from Formatting dialog box.

4. Click the **Italic** button to add italic formatting to the style.

5. Click **OK** and notice that both blocks of text formatted with My Style updated with the modification.

Remove a Style from the Quick Styles Gallery

6. In the Styles task pane, click the drop-down arrow for **My Style** again to display the menu.

7. Choose **Remove from Quick Styles Gallery** from the menu.
   Notice that removing the style from the Quick Styles gallery does not remove the formatting from the text with that style.

8. Open the **Quick Styles** gallery, and notice that your new style no longer appears in the gallery.

9. **Click** in the document to close the gallery.

Delete a Style from the Styles Task Pane

10. Display the **My Style** menu in the Styles task pane again.

11. Choose **Delete My Style** from the menu.

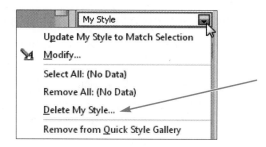

12. When the message appears verifying that you want to delete the style, click **Yes**.
    Notice that the My Style formatting has been removed from the two blocks of text in the document, and that My Style no longer appears in the Styles task pane.

13. Click the **Close** ☒ button in the upper-right corner of the Styles task pane.

14. **Save** 🖫 your file, and leave it **open** for the next topic.

7.2 Navigating with the Navigation Pane

Video Lesson labyrinthelab.com/videos

One of the options in the new Navigation pane is to use the Browse the Headings in your Document button to maneuver around in a document quickly. This option is activated only when you have assigned Heading styles to text. To do so, open the Navigation pane from the Editing group on the Home tab of the Ribbon.

Rearranging Sections

Rearranging sections is one of the most powerful uses of the Navigation pane. When you create a document, you may decide to change the order of topics later. Although you could use the Cut and Paste method to rearrange the document, using the Navigation pane is much easier because you can drag the headings up and down the pane to reposition them. When you drag a heading to a new location, all of its lower-level headings and paragraph text move right along with it. For example, you may have a Heading 1 followed by a paragraph, followed by a Heading 2 with its own paragraph. When you move the Heading 1, Word also moves the Heading 1 paragraph, the Heading 2, and the Heading 2 paragraph all as one section.

QUICK REFERENCE	REARRANGING A DOCUMENT USING THE NAVIGATION PANE
Task	**Procedure**
Display headings in the Navigation pane	■ Choose Home→Editing→Find from the Ribbon to open the Navigation pane.
	■ Click the Browse the Headings in Your Document button in the Navigation pane.
Rearrange a section	■ Click and drag a heading in the Navigation pane up or down to a new location.

DEVELOP YOUR SKILLS 7.2.1
Rearrange a Document Using the Navigation Pane

In this exercise, you will rearrange the order of sections in a document by dragging headings in the Navigation pane.

1. Choose **Home→Editing→Find** from the Ribbon to open the Navigation pane.

2. Click the **Browse the Headings in Your Document** tab to display the text that is formatted as headings.

3. Follow these steps to move the Employment Classifications section above the Employment Policies section:

Ⓐ Position the mouse pointer on the arrow next to **Employment Classifications**.

Ⓑ **Drag the heading** to above the Employment Policies heading. When you see a dark line above it, **release** the mouse button. Notice in the document that all of the subheadings and their subsequent paragraphs have been moved also.

4. **Scroll** through the document to see changes.

5. Using the same technique, **move** the *Employment Policies* heading back above the *Employment Classifications* section.

6. **Tap** Ctrl + Home to position the insertion point at the top, then close ☒ the Navigation Pane.

7. **Save** 🖫 the file and leave it **open** for the next exercise.

7.3 Changing Word Window Views

Video Lesson   labyrinthelab.com/videos

Word provides many different ways of viewing your documents on the screen. The Arrange All command arranges all open Word documents on the screen. Initially, it displays the windows horizontally, one above the other. You can also view the two windows side-by-side vertically. Whichever view the two documents are in, you can choose to scroll through them separately or simultaneously. You might use this view with the synchronous scrolling option to compare two versions of a document, as an example. The Split command splits a document's window into two individual windows that you can scroll separately. This provides the ability to compare two different parts of the same document next to each other.

QUICK REFERENCE	WORKING WITH WORD WINDOW VIEWS
View	**Procedure**
Arrange All	Choose View→Window→Arrange All from the Ribbon.
View Side by Side	Choose View→Window→View Side by Side from the Ribbon.
Split	Choose View→Window→Split from the Ribbon.

How the Split Bar Works

When you choose View→Window→Split ▭ from the Ribbon, Word displays the split bar, which spans the width of the window. The mouse pointer looks like a double-headed arrow.

The split bar moves when you move the mouse. You position the mouse pointer where you want the split bar on the screen, and then click the mouse button to anchor the bar.

DEVELOP YOUR SKILLS 7.3.1
Use the View Side By Side and Split Views

In this exercise, you will use the View Side by Side command to display both open Word documents at the same time and scroll through both documents at the same time. Finally, you will use the Split command to split your Employee Policy Manual into two windows, which you can scroll separately.

Use the View Side By Side View

1. **Open** the Original Employee Policy Manual document from the Lesson 07 folder.

2. Choose **View→Window→View Side by Side** 🕮 from the Ribbon.
   The documents now appear next to each other in separate windows. Each window has its own scroll bar.

3. **Scroll down** and then back **up** to the top using the scroll bar on the Original Employee Policy Manual.
   These are actually two separate files, each with its own title bar, Ribbon, and scroll bar. Notice that both documents scroll simultaneously instead of separately.

4. Choose **View→Window→Synchronous Scrolling** 📑 from the Ribbon on the Original Employee Policy Manual.

5. Take a moment to **scroll** through each window.
Notice that each window scrolls independently from the other.

6. Click the **Close** button in the upper-right corner of the Original Employee Policy Manual document to close it.

7. If necessary, **maximize** 🔲 the Employee Policy Manual window.

Split the Document Window

8. Choose **View→Window→Split** 🔲 from the Ribbon.
Word displays the split bar, which horizontally spans the width of the window. The mouse pointer appears as a double-headed arrow attached to the split bar.

9. Drag the **mouse pointer** up and down to change the position of the split bar.

10. Move the **split bar** to the center of the screen, and click to anchor the bar.

> ⚠️ **TIP** You can place the mouse pointer on the split bar at any time and drag to reposition it.

Notice that each part of the split window has its own scroll bar.

11. Take a moment to **scroll** both sections of the window independently.
Splits are handy for positioning separate parts of the same document next to each other for comparison purposes.

Notice that the Split command on the Ribbon changed to Remove Split.

12. Choose **View→Window→Remove Split** 🔲 to put the split bar away.

13. **Save** 💾 your file, and **close** it.

7.4 Introducing Mail Merge

Video Lesson labyrinthelab.com/videos

Word's Mail Merge feature is most often used for generating personalized form letters, mailing labels, and envelopes. However, Mail Merge is a versatile tool that can be used with any type of document. Mail Merge can be a big time-saver and is invaluable for managing large mailings. When you perform a merge, you have the option to merge directly to a printer or to a new document.

Components of a Mail Merge

Merging creates a merged document by combining information from two or more documents. The documents are known as the *main document* and the *data source*.

■ **Main Document**—This document controls the merge. It contains the fixed information into which the variable information for each contact is merged. In a typical form letter, for instance, you will have a different name and address on each letter, while the rest of the text is the same for everyone receiving the letter.

> ⚠️ **TIP** Remember that whatever text is to be included in every letter should be typed in the main document.

- **Data Source**—This can be another Word document, a spreadsheet, a database file, or a contacts list in Outlook. When creating the data source, keep in mind how you want to use the data in the merge. For example, if you want the letter to be addressed informally using the first names, then in the data source, there must be a separate column (field) for the first name.

- **Merged Document**—This document is the result after you perform the merge. It contains all of the individual letters addressed to each individual in the data source you used. You can save this document, if you wish, or simply close it without saving after you print.

You can merge an existing main document with an existing data source, or you can create the main document and data source while stepping through the merge process.

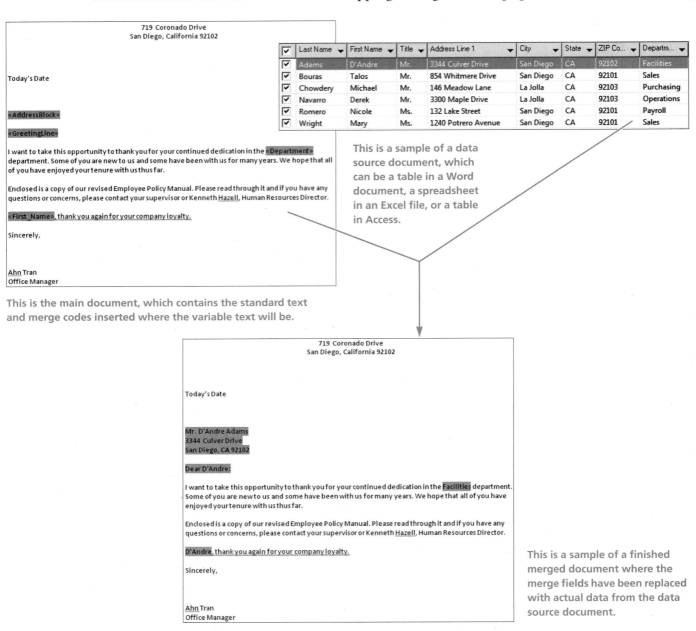

This is a sample of a data source document, which can be a table in a Word document, a spreadsheet in an Excel file, or a table in Access.

This is the main document, which contains the standard text and merge codes inserted where the variable text will be.

This is a sample of a finished merged document where the merge fields have been replaced with actual data from the data source document.

The Benefits of Using Mail Merge

Mail Merge will save you a lot of time and can help reduce errors in large mailings. For example, say you want to send a letter to 100 customers. Without using Mail Merge, you would be typing the same text in all 100 letters (or copying and pasting 100 times). However, using Mail Merge for the job, you create only one main document containing the standard text and one data source document containing the 100 customer names. You will also really appreciate Mail Merge when you later decide you want to make a change. Using Mail Merge, you can edit the main document once and remerge it with the data source to produce a new merged document. Without Mail Merge, you would need to edit each personalized letter individually.

The Mailings Tab

The Mailings tab on the Ribbon provides guidance in setting up both the main document and data source and helps you conduct the merge. The Start Mail Merge command group on the Mailings tab is the beginning point. Alternatively, you can choose Step by Step Mail Merge Wizard from the Start Mail Merge command to walk you through the process of choosing the main document, the data source document, inserting merge fields, and finally conducting the merge.

The Start Mail Merge command is where you specify the type of main document you want to use, such as letters, envelopes, or labels.  Select Recipients is where you either identify an existing data source list or create a new data source.

 The Mail Merge Wizard will be familiar to those who have conducted merges in earlier versions of Word.

7.5 Working with the Data Source

Video Lesson   labyrinthelab.com/videos

Data sources usually contain names, addresses, telephone numbers, and other contact information. However, you can include any information in a data source. For example, you may want to include inventory names, numbers, and prices of parts, if you are using Mail Merge to create a parts catalog. You can create a data source in Word, or you can use external data sources, such as an Access database or an Excel worksheet. Once a data source is created, it can be used as a source for many different main documents.

Designing Effective Data Sources

It is very important that you design effective data sources. The most important consideration is the number of fields to use. The more fields, the more flexibility you will have in the merge. An important rule to remember is that you cannot merge a portion of a field. For example, if a field contains both a first name and last name, then you will never be able to merge only the last name into a main document. This would be a problem if you needed to merge only a last name to create salutations such as Dear Ms. Alvarez. In this example, you would need to use one field for the first name and a separate field for the last name. You would also need to use a title field for the titles Mr., Ms., and Mrs.

Creating Address Lists

You can use the New Address List dialog box to set up address lists (data sources) for use in mail merges. This tool stores the addresses you enter in a table within a Microsoft Access database. This table, which becomes the data source for the merge, is linked to the mail merge main document. You can also use a Word table, an Excel worksheet, or an Access table as a data source for a mail merge. Each of these tools stores data in a table or worksheet structure.

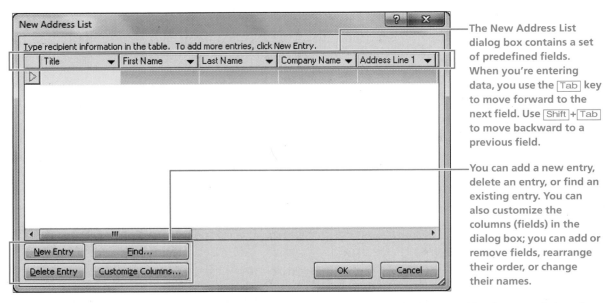

The New Address List dialog box contains a set of predefined fields. When you're entering data, you use the Tab key to move forward to the next field. Use Shift+Tab to move backward to a previous field.

You can add a new entry, delete an entry, or find an existing entry. You can also customize the columns (fields) in the dialog box; you can add or remove fields, rearrange their order, or change their names.

> **NOTE** The terms *fields* and *columns* are used interchangeably in this lesson. Each row of data is referred to as a *record*.

Customizing an Address List

The Customize Address List dialog box makes it easy to set up the mailing list just as you want it. You can easily delete unnecessary fields and add your own custom fields to the list. You can also rename an existing field name and use the Move Up and Move Down buttons to reorder the list of fields.

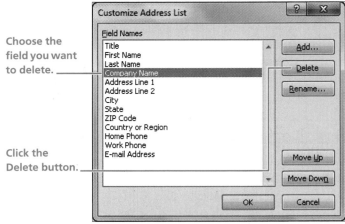

Choose the field you want to delete.

Click the Delete button.

Delete a field from the list.

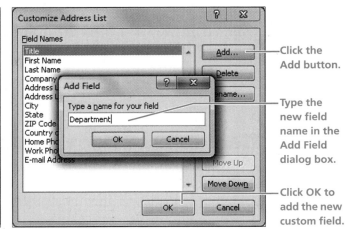

Click the Add button.

Type the new field name in the Add Field dialog box.

Click OK to add the new custom field.

Add a field to the list.

Specify the Main Document and Create a Data Source

In this exercise, you will use the Start Mail Merge group on the Mailings tab to specify a letter as your main document, to customize the data source, and to enter data.

1. **Open** the Policy Manual Letter Main from the Lesson 07 folder.

2. Choose **Mailings→Start Mail Merge→Start Mail Merge**  from the Ribbon.

3. Choose **Letters** from the menu, as shown at right.
   You are indicating here that the open document on the screen will be the main document.

Connect to the Data Source

Next you will indicate which data source will be connected to the letter. Since you don't have an existing data source, you will create one during the mail merge process.

4. Choose **Mailings→Start Mail Merge→Select Recipients** 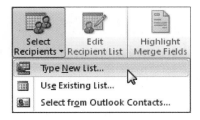 from the Ribbon.

5. Choose **Type New List** from the menu.

   The New Address List dialog box opens.

Remove Fields

You will remove unnecessary fields from the set of predefined fields.

6. Click the **Customize Columns** button in the bottom-left corner of the dialog box to display the Customize Address List dialog box.

7. Choose the **Company Name** field.

8. Click the **Delete** button, and then click **Yes** when the message appears to verify the deletion.

9. **Delete** the Address Line 2, Country or Region, Home Phone, Work Phone, and E-mail Address fields; then, click on the **Title** field name at the top of the list.

Add a Field

10. Follow these steps to add a Department field to the list:

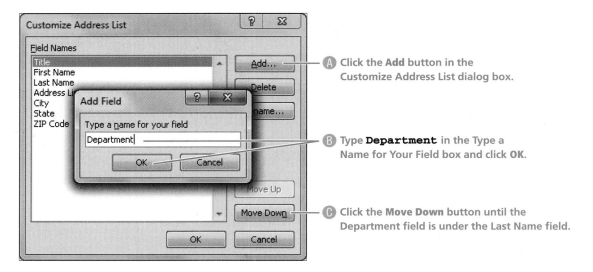

A Click the **Add** button in the Customize Address List dialog box.

B Type **Department** in the Type a Name for Your Field box and click **OK**.

C Click the **Move Down** button until the Department field is under the Last Name field.

11. Click **OK** to complete the changes.

Enter the First Record

The cursor should be in the Title field.

12. Type **Mr.**, and then **tap** Tab to move to the next field.

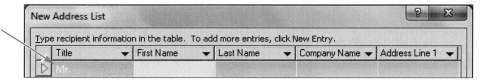

Do not type spaces after entering information in fields. Word will take care of adding the necessary spaces in the inside address and the salutation. You can always click in a field and make editing changes if necessary.

13. Type **Talos**, and then **tap** Tab to move to the next field.

14. Type **Bouras**, and then **tap** Tab to move to the next field.

15. Finish **entering** the Talos Bouras data shown in the following table, **tabbing** between fields. The list of fields will scroll as you continue to Tab and type.

16. When you complete the first record, click the **New Entry** button or **tap** Tab to generate a new blank row for the next record, and then **enter** the two remaining records shown in this table.

Mr. Talos Bouras	Ms. Nicole Romero	Mr. Michael Chowdery
Sales	Payroll	Purchasing
854 Whitmore Drive	132 Lake Street	900 C Street
San Diego, CA 92101	San Diego, CA 92101	La Jolla, CA 92103

If you accidentally tap Tab after the last record and add a blank record, just click the Delete Entry button.

17. Leave the New Address List dialog box **open**.

Reviewing Your Records

Video Lesson labyrinthelab.com/videos

It's a good idea to review your records for accuracy before saving the data source. However, if you miss an error, you can always edit it in the Edit Data Source dialog box, which you'll learn about later in this lesson.

If an entry is wider than the default field width, you can click the insertion point directly in the field and use the arrow keys to move through the entry.

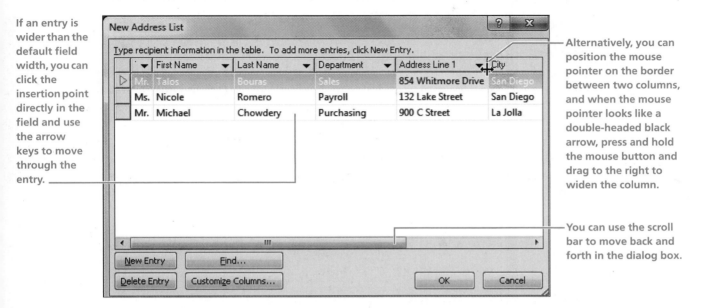

Alternatively, you can position the mouse pointer on the border between two columns, and when the mouse pointer looks like a double-headed black arrow, press and hold the mouse button and drag to the right to widen the column.

You can use the scroll bar to move back and forth in the dialog box.

DEVELOP YOUR SKILLS 7.5.2
Review and Save Your Work

In this exercise, you will take a moment to examine your records for accuracy, and then you will save your data source.

1. Position the **mouse pointer** on the scroll bar and drag left and right to view all the fields.

2. Click the **insertion point** in the Address Line 1 field for the first record, and use the **arrow keys** on the keyboard to move the insertion point through the entry.

3. Position the **mouse pointer** on the border between the Address Line 1 and City fields, and when the mouse pointer changes to a double-headed black arrow, **drag** to the **right** to display the entire *854 Whitmere Drive* entry.

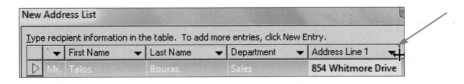

4. Make any needed revisions.

5. When you finish reviewing your records, click **OK** to open the Save Address List dialog box.

6. **Save** the data source file as **Policy Manual Letter Data** in the Lesson 07 folder. *Your data source is now connected to the main document.*

7. Leave the current document **open**, and stay in the Mailings tab on the Ribbon for the next exercise.

Managing the Address List

Video Lesson   labyrinthelab.com/videos

The Mail Merge Recipients dialog box lets you sort and filter address lists and choose records to include in a mail merge. To edit data, you click the Edit button in the Mail Merge Recipients dialog box to display the Edit Data Source dialog box, where you can add, delete, and edit entries.

 If you used a Word table, Excel spreadsheet, or other document for your data source, you can edit directly in that data source document if you wish. Since the data source is connected to the main document, any changes made are updated automatically in the main document.

You choose→Mailings→Start Mail Merge→Edit Recipient List 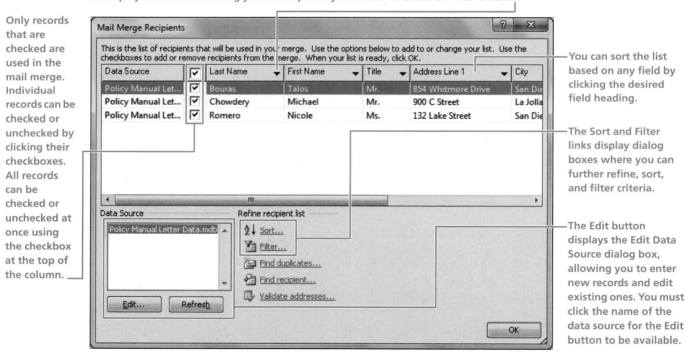 from the Ribbon to access the Mail Merge Recipients dialog box.

If there are records that you do not want to include in your mailing, use the menu ▼ buttons to display a filter list allowing you to temporarily hide records based on filter criteria.

Only records that are checked are used in the mail merge. Individual records can be checked or unchecked by clicking their checkboxes. All records can be checked or unchecked at once using the checkbox at the top of the column.

You can sort the list based on any field by clicking the desired field heading.

The Sort and Filter links display dialog boxes where you can further refine, sort, and filter criteria.

The Edit button displays the Edit Data Source dialog box, allowing you to enter new records and edit existing ones. You must click the name of the data source for the Edit button to be available.

The Edit Data Source dialog box looks and operates like the New Address List dialog box that you used to enter the original list.

Use Mail Merge Recipient Options and Edit Records

In this exercise, you will work with the Mail Merge Recipients dialog box, where you can sort, filter, and edit your mailing list.

1. Choose **Mailings→Start Mail Merge→Edit Recipient List** 📇 from the Ribbon.

2. Follow these steps to sort and filter the list and open the Edit Data Source dialog box:

Ⓐ Click the **Last Name** field heading to temporarily sort the list in ascending order by last name. Each time you click a field heading, the list toggles between ascending and descending order.

Ⓑ Click the **Last Name menu** ▼ button and notice the filtering options. Choose **Chowdery** from the menu to filter out all other entries. Click the **Last Name menu** ▼ button again, and choose **(All)** to redisplay all records.

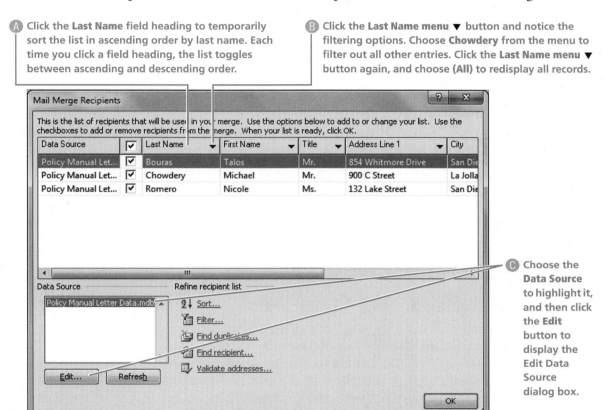

Ⓒ Choose the **Data Source** to highlight it, and then click the **Edit** button to display the Edit Data Source dialog box.

Edit a Record

Remember, the Edit Data Source dialog box looks and operates like the New Address List dialog box.

3. **Click** the *900 C Street* to highlight the text.

4. Type **146 Meadow Lane** in its place.

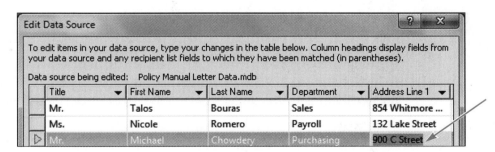

5. Follow these guidelines to enter the three records at right:

Ms. Mary Wright	Mr. Derek Navarro	Mr. D'Andre Adams
Sales	Operations	3344 Culver Drive
1240 Potrero Avenue	3300 Maple Drive	San Diego, CA 92102
San Diego, CA 92101	La Jolla, CA 92103	

- ■ Use the **New Entry** button or **tap** Tab for each new record.

- ■ **Tap** Tab to move from one field to the next.

- ■ Notice that the third record does not include a department name. **Tap** Tab to pass through the department field and leave it empty.

- ■ Make sure to **enter** the data in the correct fields.

6. Click **OK** to close the dialog box.

7. Click **Yes** when the message appears verifying your update, and then notice your changes in the Mail Merge Recipients dialog box.
Notice that Word remembers that you wanted the list sorted in alphabetical order by last name.

8. Click **OK** to close the Mail Merge Recipients dialog box.
You will create the main document in the next exercise.

7.6 Working with Main Documents

Video Lesson labyrinthelab.com/videos

You accomplish a merge by combining a main document with a data source. Typical main documents include form letters, envelopes, and mailing labels. A main document is linked to a data source that includes one or more merge fields. Merge fields inserted into a main document correspond to fields in the attached data source. Some merge fields, such as the address block, are composite fields consisting of a number of fields grouped together. For example, Title, First Name, Last Name, Address, City, State, and Zip would be included in the address block merge field.

Though not a necessity, including the word "main" in the document's name can be helpful in the future.

When you conduct a merge, a customized letter, envelope, or label is created for each record in the data source. After the merge is complete, you can save or print the merged document. The following figure shows the command buttons in the Write & Insert Fields group of the Mailings tab that you will use to insert merge fields into your letter.

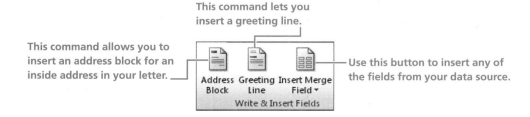

This command lets you insert a greeting line.

This command allows you to insert an address block for an inside address in your letter.

Use this button to insert any of the fields from your data source.

The following illustration shows the form letter with the location of the merge fields you will insert.

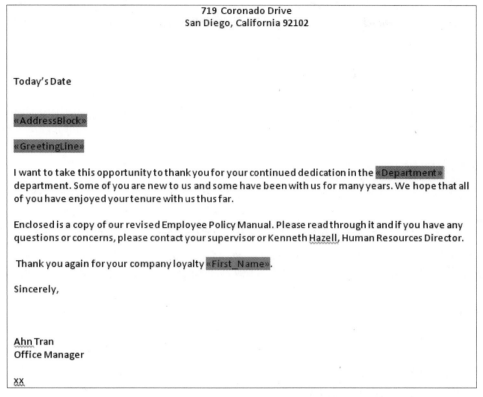

719 Coronado Drive
San Diego, California 92102

Today's Date

«AddressBlock»

«GreetingLine»

I want to take this opportunity to thank you for your continued dedication in the «Department» department. Some of you are new to us and some have been with us for many years. We hope that all of you have enjoyed your tenure with us thus far.

Enclosed is a copy of our revised Employee Policy Manual. Please read through it and if you have any questions or concerns, please contact your supervisor or Kenneth Hazell, Human Resources Director.

Thank you again for your company loyalty «First_Name».

Sincerely,

Ahn Tran
Office Manager

xx

When you execute the merge, the main document and data source are merged; the address block, greeting line, and merge fields are replaced with data from the data source.

Setting Up Main Documents

You can use any document as a mail merge main document. A document becomes a main document when you attach it to a data source and insert merge fields. In this lesson, you create a main document from the Policy Manual Letter Main document that is already open on your screen. Once a data source is attached, you can insert merge fields.

DEVELOP YOUR SKILLS 7.6.1
Set Up a Form Letter

In this exercise, you will set up a form letter. The Policy Manual Letter Main document should still be open.

1. If necessary, choose **Home→Paragraph→Show/Hide** ¶ from the Ribbon to display formatting characters.

Insert the Date

2. Using the left margin area, select the **Today's Date** line, and then **tap** Delete.

3. Choose **Insert→Text→Insert Date and Time** 🗓 from the Ribbon to display the Date and Time dialog box.

4. Choose the **third date** format on the list, check the **Update Automatically** checkbox in the bottom-right corner of the dialog box, and then click **OK**.
Checking this option instructs Word to insert the current date when the letter file is opened on a later date. The date in your letter will always be the current date, which is a convenient option for form letters that you want to use again.

5. **Tap** [Enter] four times after inserting the date.

Insert the Address Block

6. Choose **Mailings→Write & Insert Fields→Address Block** 📄 from the Ribbon.
The Insert Address Block dialog box appears, allowing you to choose a format for the address block. Notice that the Preview window is displaying the address block format of the option that is highlighted at the left side of the dialog box.

7. Follow these steps to insert an Address Block merge code:

Ⓐ **Click** on the different formats for the recipient's name, viewing the changes in the Preview box, and then choose **Mr. Joshua Randall Jr.**

Ⓑ Preview the results of removing the checkmark from the Insert Postal Address checkbox, and then **click** it again to reinsert the merge code into the document.

Ⓒ Click **OK** to accept the Address Block options.

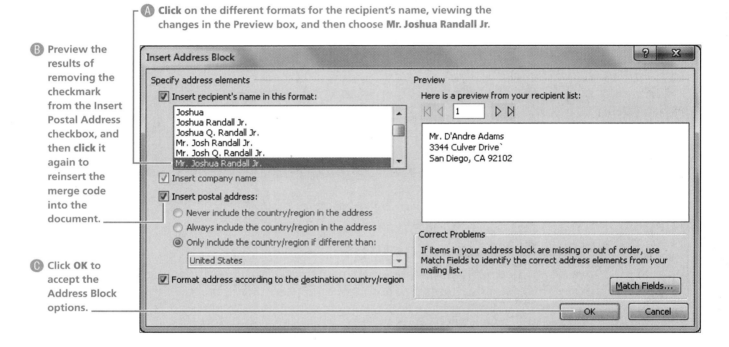

An Address Block merge code appears in the document. During the merge, Word inserts address information from the data source at the location in the customized letters.

8. **Tap** [Enter] twice.

Insert the Greeting Line

9. Choose **Mailings→Write & Insert Fields→Greeting Line** 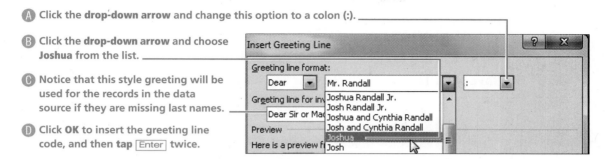 from the Ribbon.

10. Follow these steps to modify and insert the greeting line:

Ⓐ Click the **drop-down arrow** and change this option to a colon (:). _____

Ⓑ Click the **drop-down arrow** and choose **Joshua** from the list. _____

Ⓒ Notice that this style greeting will be used for the records in the data source if they are missing last names. _____

Ⓓ Click **OK** to insert the greeting line code, and then **tap** Enter twice.

Insert Another Merge Field

11. Follow these steps to insert the Department merge field code into the letter:

Ⓐ Position the **insertion point** at the end of the word *the* in the first line and **tap** Spacebar.

Ⓑ Choose **Mailings→Write & Insert Fields→Insert Merge Field menu button** from the Ribbon to display a list of merge fields in the Data Source document. _____

Ⓒ Choose **Department** from the merge field list. _____

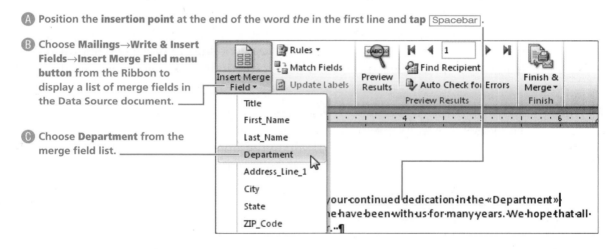

12. Position the **insertion point** at the end of the line beginning with *Thank you again*.

13. Choose the **Mailings→Write & Insert Fields→** Insert Merge Field ▾ menu button from the Ribbon.

14. Choose the **First_Name** field from the drop-down merge field list.

15. Choose **Home→Paragraph→Show/Hide** ¶ from the Ribbon to turn off the formatting marks.

16. Take a few moments to review your letter, making sure the merge fields match the preceding example. In particular, make sure you used the proper punctuation and spacing between fields and the text. Any punctuation or spacing errors that occur in your main document will appear in every merged letter.

17. **Save** 💾 the letter in the Lesson 07 folder.

7.7 Conducting a Merge

Video Lesson labyrinthelab.com/videos

Merging combines a main document with a data source to produce a merged document. If you are merging a form letter with a data source, Word produces a personalized copy of the form letter for each record in the data source. You can print one or all of the records and save the merged document if you wish. It's always a good idea to preview what the document will look like when it is merged so you can make corrections to the main document, if needed.

Previewing the Results

The Preview Results group on the Mailings tab allows you to see how your letters will look before you complete the merge. If you notice an error that needs to be fixed in the main document, simply click the Preview Results button again to return to it.

Using Auto Check for Errors

When you have many records to preview, rather than previewing each one individually, you can use Auto Check for Errors. The feature goes through the document checking for common errors such as an invalid field code. In the Auto Check for Errors dialog box, you have three options for viewing errors:

- Simulate the merge and report errors in a new document
- Complete the merge, pausing to report each error as it occurs
- Complete the merge without pausing; errors are reported in a new document

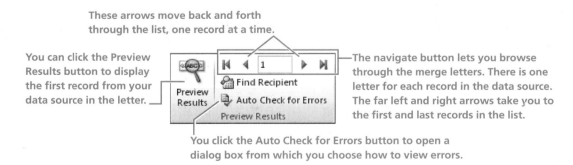

These arrows move back and forth through the list, one record at a time.

You can click the Preview Results button to display the first record from your data source in the letter.

The navigate button lets you browse through the merge letters. There is one letter for each record in the data source. The far left and right arrows take you to the first and last records in the list.

You click the Auto Check for Errors button to open a dialog box from which you choose how to view errors.

Finishing the Merge

When you feel confident that your letter and data source are accurate, you use the Finish & Merge command.

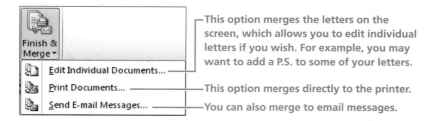

This option merges the letters on the screen, which allows you to edit individual letters if you wish. For example, you may want to add a P.S. to some of your letters.

This option merges directly to the printer.

You can also merge to email messages.

To Save or Not to Save

Merged documents are rarely saved, because they can easily be reconstructed by merging the main document with the data source. A merged document is usually previewed, printed, and closed without saving. However, you can certainly save the merged document if you wish to save a record of it. If a merged document contains errors, you can close it without saving, edit the main document or data source, and then conduct the merge again.

Conduct the Merge

In this exercise, you will use the Preview Results group on the Mailings tab to review your letters before you perform the merge. Then you will complete the merge on the screen.

1. Choose **Mailings→Preview Results→Preview Results** from the Ribbon to view the data from the first record.

2. Use the **navigation buttons** in the Preview Results group to scroll through all your merged documents.

3. Choose **Mailings→Finish→Finish & Merge** from the Ribbon.

4. Choose **Edit Individual Documents** from the menu to merge the letters on the screen.

5. Click **OK** to merge all records.

6. **Scroll** through the letters and scan their contents.
   Notice that there is one letter for each record in the data source.

7. **Close** the merged document without saving.

8. Choose **Mailings→Preview Results→Preview Results** again to display the main document instead of the preview.

9. Leave the main document **open** for the next exercise.

7.8 Working with Merge Problems

Video Lesson   labyrinthelab.com/videos

Several common errors can cause a merge to produce incorrect results. The merged document (or preview) will usually provide clues as to why a merge fails to produce the intended results. Once you identify an error in the merged document, such as leaving out a comma or space before or after a merge field, you can make changes to the main document or the data source. You can then conduct the merge again to determine if the error was fixed. Repeat this process until the merge works as intended.

Common Merge Problems

Several problems are common in merges. These problems and their solutions are described in the following Quick Reference table.

QUICK REFERENCE	DEALING WITH COMMON MERGE PROBLEMS
Problem	**Solution**
The exact same error appears in every merge letter.	The problem is in the main document, since it occurs in every merge letter. Correct the error in the main document and perform the merge again.
Some letters in the merged document are missing data.	This occurs because some records in the data source are missing data. Add data to the necessary fields in the data source, or modify the main document or merged letters to account for the missing data.
Some letters in the merged document have incorrect data.	The problem is in the data source, since it does not affect every letter in the merged document. Correct the data errors in the data source and perform the merge again.

DEVELOP YOUR SKILLS 7.8.1
Fix Merge Problems

In this exercise, you will examine your document for merge problems. Refer to the previous table if you need help solving them. The following steps are a guide to assist you. They do not address all the possible problems that you may encounter; they do, however, address one specific error that was made intentionally. You will insert a comma after the First Name field.

1. Position the **insertion point** after the <<First Name>> merge field, and then **type** a comma.

2. Conduct the **Finish & Merge** process again to review and fix problems in the merged document.

3. Browse through the entire document, from beginning to end, and look for any errors. Note errors in a separate Word document or on a piece of paper. Indicate how often the errors occur (in every merged letter or just one).

4. If you find an error that occurs in *every merged letter*, such as the one you corrected with the missing comma, **close** the merged document without saving and **edit** the main document, and then **save** it.

5. If you find a data error in *just one letter,* such as the missing *Facilities* department name for Mr. Adams, close the merged document without saving it.

- Choose **Mailings→Start Mail Merge→Edit Recipient List**  from the Ribbon.

- When the Mail Merge Recipients dialog box appears, highlight the **Data Source** in the bottom-left corner of the dialog box, and click the **Edit** button.

- After you fix any errors, click **OK**, and then click **Yes** when the message appears asking if you want to update the data.

- Click **OK** to close the Mail Merge Recipients dialog box.

6. When you have corrected any errors, execute the **merge** again.

7. **Close** the merged document without saving it.

8. **Save** and **close** Policy Manual Letter Main.

7.9 Using Envelopes and Labels with Mail Merge

Video Lesson   labyrinthelab.com/videos

When you choose Mailings→Start Mail Merge→Start Mail Merge from the Ribbon, Word presents you with options for the type of main document you want to create. In addition to form letters, you can use envelopes, labels, and other types of documents as main documents. The merged document's title bar reflects the type of merge performed. For example, when you conduct the merge for envelopes the first time, the name of the merged document is Envelopes1; you may change the name and save it if you wish.

You can use the same data source for various main documents. For example, you can use the same data source for envelopes and mailing labels that you used for the form letter.

Generating Envelopes with Mail Merge

You can use Mail Merge to generate an envelope for each record in a data source. Mail Merge lets you choose the envelope size and formats. The standard business (Size 10) envelope is the default. You will check your printer to see how to place the envelopes in it for printing. For example, you may need to know which side should be facing up and which way the flap is facing.

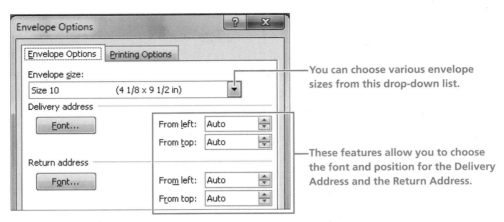

You can choose various envelope sizes from this drop-down list.

These features allow you to choose the font and position for the Delivery Address and the Return Address.

If you are using envelopes with the company name and address preprinted, then you will not use any Return Address options here.

DEVELOP YOUR SKILLS 7.9.1

Choose an Envelope Size and Attach a Data Source

In this exercise, you will choose an envelope as the main document and connect the Policy Manual Letter Data file to the envelope.

1. Start a **new** blank document.

2. Choose **Mailings→Start Mail Merge→Start Mail Merge** ![icon] from the Ribbon, and then choose **Envelopes** from the menu.

3. When the Envelope Options dialog box appears, if necessary, choose **Size 10** from the Envelope Size list.
   This is the standard envelope size for business correspondence.

4. Click **OK** to apply the settings to the document.
   The envelope main document appears in the Word window although right now, it doesn't look any different. You will set up the envelope main document in a moment, and you will see the envelope layout on the screen.

Connect the Data Source

5. Choose **Mailings→Start Mail Merge→Select Recipients** 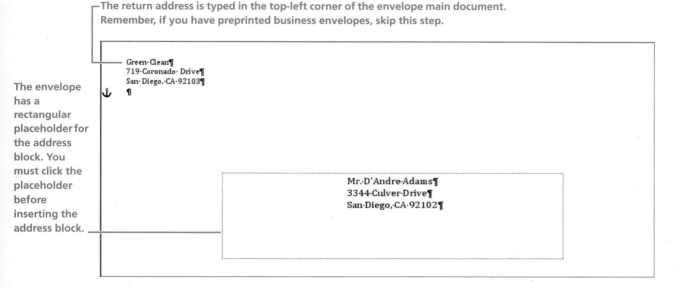 from the Ribbon, and then choose **Use Existing List** from the menu.

6. When the Select Data Source dialog box appears, navigate to your file storage location and **open** Policy Manual Letter Data from the Lesson 07 folder.

7. Stay in the **Mailings** tab for the next topic.

Arranging the Envelope

Video Lesson   labyrinthelab.com/videos

You can insert an address block in the envelope main document. An envelope main document can be saved like any other main document, allowing you to use it over and over to generate envelopes from a data source. The following illustration shows the envelope main document that you will set up in the next exercise.

⌐The return address is typed in the top-left corner of the envelope main document.
Remember, if you have preprinted business envelopes, skip this step.

The envelope has a rectangular placeholder for the address block. You must click the placeholder before inserting the address block.

Green·Clean¶
719·Coronado· Drive¶
San· Diego,·CA·92103¶
⚓   ¶

Mr.·D'Andre·Adams¶
3344·Culver·Drive¶
San·Diego,·CA·92102¶

DEVELOP YOUR SKILLS 7.9.2
Merge to Envelopes

In this exercise, you will position the return address and the address block on the envelope, and then you will merge the envelope main document with the data source.

Set Up the Envelope

1. If necessary, turn on the **formatting marks**, and then **type** the return address, starting at the first paragraph symbol in the upper-left corner of the envelope, as shown here.

Green· Clean¶
719·Coronado· Drive¶
San· Diego,·CA·92103¶
¶

2. Position the **insertion point** next to the paragraph symbol toward the center bottom half of the envelope to display the address block placeholder.

3. Choose **Mailings→Write & Insert Fields→Address Block** 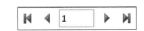 from the Ribbon.

4. Click **OK** to accept the default address block settings.
   This is the same Insert Address Block dialog box you used to insert the address block in the form letter. An Address Block field is inserted in the placeholder box. Word will merge the address information from the data source into this location when the merge is conducted.

Preview the Merge

5. Choose **Mailings→Preview Results→Preview Results** from the Ribbon to display the first record from the data source in the envelope.

6. Use the **navigation buttons** in the Preview Results group to scroll through all your merged envelopes.

7. Choose **Mailings→Finish→Finish & Merge** from the Ribbon.

8. Choose **Edit Individual Documents** from the menu, and then click **OK** to merge all the records.

9. Turn **off** the formatting marks from the Ribbon.

10. **Scroll** through the envelopes, and notice that there is one envelope for each record in the data source.
    You could use the envelopes for mailing the letters created in the previous exercises, because they are generated from the same data source.

11. If necessary, fix any problems with the mail merge.

12. When you finish, **save** the merged document as **Policy Manual Envelopes** in the Lesson 07 folder, and then **close** it.

13. Turn **off** the Preview Results button, and then **save** the envelope in the Lesson 07 folder as **Policy Manual Envelope Main** and **close** it.

Generating Labels with Mail Merge

Video Lesson   labyrinthelab.com/videos

You can use Mail Merge to generate mailing labels for each record in a data source. Mail Merge lets you choose the label format, sheet size, and other specifications. It also lets you insert an address block and other fields in the main document. Like other main documents, a labels main document, as well as the merged document, can be saved for future use. The following illustration shows a portion of the labels main document that you will set up in the next exercise.

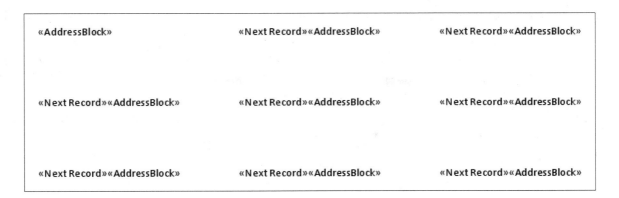

«AddressBlock»	«Next Record»«AddressBlock»	«Next Record»«AddressBlock»
«Next Record»«AddressBlock»	«Next Record»«AddressBlock»	«Next Record»«AddressBlock»
«Next Record»«AddressBlock»	«Next Record»«AddressBlock»	«Next Record»«AddressBlock»

Using Label Options

The Label Options dialog box allows you to choose printer options and the type of label you will use for your merge. You will find a number on the package of labels you purchase that may correspond to the Product Number in the Label Options dialog box. If you buy a brand name not included in the Label Vendors list, you can match your label size with the label size in the Label Information section.

Choose the appropriate printer information in this area.

Choose the product brand from this drop-down list.

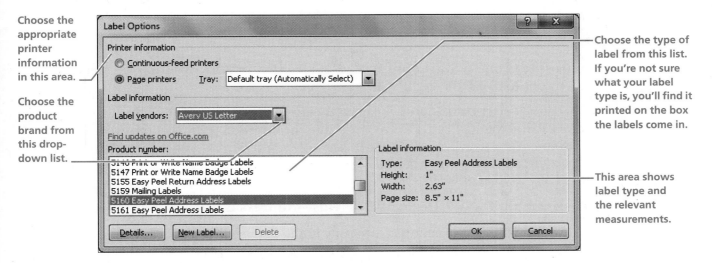

Choose the type of label from this list. If you're not sure what your label type is, you'll find it printed on the box the labels come in.

This area shows label type and the relevant measurements.

DEVELOP YOUR SKILLS 7.9.3
Use Mail Merge to Generate Mailing Labels

In this exercise, you will set up a labels main document, and then you will merge the labels main document with the data source used in the previous exercises.

1. Start a **new** blank document.

2. If necessary, choose **Home→Paragraph→Show/Hide** ¶ from the Ribbon to display formatting marks.

3. Choose **Mailings→Start Mail Merge→Start Mail Merge** from the Ribbon, and then choose **Labels** from the menu.

4. Follow these steps to choose a label:

Ⓐ Scroll through the options and choose **Avery US Letter** from the Label Vendors drop-down list.

Ⓑ Scroll through the list options and then choose **5160 Easy Peel Address Labels** from the Product Number list.

Ⓒ Click **OK**.

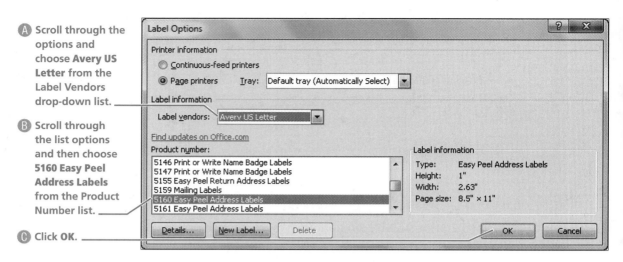

The labels main document appears in the Word window.

Labels are contained in a Word table, but don't worry. You don't have to be a table expert to create labels. By default, table grid lines don't appear when you create labels.

Connect the Data Source

5. Choose **Mailings→Start Mail Merge→Select Recipients** 📇 from the Ribbon, and then choose **Use Existing List** from the menu.

6. When the Select Data Source dialog box opens, navigate to your file storage location and **open** Policy Manual Letter Data. Make sure the insertion point is in the first address label position.
   Notice that the space for the first label is blank and all the rest have a <<Next Record>> code in them. You will add the Address Block merge fields with the next few steps.

7. Choose **Mailings→Write & Insert Fields→Address Block** 📄 from the Ribbon.

8. Click **OK** to insert the address block code in the first label.

9. Choose **Mailings→Write & Insert Fields→Update Labels** 📄 from the Ribbon to place the address block in all of the labels.
   Your addresses will fit the labels better if you remove Word's additional spacing.

10. **Press** Ctrl + A to select the entire document.

11. Choose **Home→Styles** from the Ribbon.

12. Choose the **No Spacing** style from the Quick Styles gallery.

13. Choose **Mailings→Preview Results→Preview Results** 🔍 from the Ribbon to see how the labels will look when you print them, and then turn off the Preview Results command.

Conduct the Merge

14. Choose **Mailings→Finish→Finish & Merge** ▣ from the Ribbon.

15. Choose **Edit Individual Documents** from the menu.

16. When the Merge to New Document dialog box appears, click **OK** to merge all the records.

17. **Close** your merged document without saving it.

18. **Save** ▣ the labels main document in the Lesson 07 folder as **Merge Labels**, and then **close** it.

7.10 Concepts Review

Concepts Review   labyrinthelab.com/word10

To check your knowledge of the key concepts introduced in this lesson, complete the Concepts Review quiz by going to the URL listed above. If your classroom is using Labyrinth eLab, you may complete the Concepts Review quiz from within your eLab course.

Reinforce Your Skills

Apply Quick Styles to a Document

In this exercise, you will apply Quick Styles to a document. Then you will copy a style using the Format Painter, and finally you will change the Theme color to alter the look of the style.

Change the Quick Styles Style Set

1. **Open** rs-Instructor Profiles from the Lesson 07 folder.

2. **Select** in the heading at the top of the document.

3. Choose **Home→Styles→Change Styles** from the Ribbon.

4. Choose **Fancy** from the Style Set submenu.

Apply a Style

5. Click the **More** button on the Quick Styles gallery to display the entire gallery.

6. Choose the **Title** style to format the document heading.

7. Position the **insertion point** in the heading *Tanya Walton* below the main heading.

8. Choose **Heading 2** from the Quick Styles gallery. Keep the insertion point in the heading *Tanya Walton*.

Copy the Quick Style

9. Choose **Home→Clipboard** from the Ribbon.

10. Use the **Format Painter** to copy the Heading 2 style to the other instructor headings. *Remember, double-clicking the Format Painter keeps the feature turned on until you turn it off.*

11. Turn off the Format Painter.

Change the Theme Color

You may recall that the look of Quick Styles is based on the current document theme.

12. Choose **Page Layout→Themes→Theme Colors** from the Ribbon.

13. Choose **Urban** from the list.

14. **Save** the file, and **close** it.

Create, Modify, and Delete a Character Style

In this exercise, you will create a character Quick Style. You will create the style by formatting text with the formats you want in your style. Then you will modify your new style, and finally you will delete it.

1. **Open** rs-Recycle Computers from the Lesson 07 folder.
2. **Select** *Wellsville Donation Center* in the table *Where To Take Your Computer Equipment*.

Format the Text

3. Choose **Home→Font→Font Color** **A** menu ▾ from the Ribbon.
4. Choose the color in **column 6**, **row 5**: Red, Accent 2, Darker 25%.
5. Choose **Home→Font→Bold** **B** from the Ribbon.
6. Choose **Home→Font→Font Size** 11 ▾ menu ▾ from the Ribbon, and choose **16 pt**.

Create the Style

7. Keep the text selected, and if necessary, click the **dialog box launcher** 🔲 in the bottom-right corner of the Styles group on the Home tab.
This opens the Styles task pane.
8. Click the **New Style** 🔲 button in the bottom-left corner of the Styles task pane.
Notice that the Formatting area of the dialog box has taken on the formatting from the selected text in the document, so the only thing remaining is to give the style a name.
9. Type **My Character Style** in the Name area at the top of the dialog box.
10. Choose **Character** from the Style Type drop-down list and click **OK**.

Apply the Style

11. Use the **Quick Styles** gallery to apply the new character style to *Woodridge Donation Center* in the table.
12. Use the **Styles** task pane to apply **My Character Style** to *Elk Grove Donation Center* in the table.
13. **Apply** your new style to the remaining donation center names, using either the Quick Styles gallery or the Styles task pane.

Modify the Style

You've decided that the point size in your style is too large, so you will change the point size, and all of the text formatted with that style will update with the change.

14. Hover the **mouse pointer** over My Character Style in the Styles task pane and click the drop-down arrow, and then choose **Modify**.
15. Choose **14 pt** from the Font Size drop-down menu, and then click **OK**.
Notice that all donation center names reformatted to 14 pt.

Delete the Style

16. Hover the **mouse pointer** over My Character Style in the Styles task pane to display the drop-down arrow.

17. Click the **arrow**, and choose **Delete My Character Style** from the menu.

18. When the message appears confirming the deletion, click **Yes**.
Notice that Word removed the style from the names of the donation centers and deleted the style from the Quick Styles gallery and the Styles task pane.

19. Click the **Close** ⊠ button in the upper-right corner of the Styles task pane to close it.

20. Save 🖫 the file, and **close** it.

REINFORCE YOUR SKILLS 7.3
Set Up a New Mail Merge

In this exercise, you will set up a main document and a data source. You will remove unnecessary fields from the data source, sort the data, and execute the merge.

Set Up the Data Source

1. Open the rs-Fundraiser Main document from the Lesson 07 folder.

2. Choose **Mailings→Start Mail Merge→Start Mail Merge** 🗋 from the Ribbon, and then choose **Letters** from the menu.

3. Choose **Mailings→Start Mail Merge→Select Recipients** 🗐 from the Ribbon, and then choose **Type New List** from the menu.

4. Click the **Customize Columns** button in the New Address List dialog box to display the Customize Address List dialog box.

5. Use the **Delete** button in the dialog box to remove the following fields (You must select the field names on the list before clicking Delete.):
- Address Line 2
- Country or Region
- Home Phone
- E-mail Address

6. Click **OK** to complete the changes to the data source.

Enter Data

7. **Enter** the following data into your new data source:

Mr. Sean Corn 308 Alhambra Avenue Monterey Park, CA 91754 626-555-9876	Mr. Craig Dostie Whole Life, Inc. 31200 Erwin Street Woodland Hills, CA 91367 818-555-1711	Ms. Alexia Lopez 2134 Harbor Blvd. Costa Mesa, CA 92626 714-555-9855
Ms. Winston Boey Pasadena City College Pasadena, CA 91104 626-555-1234	Ms. Phyllis Coen Pasadena City College 4745 Buffin Avenue Fremont, CA 94536 408-555-4950	Ms. Margaret Wong Popcorn Video 1308 West Ramona Blvd. Alhambra, CA 91803 818-555-8883

8. Click **OK** when you finish entering the data.

9. Use the **Save Address List** box to navigate to your exercise files.

10. **Save** the data source in the Lesson 07 folder as **rs-Address Data**.

Sort the List

11. Choose **Mailings→Start Mail Merge→Edit Recipient List** from the Ribbon.

12. Click the **Last Name** column heading to sort the records on the Last Name field, as shown here.

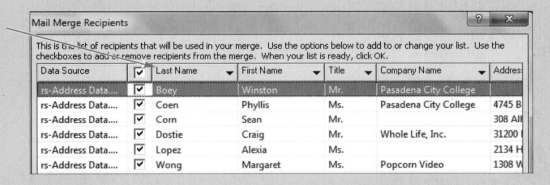

13. Click **OK** to return to the main document.

Set Up the Form Letter

14. Use the following guidelines to insert codes as shown in the following main document:

- Replace **Today's Date** with a date code that will update automatically.
- Insert the **Address Block** merge field below the date (as shown in the following illustration), using the first and last name only format.
- Insert an **appropriate greeting** line followed by a colon.
- Insert the **Work_Phone** merge field as shown in the last paragraph.

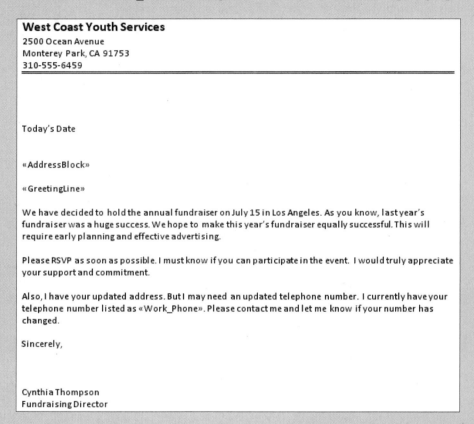

West Coast Youth Services
2500 Ocean Avenue
Monterey Park, CA 91753
310-555-6459

Today's Date

«AddressBlock»

«GreetingLine»

We have decided to hold the annual fundraiser on July 15 in Los Angeles. As you know, last year's fundraiser was a huge success. We hope to make this year's fundraiser equally successful. This will require early planning and effective advertising.

Please RSVP as soon as possible. I must know if you can participate in the event. I would truly appreciate your support and commitment.

Also, I have your updated address. But I may need an updated telephone number. I currently have your telephone number listed as «Work_Phone». Please contact me and let me know if your number has changed.

Sincerely,

Cynthia Thompson
Fundraising Director

Conduct the Merge

15. **Preview** your letters and **correct** any errors you find in the main document or data source.

16. Now **complete** the merge, using the **Edit Individual Documents** option.

17. When you finish, **close** the merged document without saving it.

18. Turn off Preview Results, and then **save and close** the document.

Generate Mailing Labels

In this exercise, you will create a labels main document. You will merge the labels document with rs-Address Data.

1. Start a **new** Word document.

2. Choose **Mailings→Start Mail Merge→Start Mail Merge** from the Ribbon.

3. Choose **Labels** from the menu.

4. If necessary, choose **5160** from the Product Number box.

5. Click **OK** to apply the settings to the document.

Attach the Data Source

6. Choose **Mailings→Start Mail Merge→Select Recipients** from the Ribbon.

7. Click **Use Existing List** from the menu.

8. Choose rs-Address Data from the Lesson 07 folder.

Arrange the Labels

9. Choose **Mailings→Write & Insert Fields→Address Block** from the Ribbon.

10. Click **OK** to insert the address block code in the first label.

11. Choose **Mailings→Write & Insert Fields→Update Labels** from the Ribbon.
    This populates the sheet with codes, ensuring that labels can be positioned at all locations on the sheet.

12. **Press** Ctrl + A to select the entire document.

13. Choose **Home→Styles** from the Ribbon.

14. Choose the **No Spacing** style from the Quick Styles gallery to remove Word's extra spacing.

Merge the Main Document and Data Source

15. Choose **Mailings→Preview Results→Preview Results** from the Ribbon.

16. **Preview** your labels, and then **complete** the merge using the **Edit Individual Documents** option from the menu.

17. Click **OK** to merge all records.

18. Observe your labels. You should see one label for each record.

19. When you finish, **close** the merged document without saving it.

20. Turn off Preview Results, and then **save and close** the file.

Apply Your Skills

Work with Views

In this exercise, you will use the Split command to view a document, and then you will open a second document and use the View Side by Side view to compare the documents.

Split a Document Window

1. **Open** the as-TrainRight Qualifications document from the Lesson 07 folder.

2. **Split** the Word window horizontally, with the split bar approximately in the middle of the screen.
   - ■ Ask your instructor to initial that this has been done successfully. _____

3. **Remove the split** from the Word window.
   - ■ Ask your instructor to initial that this has been done successfully. _____

Use the Arrange All View

4. Position the **insertion point** at the top of the document.

5. **Open** the as-Qualifications document from the Lesson 07 folder.

6. Use the View Side by Side command, and **scroll** through each window separately to compare the formatted and unformatted documents.

7. **View** the two open documents side by side.

8. **Scroll** through the document at the same time.

9. **Close** both files, and then **maximize** the Word window.

Merge a Form Letter with a Data Source

In this exercise, you will create a new main document letter. Then you will create a new address list, but you will remove any unnecessary fields first. Finally, you will execute the merge.

1. Use the **Mailings** tab and the following guidelines to set up a form letter and data source:
   - Use the as-Health Club Main document from the Lesson 07 folder.
   - Your data source should contain only the **three records** shown after the letter below. Remove any **unused fields** from the data source.
   - **Save** the data source document as **as-Health Club Data** in the Lesson 07 folder.
   - Insert the **date** in the form letter as a field that updates automatically.
   - Insert an **address block** and **greeting** of your choice.
   - Insert the **work phone number** field in the appropriate location.

Today's Date

«AddressBlock»

«GreetingLine»

The purpose of this letter is to inform you that your health club membership is about to expire. You have been an excellent member for some time, so we would like to offer you a low renewal rate of just $99 per year.

Please contact me as soon as possible. This offer will expire on March 31. Also, we currently have your phone number listed as «Work_Phone». Please return the enclosed change of phone number card and let me know if this number is still valid.

Sincerely,

Dave Nelson
Renewal Manager

Enclosure

Mr. David Roth	Mrs. Tammy Simpson	Mr. Jason Williams
760 Maple Avenue	Barkers Books	2233 Crystal Street
Fremont, CA 94538	312 Tennessee Street	San Mateo, CA 94403
510-555-9090	Richmond, VA 94804	415-555-2312
	510-555-2233	

2. **Merge** the form letter with the data source.

3. Turn off **Preview Results, save** the document, and then **close** it.

4. If necessary, **save** any changes to your main document, and then **close** it.

Generate Envelopes

In this exercise, you will create a new main envelope document and execute the merge.

1. Use the **Mailings** tab on the Ribbon and these guidelines to set up an envelope main document:
   - Use a **standard size 10** envelope.
   - Use as-Health Club Data as the **data source**.
   - Use the **return address** of your choice.
   - Position the **insertion point** in the placeholder toward the center bottom half of the envelope and insert the **default address block**.

2. **Save** the envelope main document in your Lesson 07 folder as **as-Health Club Envelope**.

3. **Merge** the envelope main document with the data source.

4. **Close** the merged document without saving it.

5. If necessary, **save** any changes to the envelope main document, and then **close** it.

Critical Thinking & Work-Readiness Skills

In the course of working through the following Microsoft Office-based Critical Thinking exercises, you will also be utilizing various work-readiness skills, some of which are listed next to each exercise. Go to labyrinthelab.com/workreadiness *to learn more about the work-readiness skills.*

7.1 Style an Employee Policy Manual

Jenna is formatting the new employee policy manual. Open ct-Employee Manual Draft from your Lesson 7 folder and, using Style tools, give it a consistent and professional look. Format the company logo as necessary. Number all of the topics. Ask yourself: Are there any missing that I might reasonably want to see covered in an employee manual? Add a note to the end of the file suggesting topics you would like to see covered. Save the file as **ct-Employee Manual Draft 2**.

WORK-READINESS SKILLS APPLIED
- Showing responsibility
- Reading
- Evaluating information

7.2 Move Sections

Jenna wants to reorganize the manual so that the information flows in a more logical way. If necessary, open ct-Employee Manual Draft 2 and save it to your Lesson 7 folder as **ct-Employee Manual Draft 3**. Use the Navigation pane to move the president's Welcome message to before Company History and move the Company Mission to before the Company Vision. Rearrange the other sections as you see fit. Use the Split Bar to keep the top portion of the manual visible as you scroll through the document in the bottom pane looking for other thing to improve. Make any changes you feel are necessary and then save and close the file. If working in a group, discuss why you decided to organize the manual as you did. If working alone, type your answer in a Word document named **ct-Questions** saved to your Lesson 7 folder.

WORK-READINESS SKILLS APPLIED
- Reading
- Evaluating information
- Organizing information

7.3 Use Mail Merge

Jenna decides to ask for help from some outside consultants who are experts in employee policy documentation. Create a mail merge data source from the ct-Consultants file in your Lesson 7 folder and save it as **ct-Consultant Data Source**. Next, create a form letter thanking the consultants for help and asking them to send you feedback at their earliest convenience. Insert the appropriate address block and greeting line, using the data source, and save the form letter to your Lesson 7 folder as **ct-Dear Consultants Merged**.

WORK-READINESS SKILLS APPLIED
- Exercising leadership
- Using computers to process information
- Writing

Creating a Research Paper

LEARNING OBJECTIVES

After studying this lesson, you will be able to:

- Insert footnotes and endnotes in a research paper
- Add headers and footers to documents
- Place captions on figures
- Generate a table of figures
- Create templates

In this lesson, you will learn about research papers, a requirement for nearly every undergraduate and graduate student, and for many professionally employed individuals. You will use Word to develop a research paper using widely accepted style conventions. Your paper will include footnotes, endnotes, a header, and a table of figures. Then you will create a research paper template to simplify writing future research papers.

Researching Internet Commerce

Brian Simpson works as a customer service representative at Green Clean while continuing his undergraduate work in marketing at a small private college. Brian was assigned the task of writing a research paper. The main topic must be on Internet commerce, and since Brian is also interested in the environment, he puts his own spin on the paper to include what effect e-commerce has had on the environment.

Brian uses Word 2010 to set up the research paper. Following the Modern Language Association's (MLA) handbook, he uses a header, footnotes, and a table of figures in his paper. Brian finds that the Footnote feature makes it easy to insert information about research sources into his paper.

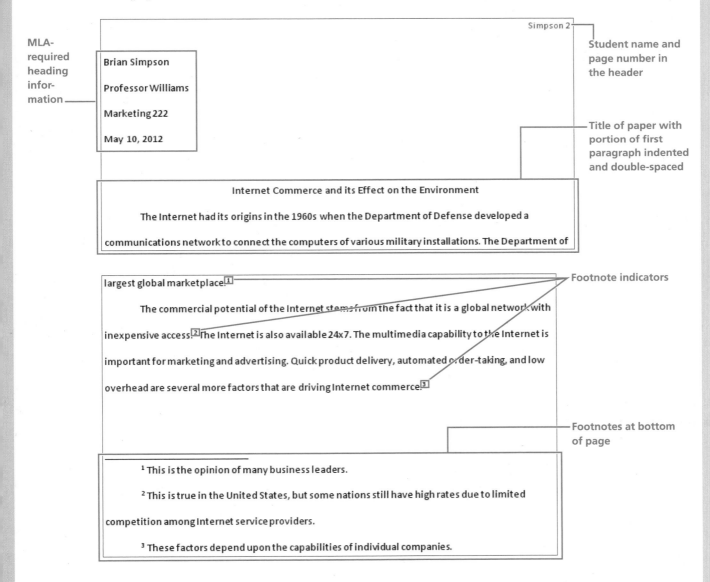

MLA-required heading information

Student name and page number in the header

Title of paper with portion of first paragraph indented and double-spaced

Footnote indicators

Footnotes at bottom of page

Simpson 2

Brian Simpson

Professor Williams

Marketing 222

May 10, 2012

Internet Commerce and its Effect on the Environment

The Internet had its origins in the 1960s when the Department of Defense developed a communications network to connect the computers of various military installations. The Department of largest global marketplace.[1]

The commercial potential of the Internet stems from the fact that it is a global network with inexpensive access.[2] The Internet is also available 24x7. The multimedia capability to the Internet is important for marketing and advertising. Quick product delivery, automated order-taking, and low overhead are several more factors that are driving Internet commerce.[3]

[1] This is the opinion of many business leaders.

[2] This is true in the United States, but some nations still have high rates due to limited competition among Internet service providers.

[3] These factors depend upon the capabilities of individual companies.

8.1 Using Research Paper Styles

There are several documentation styles, each with their own specific formatting requirements. The MLA style has been the standard for undergraduate and graduate research papers for many years.

Understanding the MLA Documentation Style

Video Lesson labyrinthelab.com/videos

The MLA publishes the *Modern Language Association Handbook for Writers of Research Papers*. The MLA style has very specific formatting requirements, some of which are already defaults within Microsoft Word. For example, all four of Word's default margins are one inch, which complies with the MLA margin requirement. You can visit the MLA website at www.mla.org for detailed information. Following is an overview of the MLA style guidelines:

- MLA style requires a header with the student's name followed by the page number aligned on the right one-half inch from the top of every page.

- The student name, professor, course, and date lines are positioned at the top-left of the first page and are double-spaced. Note that MLA does not require a separate title page for the research paper.

- The title of the paper follows the date line and extra line.

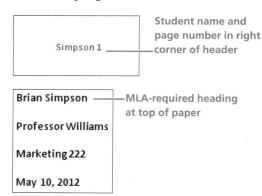

Student name and page number in right corner of header

MLA-required heading at top of paper

An extra line between the date and paper title

May·10,·2012¶

¶

Internet·Commerce·and·its·Effect·on·the·Environment¶

- The first line of each paragraph is indented one-half inch, and the line spacing requirement is double-space with the extra spacing removed after the paragraph.

Paragraph indented and double-spaced

The Internet had its origins in the 1960s when the Department of Defense developed a communications network to connect the computers of various military installations. The Department of Defense removed its computers from this network in the 1980s and turned over the control to the

- A superscript number appears at the end of the text to indicate a footnote or endnote. The actual footnote or endnote text uses the same formatting as the rest of the document.

Example of a superscript footnote indicator

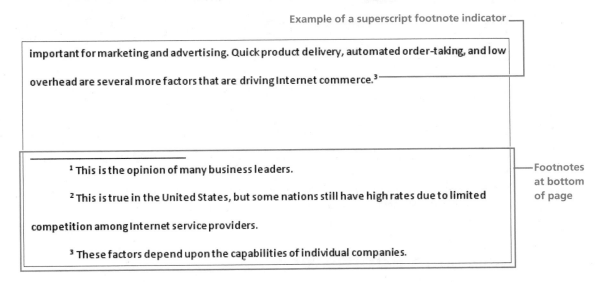

important for marketing and advertising. Quick product delivery, automated order-taking, and low

overhead are several more factors that are driving Internet commerce.³

¹ This is the opinion of many business leaders.

² This is true in the United States, but some nations still have high rates due to limited

competition among Internet service providers.

³ These factors depend upon the capabilities of individual companies.

Footnotes at bottom of page

- A citation appears in parentheses at the end of the line you are referencing, instead of a superscripted footnote or endnote indicator. The citation usually contains the author's last name and possibly a page number if referencing a page in a book.

Example of a citation

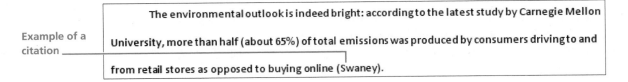

The environmental outlook is indeed bright: according to the latest study by Carnegie Mellon

University, more than half (about 65%) of total emissions was produced by consumers driving to and

from retail stores as opposed to buying online (Swaney).

- A separate Works Cited page is added to the end of the research paper, listing, in alphabetical order, all citations referenced in the document.

Example of a Works Cited page

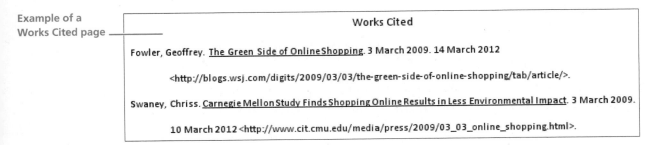

Works Cited

Fowler, Geoffrey. The Green Side of Online Shopping. 3 March 2009. 14 March 2012

<http://blogs.wsj.com/digits/2009/03/03/the-green-side-of-online-shopping/tab/article/>.

Swaney, Chriss. Carnegie Mellon Study Finds Shopping Online Results in Less Environmental Impact. 3 March 2009.

10 March 2012 <http://www.cit.cmu.edu/media/press/2009/03_03_online_shopping.html>.

Video Lesson   labyrinthelab.com/videos

Footnotes, endnotes, and citations are important parts of most research papers. You use them to comment on or cite a reference to a designated part of the text. Footnotes appear at the bottoms of pages; endnotes, as the name implies, appear at the end of a document or section; and citations appear on a separate Works Cited page at the end of the document. The Works Cited page is another name for a bibliography.

For the sake of simplicity, the following topics use the term *footnote* only. All details described for footnotes apply equally to endnotes.

Inserting Footnotes

The References tab of the Ribbon contains many of the commands you will use for this research paper project. You can insert footnotes using the buttons in the Footnotes group, keyboard shortcuts, and the Footnote and Endnote dialog box. Word automatically numbers each footnote and renumbers them if you add or remove one.

FROM THE KEYBOARD

Alt+Ctrl+F to insert a footnote

When you insert a footnote, Word automatically inserts a superscripted number for it in your text at the location of the insertion point.

Using the Footnote and Endnote Dialog Box

This dialog box offers another method for inserting notes, but additionally it provides options for controlling the position, format, and other aspects of notes. You can even create custom footnote marks.

This is where you can choose to insert either a footnote or an endnote. ——

You can choose from several formats for footnote and endnote reference marks. You can also type a custom mark or choose a custom character from the Symbol dialog box. ——

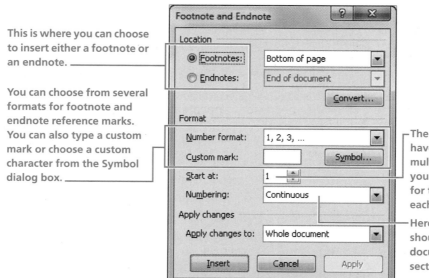

The Start At option is useful if you have a large project organized into multiple documents. In this situation, you can specify a starting number for the footnotes and endnotes in each document.

Here you specify whether numbering should be continuous throughout the document or restart at each new section or page.

Inserting Footnote Links

When you insert a footnote, Word inserts a footnote reference mark in the document, and the mark is linked to a corresponding footnote. The following illustration shows a footnote reference mark and the corresponding footnote at the bottom of the page.

This is the footnote reference mark in the main portion of the document. It matches the number or symbol in the footnote.

The footnote text is typed at the bottom of the page. Word adds a note separator line above the footnotes and inserts the appropriate numbers.

overhead are several more factors that are driving Internet commerce³

Internet commerce will be a driving force in the global economy of the twenty-first century.

There are still obstacles to overcome, but technology and market forces will propel this new commercial

medium forward at a rapid pace.

¹ This is the opinion of many business leaders.
² This is true in the United States, but some nations still have high rates due to limited competition among Internet service providers.
³ These factors depend upon the capabilities of individual companies.

Using Citations

A citation is used to refer to material you obtained from an outside source that you are using in the paper. The source information can be entered when you insert the citation, or you can insert a placeholder and edit the source data later. The citation appears inside parentheses at the end of the cited material; this notation takes the place of the superscript number that is placed for a footnote or endnote.

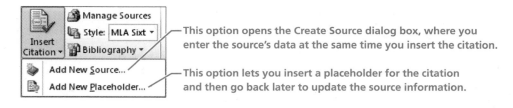

This option opens the Create Source dialog box, where you enter the source's data at the same time you insert the citation.

This option lets you insert a placeholder for the citation and then go back later to update the source information.

Inserting a Citation

The Insert Citation command is found in the Citations & Bibliography group on the References tab of the Ribbon. Immediately following the text and before the ending punctuation, a note (sometimes referred to as a p-note because it appears inside parentheses) is placed citing the author's last name, if available, or the document title. Before inserting the citation, it's a good idea to choose the style of documentation you are using, for example, MLA, APA, or Chicago. You will learn more about this later in this lesson.

In addition to the MLA documentation style, two other popular styles are American Psychological Association (APA) and The Chicago Manual of Style (CMS).

A truck delivering numerous packages along its way is the largest environmental savings, as it uses less energy per package than if the consumers had driven to the shops themselves (Fowler).

This is an example of a citation, where the author's last name is placed inside parentheses at the end of a paragraph. Notice the citation is after the text but before the period. A common mistake is to place the citation after the period.

DEVELOP YOUR SKILLS 8.2.1
Insert Footnotes and Citations

In this exercise, you will create a research paper and insert footnotes and citations in it. You will also look at the footnotes in different views.

1. **Open** the Internet Research document from the Lesson 08 folder.
   Feel free to turn the formatting marks on or off as needed during this lesson.

2. If necessary, switch to **Print Layout** ▦ view.
   Footnotes may differ in appearance depending on the view you are using, as you will see later.

3. Position the **insertion point** at the top of the document and **type** the four lines of text above the title, **tapping** ⎵Enter⎵ once after each line, including the last line:

Brian·Simpson¶

Professor·Williams¶

Marketing·222¶

May·10,·2012¶

¶

　　　　　　　Internet·Commerce·and·Its·Effect·on·the·Environment¶

　　The·Internet·had·its·origins·in·the·1960s·when·the·Department·of·Defense·developed·a·communications·network·to·connect·the·computers·of·various·military·installations.·The·Department·of·Defense·removed·its·computers·from·this·network·in·the·1980s·and·turned·over·the·control·to·the·National·Science·Foundation·(NSF).·In·1992,·the·U.S.·government·withdrew·funding·from·the·NSF·and·encouraged·private·companies·to·administer·and·control·the·"Internet."·It·was·at·this·point·that·Internet·commerce·was·born.·Companies·both·large·and·small·suddenly·realized·the·enormous·marketing·potential·of·this·global·computer·network.·In·fact,·by·2007,·the·Internet·has·no·doubt·become·the·largest·global·marketplace.¶

　　The·commercial·potential·of·the·Internet·stems·from·the·fact·that·it·is·a·global·network·with·

The additional line space between the date and the title is an MLA requirement. Notice also that the paragraph text is double-spaced and the extra space after the paragraphs has been removed, per MLA requirements.

Insert a Footnote

4. Position the **insertion point** to the right of the period at the end of the first paragraph.

5. Choose **References→Footnotes→Insert Footnote** AB¹ from the Ribbon.

6. Follow these steps to complete the footnote:

(A) The footnote area appears at the bottom of the page. Word automatically inserts both a separator line and the correct superscript number.

¹ This is the opinion of many business leaders.

(B) **Type** the text shown in the footnote area.

7. Position the **insertion point** in the appropriate places, then use **References→ Footnotes→Insert Footnote** from the Ribbon to insert the remaining two footnotes shown in the following illustration.

> The commercial potential of the Internet stems from the fact that it is a global network with inexpensive access.² The Internet is also available 24x7. The multimedia capability to the Internet is important for marketing and advertising. Quick product delivery, automated order-taking, and low overhead are several more factors that are driving Internet commerce.³
>
> Internet commerce will be a driving force in the global economy of the twenty-first century. There are still obstacles to overcome, but technology and market forces will propel this new commercial medium forward at a rapid pace.
>
> _____
> ¹ This is the opinion of many business leaders.
> ² This is true in the United States, but some nations still have high rates due to limited competition among Internet service providers.
> ³ These factors depend upon the capabilities of individual companies.

Notice that the formatting of the footnotes does not adhere to MLA requirements. You will fix this a little later in this lesson.

8. **Type** the following paragraphs after the paragraph beginning *Internet Commerce will be…*

The environmental outlook is indeed bright: according to the latest study by Carnegie Mellon University, more than half (about 65%) of total emissions was produced by consumers driving to and from retail stores as opposed to buying online.

Geoffrey Fowler, in his March 3, 2009 article on the Wall Street Journal website, cited the following environmental benefits to e-commerce shopping:

- Uses about one-third less energy than conventional retail shopping
- Uses a one-third smaller carbon footprint than a standard building
- A truck delivering numerous packages along its way is the largest environmental savings, as it uses less energy per package than if the consumers had driven to the shops themselves.

Change the Style to MLA

9. Choose **References→Citations & Bibliography→MLA Sixth Edition** from the Ribbon.

Insert a Citation as a New Source

10. Position the **insertion point** between the word *online* and the period at the end of the first paragraph on page 2 and **tap** the ⎡Spacebar⎤.

The environmental outlook is indeed br

University, more than half (about 65%) of total e

from retail stores as opposed to buying online |

---

11. Choose **References→Citations & Bibliography→Insert Citation** from the Ribbon.

12. Choose **Add New Source** from the drop-down menu to open the Create Source dialog box.

13. Follow these steps to create the new source to insert as the citation:

Ⓐ Choose **Web Site** from the Type of Source drop-down menu.

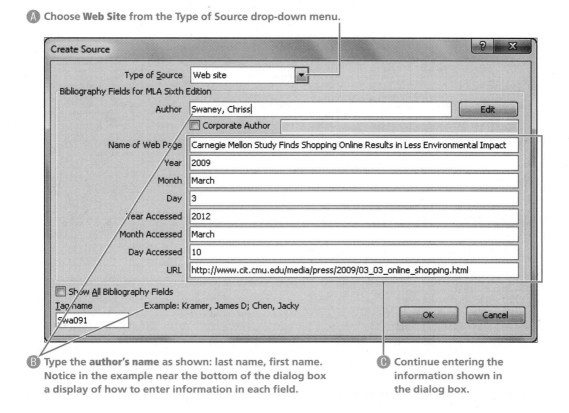

Ⓑ Type the **author's name** as shown: last name, first name. Notice in the example near the bottom of the dialog box a display of how to enter information in each field.

Ⓒ Continue entering the information shown in the dialog box.

14. When finished, click **OK**.
Notice the author's last name has been inserted automatically as the name of the citation enclosed in parentheses.

Insert a Citation Placeholder

15. Position the **insertion point** at the end of the last line of the document but before the period.

> • A truck delivering numerous packages along its way is the largest environmental savings, as it uses less energy per package than if the consumers had driven to the shops themselves

16. **Tap** the ⌨Spacebar, and then choose **References→Citations & Bibliography→Insert Citation** from the Ribbon.

17. Follow these steps to create a placeholder for a citation named *Fowler:*

Ⓐ Choose **Add New Placeholder** from the drop-down menu to open the Placeholder Name dialog box.

Ⓑ Type **Fowler** in the name box, and click **OK**.

18. **Save** 💾 the document, and then continue with the next topic.

Editing and Formatting Footnotes

Video Lesson labyrinthelab.com/videos

You can edit footnote text directly in the footnote area. In addition to editing the text of a footnote, you can also do the following:

- **Reposition**—You can change the position of a footnote reference mark in the main part of the document by dragging it to another location.
- **Format**—You can change various formatting features of footnotes. For example, you can change the numbering scheme, the starting number, or even replace a footnote number with a special symbol.

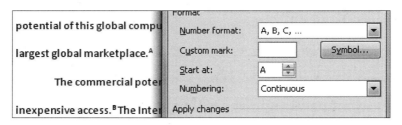

In this example, uppercase letters replace the normal numbering for this footnote.

Changing the Text Style of a Footnote

Word's default style for the footnote text does not meet the requirements of the MLA documentation style. Therefore, you need to change the formatting if you want to be in compliance with MLA. MLA requirements state the text should be the same formatting as the regular text in the document; that is, double-spaced and with first line indented. You can also change the number format and location for the footnotes using the Footnote and Endnote dialog box.

¹ This is the opinion of many business lea
² This is true in the United States, but son
service providers.
³ These factors depend upon the capabili

This is an example of Word's default
formatting of footnotes; it is single-
spaced and a smaller font size than
the other text in the document.

¹ This is the opinion of many business l

² This is true in the United States, but s

competition among Internet service providers

³ These factors depend upon the capal

This is an example after the footnote formatting has been
changed to the same format as the rest of the document.
Notice the first line of text is indented, is double-spaced,
and is the same font size as the rest of the document.

Editing a Citation

Once you insert a placeholder for a citation or create a source, you can edit the information in
the Edit Source dialog box. You choose what type of source you are using, for example, a book,
an article, a website, and so forth. You then edit all the pertinent information about the source,
such as author's name, document name, and website address. The default citation is the
author's last name; however, you could choose to suppress it and instead show the name of
the web page.

The author's name is entered
last name, first name.

You choose the type of source from this list,
for example, a book, article, or website.

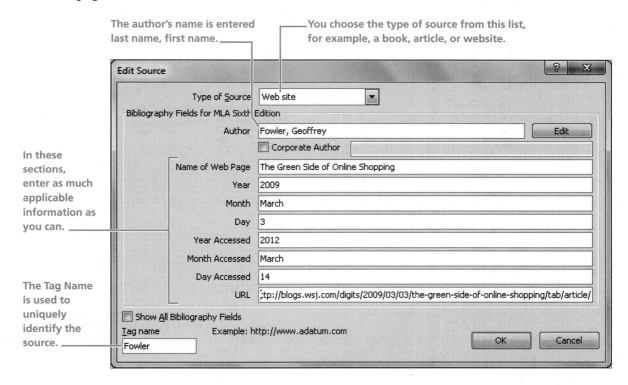

In these
sections,
enter as much
applicable
information as
you can.

The Tag Name
is used to
uniquely
identify the
source.

Edit Source

Type of Source | Web site
Bibliography Fields for MLA Sixth Edition
Author | Fowler, Geoffrey | Edit
☐ Corporate Author
Name of Web Page | The Green Side of Online Shopping
Year | 2009
Month | March
Day | 3
Year Accessed | 2012
Month Accessed | March
Day Accessed | 14
URL | :tp://blogs.wsj.com/digits/2009/03/03/the-green-side-of-online-shopping/tab/article/

☐ Show All Bibliography Fields
Tag name | Example: http://www.adatum.com
Fowler

OK | Cancel

QUICK REFERENCE	WORKING WITH FOOTNOTES AND CITATIONS
Task	**Procedure**
Insert a footnote	▪ Choose References→Footnotes→Insert Footnote from the Ribbon.
Navigate to footnotes	▪ Choose References→Footnotes→Next Footnote from the Ribbon.
Edit footnotes in Print Layout View	▪ Edit in the designated area at the bottom of the page.
Format a footnote	▪ Choose References→Footnotes from the Ribbon. ▪ Click the dialog box launcher [▣] to access the Footnote and Endnote dialog box. ▪ Make the desired formatting changes.
Change the style of footnote text	▪ Select the footnote text. ▪ Make the desired text and paragraph style changes.
Delete a footnote	▪ Select the footnote number in the document area and tap the [Delete] key. The note text associated with the mark is deleted from the footnote area simultaneously.
Insert a citation	▪ Choose References→Citations & Bibliography→Insert Citation from the Ribbon. ▪ Choose Add New Source to open the Create Source dialog box. ▪ Enter data in the Create Source dialog box and click OK.
Edit a citation source	▪ Click on the citation in the document. ▪ Click the down arrow to the right of the citation. ▪ Choose Edit Source from the drop-down menu. ▪ Make the desired changes in the dialog box and click OK.
Edit a citation	▪ Click on the citation in the document. ▪ Click the down arrow to the right of the citation. ▪ Choose Edit Citation from the drop-down menu. ▪ Make the desired changes in the dialog box and click OK.

DEVELOP YOUR SKILLS 8.2.2

Format, Edit, and Delete Footnotes and Citations

In this exercise, you will practice formatting, editing, and deleting footnotes and citations.

Format Footnotes

1. Position the **insertion point** at the beginning of the second paragraph on the first page and scroll, if necessary, so you can see the three footnote indicators and the footnote text at the bottom of the first page.

2. Choose **References→Footnotes→dialog box launcher** to display the Footnote and Endnote dialog box.

3. Choose **Footnotes** in the Location area at the top of the dialog box.

4. Click the Number Format drop-down arrow, and choose **A, B, C...** from the list.

5. Click the **Apply** button.
   Notice that the footnote numbers change to alphabetic characters. You use the same technique to change the format of endnotes.

6. Click the **Undo** ↺ button to return the footnote formatting to numbers.

7. Select the **three footnotes** at the bottom of the page.

8. Follow these steps to format the footnotes:
   - Change the line spacing to **double-space**.
   - Change the font size to **11**.
   - If necessary, display the ruler, and then drag the top triangle to **indent** the first lines **one-half inch**.

Delete a Footnote

9. Follow these steps to delete a footnote:

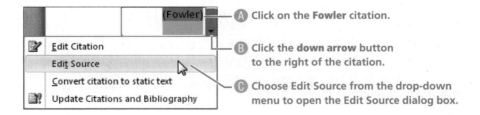

Ⓐ Select the **marker** by dragging the mouse pointer over it.

potential of this global comput

largest global marketplace.¹

Ⓑ **Tap** [Delete] to remove the marker. The footnote indicator and the footnote text are removed. Notice also that the remaining footnotes have been renumbered.

10. Click the **Undo** ↺ button to replace the footnote indicator and its text.

Edit a Footnote

11. Position the **insertion point** between the last word and the period of the first footnote.

12. **Tap** the [Spacebar] and type **and economists**.

Edit a Citation and a Source

13. Scroll to **page 2** to view the Fowler citation.

14. Follow these steps to open the Edit Source dialog box:

(Fowler)

📝 Edit Citation
Edit Source
Convert citation to static text
📄 Update Citations and Bibliography

Ⓐ Click on the **Fowler** citation.

Ⓑ Click the **down arrow** button to the right of the citation.

Ⓒ Choose Edit Source from the drop-down menu to open the Edit Source dialog box.

15. Follow these steps to edit the source information for the Fowler citation:

Ⓐ Choose **Web Site** for the source type.

Ⓑ Type **Fowler, Geoffrey** for the author's name.

Ⓒ Enter the remaining data shown in the illustration.

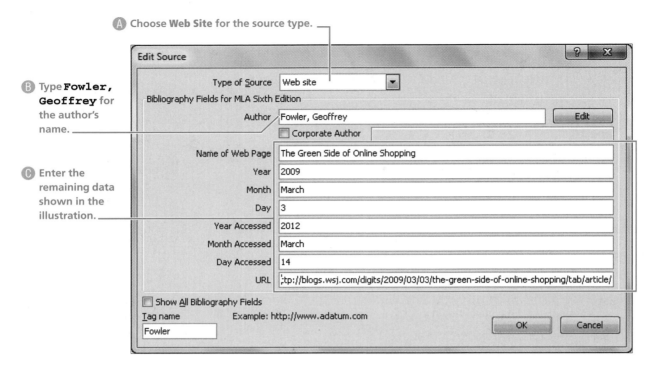

16. Click **OK** to close the Edit Source dialog box.

17. Click **Yes** if a message box appears asking if you want to update the master list and the current document.

18. **Save** 💾 the file, and leave it **open** for the next topic.

8.3 Working with Bibliographies

Video Lesson labyrinthelab.com/videos

A bibliography is a list of all the sources that were referred to in preparation of the document. This list may be called different things depending on which documentation style you are using. MLA requires a separate page at the end of the document titled Works Cited. The Works Cited page is an alphabetical listing of all sources actually referred to in citations in the document.

Changing the Bibliography Style

You choose the documentation style from the Style drop-down menu in the Citations & Bibliography group on the References tab. Different documentation styles require different bibliography formatting; therefore, the Create Source dialog box will contain different fields, depending on which documentation style is selected in the Citations & Bibliography group. One example of this is the requirement difference for a website citation for MLA versus APA documentation style. The APA style requires the name of the web page and the name of the website, whereas the MLA style requires only the name of the web page. The source data entered is used later to create the bibliography.

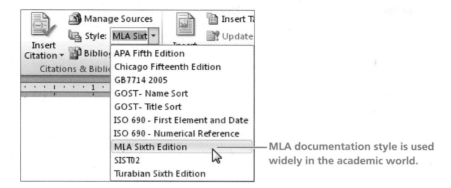

MLA documentation style is used widely in the academic world.

Creating a Bibliography

The bibliography list is created according to the document style you selected from the Style menu. It picks up the information you entered in the Create Source dialog box and creates the list with the correct punctuation in the bibliography. However, certain formatting requirements such as the title location and the double-spacing between paragraphs are not Microsoft defaults and must be done separately.

The Bibliography button in the Citations & Bibliography group on the References tab contains two built-in options: Bibliography and Works Cited. You can choose either of these; however, the paragraph formatting may or may not meet the requirements of the document style you chose. For example, the Works Cited option for the MLA style does not format the title, the paragraph spacing, or the line spacing correctly. Thus, it is advised that you type the title at the top-center of the page and then use the Insert Bibliography command rather than one of the built-in options.

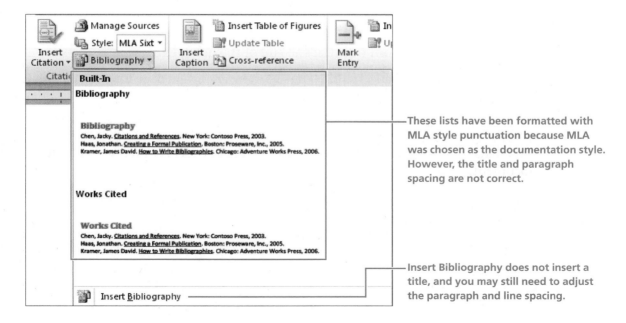

These lists have been formatted with MLA style punctuation because MLA was chosen as the documentation style. However, the title and paragraph spacing are not correct.

Insert Bibliography does not insert a title, and you may still need to adjust the paragraph and line spacing.

Creating an Alphabetic List of Citations

In a document using the MLA documentation style, the bibliography is titled Works Cited. The MLA Works Cited page has specific requirements.

Title is centered one inch from the top of the paper and created on a separate page at the end of the document.

Works Cited

Fowler, Geoffrey. The Green Side of Online Shopping. 3 March 2009. 14 March 2012

<http://blogs.wsj.com/digits/2009/03/03/the-green-side-of-online-shopping/tab/article/>.

Swaney, Chriss. Carnegie Mellon Study Finds Shopping Online Results in Less Environmental Impact. 3 March 2009.

10 March 2012 <http://www.cit.cmu.edu/media/press/2009/03_03_online_shopping.html>.

Sources are listed in alphabetical order no matter what order they appear in throughout the document. Paragraphs are double-spaced and use a hanging indent.

Updating a Bibliography

When you edit the citation source or add a new one, you can easily update the bibliography list using the Update Field command on the drop-down menu when you right-click anywhere on the list. When you use the Update Field command, it reformats the list to single-spacing again; thus, you must remember to change it to double-spacing.

DEVELOP YOUR SKILLS 8.3.1
Create a Bibliography

In this exercise, you will create a bibliography for the citations in the document. You will title the page as Works Cited since the lesson is following the MLA documentation style. Finally, you will edit an existing citation, update the bibliography list, and format the paragraphs with double-spacing.

Create a New Page and Add the Title

1. Position the **insertion point** at the end of the document.

2. **Tap** Enter twice, and **tap** Ctrl + Enter to insert a new page for the bibliography that you will insert in the next section of the exercise.

3. Choose **Home→Paragraph→Center** ☰ from the Ribbon to center the insertion point. Type **Works Cited** and **tap** Enter.

Insert the Bibliography List

4. Choose **References→Citations & Bibliography→Bibliography** from the Ribbon.

5. Choose **Insert Bibliography** from the drop-down menu.

Update a Bibliography

6. **Scroll up** and click on the **Fowler** citation at the bottom of the second page and click the **down arrow** on the right of it.

7. Open the **Edit Source** dialog box, change the Day Accessed to **10**, and then click **OK**.

8. **Scroll down** the Works Cited page, and notice nothing has changed yet in the list.

9. Follow these steps to update the bibliography:

A **Right-click** on any line of the list to display the drop-down menu.

Fowler, Geoffrey. The Green Side
<http://blogs.wsj.com/di
Swaney, Chriss. Carnegie Mellon
10 March 2012 <http://w

Cut
Copy
Paste Options:
Update Field

B Click **Update Field** from the menu. Notice the date accessed for the Fowler citation changed to March 10, 2012.

Notice after you use the Update Field command, the list is single-spaced; thus, you must manually double-space between paragraphs.

Format the List

10. Using the margin area, select the **bibliography list** (do not select the title).

11. Choose **Home→Paragraph→Line and Paragraph Spacing** from the Ribbon.

12. Choose **2.0** from the drop-down menu to double-space the selected list.

13. **Save** the document and continue with the next topic.

8.4 Introducing Headers and Footers

Video Lesson labyrinthelab.com/videos

There is a header area and a footer area at the top and bottom of every page in a document, above and below the margins. You can place text, page number codes, date codes, graphics, and other items in the header and footer areas. When you enter information in these areas, it is replicated on every page of the document, or you can specify different headers and footers for each section of a document.

You choose the Header or Footer command from the Header and Footer group on the Insert tab of the Ribbon. Word offers a variety of header and footer formatting styles that you can choose from the menu.

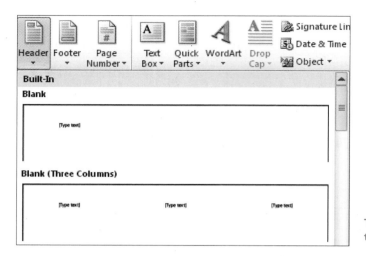

These are just two examples of the many built-in header styles.

If you wish to create your own header or footer from scratch, you can choose the Edit Header or Edit Footer commands from the Header or Footer menu, and then type and format the header or footer.

Formatting Headers and Footers

The Design tab under Header and Footer Tools on the Ribbon provides many options for formatting a header or footer. For example, you can format page numbers as alphabetic characters or Roman Numerals using the Format Page Numbers command.

Using the Insert group on the same tab, you can insert date and time codes, documents such as the author or company name, or fields such as the document's filename and path.

The Header and Footer Design contextual tab replaces the Header and Footer Custom Dialog Box found in previous versions of Word.

QUICK REFERENCE	WORKING WITH HEADERS AND FOOTERS
Task	**Procedure**
Create a header/ footer	■ Choose Insert→Header & Footer→Header/Footer from the Ribbon. ■ Choose a built-in header/footer style. *or* ■ Choose Edit Header/Footer from the menu and create your own.
Delete a header/ footer	■ Choose Insert→Header & Footer→Header/Footer from the Ribbon. ■ Choose Remove Header/Footer from the menu.
Format page numbers	■ Choose Header and Footer Tools→Design→Header and Footer→Page Number from the Ribbon. ■ Choose Format Page Numbers from the menu. ■ Choose the desired number format in the Page Number Format dialog box. ■ Click OK.
Insert a date and time code	■ Choose Header and Footer Tools→Design→Insert→Date & Time from the Ribbon. ■ Choose the desired date format in the Date and Time dialog box. ■ Click OK.

Add a Header to the Report

In this exercise, you will add a page number and the author's name to the report. As specified in the MLA guidelines, the page number and name must be right-aligned at the top of the page.

1. Position the **insertion point** at the top of the document.

2. Choose **Insert→Header & Footer→Page Number** [icon] from the Ribbon.

3. Choose **Top of Page** from the menu, and then choose **Plain Number 3** from the gallery.
   This places page number 1 right-aligned in the header area. Now you will add the writer's name.

4. Choose **Insert→Header & Footer→Header** [icon] from the Ribbon.

5. Choose **Edit Header** from the bottom of the menu.
   This positions the insertion point in the page number object to the left of the number. When you are already in the Header section, steps 4 and 5 are not required; you can just begin editing. The steps are included here as reinforcement of where the command is located.

6. Type **Simpson**, and then **tap** the ⌷Spacebar⌷.

7. **Double-click** in the document background to close the header area and to view the header text.

8. Scroll to the top of **page 2**, and observe the header.

9. **Save** [icon] the file, and leave it **open** for the next topic.

8.5 Inserting Captions and a Table of Figures

Video Lesson   labyrinthelab.com/videos

You use captions to insert text associated with figures or tables in a paper. Word then uses the captions as entries in the table of figures. Later, if you alter some of the captions, Word updates these when you regenerate the table of figures.

Inserting Captions

Word can automate or semiautomate the creation of captions for figures in a document. For example, you can standardize on the phrase *Figure x*, with Word automatically assigning a number to each caption. You can choose References→Captions→Insert Caption to open the Caption dialog box, or right-click on an object and choose Insert Caption from the drop-down menu.

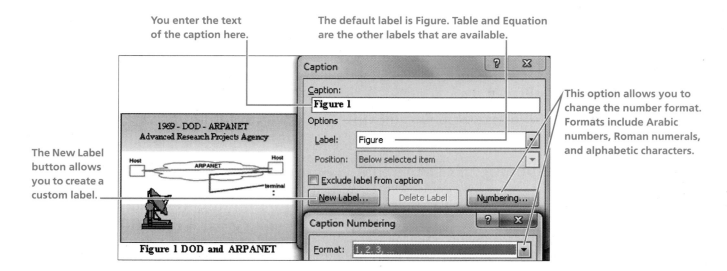

You enter the text of the caption here.

The default label is Figure. Table and Equation are the other labels that are available.

This option allows you to change the number format. Formats include Arabic numbers, Roman numerals, and alphabetic characters.

The New Label button allows you to create a custom label.

Generating a Table of Figures

A table of figures guides the reader to all tables, charts, diagrams, pictures, and other graphic elements in a document. Before creating a table of figures, you mark the figures in your document with captions.

DEVELOP YOUR SKILLS 8.5.1
Add Captions to Figures

In this exercise, you will insert a file between page 1 and 2 that contains five PowerPoint slides pasted from a presentation. You will add captions to the slides in preparation for creating a table of figures.

Insert a File

1. Position the **insertion point** after the Footnote 3 indicator at the bottom of the first page.

2. **Press** ⌨Ctrl+⌨Enter to insert a page break.

3. Choose **Insert→Text→Object** 🖼 **menu ▾** from the Ribbon, and then choose **Text from File** from the menu.

4. In the Insert File dialog box, navigate to your Lesson 08 folder, choose Internet Slides, and then click the **Insert** button.

5. If necessary, choose **Home→Paragraph→Show/Hide** ¶ from the Ribbon to display formatting marks.

6. **Tap** ⌨Delete to remove any extra paragraph marks between the last paragraph of the new file inserted and the next one.

Add Captions and Edit a Caption

7. Position the **insertion point** on the first blank line below the first slide.

8. Choose **References→Captions→Insert Caption** 🖼 from the Ribbon to open the Caption dialog box.

9. The Caption dialog box should match the following illustration. If *Figure 1* does not appear in the Caption text box at the top of the dialog box, follow these steps. Otherwise, go to step 11.

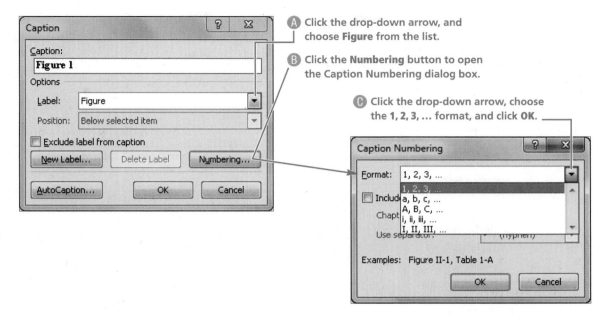

A Click the drop-down arrow, and choose **Figure** from the list.

B Click the **Numbering** button to open the Caption Numbering dialog box.

C Click the drop-down arrow, choose the **1, 2, 3, ...** format, and click **OK.**

10. If necessary, position the **insertion point** to the right of *Figure 1* in the Caption text box.

11. **Tap** the [Spacebar], type **DOD and ARPANET**, and click **OK** to insert the caption. *Notice the caption is placed on the left margin; you will fix this problem in the next step.*

12. Choose **Home→Paragraph→Center** ☰ to center the caption.

13. Position the **insertion point** in the first blank line below the second slide.

14. Choose **References→Captions→Insert Caption** ▣ from the Ribbon to open the Caption dialog box for Figure 2.

15. **Tap** the [Spacebar], type **NSF**, and click **OK**.

16. **Center** ☰ the caption.

17. Add the **captions** shown in the following table and **center** them:

Slide Number	Caption Text
3	MILNET and TCP/IP
4	First Graphical Browser
5	Netscape

Edit a Caption

18. Return to **slide 2**, select *NSF*, and type **National Science Foundation** in its place.

19. Choose **Home→Paragraph→Show/Hide** ¶ from the Ribbon to turn off the formatting marks.

20. **Save** 🖫 the file, and leave it **open** for the next exercise.

Inserting a Table of Figures

Video Lesson   labyrinthelab.com/videos

Academic papers often include a table of figures at the front, which guides the reader to illustrations, charts, tables, and other types of figures. This is particularly helpful in long documents. The table entries conveniently function as hyperlinks if you are reading the document online. You will create a table of figures like the one in the following illustration.

Table of Figures

Figure 1 DOD and ARPANET _____ 3
Figure 2 National Science Foundation _____ 3
Figure 3 MILNET and TCP/IP _____ 3
Figure 4 First Graphical Browser_____ 4
Figure 5 Netscape _____ 4

QUICK REFERENCE	CREATING CAPTIONS AND TABLES OF FIGURES
Task	**Procedure**
Insert a caption	▪ Choose References→Captions→Insert Caption from the Ribbon.
	▪ Type the text for the caption.
Insert a table of figures	▪ Choose References→Captions→Insert Table of Figures from the Ribbon.
	▪ Make formatting choices in the Table of Figures dialog box.
Update a table of figures	▪ Right-click the table, and choose Update Field from the pop-up menu.

DEVELOP YOUR SKILLS 8.5.2
Generate a Table of Figures

In this exercise, you will generate a table of figures from the captions you inserted in the preceding exercise. You will change the numbering format of your captions, and then you will update the table to reflect the change.

Insert the Table of Figures

1. Move the **insertion point** to the top of the document, and insert a **page break**.

2. Tap [Ctrl]+[Home] to position the insertion point at the top of the new page, type **Table of Figures**, and tap [Enter] twice.

3. Select the **heading** you just typed, **center** ≡ it, and format it with **bold 16 pt**.

4. Place the **insertion point** in the blank line below the heading.

5. Choose **References→Captions→Insert Table of Figures** 📑 from the Ribbon.

6. Follow these steps to set up the table:

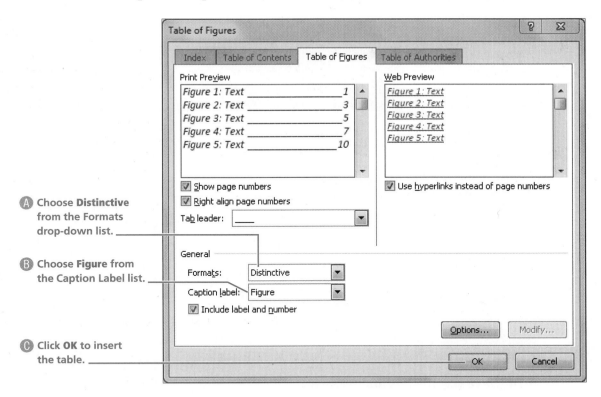

(A) Choose **Distinctive** from the Formats drop-down list.

(B) Choose **Figure** from the Caption Label list.

(C) Click **OK** to insert the table.

7. Position the **insertion point** on page 3 of the document.

Change the Numbering Format of the Captions

8. Choose **References→Captions→Insert Caption** 📄 from the Ribbon.

9. Click the **Numbering** button in the bottom-right corner of the dialog box, and the Caption Numbering dialog box appears.

10. Choose the **A, B, C,...** format, as shown at right, and then click **OK**.

11. Click the **Close** button in the Caption dialog box, and **scroll** through the slides. Notice that the figure numbers changed to alphabetic characters.

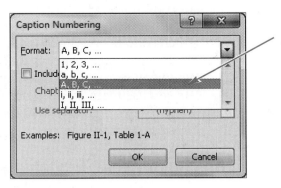

Update the Table of Figures

12. **Scroll up** to view the Table of Figures on page 1. Notice that the table is still showing the numeric figure numbers.

13. Follow these steps to update the table of figures:

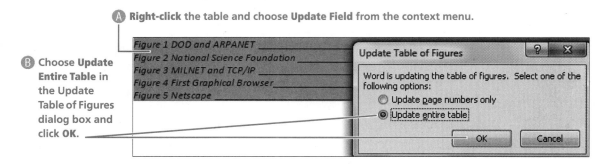

Ⓐ **Right-click** the table and choose **Update Field** from the context menu.

Ⓑ Choose **Update Entire Table** in the Update Table of Figures dialog box and click **OK.**

The table should match the following illustration.

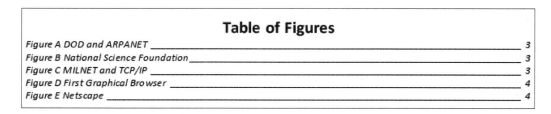

Table of Figures

Figure A DOD and ARPANET	*3*
Figure B National Science Foundation	*3*
Figure C MILNET and TCP/IP	*3*
Figure D First Graphical Browser	*4*
Figure E Netscape	*4*

The text switched from Figures 1–5 to Figures A–E.

14. **Save** 💾 the file, and **close** it.

8.6 Working with Templates

Video Lesson   labyrinthelab.com/videos

All Word documents are based on templates, which can include text, formatting, graphics, and any other objects or formats available in Word. The default Word template is named Normal, which contains one-inch margins, Calibri 11 pt font, line spacing of 1.15, and other settings. The benefit of templates is that they do not change when documents based on them change. When you start a new document based on a template, Word opens a *copy* of the template. This lets you use templates repeatedly as the basis for new documents. Word provides a variety of ready-to-use templates, and if necessary, you can modify them to suit your needs. You can also create custom templates.

Creating a Document from a Template

You choose File→New to access the Available Templates pane, from where you can use existing templates or create new custom templates. Basing a new document on a saved template can save you a lot of time since much of the formatting is already included in the template for you.

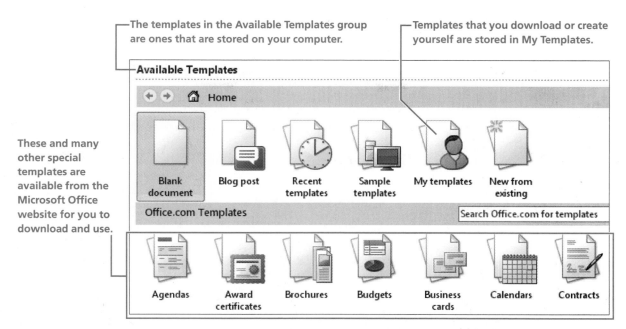

The templates in the Available Templates group are ones that are stored on your computer.

Templates that you download or create yourself are stored in My Templates.

These and many other special templates are available from the Microsoft Office website for you to download and use.

The appearance of this window may vary depending on recent actions taken here.

Saving Documents as Templates

When you create a document containing specific formatting, you can save it to use later as a template. You should save the template in the Templates folder. This is what causes your templates to appear in the My Templates folder found in the Available Templates section. You can save a template as a .dotx file type or a .dotm file type. A .dotm file is one that contains a special series of instructions, called a macro.

Create a Template from an Existing Document

In this exercise, you will open a copy of a report and save it as a template. The body text of the report has been removed; however, other elements are still in place, such as the cover page, the table of figures, and the double spacing. You will save time by starting new reports based on the template.

Save an Existing Document as a Template

1. **Open** My Report from the Lesson 08 folder.

2. **Scroll** through the document, and notice the elements that are still in place in the document that will be useful when you create a new report.

3. Choose **File→Save As**.

4. Click **Templates** in the left pane of the Save As dialog box.

You may need to expand the Microsoft icon in the left pane by pointing to it and clicking its left arrow, to display the Templates folder.

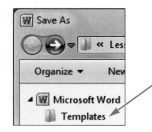

5. Choose **Word Template** from the Save As Type drop-down list at the bottom of the dialog box.

6. Name the file **My Report Template**, and then click **Save**.

7. **Close** the template file.

Create a New Document Based on the Template

8. Choose **File→New**.

9. Follow these steps start a new document based on a template:

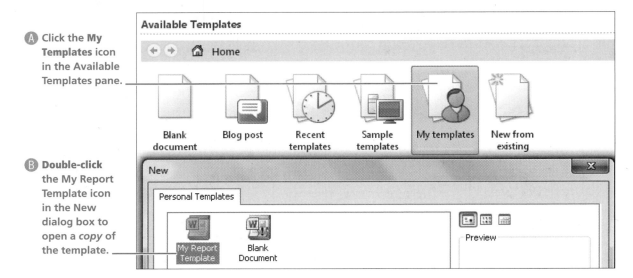

Ⓐ Click the **My Templates** icon in the Available Templates pane.

Ⓑ **Double-click** the My Report Template icon in the New dialog box to open a *copy* of the template.

Notice the title bar with the generic Document(x) name that appears at the top of the window. This indicates that this is just a regular Word document and you are not changing the actual template.

10. Scroll to **page 3**, and replace [DOCUMENT TITLE] with **The Green Life**.

11. **Save** 💾 the document as **Green Life** in the Lesson 08 folder, and then **close** it.

Deleting a Template

Video Lesson   labyrinthelab.com/videos

When a template is no longer useful, you may wish to delete it. Templates are easily removed from the New dialog box. It's a good idea to delete unwanted templates so the dialog box does not become too cluttered.

QUICK REFERENCE	CREATING AND DELETING TEMPLATES
Task	**Procedure**
Save an existing document as a template	▪ Choose File→Save. ▪ Click the Templates icon. ▪ Choose Word Template (*.dotx) from the Save As Type menu.
Delete a template	▪ Choose File→New. ▪ Choose My Templates from the pane on the left. ▪ Right-click the template you wish to delete. ▪ Choose Delete from the pop-up menu.

Delete a Template

In this exercise, you will delete the template you created.

1. Choose **File→New**.

2. Choose **My Templates** from the Available Templates dialog box to open the New dialog box.

3. Follow these steps to delete My Report Template:

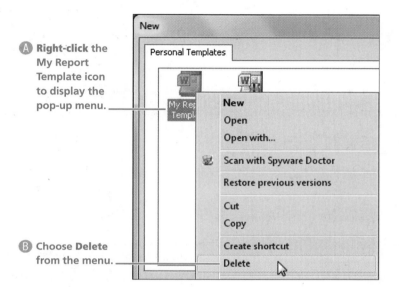

A **Right-click** the My Report Template icon to display the pop-up menu.

B Choose **Delete** from the menu.

4. When the message box appears to verify that you want to delete the template, click **Yes**. *Notice that the template was removed from the dialog box.*

5. Click **Cancel** to close the New Document dialog box.

8.7 Concepts Review

Concepts Review   labyrinthelab.com/word10

To check your knowledge of the key concepts introduced in this lesson, complete the Concepts Review quiz by going to the URL listed above. If your classroom is using Labyrinth eLab, you may complete the Concepts Review quiz from within your eLab course.

Reinforce Your Skills

Insert and Delete Footnotes

In this exercise, you will insert footnotes in a document.

1. **Open** rs-Garden Report from the Lesson 08 folder.

2. Position the **insertion point** after the word *tested* at the end of the first sentence under the *Organic Lawn Fertilizer* heading on page 2.

3. Choose **References→Footnotes→Insert Footnote** AB[1] from the Ribbon.
   The insertion point is next to the footnote number at the bottom of the page.

4. Type **Products tested by Garden Laboratories, Inc., Melville, CA** as the footnote text.
   Next you will place a footnote above the one you just inserted, which will cause renumbering of the original footnote.

5. In the *Weed Control* paragraph, position the **insertion point** to the right of the word *Rover* toward the end of the fourth line.

6. Choose **References→Footnotes→Insert Footnote** AB[1] from the Ribbon to place the next footnote marker at the bottom of the page.
   Notice that the original footnote is numbered 2.

7. Type **Products approved by the Wildlife Association of America**.

8. Position the **insertion point** at the end of the third bullet on page 3.

9. Insert a footnote marker, and type **Manufacturer's warranty is 60 days**.

10. Position the **insertion point** after the words *Mighty Mulcher* on the last page.

11. Insert a footnote marker, and type the footnote **Extended manufacturer's warranty available**.
    Next you will delete the footnote next to Rover *in the* Weed Control *paragraph.*

Delete a Footnote

12. Return to **page 2**, and **select** the footnote marker next to *Rover* in the *Weed Control* paragraph.

13. **Tap** Delete to remove the marker.

14. **Scroll** to the bottom of the page, and notice that the footnote is gone and the second footnote renumbered to 1.

15. **Scroll** through the other pages, and observe that renumbering took place.

16. **Save** 💾 the file, and **close** it.

Insert Headers and Footers

In this exercise, you will add headers and footers to a document you prepared as a handout for your meeting presentation. You will use the Edit Header command to add your header, and then you will use one of Word's predesigned footers to add page numbers to your document. You will also format the header and footer text.

Add a Header

1. **Open** rs-Options from the Lesson 08 folder.

2. Choose **Insert→Header & Footer→Header** ▯ from the Ribbon.

3. Choose **Edit Header** from the bottom of the menu.

4. Type **Options and Swaps Presentation** at the header's left margin.

5. **Tap** Tab twice to right-align the insertion point, and then type **GRCC Chapter Meeting**.

6. Select the header text and use the Mini Toolbar to change the font size to **9**.

7. **Double-click** in the body of the document to close the header area.

Add a Footer

8. Choose **Insert→Header & Footer→Footer** ▯ from the Ribbon.

9. **Scroll down** the list of preformatted footers, and choose **Alphabet** from the menu to insert page numbers in your document.

10. Replace [Type Text] with **Presented by: [Your Name]**.

11. Select the **footer** text, including the page number, and use the Mini Toolbar to change the font to **9 pt italics**.

12. **Double-click** in the body of the document to close the footer area.

13. **Scroll** through the document, and observe your headers and footers.

14. **Save** ▯ the file, and **close** it.

Insert Captions and a Table of Figures

In this exercise, you will add captions to the pictures in a document, and then you will generate a table of figures from the captions.

Insert Captions

1. **Open** rs-Rose Catalog from the Lesson 08 folder.

2. Scroll to **page 3** of the document, and position the **insertion point** on the blank line below the first rose picture.

3. Choose **References→Captions→Insert Caption** 📄 from the Ribbon to open the Caption dialog box.

4. If Figure 1 appears in the Caption text box, continue with the next step. Otherwise, click the **numbering** button, choose **1, 2, 3,...** from the Format drop-down list, and click **OK**.

5. Make sure the **insertion point** is to the right of *Figure 1* in the Caption text box.

6. **Tap** the ⌜Spacebar⌝, type **Floribunda**, and click **OK**.

7. Repeat this technique to enter **captions** below the next three pictures. Use the following captions:

   - **Glorious**
   - **Moondance**
   - **Heaven on Earth**

Generate the Table of Figures

8. Go to **page 2**, and position the **insertion point** on the second blank line below the Table of Figures heading.

9. Choose **References→Captions→Insert Table of Figures** 🗐 from the Ribbon.

10. Choose **Formal** from the list of formats to match the following illustration.

Table of Figures
FIGURE 1 FLORIBUNDA..3
FIGURE 2 GLORIOUS..3
FIGURE 3 MOONDANCE..3
FIGURE 4 HEAVEN ON EARTH..3

11. Click **OK** to insert the Table of Figures.

12. **Save** 💾 the file, and **close** it.

Create a Template from an Existing Document

In this exercise, you will open a document and save it as a template. You will then open a copy of the template, and finally you will delete the template.

1. **Open** rs-Rose Sales from the Lesson 08 folder.

2. Choose **File→Save As**.

3. Click the **Templates** icon in the left pane of the Save As dialog box to switch to the Templates folder.

4. Choose **Word Template** from the Save As Type drop-down list at the bottom of the dialog box.

5. Name the file **rs-My Rose Template**.

6. Click the **Save** button.

7. **Close** the template.

Open a Copy of the Template

8. Choose **File→New**.

9. Choose **My Templates** from Available Templates to open the New dialog box.

10. **Double-click** the rs-My Rose Template icon to open a copy of the template. *Notice the generic Document(x) name in the title bar.*

11. **Close** the document without saving.

Delete a Template

12. Choose **File→New**.

13. Choose **My Templates** from Available Templates to open the New dialog box.

14. **Right-click** the rs-My Rose Template icon, and choose **Delete** from the menu.

15. When the message box appears, click **Yes** to complete the deletion.

16. Click **Cancel** to close the New dialog box.

Apply Your Skills

Create Captions and a Table of Figures

In this exercise, you will open a real estate brochure and place captions below the pictures of the houses. Then you will generate a table of figures that lists the captions and their associated page numbers.

Add the Captions

1. **Open** as-RE Brochure from the Lesson 08 folder.

2. Create the following **captions** for each house picture in the brochure, but this time try a different method. Instead of going to the Ribbon to access the Insert Caption command, **right-click** on the picture and choose **Insert Caption** from the pop-up menu.

   Figure 1 **Pleasant Valley charming cottage**

   Figure 2 **Burgundy Valley appealing updated home**

   Figure 3 **Pleasant Valley cottage with delightful garden**

   Figure 4 **Kensington two-story charmer**

   Figure 5 **Lakeville waterfront cottage with dock**

3. **Scroll up** and position the **insertion point** at the bottom of page 1 at about the 6 ½-inch mark on the ruler, as shown in the following illustration.

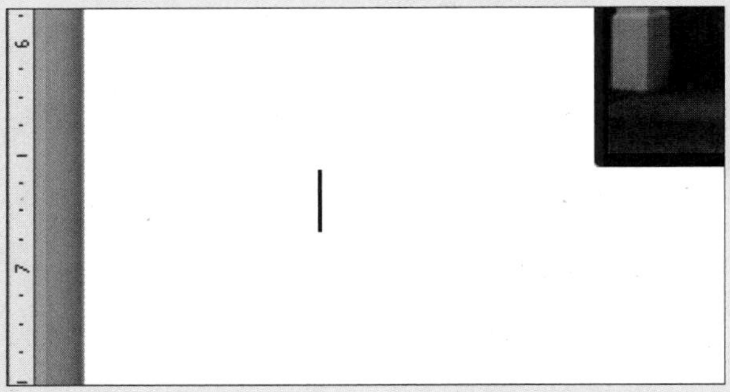

4. **Tap** Ctrl + Enter to insert a page break.

5. Type **Table of Figures** and **tap** Enter.

6. Reduce the size of the heading to **14 pt.**

Generate the Table of Figures

7. Position the **insertion point** on the first blank line below the heading.

8. Choose **References→Captions→Insert Table of Figures** ▤ from the Ribbon.

9. Choose the **Distinctive** format, and click **OK** to generate the table.
   Next you will modify one of the captions and then regenerate the table.

10. Go to the **Figure 2** caption and change *appealing* to **attractive**.

11. Scroll down to the **Figure 4** caption and insert the word **colonial** before the word *charmer*.

12. Return to the table, and **right-click** it to view the pop-up menu.

13. Choose **Update Field** from the menu, choose **Update Entire Table** in the Update Table of Figures dialog box, and then click **OK**.
    That updates the table with the Figure 2 edit you just made.

14. **Save** ▤ the file, and **close** it.

Create a Research Paper with Citations and a Bibliography

Most English and humanities classes follow the method for writing research papers dictated in the MLA handbook. Various academic disciplines use their own editorial guidelines for citing resources in research papers. Following is a list of organizations that sponsor style manuals.

- *Modern Language Association*
  http://www.mla.org
- *Council of Science Editors*
  http://www.councilscienceeditors.org
- *Linguistic Society of America*
  http://www.lsadc.org/

In this exercise, you will visit these websites (or websites of your choice with related topics) and locate the mission statement (or an overview statement) on each site. You will then copy a paragraph from each mission statement and paste it in your research paper. Then you will insert a citation for each paragraph, citing the web page of the organization in the footnote. (Results may vary due to the changing nature of the Internet.)

1. Start a **new** document, and **format** it according to the MLA guidelines outlined at the beginning of this lesson.

2. Add a **right-aligned header** with your last name and the page number.

3. **Type** the student name, professor, course, and date at the top of the first page. The student name is your name, the professor is **Professor Higgins**, and the course is **Humanities 101**. Use today's date.

4. Type **Style Guide Research** as the title of the paper.

5. Use the **URLs** provided above to visit the websites of the organizations listed (or similar organizations).

6. **Copy** a paragraph from the mission statement or overview statement of each site, and paste it into your paper.

7. **Format** the text according to your preferences but within the MLA guidelines.

8. Insert a **citation** at the end of each paragraph, and add the required **source data** from each web page.

9. Create a **new page** at the end of the document.

10. **Center** and type **Works Cited** as the title for the new page.

11. Insert a **bibliography** (do not use the built-in Bibliography or Works Cited option).

12. **Double-space** the lines in the bibliography list.

13. **Save** 📁 the file in the Lesson 08 folder as **as-Style Research** and **close** it.

Critical Thinking & Work-Readiness Skills

In the course of working through the following Microsoft Office-based Critical Thinking exercises, you will also be utilizing various work-readiness skills, some of which are listed next to each exercise. Go to labyrinthelab.com/workreadiness to learn more about the work-readiness skills.

8.1 Add Footnotes, Citations, Headers, and Footers

Jordan Stewart, a college intern working at Green Clean, has been asked to research the environmental benefits of using washable fabric napkins rather than disposable paper napkins. Her research, which was assigned by her professor, will be shared with Green Clean clients as a community service. Open the ct-Napkin Research file (Lesson 08 folder) and save a copy of it as **ct-Napkin Research Footnotes**. Insert an appropriate header, your name, your teacher's name, your course, and today's date, all formatted to MLA specifications. Format the rest of the document text with a Calibri 11 pt font. Make up three humorous footnotes with citations and add a header and footer. Save your changes.

WORK-READINESS SKILLS APPLIED

- Using computers to process information
- Organizing and maintaining information
- Thinking creatively

8.2 Work with Figures and Captions

Start with the ct-Napkin Research Footnotes document you created in the previous exercise and save a copy of it with the name **ct-Napkin Figures** to your Lesson 08 folder. Add creative captions to the two figures and create a table of figures. Insert a cover page with appropriate text and formatting. Remember, this is a research paper that will be shared with customers, so make sure it is customer appropriate. Save your changes. If working in a group, discuss what may be considered "customer appropriate" and not. If working alone, type your answers in a Word document named **ct-Questions** saved to your Lesson 08 folder.

WORK-READINESS SKILLS APPLIED

- Serving clients/ customers
- Making decisions
- Participating as a member of a team (or Writing)

8.3 Create a Template and add a Bibliography

Open the ct-Napkin Figures document you created in the previous exercise. Take one last look to verify proper MLA formatting and a professional cover page. Save it as a template to Word's Templates folder as **Research Paper [First Last] Template** (substitute your actual first and last name). Create a new document based on the template you just created and save it to your Lesson 08 folder as **ct-Child Page**. Add a bibliography page to the end of the document (there is no need to fill it in). Save your changes. If working in a group, brainstorm scenarios in which having a predesigned template can be helpful. If working alone, type your answers in a Word document named **ct-Questions2** saved to your Lesson 08 folder.

WORK-READINESS SKILLS APPLIED

- Showing responsibility
- Selecting technology
- Participating as a member of a team

Creating a Promotional Brochure

LEARNING OBJECTIVES

After studying this lesson, you will be able to:

- Use Shapes to add graphic interest
- Insert and edit pictures
- Work with SmartArt graphics
- Add page borders and background page color

In this lesson, you will learn to add graphic elements, such as Shapes, pictures, and SmartArt to your document, and then you will use Word's galleries to format these graphic images. Finally, you will format the page background with page color and a page border.

Promoting an Ergonomics Seminar

Josh DeLeone owns Ergonomic Office Solutions. He has called upon his old buddy, Tommy Choi, owner of Green Clean, with an idea to create a presentation about the benefits of using ergonomic equipment. He believes using Tommy's database of customers would be a great place to launch his seminar. He knows Tommy's customer base is already interested in the environment, and he believes those same customers would be interested in taking care of their ergonomic health.

Josh decides he will create a brochure, have Tommy review a draft of it, and then mail it to local businesses to promote this seminar and, thereby, spark interest in the ergonomic office furniture and computer equipment he sells. Josh uses product pictures as well as Word's Shapes and SmartArt to create a brochure that is both informative and visually appealing.

green clean

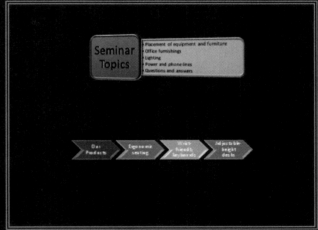

9.1 Working with Shapes

Video Lesson labyrinthelab.com/videos

Word has a large gallery of graphic shapes that you can insert into your documents. Shapes include lines; text boxes; basic shapes such as rectangles, ovals, and triangles; special shapes such as arrows, stars, callouts, and banners; and many others. They can add interest to documents such as flyers, brochures, and other graphical documents. You can also type text in most shapes.

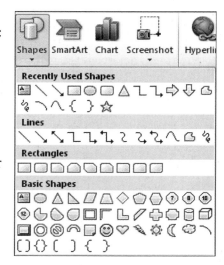

Shapes are located in the Illustrations group on the Insert tab of the Ribbon. They are found in a gallery similar to other galleries you have worked with.

You insert Shapes by choosing the desired Shape in the gallery. When the mouse pointer is in the document, it changes to a crosshair, which you click or drag in the document to create the Shape.

Rotating, Resizing, and Moving Shapes

Clicking a Shape displays the handles, which are similar to handles you've seen on clip art. If the handles are not visible, clicking the object displays them. You can move, resize, or rotate a Shape only when the handles are visible. You can insert a perfect square or circle in one of two ways: by choosing the rectangle or oval tool and clicking in the document, or by holding down the Shift key while drawing the shape.

When you place the mouse pointer on the Rotate handle, the pointer changes to a circular arrow. You can then drag left or right to rotate the object.

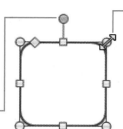

Position the mouse pointer on a handle, and it changes to a double-headed arrow; then you can drag to resize the object. If you hold the Shift key when you drag a corner handle, the object maintains its original proportions. A square remains a square, for example.

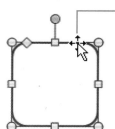

When you position the mouse pointer on the border of the selected Shape, the Move handle (four-headed arrow) indicates that you can now drag to move the Shape.

Adding and Formatting Text in Shapes

You can add text to the Shapes you draw. This can be handy if, for example, you want to create a flyer announcing an event. You can right-click a selected Shape and choose the option to add text from the pop-up menu. Alternatively, you can choose the Edit Text button in the Insert Shapes group on the Format tab of the Ribbon. Both options place the insertion point inside the drawn Shape, ready for you to type your text. Text is automatically centered both horizontally and vertically, and wraps within a shape as you type.

Selecting a Shape by the border selects all the text inside the Shape; however, it does not highlight the text, as Word normally does when you select text. You can then make character formatting changes, which will affect all of the text. If you wish to format only a portion of the text, you must drag to select it.

Formatting Shapes

When a Shape is selected, Word provides a contextual Format tab, which contains many tools you can use to add color and pizzazz to the Shape, including Shape Styles, Shadow Effects, and 3-D Effects. The Format tab also has its own Insert Shapes gallery containing the same shapes as the Shapes gallery located in the Illustrations group on the Insert tab. When multiple shapes are selected, you can align, resize, or move them.

QUICK REFERENCE	WORKING WITH SHAPES
Task	**Procedure**
Insert a perfect square	■ Choose the rectangle Shape from the Shapes gallery. ■ Click in the document. *or* ■ Hold the Shift key while dragging in the document.
Insert a perfect circle	■ Choose the oval Shape from the Shapes gallery. ■ Click in the document. *or* ■ Hold the Shift key while dragging in the document.
Maintain an object's proportions	■ Hold the Shift key while dragging a corner handle to resize.
Type text within a Shape	■ Select the Shape. ■ Begin typing.
Selecting multiple Shapes	■ Hold the Shift key down, and click on each object.
Align multiple objects	■ Select the objects using the Shift key. ■ Choose Format→Arrange→Align from the Ribbon. ■ Choose the desired alignment.
Move an object	■ Select the object. ■ Position the mouse pointer on a border to display the Move handle. ■ Drag the object to the desired location.

DEVELOP YOUR SKILLS 9.1.1
Draw Shapes and Insert Graphic Objects

In this exercise, you will draw Shapes and add text to them, and then you will insert and format WordArt and a picture into your brochure. First you will change the Theme to Office.

1. **Open** the Promo Brochure document from the Lesson 09 folder.

Change the Theme

2. Choose **Page Layout→Themes→Themes** [Aa] from the Ribbon, and then choose **Office** from the menu.
   The change of Theme won't be apparent until you enter more content into your document.

Draw a Shape

First you will experiment with a Shape, and then you will insert the Shape that you will use for your brochure.

3. Choose **Insert→Illustrations→Shapes**  from the Ribbon to display the Shapes gallery.

4. Choose the **rounded rectangle** from the **Rectangles** section of the gallery, as shown in the following illustration.

5. **Click and drag** in the document to draw a rounded rectangle.
   Notice the rectangle shape is filled with a color; that's because you applied a Theme to this document, and themes include fill colors for shapes.

6. Choose **Format→Insert Shapes** from the Ribbon, and then click the **rounded rectangle**.

7. **Hold** the ⸤Shift⸥ key and drag to draw a rounded rectangle that's larger than the last one.
   Notice this time you drew a perfect square with rounded corners instead of a rectangle even though you started with the same Shape. This happened because you held down the ⸤Shift⸥ key while drawing.

8. Make sure the **Shape** is selected (displaying handles), and then take a moment to practice resizing it using the handles.

9. Use the **Rotate** handle at the top of one of the Shapes to rotate it.

Delete the Practice Shapes

You must select a Shape before you can delete it.

10. Click one of the **Shapes** to display the handles, and then **press and hold** the ⸤Shift⸥ key and select the other **Shape**.

Holding the ⸤Shift⸥ key allows you to select multiple Shapes at once, and then you can delete, move, or format them all at once.

11. **Tap** ⸤Delete⸥ to remove both of the Shapes.

Draw a Shape for Your Brochure

12. If necessary, click the **View Ruler** 🔲 button at the top of the vertical scroll bar to display the Ruler.
    The Ruler will be helpful in sizing your Shape.

13. Choose **Insert→Illustrations→Shapes**  from the Ribbon.

14. Choose the **rounded rectangle** from the **Shapes** gallery, and draw a long narrow rectangle at the top margin that spans across the page. It should be about 1 inch high.

Remember, the Move handle appears when you place the mouse pointer on the border of a selected Shape. You press and hold down the mouse button, and then drag to move the Shape.

15. Use the **Move** handle to practice moving the shape around, placing it back in its original position when you are finished.

Add Text to the Shape

16. Make sure the **Shape** is still selected.

17. **Tap** ⌈Caps Lock⌉, begin typing **ERGONOMIC OFFICE SOLUTIONS**, tap ⌈Enter⌉, and then type **PRESENTS**.
   Notice that the text was automatically centered in the Shape.

Format the Text

18. Click the **border** of the Shape.

Selecting a Shape by the border selects everything inside the Shape as well. Thus, the text in the Shape is selected, although it is not highlighted.

19. Choose **Home→Font→Font menu** from the Ribbon, and then choose **Tahoma** from the Font list.

20. Keep the **Shape** selected, and apply **bold 22 pt** font.
   You may need to drag a resizing handle if your drawn shape is not big enough to display the larger text.

Format the Shape

Next, you will use the Shape Styles gallery to format the Shape. This gallery behaves like other galleries you have used.

21. Make sure the object is selected so the contextual **Format** tab is available.

22. Choose **Format→Shape Styles** from the Ribbon.

23. Follow these steps to format the Shape:

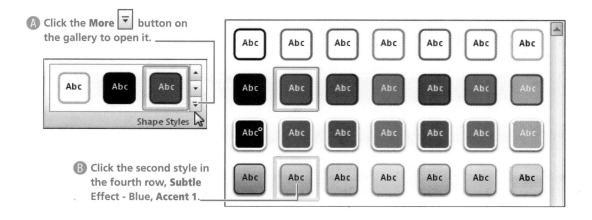

Ⓐ Click the **More** ▼ button on the gallery to open it.

Ⓑ Click the second style in the fourth row, **Subtle Effect - Blue, Accent 1.**

Add and Align Objects

Next, you will add another object and then center it.

24. Click in the document under the **rectangle**, and choose **Insert→Text→WordArt** 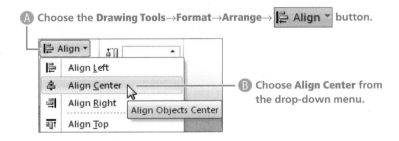 from the Ribbon.

25. Choose the fourth style in the fourth row, **Gradient Fill – Blue, Accent 1, Outline – White**, and then type **The Ergonomically Challenged Office**.

26. Position the **mouse pointer** on the bottom edge of the WordArt text box, and **drag** it down about **two inches** below the rectangle. You can use the illustration at the end of the exercise as a guide if you wish.
Don't worry about centering it under the object at the top of the document; you will align the objects in the next steps.

27. Follow these steps to select multiple objects:

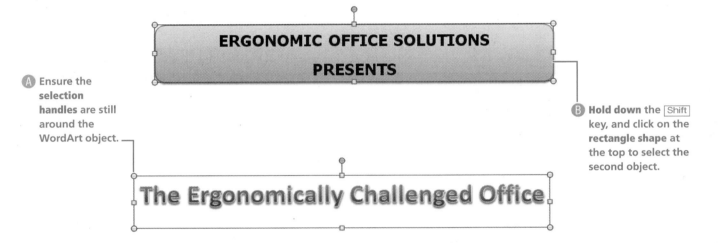

Ⓐ Ensure the selection handles are still around the WordArt object.

Ⓑ **Hold down** the ⬚Shift key, and click on the **rectangle shape** at the top to select the second object.

28. Make sure the contextual **Format** tab is activated on the Ribbon.

29. Follow these steps to center the two objects:

Ⓐ Choose the **Drawing Tools→Format→Arrange→** 🔲 **Align** button.

Ⓑ Choose **Align Center** from the drop-down menu.

30. Position the **mouse pointer** on either of the selected objects, and then **drag** them toward the center of the page, between the margins.
Notice that because both objects are selected, they both move at the same time.

31. Click on a **blank area** of the document to deselect the objects.

Insert a Picture in the Brochure

32. **Scroll down**, and click in the **left cell** of the table.

33. Choose **Insert→Illustrations→Picture**  from the Ribbon.

34. Navigate to the Lesson 09 folder, and **double-click** the Keyboard picture file to insert it.

35. Using the **left margin** area, click to select the **table row**.

36. Position the **mouse pointer** on the line between the two cells, and **double-click** to resize both columns to their best fit, as shown in the following illustration.

37. Position the pointer on the table's **move handle** ⊞, and then **drag** to the right to center the table under the other objects.

38. Select the **table** again, then choose the **Home→Paragraph→Border** menu button from the Ribbon.

39. Choose **No Border** from the drop-down menu to complete this page, as shown in the following illustration.

40. **Save** 🖫 the file, and leave it **open** for the next topic.

Working with Text Boxes

Video Lesson   labyrinthelab.com/videos

A text box is a special type of shape designed for you to insert text or graphics. You may wonder how inserting a text box is different from drawing a different shape and adding text inside it. It's because of the formatting. For example, when you apply a theme to a document, the theme includes formatting such as fill and line colors for shapes. Text boxes do not contain those formatting characteristics; you type in it, there is no fill color, and the text entered is left-aligned, starting at the top of the box. You can format all of the text by selecting the text box itself, or format only a portion of the text by selecting the part you want to change.

Adding a Text Box

You choose the text box from the Shapes gallery in the Illustrations group on the Insert tab and either click to place it in the document or drag it to the desired size. You can also use the Text Box gallery in the Text group on the same tab on the Ribbon to draw a text box, or choose a preformatted one from the gallery.

If you insert the text box by clicking in the document, when you begin typing, the text box expands to the edge of the paper and then begins to wrap the text. However, if you draw the text box, it remains the same size.

Formatting a Text Box

You can format a text box just like any other object. You must first select the text box, and then you can change the line surrounding it, change the fill color, resize it, or perform any of the other options appearing on the Format tab of the Ribbon. For example, you can also apply various styles, change the direction of text, or apply shadow or 3-D effects to text boxes using the Format contextual tab. A new text box can also be saved to the Text Box Gallery.

QUICK REFERENCE	WORKING WITH TEXT BOXES
Task	**Procedure**
Insert a text box	■ Choose Text Box from the Shapes gallery.
	■ Click in the document or drag to draw to the desired size.
	or
	■ Choose Insert→Text→Text Box ▢ from the Ribbon.
	■ Choose a preformatted text box.
	or
	■ Choose Draw Text Box from the menu.
Format a text box	■ Select the text box.
	■ Choose the desired formatting commands from the contextual Format tab on the Ribbon.
Apply a 3-D effect	■ Select the text box.
	■ Choose Text Box Tools→Format→3-D Effects.
	■ Choose the desired effect.
Apply a shadow effect	■ Select the text box.
	■ Choose Text Box Tools→Format→Shadow Effects.
	■ Choose the desired effect.

QUICK REFERENCE	WORKING WITH TEXT BOXES (continued)
Task	**Procedure**
Apply a text box style	■ Select the text box. ■ Choose Text Box Tools→Format→Styles. ■ Choose the desired style.
Change the text direction	■ Select the text box. ■ Choose Text Box Tools→Format→Text→Text Direction. ■ Choose the desired direction.
Save a text box to the text box gallery	■ Select the text box. ■ Choose Insert→Text→Text Box. ■ Choose Save Selection to the Text Box Gallery.

DEVELOP YOUR SKILLS 9.1.2
Work with Text Boxes

In this exercise, you will insert a text box, reposition it, and format the text within it.

Insert a Text Box

1. Choose **Insert→Illustrations→Shapes** 📷 from the Ribbon.

2. Choose the **Text Box** 🅰 from the Shapes gallery.

3. Position the **Text Box mouse pointer** ┼ under the center of the WordArt object.

4. Begin dragging to draw a text box about **2 inches long** and **½ inch tall**.

5. **Type** the text shown in the illustration to the right.
   Notice how the text automatically wraps within the text box and is left-aligned.

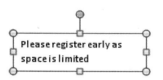

Format a Text Box

6. Follow these steps to resize the text box:

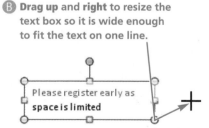

Ⓐ Position the **mouse pointer** on the bottom corner of the text box.

Ⓑ **Drag up** and **right** to resize the text box so it is wide enough to fit the text on one line.

7. Make sure the **text box** is selected so the contextual **Format** tab is displayed.

8. Follow these steps to remove the outline:

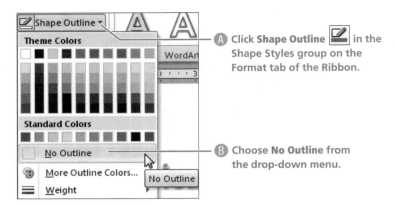

A Click **Shape Outline** [icon] in the Shape Styles group on the Format tab of the Ribbon.

B Choose **No Outline** from the drop-down menu.

9. Click the **Shape Fill menu button** in the Shape Styles group, and then choose **Orange, Accent 6, Lighter 80%**.

10. Choose **Drawing Tools→Format→Shape Styles→Shape Effects→3-D Rotation**.

11. Choose **Perspective Right** (the third column in the first row) in the menu.

Align Selected Objects

12. With the text box still selected, **hold down** the Shift key, and select the two objects **above** it.

13. Choose **Format→Arrange→Align** [icon] from the Ribbon.

14. Choose **Align Center** from the menu.

15. Click in the **document** to deselect the three objects.

16. **Save** [icon] the document, and continue with the next topic.

Video Lesson   labyrinthelab.com/videos

It is often easier to grasp concepts in business documents if information is presented graphically rather than textually. Word provides a large variety of SmartArt graphics that you can add to documents. SmartArt graphics make it easy to combine predesigned graphics with text to create sophisticated figures.

An example of a SmartArt figure

Inserting a SmartArt Graphic

When you choose Insert→Illustrations→SmartArt ⊞ from the Ribbon, the Choose a SmartArt Graphic dialog box appears. This contains a large array of categorized graphic images.

Choosing a SmartArt category in the left pane displays the associated images in the center pane.

Choosing an image displays a close-up view with a description of how the image could be used.

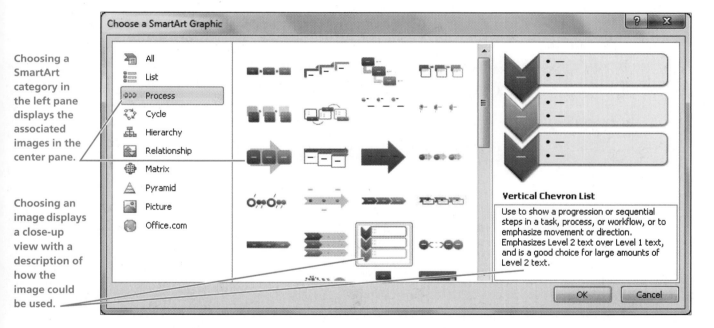

SmartArt Categories

SmartArt images are divided into the following categories:

Category	Purpose
List	Shows nonsequential data
Process	Shows steps in a process or progression
Cycle	Shows a continual process
Hierarchy	Creates a hierarchical structure or shows a decision tree
Relationship	Illustrates associations
Matrix	Shows how parts relate to a whole
Pyramid	Shows proportional relationships with the largest element on the top or bottom
Picture	Shows groups of pictures
Office.com	Shows various shapes available online

Using the SmartArt Text Pane

You use the SmartArt text pane to add text to your graphic image. When you insert the image, the text pane may or may not be open. If the pane is not open, you click the tab that appears on the left side of the image. The same tab closes the text pane. The [Text] placeholders are replaced with the text you enter in the SmartArt text pane.

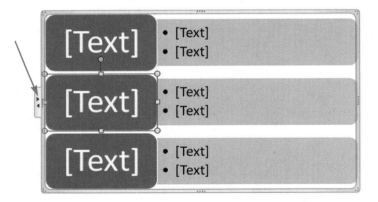

You type in a bulleted list in the Type Your Text Here pane as shown in the following illustration. As you type, the text is added to the image. Tapping Tab while entering text in the SmartArt text pane inserts the text in the right-hand column. Word adjusts the font size based on the amount of information you type. If you cannot find the exact image you want, you can modify, add, and delete Shapes within the graphic. SmartArt objects are formatted in the same way as other graphic Shapes.

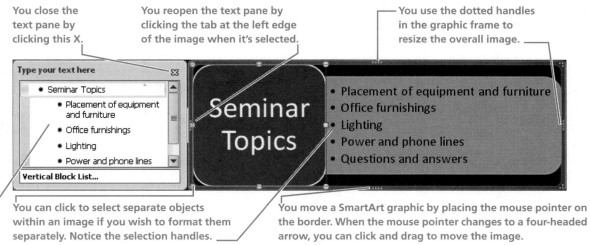

You enter the text here. You also format text in this pane, but the formatting appears only in the graphic. Sub-bullets appear in the right-hand column.

You close the text pane by clicking this X.

You reopen the text pane by clicking the tab at the left edge of the image when it's selected.

You use the dotted handles in the graphic frame to resize the overall image.

You can click to select separate objects within an image if you wish to format them separately. Notice the selection handles.

You move a SmartArt graphic by placing the mouse pointer on the border. When the mouse pointer changes to a four-headed arrow, you can click and drag to move the image.

Changing SmartArt Styles

The SmartArt Styles gallery on the contextual Design tab provides interesting variations of the original graphic. Like other galleries you have worked with, you can scroll through it, or you can use the More button to open the entire gallery. Live Preview lets you see the effect of the various styles without actually applying them.

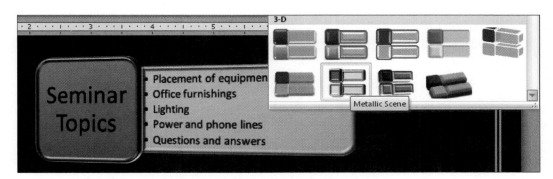

Using Live Preview to observe SmartArt Styles effects

QUICK REFERENCE	USING SMARTART
Task	**Procedure**
Insert a SmartArt image	■ Choose Insert→Illustrations→SmartArt from the Ribbon. ■ Select the desired SmartArt category. ■ Choose the SmartArt object you want to use, and then click OK.
Add text to a SmartArt object	■ If necessary, click the tab on the left side of the image to display the Type Your Text Here pane. ■ Use the pane to add text to the object. ■ To reopen the pane to add or edit text, select the object and click the tab at the left edge of the object's frame.
Apply a SmartArt Style	■ Choose Design→SmartArt Styles from the Ribbon. ■ Click a style in the gallery to apply it to the SmartArt image.

Insert SmartArt

In this exercise, you will use two SmartArt graphics: one to list the seminar topics and one to list the ergonomic products.

1. **Tap** ⌈Ctrl⌉+⌈End⌉ to move the insertion point to the bottom of the document.

2. **Press** ⌈Ctrl⌉+⌈Enter⌉ to insert a page break.

3. Choose **Home→Paragraph→Center** 🔲 from the Ribbon.
   Your image will be center-aligned when you insert it.

4. Choose **Insert→Illustrations→SmartArt** 🔲 from the Ribbon.

5. Follow these steps to insert a SmartArt object:

Ⓐ Make sure the **List** category is chosen.

Ⓑ Scroll down, and choose **Vertical Block List** in the seventh row. (Yours may be in a different location than shown in the figure.)

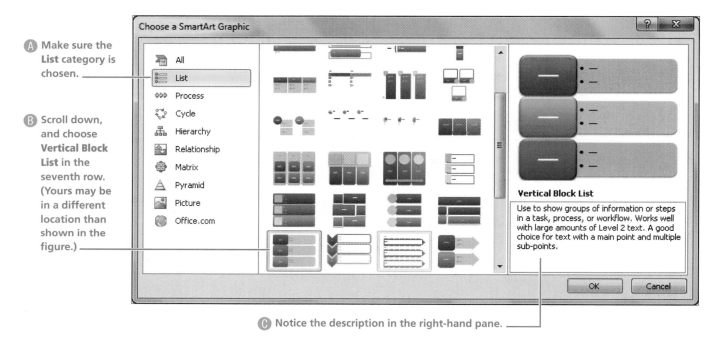

Ⓒ Notice the description in the right-hand pane.

6. Click **OK** to insert the SmartArt image in your document.

7. If the text pane is not visible, click the **tab** on the left side of the image, as shown in the following figure.

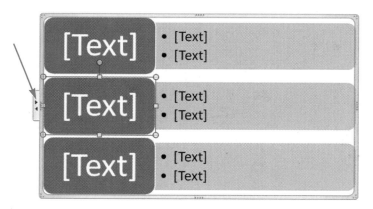

8. If necessary, reposition the **text pane** by dragging it by its top border, as shown in the following figure. In this example, it's best to position the pane to the left of the image.

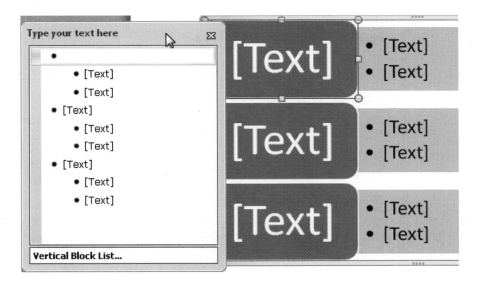

Customize the SmartArt Image

This image has three major text objects, but you will only use one.

9. If necessary, **scroll down** in the text pane until the last six bullet points are visible.

10. Follow these steps to remove two of the text objects:

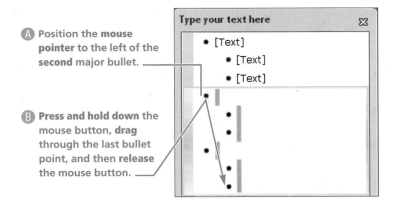

Ⓐ Position the **mouse pointer** to the left of the **second** major bullet.

Ⓑ **Press and hold down** the mouse button, **drag** through the last bullet point, and then **release** the mouse button.

11. **Tap** ⌑Delete⌑ to remove the last two objects.

12. Follow these steps to begin entering the seminar topics:

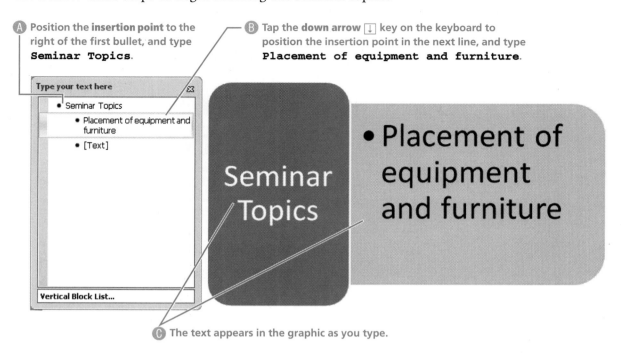

A Position the **insertion point** to the right of the first bullet, and type **Seminar Topics**.

B Tap the **down arrow** ⬇ key on the keyboard to position the insertion point in the next line, and type **Placement of equipment and furniture**.

C The text appears in the graphic as you type.

13. **Tap** the ⬇ key to go to the next line, and type **Office furnishings**.

14. **Tap** Enter to generate the next bulleted line, and type **Lighting**.

15. **Tap** Enter as necessary, and **type** the following items to complete the list:
   - **Power and phone lines**
   - **Questions and answers**

16. Click the **Close** ☒ button in the upper-right corner of the Type Your Text Here pane to close it.

17. Click the **outside border** of the image to make sure the entire image is selected and not just an individual object within the image.

18. Drag the **bottom-center sizing handle** up until the image is approximately half as tall as the original image.

Change the SmartArt Style

19. Choose **Design→SmartArt Styles→Change Colors** ⬤ from the Ribbon.

20. In the Accent 1 category, choose the fourth column, **Gradient Loop - Accent 1**.

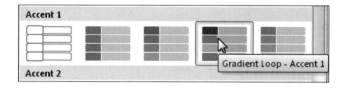

21. Choose **Drawing Tools→Design→ SmartArt Styles→More** button to display the entire gallery.

22. In the 3-D category, choose the second item in the second column, **Metallic Scene**. The Metallic Scene option may be in a different location, depending on the size of your screen.

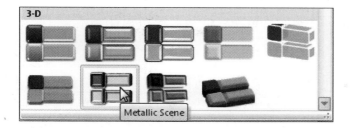

Add Another SmartArt Image

23. **Tap** [Ctrl]+[End] to position the insertion point at the end of the document.

24. **Tap** [Enter] twice.

25. Choose **Insert→Illustrations→SmartArt** ![icon] from the Ribbon.

26. Follow these steps to insert the next image:

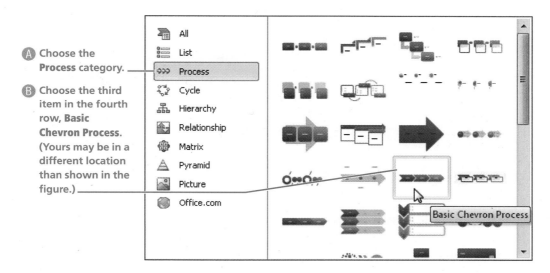

Ⓐ Choose the **Process** category.

Ⓑ Choose the third item in the fourth row, **Basic Chevron Process**. (Yours may be in a different location than shown in the figure.)

27. Click **OK** to insert the object.

28. **Click** on the [Text] placeholder in the first graphic arrow, and then type **Our Products**.

29. Click in each **arrow** to enter the text shown in the following illustration in the **middle** and **last arrows**.

30. If necessary, click on the **image** to select it.

31. Follow these steps to add a new arrow:

Ⓐ Click the tab on the **left side** of the image to display the Type Your Text Here pane.

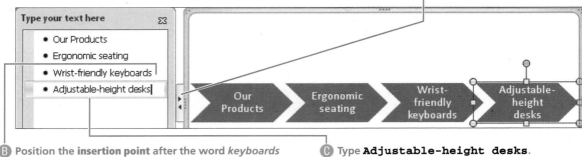

Ⓑ Position the **insertion point** after the word *keyboards* in the bulleted line, and then **tap** Enter. Notice that a new arrow was added to the end of the graphic.

Ⓒ Type **Adjustable-height desks**.

32. **Close** ☒ the text pane.

Format the Image

33. Click the **outside border** of the image to make sure the entire SmartArt graphic is selected.

34. Choose **Design→SmartArt Styles→Change Colors** 🎨 from the Ribbon.

35. Choose the fourth item in the Accent 1 category, **Gradient Loop – Accent 1**.

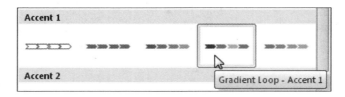

36. Click the **More** ⊽ button on the SmartArt Styles gallery, and in the 3-D category, choose the third item in the first row, **Cartoon**, and then click in the **document** to deselect the object.

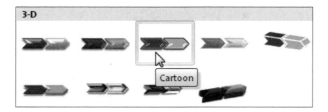

37. **Save** 💾 the document, and leave it **open** for the next topic.

Video Lesson labyrinthelab.com/videos

Word has great page background formatting features that add color and visual variety to your documents. Page colors and page borders provide the finishing touches that add professional polish and pizzazz. For example, you can add colors from a gallery specifically designed to blend with a document's theme. Border theme colors are also designed to tastefully complement page colors. These features are located in the Page Background group of the Page Layout tab on the Ribbon.

Adding Page Colors and Page Borders

The Page Colors gallery is similar to other color galleries you have worked with. The colors that appear in the Theme Colors section of the gallery, as the name implies, are based on the Theme currently in effect.

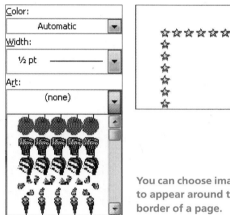

You can choose images to appear around the border of a page.

Page borders surround the outer edges of the entire page, rather than a particular object. You can adjust the color (again, based on the current Theme), line thickness, and other features of the border. There are also various graphic images available to use as page borders. A page border can be applied to the whole document, an individual section, the first page only, or all pages except the first page.

The Borders and Shading Dialog Box

This dialog box allows you to make settings similar to those you can set for paragraphs.

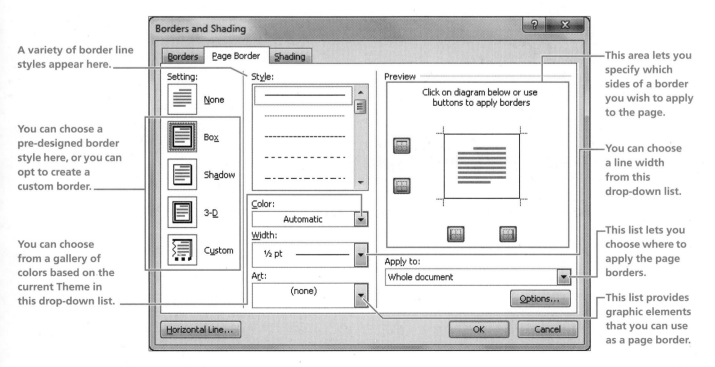

A variety of border line styles appear here.

You can choose a pre-designed border style here, or you can opt to create a custom border.

You can choose from a gallery of colors based on the current Theme in this drop-down list.

This area lets you specify which sides of a border you wish to apply to the page.

You can choose a line width from this drop-down list.

This list lets you choose where to apply the page borders.

This list provides graphic elements that you can use as a page border.

Inserting a Watermark

A watermark is text or a graphic that is placed behind the text or other objects in a document; it is visible only when in Page Layout or Full Screen Reading view and is not visible in Web, Outline, or Draft views. A watermark is inserted in the Header of a document; thus, you can apply a text watermark to the entire document or to only certain pages by inserting section breaks. Some common watermarks you may be familiar with include a faint image of the word *Draft* or *Sample* in the background or perhaps a company's logo faintly visible.

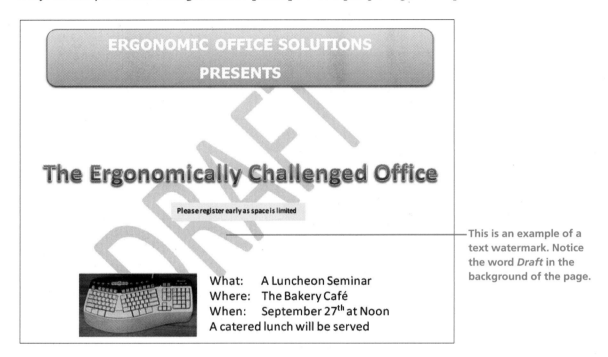

This is an example of a text watermark. Notice the word *Draft* in the background of the page.

Adding a Watermark

The watermark gallery is found in the Page Background group on the Page Layout tab of the Ribbon. There are built-in text watermarks, or you can create your own custom watermark with text or a picture. Text watermarks appear on every page, unless you specify differently. A photograph, clip art image, or picture can also be inserted by choosing Custom Watermark at the bottom of the watermark gallery, then navigating to and choosing the picture; however, the graphic will appear on every page, even if the document contains sections.

QUICK REFERENCE	FORMATTING PAGE BACKGROUNDS
Task	**Procedure**
Add a page color	■ Choose Page Layout→Page Background→Page Color from the Ribbon. ■ Choose the desired color from the gallery.

Task	Procedure
Add a page border	■ Choose Page Layout→Page Background→Page Borders from the Ribbon. ■ Choose the desired style, color, weight, and other options from the Borders and Shading dialog box.
Add a watermark	■ Choose Page Layout→Page Background→Watermark from the Ribbon. ■ Choose the desired watermark from the gallery.
Add a picture watermark	■ Choose Page Layout→Page Background→Watermark from the Ribbon. ■ Choose Custom Watermark from the gallery. ■ Click Picture Watermark and then Select Picture. ■ Navigate to the storage location for the picture. ■ Double-click the picture to insert it.

Apply Page Color and a Page Border

In this exercise, you will add a background color to your brochure and a border surrounding the page. Finally, you will add a Draft watermark to the document.

Add Page Color

1. Choose **Page Layout→Page Background→Page Color** ![icon] from the Ribbon.

2. Hover the **mouse pointer** over several colors in the Theme Colors area of the gallery, and Live Preview displays the effects of the different colors.

3. Choose the color in the fifth column, bottom row, **Blue**, **Accent 1**, **Darker 50%**.

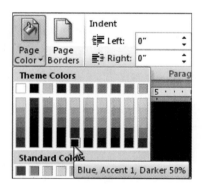

Add a Page Border

4. Choose **Page Layout→Page Background→Page Borders** ![icon] from the Ribbon.

5. Choose **Box** from the Setting area in the panel on the left.

6. Follow these steps to format the page border:

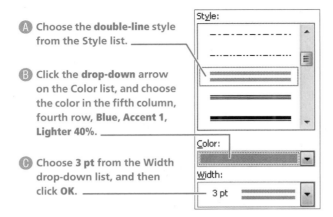

Ⓐ Choose the **double-line** style from the Style list.

Ⓑ Click the **drop-down** arrow on the Color list, and choose the color in the fifth column, fourth row, **Blue, Accent 1, Lighter 40%**.

Ⓒ Choose **3 pt** from the Width drop-down list, and then click **OK**.

Insert a Watermark

Now, you will add a Draft watermark, and then finalize the document by removing it.

7. Choose **Page Layout→Page Background→Watermark** from the Ribbon.

8. **Scroll down**, and choose **Draft 1** from the watermark gallery.

9. **Scroll** through the document to view the watermark, page border, and page color on both pages.

10. **Undo** to remove the watermark from the document.

11. **Save** the file, and **close** it.

9.4 Concepts Review

Concepts Review	labyrinthelab.com/word10

To check your knowledge of the key concepts introduced in this lesson, complete the Concepts Review quiz by going to the URL listed above. If your classroom is using Labyrinth eLab, you may complete the Concepts Review quiz from within your eLab course.

Reinforce Your Skills

Draw a Map with Shapes

In this exercise, you will use Word's Shapes to draw a map to Ergonomic Office Solutions, and you will rotate and align Shapes.

1. **Open** rs-Directions from the Lesson 09 folder.

2. Choose **View→Zoom→One Page** ▣ from the Ribbon.

Draw Lines

3. Choose **Insert→Illustrations→Shapes** ▢ from the Ribbon.

4. Choose the **first line style** in the Lines category.

5. Draw a **straight line** down the middle of the page starting about 1 inch below the rectangle and ending about 1 inch above the bottom of the page. (Remember, holding the Shift key while you draw constrains the object. This will ensure a straight line.)

6. Choose the **Line Shape** again, and draw a **horizontal line** at about the 3-inch mark on the vertical ruler, and about the same width of the rectangle.

7. Using the same method, draw **two** more **horizontal lines** of the same width at about the 5-inch and 7-inch marks on the vertical ruler.

Draw and Format a Rectangles

8. Choose **Insert→Illustrations→Shapes** ▢ from the Ribbon, and choose the **Rectangle** tool from the Rectangles category.

9. Draw a **rectangle** under the first horizontal line on the left side of the vertical line. Refer to the illustration at the end of the exercise.

10. Type **Hilliard Avenue** in the rectangle.

11. Using the same techniques, insert **two rectangles**, one below each horizontal line. *These will be used for the names of the cross streets.*

12. In the **top** rectangle, type **Brandon Road**, and in the **bottom** rectangle, type **Sycamore Avenue**.

13. Click on one rectangle, and then **hold** Shift and **click** on the other two to select all three of them.

14. Choose **Format→Shape Styles→Shape Outline** ▨ from the Ribbon, and then choose **No Outline** from the menu.

15. Choose **Page Layout→Arrange→Align** from the Ribbon, and then choose **Align Center** to align the three rectangles.

Rotate a Shape

16. Draw another **rectangle** about the same size as the others, and then type **University Avenue** in it.

17. Drag the **green rotating handle** until the rectangle is vertical.

18. Position the **mouse pointer** on an edge of the rectangle until the move handle appears, and then drag it so it is on the right side of the vertical line, similar to the illustration at the end of the exercise. Then, zoom the document back out to **100%**.

19. **Save** 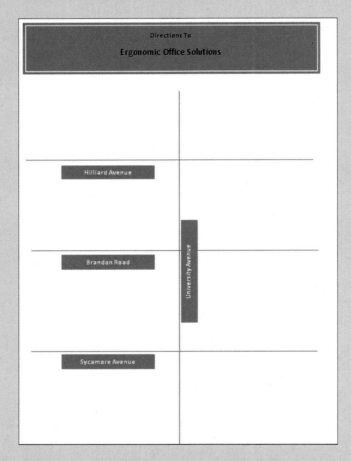 the file, and **close** it.

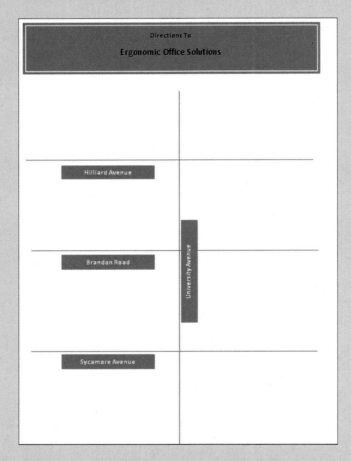

REINFORCE YOUR SKILLS 9.2

Create a Cycle Diagram Using SmartArt

In this exercise, you will create a document for your natural sciences class, picturing nature's water cycle.

1. **Open** rs-Water Cycle from the Lesson 09 folder.
2. Choose **Page Layout→Themes→Themes** from the Ribbon.
3. Choose **Solstice** from the Themes menu.
4. Position the **insertion point** in the first line of the document.
5. Choose **Title** from the **Home→Styles→QuickStyles Gallery**.
6. **Tap** Ctrl+End to position the insertion point at the end of the document.

Insert a SmartArt Graphic

7. Choose **Insert→Illustrations→SmartArt** from the Ribbon.
8. Choose the **Cycle** category in the panel on the left side of the dialog box.
9. Choose the first diagram in the first row, **Basic Cycle**, and then click **OK** to insert the SmartArt graphic in your document.
10. If necessary, click the **tab** on the left edge of the graphic to open the Type Your Text Here pane.
11. Complete the text pane, as shown in the illustration to the right.
12. **Close** the text pane.
13. Click the **outside border** of the image to select the entire image.

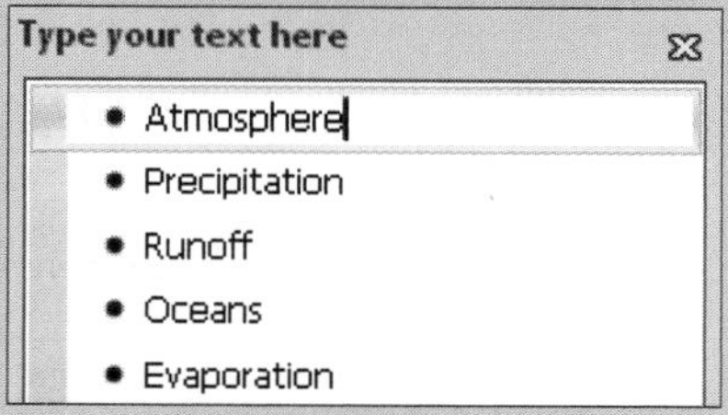
Type your text here
Atmosphere
Precipitation
Runoff
Oceans
Evaporation

Format the SmartArt Graphic

14. Choose **Design→SmartArt Styles** from the Ribbon.
15. Click the **More** button in the SmartArt Styles gallery to display the entire gallery.
16. Use **Live Preview** to examine several of the available styles, and then in the 3-D category, choose the first style in the first row, **Polished**. Finally, deselect the object.

Format the Document Background

17. Choose **Page Layout→Page Background→Page Color** from the Ribbon.
18. Choose the color in the fifth column, second row—**Aqua, Accent 1, Lighter 80%**—as the background color.
19. Choose **Page Layout→Page Background→Page Borders** from the Ribbon.
20. **Scroll down** to the black-and-white artwork, and choose the **umbrellas** from the Art drop-down list at the bottom of the center pane in the dialog box.
21. Click **OK** to place the border on the page.
22. **Save** the file, and **close** it.

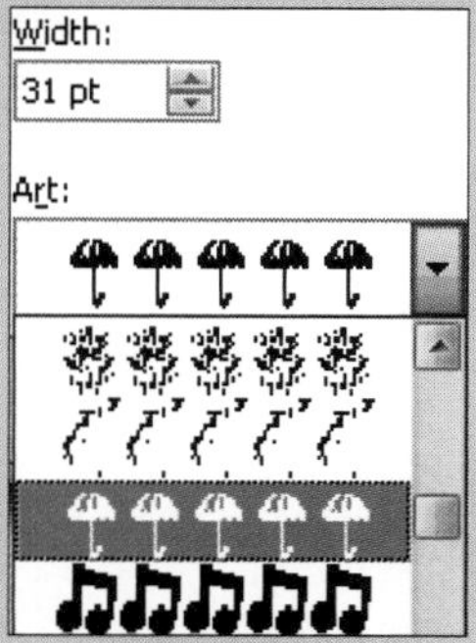
Width:
31 pt
Art:

Apply Your Skills

Create an Announcement

In this exercise, you will create an announcement that includes Landscape orientation, a photograph, a page border, and page color.

1. Create the announcement using the following guidelines, similar to the illustration at the end of this exercise:

   - Announce an upcoming concert. Include the **date**, **time**, and **location**. Also specify **where** tickets can be purchased.
   - List **two bands** that will be presented.
   - Use **Landscape** orientation.
   - Choose a **Theme** for your document.
   - **Format** the text as you desire.
   - **Insert** the as-Guitar Photo in the Lesson 09 folder. Format the photo as you wish.
   - Use a **page color** and **page border** to set off your announcement.

2. **Save** the document as **as-Announcement** in the Lesson 09 folder.

Create a Family Tree

In this exercise, you will use Shapes to create a family tree.

1. Start a **new** document, and follow these guidelines to create Helen's family tree, similar to the illustration at the end of this exercise:

   - Use a **WordArt** style of your choice to create the heading.
   - Use **rectangles, lines**, and **arrows** from the Shapes gallery to draw the family tree.
   - Use the **Shape Fill** colors of your choice to color the boxes.
   - Use the **Shape Outline** color of your choice to color the lines and arrows.
   - Use the illustration at the end of the exercise to add the **family names**.
   - Use **alignment tools** to align the boxes
   - Insert a **custom watermark** picture using the as-Tree Photo in the Lesson 09 folder.
   - Use your choice of **font formatting** for the family member names.
   - Apply a **page border**.

2. **Save** the file as **as-Family Tree** in the Lesson 09 folder.

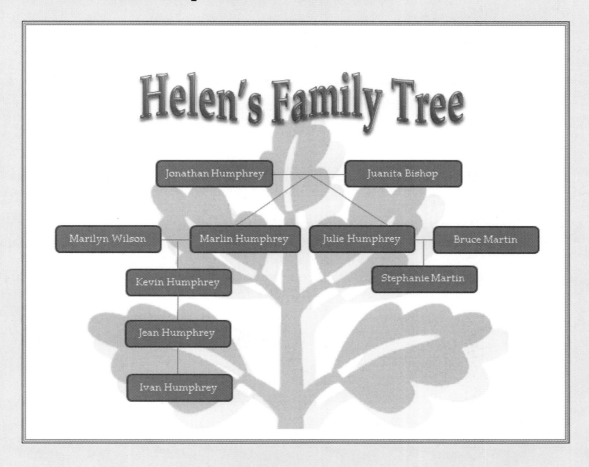

Critical Thinking & Work-Readiness Skills

In the course of working through the following Microsoft Office-based Critical Thinking exercises, you will also be utilizing various work-readiness skills, some of which are listed next to each exercise. Go to labyrinthelab.com/workreadiness *to learn more about the work-readiness skills.*

9.1 Create a Handout for a Report

WORK-READINESS SKILLS APPLIED

- Acquiring and evaluating information
- Seeing things in the mind's eye
- Thinking creatively

Green Clean's Purchasing Manager, Michael Chowdery, has asked you to create a handout about adding energy-efficient lighting to their product list. On the Internet, research information on the three bulbs in the ct-Light Bulbs document (Lesson 09 folder). Insert, format, and align text boxes next to each bulb listed to enter a description. If you copy information from a website, give credit for each in this manner: **Attribution: websitename.com**. Convert the title to a WordArt image of your choice and add page border. Insert and format a Shape next to the bulb you feel would be the most efficient. When finished, save and close the file.

9.2 Create an Announcement

WORK-READINESS SKILLS APPLIED

- Thinking creatively
- Seeing things in the mind's eye
- Writing

Green Clean is sponsoring a fundraiser for the WCA Garden Club, which promotes environmentally friendly gardening practices. The fundraiser will be a community yard sale held in the parking lot at Green Clean headquarters. Create an announcement for the fundraiser. Use a light page color and insert and format pictures into text boxes for a graphical impact. (Include pictures of object you might see at a yard sale.) Insert various shapes, including a SmartArt object emphasizing the details of the sale, such as where, when, and why. Highlight that this is a fundraiser. Move, resize, and align the shapes as needed. Use the ct-Garden image (Lesson 09 folder) as a watermark on the announcement. Save the file as **ct-Yard Sale**.

9.3 Create a Flyer

WORK-READINESS SKILLS APPLIED

- Organizing information
- Thinking creatively
- Seeing things in the mind's eye

Ken Hazell, the human resource manager at Green Clean, is responsible for employee training. He has arranged for a consultant to provide a half-day Word 2010 Basics class on September 22. Design a flyer to post on the bulletin board promoting the upcoming class. Include WordArt, pictures, shapes, fonts, colors, and other coordinating formats. Add a page border that coordinates with the shapes and text colors used. Use the photos in ct-School (Lesson 09 folder) or find others on the Internet. Use a SmartArt object to add three or four features you have learned in Word 2010. Save the flyer as **ct-Word Class** in the Lesson 09 folder.

Organizing Long Documents

LEARNING OBJECTIVES

After studying this lesson, you will be able to:

- Create a table of contents
- Add headers and footers
- Insert an index in a document
- Use cross-references

Word offers several great tools for organizing long documents. A table of contents and an index help readers locate specific topics in documents. Headers and footers are useful for displaying information such as page numbers and chapter names, and cross-references inform the reader of related material dispersed through a long document. In this lesson, you will work with these tools to organize long documents.

Refining a Clinic Policies & Procedures Manual

Raritan Clinic East

Pediatric Diagnostic Specialists

Raritan Clinic East is a pediatric medical practice. The practice serves patients ranging in ages from newborn to 18 years.

James Elliott has recently accepted a position in the human resources department with Raritan Clinic East. He has been tasked with reviewing the current policies and procedures manual, and he has identified numerous "finishing" features that need to be added to the manual to make it easier to use. By adding a table of contents, index, headers and footers, and cross-references, he believes the document will be easier to use.

Table of Contents

Table of Contents page

Index page

10.1 Creating a Table of Contents

Video Lesson   labyrinthelab.com/videos

Word's Table of Contents feature automatically builds a table of contents by gathering up the headings that are formatted with heading styles. Word organizes the headings in the order in which they appear in the document. In addition, it applies TOC styles that correspond to the heading level. The styles then format the table entries and indent them appropriately. For example, Heading 2 entries are subordinate to Heading 1 entries, so they are indented slightly.

Table of Contents Links

A table of contents is inserted as a large field composed of the various table entries. Each entry within a table of contents is formatted as a hyperlink. You can navigate to a page within the document by pressing Ctrl while clicking a particular table of contents entry. In addition, you can edit specific entries after the table of contents is generated.

You can navigate to a page by pressing Ctrl while clicking a table of contents entry.

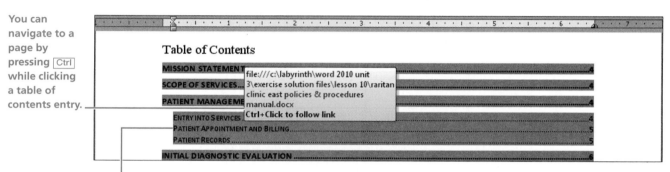

Table of contents entries are formatted with styles that show the hierarchical structure of the document. Notice that this Heading 2 entry is subordinate to the Heading 1 entry.

Using a Predesigned Table of Contents

Word 2007 introduced predesigned layouts for tables of contents. You can apply a predesigned table of contents format from the Table of Contents gallery shown in the following illustration. At the bottom of the gallery is a manual table of contents design option that you can fill out independently of the document content.

Built-In

Automatic Table 1

Contents

Heading 1 1

   Heading 2 1

      Heading 3 1

Automatic Table 2

Table of Contents

Heading 1 1

   Heading 2 1

      Heading 3 1

Manual Table

Table of Contents

Type chapter title (level 1) **1**

   Type chapter title (level 2) 2

      Type chapter title (level 3) 3

Type chapter title (level 1) **4**

📋	More Table of Contents from Office.com ▶
📄	Insert Table of Contents...
📄	Remove Table of Contents
📄	Save Selection to Table of Contents Gallery...

Creating a Page to Hold the TOC

In most documents, the table of contents appears at the beginning of the document—just after the title page in documents containing a title page. Because the table of contents is normally created after the document is complete, it is often necessary to create a new page in the document to hold the table. New pages can be created using a page break when no other features such as column layouts, headers and footers, or other document elements are involved. In addition, Word 2010 contains a new tool for inserting a new blank page within a document. You will find the new tool on the Insert tab of the Ribbon.

When headers and footers or other page layouts appear in a document, it is safer to create a page to hold the table of contents by adding a section break.

DEVELOP YOUR SKILLS 10.1.1
Insert a Table of Contents

In this exercise, you will open the Raritan Clinic East Policies & Procedures Manual and review the heading styles used in the document. Then you will create a table of contents and navigate in the document using the table of contents links.

1. Make sure the Word window is **maximized**.

2. **Open** the document Raritan Clinic East Policies & Procedures Manual from the Lesson 10 folder.

Review the Heading Styles

3. Choose **Home→Styles→dialog box launcher** ⬚ from the Ribbon.
   Word opens the Styles task pane.

4. Scroll to **page 2** and position the **insertion point** in the heading *Mission Statement*.
   Notice that a rectangle appears around Heading 1 in the Styles task pane, indicating that Heading 1 is the style used to format the heading.

5. Position the **insertion point** in several additional headings on **page 2**.
   You will notice that you have both Heading 1 and Heading 2 styles on the page.

6. **Close** ⊠ the Styles task pane.

7. Scroll to **page 2**, and position the **insertion point** in front of the heading *Mission Statement*.

Create a New Page for the Table of Contents

In the next step, you will insert a section break to create a blank page for the table of contents.

8. Choose **Page Layout→Page Setup→Breaks→Next Page** from the Ribbon.

9. If necessary, choose **Home→Paragraph→Show/Hide** ¶ from the Ribbon to display formatting marks.

10. Position the **insertion point** just in front of the section break, and **press** Enter.

Insert the Table of Contents

11. Choose **References→Table of Contents→Table of Contents** ⬚ from the Ribbon, and then choose **Automatic Table 2** from the gallery.

12. **Scroll up** and review the table of contents.
    You can see that the headings in the document are used as the table of contents entries.

Navigate Using Hyperlinks

13. Click the **Table of Contents** to select it, and then hover the **mouse pointer** over the *Initial Diagnostic Evaluation* entry in the table of contents.
    Notice the pop-up message.

14. **Press** Ctrl and click the *Initial Diagnostic Evaluation* link.
    Word jumps to the Initial Diagnostic Evaluation *heading in the document.*

15. **Press** Ctrl + Home to return to the top of the document.

16. **Save** ⬚ the document, and leave it **open**.

Adding Text to a Table of Contents

Video Lesson   labyrinthelab.com/videos

As you may already know, the advent of the Ribbon in Word 2007 increased the capabilities of special features in Microsoft Word. It is now possible to include text that is not formatted with a heading style in the table of contents. The Add Text command in the Table of Contents group on the Ribbon enables you to add important items to the table of contents that you prefer not to format with heading styles.

Using the Update Table Button

Each time you make changes to headings or text in a document or add text to a table of contents, you need to update the table of contents. Word has an automatic update feature that makes this task easy and efficient. Whenever the insertion point appears anywhere in the table of contents, Word displays two buttons in the upper-left corner of the table. One button is used to update the table of contents, while the other is used to display the Table of Contents gallery and the command to remove the table from the document.

FROM THE KEYBOARD
[F9] to update a table of contents

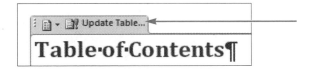

When you click the Update Table button, Word presents options for updating page numbers only or the entire table, as shown in the following illustration.

Using the Table of Contents Button

The Table of Contents button displays the Table of Contents gallery and the Remove Table of Contents command. By using this button, you can remove the current table of contents and regenerate it, if desired, using a different automatic layout or create it manually.

Add Text, Update, and Remove a Table of Contents

In this exercise, you will add text that is not formatted with a heading style to the table of contents. Then you will update the table of contents to display the added text. Finally you will remove the table of contents.

Before You Begin: Your Raritan Clinic East Policies & Procedures Manual should be open.

Add Text to the Table of Contents

1. Search for and select the heading *Scope of Services*.
   That heading is not included in the table of contents, because it is not formatted with a heading style.

2. Choose **References→Table of Contents→Add Text** 📄 from the Ribbon.

3. Choose **Level 1** from the menu.
   When you perform an update, Word will position the text at the same level in the table as a Heading 1 entry.

Update the Table of Contents

4. Scroll up to **page 2** and position the **insertion point** in the table of contents.

5. Click the **Update Table** 📄 button in the upper-left corner of the table of contents.

6. When the Update Table of Contents dialog box appears, choose the **Update Entire Table** option, and then click **OK**.

Notice that Scope of Services *now appears toward the top of the table of contents.*

Remove the Table of Contents

7. Hover the **mouse pointer** over the table.

8. Click the **Table of Contents** 📄 button in the upper-left corner of the table.

9. Choose the **Remove Table of Contents** command at the bottom of the gallery.

10. **Save** 💾 the file, and leave it **open**.

Using the Table of Contents Dialog Box

Video Lesson   labyrinthelab.com/videos

The Table of Contents gallery probably provides the fastest method for creating a table of contents, but if you wish to have more control over the formatting of your table, you can use the Table of Contents dialog box. When you use the Table of Contents dialog box to insert a table of contents, you must also manually add the title that precedes the table. In addition, when a table of contents is generated from the Table of Contents dialog box, Word displays no Table of Contents or Update buttons as it does for a table generated from the Table of Contents gallery. To update a manual table of contents, use the shortcut keystroke.

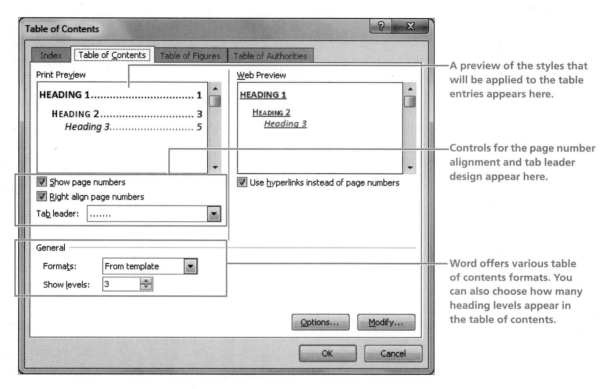

A preview of the styles that will be applied to the table entries appears here.

Controls for the page number alignment and tab leader design appear here.

Word offers various table of contents formats. You can also choose how many heading levels appear in the table of contents.

QUICK REFERENCE	CREATING AND UPDATING A TABLE OF CONTENTS
Task	**Procedure**
Create a table of contents from a predesigned format	▪ Format table of contents entries with Word's heading styles. ▪ Choose References→Table of Contents→Table of Contents ▤ from the Ribbon. ▪ Choose a predesigned table of contents style from the gallery.

CREATING AND UPDATING A TABLE OF CONTENTS (continued)

Task	Procedure
Add text to a table of contents (when text is not formatted with a heading style)	<ul><li>Select the text to be added.</li><li>Choose References→Table of Contents→Add Text ⊞ from the Ribbon.</li><li>Choose a table of contents level from the menu.</li><li>Update the table of contents.</li></ul>
Create a table of contents from the Table of Contents dialog box	<ul><li>Choose References→Table of Contents→Table of Contents ▤ from the Ribbon.</li><li>Choose the Insert Table of Contents command at the bottom of the gallery.</li></ul>
Update a table of contents	<ul><li>If you are using a predesigned table of contents, hover the mouse pointer over the table of contents, and then click the Update Table button.</li><li>If you used the Table Of Contents dialog box to generate the table of contents, select the table of contents, and then press F9.</li></ul>

DEVELOP YOUR SKILLS 10.1.3

Insert a Table of Contents Using the Dialog Box

In this exercise, you will insert a new table of contents using the Table of Contents dialog box. You will also edit a heading and then update the table of contents.

Before You Begin: Your Raritan Clinic East Policies & Procedures Manual should be open.

Add the Table of Contents Title

1. Position the **insertion point** just to the left of the section break at the top of **page 2**.

2. **Press** Enter to create a new blank line in the document.
   Notice that the paragraph symbols reflect the formatting of the first heading on page 3. When you insert a section break, the paragraph that appears before the section break takes on the formatting of the paragraph that follows the break.

3. Follow these steps to format and add the table title:

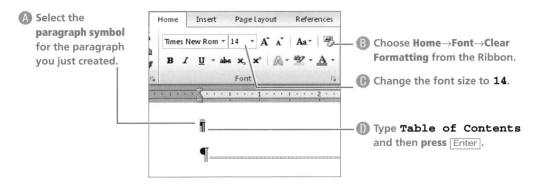

A Select the **paragraph symbol** for the paragraph you just created.

B Choose **Home→Font→Clear Formatting** from the Ribbon.

C Change the font size to **14**.

D Type **Table of Contents** and then **press** Enter.

4. Position the **insertion point** just before the paragraph on the line below the Table of Contents title, if necessary.

Table of Contents¶

Insert a Table of Contents

5. Choose **References→Table of Contents→Table of Contents** from the Ribbon.

6. Choose the **Insert Table of Contents** command at the bottom of the gallery to display the Table of Contents dialog box.

7. Follow these steps to generate a table of contents:

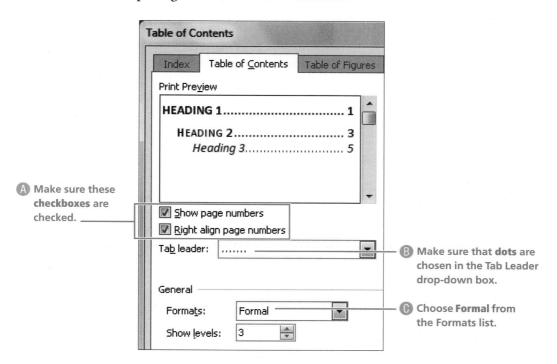

(A) Make sure these **checkboxes** are checked.

(B) Make sure that **dots** are chosen in the Tab Leader drop-down box.

(C) Choose **Formal** from the Formats list.

8. Click **OK** to insert the table of contents.
Notice that Word retained the added text Scope of Services *in the table of contents.*

Edit a Heading and Update the Table of Contents

9. Search for the heading, *Patient Attendance and Billing* and change *Attendance* to **Appointments**.

10. Scroll up to **page 2** and position the **insertion point** in the table of contents.
Notice that there is no Update Table button in the upper-left corner of the table.

11. **Press** F9 to begin the update.

12. When the Update Table of Contents dialog box appears, choose the **Update Entire Table** option, and then click **OK** to make the update.
Notice that the word Attendance *changed to* Appointment *in the table of contents.*

13. **Save** 💾 the document, and leave it **open**.

10.2 Working with Multiple Headers and Footers

Video Lesson   labyrinthelab.com/videos

By now, you may already be familiar with the headers and footers and how they are used in documents. Initially, Word uses the same header and footer throughout a document regardless of the number of pages or sections the document contains. By default, Word carries the initial header or footer on to each page or section of the document. When a document contains multiple sections, you can create a new header and footer for each document section.

For example, suppose you want to number preliminary pages of a long document using small roman numerals and the body of the document using Arabic numerals. Inserting a section break before the first page of the document body enables you to do so. Creating additional sections, therefore, is the first important step before creating multiple headers and footers within a document. It is also important to break the link between the headers and footers that Word applies to carry the initial header and footer across all document sections.

Breaking the Link Between Sections

The Link to Previous ⊞ button in the Navigation group of the contextual Design tab lets you break the links Word creates for headers and footers between sections. After the links are broken, you can edit the header or footer in one current section without affecting the headers and footers in other sections. Likewise, when you want a header or footer in a section to match the previous header and/or footer, you can activate the Link to Previous button.

Restarting and Formatting Page Numbers

When you have more than one section in a document, you may wish to control the starting page number within a section. Typically the body of a document starts page numbering with 1. You may also want to control the page number formats. The Page Number Format dialog box provides options to restart numbering and to modify the number format.

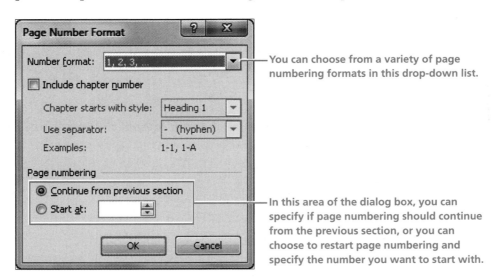

You can choose from a variety of page numbering formats in this drop-down list.

In this area of the dialog box, you can specify if page numbering should continue from the previous section, or you can choose to restart page numbering and specify the number you want to start with.

Setting Up a Different First Page Header or Footer

In addition to setting different headers and footers for different sections of a document, there may be times when all you want to do is set up a different footer or header on the first page of a document. For example, suppose you want all pages of a document numbered in the footer area of each page except for the title, or first, page. Word tools enable you to set a different first page header or footer simply by checking or clearing the checkmark for the attribute on the Header & Footer Tools Design tab of the Ribbon.

Changing Header and Footer Margins

As you review the Header & Footer Tools Design tab of the Ribbon, you will notice tools for changing the margins for the header or footer. Setting the header or footer margins lets Word know how far from the edge of the paper to place the header or footer. The margins for the body of the document are unaffected by setting the header and footer margins. Setting the header and footer margins to decrease the distance to the edge of the page simply increases the distance between the body text and the header or footer.

QUICK REFERENCE	SETTING HEADERS AND FOOTERS
Task	**Procedure**
Insert a header	■ Choose Insert→Header & Footer→Header ⬚ from the Ribbon. ■ Choose a header from the gallery, or choose Edit Header and create your own.
Insert a footer	■ Choose Insert→Header & Footer→Footer ⬚ from the Ribbon. ■ Choose a footer from the gallery, or choose Edit Footer and create your own.
Insert a page number	■ Choose Insert→Header & Footer→Page Number ⬚ from the Ribbon. ■ Choose Top of Page, Bottom of Page, or Page Margins. ■ Choose a page number design from the gallery.
Use multiple headers and footers	■ Segment the document with section breaks. ■ Choose Design→Navigation→Link to Previous ⬚ to break the link between sections. ■ Insert different headers and footers in different sections of the document.

DEVELOP YOUR SKILLS 10.2.1
Work with Multiple Headers and Footers

In this exercise, you will insert header text that will appear in both sections of the document. Then you will break the connection between footers so you can have different footers in each section and change the starting page number on the second page of the document.

Before You Begin: Your Raritan Clinic East Policies & Procedures Manual should be open.

Insert a Header that Appears in Both Sections

1. Position the **insertion point** in section 2 of the document, which begins with *Mission Statement.*

2. Choose **Insert→Header & Footer→Header** ⬚ from the Ribbon.

3. Choose the **Edit Header** command at the bottom of the gallery.

4. Take a moment to review the header area.

You will recall that you inserted a section break when you created the blank page for the table of contents. Therefore you have two sections in your document. The table of contents and title pages are section 1, and the rest of the document is section 2.

The insertion point is at the left side of the header area.

¶

Header -Section 2-   **Mission·Statement¶**   Same as Previous

This tab indicates that the insertion point is positioned in the header area of section 2.

The Same as Previous tab indicates that the text you type in section 2 will carry over to the previous section. In other words, the sections are linked together.

In this example, you want the two header sections to be linked, because the word DRAFT should appear on all pages of the document.

5. **Press** ⌈Tab⌉ to position the insertion point at the center of the header area.

6. Type **DRAFT** as the header text.

7. Use the Mini toolbar to format the header text with **bold 14 pt**.

8. **Double-click** in the body of the document to close the header area.

9. **Scroll up** to the table of contents.
Notice that the word DRAFT appears in the header. That's because the headers in both sections are linked.

Add a Footer that Appears in Only One Section

10. **Scroll down** and click in section 2.

11. Choose **Insert→Header & Footer→Footer** 🖹 from the Ribbon.

12. Choose the **Edit Footer** command at the bottom of the gallery.
Notice the Same as Previous tab in the footer area. In this example, you do not want the footer text to appear on the table of contents page, so you will break the link.

13. Choose **Design→Navigation** from the Ribbon.
The Link to Previous button is highlighted, meaning that it is turned on and the footers in sections 1 and 2 are linked.

14. Click the **Link to Previous** 🖳 button to turn it off and break the link between the two sections.
The Same as Previous tab at the right side of the footer area disappeared.

This time you will use one of Word's predesigned footers.

15. Choose **Design→Header & Footer→Footer** 🖹 from the Ribbon.

16. **Scroll down**, and choose **Pinstripes** from the gallery.

17. Click the **Type Text** object to select it, and then type **Policies & Procedures Manual**.

18. **Press** the [Tab] key to position the insertion point in the center of the footer area, and type **Raritan Clinic East**.

19. Choose **Header & Footer Tools→Design→Position→Header from Top** and type **0.3"**.

Change the Starting Page Number

You want to start numbering with a 1 on the first page of the body of the document.

20. Choose **Design→Header & Footer→Page Number** 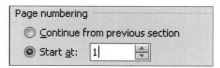 from the Ribbon.

21. Choose **Format Page Numbers** from the menu.
    The Page Number Format dialog box opens.

22. Choose the **Start At** option in the bottom of the dialog box.
    Word automatically chooses the number 1, but you could change it if you needed to.

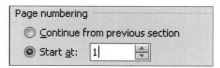

23. Click **OK** to restart page numbering with a 1, and then **double-click** in the body of the document to close the header and footer areas.

24. **Scroll up** and notice that the footer does not appear on the table of contents page, and then **scroll down** and observe the footer text in the rest of the document.

25. **Save** 💾 the changes, and continue with the next topic.

10.3 Creating an Index

Video Lesson   labyrinthelab.com/videos

Microsoft Word offers two distinct procedures for creating an index:

- Manually marking items to include in the index
- Generating the index by creating a concordance of words to be included in the index

Regardless of which procedure you use, Word automatically generates the index using the words and phrases you identify. In addition, Word sorts the words and phrases alphabetically and groups the contents of the index according to the first letter of the word or phrase. Like the Table of Contents feature, the Index feature lets you choose a style. And as in a table of contents, any changes you make directly in the index will be overwritten if you update the index. Index styles format the main entries and subentries and apply other formats to the index.

This is a main entry. → diagnostic

These are subentries. → emergency, evaluation

The index excerpt shows:

Cardiology .... → .... 1,3¶
certification .... → .... 1¶
color .... → .... 3¶
custodial .... → .... 1,2¶

D¶

diagnostic .... → .... 1,2,4,5¶
disorder .... → .... 3,4¶

E¶

emergency .... → .... 2¶
evaluation .... → .... 2,4,5¶

F¶

N¶

Neonatology .... → .... 1,3¶

O¶

Orthopedics .... → .... 1,3¶

P¶

patient .... → .... 1,2,3,4,5,6,7¶
Patient .... → .... 2¶
  files .... → .... 3¶
  records .... → .... 3¶
Pediatric-General-Medicine .... → .... 1,3¶
permanent .... → .... 3,4,5,6¶
permission .... → .... 2¶

Marking Index Entries

FROM THE KEYBOARD

Alt + Shift + X to open the Mark Index Entry dialog box

The first step in creating an index is to mark the main index entries and subentries. These are the words and phrases that will appear in the index. For example, a main entry might be *Patient Records*, and its subentries might be *Permanent Patient Files, Color Coding,* and *Check-Out Policy.*

Entries are marked using the Mark Index Entry dialog box. You can select text, and then click the Main Entry box to add the selected text to it. Alternatively you can click the main entry in the document, and then type the text of your choice in the Main Entry box. Subentry text must always be manually typed.

It is important to note that marking index entries is a case-sensitive action. As a result, if you mark all occurrences of a word such as *Billing* for inclusion in the index, Word will only mark those occurrences for the word *Billing* where the *B* is capitalized. As a result, it is important to consider what occurrences you want marked before selecting Mark All.

Marking Index Subentries

Index subentries appear in the index indented below main entries. Entering subentries in the Mark Index Entry dialog box is a bit more tedious than marking main entries. As a result, many organizations create indices using only main entries. There are two primary ways to create subentries. They include:

- Typing text for the subentry as you mark text for main entries. This procedure should be used only when the text you want to mark as main entries and subentries appear close together in the document.

- Selecting the text for the subentry, cutting the text from the Main Entry field and pasting it into the Subentry field in the Mark Index Entry dialog box and then type the text for the main entry.

As you mark text for all index entries, you can keep the Mark Index Entry dialog box open for easy access.

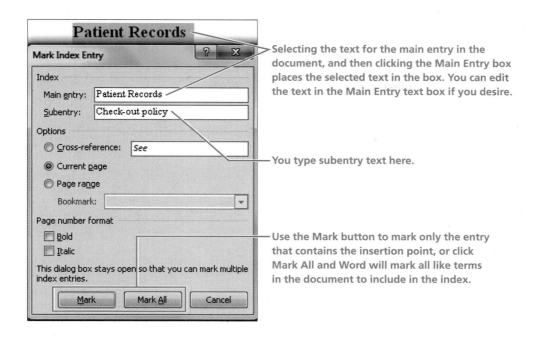

Selecting the text for the main entry in the document, and then clicking the Main Entry box places the selected text in the box. You can edit the text in the Main Entry text box if you desire.

You type subentry text here.

Use the Mark button to mark only the entry that contains the insertion point, or click Mark All and Word will mark all like terms in the document to include in the index.

QUICK REFERENCE	CREATING AN INDEX
Task	**Procedure**
Mark an index main entry	▪ Select the desired word or phrase in the document. ▪ Display the Mark Index Entry dialog box. The quickest method is using the Alt+Shift+X shortcut keystrokes. The selected text will appear in the Main Entry text box. ▪ Click the Mark button. You can also modify the text in the Main Entry box before clicking the Mark button. The modified text will appear in the index.
Mark an index subentry	▪ In the document, select the main entry text. ▪ Display the Mark Index Entry dialog box. ▪ Type the desired subentry text in the Subentry text box. ▪ Click the Mark button.
Insert an index	▪ Choose References→Index→Insert Index 📄 from the Ribbon. ▪ Choose a style from the Formats list, if desired.
Modify the index format	▪ Select the index. ▪ Choose References→Index→Insert Index 📄 from the Ribbon to open the Index dialog box. ▪ Make the desired formatting choices in the dialog box. *or* ▪ Format the index directly. (The format that is active in the Index dialog box will be reapplied if you update the index.)
Change the text of an index entry	▪ Edit the text directly in the code that was created when the entry was originally marked. (You then need to update the index.)
Delete an index entry	▪ Delete the code that was created when the entry was originally marked. (You then need to update the index.)
Update the index	▪ Select the index. ▪ Choose References→Index→Update Index 📄 from the Ribbon.

Mark Index Entries

In this exercise, you will mark index entries and subentries in preparation for generating an index.

Before You Begin: Your Raritan Clinic East Policies & Procedures Manual should be open.

Mark Main Entries

1. Go to the **first page** of the body of the manual.

2. If necessary, choose **Home→Paragraph→Show/Hide** ¶ to display the formatting marks.

3. Select the heading *Mission Statement.*

4. Choose **References→Index→Mark Entry** ⬒ from the Ribbon.
   The Mark Index Entry dialog box opens.

Edit the Main Entry Text

5. Type **Goals** in the Main Entry box, and it replaces the text that Word automatically inserted.
   The text that was in the box came from the words you selected in the document. You can always replace or edit the suggested entries in this manner.

6. Click the **Mark** button at the bottom of the dialog box.
   The Mark Index Entry dialog box remains open, allowing you to scroll through the document and mark additional entries and subentries.

Review an Index Code

7. If necessary, drag the **dialog box** to the side, and notice that Word inserted a {XE"Goals"} code in the document.
   This code identifies Goals as a main index entry.

8. Click in the **document** once to make it active.

9. Select the word *specialties*, which appears at the end of line 2 in the second paragraph under the *Mission Statement* heading.

10. Click the **Mark Index Entry** dialog box, and then click the **Mark** button to use the proposed text as the main entry.
    When you click the Mark Index Entry dialog box, Word automatically recognizes the text that you have selected and places it in the Main Entry field.

11. Repeat the procedures outlined in **steps 9 and 10** to mark each of the following as main entries.

Text	Location	Main Entry Text if Different
population	Last line of paragraph 2 under Mission Statement	
General Medicine	First line of paragraph 3 under Scope of Services	Specialty Areas
Referrals	First line of paragraph 1 under Entry into Services	
Permission	First word in sentence 2 of paragraph 1 under Entry into Service	
appointment	Line 1 of paragraph 3 under Entry into Service	
Patient	In the heading, Patient Appointments and Billing	

Mark All Entries

Depending on the nature of the document you are marking, there may be text you want to mark every time it appears.

12. Select the text *Billing* in the heading *Patient Appointments and Billing*, and then click the **Mark Index Entry** dialog box to make it active.

13. Click the **Mark All** button to mark all occurrences of the word *Billing* for inclusion in the index.

14. Repeat the procedures outlined in **steps 12 and 13** to mark all occurrences of the following text as main entries.

Text	Location	Main Entry Text if Different
receptionist	Line 1 of paragraph 1 under Patient Appointments and Billing	
billing	Last line of paragraph 3 under Patient Appointments and Billing	
Supervisors	Line 1 of paragraph 3 under Patient Appointments and Billing	
Confidentiality	Page 6, first word in paragraph above heading *Initial Diagnostic Evaluation*.	confidentiality

Mark Subentries

You will mark only a few subentries in the document—enough to give you an idea of how to mark them. If you have closed the Mark Index Entry dialog box, open it before continuing by choosing References→ Index→Mark Entry.

15. Navigate to the *Patient Records* heading and follow these steps to mark *records* as a subentry of *Patients*:

Ⓐ Select the text *Patient* in the heading *Patient Records*.

Ⓑ Click the **Mark Index Entry** dialog box to make it active.

Ⓒ Type **records** in the Subentry field.

Ⓓ Click **Mark** at the bottom of the dialog box.

16. Navigate to the second paragraph below the *Patient Records* heading and follow these steps to mark *files* as a subentry of *Patients:*

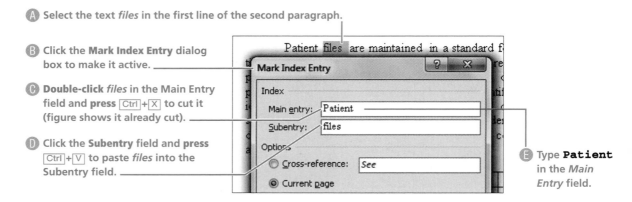

Ⓐ Select the text *files* in the first line of the second paragraph.

Ⓑ Click the **Mark Index Entry** dialog box to make it active.

Ⓒ **Double-click** *files* in the Main Entry field and **press** Ctrl+X to cut it (figure shows it already cut).

Ⓓ Click the **Subentry** field and **press** Ctrl+V to paste *files* into the Subentry field.

Ⓔ Type **Patient** in the *Main Entry* field.

17. Click the **Mark** button at the bottom of the dialog box.

Mark Additional Entries

The additional entries marked in step 18 are optional and have no impact on your ability to complete the rest of the activities in this lesson.

18. **Scroll** through the document and mark additional main entries and subentries as time permits.

19. Close the **Mark Index Entry** dialog box and turn off Show/Hide.
   Because index codes can be quite lengthy, displaying them can cause text to roll onto other pages. As a result, it is important to turn off the Show/Hide feature to ensure that page numbers in the index are accurate.

20. **Save** 🖫 changes to the document and leave it **open**.

Generating Index Entries Using a Concordance

Video Lesson   labyrinthelab.com/videos

When you are working with documents that are between five and fifty pages, marking index entries can be an effective way to identify words and phrases that you want to include in an index. When a document spans more pages, however, marking entries for an index can be overwhelming. As a result, Word offers an automatic option for marking words and phrases to be included in an index. This option allows you to create a list of words and phrases you want to include and saves it as a separate file that acts as a *concordance* file.

When you use a concordance file to generate an index, it is important to know how Word reacts. The following guidelines will provide you with some basic information.

- The list of words and phrases to be included as main entries should be typed in one column straight down the left margin of the document or in the first column of a table.
- The document should have no title at the top of the page and should contain only the words and phrases to be marked.

- To mark main entries with subentries, create the concordance using a table layout. In the first column, type the words you want to mark. In the second column, type the index entry you want to generate for the main entry followed by a colon (:) followed by the text for the subentry, without spaces, as show in this illustration:

Document text to mark | Main Entry:Subentry

- Entries can be listed in any order in the concordance—Word will sort them and group them alphabetically when you generate the index. However, sorting the words helps identify duplicate words in the concordance.

DEVELOP YOUR SKILLS 10.3.2
Mark Index Entries Using a Concordance

In this exercise, you will mark index entries using a concordance document.

Before You Begin: The Raritan Clinic East Policies & Procedures Manual should be open. Turn on Show/Hide marks if necessary.

1. **Open** the Raritan Policies & Procedures Concordance file from the Lesson 10 folder.

2. **Scroll** through the document, review the document contents, and **close** the file.

3. Make the Raritan Clinic East Policies & Procedures Manual the **active document**, and position the **insertion point** at the beginning of the document.

4. Choose **References→Index→Insert Index** 📑 to open the Index dialog box.

5. Click the **AutoMark** button at the bottom of the dialog box to open the Open Index AutoMark File dialog box.

6. Navigate to the Lesson 10 folder, and **double-click** the Raritan Policies & Procedures Concordance file to open it.
   Although nothing appears to happen, Word compares the list of words and phrases in the concordance file with text found in the Policies and Procedures manual. When it finds a word on the concordance list, it automarks the entry and completes the action very quickly!

7. **Scroll** through and review the document.
   Notice the numerous index marks Word added from the concordance as well as the individually marked items from the previous exercise.

8. **Save** 🔲 changes to the document.

Inserting an Index

Video Lesson   labyrinthelab.com/videos

After all of the index entries are marked, you can move to the location in the document where you want the index to appear and generate the index using the Index dialog box. The Index dialog box contains different tabs for formatting each reference item—the table of contents, index, table of figures, and table of authorities. On the Index tab of the dialog box, you can choose the overall format for the index and several other formatting options. The normal position for an index is at the end of a document on a new page or section.

Formatting the Index

Formatting options to be used for the index are also found on the Index tab of the dialog box. Available options enable you to specify a tab leader style, choose from a list of built-in formats, or specify the number of columns in the index.

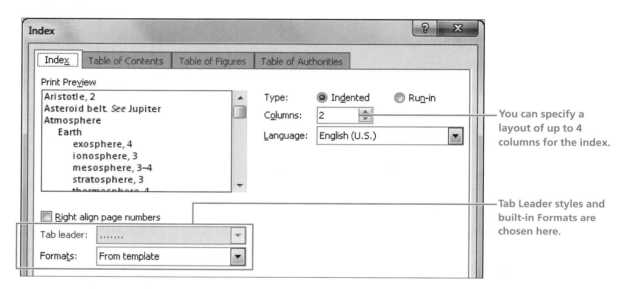

You can specify a layout of up to 4 columns for the index.

Tab Leader styles and built-in Formats are chosen here.

Modifying and Deleting an Index Entry

There are several ways to modify an index once you create it. You can select the index and display the Index dialog box and then change various formatting options. You can also format the index directly; however, the format active in the Index dialog box will be reapplied if you update the index.

The Update Index ⊞ button in the Index group of the References tab on the Ribbon lets you quickly update the index with any changes you make. You can change the text of an entry by replacing it directly in the code that was created when you originally marked it and then update the index. You can delete an index entry by selecting the index code, deleting it, and then updating the index.

Insert and Modify the Index

In this exercise, you will generate an index from the entries you marked in the previous exercises. Then you will modify the format of the index.

Before You Begin: Your Raritan Clinic East Policies & Procedures Manual should be open.

Set Up a New Page

1. **Press** Ctrl + End to position the insertion point at the end of the document.

2. **Type** the heading **Index**, and press Enter.

3. Select the *Index* heading, and format the text as **bold 16 pt**.

4. Position the **insertion point** on the blank line below the *Index* heading.

Insert the Index

5. Choose **References→Index→Insert Index** from the Ribbon.

6. Choose the **Formal** style from the Formats list at the bottom-left corner of the dialog box.

7. Click **OK**, and Word inserts the index.

Modify the Index Format

8. Click anywhere in the **index**.

9. Choose **References→Index→Insert Index** from the Ribbon.

10. Choose the **Modern** format at the bottom-left corner of the dialog box, and choose the **Run In** option at the top-right corner of the dialog box.
    Notice the effect of these choices in the preview area.

11. Click **OK**, and then click **OK** again when Word asks if you want to replace the selected index.
    The new index is inserted with the Run In number style. Notice how the Run In style affects the subentries.

12. Click **Undo** twice to reverse the change.

13. **Save** the file and leave it **open**.

10.4 Adding Cross-References

Video Lesson   labyrinthelab.com/videos

Cross-references point you to items such as headings and footnotes located in other parts of a document. The following illustrations show a cross-reference you will create in Develop Your Skills 10.4.1 and the options available through the Cross-Reference dialog box. The Cross-Reference command is located in the Links group of the Insert tab on the Ribbon.

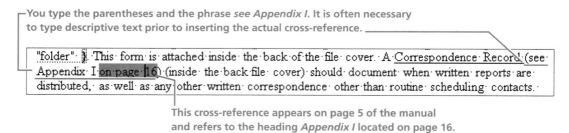

You type the parentheses and the phrase *see Appendix I*. It is often necessary to type descriptive text prior to inserting the actual cross-reference.

"folder". This form is attached inside the back of the file cover. A Correspondence Record (see Appendix I on page 16) (inside the back file cover) should document when written reports are distributed, as well as any other written correspondence other than routine scheduling contacts.

This cross-reference appears on page 5 of the manual and refers to the heading *Appendix I* located on page 16.

Reviewing the Cross-Reference Dialog Box

A cross-reference can be one of several types, such as a heading, bookmark, footnote, endnote, table, and other items. The Insert Reference To options vary, depending on the Reference Type chosen. For example a Heading can refer to a page number or another heading. Inserting a reference as a hyperlink allows the reader to electronically jump to the cross-reference target.

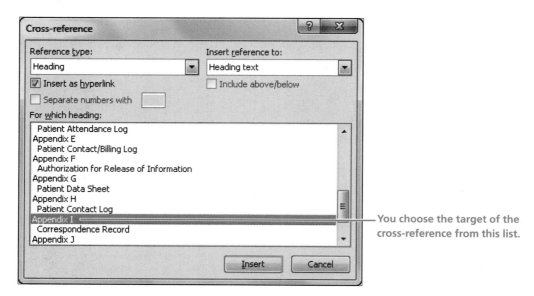

You choose the target of the cross-reference from this list.

Updating Cross-References

Cross-references need to be updated if the pagination of a document changes or if the text you refer to is modified. You can update individual cross-references and other fields by right-clicking the desired field and choosing Update Field from the pop-up menu. You can also use the F9 key to update selected fields.

QUICK REFERENCE	WORKING WITH CROSS-REFERENCES
Task	**Procedure**
Insert a cross-reference	■ Choose Insert→Links→Cross-Reference from the Ribbon. ■ Make the desired choices in the Cross-Reference dialog box. ■ Click the Insert button.
Update a cross-reference	■ Right-click the cross-reference field, and then choose Update Field from the pop-up menu. *or* ■ Click the cross-reference field to select it, and then press F9.

DEVELOP YOUR SKILLS 10.4.1

Insert Cross-References

In this exercise, you will insert a cross reference to a page number, and then you will follow the cross-reference hyperlink to the specified page. Finally, you will add a cover page to the manual.

Before You Begin: *Your Raritan Clinic East Policies & Procedures Manual should be open.*

Insert a Cross-Reference

1. Navigate to the heading *Patient Contact.*
2. Click **after** the text *Correspondence Record* in the paragraph below the heading, as shown in the following illustration.

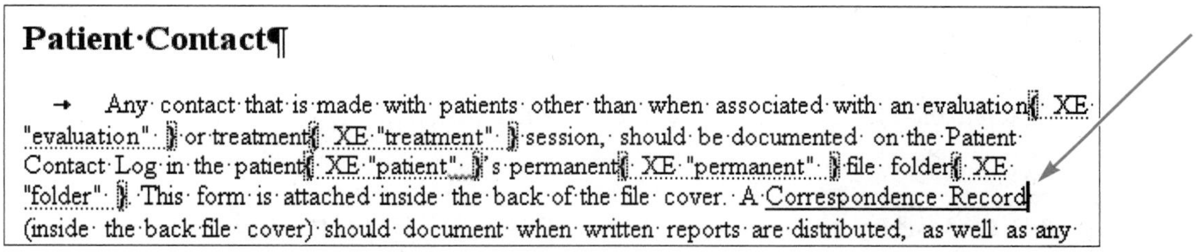

Patient·Contact¶

→ Any·contact·that·is·made·with·patients·other·than·when·associated·with·an·evaluation{·XE·"evaluation"·}·or·treatment{·XE·"treatment"·}·session,·should·be·documented·on·the·Patient·Contact·Log·in·the·patient{·XE·"patient"·}'s·permanent{·XE·"permanent"·}·file·folder{·XE·"folder"·}.·This·form·is·attached·inside·the·back·of·the·file·cover.·A·Correspondence·Record (inside·the·back·file·cover)·should·document·when·written·reports·are·distributed,·as·well·as·any·

3. **Press** the Spacebar and type **(see Appendix I** . (You will type the closing parenthesis later.)
4. Choose **References→Captions→Cross-Reference** from the Ribbon.

5. Follow these steps to insert the cross-reference:

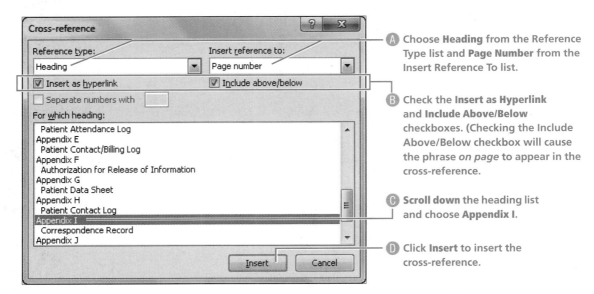

A) Choose **Heading** from the Reference Type list and **Page Number** from the Insert Reference To list.

B) Check the **Insert as Hyperlink** and **Include Above/Below** checkboxes. (Checking the Include Above/Below checkbox will cause the phrase *on page* to appear in the cross-reference.

C) **Scroll down** the heading list and choose **Appendix I**.

D) Click **Insert** to insert the cross-reference.

6. **Close** the Cross-Reference dialog box.
   The insertion point should be just to the right of the cross-reference.

7. **Type** the closing parenthesis **)** to complete the cross-reference.

Follow a Cross-Reference Hyperlink

8. Position the **mouse pointer** over *page 16* in the cross-reference you created.
   A tip appears explaining how to follow the link.

9. **Press** the Ctrl key while you click the cross-reference.
   The insertion point jumps to the referenced heading.

Add a Cover Page

10. Choose **Insert→Pages→Cover Page** [icon] from the Ribbon.

11. Choose **Pinstripes** from the gallery.

12. Copy the **clinic graphic** from the new page 2, and paste it at the **top** of the document just above the new title.

13. Remove the remaining text on the title page, and then **delete** the original title page by deleting the page break using the Delete key.

14. **Save** [icon] your changes and **close** the file.

10.5 Viewing Master Documents

Video Lesson labyrinthelab.com/videos

Sometimes the documents you create will be much longer than Word 2010 can comfortably handle. Take, for example, a 1,000-page novel or court document. Managing such long documents can become tedious. Many long documents are made up of other documents or are divided into main topics or chapters. When you are working with long documents, you may find it easier to work with pieces of the document individually and then add them to the main body of the document.

You will be excited to know that Word has a special tool for managing extremely long documents that are made up of smaller documents. It's called Master Documents. Master documents consist of a shell (the master layout) for the document and individual smaller documents called *subdocuments*. Not only does working with a master document make managing documents more efficient, it also makes updating documents that change frequently more efficient.

Master documents are accessed from the View tab of the Ribbon. They display document text differently from standard documents and outlines. Review the example of the master document shown here to identify special master document features.

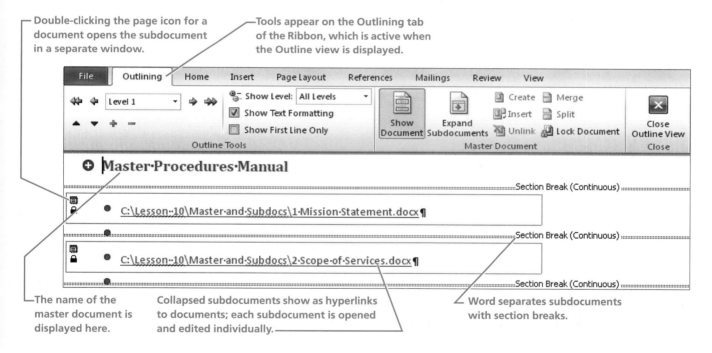

Double-clicking the page icon for a document opens the subdocument in a separate window.

Tools appear on the Outlining tab of the Ribbon, which is active when the Outline view is displayed.

The name of the master document is displayed here.

Collapsed subdocuments show as hyperlinks to documents; each subdocument is opened and edited individually.

Word separates subdocuments with section breaks.

The Master Document file and all subdocuments must be stored in the same folder.

Display Master and Subdocuments

In this exercise, you will open a master document, expand and collapse subdocuments, and review the structure of a master document.

1. **Open** the Master Procedures Manual document that is located in the Lesson 10 subfolder Master and Subdocs in your student files.

2. Choose **Outlining→Master Document→Expand Subdocuments** on the Ribbon. *Word displays the paragraphs contained in each subdocument.*

3. Choose **Outlining→Master Document→Collapse Subdocuments** on the Ribbon.

4. Use Ctrl +click on the second link in the list to open Scope of Services.docx.

5. **Close** the subdocument and then choose **Outlining→Close→Close Outline View**.

6. **Close** the file, **saving** changes if prompted.

10.6 Concepts Review

Concepts Review   labyrinthelab.com/word10

To check your knowledge of the key concepts introduced in this lesson, complete the Concepts Review quiz by going to the URL listed above. If your classroom is using Labyrinth eLab, you may complete the Concepts Review quiz from within your eLab course.

Reinforce Your Skills

Use Multiple Headers and Footers

In this exercise, you will open a document that contains only one section, insert a section break, and break the links between section headers and footers. You will then add header and footer elements for section 2 of the document.

1. **Open** the document named rs-Heart Report from the Lesson 10 folder.

2. After the date, insert a **section break** that begins on the next page.

3. Position the **insertion point** in the second page of the document.
   This is the first body page of the document.

Add a Header

4. Choose **Insert→Header & Footer→Header** 📄 from the Ribbon.

5. Choose the **Edit Header** command at the bottom of the gallery.
   The tab at the left end of the header shows that you are in section 2, and the tab at the right end of the header indicates that this header area is linked to the previous header area.

6. Choose **Design→Navigation→Link to Previous** 🖥 from the Ribbon to break the link with the previous header area.
   Notice that the Same as Previous tab disappears from the right side of the header area.

7. **Type** the following header text using the Tab key to align the word *Heart* on the right side:

Asian·Languages·133B| →   →   *HEART¶*

`Header -Section 2-`

I·am·writing·my·paper·on·Heart·by·George·Barnard,·a·novel·whose·title·is·perfect·in·describing·the·

meanings·and·messages·that·it·contains.·In·Japanese·the·word·heart·describes·the·many·feelings·and·

Add a Page Number Footer

8. Choose **Design→Navigation→Go to Footer** on the Ribbon to move to the footer.

9. Choose **Design→Navigation→Link to Previous** 🖥 on the Ribbon to break the link to the previous footer area.

10. Choose **Design→Header & Footer→Page Number** 📄 from the Ribbon.

11. Choose **Bottom of Page** from the menu, and then choose **Plain Number 2** from the gallery to add a page number to the footer.

Change the Starting Page Number

The page number starts at 2 in the first body page, and you want it to start at 1.

12. Choose **Design→Header & Footer→Page Number** from the Ribbon.

13. Choose **Format Page Numbers** from the menu to open the Page Number Format dialog box.

14. Choose the **Start At** option at the bottom of the dialog box.
    Word automatically chooses the number 1.

15. Click **OK** to restart page numbering at 1.

16. **Double-click** in the body of the document to close the header and footer areas, and then **scroll** to the first page and observe that there is no header or footer on that page.

17. **Save** 🖫 the file as **rs-Heart Report** in your Lesson 10 folder, and then **close** the file.

REINFORCE YOUR SKILLS 10.2
Create a Table of Contents

In this exercise, you will create a table of contents for a recipe book. Then you will add a Dessert chapter to the book and regenerate the table of contents. You will also include a page number footer in the document.

1. **Open** the document rs-Recipes from the Lesson 10 folder.

2. If necessary, choose **Home→Paragraph→Show/Hide** ¶ from the Ribbon to display formatting marks.
   This document starts with two blank pages followed by three chapters: Hors d'Oeuvres, Brunch, and Entrees. There is a section break before and after the second blank page. The title pages and recipe titles are formatted with heading styles.

3. On the first page of the document, add the title **Good Old Family Recipes** and format it with **Comic Sans MS bold 22 pt centered**.

Break the Link Between Two Sections

4. Position the **insertion point** in page 3 (section 2).

5. Choose **Insert→Header & Footer→Footer** 📄 from the Ribbon, and then choose **Edit Footer** at the bottom of the gallery to open the footer area.

6. Choose **Design→Navigation→Link to Previous** 🖳 from the Ribbon to break the link between the two sections.

Insert a Page Number in the Footer Area

7. Choose **Design→Header & Footer→Page Number** 📄 from the Ribbon.

8. Choose **Bottom of Page** from the menu, and then choose **Accent Bar 2** from the gallery.

Change the Starting Page Number

Notice that the page number is 3, but you want the body of the document to start numbering at 1.

9. Choose **Design→Header & Footer→Page Number** 📄 from the Ribbon.

10. Choose **Format Page Numbers** from the menu.
    This opens the Page Number Format dialog box.

11. Choose the **Start At** option at the bottom of the dialog box.
    Word automatically chooses the number 1.

12. Click **OK** to restart page numbering with 1.

13. **Double-click** in the body of the document to close the footer area.

14. **Scroll** through the document and review the footer area.
    There are no page numbers on the first two pages, and page numbering starts on the third page with number 1.

Generate the Table of Contents

15. Return to the **table of contents** page (second page of the document) and place the **insertion point** at the left end of the section break.

16. Choose **References→Table of Contents→Table of Contents** 📑 to display the gallery.

17. Choose the second option in the gallery, **Automatic Table 2**, to insert the table, and then scroll up and review the table.

Add a Chapter to the Book

18. **Press** ⌜Ctrl⌝+⌜End⌝ to move the insertion point to the end of the document, and then insert a **manual page break**.

19. Choose **Insert→Text→Object** 🖼 **menu button arrow** on the Ribbon, and select **Text from File** to open the Insert file dialog box.

20. **Double-click** the rs-Desserts file from the Lesson 10 folder.
    Since you added pages to your document, you need to regenerate the table of contents.

21. Return to the **table of contents**, and click the **mouse pointer** in the table to display the buttons in the upper-left corner of the table of contents field.

22. Click the **Update Table** 📑 button, and when the Update Table of Contents dialog box appears, choose the **Update Entire Table** option.

23. Click **OK** to regenerate the table.
    Notice that the headings from the rs-Desserts file were added to the table of contents.

24. **Save** 💾 the file, and **close** it.

Create Cross-References

In this exercise, you will use cross-references to locate information in various parts of a document, and then you will test your cross-reference links.

Create the First Cross-Reference

1. **Open** the rs-Vacation Rentals file from the Lesson 10 folder.

2. Position the **insertion point** in front of *If* in the third line of the first paragraph, as shown in the following illustration.

> The Goodspeed Company welcomes you to Palm Springs, the land of endless sunshine. Imagine yourself lounging by the pool at a luxury home overlooking lush fairways with a view of the surrounding San Jacinto Mountains rising 9,000 feet in front of you. If golf is not your thing,

3. Type **(See** and then **press** the ⌷Spacebar⌷.

4. Choose **References→Captions→Cross-Reference** 🔲 from the Ribbon.

5. If necessary, in the Cross-Reference dialog box, click the drop-down arrow for **Reference Type**, and choose **Heading**.

6. If necessary, choose **Heading Text** from the Insert Reference To drop-down list.

7. Make sure Insert as **Hyperlink** is checked.

8. Choose *Golf Resort Rentals* in the For Which Heading list, and then click the **Insert** button.

9. Leave the dialog box **open**, and position the **insertion point** to the **right** of the cross-reference. (You may need to drag the dialog box out of the way.)

10. **Type** a period and closing parenthesis **.)**, and then **press** the ⌷Spacebar⌷ if necessary.

Add the Second Cross-Reference

11. Position the **insertion point** in front of *Stroll* in the fifth line of the first paragraph, as shown in the following illustration.

> The Goodspeed Company welcomes you to Palm Springs, the land of endless sunshine. Imagine yourself lounging by the pool at a luxury home overlooking lush fairways with a view of the surrounding San Jacinto Mountains rising 9,000 feet in front of you. (See Golf Resort Rentals.) If golf is not your thing, check out our selection of in-town condominiums with tennis, pools, and spas. Stroll along Palm Canyon Drive in the historic heart of Palm Springs and discover a

12. Type **(See,** and then **press** the ⌷Spacebar⌷.

13. In the Cross-Reference dialog box, choose **Condominium Rentals** in the For Which Heading list, and then click the **Insert** button.

14. Leave the dialog box **open**, and click in the **document** to the **right** of the cross-reference.

15. **Type** a period and closing parenthesis **.)**, and then **press** the ⌷Spacebar⌷ if necessary.

Create the Remaining Cross-References

16. Repeat the procedures outlined in **steps 11–15** to create additional cross-references shown in the following table:

Position	Heading Title
After *Valley*, end of paragraph 2	Activities heading
After *more*, end of paragraph 3	Coachella Valley Dining heading

17. **Close** the Cross-Reference dialog box, and test your links. Remember, you need to press the ⌈Ctrl⌋ key while clicking the link.

18. **Save** 🖫 the file, and leave it **open** for the next exercise.

REINFORCE YOUR SKILLS 10.4

Create an Index

In this exercise, you will add an index to the document you used in Reinforce Your Skills 10.3. You will create main entries and two subentries for each main entry.

Before You Begin: Make sure that you have performed the previous exercise and that the file is still open.

1. If necessary, choose **Home→Paragraph→Show/Hide** ¶ to display formatting marks.

2. Go to **page 2**, and select the *Activities* heading at the top of the page.

3. Choose **References→Index→Mark Entry** from the Ribbon to open the Mark Index Entry dialog box.
    Activities *appears in the Main Entry text box.*

4. Position the **insertion point** in the Subentry text box, and type **Aerial Tramway**. Be careful to spell it correctly.

5. Click the **Mark** button at the bottom of the dialog box.

Create the Second Subentry

6. Replace the subentry text with the word **Bicycling,** and click the **Mark** button.

7. Scroll to **page 3**, and select the heading *Golf Resort Rentals*.

8. Click the **Mark Index Entry** dialog box to replace the existing text with the new entry.

9. Click the **Subentry** text box, and type **Barnett Golf Club**, and then click the **Mark** button.

10. Add another subentry, **Champion Golf Communities**, for the *Golf Resort Rentals* main entry.

11. Continue through the document, and add the following main entries and subentries.

Main Entry	Subentries
Condominium Rentals	Canyon View
	Casa Verde
Coachella Valley Dining	Blame It on Midnight Bar & Grill
	Canyon Bistro

12. **Close** the dialog box.

13. Use ⎡Ctrl⎤+⎡End⎤ to move to the end of the document, and insert a **manual page break**.

14. Type **Index** at the top of the page, and **press** ⎡Enter⎤ twice.

15. Format the heading with **bold 22 pt centered**.

16. Click the blank line beneath the **Index** heading and then choose **References→ Index→Insert Index** from the menu.

17. In the Index dialog box, choose **Formal** from the Formats drop-down list.
    Because this example creates a short index, you will make it a one-column index.

18. Use the **spinner controls** in the Columns box in the upper-right corner of the dialog box to change to **1** column.

19. Click **OK** to insert the index.

20. **Save** 🖫 the file, and **close** it.

Apply Your Skills

Create Multiple Headers and Footers

In this exercise, you will create a college-style research paper, insert text for the paper from another Word file, and insert new sections for End Notes and the Bibliography at the end of the paper.

1. Create a **new** document and **type** the current date at the top of the document.

2. **Insert** the text from a file named as-History of Tobacco found in the Lesson 10 folder on a new line following the date.

3. Create **section breaks** to start the *End Notes* page and the *Bibliography* page on new pages.

4. Insert a **page number** in the header area, format it using the number style of your choice, and position the number at the right side of the header.

5. Add **your name** to the header, positioning it on the left side of the header.

6. **Break the connection** between the footers in sections 1 and 2 and between sections 2 and 3.

7. Place the **page number** in the footer of sections 2 and 3, and remove it from the header area of sections 2 and 3.

8. **Save** the document as **as-Tobacco History**, and then close **it**.

Create a Table of Contents

In this exercise, you will create a table of contents.

1. **Open** the as-B&B file from the Lesson 10 folder.

2. Display **formatting marks**, and review the document, noting the headings applied to document text.

3. Insert the **table of contents** just below the heading *Table of Contents*, and format it using the **Distinctive** format.

4. **Save** the document using the filename **as-B&B TOC**.

Create an Index

In this exercise, you will mark main entries for an index using a concordance and then manually mark subentries and generate an index from those entries.

Before You Begin: *If you completed Apply Your Skills 10.2 above, continue using the as-B&B TOC file you saved. Otherwise, open the as-B&B file from the Lesson 10 folder.*

1. **Automark** all main index entries for the as-B&B file using the as-B&B Concordance file from the Lesson 10 folder.

2. Create **three** separate subentries for Northern California:
   - Emily's Inn
   - The Speck House
   - Inn on the Square

3. Create **six** separate subentries for Town by selecting the town name and moving it to the subentry text box and adding the main entry text:
   - Sonoma
   - Eureka
   - Santa Rosa
   - Carmel
   - Monterey
   - Pacific Grove

4. Create **three** separate subentries for Central Coast and Valley:
   - Wesley House
   - Carmichael Inn
   - Murphy's Inn

5. Close the **Mark Index Entry** dialog box, and **turn off** Show/Hide.

6. Generate a **one-column index** using the Formal style below the Index heading.

7. **Save** the document in the Lesson 10 folder using the filename `as-B&B Index`, and **close** the document.

Critical Thinking & Work-Readiness Skills

In the course of working through the following Microsoft Office-based Critical Thinking exercises, you will also be utilizing various work-readiness skills, some of which are listed next to each exercise. Go to labyrinthelab.com/workreadiness *to learn more about the work-readiness skills.*

10.1 Insert Sections and Generate a TOC

The Raritan Clinic East administrator has identified a pediatric reference handbook physicians in the clinic would find useful. A description of one such handbook appears in ct-Pediatric Handbook (Lesson 10 folder). The administrator would like you to review the document and add a table of contents (TOC) to it so it is more useful to others. Use the table of contents style you prefer and place the TOC on a separate page following the graphic currently located on the first page of the document. Separate the body of the document from the table using an appropriate section break. Add your name to the header of page 1 of the document body. Save your file in your Lesson 10 folder as **ct-Handbook TOC**. Print a copy of the document.

WORK-READINESS SKILLS APPLIED

- Serving clients/customers
- Reading
- Using computers to process information

10.2 Mark and Generate an Index

To add even more functionality for users, you decide to create an index for the handbook. Generate an index for the ct-Pediatric Handbook document (Lesson 10 folder). Manually mark text in the document for inclusion in the index. Include appropriate subentries for at least two of the main index entries marked. Then, create a new section at the end of the document to hold the index. Break the link between headers and footers for both sections. Add page numbers formatted as Arabic numerals in the footer of section one and small roman numerals for the index page. Insert your name in the header of the index page. Save the file in your Lesson 10 folder as **ct-Handbook Index**. Print only the page containing the index.

WORK-READINESS SKILLS APPLIED

- Organizing and maintaining information
- Using computers to process information
- Serving clients/customers

10.3 Update a Concordance and Remark Text

The concordance file used in the Develop Your Skills activities in this lesson marked all entries as main entries. Open the ct-Raritan Clinic East Policies & Procedures Manual and the ct-Raritan Policies & Procedures Concordance files (Lesson 10 folder). Review the concordance file and determine which topics would be better as subentries contained in the document. Then, edit the concordance file so both main entries and subentries can be marked automatically. Save the changes to the concordance file and close it. Then, use the revised concordance file to automark index entries in the ct-Raritan Clinic East Policies & Procedures Manual document. After marking the entries, generate the index on a separate page at the end of the document. Save your changes and print the document.

WORK-READINESS SKILLS APPLIED

- Organizing and maintaining information
- Using computers to process information
- Reading

Collaborating in Word

LESSON OUTLINE

LEARNING OBJECTIVES

After studying this lesson, you will be able to:

- Use and customize the Track Changes feature
- Track changes to documents
- Insert comments into documents
- Review tracked changes
- Use Word's Save & Send tools
- Combine and compare documents
- Use the highlighter tool
- Collaborate in Windows Live SkyDrive
- Use Office Web Apps

The Internet makes it much easier for project teams to collaborate on the drafting of documents. Team members can exchange documents across the country as easily as they can across the hall. In addition to inserting comments in a document, Word has several features that make collaboration activities more efficient. For example, Word can track all of the changes made on a document by each group member and combine these changes into a single document for review. In this lesson, you will work with these collaboration tools.

Collaborating on a Manual

Raritan Clinic East

Pediatric Diagnostic Specialists

James Elliott has been reviewing and is trying to finalize the Raritan Clinic East Policies & Procedures Manual. It is now ready for review by clinic administrators and personnel in the human resources department. As others review the manual, they will use many of Word's collaboration tools to mark suggested changes and identify topics that they believe should be revised. Some reviewers will insert comments to identify their recommendations, while others will use Word's Track Changes feature to mark suggested edits. Some will highlight text to identify wording that needs revised; others will type a list of edits that need to be made in a separate document or email message.

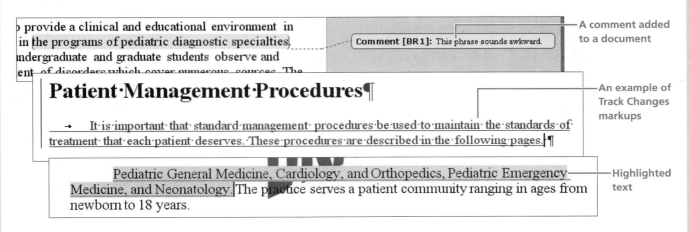

A comment added to a document

An example of Track Changes markups

Highlighted text

James' task will be to review all suggested edits and comments and finalize the document for printing.

11.1 Using the Highlighter

Video Lesson   labyrinthelab.com/videos

Word's highlighter tool works just like its real-life counterpart (except that you can easily erase this highlighter). The tool applies a transparent color to the background of the text. You apply a highlight by selecting a highlight color and dragging. Or you can select the text and then click to apply the highlight color.

FROM THE KEYBOARD

Press [Esc] on the keyboard to turn off the highlighter.

As an example, you can highlight a note you write to yourself in a document so that you don't overlook it. Or perhaps you are waiting for additional information for a report. You can highlight the area where the information will go to remind yourself that you are expecting more material.

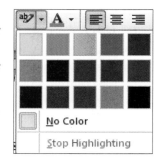

The Text Highlight Color tool offers a variety of colors for highlighting, so you can color-code the highlights you use in a document if you wish. For example, you might highlight a note to yourself in yellow and a "waiting for information" reminder in green.

DEVELOP YOUR SKILLS 11.1.1
Highlight Text in a Document

In this exercise, you will highlight a note to yourself and a reminder that you are waiting for additional information.

1. **Maximize** Word, and then **open** the Raritan Clinic East Draft Procedures Manual document from the Lesson 11 folder.
   This document contains a draft of the policies and procedures manual for Raritan Clinic East.

2. **Save** the document in the Lesson 11 folder using the filename **Revised Raritan Clinic East Procedures Manual**.

3. **Press** [Ctrl]+[Home] to move to the beginning of the document.

4. **Search** the document for the text *Pediatric General Medicine*, and position the insertion point at the beginning of the line where the text appears.

5. **Type** this note: **Chin has more information about these specialties:**

6. Choose **Home→Font→Text Highlight Color** 🖉 ▾ **menu ▾** from the Ribbon.

Change the Highlight Color

7. Choose **Bright Green** from the gallery.
   When the mouse pointer is in the body of the document, it looks like a highlighter pen.

8. Drag the **pen** across the text you just added to highlight it in green.

9. Choose **Home→Font→Text Highlight Color** 🖉 from the Ribbon to turn the pen off.
   Notice that the pen color on the button now reflects the most recently used color.

10. **Press** Ctrl + End to move to the end of the document.

11. **Type** this sentence: `Check with Finance to see if they have information to add.`

12. **Select** the sentence, and choose **Home→Font→Text Highlight Color** [aby ▾] **menu ▾** from the Ribbon.

13. Choose **Yellow** from the gallery.
    This highlights the selected text and changes the button color to yellow.

Remove Highlighting

14. Select the **note** you added to the end of the document again.

15. Choose **Home→Font→Text Highlight Color** [aby ▾] **menu ▾** from the Ribbon.

16. Choose the **No Color** command at the bottom of the gallery to remove the highlight.

17. **Save** [💾] the file, and leave it **open**.

11.2 Tracking Changes to Documents

Video Lesson labyrinthelab.com/videos

Although managing document edits from numerous printed copies of a document is one alternative to obtaining feedback from workgroup members, communicating electronically is fast becoming the preferred method for obtaining valuable feedback. This is especially true now that many software applications are including tools to make the collaboration process more efficient. Word's tools are no exception.

The Track Changes feature is one of Word's most useful collaboration tools. With Track Changes switched on, Word marks each change made to a document. Word's reviewing tools then enable you to review each change and accept or reject it. You can distribute several copies of a document to different team members and then merge changes from all copies of the document into a single document.

Reviewers can also use Word's Comment feature to leave messages in the document as a means of communicating with the originator or highlight text to call attention to it.

Identifying Steps in a Typical Editing and Reviewing Process

In a perfect world, team members working together to construct a document would all mark their recommended changes on the same printed document. Time delays using such a process can result when one reviewer holds the document or is out of town and unable to review the document. As a result, following is how a typical review process might progress in today's world of requests for instant feedback.

Step	Description	Performed by
1	You open the document in Word, activate the Track Changes feature, and save changes to the document.	You
2	You send an electronic copy of the document via email to all those who need to review it, indicating the date by which you need their edits returned.	You
3	Each reviewer makes revisions to the copy of the document he or she received. Word's Track Changes feature marks edits and identifies the date and person making the edit, as well as the type of revision made.	Reviewers
4	Reviewers return the edited document to you.	Reviewers
5	After you have received all copies of the document, you can review each change manually and accept or reject the edits, or you can combine all documents containing edits into one document so that you have one document that contains all edits from all reviewers.	You

Viewing Tracked Changes

Word offers two options for viewing edits made to documents using Track Changes.

- **Balloons**—Comments and edits appear in bubbles on the right side of the document text. Each bubble identifies the person who made the edit as well as the type of edit made— inserted text, deleted, etc. Balloons are the default setting for Word.

- **Inline**—Edits are marked directly within sentences and paragraphs. Text that is deleted by the reviewer is marked through with a line and text added appears in a different color to help identify what action the author took.

Tracked changes are shown in line with paragraph text

Patient·Management·Procedures¶

→   It·is·important·that·standard·management·procedures·be·used·to·maintain·the·standards·of· treatment·that·each·patient·deserves.·These·procedures·are·described·in·the·following·pages.¶

Full·diagnostic,·rehabilitative,·preventive,·related·counseling·services·and·screenings·are· available·to·individuals·from·birth·to·18·years·in·the·following·areas:¶

Deleted: habilitative,·

Tracked changes are marked as balloons in the margin.

QUICK REFERENCE	DISPLAYING TRACKED CHANGES
Method	**Description**
Show revisions in balloons	■ Deleted text, comments, and formatting changes appear in balloons in the Markup Area to the right of the document being reviewed. ■ Added text is underlined in the body of the document. ■ Moved text appears in a balloon at the *moved from* area; it appears underlined in the body of the document in the *moved to* area.
Show all revisions inline	■ Deleted text appears in the body of the document with a strikethrough font. ■ Added text is underlined in the body of the document. ■ Comments highlight the selected text, and you read the comment by hovering the mouse pointer over it. ■ Moved text uses a strikethrough font at the *moved from* area, and it appears underlined in the body of the document in the *moved to* area.
Show only comments and formatting in balloons	■ Comments and formatting changes appear in balloons. ■ All other changes appear inline.

The descriptions in the preceding table relate to working in a view called Final Showing Markup. Variations occur when you make other viewing choices. You will learn about viewing choices later in this lesson.

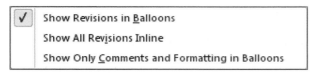

The Balloons menu provides several options for displaying marked changes.

The balloons method is the primary method used in this lesson.

Setting the Username and Initials

The Track Changes feature in Word uses information set up on your computer to identify your username and initials for edits you make to a document. As a result, whenever you collaborate on a document where Track Changes will be used, it is important to make sure your username and initials are set correctly. Track Changes also displays the reviewer's name when you hover the mouse pointer over a change.

Setting Reviewer Ink Colors

Track Changes can then use different colors to distinguish the edits of each reviewer who works on the document. Each reviewer can specify colors for his or her comments and tracked changes. This makes it easier to rapidly identify changes submitted by a specific reviewer. It also allows you to keep a consistent color for a reviewer you work with frequently, rather than settling on colors Word may assign automatically.

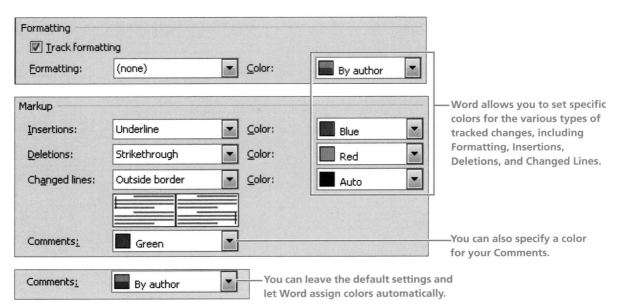

Word allows you to set specific colors for the various types of tracked changes, including Formatting, Insertions, Deletions, and Changed Lines.

You can also specify a color for your Comments.

You can leave the default settings and let Word assign colors automatically.

TIP If reviewers work on separate documents, you can combine them into a single document, as you will see later in this lesson.

QUICK REFERENCE	TRACKING CHANGES FOR A DOCUMENT
Task	**Procedure**
Turn on Track Changes	■ Choose Review→Tracking→Track Changes from the Ribbon.
Choose a method of tracking	■ Choose Review→Tracking→Show Markup→Balloons from the Ribbon. ■ Choose the desired method from the menu.
Associate your name and initials with changes	■ Choose Review→Tracking→Track Changes menu ▼ from the Ribbon. ■ Choose Change User Name from the menu. ■ Enter your name and initials, and then click OK.
Set reviewer ink colors	■ Choose Review→Tracking→Track Changes menu ▼ from the Ribbon. ■ Choose Change Tracking Options from the menu to display the Track Changes Options dialog box. ■ Make the desired choices.

DEVELOP YOUR SKILLS 11.2.1

Change Tracking Colors, Username, and Initials

In this exercise, you will turn on Track Changes, change the tracking colors, and set the user's name and initials for the Revised Raritan Clinic East Procedures Manual created in Develop Your Skills 11.1.1.

Switch on Track Changes

1. Choose **Review→Tracking→Track Changes** 📝 from the Ribbon.
   Notice that the Track Changes button is active. Word is now set to track every change to the document.

Change Tracking Colors

2. Choose **Review→Tracking→Track Changes** ![menu icon] **menu ▾** from the Ribbon.

3. Choose **Change Tracking Options** from the menu.

4. Follow these steps to choose options for your reviewer ink color settings:

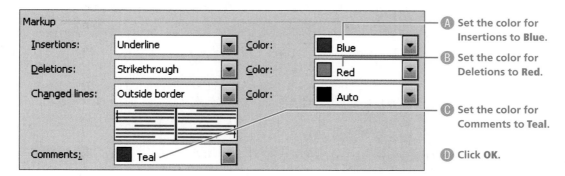

A) Set the color for Insertions to **Blue**.

B) Set the color for Deletions to **Red**.

C) Set the color for Comments to **Teal**.

D) Click **OK**.

Set the Username and Initials

Since Word can keep track of each reviewer who makes revisions to a document, you should make sure that your name and initials are set properly.

5. Choose **Review→Tracking→Track Changes** ![menu icon] **menu ▾** from the Ribbon.

6. Choose **Change User Name** from the menu.

7. Enter your username and initials, and then click **OK**.

8. **Save** the file, and leave it **open** for the next exercise.

Adding Comments to a Document

Video Lesson   labyrinthelab.com/videos

Word's Comment feature is a great collaboration tool. It allows reviewers and originators to communicate about the document by sending notes back and forth. A reviewer might want to point out the reason for a deletion, for example. You can place comments in the body of a document or in a balloon in the Markup Area to the right of the document. When you hover the mouse pointer over a comment, Word displays the name of the comment's author and the date and time the comment was inserted.

This is an example of a comment balloon in the Markup Area. It contains the note written for the originator's attention.

This is an example of a comment inline in the body of the text. By double-clicking on the initials of the person who recorded the comment, a Summary panel opens on the left side of the screen or at the bottom of the screen to enable you to view the comment, reply to the comment, or edit the comment.

WORKING WITH COMMENTS

Task	Procedure
Insert a comment	■ Choose Review→Comments→New Comment from the Ribbon.
Display comments inline or in a balloon in the Markup Area	■ Choose Review→Tracking→Show Markup→Balloons from the Ribbon. ■ Choose the desired method from the menu.
Edit a comment	■ If the comment is in a balloon, click in the balloon, and make editing changes. *or* ■ If the comment is inline, right-click the comment, and choose Edit Comment from the menu to display an editing pane on the left side of the screen. ■ Make changes in the editing pane.
Delete a comment	■ Whether the comment is inline or in a balloon, right-click the comment, and choose Delete Comment from the menu. *or* ■ Choose Review→Comments→Delete on the Ribbon.

DEVELOP YOUR SKILLS 11.2.2
Work with Track Changes

In this exercise, you will choose the balloon display for tracking changes, and then you will insert a comment and make revisions in the document.

Before You Begin: Your Revised Raritan Clinic East Procedures Manual should be open.

Choose the Tracking Method

1. Choose **Review→Tracking→Show Markup→Balloons** from the Ribbon.

2. Ensure that **Show Revisions in Balloons** is active and **click** to select it if it is not.

3. **Press** Ctrl + G to display the Go To dialog box, enter **2** as the page number, and then click the **Go To** button.
   Page 2 displays.

4. **Close** the Go To dialog box.

Insert a Comment

5. Scroll to the **last paragraph** on the page, and select the **first word**, *Referral*, of the paragraph.

6. Choose **Review→Comments→New Comment** from the Ribbon.
   Notice the Markup Area that appears to the right of the document. This is where comment balloons and editing balloons appear.

7. **Type** the following text in the comment balloon:

   Comment [BR2]: Indent·to·match·other· paragraphs.¶

8. Locate the text *(see Appendix A)* in the next line, **select** the text, and **delete** it.
   Word places deleted text in a balloon in the Markup Area, as shown in the following illustration, and places a black bar in the left margin to help reviewers locate changes.

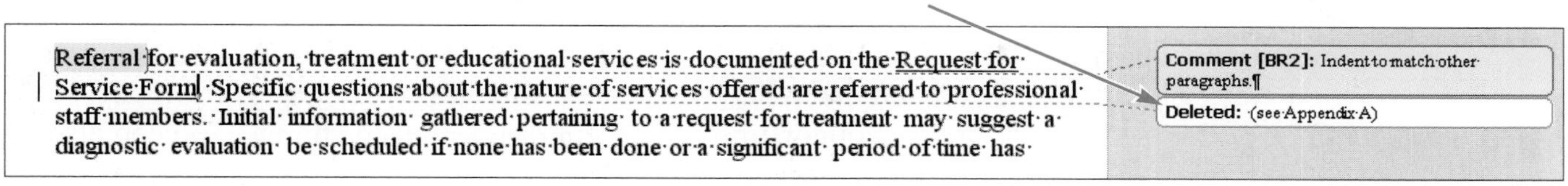

Referral·for·evaluation,·treatment·or·educational·services·is·documented·on·the·Request·for· Service·Form|·Specific·questions·about·the·nature·of·services·offered·are·referred·to·professional· staff·members.·Initial·information·gathered·pertaining·to·a·request·for·treatment·may·suggest·a· diagnostic·evaluation·be·scheduled·if·none·has·been·done·or·a·significant·period·of·time·has·

Comment [BR2]: Indent to match other paragraphs.¶

Deleted: (see·Appendix·A)

9. **Search** for the text *see* to locate each additional cross-reference to an appendix and delete the cross-references for Appendix B through Appendix K.

10. **Search** for the text *Patient Management Procedures,* and then **close** the Find and Replace dialog box.

11. Follow these steps to insert introductory text for the main heading:

Ⓐ Position the **insertion point** at the end of the heading, and **press** Enter.

Ⓑ **Press** Tab to indent the first line of the paragraph, and **type** the text shown.

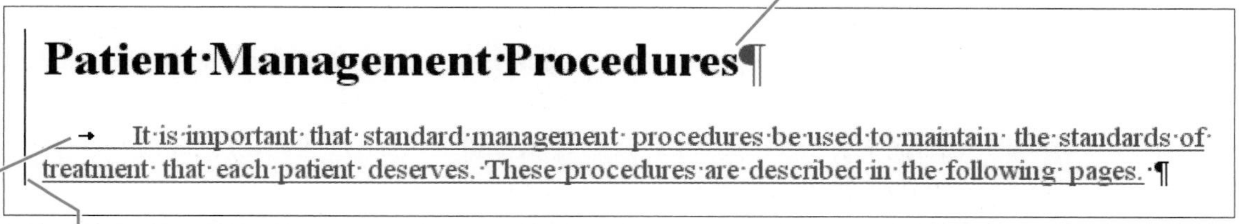

Patient·Management·Procedures¶

→ It·is·important·that·standard·management·procedures·be·used·to·maintain·the·standards·of· treatment·that·each·patient·deserves.·These·procedures·are·described·in·the·following·pages.·¶

Ⓒ Notice the black bar in the left margin that helps locate places in the document where changes are made.

12. **Save** 🖫 changes to the document, and leave it **open**.

11.3 Reviewing Tracked Changes

Video Lesson   labyrinthelab.com/videos

Word makes it easy to find and review changes to a document. You can review changes even when Track Changes is not turned on. When you review changes, Word jumps from one change to the next, giving you the opportunity to accept or reject each change. You can also accept or reject all changes at once. After you accept or reject a change, Word removes the revision marks.

ACCEPTING AND REJECTING CHANGES	
Ribbon Menu Option	**Description**
Review→Changes→Accept→ Accept and Move to Next	Accepts the change at the insertion point and moves to the next change or comment. This is the default acceptance setting.
Review→Changes→Accept→ Accept Change	Accepts the change at the insertion point and waits for you to advance to the next change or return to the previous change.
Review→Changes→Accept→ Accept All Changes Shown	Accepts only the changes that are visible onscreen at the time the command is given.
Review→Changes→Accept→ Accept All Changes in Document	Accepts all changes in the document whether they are visible or not.
Review→Changes→Reject→ Reject and Move to Next	Rejects the change at the insertion point and moves to the next change or comment. This is the default rejection setting.
Review→Changes→Reject→ Reject Change	Rejects the change at the insertion point and waits for you to advance to the next change or return to the previous change.
Review→Changes→Reject→ Reject All Changes Shown	Rejects only the changes that are visible onscreen at the time the command is given.
Review→Changes→Reject→ Reject All Changes in Document	Rejects all changes in the document whether they are visible or hidden.

This button accepts the currently selected change. ──

This button rejects the currently selected change. ──

──These buttons navigate you to the next and previous tracked change.

You can also right-click a proposed change and choose an Accept or a Reject command from the pop-up menu.

Options for Displaying Tracked Changes

Word allows you to display tracked changes in four distinctive views. Depending on the type of detail you want to focus on, each view offers specific advantages. For example, you may want to view how the document would look after the changes are incorporated. In this case, you would choose the Final option. If you want to see how the document looked before any changes were made, you would choose Original.

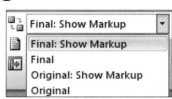

View	Why Use This View	Example
Final Show Markup	To see all tracked changes relative to the final document	Acme continues to Deleted: has continued
Final	To see the final document appearance if all pending tracked changes were accepted	Acme continues to
Original Show Markup	To see all tracked changes relative to the original document	Acme has continued to Inserted: continues
Original	To see the original document appearance without the changes	Acme has continued to

DEVELOP YOUR SKILLS 11.3.1
Review Tracked Changes

In this exercise, you will review tracked changes to the document, accepting some changes and rejecting others, and displaying the document in markup display views.

Before You Begin: Your Revised Raritan Clinic East Procedures Manual should be open.

1. **Press** Ctrl + Home to move the **insertion point** to the beginning of the document.
   Starting at page 1 allows you to review tracked changes in sequence. Otherwise, the Next button begins searching from the current insertion point location.

Cycle Through the Reviewing Views

2. Choose **Review→Tracking→Display for Review** 📋 from the Ribbon.

3. Click the drop-down list, choose **Original**, and **scroll** through the document.
   The document now appears as it did before you made changes.

4. Choose **Original: Show Markup** in the Display for Review box and **scroll** through the document.
   Notice the Inserted balloon in the Markup Area on the right. With the original displayed and markups shown, Word moves inserted text to the Markup Area.

5. Choose **Final** in the Display for Review box and **scroll** through the document.
   The change balloon disappears, and you see the document as it would appear if the revisions were approved.

6. Choose **Final: Show Markup** in the Display for Review box and **scroll** through the document.
   Now Word displays the insertion inline, as it would appear in the final version. However, the insertion is marked in blue and underscored, to indicate that it has not yet been accepted.

7. Choose **Review→Changes→Next** 📝 from the Ribbon.
   Word jumps to and highlights the paragraph you added to the document. This is a good addition to the document so you will accept it.

8. Choose **Review→Changes→Accept** [icon] from the Ribbon.
   Word removes the change marks from the new paragraph and moves to the next tracked change—the comment you added.

9. Choose **Review→Changes→Next** [icon] to skip the comment and move to the next change, the deleted reference to Appendix A.

10. Choose **Review→Changes→Reject** [icon] from the Ribbon.
    Word rejects the change and moves to the next tracked change.

11. Repeat the procedure outlined in **step 10** to reject each deleted reference to an appendix.
    These appendices will be added to the document before it is distributed. Word displays a prompt about continuing at the beginning of the document.

12. Choose **Yes** to return to the skipped comment, and then choose **Review→Tracking→ Track Changes** from the Ribbon to turn the feature off.

13. Choose **Review→Comments→Delete** [icon] on the Ribbon to remove the comment.

14. Position the **insertion point** at the beginning of the paragraph referenced by the comment deleted in **step 13**, and **press** ⎯Tab⎯ to indent the first line of the paragraph.

15. **Save** [icon] the file, leave it **open**, and continue with the next topic.

11.4 Saving and Sending Files

Video Lesson labyrinthelab.com/videos

Before reviewers can do their job and edit or comment on a document, you must decide how to get the document to them. Copying a document to CD and mailing it is slow. Instead, you can use the speed of the Internet to share your document several ways, including:

- Email
- SkyDrive and Office Web Apps 2010
- Internet Fax
- Blog Post

Sharing Files via Email

Sharing files via email is a simple procedure, but as with any process, it has its own strengths and weaknesses.

STRENGTHS AND WEAKNESSES OF SHARING FILES VIA EMAIL	
Strengths	**Weaknesses**
■ No Windows Live ID is required	■ There are potentially several versions of the same document to keep track of
■ Using email is already familiar to most users	
■ It is a simple process to attach a document to an email	■ Large documents containing video, audio, or other linked files can be problematic to email
■ As reviewers must have Word, comments can be added directly to the document	■ Each reviewer must have Word installed to edit the document or insert comments

Selecting an Email Program

When you use the Send Using E-mail command in Word, your email message is automatically created and the document automatically attached to the message. Word works with any email program or webmail service that you can select from the Programs tab of the Internet Options menu in Internet Explorer (Win XP) or in the Windows Control Panel (Win 7/Vista). If you want to change the email service, you should make this selection before starting Word. Some email services (for example, most webmail services) don't support attaching the document automatically, so you must do so manually.

QUICK REFERENCE	SETTING THE DEFAULT EMAIL PROGRAM
Operating System	**Procedure**
Set the default email program (Win 7/Vista)	■ Choose Start→Control Panel ■ Click Programs. ■ Click Set Your Default Programs. ■ Select your preferred email program from the list at the left. ■ Click Set This Program as Default in the right column.
Set the default email program (Win XP)	■ Start Internet Explorer. ■ Choose Tools→Internet Options from the Command Bar. ■ Select the Programs tab. ■ Select your preferred email program from the E-mail drop-down menu.

Using the Send Using E-mail Pane

TIP

Clicking the Send button in the Outlook window does not actually send the message. It simply saves it to your Outlook Outbox, where it will sit until you start Outlook.

The Save & Send tab of Backstage view contains a Send Using E-mail pane that includes commands to attach the current document as a regular Word file, a PDF file, an XPS document, or as an Internet FAX. When you choose this command, Word immediately displays an email window with the file attached. You just need to address the email and type your message. You can also change the Subject line, which defaults to the name of the file you are sending.

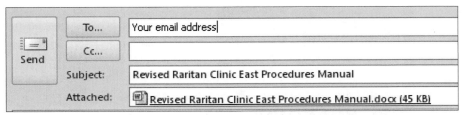

The Outlook 2010 message window (with document automatically attached) waiting to be addressed

SEND USING E-MAIL OPTIONS

Option	Explanation
Send as Attachment	▪ The file is attached in its current format. For example, if you have a DOCX file open (the default file format for Word), a DOCX file is attached to the email.
Send as PDF	▪ The document is converted to the PDF file format and the PDF file is attached to the email. ▪ The recipient must have the free Adobe Acrobat Reader or another PDF reader to open the attached PDF file.
Send as XPS	▪ The document is converted to the XPS file format and the XPS is attached to the email. ▪ XPS files can be opened with Internet Explorer.
Send as Internet Fax	▪ You must sign up with a fax service provider before using this option.

Naming Reviewer Copies

Experience shows that it works best to name each copy of a document sent out for review with the reviewer's name. Then, as the documents are returned from review, it's easy to track which came from which reviewer.

QUICK REFERENCE	SENDING A DOCUMENT FOR REVIEW VIA EMAIL
Task	**Procedure**
Send a document for review with Outlook, Outlook Express, Windows Mail, or Windows Live Mail	▪ Open the document in Word. ▪ (Optional but recommended) Choose Review→Tracking→Track Changes to turn on Track Changes so Word will track edits made by reviewers. ▪ (Optional but recommended) Choose File→Save As, rename the document, indicating which reviewer is to review this copy, and click Save. (A copy of the document is now saved with a new name and is currently open in Word.) ▪ Choose File→Save & Send→Send Using E-mail→Send as Attachment. (The document is automatically attached to the email.) ▪ Enter the recipient's email address and, if desired, revise the subject line. ▪ Click the Send button in the message window. ▪ Open your email program to actually send the message. ▪ Repeat the preceding steps for each reviewer.
Send a document for review using another email program	▪ Open your email program and address a message to the first reviewer. ▪ Use your email program's procedure to attach the saved copy of the document and click Send.

 Save all reviewer copies in a special folder to keep them together.

Send a Document for Review

In this exercise, you will send an email with a copy of the Revised Raritan Clinic East Procedures Manual document attached. You will actually send the attachment to your own email address for practice.

Before You Begin: Your Revised Raritan Clinic East Procedures Manual document should be open.

1. Turn on **Track Changes**, and **save** the document.

2. Choose **File→Save & Send→Send Using E-mail** [icon]**→Send as Attachment**.
   If your user ID was not set up as a user with an Outlook account, you will see a message saying that no profiles have been created. If so, just dismiss the message, turn off track changes, and read through the rest of this exercise.

3. Follow these steps to complete the email form, if possible:

Ⓐ Enter your **email address** and the **reviewer email addresses** here.

Ⓑ Word automatically uses the document name as the subject. You can change the subject if you wish.

Ⓒ The attachment appears here.

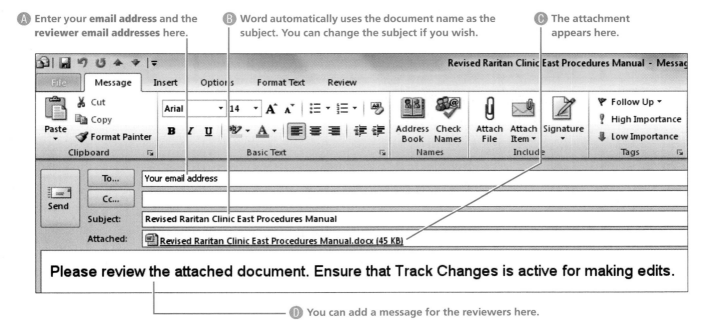

Ⓓ You can add a message for the reviewers here.

4. **Send** the document, if you are using Outlook, or click the **Close** [X] button in the upper-right corner of the email form to close it.

5. Choose **Review→Tracking→Track Changes** [icon] to turn off the feature.

Sending an Internet Fax

Microsoft Office 2010 has a tool that enables you to send Outlook, Word, Excel, and Power-Point files as Internet faxes. As a result, you can create a document and fax it directly from Word to the appropriate recipient.

This feature requires that the Windows Fax Printer Driver or Fax Services be installed on the computer. The Windows Fax feature is turned off by default for some versions of Windows. If your edition of Windows includes this driver or service, you must install it before you can send Internet faxes.

11.5 Reviewing Changes from Multiple Reviewers

Video Lesson   labyrinthelab.com/videos

If you set up a document to track changes, you can send out copies of the document for review by others. As these reviewers make revisions, Word tracks their changes in each individual copy of the document. When the reviewers send you their edited copies of the document, you can combine the tracked changes into a single document. Word marks each reviewer's changes in a different color, so you can easily recognize input from different reviewers. After the changes are merged, you can navigate through one document and accept and reject edits from all users at one time. In fact, by seeing the edits from all reviewers in one document, you will be able to identify the trouble spots in the document because many reviewers will try to modify the same area of the document.

Combining Documents

If you send a document to several people for review, you can combine two documents at once with the original. This makes it easy to see the proposed changes next to the original text. If there are more than two reviewers, repeat the process until all reviewers' changes have been accepted or rejected.

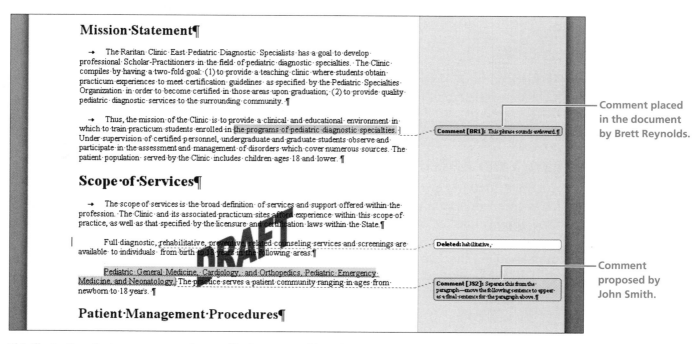

This illustration displays a comment inserted by Brett Reynolds and a comment inserted by John Smith.

Reviewing a Summary of Proposed Changes

The Reviewing Pane summarizes reviewer changes in a window that you can scroll through to examine the proposed changes. When you click a change in the Reviewing Pane, the document pane scrolls to that part of the document so you can see the change in context.

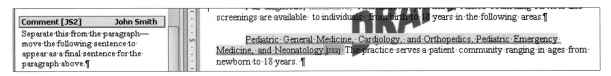

This figure shows the Reviewing Pane on the left, with the document scrolled to the displayed change.

Showing Source Documents

The following table describes different views you can use for comparing the original with reviewed documents. The view you choose is a matter of personal preference. You may find that you switch views depending on the type and extent of a reviewer's changes. It may be helpful, for example, to display the original and the marked document side by side for comparison purposes, or hide the summary of changes list to get a larger view of the combined documents.

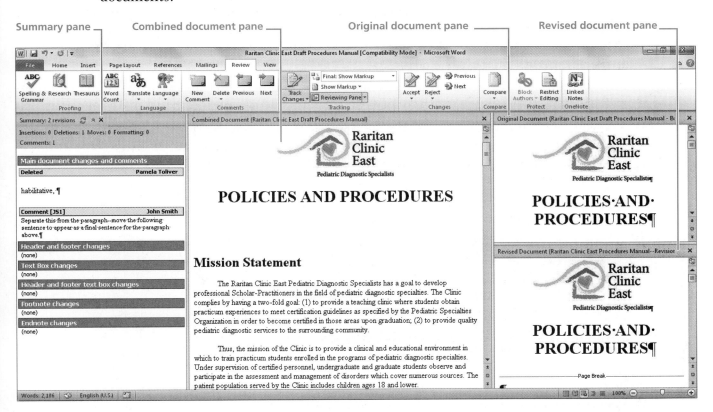

QUICK REFERENCE	**USING SOURCE DOCUMENT VIEWS**
Option	**Description**
Hide source documents	Displays the original document with the reviewer's changes embedded in it.
Show original	This choice displays the original side by side with the marked document. The documents scroll simultaneously for easy comparison.
Show revised	This view displays the original with the reviewer's changes embedded in the original next to the reviewer's tracked changes document.
Show both	This view displays the unmarked original, the marked reviewer document, and the original with the reviewer's changes embedded.

Displaying Specific Markups

Word offers numerous options for displaying tracked changes for combined documents. For example, you may only want to look at the insertions and deletions suggested by reviewers. Word stores only one set of formatting changes at a time. If you don't need to keep track of formatting changes, you may wish to turn off the Formatting option, so Word won't prompt you to choose whether to keep the original formatting or the formatting from the reviewer's copy.

Display Specific Reviewers

If you combine two reviewer documents with the original, you can choose to see changes from both at once, or you may wish to focus on the proposed changes from just one reviewer, which you can do by removing the checkmark in front of the other reviewer's name.

This command appears toward the bottom of the Show Markup menu in the Tracking group of the Review tab. The original author's name also appears in the list.

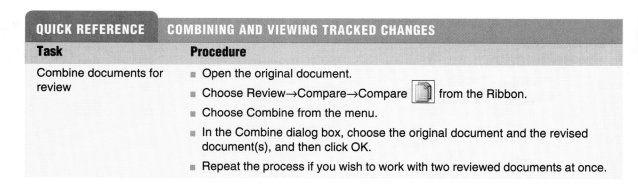

QUICK REFERENCE	**COMBINING AND VIEWING TRACKED CHANGES**
Task	**Procedure**
Combine documents for review	■ Open the original document. ■ Choose Review→Compare→Compare  from the Ribbon. ■ Choose Combine from the menu. ■ In the Combine dialog box, choose the original document and the revised document(s), and then click OK. ■ Repeat the process if you wish to work with two reviewed documents at once.

Task	Procedure
Display the Reviewing Pane	■ Choose Review→Tracking→Reviewing Pane 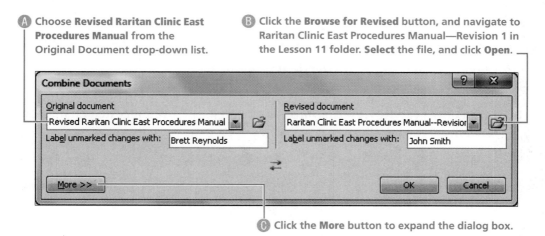 from the Ribbon. ■ Choose the desired orientation for the pane from the menu (horizontal or vertical).
Choose source documents to display	■ Choose Review→Compare→Compare →Show Source Documents from the Ribbon. ■ Make the desired choice from the menu.
Display specific types of changes and choose which reviewers' change marks should appear	■ Choose Review→Tracking→Show Markup from the Ribbon. ■ Make the desired menu choices.

DEVELOP YOUR SKILLS 11.5.1

Combine Tracked Changes from Two Reviewers

In this exercise, you will combine proposed changes from two reviewers with the original document. You will then explore additional features used for working with combined documents.

Before You Begin: Your Revised Raritan Clinic East Procedures Manual should be open.

Choose the First Document to Combine with the Original

1. Choose **Review→Compare→Compare** from the Ribbon.

2. Choose **Combine** from the menu to open the Combine Documents dialog box.

3. Follow these steps to begin combining documents:

Ⓐ Choose **Revised Raritan Clinic East Procedures Manual** from the Original Document drop-down list.

Ⓑ Click the **Browse for Revised** button, and navigate to Raritan Clinic East Procedures Manual—Revision 1 in the Lesson 11 folder. **Select** the file, and click **Open**.

Ⓒ Click the **More** button to expand the dialog box.

4. Follow these steps to control document display:

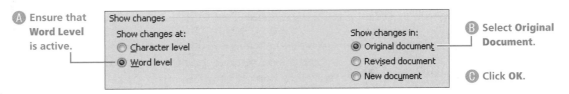

The Show Changes list of options should default to Word Level. This means that Word highlights the entire word, even if only one character or punctuation mark changes. This makes it easier to spot small edits during the review cycle. After you click OK, John Smith's proposed edits will be embedded in the original document, ready for review.

5. Select **Your Document** and then click the **Continue with Merge** button, if presented.

Hide Source Documents

6. Choose **Review→Compare→Compare** and select **Show Source Documents** ▦ from the Ribbon.

7. If necessary, choose **Hide Source Documents** from the menu.
   John's proposed changes are embedded in the original.

Choose the Second Document to Combine

8. Repeat the procedures outlined in **steps 3–5** to combine the second reviewed document named Raritan Clinic East Procedures Manual—Revision 2 with the original document.
   Brett Reynold's edits are now displayed with the original and John Smith's edits.

Turn On the Reviewing Pane

You can position the Reviewing Pane horizontally across the bottom of the screen or vertically down the side of the screen.

9. Choose **Review→Tracking→Reviewing Pane** ▣ **menu** ▾ from the Ribbon.

10. Choose **Reviewing Pane Vertical** from the menu.
    The Reviewing Pane summarizes the proposed changes from both reviewers.

11. Scroll down the **Reviewing Pane** until you locate the suggested change by Brett Reynolds, where he has inserted text.

12. Click the suggested change in the Reviewing Pane, and observe that Word scrolls the document to the location of the change.

13. Click the **Close** ⊠ button at the top of the Reviewing Pane.

14. Use ⌈Ctrl⌉+⌈Home⌉ to move to the top of the document.

15. Use techniques learned earlier in this lesson to review all changes to the document, **delete** all comments, and **accept** all edits by John and Brett.

16. **Save** the file as a new document named **Combined Manuals** in your Lesson 11 folder, and then **close** it.

Comparing Documents

Video Lesson labyrinthelab.com/videos

Sometimes documents that are sent for review are returned with no visible edits made to the document. While this is, at first, thought to be a good sign that the document is in great shape, that is not always the case. Sometimes, reviewers turn off or disable Track Changes so that the edits they make are not immediately evident. To determine whether edits have been made to the document, you can use Word's other collaboration tool for reviewing documents—Compare.

The Compare feature in Word enables you to merge two seemingly identical documents into one file. When you use Word's Compare tool, Word examines each document and automatically marks up the document using Track Changes so that you can locate edits made to the document.

Combining or Comparing Documents?

The Combine and Compare features are similar in many ways, and the differences between them are rather subtle. Essentially, the Compare feature is designed for comparing two documents: an edited version of a document, where the reviewer did not use the Track Changes feature, and the original. On the other hand, the Combine feature will accomplish the same task.

The basic procedures for comparing documents are the same as those for combining documents. A primary difference is that the Combine feature allows you to combine the tracked changes from multiple reviewers in one document, and then you can go through the single document to accept or reject the changes. If you attempt to use the Compare feature to add a second reviewer's document, Word will advise you that it will automatically accept the first person's changes before comparing the second edited document. Thus you won't have the option of accepting or rejecting changes from the first reviewer.

QUICK REFERENCE	COMBINING DOCUMENTS
Task	**Procedure**
Combine documents	■ Choose Review→Compare→Compare from the Ribbon. ■ Choose Combine from the menu. ■ Choose the original and the revised documents. ■ Click the More button, and change any defaults you desire. ■ Click OK to combine the documents.
Compare documents	■ Choose Review→Compare→Compare from the Ribbon. ■ Choose Compare from the menu. ■ Choose the original and revised documents. ■ Click the More button, and change any defaults you desire. ■ Click OK to compare the documents.

Compare Two Unmarked Documents

In this exercise, you will compare the Revised Raritan Clinic East Procedures Manual with a document received from a reviewer that appears to have no changes in it.

1. **Open** your Revised Raritan Clinic East Procedures Manual from the Lesson 11 folder and choose **Review→Compare→Compare→Compare** on the Ribbon.

2. Follow these steps to compare this file with another document:

Ⓐ Select the **Revised Raritan Clinic East Procedures Manual** from the Original Document list.

Ⓑ Click the **Browse** button, and navigate to the Lesson 11 folder to open the Edited Manual without Marks document.

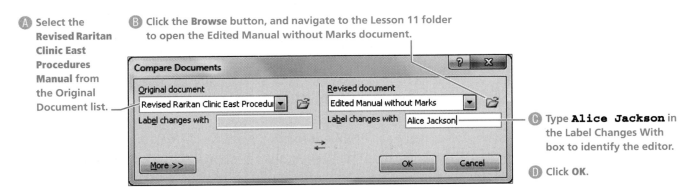

Ⓒ Type **Alice Jackson** in the Label Changes With box to identify the editor.

Ⓓ Click **OK**.

Because Track Changes was not on, no one's name appears in the Label Changes With box, so it is important to identify the editor.

3. **Scroll** through the document to locate the edits, if any.

4. **Save** the file using the filename **RCE Manual with Alice's Edits**. Then, **close** the Edited Manual without Marks document.

11.6 Managing Versions of Documents

| Video Lesson | labyrinthelab.com/videos |

As you work in Word or any other computer program, it is important to save your work regularly to prevent unwanted loss of data. Word 2010 contains tools that make it easier to recover a document, whether you close the file without saving, want to review or return to an earlier version of the file you're already working on, or something causes Word to close before you complete your work. As you work with others to modify and finish documents, retrieving work that might be lost becomes even more important.

Enabling AutoRecover and AutoSave

AutoRecover and AutoSave are features in Word that, when turned on, save versions of documents at regular intervals as you work on them. This feature has been available for several versions of Word. In Word 2010, the feature has been enhanced to enable you to store the last autosaved version of a document in the event that you need it. As a result, whether you close without saving changes, want to return to a previous editing point, or for some reason lose the most recent edits, you can restore the last autosaved copy of the document the next time you open the file.

AutoSave and AutoRecover are set in Word Options→Save options. These options are turned on by default.

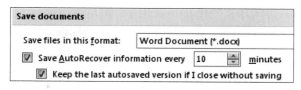

Save Documents options in Word.

 Word saves the last autosaved document for four days or until you modify the original file, whichever occurs first.

Using Manage Versions

After ensuring that the AutoSave and AutoRecover options are turned on, Word saves each open document as you work and tracks the versions autosaved. You can access a listing of autosaved document versions at any time while you are working on a document using the Manage Versions feature in Backstage View.

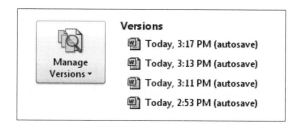

This document has been autosaved four times in the last hour.

It is important to remember that the AutoRecover feature is not a substitute for manually saving your work regularly. Saving files is the surest way to preserve your work—you should rely on automated tools in Word to recover work in extreme circumstances. When you open an autosaved version of a document from Backstage View, Word displays a business bar that enables you to restore the earlier version or compare it to the active document you were working on.

Click Compare to compare the selected autosaved version to the copy of the document you are working on. Word marks changes between the versions using Tracked Changes. ──────────

⚠ **Autosaved Version** A newer version is available. [Compare] [Restore]

Click Restore to open the autosaved version of the document and abandon the copy you were working on. ──────────

 Word presents a warning message notifying you that you are about to overwrite the later version of the document.

Recovering Unsaved Documents

You can also recover unsaved documents using the Word Recover feature. As a result, if you are working in Word creating or editing documents and you accidentally lose your connection to Word due to a power outage or some other computer error, you can still recover all edits made to the documents up to the last autosave. Word temporarily saves the last autosaved version of a document so that you can retrieve it. Here are some guildelines for recovering these files.

- If the document was one that had already been saved and named, Word displays a link to the autosaved version of the file when you open the original file again. You can review the autosaved version to determine whether it is more recent than the original or not to help determine which version to keep.

- If the document is a new document that has not yet been saved, you can use the Recover Unsaved Documents command on the File→Recent list in Backstage View. Word displays a folder containing all unsaved files, and you can open each one to determine if it is the document you created and lost.

WARNING

When you close a document and specifically choose Don't Save when prompted to save a document, Word does *not* save the latest autosaved version of the document.

QUICK REFERENCE	MANAGING VERSIONS USING AUTOSAVE AND AUTORECOVER
Task	**Procedure**
Set AutoSave and AutoCorrect options	■ Choose File→Options, and click the Save group. ■ Select the Save AutoRecover Information Every ___ Minutes checkbox. ■ Enter the number of minutes between autosaves in the Minutes value box. ■ Select the Keep the Last Autosaved Version If I Close Without Saving checkbox.
Open an AutoSaved version of a document	■ Choose File→Info→Manage Versions. ■ Double-click the version you want to restore.
Recover never-saved files	■ Choose File→Recent to display the list of recent files. ■ Click the Recover Unsaved Documents button at the bottom of the right pane of Backstage View. ■ Navigate to the folder containing autosaved files if different from the default. ■ Open the autosaved temporary file. ■ Click the Save As button at the top of the document window, and save the file. *or* ■ Choose File→Info→Manage Versions. ■ Select Recover Unsaved Documents. ■ Open the autosaved temporary file. ■ Click the Save As button at the top of the document window, and save the file.

Task	Procedure
Recover previously saved files	■ Choose File→Info.
	■ Locate the Versions section and select the version labeled *(when I closed without saving)*.
	■ Click the Restore button in the business bar to overwrite any previously saved versions of the document and replace them with the autosaved version.
Compare an AutoSaved version to the original	■ With the original document open, choose File→Info.
	■ Locate the Versions box, and double-click the autosaved version of the document you want to compare to the original.
	■ Accept and reject tracked changes using standard procedures.
Delete all unsaved documents	■ Choose File→Info.
	■ Click the Manager Versions button.
	■ Select Delete All Unsaved Documents.

DEVELOP YOUR SKILLS 11.6.1

Work with Versions

In this exercise, you will ensure that the AutoSave and AutoRecover settings are active and work with versions of the Raritan Clinic East Draft Procedures Manual.

1. **Open** the Raritan Clinic East Draft Procedures Manual.

2. Choose **File→Options** to display the Word Options dialog box.

3. Click the **Save** category in the pane on the left.

4. Follow these steps to ensure options are set:

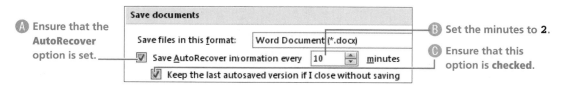

Ⓐ Ensure that the **AutoRecover** option is set.

Save documents

Save files in this format: Word Document (*.docx)

☑ Save AutoRecover information every   10   minutes

☑ Keep the last autosaved version if I close without saving

Ⓑ Set the minutes to **2**.

Ⓒ Ensure that this option is **checked**.

5. Click **OK**, change the word *AND* in the title to an ampersand (&), and wait for at least two minutes.

6. Choose **File→Info**, and locate the **Versions** area at the bottom center of the Backstage view.

7. Review the information presented by the Versions.

11.7 Introducing SkyDrive and Office Web Apps 2010

Video Lesson   labyrinthelab.com/videos

You may not always be at your computer or have access to your hard drive when you need to edit a file. For example, you may need to edit an important work document from home, but have no access to your work computer. With Microsoft Windows Live™ SkyDrive, you can store files online so they are available from any computer with an Internet connection. With Office Web Apps 2010, you can edit those files residing on SkyDrive even if you don't have the actual Microsoft Office programs installed on your computer.

Windows Live ID

SkyDrive and Office Web Apps 2010 require a Windows Live ID to sign in before the service can be used. A Windows Live ID is simply a free account with a Microsoft service such as Hotmail (email), Messenger (instant messaging), or Xbox LIVE (online gaming).

QUICK REFERENCE	CREATING A WINDOWS LIVE ID
Task	**Procedure**
Create a free Windows Live ID	▪ Start your web browser and navigate to www.live.com. ▪ Click the Sign Up button. ▪ Fill out the form to create a free Windows Live ID.

Storing Files on SkyDrive

SkyDrive is a free service provided by Microsoft that allows you to store your files online. There are several benefits to this.

- You can access your files from any computer with an Internet connection.
- You don't need to worry about your hard drive crashing or USB drive breaking because your files are stored on the SkyDrive servers.

QUICK REFERENCE	SAVING A FILE TO SKYDRIVE
Task	**Procedure**
Save a document to SkyDrive	■ Open the document in Word. ■ Choose File→Save & Send→Save to Web. ■ Click Sign In and sign in with your Windows Live ID. ■ Select the SkyDrive folder in which you'd like to save the document. ■ Click Save As. ■ Name the file, click Save, and wait as the document is uploaded.
Access a file stored on SkyDrive	■ Start your web browser and navigate to www.SkyDrive.com. ■ Sign in with your Windows Live ID. ■ Click the folder containing the file you want access. ■ Click a file to view it. *or* ■ Point to the file you want to access and click an action, such as Edit in Browser, Share, or More.

DEVELOP YOUR SKILLS 11.7.1
Save a Document to SkyDrive

WebSim	labyrinthelab.com/word10

In this exercise, you will save a document to SkyDrive.

1. **Type** the URL for the student web page (listed above) in the address bar of your web browser and **tap** [Enter].

2. From the left navigation bar, click **Lessons 10–14** and then **Lesson 11**; then, click the **Develop Your Skills 11.7.1: Save a Document to SkyDrive** link.
   The WebSim loads. The Revised Raritan Clinic East Procedures Manual is open in Word.

3. Work your way through the **on-screen exercise instructions**.

4. **Scroll** back to the top of the page and click the **Back to Course** link at the top-right corner of your screen.

Editing Files with Office Web Apps 2010

Video Lesson	labyrinthelab.com/videos

Files that have been saved to SkyDrive can be edited online using Office Web Apps 2010. Office Web Apps 2010 can be thought of as free online versions of Microsoft Office programs, but with limited functionality. Currently, Microsoft plans to support editing only Word, Excel, and OneNote documents with Office Web Apps 2010.

The Word Web App features a similar Ribbon to the full version of Word, but lacks much of the functionality.

STRENGTHS AND WEAKNESSES OF OFFICE WEB APPS 2010

Strengths	Weaknesses
■ Files can be edited from any computer with an Internet connection	■ Requires a Windows Live ID
■ No need for Microsoft Office to be installed	■ Fewer features and capabilities than the full Microsoft Office
■ Documents display full color, backgrounds, and fonts	

DEVELOP YOUR SKILLS 11.7.2
Edit a Document with Office Web Apps 2010

WebSim   labyrinthelab.com/word10

In this exercise, you will edit a document with Office Web Apps 2010.

1. If necessary, **type** the URL listed above into the address bar of your web browser and **tap** Enter.

2. From the left navigation bar, click **Lessons 10–14** and then **Lesson 11**; then, click the **Develop Your Skills 11.7.2: Edit a Document with Office Web Apps 2010** link.
   The WebSim loads and the SkyDrive start page appears. The computer represented in the WebSim does not have Word installed. You will edit the document using Office Web Apps 2010.

3. Work your way through the **on-screen exercise instructions**.

4. **Scroll** back to the top of the page and click the **Back to Course** link at the top-right corner of your screen.

Sharing Files with SkyDrive

Video Lesson   labyrinthelab.com/videos

In addition to editing files stored on SkyDrive yourself with Office Web Apps 2010, you can share files and allow others to edit or comment on them. Alternatively, you can share files and allow others to only view or comment on them.

SkyDrive Folders

When you share a file on SkyDrive, you actually share the SkyDrive folder containing the file. Therefore, all files stored in the SkyDrive folder are shared. You can easily create additional SkyDrive folders to more easily manage permissions. For example, you can create one folder that stores files you allow others to edit and create another folder that stores files you allow the same people to only view.

Folders that are shared display the shared icon (two people).

Folders that are not shared display a padlock icon.

QUICK REFERENCE	WORKING WITH SKYDRIVE FOLDERS
Task	**Procedure**
Create a folder	▪ Use your web browser to log in to SkyDrive.
	▪ Choose New→Folder from the web page menu bar above the SkyDrive folder icons.
	▪ Type a name for your new folder and click Next.
	▪ Drag documents from your computer into the web page window to upload them to the new SkyDrive folder and click Continue.
	▪ Edit the share permissions on the folder as necessary.
Share a folder	▪ Use the web browser to log in to SkyDrive.
	▪ Click the folder you want to share.
	▪ Click the link to the right of Shared With to edit the permissions.
	▪ Click Edit Permissions at the top of the web page.
	▪ Enter the email address of the person with whom you would like to share the folder and click Save.
	▪ Type a message to include in the invitation email and click Send.
Access a shared file	▪ Click the link to the shared folder in the invitation email you received from the file's owner.
	▪ Click the View Folder button in the email.
	▪ Point to the file you wish to view or edit and choose an action.

Create a SkyDrive Folder

WebSim	labyrinthelab.com/word10

In this exercise, you will create a SkyDrive folder to store shared documents.

1. If necessary, **type** the URL listed above into the address bar of your web browser and **tap** Enter.

2. From the left navigation bar, click **Lessons 10–14** and then **Lesson 11**; then, click the **Develop Your Skills 11.7.3: Create a SkyDrive Folder** link.
   The WebSim loads and the SkyDrive start page appears. You are already logged in as DrJacksonRaritan@hotmail.com.

3. Work your way through the **on-screen exercise instructions**.

4. **Scroll** back to the top of the page and click the **Back to Course** link at the top-right corner of your screen.

Moving Files

Video Lesson	labyrinthelab.com/videos

Since permissions are set on folders and not individual files, you may find it necessary to move files from one SkyDrive folder to another.

Move Files

WebSim	labyrinthelab.com/word10

In this exercise, you will move a file from one SkyDrive folder to another.

1. If necessary, **type** the URL listed above into the address bar of your web browser and **tap** Enter.

2. From the left navigation bar, click **Lessons 10–14** and then **Lesson 11**; then, click the **Develop Your Skills 11.7.4: Move Files** link.
   The WebSim loads and the SkyDrive start page appears. You are already logged in as DrJacksonRaritan@hotmail.com.

3. Work your way through the **on-screen exercise instructions**.

4. **Scroll** back to the top of the page and click the **Back to Course** link at the top-right corner of your screen.

Setting Folder Permissions

Video Lesson	labyrinthelab.com/videos

After a folder is created, you can set its permissions, allowing others to view or edit the files inside. SkyDrive lets you set global permissions and share a folder with the general public, or you can specify individuals by their email address. Any files stored in the folder will inherit the folder's permissions.

Share a Folder

WebSim   labyrinthelab.com/word10

In this exercise, you will share a SkyDrive folder and all the files within.

1. If necessary, **type** the URL listed above into the address bar of your web browser and **tap** Enter.

2. From the left navigation bar, click **Lessons 10–14** and then **Lesson 11**; then, click the **Develop Your Skills 11.7.5: Share a Folder** link.
   The WebSim loads and the SkyDrive page appears, displaying the contents of the For Review folder. You are already logged in as DrJacksonRaritan@hotmail.com.

3. Work your way through the **on-screen exercise instructions**.

4. **Scroll** back to the top of the page and click the **Back to Course** link at the top-right corner of your screen.

Accessing Shared Files

Once a file has been shared with you, accessing it is simple. You click the View folder button in the invitation email, log in with your Windows Live ID if prompted, and edit the file just as if it were one of your own files on SkyDrive. Make sure you save the invitation email as the View folder button in the easiest way to access the files.

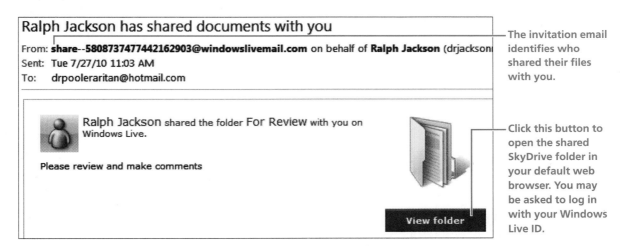

Ralph Jackson has shared documents with you

From: **share--5808737477442162903@windowslivemail.com** on behalf of **Ralph Jackson** (drjackson
Sent: Tue 7/27/10 11:03 AM
To: drpooleraritan@hotmail.com

Ralph Jackson shared the folder For Review with you on Windows Live.

Please review and make comments

View folder

The invitation email identifies who shared their files with you.

Click this button to open the shared SkyDrive folder in your default web browser. You may be asked to log in with your Windows Live ID.

Publishing a Blog Post

In addition to posting files to folders on SkyDrive, Word 2010 contains additional tools that enable users to post documents as blogs. To use the tool, you must already have a blog account to which to post the file. The first time you use the tool in Word 2010, you will be prompted to register for the blog.

Windows Live, the site to which you connected to access SkyDrive, enables you to post blogs as well as to store files in folders. To publish a file as a blog post requires that you also create a new email address for the service you choose so that you can receive notifications about blog responses.

11.8 Concepts Review

Concepts Review   labyrinthelab.com/word10

To check your knowledge of the key concepts introduced in this lesson, complete the Concepts Review quiz by going to the URL listed above. If your classroom is using Labyrinth eLab, you may complete the Concepts Review quiz from within your eLab course.

Reinforce Your Skills

Work with Track Changes

In this exercise, you will switch on Track Changes and edit a document that has been reviewed by one person. You will add your changes to the document, and then you will review and accept or reject the changes.

1. **Open** the document rs-How the Internet Works from the Lesson 11 folder.

2. Choose **Review→Tracking→Track Changes** from the Ribbon to turn the feature on.

Check the Username and Initials

3. Choose **Review→Tracking→Track Changes** menu ▼ from the Ribbon.

4. Choose **Change User Name** from the menu, and make sure your username and initials are listed, and then click **OK**.

5. Choose **Home→Editing→Find** from the Ribbon, and search for the word *united*.

6. **Close** the Navigation pane after Word locates the term.

7. Select *United Parcel Service*, and replace it with **Airborne Express (AE)**.
   You were able to replace a previous tracked change with one of your own.

8. Choose **Home→Editing→Replace** from the Ribbon, globally replace each instance of *UPS* with **AE**, and **close** the dialog box when you finish.

Review and Approve Tracked Changes

9. Use Ctrl + Home to jump to the beginning of the document.

10. Choose **Review→Changes→Next** from the Ribbon.

11. Choose **Review→Changes→Accept** from the Ribbon.

12. **Accept** the next two revisions.

13. **Reject** the replacement of *critical* with *important* twice.

14. **Accept** the deletion of the word *ideally.*

15. **Scroll** the page until the last three paragraphs are visible.

Switch Off the Display of One Reviewer's Edits

It would require quite a few commands to accept all of these tracked changes individually. It is also potentially confusing to see the other reviewer's edits along with your own. Let's switch off the display of the other reviewer's edits.

16. Choose **Review→Tracking→Show Markup** 📄 **menu ▾** from the Ribbon.

17. Choose **Reviewers** at the bottom of the menu, and choose **Ariana Blakely** from the submenu.
    Ariana Blakely's edits are now hidden. This allows you to focus on your own tracked changes. In this case, you decide to approve all of the edits that change the name of the shipping carrier.

18. Choose **Review→Changes→Accept** 📝 **menu ▾** from the Ribbon.

19. Choose **Accept All Changes Shown** from the menu.
    All of the visible tracked changes are approved.

20. Choose **Review→Tracking→Show Markup** 📄 from the Ribbon.

21. Choose **Reviewers** from the menu, and click **Ariana Blakely** in the submenu.
    The tracked changes for Ariana Blakely reappear.

22. Choose **Review→Changes→Accept** 📝 menu ▾ from the Ribbon.

23. Choose **Accept All Changes in Document** from the menu.
    The deletions are accepted and disappear.

24. **Save** 💾 the document, and **close** it.

REINFORCE YOUR SKILLS 11.2
Combine Tracked Changes

In this exercise, you will combine tracked changes from two documents into a third document.

1. **Open** the document rs-Internet History from Lesson 11 folder.
   This is the original version of a document sent out for review.

2. Choose **Review→Compare→Compare** 📄 from the Ribbon.

3. Choose **Combine** from the menu.

Combine the Edits from Reviewer A

4. Choose rs-Internet History from the Original Document drop-down list.

5. On the right side of the dialog box, click the **Browse for Revised** button and navigate to the Lesson 11 folder.

   > Revised document
   > rs-Internet History (Reviewer A) ▾ 📂
   > La_bel unmarked changes with: Ariana Brod

6. **Open** the document rs-Internet History (Reviewer A), and then click **OK**.

7. Choose **Review Compare→Show Source Documents** 📑 from the Ribbon.

8. If necessary, choose **Hide Source Documents** from the menu.
   This means that the original document is the only open document, and the tracked changes from Reviewer A are embedded in the original document.

Observe the Final Before Combining Changes

9. Choose **Review→Tracking→Display for Review** 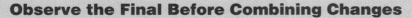 from the Ribbon.

10. Choose **Final** from the menu.
    This view of the original displays how the document will look if you accept all changes.

11. Choose **Review→Tracking→Display for Review** from the Ribbon.

12. Choose **Final: Show Markup** from the menu.

Combine the Edits with the Original Document

13. Choose **Review→Changes→Accept** **menu ▾** from the Ribbon.

14. Choose **Accept All Changes in the Document** from the menu to merge the changes into the original document.

Combine the Tracked Changes from Reviewer B

15. Choose **Review→Compare→Compare** from the Ribbon.

16. Choose **Combine** from the menu.

17. Choose rs-Internet History from the **Original Document** drop-down list.

18. Click the **Browse for Revised** button on the right side of the dialog box, and **open** rs-Internet History (Reviewer B).

19. Click **OK**.

20. **Accept** all changes in Internet History (Reviewer B) as you did for Internet History (Reviewer A).
    Word merges these changes as well.

21. **Save** the document, and **close** it.

REINFORCE YOUR SKILLS 11.3

Email a Document for Review

In this exercise, you will turn on Track Changes. Then you will simulate the steps to send an email with a copy of your document attached.

1. **Open** rs-Email Annual Report from the Lesson 11 folder.

2. Choose **Review→Tracking→Track Changes** from the Ribbon.

3. **Save** the document.

4. Choose **File→Save & Send→Send Using E-mail→Send as Attachment**.
   If you receive a message indicating no profiles have been created, dismiss the message, turn off Track Changes, and read through the rest of the exercise.

5. Follow these steps to review the email form:

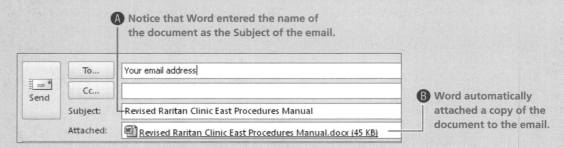

A Notice that Word entered the name of the document as the Subject of the email.

To... | Your email address

Cc...

Send

Subject: | Revised Raritan Clinic East Procedures Manual

Attached: | Revised Raritan Clinic East Procedures Manual.docx (45 KB)

B Word automatically attached a copy of the document to the email.

6. Click the **Close** ⊠ button in the upper-right corner of the email form to close it.

7. Choose **Review→Tracking→Track Changes** to turn off the feature.

8. **Close** the document without saving it.

REINFORCE YOUR SKILLS 11.4

Compare Documents and Highlight Text

In this exercise, you will compare two documents to locate edits made without Tracked Changes turned on. You will also add highlighting to the document.

1. Open rs-Components of Web Pages (Reviewer) from the Lesson 11 folder.

2. Scroll through the document, and notice that the reviewer did not use Track Changes.

3. Close the file.

4. Open rs-Components of Web Pages from the Lesson 11 folder.
This is the original document.

5. Choose **Review→Compare→Compare** from the Ribbon.

6. Choose **Compare** from the menu to open the Compare Documents dialog box.

7. Choose rs-Components of Web Pages from the **Original Document** drop-down list.

8. Click the **Browse for Revised** button on the right side of the dialog box, and navigate to the Lesson 11 folder.

9. Open rs-Components of Web Pages (Reviewer).

10. Click the **More** button, and make sure the **Original Document** option is chosen in the Show Changes In area at the bottom-right corner of the dialog box.

11. Click the **Less** button to collapse the dialog box, and then click **OK**.
Observe the changes in the document.

12. Choose **Review→Changes→Accept** menu ▼ from the Ribbon.

13. Choose **Accept All Changes in Document** from the menu.
Word combines the reviewer's changes into the original document.

14. Position the **insertion point** in front of the first paragraph beginning *In order to create*....

15. **Press** Enter to create a blank line.

16. Position the **insertion point** in the blank line, and **type** the following statement:
    `I've incorporated the changes. Please turn on Track`
    `Changes if you make any additional edits.`

Highlight the Statement

17. Choose **Home→Font→Text Highlight Color** aby ▾ **menu ▾** from the Ribbon.

18. Choose **Pink** from the gallery.
    The mouse pointer changes to a highlighter shape.

19. Drag the **highlighter** over the statement you just typed.
    The reviewer will be sure to notice the statement.

20. Choose **Home→Font→Text Highlight Color** aby to turn the highlighter off.

21. **Save** 💾 the file, and **close** it.

REINFORCE YOUR SKILLS 11.5

Create a New SkyDrive Folder and Add a Document

WebSim labyrinthelab.com/word10

In this exercise, you will access the Windows Live SkyDrive, create a new shared folder, and add a document to the folder.

1. **Type** the URL for the student web page (listed above) in the address bar of your web browser and **tap** Enter.

2. From the left navigation bar, click **Lessons 10–14** and then **Lesson 11**; then, click the **Reinforce Your Skills 11.5: Create a New SkyDrive Folder and Add a Document** link.
    The WebSim loads and the SkyDrive page appears. You are already logged in as LabyrinthWord@yahoo.com.

3. Work your way through the **on-screen exercise instructions**.

4. **Scroll** back to the top of the page and click the **Back to Course** link at the top-right corner of your screen.

Apply Your Skills

Create Tracked Changes

In this exercise, you will make several edits to a document and set Word to track your changes.

1. **Open** the document as-Images for the Web from the Lesson 11 folder.

2. Set Word to **track changes**.

3. Enter the **current date** in place of *Today's Date* at the top of the document.

4. Toward the end of the fourth line of the first main paragraph, change *14* to **7**.

5. In the next line, change *28.8* to **56**.

6. At the beginning of the **second bullet point**, change *JPG* to **JPEG**.

7. Use Ctrl + End to jump to the bottom of the document, and then type **[Your Name]**.

8. **Save** 🖫 and **close** the document.

Review Tracked Changes

In this exercise, you will review tracked changes in a document and accept or reject specific changes.

1. **Open** the document as-Internet Service Provider from the Lesson 11 folder.

2. Turn on the **reviewing pane** in the **vertical** position.

3. **Scroll** through and examine the changes, and then **close** the reviewing pane.

4. Display the document in **Final** view, and then change the view to **Final: Show Markup**.

5. **Find** and **accept** the first three tracked changes.

6. **Reject** the rest of the changes *except* the very last one.

7. **Save** 🖫 and **close** the document.

Send a Document for Review by Email

In this exercise, you will send a document via email for review.

Skip this exercise if your computer is not set up with an email account.

1. **Open** the document as-Website Makeover from the Lesson 11 folder.

2. Turn on **Track Changes**.

3. **Save** 🖫 the document.

4. **Send** the document to yourself for review and then **close** the document.

5. Open the **email** containing the attachment, and then open the **document**.

6. Make **three edits** to the document to change text you think you can clarify.

7. **Save** changes to the document using the filename **as-Revised Website Makeover** in your Lesson 11 folder.

8. Insert a **comment** at the beginning of the document that informs the author of the file that you have made changes to the document.

9. **Close** the file.

Combine Original and Edited Documents

In this exercise, you will combine the file you edited in Apply Your Skills 11.3 with the original document.

1. **Open** the file as-Website Makeover from the **Lesson 11** folder.

2. **Combine** the original file with the as-Revised Website Makeover file edited in Apply Your Skills 11.3.

3. **Save** the combined file in the **Lesson** 11 folder using the filename **as-Combined Makeover**.

4. **Print** a copy of the document, and then **close** it.

Post Files on SkyDrive

WebSim   labyrinthelab.com/word10

In this exercise, you will sign onto Windows Live SkyDrive, create a new shared folder, and add a file to the folder. You will then access the file from your inbox, make edits to the file, and save the edits to the Windows Live SkyDrive.

1. **Type** the URL for the student web page (listed above) in the address bar of your web browser and **tap** Enter.

2. From the left navigation bar, click **Lessons 10–14** and then **Lesson 11**; then, click the **Apply Your Skills 11.5: Post Files on SkyDrive** link.

3. Work your way through the **on-screen exercise instructions**.

4. **Scroll** back to the top of the page and click the **Back to Course** link at the top-right corner of your screen.

Critical Thinking & Work-Readiness Skills

In the course of working through the following Microsoft Office-based Critical Thinking exercises, you will also be utilizing various work-readiness skills, some of which are listed next to each exercise. Go to labyrinthelab.com/workreadiness *to learn more about the work-readiness skills.*

11.1 Email-Based Collaborative Writing

The director of Raritan Clinic East has suggested that all employees work together to create a completely new mission statement for the clinic that concisely states the company's purpose for its staff and patients. Simulate the process of passing a draft to department members. You may play the role of each group member by emailing the document to yourself, or work with others in an instructor-assigned group. Start the mission statement in a Word document named **ct-Department Mission Statement**, add one sentence, and then pass the document to the next person in the group via email. The next person will use Track Changes to edit the first sentence and then add another sentence and so on until the document is complete. The last person should email the document to all group members.

WORK-READINESS SKILLS APPLIED

- Selecting technology
- Writing
- Participating as a member of a team

11.2 Combine and Review Documents

The new mission statement you created in the previous exercise is ready for review. Combine the document you receive from the last person in your group with your original document. Review the tracked changes and accept or reject them to create what you believe to be a good mission statement for the clinic. Forward your last version, showing the tracked changes, to your instructor by email with a short paragraph explaining why you made the choices you did.

WORK-READINESS SKILLS APPLIED

- Reasoning
- Writing
- Managing the self

11.3 Post to Office Live Workspace

Post the final version of the ct-Department Mission Statement to SkyDrive named **Final Mission**. Ensure that Track Changes is on within the document so additional edits will be easy to identify. Share the workspace with your instructor so he or she can review the statement, make comments or edits, and return the final copy to you. When you receive the review, accept or reject changes and print a final copy of the document.

WORK-READINESS SKILLS APPLIED

- Reasoning
- Selecting technology
- Participating as a member of a team

Sharing and Securing Content Using Backstage View

LEARNING OBJECTIVES

After studying this lesson, you will be able to:
- Use Word's file compatibility features
- Check documents with the Document Inspector
- Restrict formatting and editing in a document
- Secure documents with passwords and digital signatures
- Mark a document as final

In today's world, documents fly around electronically at speeds only dreamed about by our forefathers. Knowing that your documents can be opened and read by those who receive them without giving away a great deal of personal information is important in this electronic age. Virtual collaboration means that your documents are often in others' hands.

In Word 2010, Microsoft has grouped tools and features to help you control the formatting and content of documents, as well as document security and access together in what the company is calling the Backstage view. Microsoft has also introduced a new online storage feature that allows you to store documents for retrieval from any computer with Internet access, making document security even more important.

In this lesson, you will learn to work with Backstage view to control document access. This will help you assure those who receive your documents that they were created and are protected by you, whether the documents are stored locally or online.

Securing Confidential Information

At Raritan Clinic East, privacy and security of patient records are vitally important. As a result, James Elliott wants to explore Word's features that ensure that documents sent outside the clinic remain confidential and contain no information that could enable those receiving the documents to learn more about the Clinic than they need to know. The knowledge he gains will be added to the Policies & Procedures Manual that he has been developing. James will learn how to use Backstage view and identify some of the security features he can use.

Raritan Clinic East
Pediatric Diagnostic Specialists

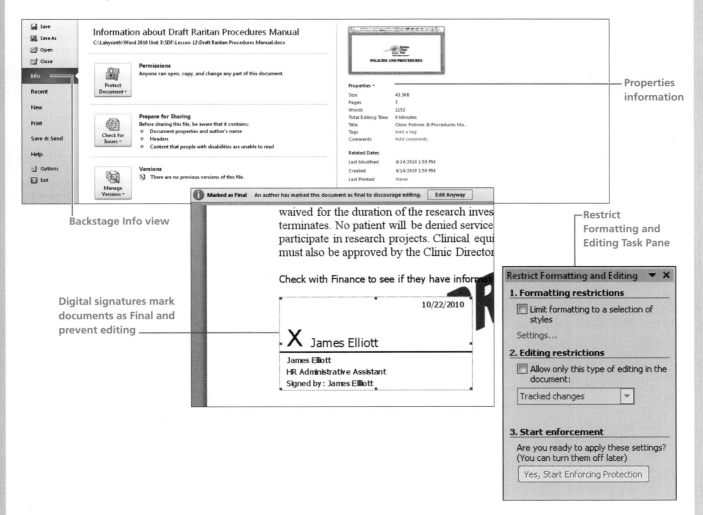

Backstage Info view

Properties information

Digital signatures mark documents as Final and prevent editing

Restrict Formatting and Editing Task Pane

12.1 Preparing Documents for Sharing

Video Lesson   labyrinthelab.com/videos

There are a number of things to think about when sharing documents with colleagues or team members. Compatibility issues between Word 2010 and earlier versions of Word should be considered. Additionally, Word documents can contain hidden or personal information about your organization or about a document that you do not want to share publicly. The Document Inspector can help you deal with these items.

Considering Compatibility Issues

Word 2010 uses a new file format (*.docx) which was introduced in Word 2007. Previous versions of Word used a *.doc file format. The benefits of the new format include smaller file size, improved damaged-file recovery, and more control of personal information. It is important to understand how Word 2010 behaves with documents created in earlier versions. Likewise, you need to make sure your Word 2010 documents can be read by people using Word 97-2003. There are several approaches for dealing with these compatibility issues. Word 2010 saves documents, by default, in Word 2007 format.

Opening Documents in Compatibility Mode

If you open a document in Word 2010 that was created in a version that came out prior to Word 2007, it opens in Compatibility Mode. The words *Compatibility Mode* appear in Word's title bar.

> 2003 Draft RCE Procedures Manual [Compatibility Mode] - Microsoft Word

Limitations of Compatibility Mode

When creating documents in Word 2010, you can save them in the Word 97-2003 format, but the new features of Word 2007/2010 either won't be available or they will be modified in a manner more compatible with older versions.

DEVELOP YOUR SKILLS 12.1.1
Open a Document in Compatibility Mode

In this exercise, you will open a Word 2003 document in Word 2010 in Compatibility Mode. You will then try to insert a Word 2010 SmartArt graphic in the Word 2003 Compatibility Mode document, and you will see how Word deals with the feature.

Open a Document in Compatibility Mode

1. Launch **Word**, and maximize the window.

2. Choose **File→Open**, and navigate to your Lesson 12 folder.

3. **Open** the 2003 Draft RCE Procedures Manual document.
   Notice the term Compatibility Mode *in Word's title bar.*

> 2003 Draft RCE Procedures Manual [Compatibility Mode] - Microsoft Word

Attempt to Insert SmartArt

Next you will attempt to add a Word 2010 SmartArt graphic to the Word 2003 Compatibility Mode document.

4. If necessary, choose **Home→Paragraph→Show/Hide** ¶ from the Ribbon to display formatting marks.

5. Position the **insertion point** before the paragraph marker for the blank line at the top of **page 2**.

6. Type **Organization**, and then **press** ⌈Enter⌋ twice.

7. Ensure that the **insertion point** appears in the second blank line below the heading.

8. Choose **Insert→Illustrations→SmartArt**  from the Ribbon.
   Note that Word opens the Word 2003 Diagram Gallery, rather then the Word 2010 SmartArt gallery because the Compatibility Mode document is not capable of working with Word 2010's SmartArt feature.

9. Click **Cancel** to close the Diagram Gallery.

Observe How Word Saves the Compatibility Mode Document

10. Choose **File→Save As** to open the Save As dialog box.
    Notice that Word 2010 defaults to the Word 97-2003 Save as Type option, as shown in the illustration.

    Word 2010 will default to the older format unless you purposely convert a document to Word *.docx format or save it as a Word document (*.docx) via the Save As command.

11. Click **Cancel** to close the Save As dialog box, and leave the document **open**.

To Convert or Not to Convert

Video Lesson   labyrinthelab.com/videos

If most of the people you share documents with are using older versions of Word, it's a good idea to keep their documents in Compatibility Mode. This ensures that documents will look the same in Word 2010 as they do in the older version. It also ensures that the features available in Word 2010 will be limited to or similar to the features available in older versions. For example, some functionality will be limited. As you saw in the previous exercise, when you attempt to insert a SmartArt graphic in a Compatibility Mode document, rather than being presented with the large gallery of SmartArt graphics, you were limited to the six graphics available in the Diagram Gallery from earlier Word versions. Compare these two figures.

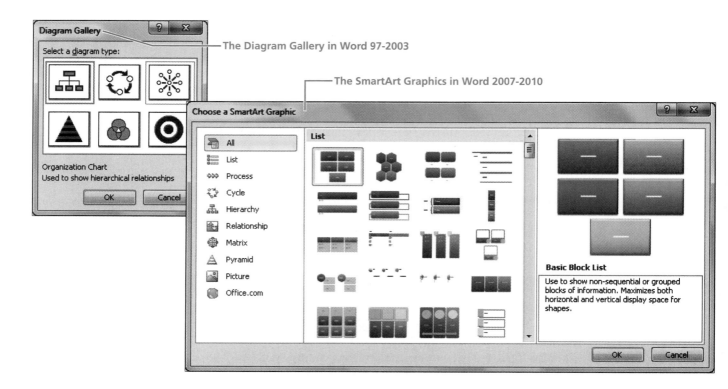

The Diagram Gallery in Word 97-2003

The SmartArt Graphics in Word 2007-2010

Other features introduced in 2007 or 2010 that are unavailable for use with the Compatibility Mode include Themes, Screenshot, Drop Cap, and Equations. Some additional object-specific features are also unavailable in Compatibility Mode.

Choosing Conversion

If you are working with a Compatibility Mode document that would benefit from the full functionality of Word 2010 features that are currently disabled or limited, you have a candidate for conversion. When you convert the document, Word 2010 turns on the new and enhanced features.

There are two ways to convert an older version (*.doc) document to a Word 2007/2010 (*.docx) document:

- Use the Convert command on the File→Info menu
- Save a copy of the document in the new format

Using Convert

The Convert command appears on the File→Info menu when a document is open in Compatibility Mode. Using this command literally converts the Compatibility Mode document to a Word 2007/2010 document. Using the File→Info→Convert command performs a conversion of the original document and overwrites the original document. As a result, the Word 97-2003 document is no longer available.

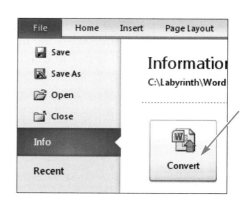

One important reminder is to always keep the person who sent you the document or the person to whom you are sending a document in mind before converting. If you are editing a document that needs to be returned to someone who is using an earlier version of Word, leave the document in its original format rather than converting it. Some organizations have installed a Compatibility Pack on systems that are running Office 2003 that enables them to open documents saved in the *.docx format. However, some features would not be available.

Using Save As

When you resave and rename an existing document using the Save As command, you are actually making a copy of the document. When you perform a Save As with a Compatibility Mode document, you still have the original (*.doc) file, and you create a new second document, a (*.docx) file.

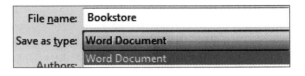

Saving in Word 2010 Format While Maintaining Compatibility

Another alternative to converting compatible documents to Word 2010 format is to use a feature new to Word in 2010. This new feature enables you to save a document created using Word 97-2003 using Word 2010 and check an option to maintain compatibility with previous versions of Word. Saving a document with this option checked prevents those who work with the document from using features that were unavailable in the earlier versions of Word. Saving a compatible document in 2010 format and maintaining compatibility with previous versions of Word creates a new document and leaves the original compatible document as a separate file. The option appears in the Save As dialog box only when you are saving a *compatible* document as a *Word Document* as the Save As Type, as shown here:

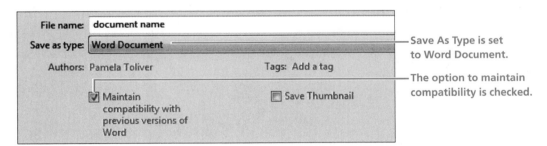

Convert a .doc Document to .docx Format

In this exercise, you will save a document in 2007 format and maintain compatibility with previous versions of Word. You will also convert a Word 2003 document to .docx format, and then you will add Word 2010 features to the document.

Before You Begin: The 2003 Draft RCE Procedures Manual should be open.

Save Maintaining Compatibility

1. Choose **File→Save As** to open the Save As dialog box, and navigate to the folder in which you are saving your data files.

2. Click the **Save As Type** drop-down arrow, and select **Word Document**.

3. Ensure that there is a **checkmark** in the **Maintain Compatibility With Previous Versions of Word** checkbox.

4. Replace 2003 in the **File Name** field with `Compatible`, and then click **Save**.

5. **Close** the document, and **open** the 2003 Draft RCE Procedures Manual compatible document from the Lesson 12 folder again.

Convert the Document

6. Choose **File→Info→Convert**.
   Word displays an information box advising you that format may change with the conversion and provides additional information. Be careful about checking the Do Not Ask Me Again About Converting Documents checkbox. It serves as a reminder that the document may change significantly.

7. Click **OK** to acknowledge the message.
   Word completes the conversion. Notice that the words Compatibility Mode disappear from the title bar.

8. Position the **insertion point** on page 2 at the beginning of paragraph 3 under the *Scope of Services* heading, and **press** Enter twice.

9. Reposition the **insertion point** just before the paragraph mark for the first blank line.

Add a Word 2010 Feature

10. Choose **Insert→Illustrations→SmartArt** ⬚ from the Ribbon.
    Since you converted the document, the SmartArt gallery is now available.

11. Follow these steps to insert a SmartArt graphic:

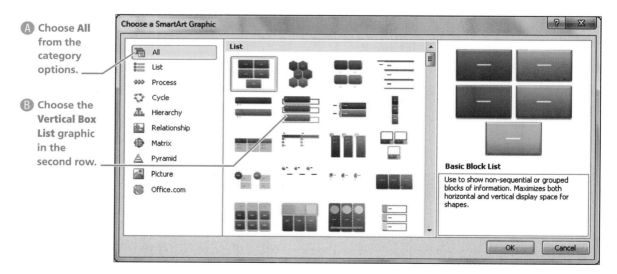

Ⓐ Choose **All** from the category options.

Ⓑ Choose the **Vertical Box List** graphic in the second row.

12. Click **OK** to insert the object.
    The graphic shows three boxes into which you can type text. Though it is large, as you add text in the following steps, the size of the graphic will adjust to fit the document.

13. Click the **tab** on the left side of the image box to display the Type Your Text Here pane, as shown at right.

14. **Type** the text shown in the following figure.

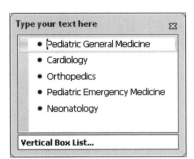

15. Click the text panel **Close** ⊠ button to close the pane.

16. **Save** 🖫 the document, and **close** it.

Notice that Word added the docx extension to the file name in the title bar. This indicates that the file format was converted.

Preparing Backward-Compatible Documents in Word 2010

Video Lesson   labyrinthelab.com/videos

If you know that you'll be working with people who have older versions of Word, and if it's important that all features are compatible among the versions, you might start your new document by saving it as a Word 97-2003 document. That way, you can avoid using features unavailable in older versions.

If you *always* want to save your documents in an earlier version, you can choose the options shown in the Word Options dialog box to save documents down to an earlier version.

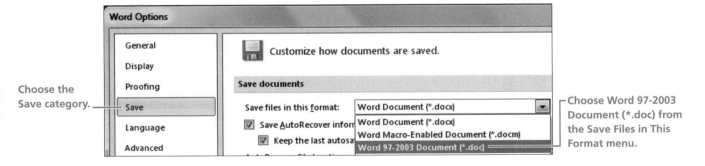

Choose the Save category.

Choose Word 97-2003 Document (*.doc) from the Save Files in This Format menu.

Using the Compatibility Checker

If you save a Word 2010 document that contains features new in Word 2007 or 2010 down to an older Word version, the Compatibility Checker notifies you that the document contains features unique to newer versions of Word. You can also manually run the Compatibility Checker before saving the document in older versions of Word.

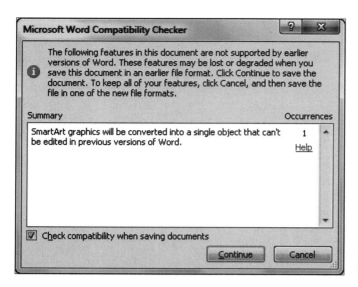

The Compatibility Checker alerts you to how Word 2010 features will be handled if you save a document to an earlier version of Word.

Round-Tripping Documents

Round-tripping is a term that you may hear as you work with documents created in various versions of Word. Round-tripping refers to the practice of opening a document in a later version of Word, such as Word 2010, that was created in an earlier version of Word, such as Word 2003, converting the document to Word 2010 format and then saving it back to Word 2003 format. Round-tripping can create issues with the document that corrupt it so that it acts weirdly or is damaged beyond repair. Avoid round-tripping your documents to prevent unwanted loss of time and data.

DEVELOP YOUR SKILLS 12.1.3

Save a Word 2010 Document to 97-2003 Format

In this exercise, you will save the document, which is now in Word 2010 mode, to Word 97-2003 format version, for people who have not yet upgraded to Word 2007.

1. **Open** the Draft Raritan Procedures Manual document from the Lesson 12 folder.

2. Choose **File→Save As**.

3. Click the **Save as Type** list arrow, and choose **Word 97-2003 Document**.

4. Click the **Save** button.
   Word saves the document without opening the Compatibility Checker. The document contained no features unavailable in earlier versions of Word. Notice that Compatibility Mode now appears in the title bar.

The Office 2010 Compatibility Pack

Video Lesson   labyrinthelab.com/videos

Users who have earlier versions of Word and who need to work with Word 2010 documents can download a Compatibility Pack from the Microsoft website to open, edit, and save Word 2010 documents. You must install updates for the earlier Word versions prior to installing the Compatibility Pack. Updates vary depending on which version of Word you are using.

Do a search in your favorite search engine for "office 2010 compatibility pack" for the latest information on this free software.

QUICK REFERENCE	USING WORD'S COMPATIBILITY FEATURES
Task	**Description**
Open a document in Compatibility Mode	▪ In Word 2010, open a document created in an earlier version. (Word 2010 automatically displays the document in Compatibility Mode.)
Convert a Word 97-2003 document to a Word 2010 document	▪ Open an earlier version document in Word 2010. ▪ Choose File→Info→Convert. ▪ When the message appears about converting the document, click OK. *or* ▪ Open the earlier version document in Word 2010. ▪ Choose Office→Save As. ▪ Choose Word Document (*.docx) from the Save as Type list. This retains the original (*.doc) document and creates a new (*.docx) document.
Prepare a backward-compatible document	▪ Create a document in Word 2010. ▪ Choose File→Save As. ▪ Choose Word 97-2003 Document (*.doc) from the Save as Type list. ▪ If the Compatibility Checker appears, click Continue.
Install the Compatibility Pack	▪ Download the Compatibility Pack from the Microsoft website and follow the prompts to install it.

Working with the Document Inspector

If you intend to share a document with colleagues or clients, you may want to use the Document Inspector to ensure that your documents contain no hidden or personal information that might be stored in the document or in the document properties. For example, a document could contain comments and tracked changes that are hidden from view. Document properties could contain information such as the author's name and the company name.

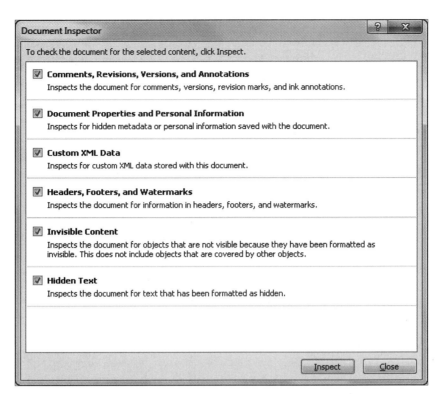

You can choose various categories of information to be inspected in the Document Inspector dialog box. Each of these categories would be cleaned separately if the Inspector discovers information you might want to remove.

Inspecting Document Properties

Valuable information about a document appears in the Properties panel in Backstage view. Among the data Word stores within a document are the author's name, dates for file creation and editing, the template used to create the file, and the file storage location on the computer or network drive. Sending this data along with a document can inadvertently reveal to document recipients data that you would rather protect.

You can inspect document properties to determine what data is available to anyone who receives the document by choosing File→Info to show the data in the Word Backstage view window.

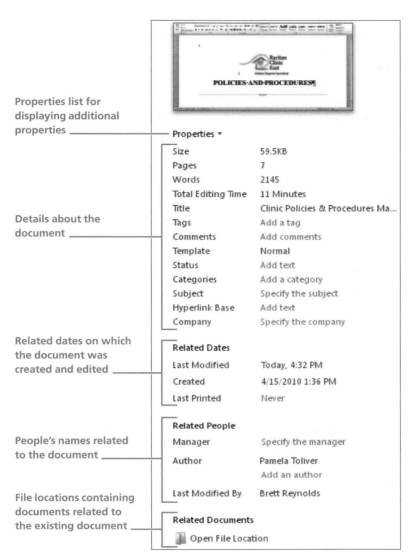

Properties list for displaying additional properties —————

Properties ▾

Size	59.5KB
Pages	7
Words	2145
Total Editing Time	11 Minutes
Title	Clinic Policies & Procedures Ma...
Tags	Add a tag
Comments	Add comments
Template	Normal
Status	Add text
Categories	Add a category
Subject	Specify the subject
Hyperlink Base	Add text
Company	Specify the company

Details about the document —————

Related Dates

Last Modified	Today, 4:32 PM
Created	4/15/2010 1:36 PM
Last Printed	Never

Related dates on which the document was created and edited —————

Related People

Manager	Specify the manager
Author	Pamela Toliver
	Add an author
Last Modified By	Brett Reynolds

People's names related to the document —————

Related Documents

📄 Open File Location

File locations containing documents related to the existing document —————

Properties provide details about a document. The dates are shown on the Related Dates section, the Related People section shows you as the author, and the Related Documents section could give away secure file location information if left in the document.

The Document Inspector displays a list of issues found in a document. The only option for removing data for each category of information is to remove all data that falls into that category. Sometimes you may want to manually review information before deciding which data to remove. To use the automatic Remove All option for a category, it may be wise to make a copy of a document, run the Document Inspector on the copy, and remove all issues to see what effect data removal has on the document. This will help prevent unwanted loss of data.

QUICK REFERENCE	INSPECTING A DOCUMENT FOR HIDDEN OR PERSONAL INFORMATION
Task	**Description**
Use the Document Inspector	▪ Choose File→Info→Check for Issues→Inspect Document.
	▪ Uncheck any categories you do not want inspected.
	▪ Click the Inspect button.
	▪ Click the Remove All button for the category you want to clean.

Inspect a Document

In this exercise, you will run the Document Inspector on the document you just saved in Word 97-2003 format and remove all personal data from the document.

Before You Begin: The Draft Raritan Procedures Manual (Compatibility Mode) document should be open.

Review Document Properties

1. Choose **File→Info**, and review the Properties listed below the document image in the pane on the right side of the window.
   Notice that the title of the document may be different from the document filename. The dates are shown in the Related Dates section, the Related People section shows you as the author, and the Related Documents section could give away secure file location information if left in the document.

Use the Document Inspector

2. Choose **File→Info→Check for Issues→Inspect Document**.
   At this point you can remove the checkmark from any item you don't want the Document Inspector to inspect.

3. Click the **Inspect** button at the bottom of the dialog box, and review the results of the inspection.

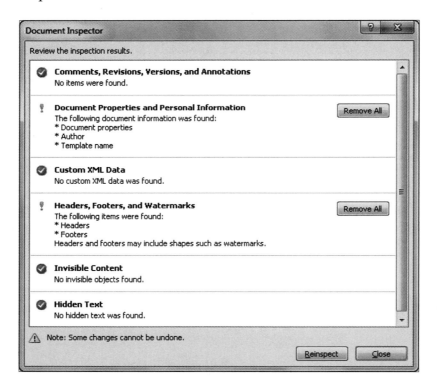

The inspector found document properties and/or personal information along with Headers and Footers. In this example, you will remove only the properties and personal information.

4. Click the **Remove All** button to the right of *Document Properties and Personal Information*, and then click the **Close** button at the bottom of the dialog box.

Review Document Properties

Now you will look at the document properties to ensure that the personal information was removed.

5. Review the Properties pane.
   Notice that the personal information is now gone.

6. **Save** the file, and leave it **open**.

12.2 Controlling Document Access

Video Lesson   labyrinthelab.com/videos

When you share documents with colleagues and team members, it can be helpful to control the changes that others can make. Word provides several features to assist you with protecting documents. For example, you can restrict the kinds of formatting and editing changes a reviewer can make. You can add a password to a document, and you can mark a document as final, thereby preventing any changes to it.

Restricting Formatting and Editing

The Restrict Formatting and Editing task pane enables you to limit the formatting reviewers can apply to text in a document as well as the edits others can make to document text. When you share a document with unrestricted formatting and editing allowed with multiple reviewers, it is easy to imagine the jumble of formats and edits they will add. By restricting formatting and editing by adding a password, only those who know the password will be able to format and edit the file. Restricting formatting enables you to:

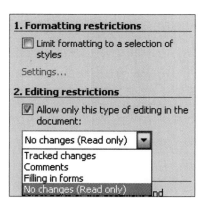

Word's Restrict Editing command allows you to set various restrictions on the editing of a document.

- **Restrict Formatting**—This setting protects a document from the use of any styles not approved for use and prevents reviewers from modifying any styles in the document. This restriction helps to enforce consistent formatting when multiple people edit a document.

- **Restrict for Tracked Changes**—This setting protects a document from having the Track Changes command disabled. This means that every change to the document will be recorded and highlighted according to the options chosen in the Track Changes dialog box. In addition, no one can execute the Accept Change or Reject Change commands while the document is protected.

- **Restrict for Comments**—This setting permits reviewers to insert and edit comments in the document but not to edit the document itself. Reviewers can comment on the text of the document, but they cannot make changes to it.

- **Restrict for Filling In Forms**—This setting permits users to only insert data in unrestricted areas of a form.

You can protect a document for tracked changes or comments, but not for both simultaneously.

Working with Passwords

Another option on the Protect Document list enables you to encrypt the document with a password. However, when you restrict editing of a document, you are also given the opportunity to enter a password. Only users who know the password will be able to switch off this feature. When you use a password with document protection, keep a few facts in mind:

- **Passwords are case sensitive**—If you use capital letters in the password, they must be typed identically when entering the password to open a document. The passwords *ProStart* and *prostart* are not identical.

- **Don't forget the password**—If you set a password and then later forget it, you will be unable to remove the document protection setting. When you create a new password, it is a good idea to write it down and keep it in a secure place where you will be able to locate it easily.

- **Don't use obvious passwords**—The name of a spouse, a birthday, and other items that may be common knowledge are not good choices for passwords. The most effective passwords usually include one or more numbers as well as uppercase and lowercase letters.

The Encrypt Document and Confirm Password dialog boxes appear when you set only a password with no document restrictions. The word *encrypt* means to encode or protect so that others are unable to access the file.

The Start Enforcing Protection dialog box displays the two fields for entering and confirming a password in the same dialog box. It appears when you set document restrictions for formatting and editing.

Protect a Document

In this exercise, you will set document protection options to allow tracked changes and assign a password to the document to prevent unauthorized users from editing the file.

1. Choose **File→Info→Protect Document**.

2. Select **Restrict Editing** from the menu, and then follow these steps to switch on document protection for tracked changes:

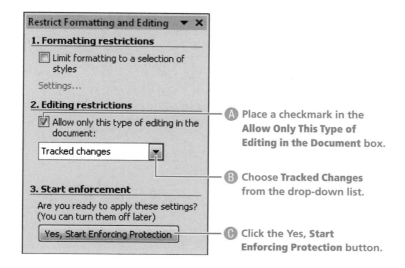

Ⓐ Place a checkmark in the **Allow Only This Type of Editing in the Document** box.

Ⓑ Choose **Tracked Changes** from the drop-down list.

Ⓒ Click the Yes, **Start Enforcing Protection** button.

Word displays the Start Enforcing Protection dialog box. At this point, you can either click OK to protect the document without a password or enter the desired password twice to apply a password to document protection.

3. Follow these steps to add a password:

Ⓐ Enter **Labyrinth11** as the password for the **Protect Document** command. Notice that Word displays the password as dots to prevent passersby from seeing your password.

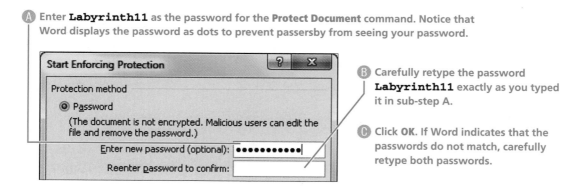

Ⓑ Carefully retype the password **Labyrinth11** exactly as you typed it in sub-step A.

Ⓒ Click **OK**. If Word indicates that the passwords do not match, carefully retype both passwords.

Notice that the Track Changes button is grayed out. You cannot switch off change tracking. Notice that the Accept and Reject buttons are also grayed out.

4. Move to **page 2** of the document.

5. Select the text *Mission Statement*, and **type** the text **Our Mission**.
Word marks the tracked change. No one can alter this document without changes being marked.

6. **Press** the [Home] key to place the insertion point at the beginning of the line.

7. Choose **Review→Changes→Next** 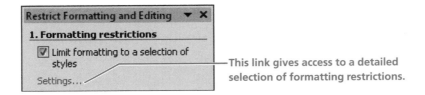 from the Ribbon.
   Word highlights the change you just made. Again, notice that the Accept and Reject buttons are grayed out. You cannot accept or reject changes while the document is protected.

Unprotect the Document

8. Click the **Stop Protection** button at the bottom of the Restrict Formatting and Editing task pane.
   Word prompts you to enter the password in order to switch off document protection.

9. Type **Labyrinth11** in the Password field, and **press** [Enter].
   Notice that the Track Changes feature is active again.

10. **Accept** the edit you made to the document.

11. Click the **Close** [X] button in the upper-right corner of the Restrict Formatting and Editing task pane.

12. **Save** [💾] the document, and leave it **open**.

Applying Formatting Restrictions

Video Lesson   labyrinthelab.com/videos

Formatting is restricted to a list of specified Word styles, thus preventing anyone from indiscriminately applying bold, italics, or other manual formatting.

This link gives access to a detailed selection of formatting restrictions.

The Formatting Restrictions dialog box lets you specify which of Word's styles a reviewer can use in modifying a document. This also prevents reviewers from applying direct formatting, such as bold or italics, to the document.

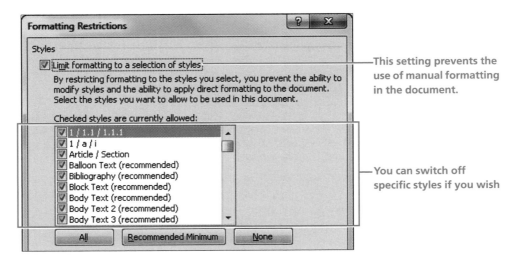

This setting prevents the use of manual formatting in the document.

You can switch off specific styles if you wish

Set Formatting Restrictions

In this exercise, you will use the Restrict Formatting and Editing task pane to apply formatting restrictions.

Before You Begin: The Draft Raritan Procedures Manual (Compatibility Mode) document should be open.

1. Choose **File→Info→Protect Document→Restrict Editing** 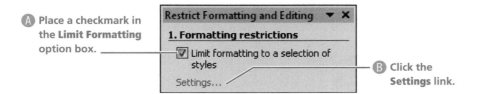 from the Ribbon.
   The Restrict Formatting and Editing task pane appears.

2. Follow these steps to limit formatting and open the Formatting Restrictions dialog box:

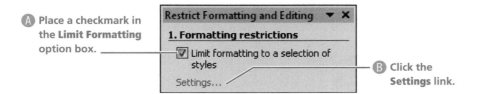

Ⓐ Place a checkmark in the **Limit Formatting** option box.

Ⓑ Click the **Settings** link.

   Word displays the Formatting Restrictions dialog box.

3. Follow these steps to set specific restrictions:

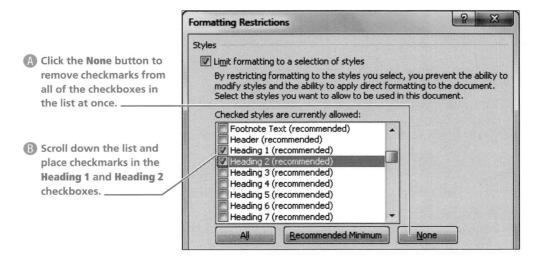

Ⓐ Click the **None** button to remove checkmarks from all of the checkboxes in the list at once.

Ⓑ Scroll down the list and place checkmarks in the **Heading 1** and **Heading 2** checkboxes.

   The only formatting change a reviewer can make is to add Heading 1 or Heading 2 formatting.

4. Click **OK** to close the dialog box.
   Word displays a message asking if you want to remove other styles.

5. Choose **No** in response to the prompt.
   Removing other styles from the document would reformat the entire document with sometimes unexpected results.

6. Click the **Yes, Start Enforcing Protection** button in the task pane.
   You could add password protection so that a person must know the password in order to change any of the task pane settings. In this example, you will not add a password.

7. Click **OK** to dismiss the password dialog box.
Notice that the task pane now contains a link to Available Styles.

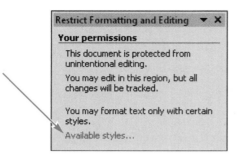

8. Click the **Available Styles** link to display the Styles task pane.
In addition to the Normal style, the only special styles available are Heading 1 and Heading 2.

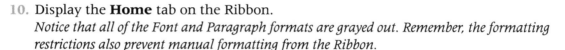

9. **Close** ☒ the Styles task pane.

10. Display the **Home** tab on the Ribbon.
Notice that all of the Font and Paragraph formats are grayed out. Remember, the formatting restrictions also prevent manual formatting from the Ribbon.

11. Click the **Stop Protection** button at the bottom of the Restrict Formatting and Editing task pane.
Word restores normal formatting capabilities. Notice that the Font and Paragraph controls are restored.

Leave the document open for the next exercise.

Applying Editing Exceptions

Video Lesson labyrinthelab.com/videos

You can restrict a person's ability to make editing changes in a document, but with the Exceptions option you can specify certain areas of a document that a person can edit freely. As a result, if a document is in its final version except for one section, you can exempt the incomplete section of the document so that it can be edited.

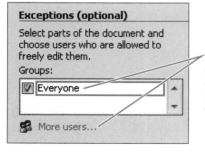

By checking the Everyone checkbox, no one can make edits to the file. To allow specific people to make edits, choose the More users link and select those who can make edits. Users are identified by their Microsoft Windows user account names or email addresses.

Task	Description
Set formatting restrictions	■ Choose File→Info→Protect Document→Restrict Editing or Review→Protect→Restrict Editing from the Ribbon to display the Restrict Formatting and Editing task pane.
	■ Place a checkmark in Formatting Restrictions area of the task pane.
	■ Click the Settings link.
	■ Remove checkmarks from Word styles you want to prevent from being used.
	■ Checkmark styles you want available to reviewers.
	■ Click the Yes, Start Enforcing Protection button in the task pane.
Set editing restrictions	■ Choose File→Info→Protect Document→Restrict Editing or Review→Protect→Restrict Editing from the Ribbon to display the Restrict Formatting and Editing task pane.
	■ Place a checkmark in the Editing Restrictions section of the task pane.
	■ Choose the type of editing permitted from the drop-down list.
	■ Click the Yes, Start Enforcing Protection button in the task pane.
Apply exceptions to editing restrictions	■ Select the text that will be an exception to the restrictions.
	■ Under Groups, click Everyone, or click the More Users link, and enter the email addresses or Windows login to identify specific users.

DEVELOP YOUR SKILLS 12.2.3

Apply Editing Exceptions

In this exercise, you will specify the document as read-only; however, you will apply an exception to one paragraph so the reviewer can make changes to it.

Before You Begin: The document Draft Raritan Procedures Manual (Compatibility Mode) should be open, and the Restrict Formatting and Editing pane should be visible on the right side of the Word window.

Place Editing Restrictions in the Document

1. Follow these steps to restrict editing the document.

Ⓐ Place a checkmark in the **Editing Restrictions** option box.

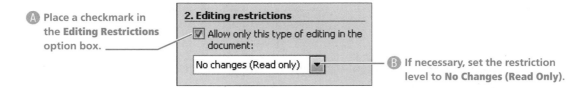

2. Editing restrictions

☑ Allow only this type of editing in the document:

No changes (Read only) ▼

Ⓑ If necessary, set the restriction level to **No Changes (Read Only)**.

Apply Exceptions to the Restrictions

2. Scroll to the **third page** of the document, and select the **three paragraphs** below the heading *Patient Appointment and Billing*.

3. Place a checkmark in the **Everyone** option box under Exceptions (Optional), as shown at right.
This specifies that all reviewers will be able to edit these paragraphs.

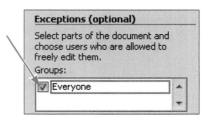

Exceptions (optional)

Select parts of the document and choose users who are allowed to freely edit them.
Groups:

☑ Everyone

4. Click the **Yes, Start Enforcing Protection** button at the bottom of the task pane.
   Word prompts you for a password.

5. Type **pass** in both boxes in the Start Enforcing Protection dialog box, and then click **OK**.
   The password appears as dots, to prevent others from viewing it as you type. You type the password twice to avoid a typo.

6. **Click** to deselect the paragraph.
   Notice that the editable paragraph is shaded to make it readily visible to reviewers.

Attempt to Edit in a Restricted Area

7. Select a word in any paragraph where there is no shading.

8. **Press** the ⌈Delete⌋ key.
   Nothing happens because you are restricted to editing only the shaded paragraphs.

9. Click the **Stop Protection** button at the bottom of the task pane.

10. Type **pass** in the Unprotect Document dialog box, and then click **OK**.

11. Select the **three exception** paragraphs, and then remove the checkmark from the **Everyone** option box in the task pane to remove the shading.

12. **Close** ⊠ the Restrict Formatting and Editing task pane.

13. **Save** 🖫 the file, and leave it **open**.

Setting Document Passwords

Video Lesson   labyrinthelab.com/videos

By using commands on the Backstage view Info tab, you can set two passwords for a document. If you use both passwords, the reviewer would need a password to open the document as well as another password to edit the document.

■ **Password to Open**—Reviewers are able to open the document only if they have the password. Document passwords are set using the File→Info→Protect Document→Encrypt with a Password feature.

■ **Password to Modify**—The reviewer can open the document but is restricted from editing the document unless he or she has the password. Editing passwords are set using the File→Info→Protect Document→Restrict Editing feature.

In this section, the focus will be on encrypting a document with a password so that unauthorized readers are unable to open the document.

Encrypting Documents

Adding a document password also enables you to *encrypt* the document. Encrypting a document simply means to alter information using a code or mathematical algorithm so as to be inaccessible to unauthorized readers. By applying this feature to a Word 2010 document, you are protecting it by applying a password others will need to use to open the file. Therefore, the document is inaccessible to unauthorized readers. When you encrypt a document, Word prompts you for a password. After you enter the password one time, Word presents a second prompt so that you can enter the password again. This practice of entering a password twice helps Word ensure that you have typed the password as you planned to type it, without any typographical errors.

Word displays
raised dots to
protect your
password.

┌The first dialog box prompts you for a password.

┌The second dialog box prompts you to confirm the password.

Opening an Encrypted Document

If you try to open a document that is encrypted with a password and enter an inaccurate password, Word displays a message box advising you that the file cannot be opened.

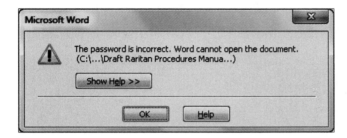

Removing Passwords

After a document has been reviewed and returned to you, you can remove the password after first opening the document. You simply remove the password from the Encrypt with Password prompt to remove the protection from the document.

Reviewing Protect Settings

When you assign a password to control who edits a document, encrypt a file to prevent unwanted access, or mark a document as final, Word displays the security settings on the Info panel in Backstage view. You will notice, after setting these protections, that active permissions are displayed in the Permissions list for the file.

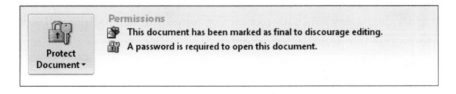

SETTING AND REMOVING DOCUMENT PASSWORDS	
Task	**Description**
Set a document password	▪ Choose File→Info→Protect Document→Encrypt with a Password.
	▪ Type the password in the Encrypt Document dialog box, and click OK.
	▪ Type the password again in the Confirm Password dialog box, and click OK.
Remove a document password	▪ Open the document using the password.
	▪ Choose File→Info→Protect→Document→Encrypt with a Password.
	▪ Remove the password from the Encrypt Document dialog box, and click OK.

DEVELOP YOUR SKILLS 12.2.4

Set and Remove a Document Password

In this exercise, you will set a document password.

Before You Begin: The document Draft Raritan Procedures Manual (Compatibility Mode) should be open.

1. Choose **File→Info→Protect Document→Encrypt with a Password**.

2. Type **pass** in the Encrypt Document dialog box, and click **OK**.

3. Type **pass** in the Confirm Password dialog box, and click **OK**.

4. **Save** the document, and then **close** it.

 Depending on the security settings active on your computer, you may receive a message asking if you would like to increase the security of the document by converting it to an Office Open XML format. Respond to the message by clicking the No button.

Open a Password-Protected Document

5. Choose **File→Recent**, and click the Draft Raritan Procedures Manual document at the top of the recent documents list.
   Word prompts you for the password to open the document.

6. Type **pass** in the password box, and click **OK**.

Remove the Password

7. Choose **File→Info→Protect Document→Encrypt with a Password**.

8. Select the text in the password field, **press** Delete on the keyboard to remove it, and click **OK**.

9. **Save** changes to the document, and **close** it.

10. **Open** the document, and leave it **open** for the next exercise.

Marking a Document as Final

Video Lesson   labyrinthelab.com/videos

One additional way to control edits and access to the content of a document is to mark the document as "final." Using the Mark as Final command makes a document *read-only.* As a result, readers and reviewers will know that this document appears as it did when it went to a client, was filed electronically, or was in some other way beyond the reach where edits would be useful. Marking as final also prevents accidental altering of the document.

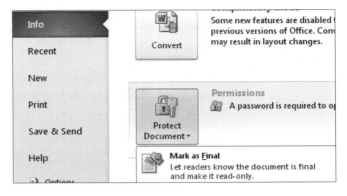

The Mark as Final command is found in Backstage view under the Info→Protect Document list.

Editing Documents Marked as Final

When the Mark as Final feature is turned on for a document, a gold business bar appears above the document screen each time you open the document. The message in the bar lets you know that the document has been marked as final to discourage editing and the Ribbon is hidden. A button in the message bar enables you to edit the document anyway.

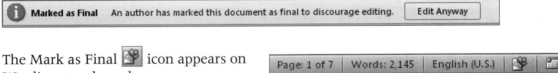

The Mark as Final 🖉 icon appears on Word's status bar when you open a document that is marked as final.

| Page: 1 of 7 | Words: 2,145 | English (U.S.) | 🖉 | 📝 |

Reversing Mark as Final Status

If you want to reenable editing for a document marked as final, you choose the Mark as Final command again. This turns off the feature and removes the Mark as Final button from the status bar. You can also simply click the Edit Anyway button on the business bar to enable editing.

QUICK REFERENCE	MARKING A DOCUMENT AS FINAL
Task	**Description**
Mark a document as final	■ Choose File→Info→Protect Document→Mark as Final.
Enable the document for editing	■ Choose File→Info→Protect Document→Mark as Final to turn the feature off.
	or
	■ Click the Edit Anyway button on the business bar.

Mark a Document as Final

In this exercise, you will mark a document as final, and then you will remove the designation in order to re-enable editing.

Before You Begin: The document Draft Raritan Procedures Manual (Compatibility Mode) should be open.

1. Choose **File→Info→Protect Document→Mark as Final**.
   Word displays a message that the document will be marked as final and saved.

2. Click **OK** to confirm marking the document as final.
   Word displays additional information about this setting.

3. Click **OK** to complete the Mark as Final command, and then **tap** [Esc] on the keyboard to return to the document.
   Notice the Mark as Final icon on the status bar at the bottom-left corner of the screen.

Test the Document

4. Select the heading Our Mission on **page 2**.

5. **Press** the [Delete] key, and the text is not deleted.
   Notice the message on the status bar at the bottom of the screen.

> This modification is not allowed because the selection is locked.

The message disappears after a few seconds. Press [Delete] again to redisplay the message if you missed it.

Enable the Document for Editing

6. Choose **File→Info→Protect Document→Mark as Final**, and then **tap** [Esc] on the keyboard to return to the document.
   The Mark as Final icon no longer appears on the status bar.

7. Leave the document **open** for the next exercise.

12.3 Attaching Digital Signatures to Documents

Video Lesson labyrinthelab.com/videos

With the capability to pass documents globally within seconds via email, security concerns may arise. For example, how can a coworker know for certain that a critical document originated at your office? Although it is unlikely that an imposter might alter and then transmit a document you created, it is a possibility. A digital signature is a secure means of stamping a document as authentic and originating only from you. You cannot modify a signed document.

Adding a Digital Signature

There are two ways to add a digital signature to a document:

- You can add a *visible signature line* to a document and then capture the digital signature when the document is signed.
- If a visible signature line is not necessary, you can add an *invisible digital signature*. A signature button appears on the status bar at the bottom of the screen, so the recipient can verify that the document has a digital signature.

Obtaining a Digital Signature

In order to apply a digital signature, you must either create or purchase one.

- **Create a self-signature**—You can create a digital signature for yourself; however, it is not verified by any outside agency. Therefore, it is not necessarily a reliable measure, but it is the most convenient.
- **Purchase a digital signature**—Commercial providers specialize in the creation, verification, and administration of digital signatures. Digital signature providers are available on the Microsoft website.

QUICK REFERENCE	ADDING AND REMOVING DIGITAL SIGNATURES
Task	**Procedure**
Add a signature line to a document	■ Choose Insert→Text→Signature Line from the Ribbon. ■ Complete the information in the Signature Setup dialog box.
Add a signature to a signature line	■ Right-click the signature line, and choose Sign from the pop-up menu. ■ Type your name or click the Select Image link to select a signature image file.

QUICK REFERENCE	ADDING AND REMOVING DIGITAL SIGNATURES (continued)
Task	**Procedure**
Remove a signature and signature line from a document	■ Click the This Document Contains Signatures button on the status bar to display the Signatures task pane.
	■ Right-click the signature and choose Remove Signature from the menu.
	■ Click the signature line to select it, and then press [Delete] to remove it.
Add an invisible digital signature	■ Choose File→Info→Protect Document→Add a Digital Signature.
	■ When the Sign dialog box appears, add any information you wish, then click the Sign button.
Remove an invisible signature	■ Click the This Document Contains Signatures button on the status bar to display the Signatures task pane.
	■ Right-click the signature in the task pane, and choose Remove Signature from the menu.

DEVELOP YOUR SKILLS 12.3.1

Add a Digital Signature to a Document

In this exercise, you will add a signature line to a document, and then you will add a digital signature. You will then attempt to modify the signed document. Finally, you will remove the visible signature and add an invisible digital signature.

Before You Begin: The document Draft Raritan Procedures Manual (Compatibility Mode) should be open.

1. **Press** [Ctrl]+[End] to position the insertion point at the end of the document and **press** [Enter] twice.

2. Choose **Insert→Text→Signature Line**  from the Ribbon.
   Word displays a message about digital signatures. The Signature Services from the Microsoft Office Marketplace button would open a Microsoft web page where commercial signature services are available. In this exercise, you will use a self-created signature.

3. Click **OK** to continue.
   Word displays the Signature Setup dialog box.

4. Complete the information, as shown in the illustration at right. *The Instructions to the Signer text is provided by default. You can modify it, if necessary.*

5. Click **OK** to complete the signature setup.
   A signature line appears with the signer's name and title below. At this point, you can email the document if someone else needs to sign it.

6. **Right-click** the signature line, and choose **Sign** from the pop-up menu.
   A message box appears with information about digital signatures.

NOTE

7. Click **OK**.

If a message box appears asking if you want to get a digital ID or create your own digital ID, choose to create your own digital ID.

Sign the Document

8. Follow these steps to sign the document:

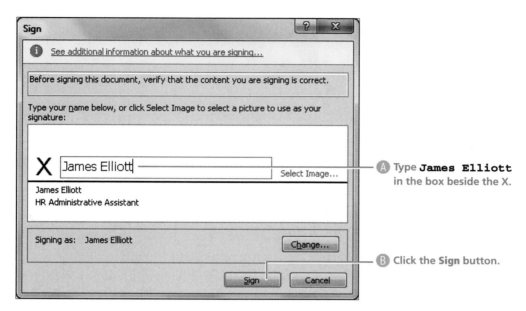

(A) Type **James Elliott** in the box beside the X.

(B) Click the **Sign** button.

A message appears indicating that your signature has been saved.

9. Click **OK** to close the message box.
Notice the Signature button that appears on the status bar at the bottom of the screen indicating that there is a signature in the document. Clicking this button turns the Signatures task pane on and off. Also notice that the Business Bar contains a message telling you that Word has marked this document as Final.

Attempt to Modify the Document

10. **Scroll up** to a paragraph above the signature, and attempt to **delete** a word in the last line.
Notice the message that appears on the status bar when you try to make the change.

This modification is not allowed because the selection is locked.

Remove the Signature

Now you will remove the signature so you can add an invisible signature.

11. Click the **This Document Contains Signatures** 🖺 button on the status bar to display the Signatures task pane.

12. **Right-click** the James Elliott signature in the task pane, and choose **Remove Signature** from the menu.
   A message appears verifying that you want to remove the signature.

13. Click **Yes** to remove the signature.
   A message appears indicating that the signature was removed.

14. Click **OK** to dismiss the message.

Remove the Signature Line

15. Click the **signature line** to select it, and then **press** ⌷Delete⌷ to remove it from the document.

16. Click the **Close** ⌧ button in the upper-right corner of the Signatures task pane.

Add an Invisible Digital Signature

When you display the Protect Document command list, notice the description for the Add a Digital Signature command. It indicates that Word will add an invisible signature.

17. Choose **File→Info→Protect Document→Add a Digital Signature**.
   A message about digital signatures appears after you click Add a Digital Signature.

18. Click **OK** to close the message box.
   When the Sign dialog box appears, notice the field where you can include a reason for signing the document if you desire. The active signature is James Elliott's.

19. Click the **Sign** button to add the signature, and then click **OK**.
   Notice the signature button on the status bar and the Marked as Final note in the Business Bar.

20. **Close** ⌧ the document.

12.4 Concepts Review

Concepts Review	labyrinthelab.com/word10

To check your knowledge of the key concepts introduced in this lesson, complete the Concepts Review quiz by going to the URL listed above. If your classroom is using Labyrinth eLab, you may complete the Concepts Review quiz from within your eLab course.

Reinforce Your Skills

REINFORCE YOUR SKILLS 12.1

Save a Word 2003 File as a Word 2010 File

In this exercise, you will open a document that was created in Word 2003, and you will use the Save As dialog box to make a Word 2010 copy of the document.

1. **Open** rs-Internet Images from the Lesson 12 folder.
   Observe the title bar, and notice that the Word 2003 document opens in Compatibility Mode. Next you will save the document as a Word 2010 file.

2. Choose **File→Save As** to open the Save As dialog box.

3. At the bottom of the dialog box, choose **Word Document** from the Save as Type list.

4. Clear the **Maintain Compatibility with Previous Versions of Word** checkbox and then click the **Save** button to create a copy of the document in Word 2010 format.

5. Click **OK** to acknowledge the message.

Verify the Word Format

You'll recall that the SmartArt feature is not available in Word 2003 documents. Next you'll access the SmartArt feature to prove that Word 2010 features are available.

6. Choose **Insert→Illustrations→SmartArt** ![icon] from the Ribbon.
   The Choose SmartArt Graphic dialog box opens, verifying that this document is Word 2010 capable.

7. Click **Cancel** to close the dialog box.

8. **Close** the file.

REINFORCE YOUR SKILLS 12.2

Save a Word File as an Earlier Version

In this exercise, you will save a document created in Word 2010 as a Word 97-2003 document.

1. **Open** rs-Components of Web Pages from the Lesson 12 folder.

2. Choose **File→Save As** to open the Save As dialog box.

3. At the bottom of the dialog box, choose **Word 97-2003 Document** from the Save as Type menu.

4. Click the **Save** button to finish saving the document as an earlier Word version.

Verify the Version

You will attempt to open the Choose a SmartArt Graphic dialog box to see if the document is Word 2010 capable.

5. Choose **Insert→Illustrations→SmartArt** from the Ribbon.
   The Diagram Gallery, which provides graphic images for earlier versions of Word, appears. The Choose a SmartArt Graphic dialog box did not open, as it would for a Word 2010 document.

6. Click the **Cancel** button to close the Diagram Gallery dialog box.

7. **Save** and **close** the file.

REINFORCE YOUR SKILLS 12.3

Inspect Your Document

In this exercise, you will open a document and make a copy of it, and then you will use the Document Inspector to see if the document includes any information you wish to remove before distributing it to coworkers.

Copy the Document

1. **Open** the document rs-Savvy Dining from the Lesson 12 folder.

2. Choose **File→Save As**, and then save the document as **rs-My Savvy Dining** in the Lesson 12 folder.

Review Tracked Changes and Document Properties

3. Scroll to the **bottom** of the document.
   Notice that additions were made to the document, and the changes were tracked. The Document Inspector will prompt you to remove the tracked changes, because the changed items can reveal who worked on the document.

4. Choose **File→Info**, and then review the **Properties** shown in the right-hand pane.

5. Review the author's name, click the **Properties menu ▾** button, and choose **Advanced Properties** from the list.

6. In the Properties dialog box, click the **Summary** tab, and review the information there.

7. Click the **Cancel** button to close the dialog box.

Inspect the Document

8. Choose **File→Info→Check for Issues**, and then choose **Inspect Document** from the menu.

9. Click the **Inspect** button at the bottom of the dialog box.
   The Document Inspector proposes removal of items in two categories. If you choose to remove Comments, Revisions, Versions, and Annotations, Word will incorporate the tracked changes in the document.

10. Click the **Remove All** button for each category, and then click the **Close** button at the bottom of the dialog box.

Review the Changes the Inspector Made

11. **Tap** Esc on the keyboard to return to the document, and then, if necessary, scroll to the **bottom** of the document.
    The tracked changes have been incorporated in the document.

12. Choose **File→Info**, and then review the **Properties** from the right-hand pane.
    Notice that the author's name was removed from the Document Properties pane. If your name still appears, repeat steps 8–10 to remove additional metadata.

13. Click the **Properties** menu ▾ button and choose **Advanced Properties** from the menu.

14. Click the **Summary** tab.
    The personal information has been removed.

15. Click the **Cancel** button to close the dialog box.

16. **Save** 🖫 the file, and leave it **open** for the next exercise.

REINFORCE YOUR SKILLS 12.4

Restrict Formatting in a Document

In this exercise, you will restrict the formats a reviewer can use in a document.

Before you begin: Complete Reinforce Your Skills 12.3, and rs-My Savvy Dining should be open on the screen.

1. Choose **Review→Protect→Restrict Editing** 🔒 from the Ribbon to open the Restrict Formatting and Editing task pane.

2. Place a checkmark in the **Limit Formatting to a Selection of Styles** checkbox.

3. Click the **Settings** link in the Formatting Restrictions area of the task pane.

Restrict Formatting

4. In the Formatting Restrictions dialog box, click the **None** button to remove all checkmarks from the list.

5. Scroll down and check the **Heading 1** and **Heading 2** styles, and then click **OK**.

6. When the message appears asking if you want to remove other styles, click **No**.

7. Click the **Yes, Start Enforcing Protection** button in the task pane.

8. Click **OK** to dismiss the password dialog box.

Test the Restrictions

9. In the task pane, click the **Available Styles** link.
   Notice that Heading 1 and Heading 2 are the only special styles available.

10. **Close** ☒ the Styles task pane.

11. Choose the **Home** tab on the Ribbon.
    Notice that the Font and Paragraph formats are not available. Remember, Formatting Restrictions prevent direct formatting in a document.

12. Click the **Stop Protection** button at the bottom of the task pane.

13. **Save** 🖫 the document, and leave it **open** for the next exercise.

REINFORCE YOUR SKILLS 12.5

Restrict Editing in a Document

In this exercise, you will restrict the document to read-only, but you'll add an exception to allow editing in the second page of the document.

Before you begin: You should complete Reinforce Your Skills 12.4, and rs-My Savvy Dining should be open on the screen.

1. Place a checkmark in the **Editing Restrictions** part of the task pane.

2. If necessary, click the **drop-down arrow** below the checkbox, and choose **No Changes (Read Only)** from the menu.

3. If necessary, scroll to **page 2** and select all of the text on the page.

4. Click the **Everyone** checkbox in the Exceptions portion of the task pane.

5. Click the **Yes, Start Enforcing Protection** button at the bottom of the task pane.

6. Click **OK** to dismiss the password dialog box.

7. Scroll up to the bottom of **page 1**, and attempt to **delete** the heading *Who Pays and How?*
   The deletion did not work because this part of the document is restricted to read-only.

8. Scroll back to **page 2** and select the word *Avoid* in the first bullet point, and type **Stay away from** to replace it.
   This part of the document was selected as an exception to the read-only restriction.

9. Click the **Stop Protection** button at the bottom of the task pane.

10. **Save** 🖫 the file, and **close** it.

Mark a Document as Final

In this exercise, you will mark a document as final, and then you will attempt to make an editing change. Finally, you will re-enable the document for editing.

1. **Open** rs-Acme Tax Services from the Lesson 12 folder.

2. Choose **File→Info→Protect Document**, and then choose **Mark as Final**.

3. When the message appears indicating that the document will be marked as final, click **OK**.

4. When the next message appears with more detail about marking as final, click **OK**.
   Notice the Mark as Final button on the status bar at the bottom of the screen.

Attempt to Modify the Document

5. Select the heading word *Reliability* and attempt to change it to **Dependability**.
   No change occurs because you cannot edit a document marked as final.

Enable the Document for Editing

6. Choose **File→Info→Protect Document**, and then choose **Mark as Final**.
   Notice that the Mark as Final button no longer appears on the status bar.

7. Select the heading word *Reliability* and change it to **Dependability**.
   This time the change occurs, because the document is no longer marked as final.

8. **Save** the document and leave it **open** for the next exercise.

Use a Signature Line and a Digital Signature

In this exercise, you will add a signature line and a digital signature to a document, and then you will attempt to modify it.

Before you begin: You should complete Reinforce Your Skills 12.6, and rs-Acme Tax Services should be open on the screen.

1. **Press** Ctrl + End to place the insertion point at the bottom of the document.

2. Choose **Insert→Text→Signature Line** 📝 from the Ribbon.

3. When the message box appears, click **OK**.

4. When the Signature Setup dialog box appears, type **Tom Chang** as the Suggested Signer, and type **Marketing Manager** as the Suggested Signer's Title.

5. Click **OK** to complete the signature setup.

6. **Right-click** the signature line, and choose **Sign** from the pop-up menu.

7. When the message box appears, click **OK** to display the Sign dialog box.

8. Type **Tom Chang** next to the X, and then click the **Sign** button at the bottom of the dialog box.

9. When the message appears stating that your signature was saved, click **OK**.

10. Select the *Dependability* heading at the top of the document, and **press** Delete . *The deletion does not occur, because you cannot modify a signed document.*

11. **Close** the file.

Apply Your Skills

Save a File in Different Versions

A Portable Data File (PDF) is a document format free of unwanted metadata such as author name, dates, and so forth. PDF files are also more difficult to edit. You can save files in PDF format using the same techniques you use to save Word 2010 in compatibility format. In this exercise, you will open a document created in Word 2010 and save it as a PDF file. If Adobe Reader is not installed on your computer, you will be unable to view the converted document.

1. **Open** as-Riley Resume from the Lesson 12 folder.

2. Use the **Save As** command to save the document in PDF format, storing it in your Lesson 12 folder.

3. **Print** a copy of the PDF document.

4. **Close** both the Word and PDF documents, **saving** changes if prompted.

Apply Editing Restrictions and an Exception

In this exercise, you will restrict the editing of a document to the ability to add comments, and you will apply an exception to the restriction.

1. **Open** as-Riley Memo from the Lesson 12 folder.

2. Set editing restrictions so that reviewers can:
   - Add comments to the document.
   - Modify the body of the memo without having to supply a password.

3. **Save** changes to the document and then make the following edits to the memo:
   - Add a comment asking if Marion Patel should be copied on the memo.
   - Change *next week* to read **the week after next**.

4. **Stop** the document protection, and **save** changes to the file, leaving it **open** for the next exercise.

Use the Document Inspector

In this exercise, you will inspect the document before distributing it in case it contains private information.

Before you begin: You should complete Apply Your Skills 12.2, and as-Riley Memo should be open.

1. Review the **document properties**, and then use the **Document Inspector** to inspect the document.

2. **Remove** all the items in each category that the inspector finds.

3. Review the **Document Properties**, including those in the Properties dialog box, to verify that personal information was removed.

4. **Save** 🖫 the file, and **close** it.

Add a Password to Modify to a Document

In this exercise, you will add a password to a document that specifies that a reviewer must provide a password in order to modify the document.

1. **Open** as-New Year News from the Lesson 12 folder.

2. Apply a **Password to Modify** to the document; use **pass** as the password.

3. **Close** the document and **reopen** it, entering the password.

4. In the heading *Our Fifth Year,* change *Fifth* to **Eighth**.

5. In the fourth line of the following paragraph, change *fifth* to **eighth**.

6. **Delete** the password, and then **close** and **reopen** the document to verify that a password is no longer required.

7. **Save** 🖫 the file, and **close** it.

Add a Digital Signature to a Document

In this exercise, you will add a signature line and a digital signature to a document, and then you will mark it as final.

1. **Open** as-Retirement Party from the Lesson 12 folder.

2. **Press** Ctrl + End to position the insertion point at the bottom of the document.

3. Add a signature line, using **Tory Noletti, Administrative Assistant** as the Suggested Signer and the Suggested Signer's Title.

4. Sign the letter as **Tory Noletti**.

5. **Close** the file.

Mark a Document as Final

In this exercise, you will mark a document as final. The document will be placed on your company's intranet as a tool for training new sales representatives, and you don't want anyone to accidentally make a change to the document. Marking it as final will prevent that.

1. **Open** as-Electronic Etiquette from the Lesson 12 folder.

2. Mark the document as **final**.

3. Attempt to **delete** the document heading.

4. **Save** the file, and **close** it.

Critical Thinking & Work-Readiness Skills

In the course of working through the following Microsoft Office-based Critical Thinking exercises, you will also be utilizing various work-readiness skills, some of which are listed next to each exercise. Go to labyrinthelab.com/ workreadiness *to learn more about the work-readiness skills.*

12.1 Facilitate a Conversion

WORK-READINESS SKILLS APPLIED

- Serving clients/ customers
- Writing
- Teaching others new skills

As Raritan Clinic East prepares for their conversion to Office 2010, James Elliott wants to ensure that workers using different versions of Word can use documents created in Word 2010. Word 2003 users will need to download and install the Compatibility Pack from the Microsoft website. James asks for your help. Go to microsoft.com, search for the **Compatibility Pack**, and copy the instructions for downloading and installing the software into a memo to be distributed to all employees. Create the memo using Word 2010 and include an introductory paragraph explaining the purpose of the Compatibility Pack. Save the document as a Word 97–2003 document as **ct-Compatibility Memo** in the Lesson 12 folder. Mark the document as final so it won't be altered accidentally.

12.2 Protect Document Text

WORK-READINESS SKILLS APPLIED

- Solving problems
- Understanding systems
- Applying technology to a task

Text that will appear in the Raritan Clinic East Annual Report is contained in a document named ct-Annual Report Text (Lesson 12 folder). The first paragraph of the document needs to be revised, but the rest of the document is in good condition. Open the document and run the Document Inspector to determine how much metadata it includes. Clean all metadata that Word finds. Restrict editing on all document text except the first paragraph. Assign a password to the document and save the document in the Lesson 12 folder.

12.3 Add Files to SkyDrive

WORK-READINESS SKILLS APPLIED

- Showing responsibility
- Organizing and maintaining information
- Applying technology to a task

James has decided to post the memo and the annual report text to the Public folder on SkyDrive to make it more accessible to others. By making the files public, he realizes that he needs to secure the documents with passwords and then send the password information via email to reviewers so they can access the documents. The annual report document has already been secured using a password. The memo containing the instructions for downloading and installing the Compatibility Pack does not. Secure the memo using the password **report**. Then add a digital signature for James to each document. Post both files to the Public folder in SkyDrive, if available. If you do not have a SkyDrive account, save the file according to your instructor's directions.

Personalizing Word

LEARNING OBJECTIVES

After studying this lesson, you will be able to:

- Customize Word options
- Modify document properties
- Customize research options
- Create and run macros
- Edit macros

Just as organizations often customize Word to meet the needs of their businesses, individual users also personalize Word for the way they work. They change Word options, modify document properties, and customize research options to better meet their needs. In addition, users frequently automate repetitive tasks by creating macros, and then they assign the macros to buttons or shortcut keys for quick access! Each of these features helps increase the efficiency with which users work. In this lesson, you will work with Word options, document properties, research options, and macros to learn how you might set up Word to enhance the way you work.

Student Resources   labyrinthelab.com/word10

Setting Up Word for the Way You Work

Raritan Clinic East

Pediatric Diagnostic Specialists

James Elliott has been working with Raritan Clinic East, a pediatric diagnostic clinic, for several months. By examining the types of documents he has created during this time, he has some ideas for trying to set up Word to make it more efficient for the way he works. He has noticed that the author name for many of his documents shows just the company name, and he would like for it to show his name. In addition, he has learned that most of his documents are saved to folders in a specific location, and he wants to set the default directory to access the main folder. He also wants to be able to search documents using specific words, change the way Word saves email attachments, and add technical terms to the dictionary. Finally, he has identified several tasks that he performs repeatedly and wants to automate the tasks so that they are easier to perform. As he works through the tasks to personalize his Word environment, he will use each of the following tools.

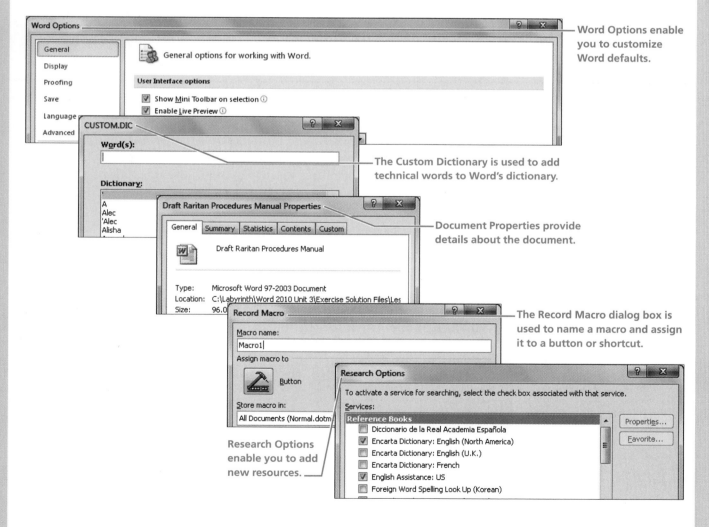

Word Options enable you to customize Word defaults.

The Custom Dictionary is used to add technical words to Word's dictionary.

Document Properties provide details about the document.

The Record Macro dialog box is used to name a macro and assign it to a button or shortcut.

Research Options enable you to add new resources.

13.1 Customizing Word Options

Video Lesson labyrinthelab.com/videos

The Word Options dialog box contains numerous categories of options that enable you to control the way Word acts. For example, the setting for the file locations controls where Word looks for templates and identifies the folder you want to use to store files. In this section, you will change some of the more common options. You will:

■ Set user name and initials

■ Change the default file location

■ Set the number of documents that appear in the Recent Documents list

■ Disable email attachments

■ Add words to the Custom dictionary

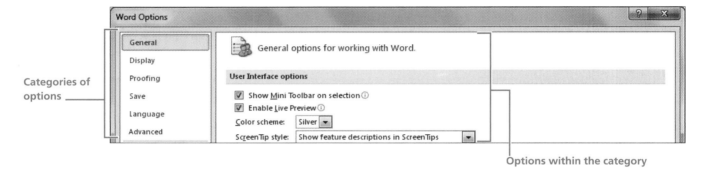

Categories of options

Options within the category

No document needs to be open when you set Word options. The changes made become part of the Normal.dotx template that Word uses for each document created. Regardless which option you want to set or change, the procedures for displaying the Word Options dialog box are the same.

Personalizing the Username and Initials

Many businesses set their business name as the username for documents that are created and saved using company computers. As a result, it is often challenging to determine who the author of a document actually is. You can change the author name for each document using the document Properties dialog box or set the default username and initials using the Word Options dialog box so Word automatically assigns the correct name to each document created and saved. After personalizing these settings, initials and username appear in properties for the document as well as in comments added to documents.

QUICK REFERENCE	CUSTOMIZING WORD OPTIONS
Task	**Procedures**
Display the Word Options dialog box	■ Choose File→Options 📇.
Set the username and initials	■ Display the Word Options dialog box. ■ Click the General category. ■ Change the User Name text. ■ Change the Initials text. ■ Click OK.
Modify the default file location	■ Display the Word Options dialog box. ■ Click the Advanced category. ■ Scroll to the General options. ■ Click the File Locations button. ■ Select the file type you want to modify, and click the Modify button. ■ Navigate to the folder you want to use to store files. ■ Click OK. ■ Close all open dialog boxes.
Set the number of recent documents	■ Display the Word Options dialog box. ■ Click the Advanced category. ■ Scroll to the Display options. ■ Change the number of documents to list in the Show this number of Recent Documents value box.

Although space does not allow coverage of each setting you can change in each category of the Word Options dialog box, feel free to explore on your own. Additional settings will be explored in exercises at the end of this lesson.

DEVELOP YOUR SKILLS 13.1.1

Set the Username and Initials

In this exercise, you will open the Word Options dialog box and set the author name and initials using the Word Options dialog box.

1. **Open** the Draft Raritan Procedures Manual from the Lesson 13 folder.

2. Choose **File→Options** 📇 to open the Word Options dialog box.

3. Click the **General** category and then write down the text in the **User Name** and **Initials** text boxes for future reference.

    User Name: _____

    Initials: _____

4. Follow these steps to change the username and enter initials:

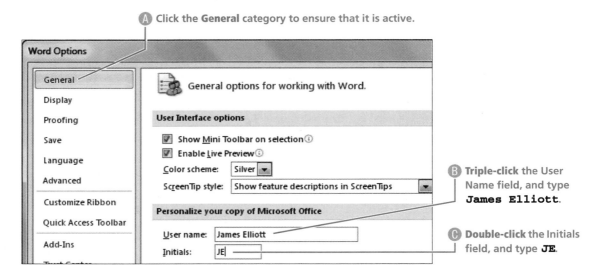

Ⓐ Click the **General** category to ensure that it is active.

Ⓑ **Triple-click** the User Name field, and type **James Elliott**.

Ⓒ **Double-click** the Initials field, and type **JE**.

5. Click **OK** to close the Word Options dialog box.
   Clicking the OK button saves the changes made to the options settings.

   Clicking the Close ▧ *button will abandon any changes made.*

Changing the Default File Location

Video Lesson labyrinthelab.com/videos

When Word and other Office programs are installed on computers, default file locations that are normally available on all computers are set up. Templates are stored in a standard location, and Word sets up a general folder for storing documents created on the machine. Many businesses provide access to network drives where company documents are stored so that they are backed up each night. By changing the default file locations, you reduce the time it takes to navigate to the correct drive and folder.

Set the Documents Default File Location

In this exercise, you will change the default file locations for documents to your student folder using the Word Options dialog box.

1. Choose **File→Options** 🖼 to display the Word Options dialog box.

2. Follow these steps to display the File Locations dialog box:

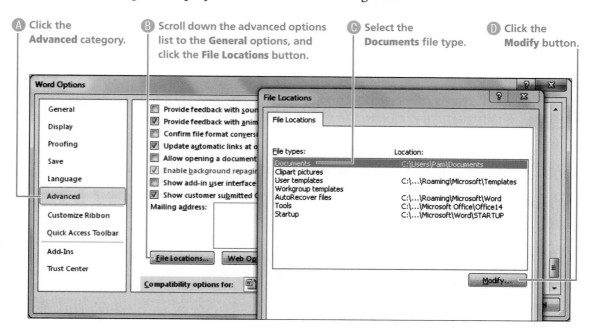

Ⓐ Click the **Advanced** category.

Ⓑ Scroll down the advanced options list to the **General** options, and click the **File Locations** button.

Ⓒ Select the **Documents** file type.

Ⓓ Click the **Modify** button.

Word opens the Modify Locations dialog box so that you can identify the drive and folder you want to use.

3. Write down the **current default file location** for Documents for future reference.

4. Navigate to the location where you are saving your student data files, and select the Lesson 13 folder.

5. Click **OK** to close the Modify Location dialog box.

6. Click **OK** to close the File Locations dialog box.

7. Click **OK** to close the Word Options dialog box.

Modifying the Recent Documents List

Video Lesson labyrinthelab.com/videos

Backstage view displays a list of recent documents used on the computer when you choose File→Recent. This Recent Documents list shows the last 22 documents opened on the computer. When a document is listed on the Recent Documents list, you can open the file simply by clicking the document name on the list. Displaying recent documents is a feature that is turned on in Word 2010 and other Office 2010 applications. You can turn the feature off so that no documents are listed, turn the feature back on, clear the list, or change the number of documents shown on the list using the Word Options dialog box. Other options are available from the Recent Documents list.

If you move a document to a different folder using an application such as Windows Explorer, the link to the document from the document name on the Recent Documents list is broken. After moving a document to a new folder, you would use the Open command to open the file.

Changing the Number of Files Shown on the Recent Documents List

When you work with only a few documents in Word, the documents you need will always appear on the Recent Documents list. If you find that you primarily work with the last few documents before moving onto new documents, you may want to change the number of documents shown on the list to reduce the number of documents you have to select from. Setting the number of documents to show on the Recent Documents list is controlled by settings in the Word Options dialog box.

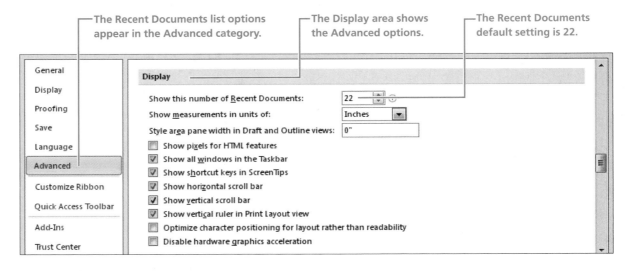

Pinning a File to the Recent Documents List

Periodically, you may find yourself modifying a specific document over an extended period of time. To ensure that the document appears in the Recent Documents list, you can pin the document to the list. Pinned documents remain on the list regardless of how many additional documents you access. They remain on the list until you unpin them. Pinning documents to the Recent Documents list is accessed using the Recent Documents shortcut menu.

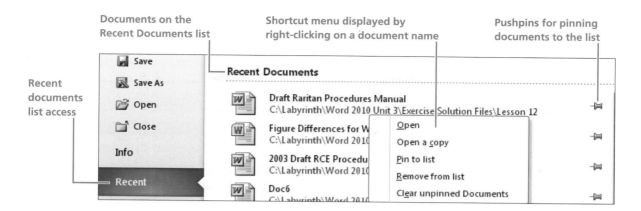

Documents on the Recent Documents list

Shortcut menu displayed by right-clicking on a document name

Pushpins for pinning documents to the list

Recent documents list access

When a document is pinned to the Recent Documents list, Word moves the document name to the top of the list and shows it as pinned. A dotted line separates pinned items from other documents on the list.

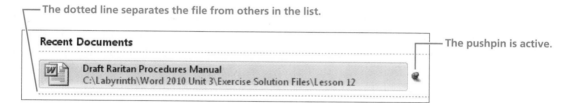

The dotted line separates the file from others in the list.

Recent Documents

Draft Raritan Procedures Manual
C:\Labyrinth\Word 2010 Unit 3\Exercise Solution Files\Lesson 12

The pushpin is active.

Adding a Quick Access List to the Backstage File Navigation Bar

In addition to the Recent Documents list that holds a set number of documents, you can also add a Quick Access List to the Backstage file navigation bar. Documents that appear on the quick access list include the most recent few documents you have accessed. You set the number of documents you want listed when you turn on the quick access list feature. Turn the feature on and off using the checkbox at the bottom of the Recent Documents list.

Quick Access List on the Backstage File Navigation Bar

Links to files on a quick access list will appear above the Info command on the navigation bar, regardless of where you are in the Backstage view. Clearing the checkbox removes the list.

Clearing the List of Recently Used Files

Workers who perform tasks associated with specific projects will enjoy the capability of clearing all unpinned items from the Recent Documents list. In addition, if you are using a public computer to create documents, you may want to clear the list so that others will be unable to identify the documents you used.

Setting the number of recent files to zero also clears the list. To turn the feature back on, set the number to something other than zero. Update the list by opening the files again and resetting the pins.

Task	Procedure
Pin a file to the Recent Documents list	■ Choose File→Recent. ■ Right-click the file you want to pin to the list. ■ Select Pin to List. *or* ■ Click the pin icon: 📌. ■ Click the pin button again to unpin the file.
Add a Quick Access List to the Backstage File Navigation Bar	■ Choose File→Recent. ■ Select the checkbox to Quickly Access This Number of Recent Documents, and choose how many files you want to see.
Clear the Recent Documents list	■ Choose File→Recent. ■ Right-click a file in the list, and select *Clear Unpinned Items*. ■ Click Yes to clear the list.
Edit the custom dictionary	■ Choose File→Options 📄 to display the Word Options dialog box. ■ Click the Proofing category. ■ Click the Custom Dictionaries button. ■ Click the Edit Word List button. ■ Type the word to add into the Word(s) text box. ■ Click Add.

DEVELOP YOUR SKILLS 13.1.3

Customize the Recent Documents List

In this exercise, you will work with the Recent Documents list to customize it using both the Word Options dialog box and the shortcut menu.

Change Number of Files on Recent Documents List

1. Choose **File→Options** 📄 to display the Word Options dialog box.

2. Follow these steps to change the number of documents shown on the Recent Documents list:

Ⓐ Click **Advanced** to display the advanced options.

Ⓑ Scroll down the advanced options list to the **Display** options.

Language		Display		
Advanced		Show this number of Recent Documents:	15	⌄ ⓘ
Customize Ribbon		Show measurements in units of:	Inches	▼

Ⓒ Write down the **default value** in this box, and then change the number of documents shown to **15**.

3. Click **OK**.

Pin a Document to the List

4. Choose **File→Recent** to display the Recent Documents List.

5. Locate the Draft Raritan Procedures Manual on the list, and **right-click** the document name.
   The shortcut menu appears.

6. Choose **Pin to List** from the shortcut menu.
   Word moves the document name to the top of the list and shows it as pinned.

Clear Unpinned Documents

7. Choose **File→Recent** to display the Recent Documents list, if necessary.

8. **Right-click** any filename shown on the list.

9. Choose **Clear Unpinned Items**.

10. Click the **Yes** button to acknowledge the message.
    All documents shown on the Recent Documents list disappear with the exception of the Draft Raritan Procedures Manual that is pinned to the list.

Unpin a Document

11. Choose **File→Recent** to display the pinned document, if necessary.

12. Click the **blue pushpin** to unpin the document from the Recent Documents list.
    After unpinning the document, you could repeat the procedures outlined in steps 8–10 to remove it from the list.

Adding Words to the Custom Dictionary

Video Lesson   labyrinthelab.com/videos

By now, you have most likely already learned that you can add words to the Custom Dictionary as the spell check feature checks for spelling. This is a great way to add words used frequently to the dictionary "on the fly." In addition to adding words using the spell check dialog box, you can also install dictionaries in Word that are suited for specific types of offices such as legal firms and medical facilities.

Even though some people work in offices related to special types of services, they may have no need for a fully developed dictionary. Sometimes there is a list of specific words within a business that need to be added to the dictionary. You can add such a list of words using the Custom.DIC dialog box.

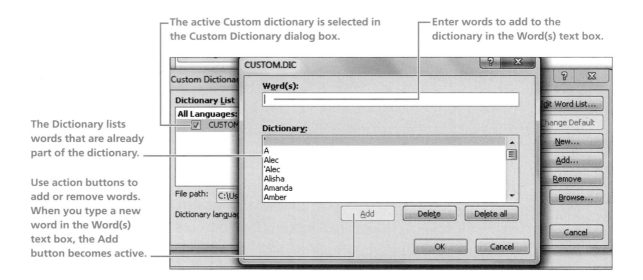

The active Custom dictionary is selected in the Custom Dictionary dialog box.

Enter words to add to the dictionary in the Word(s) text box.

The Dictionary lists words that are already part of the dictionary.

Use action buttons to add or remove words. When you type a new word in the Word(s) text box, the Add button becomes active.

Add Words to the Custom Dictionary

In this exercise, you will add words to the custom dictionary.

1. Choose **File→Options** 🗒 to display the Word Options dialog box.

2. Follow these steps to display the CUSTOM.DIC dialog box:

Ⓐ Click the **Proofing** category. Ⓑ Click the **Custom Dictionaries** button. Ⓒ Click the **Edit Word List** button.

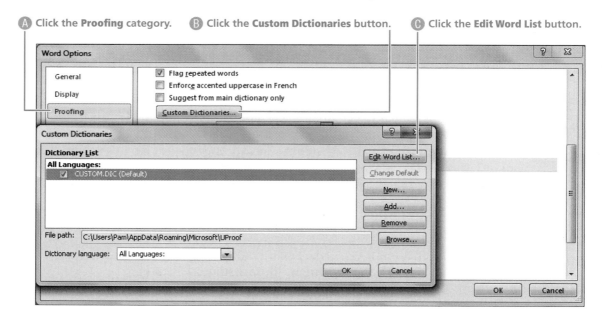

3. Follow these steps to add the first new word to the dictionary:

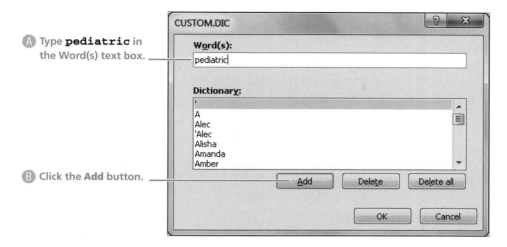

Ⓐ Type **pediatric** in the Word(s) text box.

Ⓑ Click the **Add** button.

4. Repeat the procedures outlined in **step 3** to add the following words to the dictionary:
   - cardiology
   - orthopedics
   - neonatology

5. Click the **OK** button at the bottom of all dialog boxes to return to the Word document.

13.2 Modifying Document Properties

Video Lesson labyrinthelab.com/videos

Each time you create a new document, Word pulls information from the options that you have set as well as from default options that are active. This information is stored in the Document Properties to identify details about the document. These details include such information as the date on which the document is created, the author name, the number of words contained in the document, and the path that identifies where the document is stored. Document properties display with the document in Backstage view when the Info command is active.

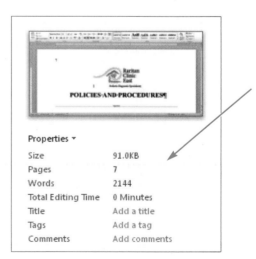

The default details are stored for every document to save you the time of entering the data. There are some details, however, that you may find it convenient to add to each document so that you can use them to search for specific documents. Among these details are keywords and comments. In addition, you can create a custom property—a property that holds document details that don't really fit into existing properties—and create a link between the active document and other documents that contain similar information or that are related in some way.

Adding Keywords and Comments

Keywords that you add to document properties enable users who are searching for documents to locate the document more easily and quickly. Keywords commonly identify words associated with the document whether the words are actually part of the document or not. They often include words related to the person who might use the document as well as specific words that provide information about a topic that could be useful to those searching for the information.

Comments, on the other hand, are descriptions about the document that you add manually.

Identifying Tools for Adding Keywords and Comments

As you have most likely discovered, Microsoft usually creates numerous tools or techniques for completing tasks. The procedure you choose depends on the way you work. There are basically three procedures that you can use to add keywords and comments to document properties:

- The Document Panel
- The Document Properties dialog box
- The Properties panel of the Info screen in Backstage view

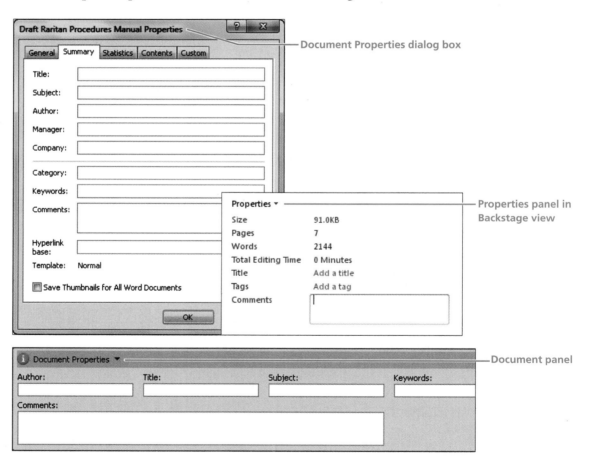

Add Keywords and Comments to Document Properties

In this exercise, you will use all three tools to add keywords and comments to the Draft Raritan Procedures Manual.

Use the Properties Panel in Backstage View

1. **Open** the Draft Raritan Procedures Manual found in the Lesson 13 folder, if it is closed.

2. Click the **File** tab, and review the document properties shown in the Properties panel on the right side of Info.

3. Click the **Comments** box, and type the following text into the box:

Ⓐ Locate the Comments, and click the box next to **Comments.**

Title	Add a title
Tags	Add a tag
Comments	Sent for review early in April.

Ⓑ **Type** the following in the Comments text box: **Sent for review early in April.**

Display the Document Panel

4. Follow these steps to display the Document Panel:

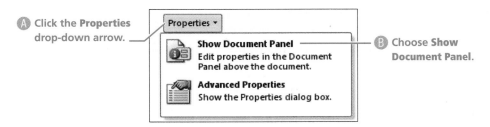

Ⓐ Click the **Properties** drop-down arrow.

Properties ▾

Show Document Panel
Edit properties in the Document Panel above the document.

Advanced Properties
Show the Properties dialog box.

Ⓑ Choose **Show Document Panel.**

5. Follow these steps to enter properties in the Document Panel:

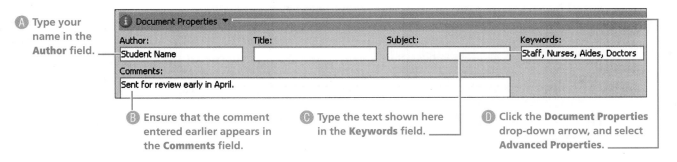

Ⓐ Type your name in the **Author** field.

ⓘ Document Properties ▾

Author: Student Name
Title:
Subject:
Keywords: Staff, Nurses, Aides, Doctors
Comments: Sent for review early in April.

Ⓑ Ensure that the comment entered earlier appears in the **Comments** field.

Ⓒ Type the text shown here in the **Keywords** field.

Ⓓ Click the **Document Properties** drop-down arrow, and select **Advanced Properties.**

6. Follow these steps to review properties and set an additional property:

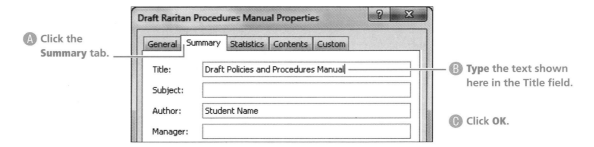

Ⓐ Click the **Summary** tab.

Ⓑ **Type** the text shown here in the Title field.

Ⓒ Click **OK**.

7. Click the **close** button at the right end of the Document Panel to close it.

8. **Save** 💾 changes to the document, and leave it **open**.

Creating a Custom Property

Video Lesson   labyrinthelab.com/videos

Though the properties available for Word are sufficient to record data for most documents, there may be times when you want to store additional data within the document. When there is no existing property to meet your needs, you can create a custom property and define the type of data you plan to place in the field. For example, if you want to include a due date for a document or the version of Word used to create a specific document, you can create a new property and enter the information. You can assign a text, time, or numeric value to custom properties, and you can also assign them the values *yes* or *no* when appropriate. Word provides a list of suggested names for custom fields, but you can also define your own property name.

DEVELOP YOUR SKILLS 13.2.2
Create a Custom Property

In this exercise, you will create a custom property for the Draft Raritan Procedures Manual *to hold the due date for the final version of the document.*

Before You Begin: The Draft Raritan Procedures Manual *should be open.*

1. Choose **File→Info**.

2. Click the **Properties** drop-down arrow, and select **Advanced Properties**.

3. Follow these steps to create a new custom property:

Ⓐ Click the Custom tab.

Ⓑ Type **Due Date** in the **Name** field.

Ⓒ Select **Date** from the **Type** list.

Ⓓ Type **7/31/2011** in the **Value** field.

Ⓔ Click **OK**.

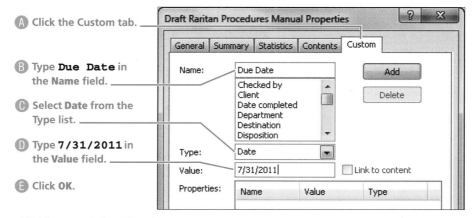

4. **Save** changes to the document and **close** it.

QUICK REFERENCE	MODIFYING PROPERTIES
Task	**Procedures**
Display the Document Panel	▪ Choose File→Info. ▪ Click the Properties list arrow. ▪ Select Show Document Panel.
Display the Document Properties dialog box	▪ Choose File→Info. ▪ Click the Properties list arrow. ▪ Select Advanced Properties. *or* ▪ Display the Document Panel. ▪ Click the Document Properties list arrow in the Document Panel title bar. ▪ Select Advanced Properties.
Add keywords	▪ Display the Document Panel or Document Properties dialog box. ▪ Click the Keywords field, and type the appropriate key words.
Add comments	▪ Display the Document Panel, Document Properties dialog box of Info Properties panel. ▪ Click the Comments field, and type the appropriate text.
Create a custom property	▪ Choose File→Info. ▪ Click Properties, and select Advanced Properties. ▪ Click the Custom tab. ▪ Type a name for the custom field, or select one from the list. ▪ Select a data type from the Type list. ▪ Type the value to assign to the property in the Value box. ▪ Click OK, and then click the File tab to return to the document.

Modifying Document Properties   **509**

13.3 Identifying Research Options

Video Lesson   labyrinthelab.com/videos

Research options in Word enable you to identify reference books and research sites that are available from Microsoft as well as those that are installed on the computer. By default the custom dictionary and thesaurus are active. By setting research options, you can select additional dictionaries, thesauruses, and Internet research sites you need to do your work. Not only do these resources help with standard day-to-day activities, but they can also help with multilingual needs. The Research Options services available depend on the language of the Office 2010 version you are using and any services that have been added to the Office Suite using the Research Options dialog box.

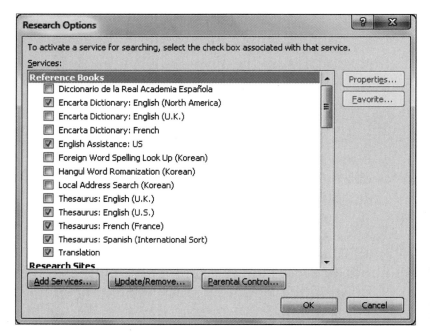

The Research Options dialog box identifies features that are installed as well as other options that are available.

QUICK REFERENCE	ACCESSING RESEARCH OPTIONS
Task	**Procedures**
Display the Research Options Dialog Box	■ Choose Review→Proofing→Research on the Ribbon. ■ Click the Research Options link at the bottom of the Research task pane.

Review Research Options

In this exercise, you will display the Research Options dialog box and identify settings active on your Word installation.

1. Create a **new** blank document and choose **Review→Proofing→Research** on the Ribbon.
   Word displays the Research task pane. The link at the bottom of the task pane is used to open the Research Options dialog box.

2. Click the **Research Options** hyperlink at the bottom of the Research task pane.

3. **Scroll** the dialog box, and review the research options available on your computer.

4. Click the **Cancel** button to close the dialog box and then close the **Research** pane.

13.4 Automating Word Tasks Using Macros

Video Lesson labyrinthelab.com/videos

As you work in Word performing daily tasks, you will soon discover that you repeat the same tasks each day—and sometimes many times during the day. When tasks involve many steps, it is very helpful to automate the tasks. Word and other Microsoft applications contain the Macro tool for capturing steps involved in performing routine tasks. Macros, then, are recorded and saved steps for performing routine tasks. After recording the steps and saving them in a macro, you can run the macro to perform the steps automatically.

For example, you may need to switch to a color printer frequently. You can record the steps of the process in a macro, and when it's time to switch printers, the macro can quickly perform the steps.

Recording Macros

Word's macro recorder records your keystrokes and the commands you issue in much the same way the automatic speed dial feature on telephones records frequently called phone numbers. When you want to call a recorded phone number, you press one or two keys, and the phone dials the number. Similarly, macros can easily play back recorded keystrokes and commands.

The Developer Tab

Basic macro recording and playing tools appear on the View tab of the Ribbon. In addition, a full set of macro tools along with the Visual Basic code access appear on the Developer tab. The Developer tab must be added to the Ribbon using the Word Options dialog box if you want to use it. As you become more familiar with macros and their benefits, you may want to add the Developer tab of the Ribbon.

Macro Storage Locations

Each macro you create will have a name and will be saved for future use. Macros can be stored in documents or templates, including the Normal template. (Remember, the Normal template is Word's default built-in template upon which all new documents are based unless you choose a different template.) The default storage location for macros is the Normal template. Macros stored there are available to all documents on the system.

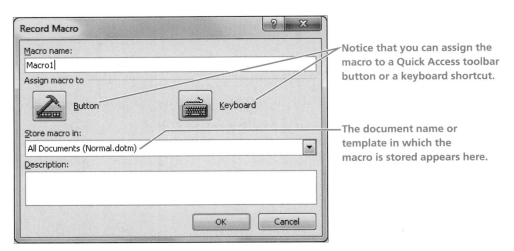

Notice that you can assign the macro to a Quick Access toolbar button or a keyboard shortcut.

The document name or template in which the macro is stored appears here.

The file extension for the Normal template is .dotm. This indicates that the template is macro-enabled.

Recording Limitations

Certain mouse motions such as scrolling, selecting, and resizing windows cannot be recorded in macros. You may also find that certain commands are not available while recording macros; however, you can often overcome these limitations with alternative techniques. For example, instead of scrolling with the mouse (which cannot be recorded), you can use the arrow keys on the keyboard. Macros can record the movement of the insertion point when you use the keyboard. Likewise, instead of selecting text with the mouse, you can press the [Shift] key and use the arrow keys on the keyboard to select text.

When you record a macro that changes settings within a dialog box, the setting normally sticks until you exit Word. As a result, running macros repeatedly using arrow keys to activate an option may, in fact, change the setting to the next option in the dialog box. Care should be taken to record within the macro a return to the original option when necessary.

QUICK REFERENCE	BUILDING MACROS IN WORD
Task	**Procedure**
View Word's built-in macros	▪ Choose View→Macros→Macros from the Ribbon.
	▪ Click the Macros In drop-down list, and choose Word Commands.
	▪ Scroll through the list of commands to ensure that you do not use one of these names for your macros.
Record a macro	▪ Choose View→Macros→Macros→Record Macro from the Ribbon.
	▪ Name the macro. (Macro names cannot contain spaces.)
	▪ Click OK to begin recording.
	▪ Execute the steps you want to include in the macro.
	▪ Choose View→Macros→Macros→Record Macro from the Ribbon.
Display the Developer tab	▪ Choose File→Options→Customize Ribbon.
	▪ Click the Choose Commands From drop-down list, and select Popular Commands.
	▪ Click the Customize the Ribbon drop-down list, and select Main Tabs.
	▪ Place a checkmark in the Developer checkbox, and click OK.

DEVELOP YOUR SKILLS 13.4.1
Record a Macro

In this exercise, you will record a macro that sets up the orientation, margins, and page size for a survey form and insert and format text.

Set Up the Macro

1. If necessary, create a **new** blank document.

2. Choose **View→Macros→Macros menu button→Record Macro** 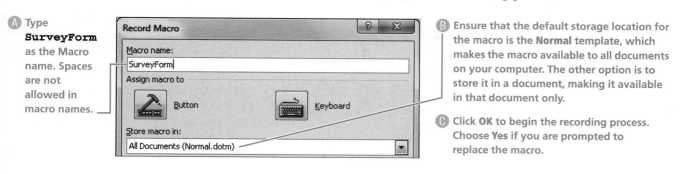 from the Ribbon.

3. Follow these steps to name the macro and begin the recording process:

A Type **SurveyForm** as the Macro name. Spaces are not allowed in macro names.

B Ensure that the default storage location for the macro is the **Normal** template, which makes the macro available to all documents on your computer. The other option is to store it in a document, making it available in that document only.

C Click **OK** to begin the recording process. Choose **Yes** if you are prompted to replace the macro.

The mouse pointer now has a cassette tape attached to it, indicating that Word is recording your steps.

Record the Macro

Now you will simply perform the manual steps you wish to record.

4. Locate **Styles** on the Home tab of the Ribbon, and click the **No Spacing** style in the Quick Styles gallery, as shown in the illustration to the right.
This sets line spacing at 1.0 and removes the after-paragraph spacing.

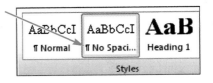

5. Choose **Home→Font→Bold** **B** from the Ribbon.

6. **Type** the title `Raritan Clinic East Pediatric Diagnostic Specialties`.

7. Choose **Page Layout→Page Setup→Orientation** from the Ribbon, and then choose **Landscape** from the menu.

8. Choose **Page Layout→Page Setup→Margins** from the Ribbon, and then choose the **Custom Margins** command at the bottom of the gallery.

9. Set the top and bottom margins to **0.4"** and the left and right margins to **0.5"**.

10. Click the **Paper** tab at the top of the dialog box, and set the width to **7"**, and set the height to **5"**.

11. Click **OK** to apply the settings to the document.

Stop Recording

12. Choose **View→Macros→Macros menu button→Stop Recording** from the Ribbon to turn off the macro recorder.
The macro is now ready for playback.

13. **Close** the document without saving it, and continue with the next topic.

Running Macros

Video Lesson	labyrinthelab.com/videos

FROM THE KEYBOARD

Alt + F8 to open the Macros dialog box

You can run macros in a variety of ways. The method used to run a macro depends on how the macro was assigned during the recording process. You created a macro without assigning it to a toolbar button or shortcut key. For that reason, you must run the macro with the standard procedure shown in the following Quick Reference table. This procedure can be used to run any macro.

QUICK REFERENCE	RUNNING MACROS
Task	**Procedure**
Run a macro from the View tab	■ Choose View→Macros→Macros→View Macros from the Ribbon to open the Macros dialog box.
	■ Choose All Active Templates and Documents from the Macros In drop-down list.
	■ Choose the macro you want to run from the Macro Name list.
	■ Click the Run button to execute the macro.

Run the Macro

In this exercise, you will create a new document and run your macro to change the page setup and enter the title text.

1. Create a **new** blank document.

2. Choose **View→Macros→Macros menu button→View Macros** 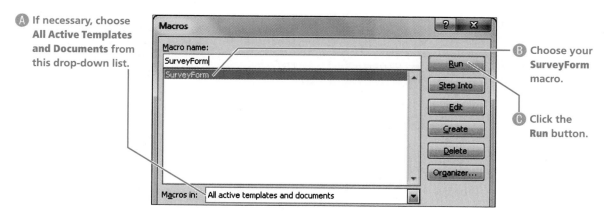 from the Ribbon. *The Macros dialog box opens.*

3. Follow these steps to execute the macro:

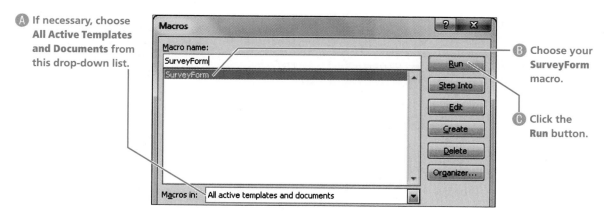

A If necessary, choose **All Active Templates and Documents** from this drop-down list.

B Choose your **SurveyForm** macro.

C Click the **Run** button.

The macro sets up the special paper size and margins and prints the title of the document.

4. **Close** the document without saving it, and create a **new** blank document.

13.5 Using the VBA Editor to Edit Macros

Video Lesson labyrinthelab.com/videos

Visual Basic for Applications (VBA) is a macro programming language that runs in Office 2010 applications. When you record a macro, you are creating a Visual Basic module containing program instructions that execute when you run the macro. This topic provides a brief introduction to Visual Basic, but a complete discussion is beyond the scope of this course.

You can edit a macro by displaying the Visual Basic module and modifying the code. The editor has its own menus, toolbars, and commands which allow you to develop, edit, and test Visual Basic applications. The following illustration shows the programming code from the Survey-Form macro that you just recorded.

Visual Basic Editor menu bar and toolbar

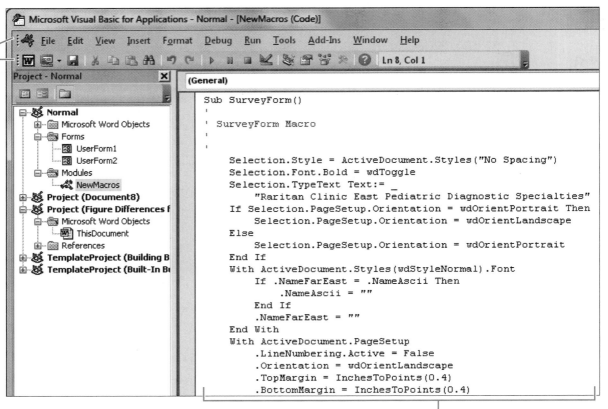

Code compiled as you recorded the macro

QUICK REFERENCE	EDITING A MACRO IN THE VISUAL BASIC MODULE
Task	**Procedure**
Edit a macro	■ Choose View→Macros→Macros→View Macros ⬛ from the Ribbon.
	■ Choose All Active Templates and Documents from the Macros In drop-down list.
	■ Choose the macro you want to edit from the Macro Name list.
	■ Click the Edit button to open the Visual Basic editor window.
	■ Make the editing changes.
	■ Choose File→Close, and Return to Microsoft Word from the menu bar. (The macro is saved automatically.)

Open the Editor and Modify the Code

In this exercise, you will open the Visual Basic editor and revise your macro. Then you will run the modified macro.

1. Choose **View→Macros→Macros menu button→View Macros** ⬚ from the Ribbon to open the Macros dialog box.

2. Follow these steps to begin the editing process:

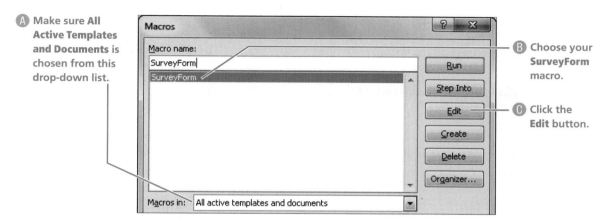

Ⓐ Make sure **All Active Templates and Documents** is chosen from this drop-down list.

Ⓑ Choose your **SurveyForm** macro.

Ⓒ Click the **Edit** button.

3. Follow these steps to modify the code:

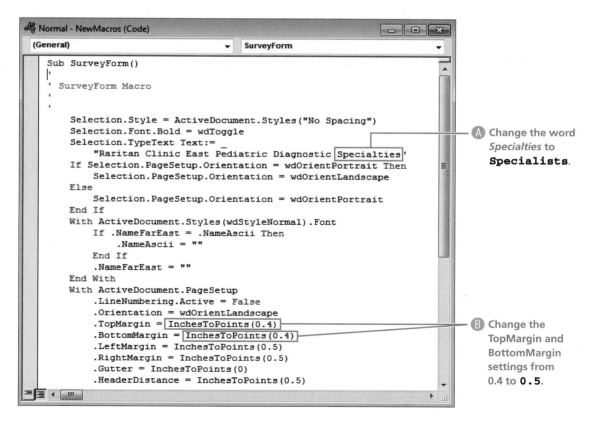

Ⓐ Change the word *Specialties* to **Specialists**.

Ⓑ Change the TopMargin and BottomMargin settings from 0.4 to **0.5**.

4. Choose **File→Close and Return to Microsoft Word** from the menu bar.
   The changes are saved automatically.

Run the Edited Macro

5. Create a **new** blank document and choose **View→Macros→Macros menu button→View Macros** from the Ribbon.

6. Choose **SurveyForm** in the Macro Name list, and then click the **Run** button.
   Notice that the word Specialties *was changed to* Specialists.

7. Choose **Page Layout→Page Setup→Margins** [ ] from the Ribbon.

8. Choose the **Custom Margins** command at the bottom of the gallery.
   Notice that the top and bottom margins are now set to 0.5".

9. **Close** the dialog box.

10. **Close** the document without saving it, and create a **new** blank document.

Running Macros from the Quick Access Toolbar

Video Lesson   labyrinthelab.com/videos

When you create a macro to automate repetitive tasks, you are trying to increase the efficiency with which you work. To make running macros more efficient, you can assign them to a button on the Quick Access Toolbar or to a shortcut combination keystroke. By taking advantage of these time-saving tools, you alleviate the tedium of displaying the Macros dialog box and selecting the macro each time you want to run it.

You can assign a toolbar button or keyboard shortcut to a macro as you record it. In addition, you can assign a button to an existing macro using the Quick Access Toolbar commands in the Word Options dialog box. Word offers numerous button images that you can choose to help keep buttons you create straight.

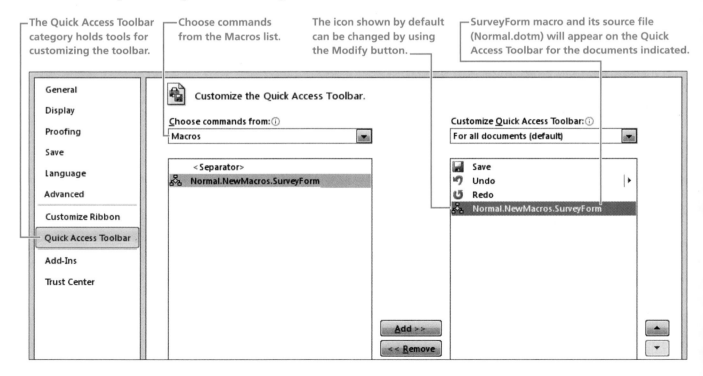

The Quick Access Toolbar category holds tools for customizing the toolbar.

Choose commands from the Macros list.

The icon shown by default can be changed by using the Modify button.

SurveyForm macro and its source file (Normal.dotm) will appear on the Quick Access Toolbar for the documents indicated.

ASSIGNING A MACRO TO A TOOLBAR BUTTON OR TO A KEYBOARD SHORTCUT

Task	Procedure
Record a macro and assign it to a Quick Access toolbar button	■ Choose View→Macros→Macros→Record Macro 🖼 from the Ribbon. ■ Name the macro. ■ Click the Button icon in the Assign Macro To area of the dialog box. ■ Click the macro in the left column to select it. ■ Click the Add button to add the macro to the right column. ■ To change the button image, click the Modify button, choose an icon, modify the Display Name if desired, and click OK twice. ■ Execute the steps you want to include in the macro. ■ Choose Developer→Code→Stop Recording 🖼 from the Ribbon.
Remove a macro button from the Quick Access toolbar	■ Right-click the macro button and choose Remove from Quick Access Toolbar from the menu.
Record a macro and assign it to a keyboard shortcut	■ Choose View→Macros→Macros→Record Macro 🖼 from the Ribbon. ■ Name the macro. ■ Click the Keyboard icon in the Assign Macro To area of the dialog box. ■ In the Commands box, click the macro name to select it. ■ In the Press New Shortcut Key box, type the keystrokes that you want to use as your shortcut. ■ Click the Assign button, and then click the Close button. ■ Execute the steps you want to include in the macro. ■ Choose View→Macros→Macros→Stop Recording 🖼 from the Ribbon.

DEVELOP YOUR SKILLS 13.5.2

Place a Macro Button on the Quick Access Toolbar

In this exercise, you will add the SurveyForm macro to a Quick Access Toolbar button and modify the icon for the macro.

1. Choose **File→Options** 🖼 to open the Word Options dialog box.

2. Click the **Quick Access Toolbar** category.

3. Follow these steps to assign the macro button to the Quick Access toolbar:

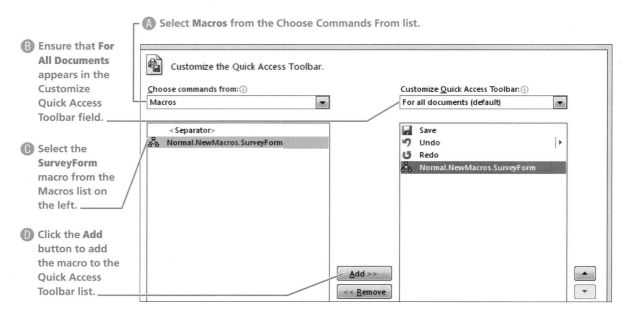

Ⓐ Select **Macros** from the Choose Commands From list.

Ⓑ Ensure that **For All Documents** appears in the Customize Quick Access Toolbar field.

Ⓒ Select the **SurveyForm** macro from the Macros list on the left.

Ⓓ Click the **Add** button to add the macro to the Quick Access Toolbar list.

4. Click the **Modify** button at the bottom of the dialog box to open the Modify Button dialog box.

5. Follow these steps to assign a button image:

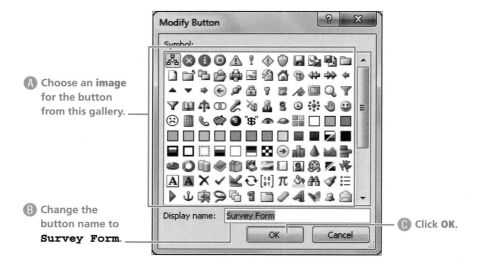

Ⓐ Choose an **image** for the button from this gallery.

Ⓑ Change the button name to **Survey Form**.

Ⓒ Click **OK**.

6. Click **OK** again to close the Word Options dialog box.
   Notice that your button appears on the Quick Access toolbar.

Test the Macro Button

7. Create a **new** document.

8. Hover the **mouse pointer** over the new macro button on the Quick Access toolbar.
   Notice that the name for the macro appears in a pop-up.

9. Click the **button** to execute the macro.
   The macro formats the document.

10. Leave the document **open** for the next exercise.

Deleting Macros

Video Lesson   labyrinthelab.com/videos

You may create a macro for use in a special project, and when the project is complete, you no longer need the macro. Deleting a macro when it's no longer required helps keep the list of macros in the Macros dialog box from becoming unwieldy.

QUICK REFERENCE	DELETING A MACRO
Task	**Procedure**
Deleting a macro	■ Choose View→Macros→Macro→View Macros 📇 from the Ribbon.
	■ Choose All Active Templates and Documents from the Macros In drop-down list.
	■ Choose the macro to be deleted.
	■ Click the Delete button.

DEVELOP YOUR SKILLS 13.5.3
Delete a Macro

In this exercise, you will delete the macro you created in the last exercise.

1. Choose **View→Macros→Macros menu button→ViewMacros** 📇 from the Ribbon to open the Macros dialog box.

2. Choose **All Active Templates and Documents** from the Macros In drop-down list.

3. Choose the **SurveyForm** macro in the Macro Name list.

4. Click the **Delete** button.

5. Click **Yes** to verify that you want to delete the macro.

6. **Close** the dialog box.

Remove the Button from the Quick Access Toolbar

7. **Right-click** the macro button on the Quick Access toolbar, and choose **Remove from Quick Access Toolbar**.

Restoring Default Settings

Video Lesson   labyrinthelab.com/videos

Setting custom options for the way you work is a great practice for a computer that is devoted to you and your work. However, when you are working on a public computer or share a computer with others, it is generally a good idea to restore the default settings you have changed. By restoring the options to their original status, you also get a quick review of the features just covered.

Retrieve the list of default settings you wrote down as you modified the Word options earlier in this lesson.

DEVELOP YOUR SKILLS 13.5.4
Restore Default Settings

In this exercise, you restore default settings for Word options and Backstage view.

1. Choose **File→Recent**, and ensure that the **Quickly Access This Number of Recent Documents** checkbox at the bottom of the list is unchecked.

2. Choose **File→Options**, and click the **General** category.

3. Remove the text from the **User Name** and **Initials** text boxes, and **type** the original text replaced earlier.

4. Click the **Advanced** category, and scroll down advanced options to the **Display** area.

5. Change the **Show This Number of Recent Documents** setting to 22 or the number you replaced earlier in this lesson.

6. Scroll further down the advanced options list to the **General** area, and click the **File Locations** button.

7. Follow these steps to reset the file location for documents:

Ⓐ Ensure that **Documents** is selected.

Ⓑ Click **Modify**.

Ⓒ Navigate to **Desktop→ Documents→My Documents** or the original file locations replaced earlier in this lesson.

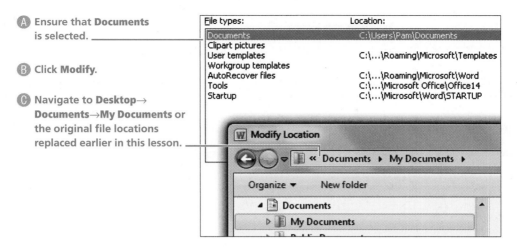

8. Click **OK** to close each of the dialog boxes that are open, **close** all open documents, and **exit** Word.

13.6 Concepts Review

Concepts Review   labyrinthelab.com/word10

To check your knowledge of the key concepts introduced in this lesson, complete the Concepts Review quiz by going to the URL listed above. If your classroom is using Labyrinth eLab, you may complete the Concepts Review quiz from within your eLab course.

Reinforce Your Skills

Record a Section Break Macro

In this exercise, you will create a macro that inserts a section break and formats the title page with different page setup options than the remaining pages. You will assign the macro to shortcut keys.

Assign the Macro to a Keyboard Shortcut

1. Create a **new** document.

2. If necessary, choose **Home→Paragraph→Show/Hide** ¶ from the Ribbon to display formatting characters.

3. Choose **View→Macros→Macros menu button→Record Macro** 📇 from the Ribbon.

4. Follow these steps to name the macro and begin assigning it to a keyboard shortcut:

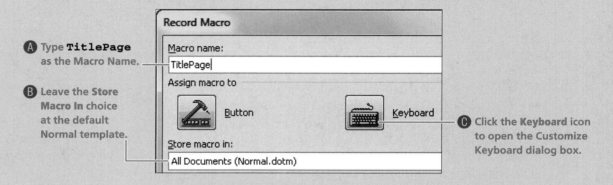

A Type **TitlePage** as the Macro Name.

B Leave the **Store Macro In** choice at the default Normal template.

C Click the **Keyboard** icon to open the Customize Keyboard dialog box.

5. Follow these steps to assign shortcut keys to the macro:

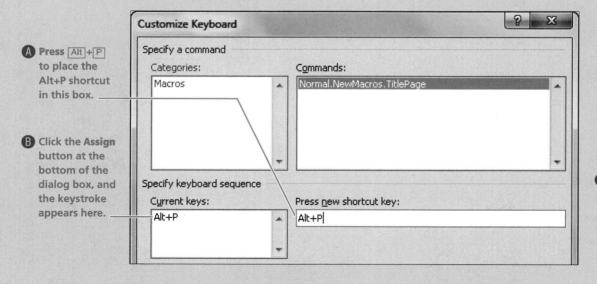

A Press Alt + P to place the Alt+P shortcut in this box.

B Click the **Assign** button at the bottom of the dialog box, and the keystroke appears here.

C Click the **Close** button, and the macro recorder begins recording your actions.

Record the Macro

6. Choose **Page Layout→Page Setup→Breaks** 📇 from the Ribbon, and then choose **Next Page** from the menu.

7. **Press** [Ctrl]+[Home] to position the insertion point on the first page.

8. Choose **Page Layout→Page Setup**, and click the **dialog box launcher** 🔲 in the bottom-right corner of the Page Setup group.
   The Page Setup dialog box appears.

9. Make the following settings in the dialog box:
   - Ensure that the **Margins** tab is in the foreground, and type **1.25** in the left and right margin boxes.
   - Switch to the **Layout** tab, and in the Headers and Footers section of the Layout tab, click the **Different First Page** checkbox. (This breaks the link between the two sections.)
   - Click the **Page Vertical Alignment** drop-down list, and select **Center**.

10. Click **OK** in the Page Setup dialog box to apply the changes to the document.

11. Locate **Styles** on the Ribbon, and then choose the **Title** style from the Quick Styles gallery.

12. Choose **View→Macros→Macros menu button→Stop Recording** ⬜ from the Ribbon.

Run the Macro

13. **Close** the document without saving it, and create a new document.

14. **Press** [Alt]+[P] to run the TitlePage macro.
    Remember, macros saved in the Normal template are available to all new documents that are based on the Normal template.

15. Type **Quarterly Report** on the title page.
    The title should be formatted with the Title style.

Add a Header in Section Two

16. **Press** [Ctrl]+[End] to position the insertion point in the second section.

17. Choose **Insert→Header & Footer→Header** 📄 from the Ribbon, and then choose **Edit Header** at the bottom of the gallery.

18. Type **Vogel Corporation** in the header area, and then **press** [Esc] to close the header area.

19. Scroll to the **title page**, and notice that the header does not appear there.
    With the Different First Page option set by the macro, this macro could be conveniently used to set up documents requiring a title page.

Delete the Macro

20. Choose **View→Macros→Macros menu button→View Macros** 📇 from the Ribbon.

21. Choose **TitlePage** from the list, and then click the **Delete** button.

22. Click **Yes** to verify that you want to delete the macro, and then **close** the dialog box.

23. **Save** 💾 the file as **rs-Vogel Quarterly Report** in your Lesson 13 folder, and then **close** it.

Record a Page Border Macro

In this exercise, you will record a macro that applies a page border to a document, and you will assign the macro to a shortcut key.

Record the Macro

1. If necessary, create a **new** document.

2. Choose **View→Macros→Macros menu button→Record Macro** 🔳 from the Ribbon.

3. Name the macro **PageBorder**, and click the **Keyboard** icon in the dialog box to open the Customize Keyboard dialog box.

Assign Shortcut Keys

4. **Press** Alt + M in the Press New Shortcut Key box, and then click the **Assign** button at the bottom of the dialog box.

5. **Close** the dialog box.

Record the Macro

6. Choose **Home→Paragraph→Borders** 🔳 ▾ **menu ▾** from the Ribbon, and choose the **Borders and Shading** command at the bottom of the gallery.

7. When the Borders and Shading dialog box appears, click the **Page Border** tab.

8. Scroll down the Style list, and choose the **first** double line style in the gallery.

9. Choose a border color from the **Color** drop-down list, and choose $1^1/_2$ pt from the **Width** drop-down list.

10. Click **OK** to close the dialog box and apply the border.

Stop the Recorder and Test the Macro

11. Choose **View→Macros→Macros menu button→Stop Recording** 🔳 from the Ribbon.

12. **Close** the document without saving it.

13. Create a **new** document, and then **press** Alt + M to execute the macro and apply the border.

14. **Save** the document as **rs-Border Macro** in the Lesson 13 folder.

Delete the Macro

15. Choose **View→Macros→Macros menu button→View Macros** 🔳 from the Ribbon.

16. Choose **PageBorder** from the list, and then click the **Delete** button.

17. Click **Yes** to confirm the deletion.

18. **Close** the dialog box, and **close** the document.

Customize Show/Hide and Add Language

In this exercise, you will set the Show/Hide feature so that paragraph symbols are automatically shown and also add a new language to Word.

1. Choose **File→Options** to open the Word Options dialog box.

2. Click the **Display** category, and check the **Paragraph Marks** checkbox.

3. Click the **Languages** category, and locate the **Choose Editing Languages** settings.

4. Click the **Add Additional Editing Language** drop-down arrow.

5. Scroll the list of languages, and select **French (France)**.

6. Click the **Add** button to add the language.

7. Click **OK** to set the changes, and then click **OK** to acknowledge the message box.

8. Follow the directions of your instructor to restore default settings, if necessary.

Enter Comments and Other Document Properties

In this exercise, you will add a comment to the document properties for a document you created.

1. Open the rs-Vogel Quarterly Report document you created in Reinforce Your Skills 13.1.

2. Choose **File→Info**, and review document properties.

3. Add the following comment to the **Comments** field in the Properties pane of the Info window: **This document was formatted using a macro**.

4. Click the **Title** property box, and type **Quarterly Report** in the text box.

5. Ensure that your name is shown as the author, and then click the **Add an Author** text box and type your instructor's name as another author.

6. **Save** changes to the document.

7. Choose **File→Print**, click the **Print All Pages** drop-down list, and select **Document Properties**.

8. Click the **Print** button to print the properties in a table.

Apply Your Skills

Record and Play a Macro

In this exercise, you will create a macro to set up legal-size paper.

1. **Record** a macro named **LegalPage** which records the following options:
   - Set up the paper to Legal 8.5 × 14.
   - Use the ruler to set a custom center-aligned tab stop at the 3.25-inch position and a right-aligned custom tab stop at the 6.5 position.

2. **Stop** the macro recording, and **close** the document without saving it.

3. **Play** back the macro, verify that it functions correctly, and then close the file without saving it.

4. Ask your instructor or a lab assistant to watch as you run the macro, and then initial that the macro works as it should. _____

5. **Delete** the macro.

Record a Header Macro and Assign to a Button

In this exercise, you will create a new macro that is designed to create a header and enter header text. You will assign the macro to a Quick Access Toolbar button.

1. Create a **new** blank document, create a new macro named **Header**, and assign the macro to the Quick Access Toolbar using the icon of your choice.

2. Store the macro in the **Normal** template, and record the macro so that it performs these actions:
   - Inserts a header containing the text **Geneva Health Care** on the left and **Human Resources** on the right.
   - Formats the header text using a dark red color and places a border below the header text.

3. Test the macro on a new blank document, and ask your instructor or lab assistant to test the macro for you and initial this exercise. _____

4. **Print** a copy of the document created using the macro, and then **close** the document without saving it.

5. **Delete** the macro.

Exploring Additional Customizations

In this exercise, you will explore additional Word options and identify which settings you would change.

1. Display the **Word Options** dialog box and explore each category of options.

2. Identify at least three categories containing settings that you would like to change.

3. Create a **new** document named **as-Personal Customizations for Your Name**, substituting your name as indicated, and save the document in the Lesson 13 folder.

4. List at least **three** categories containing settings you would change, and enter the settings within each category that you would like to change. Include a reason for your choices.

5. **Print** a copy of the document you create.

Critical Thinking & Work-Readiness Skills

In the course of working through the following Microsoft Office-based Critical Thinking exercises, you will also be utilizing various work-readiness skills, some of which are listed next to each exercise. Go to labyrinthelab.com/workreadiness *to learn more about the work-readiness skills.*

13.1 Locate Medical Research Sources

WORK-READINESS SKILLS APPLIED

- Acquiring and evaluating information
- Improving or designing systems
- Selecting technology

Secretaries and other staff at Raritan Clinic East have asked to have medical terms, equipment names, and medications added to their custom dictionaries. To reduce the time required to enter numerous terms, James Elliott has asked that you search online for available medical dictionaries that might be integrated with Word 2010 to accomplish the task. Locate at least three medical dictionary resources that can be integrated with Word to provide the information the office staff needs. Create a new Word document named **ct-Word Research Resources** listing the three resources and save it to the Lesson 13 folder. Include a description of each resource along with specific instructions for adding the resource to Word's Research Options. Print a copy of the document.

13.2 Creating a Macro

WORK-READINESS SKILLS APPLIED

- Improving or designing systems
- Applying technology to a task
- Using computers to process information

James Elliott discovers that he can create his own letterhead on the letters he sends that includes the Raritan Clinic East logo. He wants to automate this task using a macro and asks for your help. Create a macro named **Letterhead** that places letterhead information into the header of a standard sheet of paper. Include the RaritanClinic.jpg logo (Lesson 13 folder) and the company name, address, and telephone number in the letterhead. Use your school address as the clinic address and your phone number as the clinic phone number. Print a copy of the document and email the electronic file to your instructor for testing of the macro. Delete the macro when you are finished.

13.3 Create Table Macros

WORK-READINESS SKILLS APPLIED

- Improving or designing systems
- Applying technology to a task
- Using computers to process information

Each week James Elliott sets up a work schedule for the Raritan Clinic East office staff using a Word table. He wants you to set up a macro to generate the table automatically each week. Create the macro named **Schedule** that meets the following criteria:

- Use landscape orientation with the title **Work Schedule** centered across the first table row and the words **Week of** in the second row below the title.

- **Sunday** through **Saturday** should appear in additional columns for row three with employee names down the first column for **Cesar, Javier, Max, Angel, Karen, Ana**.

Verify that the macro works and save the document generated by the macro as **ct-Schedule** in the Lesson 13 folder. Print a copy of the document and then delete the Schedule macro.

Integrating Word with Excel, PowerPoint, and the Web

LESSON OUTLINE

LEARNING OBJECTIVES

After studying this lesson, you will be able to:

- Embed and link Excel objects in Word
- Use an Excel worksheet as a Mail Merge data file
- Create Word outlines from PowerPoint presentations
- Create PowerPoint presentations from Word outlines
- Convert Word documents to web pages

One advantage to using a suite of applications is that they are designed to share data and information and to work together seamlessly. This advantage enables you to save time by using data that was created in one application in other documents or files. As a result, you can display data originally stored in an Excel worksheet in a Word document or send an outline of a Word document to PowerPoint to create a new presentation. You can also send data from a Word document to create an Excel worksheet or open a Word document in PowerPoint to create a new presentation and use the text to create and format a supporting document. In addition, you can use Word to format data for posting on the web so that it can be viewed using a web browser. In this lesson, you will explore the features available in Word that make integrating data from other Office applications more efficient and format documents as web pages.

Multitasking Using Word, Excel, and PowerPoint

James Elliott is an administrative assistant at Raritan Clinic East. A clinic advisory committee meets quarterly to review the budget and clinic activities. In preparation for an upcoming meeting, James will help prepare the quarterly expense report. The data is in an Excel worksheet, so James plans to use the Excel data in the report he prepares in Word. He plans to add the chart contained in the Excel file to the report and to prepare a PowerPoint presentation using the clinic's Annual Report. He will generate a letter to all committee members and use the Excel name and address file to address the letters. Finally, he will format the report for posting to the clinic website for others to review.

Pediatric Diagnostic Specialists

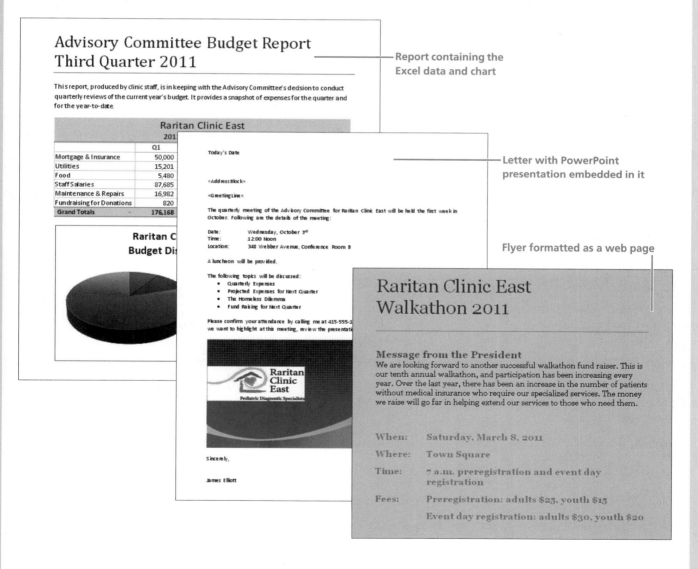

Report containing the Excel data and chart

Letter with PowerPoint presentation embedded in it

Flyer formatted as a web page

14.1 Embedding and Linking Excel Objects

Video Lesson labyrinthelab.com/videos

In the early days of sophisticated personal computer software, some programs tried to combine the capabilities of word processing, database, worksheet, and presentation programs into one application. Inevitably, these programs could rarely perform all of their functions as well as programs dedicated to one purpose.

When you use individual programs that are part of a suite distributed by the same company, you will find that you can share data and information among other programs in a suite as well as with select programs created by other companies. As a result, you will be able to create and store data using a program designed to perform the specialized task and then use the data from the file in other programs. With Office 2010 and most earlier Office applications, you can, for example, place Excel data in Word documents as separate objects and then edit the data in Word.

Defining *Objects*

Object is a term for an element that you share between files and applications. For example, you can embed or link an Excel worksheet object or chart object in a Word document, which may be helpful if you are writing a financial report.

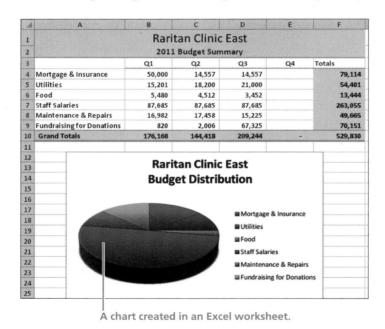

A chart created in an Excel worksheet.

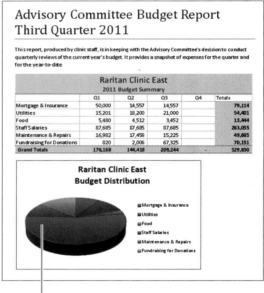

The same chart placed in a Word document.

Comparing Linking to Embedding

Two terms often associated with data sharing between computer programs are *linking* and *embedding*. While these two terms both indicate a sharing of data, they are distinctly different.

- *Embedded objects* are static copies of the data or information contained in the original or source file, such as an Excel chart. Changes that occur in the original file have no effect on the embedded chart or data.

- Linked objects are data, information, charts, etc., created in other applications (such as Excel) and placed in files created in other applications (such as Word) maintaining the tie between the object and its original source. Changes made to the original file can be reflected in the file to which they are linked.

This·report,·produced·by·clinic·staff,·is·in·keeping·with·the·Adv
quarterly·reviews·of·the·current·year's·budget.··It·provides·a·s
for·the·year·to·date.¶

	Raritan Clinic E	
	2011 Budget Summ	
	Q1	Q2
Mortgage & Insurance	50,000	14,557
Utilities	15,201	18,200
Food	5,480	4,512
Staff Salaries	87,685	87,685
Maintenance & Repairs	16,982	17,458
Fundraising for Donations	820	2,006
Grand Totals	176,168	144,418

Linked and embedded objects appear in documents as objects with sizing handles on the corners and sides.

Embedding Objects

When you are working on a Word document and want to include data from a file created in another application or from another Word document, you can embed the object so that the data included will remain the same regardless of changes made to the original (source) file. Embedded data in a Word document affects the size of the document. Embedded files eliminate worry about where the source file is stored. Linked files require that the source file be available each time you open the Word document for easy access to the data.

Linking or Embedding Procedures

Whether you are linking to or embedding files in Word documents, Word offers two basic techniques for inserting data from other files.

- **Copy/Paste**—Using this procedure, you open the file in its source application (such as Excel), select the data you want to include in the Word document, and copy the data to the clipboard. You can then paste it directly into the Word document at the position it should occupy. This procedure is useful when you want to include only a portion of a file in a document.

- **Insert Object**—Using the Insert Object command on the Insert→Text tab of the Ribbon, you actually select the file that contains the data you want to include. If you are embedding the data, you can then delete any extraneous data you want to omit when the data appears in Word. If you are linking, however, you would want to make no changes to the file in Word because it would modify the source file as well. This procedure is useful when you want to include an entire file in a document.

USING LINKING OR EMBEDDING	
Feature	**When to Use**
Linking	When you want to show the most up-to-date data in a presentation or document and the data source file changes regularly
Embedding	When you want to show the data from another source file as a snapshot of the data on a specific date or time

Embed an Excel Object in a Word Document

In this exercise, you will embed *an Excel worksheet in a Word document and test its static nature.*

1. **Maximize** Word, and create a **new** blank document.

2. **Type** the following heading lines:

   Advisory Committee Budget Report

   Third Quarter 2011

3. **Press** ⌷Enter⌷ after typing the heading lines, and then select both heading lines.

4. Choose **Home→Styles→More** ⌷▼⌷ button on the Quick Styles gallery, and choose the **Title** style.

5. Position the **insertion point** in the blank line below the heading lines, and **type** the following introductory paragraph:

   This report, produced by Clinic staff, is in keeping with the Advisory Committee's decision to conduct quarterly reviews of the current year's budget. It provides a snapshot of expenses for the quarter and for the year-to-date.

6. **Press** ⌷Enter⌷ after typing the paragraph.

Insert an Excel Object

7. Choose **Insert→Text→Object** 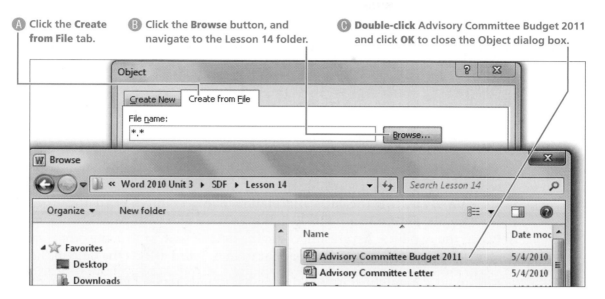 to display the Object dialog box.

8. Follow these steps to identify the Excel file from which to embed the data:

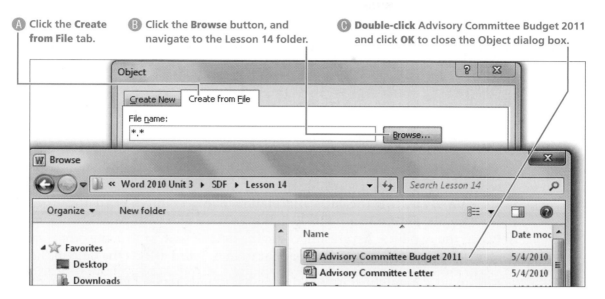

Ⓐ Click the **Create from File** tab. Ⓑ Click the **Browse** button, and navigate to the Lesson 14 folder. Ⓒ **Double-click** Advisory Committee Budget 2011 and click **OK** to close the Object dialog box.

9. **Save** the document in the Lesson 14 folder using the filename **Advisory Committee Budget Report**.

Modify the Source File

10. Launch **Excel**, and **open** the Advisory Committee Budget 2011.xlsx file.

11. Follow these steps to edit a value in the source Excel file:

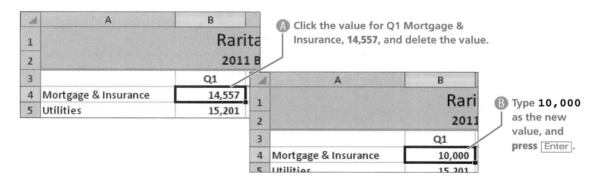

Ⓐ Click the value for Q1 Mortgage & Insurance, **14,557**, and delete the value.

Ⓑ Type **10,000** as the new value, and press ⌷Enter⌷.

12. Switch to **Word**, and verify that the value for Q1 Mortgage & Insurance remains 14,557. *Because the table is embedded in the document, the data in Word is not affected by changes made to the Excel file in Excel.*

13. Switch back to **Excel**, and click the **Undo** 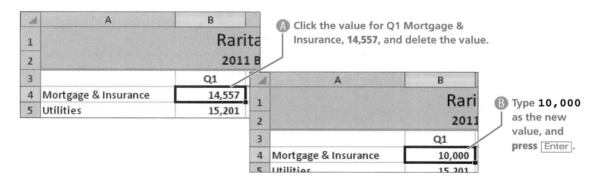 button to return the value for Q1 to its original amount.

Delete the Embedded Data

Because you want the report to reflect the most recent data contained in the worksheet, you will now delete the embedded object and link a file in the next exercise.

14. Switch back to **Word**, click the **embedded worksheet and chart objects** in the document, and **press** [Delete] to remove it from the document.

15. **Save** changes to the document, and leave it and the Excel file **open** for the next exercise.

Linking Objects

Video Lesson   labyrinthelab.com/videos

When you *link* data from another application such as Excel or PowerPoint to a Word document, the original data or information resides in Excel or PowerPoint or whatever program was used to create the original file. This file is known as the *source* file because it is the source of the data. By placing the data, information, or object into a Word document, the Word document becomes the *destination* file. By linking source files with Word documents, you create a tie between the two files. As a result, changing data or text, or in some other way modifying the source data from either the source application or Word affects the data in the other file.

For example, you might start working on a quarterly report before the end of the quarter, and if there is a linked chart in the report, it updates with the current information as the numbers change in Excel. That way, updates are centralized, and you don't have to keep track of making changes in two places.

Word offers three distinct ways to link files added to Word documents. They include:

- Inserting Objects and checking the Link checkbox
- Using Paste Special
- Using the Paste Options Smart Tag

Inserting a Linked Object

When you want to link an entire object to a Word document, you can use the Insert Object command on the Ribbon. The link option appears in the Object dialog box, as shown here.

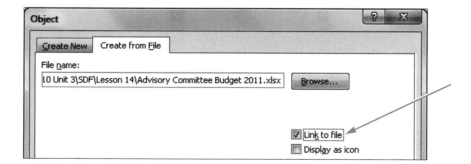

Linking Objects with Paste Special

The second procedure for linking files is to use the Paste Special command, as shown in the following illustration.

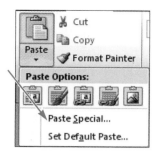

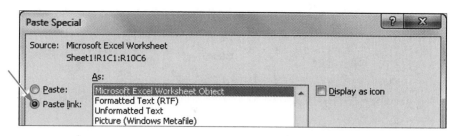

Choosing the Paste Special command opens the Paste Special dialog box.

The Paste Special dialog box contains the Paste Link command, which links the pasted object to the document in which it was created, the source document.

Linking Objects Using Paste Options Smart Tags

The Paste Options smart tags contain menu options for linking objects to their original documents. These paste options vary, depending on the object you are pasting. For example, when you paste *Excel data* into a Word document, the following Paste Options buttons and menu appears.

Numerous Paste Options are available.

Icons containing the link chain identify options for linking.

Icons that display vary depending on which program was used to create the source file. Point to each Paste Options button shown in the menu and read the ToolTip to determine which button to choose.

When you paste an *Excel chart,* the Paste Options smart tags offer a different series of menu choices.

Numerous Paste Options are available.

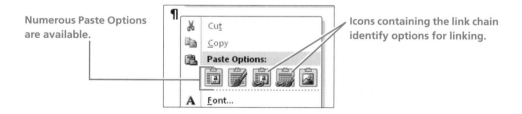

Icons containing the link chain identify options for linking.

Regardless of what you are pasting, Word displays the data or object in the document as you point to each Paste Options button. This enables you to view the data as it would appear if you click that button.

Task	Procedure
Insert an embedded object	■ In Word, choose Insert→Text→Object [icon]. ■ Click the Create from File tab, and then click the Browse button. ■ Navigate to the file you want to insert, and double-click the filename. ■ Click OK
Insert a linked object	■ In Word, choose Insert→Text→Object [icon]. ■ Click the Create from File tab, and then click the Browse button. ■ Navigate to the file you want to insert, and double-click the file name. ■ Check the Link to File checkbox, and click OK.
Link an object using Paste Special	■ In the source document, select and copy the data or object to be linked. ■ Switch to the destination document, and choose Home→Clipboard→Paste menu ▼ from the Ribbon. ■ Choose Paste Special from the menu. ■ Choose Paste Link in the Paste Special dialog box.
Link Excel data in Word using the Paste Options smart tag	■ In the source document, select and copy the data to be linked. ■ Switch to the destination document, and right-click the location where the file should appear. ■ Click the Link & Keep Source Formatting paste option button. *or* ■ Click the Link & Use Destination Styles paste option button.
Link an Excel chart in Word using the Paste Options smart tag	■ In the source document, select and copy the chart to be linked. ■ Switch to the destination document, and right-click the location where the chart should appear. ■ Click the Keep Source Formatting and Link Data paste option button. *or* ■ Click the Use Destination Theme & Link Data paste options button.

Link Excel Data to a Word Document

In this exercise, you will link Excel worksheet data to a Word document using Paste Special. You will then modify the Excel worksheet and review how the changes update the Word document. Then you will link an Excel chart to a Word document using the Paste Options smart tag.

Before You Begin: The Advisory Committee Budget 2011.xlsx file should be open in Excel, and the Advisory Committee Budget Report should be open in Word.

1. Switch to **Excel** and then follow these steps to select and copy the Excel data to add to the Word document:

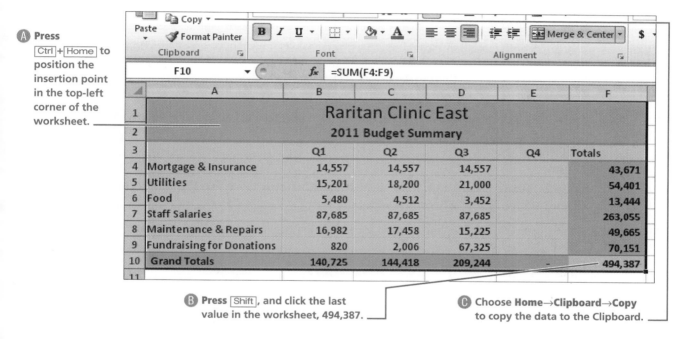

A Press
Ctrl+Home to position the insertion point in the top-left corner of the worksheet.

B Press Shift, and click the last value in the worksheet, 494,387.

C Choose **Home→Clipboard→Copy** to copy the data to the Clipboard.

2. Switch to **Word,** and position the **insertion point** at the end of the document.

Link an Excel Table in Word

3. Choose **Home→Clipboard→Paste** menu ▼ from the Ribbon, and choose **Paste Special** from the menu.
   The Paste special dialog box appears.

4. Follow these steps to paste the object:

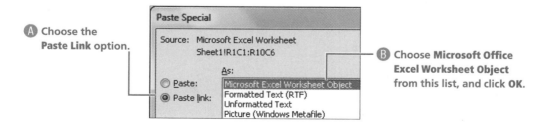

A Choose the **Paste Link** option.

B Choose **Microsoft Office Excel Worksheet Object** from this list, and click **OK.**

Edit the Excel Worksheet

5. Switch to **Excel**, and **press** Esc to remove the marquee surrounding the table.
   The marquee in Excel identifies the cells copied.

6. Click the **cell** containing the Q4 data for Mortgage & Insurance (E4).

7. Type the Q4 projections shown at right, **pressing** Enter after typing each number.
   The formulas in the Totals cells automatically update as you enter the data.

Q4
11,337
1,750
4,975
17,685
2,543
1,529

8. Switch back to **Word**.
   Notice that the linked table updated with the additions you made in the Q4 column. If the Excel table failed to update on your computer, right-click the Excel object, and select Update Link.

9. Position the **insertion point** on the blank line below the worksheet data, and **press** Enter twice.

Link an Excel Chart in Word

10. Switch to **Excel**, click the **Sheet2** tab at the bottom of the Excel window, and click the border of the **pie chart** once to select it.

11. Choose **Home→Clipboard→Copy** from the Ribbon.

12. Choose **Home→Clipboard→Paste menu button** from the Ribbon and then choose **Paste Special** from the menu.

13. Follow these steps to paste a link for the chart object:

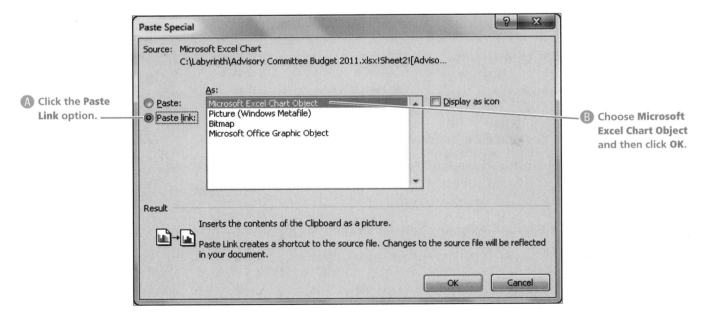

Ⓐ Click the **Paste Link** option.

Ⓑ Choose **Microsoft Excel Chart Object** and then click **OK**.

No noticeable difference will show when you paste the chart because the theme used in the Excel worksheet is similar to the one used in the Word document.

14. **Save** the Word document, and leave it **open** for the next topic.

15. **Exit** Excel, **saving** changes if prompted.

Opening Excel Objects from Word Documents

Video Lesson   labyrinthelab.com/videos

When data or objects from other sources are linked to Word documents, you can open source application tools directly from the Word document and use these tools to edit the object. There are several ways to activate these tools. These procedures assume that an Excel object and chart are linked to a document.

- Double-click either the worksheet data object or the chart to launch or switch to Excel for making edits.

- Right-click the chart and choose Edit Data to launch or switch to Excel for editing data in Excel.

- Click the chart to open the Excel Chart Tools in the Word Ribbon to make formatting changes to the chart directly in Word without modifying the look of the chart in Excel.

DEVELOP YOUR SKILLS 14.1.3
Launch Excel from Objects in Word

In this exercise, you will launch Excel from within Word, and then you will use Live Preview with the Excel Chart Tools from within Word to review potential formatting changes.

Open the Excel Window from the Worksheet Object

1. **Double-click** anywhere in the Excel worksheet object to switch to the Excel file.
   At this stage, you could make editing changes that would be reflected in the Word document.

2. In **Excel**, click in the Q1 cell for Staff Salaries (cell B7), type **1000**, and **press** ⎡Enter⎤.

3. Switch to **Word** and ensure that the data and chart both updated.
   If your table or chart failed to update, right-click the Excel object and choose Update Link from the menu.

4. Switch to **Excel** and click **Undo** 🔙 on the Quick Access toolbar.
   The chart and the worksheet data update to their original values.

Live Preview Format Changes in the Chart in Word

5. Switch to **Word,** and click the frame surrounding the chart to **select** the chart area background.
   Observe the Chart Tools tabs—Design, Layout, and Format—on the Ribbon.

6. Choose **Format→Shape Styles→Shape Fill** 🎨 **menu ▾** from the Ribbon.

7. Hover the **mouse pointer** over several different colors, and Live Preview displays the effects as they impact the chart area background color.

8. **Press** ⎡Esc⎤ to close the gallery.

9. **Press** ⎡Esc⎤ again to close the Chart Tools tabs on the Ribbon.

10. **Save** changes to the Word document, and **close** it.

Using the Links Dialog Box

Video Lesson labyrinthelab.com/videos

As you have already seen, when data in a linked object changes and the Word document containing the data is open on your computer, you must update the linked data. As you might imagine, edits to Excel files and other files containing data you may have linked to a document will often be edited without thinking about having to update the links contained in the documents. To remind you that data is linked to a document, each time you open a document containing linked data, you are prompted to update the data. When the data source file is unavailable, you may need to break the link so that the data contained in the document is the data that is shown. Breaking a link prevents further updates to the data in the document.

In addition, sometimes the data you link to a document may come from the wrong source file. In this case, the link to the data you want to include in the document needs to be modified to pull the data from the correct source file.

The Links dialog box makes editing links, breaking links, and updating links more efficient.

This option allows you to break the link when you no longer want to keep the destination document updated.

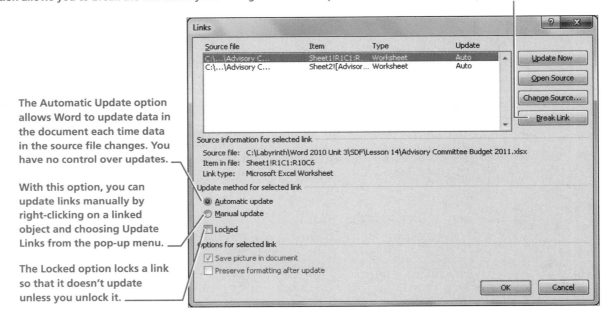

The Automatic Update option allows Word to update data in the document each time data in the source file changes. You have no control over updates.

With this option, you can update links manually by right-clicking on a linked object and choosing Update Links from the pop-up menu.

The Locked option locks a link so that it doesn't update unless you unlock it.

Task	Procedure
Open the Links dialog box via a pop-up menu	■ Right-click a linked worksheet object, and choose Linked Worksheet Object from the menu and Links from the submenu.
Automatic update	■ In the destination document, right-click the linked worksheet, and choose Linked Worksheet Object→Links.
	■ Choose a link in the Source File list.
	■ Choose the Automatic Update option button in the Update Method for Selected Link area of the dialog box.
	or
	■ Open the destination document after changes are made in the source document, and when the message appears asking if you want to update links, click Yes.
Manual update	■ In the destination document, right-click the linked worksheet, and choose Linked Worksheet Object→Links.
	■ Choose a link in the Source File list.
	■ Choose Manual Update in the Update Method for Selected Link area of the dialog box.
	■ To update the destination document, right-click the linked worksheet object, and choose Update Link from the menu.
	NOTE! Because the chart in Excel is automatically linked to the data from which it was generated, it will update when changes are made in the associated data; therefore, the linked chart image in the destination document will update.
Update locked	■ In the destination document, right-click the linked worksheet, and choose Linked Worksheet Object→Links.
	■ Choose a link in the Source File list.
	■ Choose Locked in the Update Method for Selected Link area of the dialog box. (The selected link will not update unless you unlock it.)

DEVELOP YOUR SKILLS 14.1.4

Update Links When Opening a Word Document

In this exercise, you will modify the linked Excel file and observe the prompt to update links when you open the Word document.

1. Switch to **Excel**, click **cell C4** to select it, type **50000**, and **press** Enter.
   You're typing an overly large number so that changes in the associated charts will be easy to see.

2. **Open** the Advisory Committee Budget Report document containing the linked objects.

3. When the message appears prompting you to update links, click **Yes**.
   Observe the change in the worksheet data and in the chart.

4. **Save** the Word file, and leave it **open** for the next topic. Also leave Excel **open**.

Breaking the Link

Video Lesson   labyrinthelab.com/videos

You can break the link between a linked object and its source document. Once the final figures for a period are in, you may want to break the link between Word and Excel so that the Word report always reflects the closing numbers for that period. The Break Link button in the Links dialog box provides that option.

DEVELOP YOUR SKILLS 14.1.5
Break the Link to Excel

In this exercise, you will break the links in Word that link to the worksheet data and the chart. Then you will test to see that the links are broken.

1. In Word, **right-click** in the worksheet data to display a pop-up menu.

2. Choose **Linked Worksheet Object** from the menu, and choose **Links** from the submenu to open the Links dialog box.

3. Follow these steps to break the link for the table:

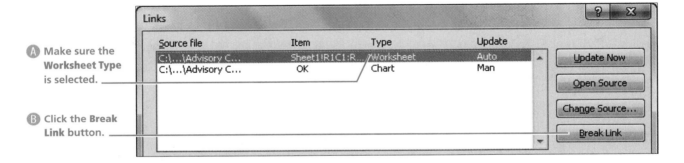

Ⓐ Make sure the **Worksheet Type** is selected.

Ⓑ Click the **Break Link** button.

4. When the message appears asking if you want to break the link, click **Yes**.
   The link disappears from the Links dialog box.

Break the Link to the Chart

The remaining link is already highlighted.

5. Click the **Break Link** button to break the link between Excel and the chart.

6. When the message box appears, click **Yes**.

7. Click **OK** to close the Links dialog box.

Test to See if the Links Are Broken

8. **Right-click** the worksheet object, and review options on the menu to note that the Update Links option is gone.

9. **Save** 💾 and **close** the Word document.

14.2 Using Excel as a Mail Merge Data Source

Video Lesson   labyrinthelab.com/videos

Word's Mail Merge feature can use a variety of file types as data sources, including Excel files. Whether you type a new data source list from within Word or you create your data source in Excel, the rules for effective data sources apply.

The more fields you have, the more flexibility you will have in the merge. A rule to remember is that you cannot merge part of a field. If the name field, for example, contains the title, first name, and last name, you will not be able to use those elements separately. For instance, in the greeting line, you will not be able to drop the first name and use *Dear Title Last Name* as a greeting.

In Excel, the columns are treated as separate fields in a mail merge. Therefore, in a name and address list, it is a good idea to place the title, first name, and last name in separate columns, as shown in the following illustration.

⬦	A	B	C	D	E	F	G
1	Title	First Name	Last Name	Address	City	State	Zip
2	Ms.	Sally	Redding	756 Locust Street	Los Angeles	CA	91025
3	Mr.	Jose	Lopez	7812 Olive Road	Los Angeles	CA	91357
4	Mr.	Charles	Douglas	91 Sycamore Ave.	Los Angeles	CA	91642
5	Mr.	Gregor	Alexandre	38 Alder Street	Los Angeles	CA	92564
6	Ms.	Ellen	Rosario	1748 Oak Street	San Francisco	CA	90256
7	Ms.	Grace	Melrose	852 Willow Way	San Francisco	CA	94612
8	Ms.	Olivia	Morales	9577 Chestnut Street	San Francisco	CA	94621
9	Mr.	James	Washington	2453 Dogwood Lane	San Francisco	CA	94652

When an Excel file is used as a merge data source file, the first row of the worksheet must contain the field names. In addition, all columns and rows must be adjacent to each other in order for Mail Merge to identify all entries as part of the same data source. You cannot have blank rows and columns within an Excel worksheet.

QUICK REFERENCE: USING EXCEL AS A MAIL MERGE DATA SOURCE

Task	Procedure
Open the main document	▪ Choose Mailings→Start Mail Merge→Start Mail Merge ▦ from the Ribbon. ▪ Choose the type of main document from the menu.
Connect to the data source	▪ Choose Mailings→Start Mail Merge→Select Recipients ▦ from the Ribbon. ▪ Choose Use Existing List from the menu. ▪ Open the Excel file. ▪ In the Select Table dialog box, choose the desired Excel file from the list. ▪ Choose Mailings→Write & Insert Fields from the Ribbon. ▪ Insert the merge fields in the main document as appropriate.
Conduct the merge	▪ Choose Mailings→Finish→Finish & Merge ▦ from the Ribbon. ▪ Choose Edit Individual Documents from the menu. ▪ Make the desired choices in the Merge to New Document dialog box, and then click OK.

Use an Excel Worksheet with Mail Merge

In this exercise, you will begin by examining the Excel worksheet that you will use as the data source. Next you will open a letter and connect the Excel data source to it, and then you will conduct the merge.

Examine the Data Source

1. Launch **Excel** if it is closed, and then **open** Committee Address List from the Lesson 14 folder.
   Each column designates a mail merge field; Title is a field, First Name is a field, and so on.

2. Look at the bottom of the Excel worksheet, and notice the tab labeled Sheet 1.
   This is the name of the page in the Excel workbook that contains the address list. You will see Sheet 1 again later in this exercise.

3. **Close** the Excel file, and then **close** the Excel program.

Open the Main Document

4. In **Word**, open Advisory Committee Letter from the Lesson 14 folder.

5. Choose **Mailings→Start Mail Merge→Start Mail Merge** from the Ribbon, and then choose **Letters** from the menu.
   This designates Advisory Committee Letter as the main document.

6. If necessary, choose **Home→Paragraph→Show/Hide** ¶ from the Ribbon to display formatting characters.
   Being able to see the formatting characters will be helpful later in this exercise.

Connect to the Data Source

Next you will indicate what data source to connect to. In this example, you will connect to the name and address list created in Excel.

7. Choose **Mailings→Start Mail Merge→Select Recipients** from the Ribbon, and then choose **Use Existing List** from the menu.

8. Navigate to the Lesson 14 folder, and **open** the Excel file Committee Address List.

9. When the Select Table dialog box appears, notice that Sheet 1 is highlighted.
   Earlier you observed Sheet 1 as the name of the page in the Excel workbook that contains the address list.

10. Click **OK** to complete selecting the list.

11. In the letter, select the line **Today's Date**, and **type** the current date in its place.

Insert the Merge Codes

12. Select the **Address Block** text and **delete** it, but do not delete the paragraph symbol at the end of the line.
    Deleting the paragraph symbol would throw off proper business letter spacing.

13. Choose **Mailings→Write & Insert Fields→Address Block** from the Ribbon.

14. When the Insert Address Block dialog box appears, click **OK** to accept the default formats for the inside address.

15. Delete the **Greeting Line** text but not the paragraph symbol at the end of the line.

16. Choose **Mailings→Write & Insert Fields→Greeting Line** 📄 from the Ribbon.

17. When the Insert Greeting Line dialog box appears, click **OK** to insert the greeting line code.

Conduct the Merge

18. Choose **Mailings→Finish→Finish & Merge** 📑 from the Ribbon, and then choose **Edit Individual Documents** from the menu.

19. When the Merge to New Document dialog box opens, click **OK** to merge all of the records from the Excel file.

20. Choose **Home→Paragraph→Show/Hide** ¶ from the Ribbon to turn off the display of formatting characters.

21. **Scroll** through the letters to see the results of the merge, and then **close** the merge document without saving it.

22. **Save** 💾 and close the Advisory Committee Letter file.

14.3 Integrating Word with PowerPoint

Video Lesson   labyrinthelab.com/videos

Word and PowerPoint are two other programs that are able to share files. One feature that exists in both applications that makes sharing files easier is that they both contain an outline view that uses heading styles. Word outlines can be used to create PowerPoint presentations. Outline view works with Word's heading styles, such as Heading 1, Heading 2, and so forth. If you want to prepare a PowerPoint presentation based on an existing report or outline, you can use the heading structure of the Word document to generate slides. This structure uses Heading 1 topics as the slide's title and headings such as Heading 2, Heading 3, and so forth as the bullet and subbullet entries in the slide.

Using Word Outline View

The Outline view in Word is an often neglected view that can be very beneficial when you become accustomed to how Outline view displays text. Study the following figure to identify basic features of the Outline view in Word.

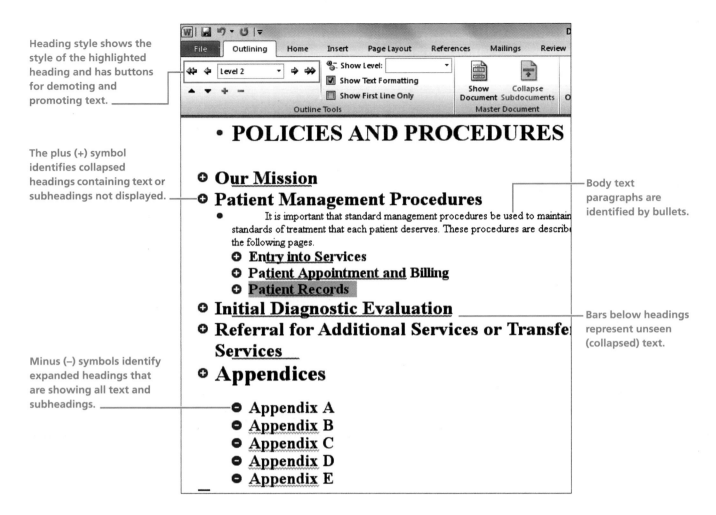

Heading style shows the style of the highlighted heading and has buttons for demoting and promoting text.

The plus (+) symbol identifies collapsed headings containing text or subheadings not displayed.

Body text paragraphs are identified by bullets.

Bars below headings represent unseen (collapsed) text.

Minus (–) symbols identify expanded headings that are showing all text and subheadings.

Whether you create a special outline to use for building a PowerPoint presentation or use an existing document and format it appropriately, creating the presentation from the outline saves having to rebuild an entire presentation structure to parallel the report. It also ensures that the flow of your PowerPoint presentation will parallel the information contained in a report.

The procedures used to launch PowerPoint are the same procedures used to launch Word. No special knowledge of PowerPoint is required to complete the following exercise.

Create a PowerPoint Presentation from a Word Outline

In this exercise, you will display the Outline view for the Draft Raritan Procedures Manual and use the outline to create a PowerPoint presentation.

1. **Open** the Draft Raritan Procedures Manual from the Lesson 14 folder.

Work with Outline View

2. Choose **View→Document Views→Outline** 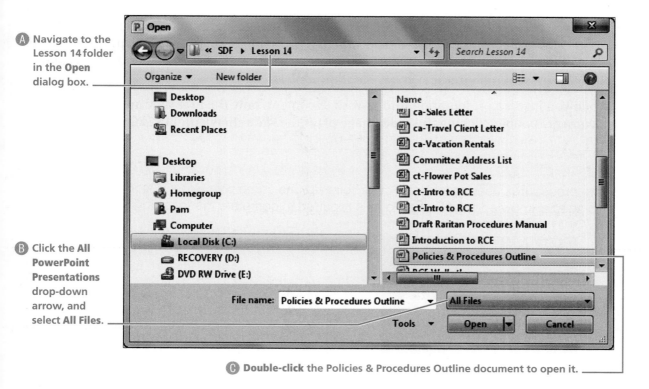 to display the outline of the document.

3. Review the outline, **double-clicking** the expand (+) button to display collapsed text.

4. Review the expanded text, and **double-click** the collapse (–) button to collapse it.

5. **Close** the document.
   The Outline view of this document was saved as an outline that you will use to create the PowerPoint presentation.

Create a PowerPoint Presentation

6. Choose **Start→All Programs→Microsoft Office→Microsoft PowerPoint 2010** to launch PowerPoint, or follow the directions of your instructor for launch shortcuts.

7. Choose **File→Open**, and then follow these steps to create a new PowerPoint presentation from a Word Outline:

A Navigate to the Lesson 14 folder in the **Open** dialog box.

B Click the **All PowerPoint Presentations** drop-down arrow, and select **All Files**.

C **Double-click** the Policies & Procedures Outline document to open it.

8. Follow these steps to display a slide containing a title and bullet points:

Ⓐ Click the **third slide** in the panel on the left.

Ⓑ Review slide contents. Note that the title is formatted using Heading 1 style, and the bullet points are formatted using Heading 2 style.

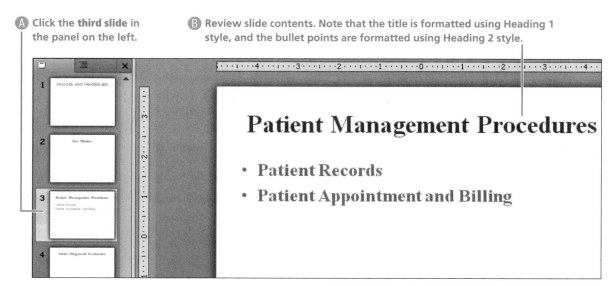

9. **Exit** PowerPoint without saving changes to the file.

Adding a PowerPoint Presentation to a Word Document

Video Lesson   labyrinthelab.com/videos

When you create a report that will be distributed electronically, it can be effective to include a PowerPoint presentation within the document. For example, suppose you want to distribute a presentation and include a letter or memo with it. You can create the letter or memo and place the presentation in the body of the communication.

When you insert a presentation into a Word document, only the first slide appears in the document. Double-clicking the slide image plays the slide show automatically.

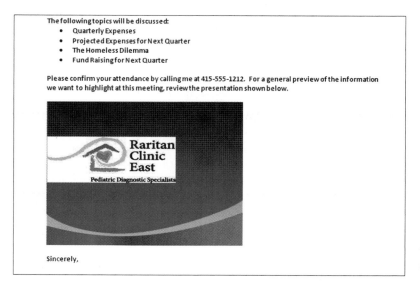

The first slide of a presentation appears as a graphic in a letter.

Task	Procedure
Create a PowerPoint presentation from a Word outline	■ Launch the PowerPoint program. ■ Create a new presentation. ■ Choose File→Open. ■ Change the file type to open to All Files. ■ Navigate to the folder containing the outline. ■ Double-click the document outline to open it in PowerPoint.
Add a PowerPoint presentation to Word and view the slide show	■ Position the insertion point in the document where you want the picture of the presentation to appear. ■ Choose Insert→Text→Object to open the Insert Object dialog box. ■ Click the Create from File tab. ■ Click the Browse button, and navigate to the folder containing the presentation. ■ Double-click the filename to insert a picture of the first slide into the document. ■ Double-click the slide to start the slide show.

DEVELOP YOUR SKILLS 14.3.2

Add a PowerPoint Presentation to a Word Document

In this exercise, you will insert a PowerPoint presentation into the letter being sent to board members.

1. **Open** the Advisory Committee Letter from the Lesson 14 folder.
   Notice that this is the letter you used to create a mail merge earlier.

2. Choose **Yes** to indicate that you want to continue.

3. Display the **Show/Hide** ¶ characters, and then position the **insertion point** on the middle paragraph symbol just before the complimentary closing for the letter.

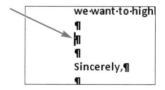

4. Choose **Insert→Text→Object** and click the **Create from File** tab.

5. Click the **Browse** button, and navigate to the Lesson 14 folder.

6. **Double-click** the Introduction to RCE.pptx file to activate it.

7. Click **OK**.
   Word adds a picture of the first slide to the position in the letter. Notice that the image is large and makes the letter extend to two pages. Next you will size the image so that the letter remains one page long.

8. Follow these steps to size the graphic appropriately:

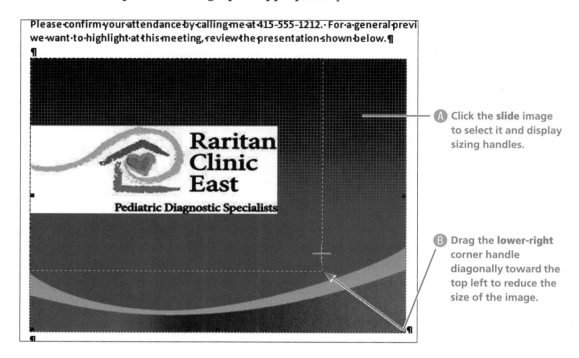

Please·confirm·your·attendance·by·calling·me·at·415-555-1212.·For·a·general·previ
we·want·to·highlight·at·this·meeting,·review·the·presentation·shown·below.¶

A Click the **slide** image to select it and display sizing handles.

B Drag the **lower-right** corner handle diagonally toward the top left to reduce the size of the image.

Repeat this procedure until both the complimentary close and author name appear on the page with the image.

Plan the Presentation

9. **Double-click** the slide image in the letter to start the presentation show.

10. Click the **mouse pointer** anywhere onscreen to advance slides and to end the show.

11. **Save** changes to the file, and **close** it.

14.4 Creating Web Pages from Word Documents

Video Lesson   labyrinthelab.com/videos

The last several versions of Word have contained a tool for creating web pages from Word documents. As you might imagine, this is a great tool because it saves you the need of learning a more specialized web design or coding program. Another advantage is that Word and other Office 2010 programs can display a document in Web Layout view so that you can make edits before posting the file on the web.

Formatting Web Pages

Web pages are often set up in tables to help align text in multiple columns, and Word's table feature works well for this purpose. When you save a document as a web page, Word converts it to hypertext markup language (HTML), the authoring language for creating web pages. When you convert a document to HTML, some formatting features may be lost. However, most of your documents should translate cleanly into attractive web pages.

QUICK REFERENCE	SAVING AND DISPLAYING A WORD DOCUMENT AS A WEB PAGE
Task	**Procedure**
Save a Word document as a web page	■ Choose File→Save As.
	■ In the Save As dialog box, choose Web Page (*.htm; *.html) from the Save as Type drop-down list.
	■ (Optional) Click the Change Title button, and type a new title to appear in the title bar of the browser.
	■ Click OK, and then click Save.
Open a web page in Internet Explorer	■ Launch Internet Explorer.
	■ Choose File→Open from the browser menu bar.
	■ In the Open dialog box, click the Browse button, and navigate to the location of the web page.
	■ Open the file.

DEVELOP YOUR SKILLS 14.4.1
Save a Document as a Web Page

In this exercise, you will examine the format of a document to be saved as a web page and then save the document.

1. **Open** the RCE Walkathon.docx file from the Lesson 14 folder.
   Notice that the document is set up in a table. The borders are visible so that you can see the column with no content on the left side of the table. Web pages may appear too far to the left in a browser window, so the blank column is acting as a spacer to position the content farther to the right on the page.

2. Choose **File→Save As** to open the Save As dialog box.

3. Follow these steps to set the format and title of the web page document:

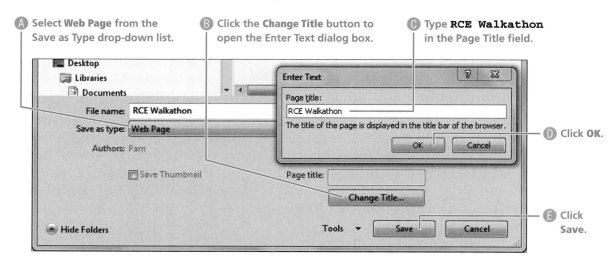

A Select **Web Page** from the Save as Type drop-down list.

B Click the **Change Title** button to open the Enter Text dialog box.

C Type **RCE Walkathon** in the Page Title field.

D Click **OK**.

E Click Save.

The page title appears in the web browser title bar when the file is open in a browser. After you click the Save button, Word automatically switches the view to Web Layout view so that you can see how the document will appear in a browser window.

4. Follow these steps to review screen elements of the figure shown in Web Layout view:

A Notice that the blank column helps align the document text toward the center of the screen.

B Borders will be hidden when the page is viewed in a web browser.

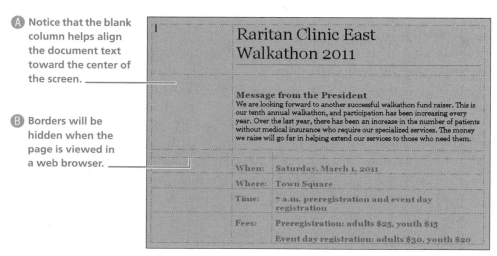

If no gridlines appear on your document, choose Table Tools→Layout→Table→View Gridlines to display them.

Open the Document in a Web Browser

5. Launch **Internet Explorer** or your default browser.

6. **Press** Ctrl + O on the keyboard, and then click the **Browse** button.

7. Navigate to the Lesson 14 folder containing the web page you just saved.

8. **Double-click** the file, and then click **OK** to open it in the browser.
   If you do not see the .htm file extension, look closely, and you will see that the web page file has a slightly different icon from a Word file icon.

9. Review the document layout shown here, and then **close** the browser and **exit** Word.

Raritan Clinic East
Walkathon 2011

Message from the President

We are looking forward to another successful walkathon fund raiser. This is our tenth annual walkathon, and participation has been increasing every year. Over the last year, there has been an increase in the number of patients without medical insurance who require our specialized services. The money we raise will go far in helping extend our services to those who need them.

When:	Saturday, March 8, 2011
Where:	Town Square
Time:	7 a.m. preregistration and event day registration
Fees:	Preregistration: adults $25, youth $15
	Event day registration: adults $30, youth $20

The Walkathon flyer displayed in the web browser.

Notice that no table borders appear, and the document looks neat and well organized.

Editing Web Pages in Word

Video Lesson   labyrinthelab.com/videos

When you create a web page in Word, you can use Word to edit the page as well. You open the *.htm page from within Word, make the necessary changes, and then resave the file. When you open it in the browser again, you will see the editing changes that you made in Word.

DEVELOP YOUR SKILLS 14.4.2
Edit a Web Page in Word

In this exercise, you will open the web page you created in the previous exercise and edit it. Then you will reopen the page in Internet Explorer and observe the change.

1. **Open** RCE Walkathon.htm from the Lesson 14 folder.

 If Windows Is not set up to display the .htm file extension, look very carefully and notice that the web page version of the file has a slightly different icon than a Word file.

2. Change the walkathon date from March 1 to March **8**.

3. **Save** the file and **close** it.

4. Restart **Internet Explorer**.

5. **Press** Ctr + O on the keyboard, click the **Browse** button, and then navigate to the Lesson 14 folder.

6. **Double-click** RCE Walkathon.htm, and then click **OK** in the Open dialog box to open the web page.

7. Observe the date change you made in the web page.

8. **Close** Internet Explorer.

14.5 Concepts Review

Concepts Review   labyrinthelab.com/word10

To check your knowledge of the key concepts introduced in this lesson, complete the Concepts Review quiz by going to the URL listed above. If your classroom is using Labyrinth eLab, you may complete the Concepts Review quiz from within your eLab course.

Reinforce Your Skills

Link Excel Objects in Word

In this exercise, you will open an Excel file and link data and a chart to a Word document. You will make changes to the Excel source document and update the changes in Word. Then you will break the link between the objects in Word and the source document.

1. **Open** rs-Collectibles Sales Report from the Lesson 14 folder.

2. If necessary, choose **Home→Paragraph→Show/Hide ¶** from the Ribbon to display formatting characters.

3. Launch **Excel**, and then **open** the rs-Collectibles file from the Lesson 14 folder.

Select and Copy the Excel Data

4. Follow these steps to select the Excel data that you will link to the Word document:

Ⓐ Position the **mouse pointer** in cell A4. The pointer should look like a thick white cross.

Ⓑ Press ⇧Shift, and click cell E8.

	A	B	C	D	E
1	Collectibles & Curiosities - Quarter 1				
2					
3					
4		Glass & Crystal	Porcelain & China	Vintage Jewelry	Art Nouveau
5	January	2,350.00	1,389.00	546.00	479.00
6	February	1,502.00	1,546.00	976.00	461.00
7	March	2,000.00	1,348.00	1,126.00	524.00
8	Total Sales	$5,852.00	$4,283.00	$2,648.00	$1,464.00

5. Choose **Home→Clipboard→Copy** from the Ribbon.

6. Click the **Word** button on the taskbar to switch to Word.

7. Position the **insertion point** in the first blank line below the main paragraph.

Paste and Link the Excel Data in Word

8. Choose **Home→Clipboard→Paste** menu ▾ from the Ribbon.

9. Choose **Paste Special** from the menu.

10. Follow these steps to paste and link the data in Word:

Ⓐ Choose the Paste Link option.

Ⓑ Choose **Microsoft Office Excel Worksheet Object** from this list.

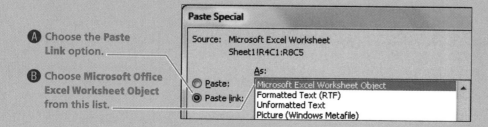

11. Click **OK** to finish pasting the data.

Copy, Paste, and Link the Chart in the Word Document

12. **Double-click** the data you just pasted in Word to switch to Excel.

13. **Press** Esc to deselect the data, and then click the **chart** to select it.

14. Choose **Home→Clipboard→Copy** from the Ribbon.

15. Use the **Word** button on the taskbar to switch to Word.

16. Position the **insertion point** next to the last paragraph symbol in the document.

17. **Right-click** the last paragraph symbol, and click the **Keep Source Formatting & Link Data Paste Option** button.

18. Click the **chart**, and **press** F9 to update the bars, if necessary.

Edit the Excel Data and Update the Data in Word

19. **Double-click** the Excel data table in the Word document to switch to Excel.

20. Follow these steps to edit the data:

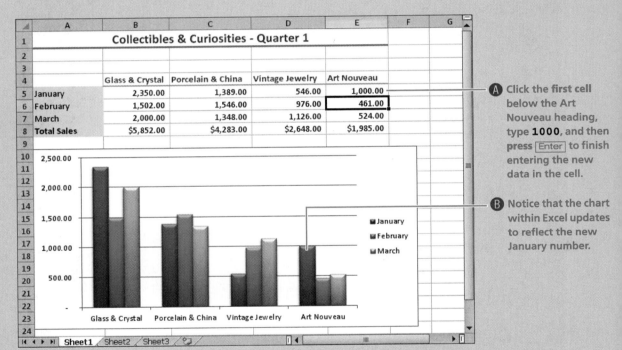

Ⓐ Click the **first cell** below the Art Nouveau heading, type **1000**, and then **press** Enter to finish entering the new data in the cell.

Ⓑ Notice that the chart within Excel updates to reflect the new January number.

21. Switch to Word, **right-click** the data table, and select **Update Link**.

22. Click the **chart**, and **press** F9 to update the chart, if necessary.

23. **Save** the Word file, and leave it **open** for the next exercise.

Break the Link Between Excel and Word

In this exercise, you will break the link between the Excel file and the Word document.

1. **Right-click** the data in the Word document, and choose Linked Worksheet Object→Links.

2. Follow these steps to break the link:

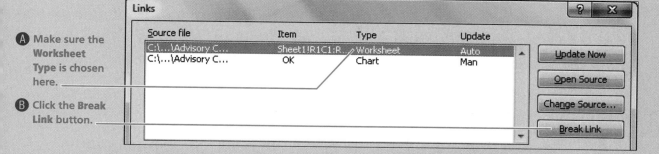

A Make sure the **Worksheet Type** is chosen here.

B Click the **Break Link** button.

3. When the message appears verifying that you want to break the link, click **Yes**.
   The Chart Type row is highlighted.

4. Click the **Break Link** button.

5. When the message appears verifying that you want to break the link, click **Yes**.

6. Click **OK** to close the Links dialog box.

7. **Save** 💾 and **close** the Word document.

8. Switch to **Excel**, and **close** the file without saving the changes, but leave the Excel program **open** for the next exercise.

Use an Excel Database with Mail Merge

In this exercise, you will use an Excel database as the source document in a mail merge.

Review the Excel File

1. In Excel, **open** rs-Interview Address List from the Lesson 14 folder.
   Notice that the data structure follows the recommendation to place Title, First Name, and Last Name in separate columns (fields), which provides more flexibility for the merge.

2. **Close** the Excel program.

3. **Open** rs-Interview Letter from the Lesson 14 folder.

4. Choose **Mailings→Start Mail Merge→Start Mail Merge** 📄 from the Ribbon, and then choose **Letters** from the menu.
   This specifies that rs-Interview Letter is the main document.

5. If necessary, choose **Home→Paragraph→Show/Hide** ¶ from the Ribbon to display formatting characters.

Connect to the Data Source

6. Choose **Mailings→Start Mail Merge→Select Recipients** 🖼 from the Ribbon, and then choose **Use Existing List** from the menu.

7. Navigate to the Lesson 14 folder, and **open** the Excel file rs-Interview Address List.
When the Select Table dialog box appears, Sheet 1 is highlighted. This is the page in the Excel workbook that contains the mailing list.

8. Click **OK** to finish selecting the list on Sheet 1.

9. In the letter, select the **ADDRESS BLOCK** and **delete** it, but do not delete the paragraph symbol at the end of the line.

10. Choose **Mailings→Write & Insert Fields→Address Block** 🖼 from the Ribbon.

11. When the Insert Address Block dialog box opens, click **OK** to insert the Address Block code.

12. In the letter, **delete** GREETING LINE but not the paragraph symbol at the end of the line.

13. Choose **Mailings→Write & Insert Fields→Greeting Line** 🖼 from the Ribbon to open the Insert Greeting Line dialog box.

14. Click **OK** to insert the Greeting Line code.

Conduct the Merge

15. Choose **Mailings→Finish→Finish & Merge** 🖼 from the Ribbon, and then choose **Edit Individual Documents** from the menu.
The Merge to New document dialog box appears.

16. Click **OK** to merge all of the records.

17. Choose **Home→Paragraph→Show/Hide** ¶ from the Ribbon to turn off the display of formatting characters.

18. **Scroll** through the letter to see the results of the merge, and then **close** the merge document without saving it.

19. **Save** 🖼 and **close** rs-Interview Letter.

Create a PowerPoint Presentation from a Word Document

In this exercise, you will open an outline in Word and then you will use the outline to create new slides in an existing a PowerPoint presentation.

1. **Open** rs-Magic Web in the Lesson 14 folder, review it, and then close it.

Import the Outline into a PowerPoint Presentation

2. Launch **PowerPoint**, and **open** rs-Magic Vision from the Lesson 14 folder.

3. Choose **Home→Slides→New Slide** [icon] **menu ▾** from the Ribbon, and then choose the **Slides from Outline** command at the bottom of the gallery.

4. Navigate to the Lesson 14 folder, and **double-click** rs-Magic Web to insert it into the presentation.

View the Slide Show

5. **Press** [F5] to start the presentation, and click the **mouse button** to move through the slide show.

6. End the show and **save** the PowerPoint file, but leave it **open** for the next exercise.

Copy a PowerPoint Presentation and Paste into Word

In this exercise, you will copy the presentation you created in the last exercise and paste it into a Word document.

1. Switch to **Word,** and **open** rs-Promotion Letter from the Lesson 14 folder.

2. Switch to **PowerPoint**.

3. Click the **first slide** in the Slides tab on the left side of the PowerPoint window to select it.

4. **Press** [Ctrl]+[A] to select all slides, and then **press** [Ctrl]+[C] to copy the slides.

5. Switch back to **Word,** and then **press** [Ctrl]+[End] to position the insertion point at the bottom of the document.

6. Choose **Home→Clipboard→Paste menu** and select **Paste Special**.

7. Select the **Microsoft PowerPoint Presentation Object** item in the As list and click **OK.** *Only the first slide in the presentation will be visible in Word.*

8. **Center** the slide in the Word document.

9. **Double-click** the slide to start the slide show.

10. Click the **mouse button** to move through the presentation and then end the show.

11. **Save** [icon], **exit** PowerPoint, and **close** the Word file.

Save a Word Document as a Web Page

In this exercise, you will open a document, view it in Web Layout view, and save it as a web page. Then you will open it in Internet Explorer.

1. **Open** rs-Retirement from the Lesson 14 folder.
   The document is set up in a table, a technique often used for aligning information on web pages.

Save the Document as a Web Page

2. Choose **File→Save As**.

3. When the Save As dialog box appears, choose **Web Page** from the Save as Type drop-down list.

4. Click the **Save** button to finish saving the web page, and notice that Word automatically displays the new document in Web Layout view.

5. **Close** the file.

Open the Web Page in Internet Explorer

6. Start **Internet Explorer**, and then **press** Ctrl+O on the keyboard.

7. In the Open dialog box, click the **Browse** button and navigate to the Lesson 14 folder.

8. **Double-click** the rs-Retirement web page file.

9. In the Open dialog box, click **OK** to open the web page.

10. **Close** Internet Explorer.

Apply Your Skills

Link Excel Data and a Chart to a Word Document

In this exercise, you will open a Word file and an Excel file and link the Excel data and chart into a Word document.

1. **Open** the Word document as-Great Year from the Lesson 14 folder.

2. Position the **insertion point** in the second blank line below the main paragraph.

3. Insert **Sheet1** of the Excel worksheet as-Store Sales file contained in Lesson 14 folder as an object at the insertion point, **linking** the data to the Excel file.

4. Ensure that the data table is linked to the Excel file by **right-clicking** the table and noting the Update Link command on the menu.

5. **Copy and paste** the chart contained on Sheet2 of the Excel worksheet as an object below the data table without linking the chart to the document.

6. **Save** 🖫 and **close** the Word document.

7. **Save** 🖫 and **close** the Excel worksheet, and then **close** the Excel program.

Use an Excel Database with Mail Merge

In this exercise, you will open a letter and create a mail merge using an Excel file as the data source.

1. **Open** as-Customer Relations Letter from the Lesson 014 folder.

2. Conduct a **merge** with an Excel file, using the following guidelines:

   - Specify as-Customer Relations Letter as the main document.
   - Identify the Excel file as-Customer Relations Address List in the Lesson 14 folder as the data source.
   - Replace the ADDRESS BLOCK and GREETING LINE text in the letter with the Address Block and Greeting Line codes.
   - Finish and merge the results to a new document (there should be four letters), and then complete the merge.
   - **Close** the merge document without saving it.
   - **Save** the letter, and then **close** it.

Create an Outline to Use in PowerPoint

In this exercise, you will create a PowerPoint presentation using a Word outline.

1. Follow these guidelines to import the outline into PowerPoint:
   - Launch **PowerPoint**, and **open** the PowerPoint presentation as-Elegant Software.
   - Insert **new slides** from the Word outline as-Software Solutions located in the Lesson 14 folder.
   - **View** the slide show.
   - **Save** 🖫 and **close** the file and **exit** PowerPoint.

Critical Thinking & Work-Readiness Skills

In the course of working through the following Microsoft Office-based Critical Thinking exercises, you will also be utilizing various work-readiness skills, some of which are listed next to each exercise. Go to labyrinthelab.com/workreadiness *to learn more about the work-readiness skills.*

14.1 Link Excel Sales Data to a Report

The manager of The Flower Pot gift shop in the Raritan Clinic East lobby is requesting a report on sales for second quarter. Create a memo for The Flower Pot in Word and include the quarterly sales. Use the Excel file ct-The Flower Pot Sales (Lesson 14 folder) for the sales data. Link the data and chart from Excel into the report. In Excel, change the April sales of Gifts from $356 to $450, and update the data and chart in the Word document. Address the memo to Dr. Jackson. Save the changes to the Excel file and close it. Save the Word file as **ct-Flower Pot Sales** in the Lesson 14 folder and then close it.

WORK-READINESS SKILLS APPLIED
- Writing
- Acquiring and evaluating information
- Reasoning

14.2 Create a PowerPoint Presentation Using a Word Outline

Dr. Edward Jackson, COO of Raritan Clinic East, works closely with the universities in his community to provide interested students the opportunity to intern with the clinic. He has been asked to give students a presentation about the clinic's different practice areas as well as other clinic opportunities such as laboratory, nursing, research, and so forth. Prepare a PowerPoint presentation for his presentation. Use the ct-Intro to RCE document (Lesson 14 folder) to add slides to the ct-Intro to RCE presentation (Lesson 14 folder) in PowerPoint. Save changes to the presentation.

WORK-READINESS SKILLS APPLIED
- Serving clients/customers
- Organizing and maintaining information
- Thinking creatively

14.3 Embed a Presentation in a Memo

Before making the presentation to the university students, Dr. Jackson wants some of his colleagues to review it. Create a memo addressed to clinic doctors asking them to review the presentation. Then, insert the ct-Intro to RCE presentation you created in the previous exercise into the memo, placing it at the bottom of the memo. Save the entire file as a web page named **ct-RCE Draft Presentation** for posting on their clinic intranet and print a copy of the memo web page.

WORK-READINESS SKILLS APPLIED
- Writing
- Using computers to process information
- Serving clients/customers

Glossary

Active X Controls
A set of controls used on web forms

Alignment
Refers to the placement of text relative to the left and right margins; text is left, right, center, or justify (evenly spaced) aligned

AutoComplete
Word recognizes certain words and phrases, such as months and days of the week as you type them; a ScreenTip appears offering to complete the typing for you

AutoCorrect
Predefined text used for automatically correcting common spelling and capitalization errors; can be customized with user-defined entries

Backstage view
Provides access to tools and other features found on the File tab of the Ribbon

Block style
A letter style that aligns all parts of a letter at the left margin

Bookmark
Selection of text identified by a name and location; a cross-reference can be made to a bookmark

Building Block
Feature that allows you to insert pre-designed content into your documents; you can create your own Building Blocks

Caption
Text added to a figure to describe or explain the figure; text formatted as captions can be used to create a table of figures

Cells
Rectangles that make up a table; the intersection of a column and row

Character Style
A style used to format a single word or selected group of words with text formatting such as font, bold, font size, etc.; no paragraph formatting is included

Clip art
Pre-designed graphic images you can place in documents

Clipboard
Task pane that lets you collect multiple items and paste them in a document; holds up to 24 entries

Collaborating
Working together with a team of people to edit and complete a document

Column
The vertical arrangement of cells in a table or the text in a document separated from other text by a space known as a gutter

Column break
Manual break of a column at a specified location; moves text at the break point to the top of the next column

Comment
An electronic note attached to a document

Compatibility Checker
When a Word 2010 document is saved down to an earlier version, the Compatibility Checker notifies the user how features specific to Word 2010 will be handled in the earlier version

Compatibility Mode
Documents created in earlier versions of Word open in Word 2010 in Compatibility Mode; this limits Word 2010 to using only features available in earlier versions

Compress
To reduce the size of graphics contained in a document to reduce the size of a document and the time it takes to display graphics on web pages

Concordance
A list of terms used to mark words or phrases in a document that are to be contained in an index

Content Controls
Controls that can be used on forms created using Word 2007 or 2010

Contextual tabs
Tabs on the Ribbon that appear in context with the task being performed

Crop
Cutting off parts of a picture to make certain other elements stand out or to remove unwanted elements

Data Source
In Mail Merge, the variable data that merges with the main document; controlled by merge fields

Default
Setting that a computer program assumes you will use unless you specify a different setting

Demote text
Increase the indentation for a paragraph so it appears farther away from the left margin and, if numbered, reduces the numbering level to the next lower level

Destination file
The file into which date copied from another document is pasted

Dialog box launcher
The small box and arrow that appear in the lower-right corner of some Ribbon groups that enable you to open a dialog box or task pane related to the group

Digital signature
Means of authenticating the identity of the originator of a document; a signed document cannot be modified

Document inspector
Reviews documents for hidden data or personal information that might be stored in the document

Drag and drop
Method for copying and moving text or objects; most useful when copying or moving a short distance within a page

Drop Cap
Formatting the first letter in a paragraph so it is significantly larger than other text in the paragraph and select options for text wrapping around the first character

Embedded object
Object from a source file that is inserted in a destination file; the object then becomes part of the destination file

See also Linked object

Encryption
Technique for encoding a document so it can only be read by the sender and the intended recipient

Endnotes
Resource reference details that appear at the end of the body of a document in which the reference is made; endnotes are numbered sequentially throughout a document

File format
Technique for storing information in a computer file; application programs normally have a special file format that they use by default

Find and Replace
Feature that finds a word, phrase, or formatting that you specify and, optionally, replaces it with another word, phrase, or formatting

Footer
Text located within the bottom margin of a document that repeats on all pages within a section

Footnote
Resource reference details that appear at the bottom of the page on which reference to the resource appears; footnote numbers can start with one on each page or may be numbered sequentially throughout a document or individually

Format painter
Allows you to copy formats from a block of text and apply them to another block of text

Formatting marks
Special characters that Word uses to control the look and layout of documents; also referred to as non-printing characters; the marks are visible when the Show/Hide button is turned on

Form fields
Text boxes, checkboxes, and other controls added to forms to limit or control the data entered in the form

Form field properties
The characteristics associated with a form field that are used to restrict the length, type, and format of data entered in the form field

Function
Predefined formula that performs calculations on table cells

Graphical User Interface (GUI)
Group of graphic screen elements that make software programs easier to use; eliminates the need to memorize command languages

Gutter
The space between two columns of text in a multicolumn layout

Header
Text located within the top margin of a document that repeats on all pages within a section

Hyperlink
Block of text or a graphic that jumps you to another location in a document to another document, or to a web page when clicked

Indent
Offsets text from the left or right margin

Legacy Forms
An older set of form fields that can be used in forms along with the Content and Active X controls

Linked object
Object created in a source file and inserted in a destination file; the object retains a link to the source file; the destination file can be updated when the source file is modified

Line break
A forced new line within a paragraph that keeps the new line as part of the paragraph

Linked style
A style that can act as either a character or paragraph format, depending on whether or not text is selected; if no text is selected, a linked style formats the entire paragraph; if text is selected, it formats only the selected text

List style
A style applied to text to convert the text to a list

Live Preview
Display of formats on selected text for some formatting commands on the Ribbon

MLA style
Modern Language Association Handbook for Writers of Research Papers; style guide for formatting research papers

Macro
Series of frequently used commands grouped together and saved as a single command; used to speed up repetitive tasks

Mail Merge
Feature used to personalize standard letters, envelopes, mailing labels, and other documents by merging a main document with a data source

Main document
In a mail merge, the document that contains the content that remains the same for each recipient; controls the merge with merge fields

Manual Page Break
A forced page break created by pressing Ctrl + Enter or choosing Insert→Pages→ Page Break

Mark as Final
Command that makes a document read-only; places an icon on the status bar to let readers know they are viewing the final form of the document

Merge cells
Combine the contents of two or more table cells to create a single table cell

Merge fields
Placeholder in a mail merge main document that instructs Word to insert information from a data source

Mini toolbar
A toolbar containing common formatting commands that appears when text is selected, pasted, or in some other way acted upon

Modified Block style
A letter style that aligns the date and signature lines at the center of the page and all other lines at the left margin; the first line of paragraphs may be indented

Navigation Pane
The panel on the left side of the Word window to help navigate to places in a document using headings, pages, or search tools

Nonbreaking space
A space inserted between two or more words to keep the words together on the same line

Normal style
A paragraph style that, by default, sets the font (Calibri), point size (11pt), alignment (left) and other standards for all new documents unless the style format is changed

Object
Element shared between documents, such as an Excel spreadsheet or chart

Office Web Apps
Versions of Word, Excel, OneNote, and PowerPoint available online for reviewing documents stored on SkyDrive; Web Apps have less-than-full application function

Page orientation
The direction that text appears on a page: Portrait (vertical) or Landscape (horizontal)

Paragraph
A group of one or more sentences separated from other sentences by pressing the Enter key on the keyboard

Paragraph style
A style used to format a paragraph or selected group of paragraphs; both paragraph formatting and character formatting can be included

Print Preview
Feature that allow you to see how a document will look when it is printed

Promote text
Reduce the indentation of text so it appears closer to the left margin and, if numbered, elevates the text to the next higher number level

Quick Access toolbar
A toolbar that appears at the left end of the title bar and contains buttons for performing common tasks regardless of which tab of the Ribbon is active

Quick Styles
Styles that appear in the Styles group of the Home tab on the Ribbon

Ribbon
The strip at the top of an application window that contains commands that help you perform tasks; organized in tabs that relate to a particular type of activity, and groups that contain related commands

Round-tripping
Converting a document created in Word 97-2003 to Word 2010 format and then saving the document back to the Word 97-2003 document format

Row
The horizontal group of cells in a table

Section break
A position in a document where the page formatting is going to change such as from single to multiple-column layout

Select text
Highlight text by dragging it with the mouse pointer or other techniques; used in preparation for certain tasks, such as formatting or copying text

Shapes
Graphic tools for drawing graphics in documents

Show/Hide
Displays nonprinting characters such as tabs and paragraph marks onscreen for easy access

Sizing handles
Small squares that appear on the corners and centers of selected graphics that can be dragged to make the graphic larger or smaller

SkyDrive
A new service offered by Microsoft that provides 25 gigabytes of online storage to persons who have a Windows Live ID

SmartArt
Pre-designed graphic designs added to a document; categories include List, Hierarchy, Pyramid, and so forth

Smart Tags
Context-sensitive option buttons that appear on menus to provide easy access to commonly used tasks

Sort
Arrangement of data in alphabetic or numeric order; can be in ascending (low to high) or descending (high to low) order

Source file
The document in which copied test originally appeared

Split cells
Create two or more table cells from a single table cell

Split View
Divide the window for the active document in horizontally so two different parts of the document can be viewed on screen at the same time

Style
A group of formats saved together to make them easier to apply to additional text in a document; allows easy update to all text formatted with the style by modifying the characteristics of the style

Table style
A style applied to cells, rows, or columns of a table to ensure consistency

Tab stops
Preset stops along the horizontal ruler at every half inch, to control and align text; can be placed anywhere on the ruler

Template
Preformatted document layout is saved so it can be used to create additional documents and maintain consistency among the documents; usually contains text, paragraph, table, graphics, and other formats

Theme
Set of formatting selections you can apply to a document; includes colors, graphic elements, and fonts all designed to work well together

Title bar
Appears across the top of the Word window, contains the name of the application (Word) and the name of the current document

Track Changes
Feature that, when activated, marks each change to a document; the changes can then be reviewed and either accepted or rejected

Views
On-screen layout of a document optimized for performing specific tasks or for determining how the document will look when deployed in final form

Visual Basic for Applications
A programming language used by Office programs that creates modules containing macros

Watermark
Text or images placed in the header of a document so it appears faintly behind document text and graphics

Windows Live ID
An electronic ID used to access personal account files on SkyDrive and other Microsoft sources

WordArt
Feature for creating stylized formatting of text; typically used for headings

Word Wrap
The automatic moving of text to a new line when it extends beyond the right margin of a paragraph; eliminates the need to tap Enter at the end of lines within a paragraph

Zoom
Command that changes the on-screen levels of magnification

Index

Notes

Notes